S0-ADH-539

Developing with Ada

Life-Cycle Methods

Dr. Bruce E. Krell

Hughes Aircraft Company

BANTAM BOOKS
NEW YORK • TORONTO • LONDON • SYDNEY • AUCKLAND

Developing with Ada: Life-Cycle Methods

A Bantam Book/September1992

This book was produced by Horizon Publications, San Diego
Cover Design by
Edward Smith Desigh, Inc.

ISBN 0-553-09102-6
Library of Congress Catalog Card Number 92-73263

Published simultaneously in the United States and Canada

Bantam Books are published by Bantam Books, a division of Bantam Doubleday Dell Publishing Group, Inc. Its trademark, consisting of the words "Bantam Books" and the portrayal of a rooster, is Registered in U.S. Patent and Trademark Office and in other countries. Marca Registrada, Bantam Books, 666 Fifth Avenue, New York, New York 10103.

PRINTED IN THE UNITED STATES OF AMERICA

0 9 8 7 6 5 4 3 2 1

To

my wife, Michiko,

and

my dad, George

Contents

Acknowledgments

Any text such as this is really a collaborative effort by numerous individuals and groups. I would like to expressly thank everyone who contributed in any way. This would probably require an extra book. Therefore, I am limited to very specific acknowledgments. If I missed anyone, please accept my apologies. The individuals and groups below deserve special thanks, for the reasons indicated.

Gary Billerbeck, for constructive criticism that significantly improved readability of the text;

Bryce Bardin, for an unceasing intellect and his lecture notes on the Layered Virtual Machines/Object-Oriented Design methodology employed in the text;

Tom Corth, for frank, insightful, and illuminating discussions about the pragmatics of software project management;

Mike Deutsch, for motivating usage of the operational view of the system from the start;

Steve Grimaldi, for the invitation to give my first Tri-Ada tutorial, which initiated the formalization of the methodology;

Ron Hinker, whose years of integration and test experience provided the basis for strategies described in the text;

Randy Jensen, for his precise formalization of the hierarchical control concept during an in-company seminar;

Karen Kawakami, for her patience in proofreading the text and for suggesting changes to improve the readability of the text;

Rick Mazzarella, for teaching me how to plan software projects in great detail and for his partnership;

Bill McAuley, for providing a fertile experimentation environment and for tolerating my floundering in that environment;

Mike Mahoney, for encouraging me to teach graduate classes at CA State University, Long Beach, and allowing me to use drafts of the text;

Jack Mogg, for believing in my technical capabilities and for defending me against an attack by a community of ogres;

Kjell Nielsen, for his sponsorship, editorial guidance and support, and his suggestions, which enhanced the content of the text;

Imtiaz Pirbhai, for his workshops that provided my initial insight into the value of a structured approach to development;

Joel Shafran, for proving that projects with short schedules can be intelligently managed and for allowing me to develop the Lightweight Helicopter Target Acquisition Software methodically;

Pat Schuler, for her continuous constructive criticism, which significantly improved the illustrations;

Ken Shumate, for continued friendship, peer acceptance, and for always being one step ahead and making me work to keep up;

Dave Smith, for his extensive experience with the Ada language, captured in his lecture notes on Ada, and for keeping me restrained under adversity;

Bob Wells, for knowing why a certain Australian beer is named "XXXX", and for his excellent knowledge of Ada run-time environments;

Ray Wolverton, for his training support over the past years at Hughes;

Advanced Technical Education Program (ATEP) at Hughes, for the many opportunities to refine the text material in after hours classes;

Students in my ATEP classes, who suffered through, criticized, and generally helped to shape and hone the text materials;

Corporate Software Initiatives Program at Hughes (Paul Stephens, Thomas Winfield, and Dennis Kane), who financed portions of the technical work described in the text;

Graduate classes at CA State University, Long Beach, who carried the student exercises rigorously through the methodology to complete implementation;

Hardware, Software, and Support Software personnel of the Lightweight Helicopter Target Acquisition System prototype effort, for the most enjoyable project and for their patience in teaching me;

Division Management of the Information Systems Division (Dick Loftus, Terry Court, and Gerry Hoshijo), for support and encouragement in my work environment;

Publications Department, Space and Communications Group at Hughes, for the high quality work and rapid response times in generating all of the art work for my projects/ATEP classes;

Chuck Swerdlow, for his excellent management of my own personal real-time system; and

Albert King, Son Seals, and Buddy Guy, for hours of incredible listening pleasure;

A special note of appreciation goes to Alan Rose, Intertext Publications and Kim Fryer, Bantam Professional Books, for making the publication of this book both enjoyable and informative.

Preface

Over the last several decades, computer hardware has made tremendous strides in capability. Technologies that were unimaginable seem to proliferate almost overnight. Hardware engineers have appeared to effectively and rapidly design systems that harness these emerging technologies. Unfortunately, software engineering has not kept pace. In recent years, however, a software language has been developed to provide a state-of-the-art development platform for software engineers. This language is named Ada, in honor of Ada Lovelace.

Many software engineers, computer scientists, and university faculty make deprecating remarks about Ada and its capabilities. After having employed a wide range of languages for real-time system development (assembly, Fortran, Cobol, and C), I decided to give Ada a try. Several years later, I implemented a complex, distributed, embedded Ada system (the Lightweight Helicopter Target Acquisition System described in the text) under an extremely short schedule. At the end of this development, I came to several important conclusions:

If properly used, Ada stands head and shoulders above other languages that I had used in the past;

Knowing how to use Ada properly is nontrivial;

Ada can be used for development of real-time systems under short schedules;

Ada is the language of preference for real-time systems development; and

I should capture my experiences regarding proper usage and potential abuses of Ada.

For these reasons, this book was developed. Within its pages, I provide a complete methodology for carrying real-time development in Ada from scratch to operations and maintenance in Ada. I have attempted to give a balanced treatment of concepts and pragmatic issues, while providing examples of what worked and what failed, with detailed explanations.

A basic tenet in the use of this methodology is that you will have to employ it on a regular basis, acknowledging the uncertainty under which most software developments occur. Every method, technique, programming guideline, and code segment described has been used on one or more actual Ada real-time projects. Additionally, I have tried to elaborate my own insights and heuristics concerning implications and alternatives to show why a particular approach was employed.

Many of the principles and techniques given in the text have been employed for systems whose software target was an environment other than Ada (C, Microsoft Windows, and even expert systems). While the transition from design to code was tortuous with other languages, the approaches shown here tend to generalize well for real-time systems, which are driven by intensive scenarios of randomly ordered events. Therefore, this book is of potential interest to a wide range of software professionals working on a large class of real-time systems.

Since practical application is the best approach to internalizing the methods described, several lengthy and detailed case studies are presented. Also included in an appendix are all the details associated with an actual project. This serves to reinforce the pragmatic foundation of the methods described in the text and case studies. While the case studies employ prototypical systems, discussions within a case study are not limited by the methodology diagrams, which are covered extensively. However, much of this discussion serves as a foundation for relating details of the prototype to actual development experiences. At the end of the book, several exercises are described. Those wanting to gain practical experience with application of the methodology are encouraged to work these exercises through the complete methodology.

I sincerely hope you will find this book to be useful, informative, and interesting. More important, I hope you gain enough insight to begin to enjoy using Ada on short deadline, real-time developments. Then, perhaps, your enjoyment will equal the pleasure I have experienced over the years using Ada and writing this book.

Bruce Krell, Ph.D.
Manhattan Beach, CA

1

Introduction

Perhaps you are facing your first Ada development with trepidation. Or maybe you've been burned in an attempt to deliver a working Ada system. In either case, you, your colleagues, and your customers have strong negative feelings regarding the use of Ada in real-time systems development. A bad experience with Ada as a development language is *not* the fault of the Ada language. In fact, Ada, when combined with methods and techniques described in this book, has been used successfully on several real-time projects. Moreover, many of the techniques, design heuristics, and code templates have been successfully adapted to event-driven systems in other environments, such as C, Microsoft Windows, expert systems, etc.

Developers who have failed to deliver working Ada systems within cost and schedule constraints usually blame the Ada language for their failure. As William Shakespeare stated in *Julius Caesar*, "The fault, dear Brutus, is not in our stars, but ourselves."

Ada (our stars) is not the reason that the development fails to meet its schedules and costs. Ada is, first and foremost, a technology. Successful system development requires that this technology be effectively harnessed. Ineffective and inappropriate application of technological capabilities in Ada (by ourselves) cause difficulties in development, not the language or its characteristics!

After significant real-time Ada development experience, I believe that:

Ada is the preferred language for real-time system development and
Ada can be effectively used for real-time system development.

I make these assertions after using a number of programming languages (assembly, Fortran, Cobol, C, and Ada) on real-time system development projects during my career as a software engineer.

Contrary to the belief of some software developers, Ada's capabilities are *not* hindrances, but instead provide strong support for these assertions. Specifically, the Ada tasking model is a natural representation of concurrent activities within a real-time system. Moreover, successful employment of Ada tasking leads to reduced hardware dependency, constraining both system complexity and development costs. Support for data abstraction as encapsulated objects or private types within Ada allows a problem-oriented representation for algorithms that can be easily translated into code. These programming paradigms, designed into the Ada language, allow programmers to develop both designs and code that look like the problem that is being solved, enhancing traceability from requirements to code. Moreover, effective utilization of both tasking and data abstraction localizes potential software problems into very small code segments and, further, halts many errors during the compilation of individual, small code segments. In this way, problems do not escape into your integrated system and run rampant. Resulting reductions in integration and test grind and improved requirements traceability are the primary reasons for asserting that Ada is the language of preference for real-time system development.

All right, you cynically inquire, then how does one effectively employ Ada's capabilities to develop a real-time system? To answer this question, three important areas of concern must be addressed. In generating code that reads like requirements, you must employ a rigorous methodology that effectively correlates requirements through design to code. In this manner, neither too little nor too much code is generated, ensuring real-time performance. Moreover, testing and integration strategies must employ results generated during the methodical development. Effective usage of tasking and data abstraction, the second area of concern, is best achieved by employing a combination of design heuristics and code templates that have proved to be effective design and implementation approaches. Finally, to assure the correct usage of methodology, heuristics, and templates, you must use a realistic development plan (and management style) that allows and encourages these activities. Thus, project management is the third important area of concern.

Developing with Ada introduces a realistic development methodology that addresses software engineering, code and unit test, and integration and testing. Copious and detailed case studies are provided, including one study in which the methodologies are applied to an actual system. Realistic insights are freely intermixed with conceptual descriptions. In this way, the reader gains knowledge of both why and how of these methods and techniques are used. Case studies for prototypical real-time systems follow this same approach of intermixed conceptual and pragmatic discussions.

A range of readers will find this book highly informative. Managers will be interested in real-time development principles (Chapter 1) and programmatic issues (Chapter 9), while software engineers will learn of methodologies in software engineering (Chapters 2–7) and integration and test (Chapter 8). Both will benefit from the case studies presented (Chapters 10–13).

Moreover, many of the principles and approaches apply to real-time systems in general. For this reason, this book is informative for the real-time community, regardless of the development language to be employed.

1.1 UNIQUE CHARACTERISTICS OF THIS BOOK

As you read *Developing with Ada*, you may wonder how this book differs from other books on this same topic. First and foremost, the contents reflect the author's successful experiences in the development, integration, and operation of real-time Ada systems. These experiences led to insights that are reflected in the contents of the book. All of the examples are uniquely developed, based on the author's experience. Specifically, generic examples in methodology and design chapters have never appeared in other texts and realistically reflect the general characteristics of real-time systems.

More than any other language, Ada requires that a life-cycle emphasis be adopted early in a project and that this emphasis be accepted by all project team members. Therefore, this text also addresses the whole life-cycle. Methodology approaches described begin with a user interface and operations model and end with actual code and documentation, covering software engineering activities. Moreover, integration and test strategies that employ products generated during software engineering are explicitly addressed.

Approaches and principles described in the remainder of this text have been thoroughly tested, refined, and evaluated. Specific real development projects have employed much of the information. Hundreds of classroom lecture hours have been consumed honing the approaches, philosophies, and examples into a communicable and logically defensible format. Many of the principles and practices apply to real-time systems in general. Case studies are provided to demonstrate successful methodology applications and to illustrate the way in which methodology application can identify and eliminate flaws.

1.2 PRINCIPLES OF REAL-TIME ADA SYSTEM DEVELOPMENT

By way of introducing the detailed contents of the text, several principles of real-time Ada development are described and discussed. Some of these principles are generally applicable to real-time systems. Other principles are reinforced by using Ada. Still others are unique to employing Ada within a real-time context. Each of the principles, however, is important and helps to explain the appearance of the chapters in the text.

Principle #1

Methodically develop requirements and design in a traceable manner. Avoid the rush; pay now, not later.

- Do *not* rush to the keyboard.
- Emphasize requirements to obtain end-to-end data flow.

- Address events and responses as well as data flows.
- Use methodology steps to assure that software works prior to coding.
- Use methodology products as a basis for integration and test.
- Treat methodology as a guiding framework, not a religion.

In most real-time software developments, programmers are under intense pressure to rush to their keyboards. Project managers want to see code now. Programmers want to develop code. (Interacting with a machine provides instantaneous gratification, while thinking requires effort.) This approach is usually justified by the philosophy that poor decisions, problems, and limitations can be fixed later. With Ada, this approach does not work. Due to the characteristics of the language and a typically short development schedule, fixes are never done. Moreover, integration and testing becomes a nightmare, involving unpaid overtime, programmer burnout, missed schedules, poor performance, and cost overruns.

A major key in the successful development of real-time Ada systems is to take the time to develop requirements and design methodically in a traceable manner. This book provides an effective, useful, and tested methodology for Ada software development, employing a life-cycle perspective, which combines software engineering results with integration and testing activities. Several case studies demonstrate explicit and detailed application of this methodology. Finally, examples of methodology application to the Lightweight Helicopter Target Acquisition Subsystem are included. (See Chapter 9.)

This principle requires recognition that Ada software development, more than any other language, is life-cycle oriented. In this chapter, all aspects of development (methodologies, tools, activities, and configuration management) are integrated into a combined and consistent view of the real-time system/software development process.

Principle #2

Design your Ada application to take best advantage of Ada capabilities. Get an experienced Ada software architect.

- Recognize that software is a system that exhibits unique behavior.
- Acknowledge the effect of design decisions upon flexibility and integration and test efforts.
- Establish hierarchical, centralized control in your software architecture.
- Make sound engineering decisions regarding the use of tasking.
- Employ entrance procedures to enforce task caller protocols.
- Identify caller/callee relationships that maximize throughput.
- Use intermediaries to control blocking while limiting overhead.
- Manage external interfaces with at least one Ada task.
- Hide hardware interfaces under functional abstractions.
- Use strong typing and data abstraction effectively with private types.

This principle is both difficult and problematic to adopt. As with most people, project managers tend to be loyal to those software engineers and architects that have helped them "muddle through" in the past. Unfortunately, those individuals are not familiar with effective design and development strategies peculiar to Ada development as characterized above. Quite often, these "other language" software engineers approach an Ada development using techniques that worked (albeit painfully and slowly) in previous developments. Ada provides significant penalties in the form of painful integration and test, poor flexibility, and reduced performance when these "other language" strategies are employed. In fact, Ada simply performs worse than "other languages" when inappropriate design principles are adopted. Project managers must abandon those time-worn loyalties.

Finding a qualified Ada software architect is a real problem. Qualified architects are few and far between. Understanding Ada design principles is different from knowing Ada syntax and semantics. Design principles emerge due to interactions of large combinations of Ada semantics, which result when complex code is implemented. An individual who knows Ada syntax and semantics well (commonly referred to as a "language lawyer") may or may not be an effective Ada designer. Certainly, an individual who has taken a single course introducing the language and semantics is not sufficiently experienced to provide effective Ada designs.

A corollary to Principle #2 requires that this lead software architect be given complete control over the day-to-day assignment and monitoring of technical tasks. An effective approach is to have the project manager deal with the external interactions with program management while the architect is the internal manager. Software architects can not enforce rigorous Ada design methods without authority.

For aspiring Ada software architects, this book contains several chapters that should prove to be informative. Detailed software engineering and test methodologies are described and illustrated here.

Principle #3

Provide technical staff with appropriate training and expertise. Know the Ada language, its strengths and weaknesses.

- Encourage participation in both Ada programming and design courses.
- Emphasize importance of hands-on experience through lab exercises.
- Provide experience paths from small to increasingly larger projects.

Many people fear the Ada language. Other individuals are so uninformed as to believe they can simply read a book and step up to a terminal. This language is as much a technology as a language. A new hardware capability is not automatically incorporated into a system. Extensive evaluation is performed to identify interfaces, capabilities, and performance within a larger system context. New hardware is selectively introduced in small increments into newly developed systems. Effective usage of Ada depends upon utilizing these same strategies.

Acquiring an Ada capability is not a short-term activity. Most organizations develop an approach that incorporates lectures and a practical experience path of continuously increasing complexity.

Principle #4

Software development is more than a lot of fancy coding. Develop your software with the goals of achieving the following factors governing software success:

- Supportive project management.
- Clear, ego-less communications among the algorithms, hardware, software, and support software development teams.
- Communicate with your customer.
- Recognize that Ada developments differ programmatically from others.
- Establish realistic review dates.
- Do not begin coding prior to reviews.
- Use methodology products to foster communications.
- Listen to and trust software leaders.

Effective software development requires at least an intuitive understanding of technical issues and their effects and impacts on both schedule and costs. Of specific importance is the establishment of realistic schedule milestones at appropriate times. Actual delivery date is not as important as exact timing of reviews in the development process (this statement might come as a surprise to some readers). Reviews that are scheduled too early do not allow sufficient time to perform all work necessary under the requirements and design specification approaches dictated by the Ada language.

Many readers will ignore these cost and scheduling implications. Typically, they say, "I don't have time to follow these approaches—my schedule is too short!" In fact, following the development methods in this book is a key to developing systems under short schedules without pain. When using Ada as a development language under tight schedules, project managers must employ milestones and methodologies that effectively utilize Ada's strengths and that take into account Ada's technology constraints.

Unfortunately, supportive schedules are necessary but not sufficient for insuring painless crunch-mode development. Additional strategies are required. These strategies deal with concepts such as incremental builds, concurrent hardware development, and integration and testing methods by which a reliable, high throughput operational software system can be delivered.

As with any project, successful development depends very heavily upon communications among the participants. With an Ada development, this factor becomes increasingly important (or deadly, as the case may be). Customers must be presented with a clear and precise formulation of their requirements and a developer's knowledge relating implementor's requirements necessary to meet customer requirements. This translation from a customer's view of the system into a developer's view reflecting experience and understanding is a key element of the offered software engineering and integration methodologies. Experience on multiple, real-time Ada developments has demonstrated that in the hands of a knowledgeable practitioner, these specific methodical approaches rapidly eliminate customer confusion and lack of commitment. Customer confusion *must* be eliminated prior to any real design work. By providing a rigorous, indisputable mechanism for translating customer requirements into functional and control requirements, little effort is required to "try to fix the problems later." Attempts to fix the problem after employing vague requirements are prone to failure. Moreover, rigor in translating customer requirements into functional and control requirements also translates into flexibility necessary to incorporate new requirements as they evolve. And, as all developers know, requirements do evolve!

Another aspect of communication which benefits from the methodical approach described is the interaction among algorithm, hardware, software, and support software development teams. Specific methodology steps encourage the inclusion of these various perspectives prior to development of any design details. If management can imbue an ego-less, cooperative spirit into the interaction of these important team members, development of real-time Ada systems is likely to be more successful. Moreover, by employing a methodology that accepts interface requirements early in the specification process, problems typically resolved by programmers at implementation time are raised and solved during specification. A resultant design that employs features of Ada to encapsulate these interfacing requirements assures that problems occur during implementation can be easily isolated, then fixed, with minimal effect on the cost and schedule.

Principle #5

Provide integrated software engineering and integration environments. Give developers and integrators the necessary and proper tools to accomplish the job.

- Do not develop software-engineering environments on an ad-hoc basis.
- Do not shortchange funding for integration and test environments.
- Treat both as serious, full scale system developments.
- Know the capabilities and limitations of off-the-shelf CASE tools.
- Recognize that integration of software tools is not trivial, regardless of vendor claims.

When hardware developers and integrators begin a complex development, their development tools and integration and test capabilities are often in place, integrated, and proceduralized. For this reason, hardware developments are predictable, repeatable, and reliable. Software development and integration environments are developed ad-hoc, usually employing tools that are insufficient in capability and inappropriate to support the particular problems that face developers and integrators. With greater emphasis on methodology and traceability from requirements to code, Ada developments must have the appropriate tools integrated and operational before development begins. Concurrent development of software engineering environments and integration and test environments spells doom (or at least great pain) for real-time Ada developments.

Both software engineering environments and integration and test environments must be treated as full-scale system developments. User needs are canvassed and are based upon operational scenarios depicting usage strategies and philosophies. From these user needs, requirements, design, development and/or acquisition, integration and test plans are developed. An integrated system is developed and tested to assure support for the user scenarios. All of this is done prior to actual software development.

Software engineering environments are most often read as CASE tools. Choice of an appropriate CASE tool is a critical decision for a real-time Ada development. Improper selection of a tool hampers an Ada development by failing to provide capabilities that effectively support good Ada design and methodical software development approaches. CASE tools promise so much but typically deliver so little when required to support a complete development methodology. Therefore, when choosing a CASE tool, a clear knowledge of the tool's capabilities is necessary to make effective use of the tool. CASE tool selection does not imply automatic integration of CASE tools within a software engineering environment. Integrating the CASE tool with other tools, such as document processors, assumes an operations concept as well as some complex software system integration effort.

Typically, real-time Ada systems employ target platforms that differ from the host platform that supports the software engineering environment. Separate host and target platforms require a serious effort to specify, design, and implement an appropriate integration and test environment. Properly developed integration and test environments allow easy transition into operational systems. Debugging is simple, if effective Ada design methods are employed and the environment is specifically established to be cognizant of this approach.

Summary of Principles

Use the principles and detailed methods to create a repeatable software manufacturing process. Plan your development; develop your plan. Work smart, not hard.

- Do not simply pay lip service to the principles and methods.
- Translate them into actual practice on your developments.
- Recognize that effective use of methods leads to:
  - elimination of integration and test grind;
  - reliability and performance of delivered software;
  - greater room for creativity by designers;
  - coding that is reduced to a minimal effort;

- elimination of cost and schedule overruns;
- and increased competitive status of your organization.

These summary principles reflect the emergence of software engineering as a true engineering discipline. As a knowledgeable reader might guess, they are appropriate for all real-time systems and perhaps software systems in general. However, within a combined Ada and real-time context, they become almost sacrosanct. Simply stated, these last principles are meant to suggest that the principles described above and the practices, guidelines, and approaches described in the remainder of the text form an effective approach to development of high throughput, flexible, easily integrated Ada systems within cost and schedule constraints. Working smart implies use of development methods and design principles described within the remainder of the text. Planning a development stresses employment of management strategies which reflect usage of these principles. Working smart, not hard, embodies the spirit and philosophy that was intended by the original designers of the Ada language. Successful and effective use of the approaches in this book on multiple Ada projects strongly supports this belief.

More importantly, experience with the approaches reflected in this text implies that Ada can, if properly utilized, lead to software development becoming a dependable, repeatable, reliable, cost-effective manufacturing process. Moreover, software development becomes a more creative process by allowing software engineers to focus considerable effort on design while minimizing effort placed on implementation. Organizations that can capitalize on the combined Ada/software manufacturing process will be the surviving developers of the coming decade.

Bottom Line

Implementation of real-time Ada systems is best accomplished by:

1. Starting with a user's view of software system operations;
2. Implementing only those requirements needed to satisfy the user's view;
3. Effectively using tasking and data abstraction to meet those limited requirements;
4. Maintaining flexibility in the design to accommodate changing requirements; and
5. Assuring that specification and design decisions do not adversely affect integration and test efforts.

In short, success depends on producing only the code required to exactly meet user operations, no more, no less, while maintaining flexibility of design. If these basic guidelines are followed, several important results are obtained. Integration and test grind is significantly reduced. Developed software exhibits high performance and tremendous reliability. Short schedules are easily met.

Ability to develop according to these bottom-line principles requires that software be treated as a system development activity. Tacitly incorporated into the system development methodologies in this text is a life-cycle perspective that can be associated with any system development. Each step is characterized according to its benefit over the life-cycle of software system development. Emphasis is placed upon the fact that additional effort during requirements and design capitalizes on the characteristics of Ada to reduce effort and to save schedule over the life-cycle of a software development. Specific requirements and design activities are characterized as to their impact upon integration and testing activity. Integration and test methodologies are described that assume the rigorous generation of earlier methodology products. Effective real-time Ada development is accomplished by applying this integrated life-cycle perspective to effectively utilize Ada's strong support for tasking and data abstraction to ease the transition from design to coding.

2

Development Methods

Ada has constantly been publicized as a language that is most effectively employed with a rigorous methodology. Recent experience by practitioners seems to support this claim. In this section, a specific and rigorous methodology is described that has been employed successfully on several real-time Ada projects. Many of Ada's characteristics and capabilities are what make a methodology such as the one described here an effective approach to software development. By comparison, Ada projects that do not rigorously follow a methodology tend to exhibit painful integration and test activities and have significant schedule slips and cost overruns, poor software productivity rates, and difficult maintenance.

Methodologies are only effective and useful if they serve several important goals. First, a methodology must provide an effective mechanism for tracing requirements to actual code. Graphic notations are not particularly effective in helping to meet this goal. More importantly, an analytical framework must be exhibited by the methodology to achieve this, which implies that certain activities occur in a specific order appropriate to the system being methodically developed. An important aspect of methodical software development is the phase in which design is translated into code. A programming language and its capabilities can either aid in this transition or detract from it. This is where Ada actually shines. Due to its basic capabilities, transition from a strong methodological framework (which tracks requirements through the design process) into Ada code is a natural and almost simple task, if proper engineering discipline is enforced.

A second and important goal of a methodology is to enhance and standardize communications among various participants in a software development effort. Using diagramming notations that are easy to understand and interpret ensures effective communications among algorithm developers, hardware engineers, software engineers, and support software development teams. Many real-time projects fail due to a significant lack of communication among relevant players. An added benefit to a properly structured methodical approach is to help stabilize some core set of requirements early in the development process. Many methodologies do not accomplish early requirements stabilization. Since the methodology described in this text requires—first and foremost—communication with your customer, requirements stabilization can usually be achieved.

Additionally, rigorous software development methodology serves to accommodate changing requirements. Unfortunately, many methodology practitioners and students tend to equate rigorous methodology with concepts such as "perform each step only once." No such interpretation is implied here. In fact, incorporation of new requirements is eased by rigorous application of an effective methodology. This effect occurs because new requirements can easily be factored into the development process. However, incorporation of new requirements typically consumes less time and effort than has been observed in the past. Every step of the development process must be accomplished again to incorporate any new requirement. Examples will be shown later that illustrate the case with which new requirements can be assimilated during a methodical development approach.

In the past, software has been a chaotic, hectic, and painful experimental process. Rigorous employment of a development methodology serves to convert this caustic experimental activity into a repeatable, reliable manufacturing process. By establishing rigor and focus to the software development effort, software developers can emphasize the more creative and greater leverage aspects of design rather than having to emphasize code generation. Emphasis on code generation to the exclusion of design has been a major factor contributing to the unreliability of software development in the past.

When rigorously and effectively followed, software development methodologies can reduce code and unit test phase schedules and ease the burden of integration and test. However, a methodology is not to be treated as a panacea. Some things can not be accomplished by a methodology. For instance, generating effective designs depends upon individual capabilities and experience. Even experience with the application domain (or the methodology, for that matter) can not be automatically supplied by a methodical approach. An effective methodology under the control of an inexperienced or poor architect will still fail to accomplish most of the goals suggested above. In other words, methodologies, even if rigorously applied, can not guarantee success. However, failure to employ a rigorous and effective methodology will significantly increase the likelihood of failure, especially if the software is coded in Ada.

While this methodology has been effectively employed on multiple Ada projects, no assertion is made as to its applicability to all Ada projects. Projects that successfully employed the methodology described in this section exhibited several specific characteristics. Primary hardware devices used in the systems developed typically include sensors (raw data collection), actuators (physical reconfiguration of the hardware system), and/or display devices (communicate results of analyzing raw data). Management of these devices and analysis of collected data requires multiple threads of control, real-time response to events (less than 150 msec per event), and management of embedded hardware interfaces. All interfaces are digital in format. Conspicuously missing is intensive utilization of complex data structuring techniques or database management systems. Access to or utilization of analog devices are also not involved in the developments.

Detailed explication of the methodology spans several chapters. First, a typical software development methodology is presented. Shortcomings of this approach are identified. Next, a more realistic methodology is presented. Each step of the methodical development process is described in terms of its goals, guidelines for employing the step, and examples of employing the step. Examples of diagramming techniques in terms of a prototypical real-time system exhibiting characteristics described in the previous section are provided. Moreover, they can be used as a starting point in performing your own real-time Ada system development as long your system exhibits appropriate characteristics.

2.1 A TYPICAL SOFTWARE DEVELOPMENT METHODOLOGY

Most software developments and corresponding system integrations employ the "big bang" approach, in which software developers are placed in a lab and instructed to start coding while hardware developers begin building. Eventually, an attempt is made to get the system to work as an integrated whole, with no documented system concept.

This process can be summarized as follows:

1. Announce a delivery date;
2. Write the code;
3. Write a user's manual;
4. Write the software requirements specification;
5. Ship the product to the customer;
6. Allow users at the customer site to test the product;
7. Identify bugs/shortcomings as potential enhancements; and
8. Announce the upgrade program.

While the viewpoint here is admittedly acerbic, a large measure of truth is apparent. Poorly tested code is delivered to customers for more realistic testing. After all, customers can pay for upgrades to software.

Shortcomings of this approach are easily identified. Developers fool themselves into thinking they are clever. After all, requirements match actual code delivered. Unfortunately, customers are usually unhappy with this approach. Once a customer attempts to use the combined hardware/software system, failure is almost guaranteed. In the short run, if system failure is not disastrous, the customer will return to you for the fixes, since a large investment has been made. If system failure destroys his $40 million satellite, short run fixes may not be possible. Over the long run, the customer will surely find new developers.

Another side effect of this particular development approach is an extensively painful attempt to fix software. Costs are quite high, and effort expended is great. All members of the development team are likely to become frustrated and burnout rapidly overcomes team members, especially those developing and integrating new software. Fixes may even require significant redesign, recoding, and retesting of existing software rather than simple add-on and integration efforts.

In fact, developments approached in this manner are penalized by Ada implementation. Features such as exporting by package specification may necessitate significant debugging efforts to accommodate simple changes. Due to the visibility of items in a package specification, significant design changes may be required, and coding changes within the package specification may not be sufficient to incorporate simple modifications to the software.

For all these reasons, developing software by such a haphazard approach no longer constitutes a professional software development. A more rigorous approach that exhibits an understandable and useful analytic framework must be employed.

2.2 OVERVIEW OF A MORE REALISTIC METHODOLOGY

During the past few years, a number of methodology-oriented texts have been published. Some of these dealt with real-time systems in general; some specifically addressed Ada developments. Published works include the following:

1. *Strategies for Real-Time System Specification* by D. J. Hatley and I. A. Pirbhai, Dorset House, 1988;
2. *Structured Development for Real-Time Systems* by P. T. Ward and S. J. Mellor, Prentice Hall, 1985;
3. *Designing Large Real-Time Systems with Ada* by K. Nielsen and K. Shumate, McGraw-Hill, 1988;
4. *Ada in Distributed Real-Time Systems* by K. Nielsen, McGraw-Hill, 1990;
5. *Notes on Layered Virtual Machines/Object Oriented Design* by B. Bardin, Hughes Aircraft Company (course material); and
6. *Software Engineering with Ada* by G. Booch, Benjamin/Cummings, 1987.

These works have been invaluable in the derivation of the methodology described in this text. They all were pioneers in developing a methodical framework. Each addresses many important aspects of real-time system development with an Ada implementation. All employ realistic case studies.

Methodical approaches in these texts proved to be useful but not sufficient for systems developed by this author. While the methodology described in this text borrows ideas heavily from these sources, both justifications and examples of use of these ideas have been developed from a different perspective. Moreover, to integrate these ideas, I have added a large number of "missing pieces." As any of these authors would most likely admit, no single methodology serves every user's purpose. Adopting appropriate pieces for integration is an explicit recognition of the value and applicability of the efforts by these authors and myself to create a workable methodology.

Methodologies for software development are usually established in order to achieve several specific goals. Perhaps the primary goal is to establish traceability from requirements to actual code. This is necessary to assure that the delivered software meets the customer's needs. An important side effect of achieving this goal is that the software is more likely to obtain real-time time performance. Traceability tends to produce minimal amounts of code. This occurs because support for traceability results in only the code necessary to meet the requirements—nothing more, nothing less.

Communications within some standard format is another goal of adopting a methodological approach. Standard formats cause software engineers to interact with each other to communicate, to justify, and to record decision processes applied during software development. A major benefit of using standard formats is the increase in development staff productivity. Time is not wasted attempting to decipher each developer's notational scheme. Common formats and products are immediately understandable by all development staff members.

Another important goal associated with methodical development processes is to transform a development organization into a "software manufacturing" facility. Internalized methodologies provide a development framework within which work on any system can be immediately started. Routine use of the same methodical framework usually means that no learning curve (for the methodology) is necessary to begin addressing a specific problem domain. As a result, short schedules can be readily met.

Recognizing the volatile environment in which modern software is developed, a methodical development process provides a framework in which flexibility is emphasized. Incorporating rapidly changing requirements with minimal effort is an important goal. Having established a development path in which specific products describe the state of the development, incorporation of new requirements is usually a simple process. Effects of new requirements are immediately apparent due to the formats of products required by the methodical development process.

Last, but not least, enforced software methodologies provide rigor, discipline, and focus to the development process. These goals are usually accomplished in the form of a sequence of steps, in which the results of each step are clearly interrelated. By emphasizing one step at a time, a methodology forces developers to concentrate on a specific aspect of the system to the exclusion of other aspects. Thus, focus and engineering discipline are obtained.

An effective software development methodology consists of a sequence of steps or actions. These steps or actions are performed in a specific order appropriate to the problem. Recognizing the fallibility of humans, the general methodical approach readily admits to the need for iteration of previous steps as subsequent steps are performed. In support of effective communications, each step encompasses a graphical and/or textual notation appropriate to the type of system or aspect of the problem under investigation. Finally, focus is provided by establishing expected results in a desired format as the result of application of each step in the methodology.

While the above elements describe mechanics associated with a methodical development process, they do not provide a complete description. These elements (a sequence of interrelated steps) compose a framework within which developers can apply their own experience. Inclusion of development experience requires several sets of heuristics (within each step and in transitioning across steps) and a mechanism for recording application of heuristics. Moreover, decisions resulting from the application of heuristics must be correlated to a common basis—a user's view of how the system is to operate. Successful application of a development methodology consists of intelligent usage of heuristics with a simultaneous view backward to a user's concept and forward to implementation issues.

Experience dictates a number of important criteria for assuring intelligent use of heuristics at each methodology step. Of course, performance impacts are a key issue in evaluating effectiveness of heuristics/guidelines. Decisions that build flexibility into the system are preferred to accommodate iterations through the methodical development process. Effects of heuristic application are carefully assessed to assure minimal integration and test effort. Incorporation of additional complexity into a system can cause heuristics to have severe variations in integration and test effort. For these reasons, guidelines and heuristics described within the text are not blindly applied. Every effort is made to extrapolate heuristic alternatives to assess the impact upon integration and test activities.

Unfortunately, methodologies are often grasped as a panacea. An understanding of exactly what a methodical approach can or can not accomplish for you is of paramount importance to obtaining its full benefits. When sufficiently internalized to the development organization and rigorously enforced, a software development methodology can usually accomplish the following:

1. Aid reliability and performance of delivered software;
2. Reduce the integration and test grind;
3. Allow designers to be more creative; and
4. Reduce effort in coding to the minimal.

In short, a well executed methodology can significantly increase the likelihood of development success, measured in terms of meeting both cost and schedule goals. Obtaining these goals is predominantly a result of the support for requirements traceability. Careful identification and traceability of requirements usually results in code whose design is optimized to meet requirements yet is flexible.

However, methodologies do have some important limitations. They can not think for a developer. Nor can a methodology replace experience in a particular application domain. In fact, lack of experience will often be highlighted when a methodology is applied. A methodology is nothing more than a rigorous framework within which developers can address problems. Their ability to successfully address problems within the framework is not guaranteed; therefore, development success is not guaranteed.

Successful application of a development methodology depends upon a number of important factors. The methodology must be rigorously followed. Its use must be internalized within the development organization, led by a small number of key individuals and followed by all other developers. The leaders must have some reasonable experience base with the problem domain. Key documents and reviews are organized around methodology products. Finally, key individuals *must be competent.*

Several important philosophies are incorporated into this methodology. Usually, software is developed according to the "big bang" approach. This essentially bottom-up methodology consists of putting software and hardware developers in a lab with instructions to start building. The approach advocated in the text, assumes that *software is a system whose global behavior must be understood.*

It also implies that a top-down, systematic approach must be employed to develop a complex, software intensive system successfully. Another important aspect of the methodology described below is that *every effort is made to determine that software works prior to implementation.*

Imparting this foundation to a methodology requires a precise dynamic aspect that is usually not incorporated into most methodologies. Finally, since real-time systems are the concern of this book, the methodology described below stresses that *developed software must meet only those requirements needed to do the user's job.*

Strong emphasis is placed upon both requirements traceability and justification of all software development decisions to support this principle.

Consistent with treating software systematically, this methodology employs a traditional model of a life-cycle—requirements, design, code and unit test, and integration and test. Experience with real-time systems has shown that this life-cycle model is extremely effective. A software engineering methodology that covers requirements and design phases is characterized in Figure 2.1. Most important, development begins by attempting to understand a typical user's needs when operating the intended combined hardware/software system. An effective Ada development methodology can be simply described in the following terms:

1. Assess what the software will have to do to meet a typical user's operational needs;
2. Determine what the software will need to do to meet those needs, based upon your experience as a developer of systems of this type;
3. Check your specified requirements against customer requirements for consistency and completeness;
4. Determine how software will do what needs to be done to meet your specified requirements;
5. Check this design against both your requirements and customer requirements for consistency and completeness;
6. Perform code and unit test on the software; and
7. Perform integration and test on the software by testing against customer requirements.

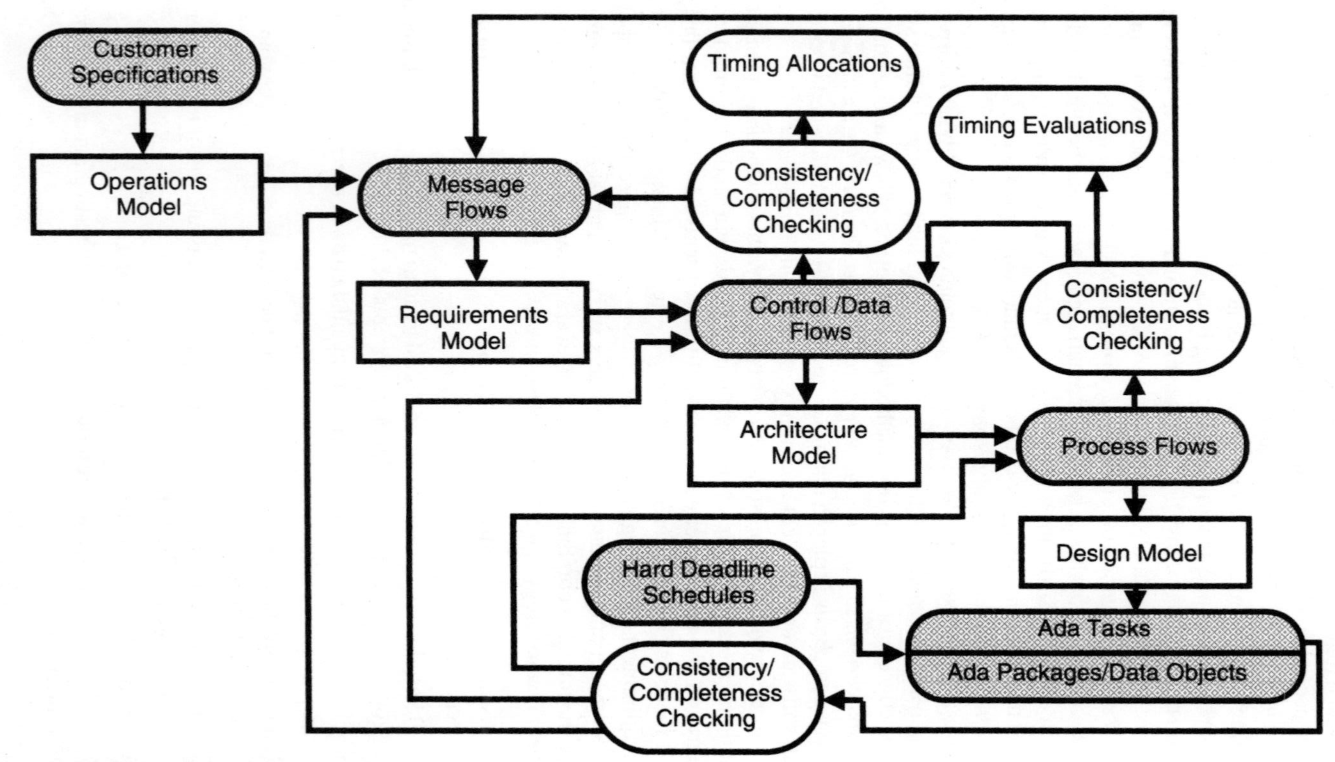

Figure 2.1 Software Engineering Methodology

While these steps may seem obvious to a reader, this approach reflects a greater life-cycle orientation than most methodologies published today. This orientation occurs because of the incorporation of several "new pieces," labeled 1, 3, 5, and 7 above. Regularly resolving consistency between any of your development activities and customer needs has been a major determinant of success in developing software intensive Ada systems with this methodology.

Initially, an operations model of the system/software is formulated (see Figure 2.2). User interface specification is delineated by a notational scheme appropriate for user-friendly interfaces. Employing an interface transition graph (ITG), one can generate a concept of user interaction and a set of messages representing that concept (translating order of operations). This message set is enhanced to represent realistic interaction with other hardware interfaces during real-time operations. A complete set of messages, called the message scenario, now represents a typical user's concept of how the system and/or software must work. These messages are listed in the order in which they occur (and, thus, each message will appear in a given context). All consistency and completeness checking described above must be accomplished against this operational message scenario.

Establishing a set of functional and control requirements that can accommodate the message scenario is an important next step. Figure 2.3 characterizes the requirements modeling step described here. Messages are first collected into a context diagram that summarizes all external interfaces. Functional decomposition is iteratively performed to generate a set of leveled and balanced data flow diagrams. By definition, a data flow is a functional transformation of one or more data flows into one or more data flows. At the lowest level of decomposition, data flow processes are specified in the form of PSPECs or process specifications. These are English-like descriptions of data transformations occurring at a primitive level.

A second pass through the data flow diagrams is accomplished to attach appropriate control flows. Control flows are defined as any data movement that requires that a decision be made (i.e., events). Many developers of real-time systems ignore control flows. Often excuses such as, "We don't need any of that control stuff," are offered. However, control flow specification is critical to successful development of real-time systems. Simply stated, control flows specify conditions under which decisions are made, the decision alternatives that are available, and effects of decisions on underlying functional processing. If these specifications are not initially detailed, individual programmers are allowed to determine system response at software implementation time. This practice can lead to several major development problems. Distributed software is difficult to debug or to integrate and test because one can not isolate and identify incorrect decision implementations. Programmers with no system awareness are not likely to make responses appropriate for a system. Experience with real-time systems has demonstrated that those systems that do not explicitly address control requirements as a first step in the development process are likely to exhibit poor performance and to require excessive and painful integration and test activity.

These last two steps—data flow and control flow generation—must reflect a developer's experience. They represent functional processing and decision making which are necessary to respond to each of the message flows presented at the

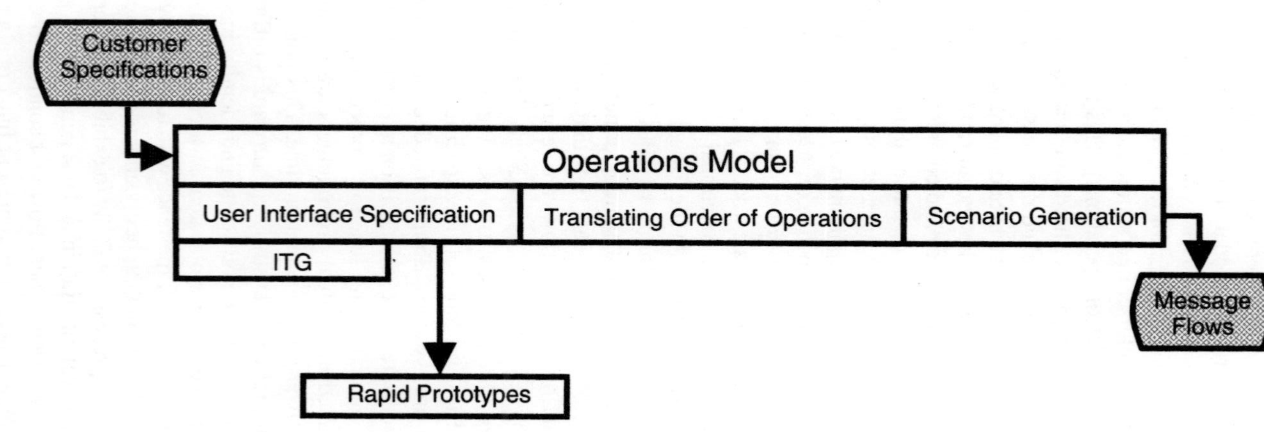

Figure 2.2 Operations Model Generation

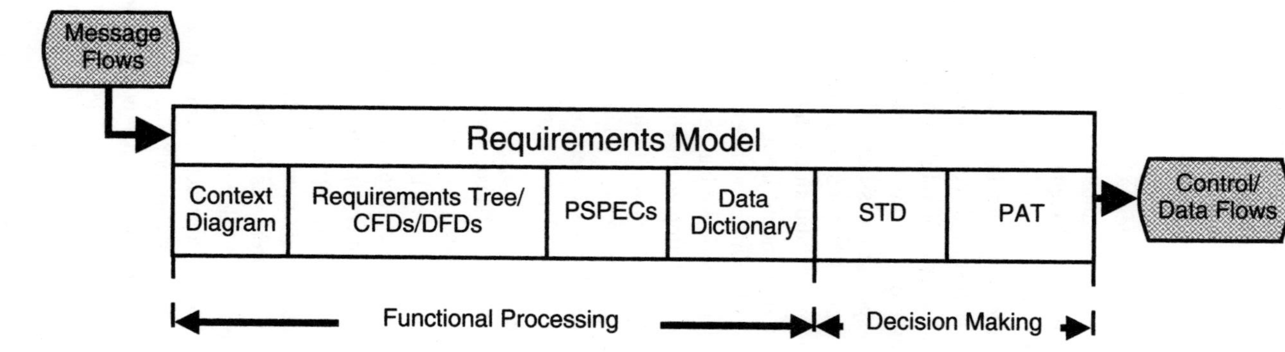

Figure 2.3 Requirements Model Generation

interface, regardless of whether a message is from a user interface or from a hardware interface. If a developer's results in accomplishing this step are vague, little or no customer confidence in the developer or the system is likely to emerge.

Much confusion regarding requirements can be eliminated if common data definitions are employed. For this reason, a data dictionary must be compiled concurrently with the above requirements specification. A formal mechanism with a general purpose language is provided to define data elements. Careful checking is accomplished to ensure that all data and control flows are uniquely defined within a common data dictionary.

Now comes the most important step. All control and data flows must be checked for consistency and completeness against the user's operational message scenario. If every message in the operational scenario leads to a consistent set of decisions and functional processing, then requirements completeness will have been demonstrated. An approach called requirements simulation, involving tracing messages in the scenario through the specified requirements, is employed and will be discussed later. An important impact of validation of requirements is enabling a developer to allocate timing requirements to functional and control flow processes, which are necessary to respond to messages. Time-line allocation from customer requirements is described and illustrated later in the text.

This process of requirements validation can have a major impact on customers and their commitment to requirements. Understanding of their use of the system is demonstrated. Application of your experience to meet their needs is accomplished. Finally, evidence that your experience has been effectively applied to determine what needs to be done by your implementation has been provided. Ultimately, proof of experience leads to customer acceptance of concrete requirements, as well as confidence in the developer. Notice that no implementation decisions have been made up to this point; the developer's system requirements have been derived from a user's operational requirements. This is significant, but usually implies no premature design on your part.

Top level design is accomplished next. Architecture model generation is summarized in Figure 2.4. An initial step is to acknowledge any requirements dictated by interacting with specific hardware interfaces. Failure to accomplish this can result in problems similar to those encountered due to lack of control specification, such as individual programmers incorrectly choosing a protocol for managing a hardware interface. Moreover, fixing an incorrect implementation can cause major design changes. Thus, requirements specification is necessary to make the transition effectively from requirements to design.

As a medium for specifying top level design, referred to as architecture, this methodology employs a process abstraction concept. Processes are defined to be system or software abstractions whose purpose is to provide a repository for requirements that must operate concurrently. Choice of an appropriate mapping from requirements to processes depends upon developer experience and the target implementation domain. A number of guidelines for translating requirements into architecture are provided later in the text. These guidelines have been derived by observing a wide range of successfully operating real-time systems. Several architectural alternatives are also formulated. These alternatives are then eval-

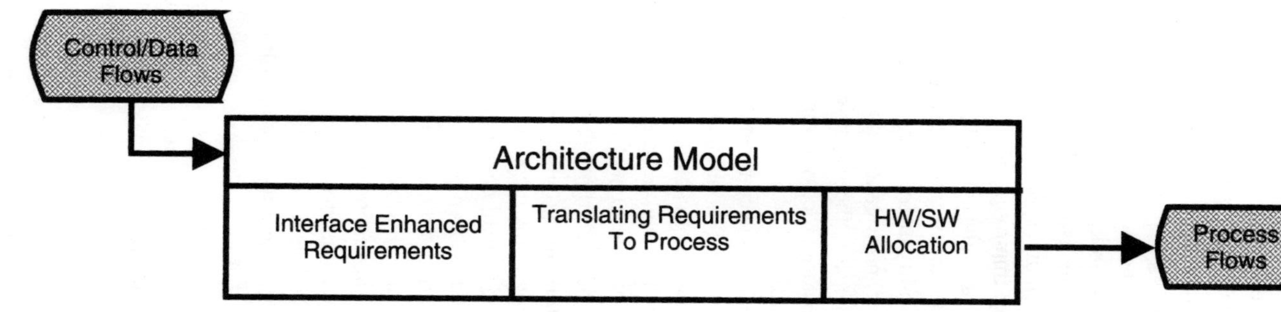

Figure 2.4 Architecture Model Generation

uated based on a set of precise criteria. An appropriate implementation architecture is then chosen.

Once a process architecture flow diagram has been generated, several levels of consistency and completeness checking must occur. First, each message in the operational message scenario is traced through all subsequent paths in the process architecture. Each design response path ends in one of two conditions—either a data store is updated or a message is generated across an external system interface. This can be a time-consuming effort, since each operational message can result in multiple data flow paths through a process architecture flow diagram. Again, however, the ultimate goal of demonstrating design consistency from a user's operational view has extensive credibility and integration and test leverage. Process invocation paths provide a mechanism for analyzing anticipated response times generated by the top level design in response to any external event. Moreover, testing threads can be generated by employing invocation paths. Examples of design timing analysis using invocation paths appear later in the text.

After demonstrating consistency and completeness against operational requirements, requirements traceability matrices are generated. In these matrices, all control and data flows and their specifications must be correlated against architecture processes. Along one dimension, these matrices clarify which requirements are satisfied by a given architecture process. From the other table dimension, unsatisfied requirements are identified.

Thus, two sets of consistency and completeness checks have been accomplished to ensure effective transition from requirements to architecture. Incorporation of a process to check architecture/design against operational message flow is a unique aspect of this methodology that makes its usage more successful. A more traditional consistency and completeness check is correlating architecture to functional and control requirements. By performing both checks, architecture credibility is obtained. Moreover, potential integration and test problems are greatly reduced, since the process invocation paths increase the probability that the architecture provides reliable end-to-end flow of data during real-time operations.

Now that an architecture has been generated, requirements within a single architectural process can be allocated between hardware and software. This allocation step is extremely critical at this point in the development process. System engineers often make process allocation decisions without explicit participation by either hardware or software engineers, resulting in cost and/or performance decisions that are suboptimal. Conscientious deliberation among system, hardware, and software engineers serves to ensure that optimal allocation decisions occur. Misconceptions such as, "Oh, that's easy to do with a little tricky software," can be eliminated if system, hardware, and software engineers meet to perform a hardware/software partitioning of requirements. If all hardware decisions have been made, of course, this allocation process can be skipped, but all of the requirements within a single architectural process must be accommodated safely by the software design.

Next, a detailed software design is produced for each architectural process. Requirements that have been allocated to software must be satisfied. As indicated in Figure 2.5, a detailed software design is first accomplished by choosing an appro-

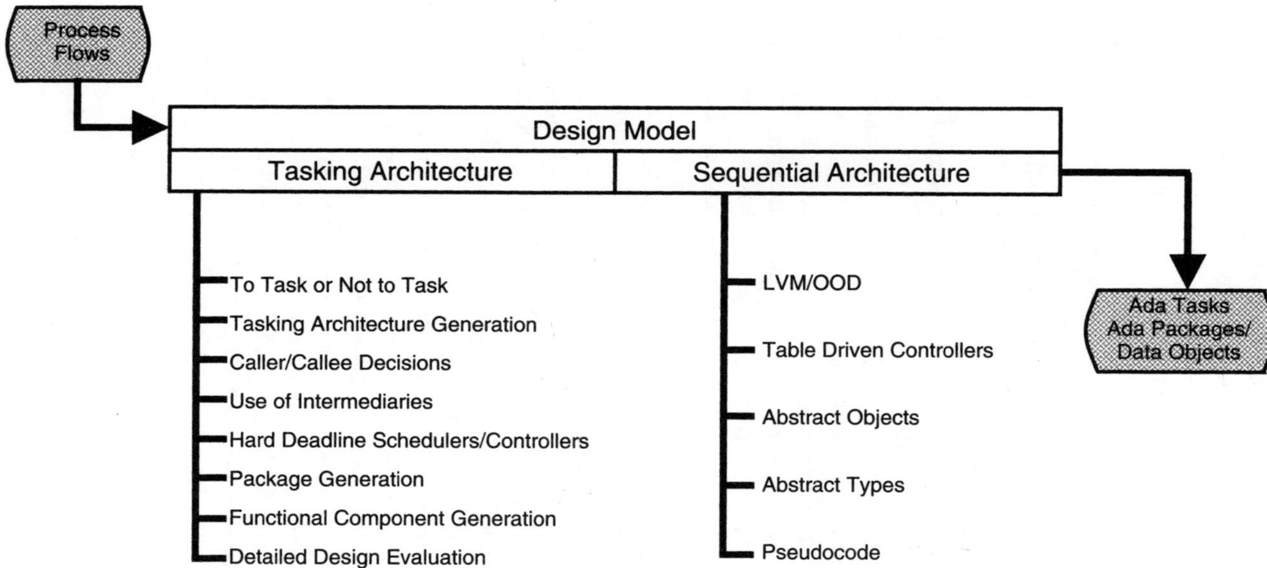

Figure 2.5 Design Model Generation

priate tasking implementation. Requirements within the architecture process are further partitioned according to the task in which they are accommodated. Determination of a specific tasking design within an architecture module requires that a number of very important decisions be explicitly made. First, each task interaction within an architectural process and across architectural processes must be assigned a caller/callee role. Second, each task interaction must be assessed as to the need for decouplers or intermediaries to eliminate or reduce potential blockage resulting from the assigned caller/callee roles (under the Ada tasking model). Unfortunately, all of these decisions interrelate at a system architecture level in a manner that can radically affect throughput. Adjustment of both sets of decisions to maximize throughput must be accomplished. Finally, if some tasks must receive CPU time periodically or aperiodically within hard deadlines, tasking design within a single architectural process must be modified to incorporate additional tasks to assure that hard deadlines will be met.

Tasks are next collected into specific packages. A number of guidelines are suggested to aid this collection process. For the most part, packaging allocations are accomplished in a manner that achieves some form of cohesion, visibility, or run-time performance. Pursuant to packaging allocation, functional components are identified within each package. These provide detailed software components for initial development and serve to identify and define specific package interfaces. A graphic depiction of detailed design ensues which is evaluated for consistency with the tasking architecture. This detailed design is also evaluated for its use of principles for a good Ada design.

Every task within an architectural process now has a set of requirements that must be met by an internal sequential software design. Generating an internal task design is accomplished by employing a layered virtual machine/object-oriented design approach (LVM/OOD). This employs stepwise refinement while identifying and extracting objects prior to each refinement of the detailed design. As the design is generated, care is exercised to record exactly which requirements are satisfied by each component.

Use of a layered virtual machine/object-oriented design approach for sequential software design leads directly to pseudocode for those detailed design constructs that were generated. Generated pseudocode consists of compilable and executable Ada. Compilation forces evaluation of syntax and type conventions at interfaces. Execution requires each pseudocoded element to print an appropriate message upon entry. As a result, the detailed design is translated into an operational description. If pseudocode is executed in response to an operations message scenario, its execution demonstrates that the attendant detailed design can meet a typical user's intended operational needs.

As development is taking place, concurrent documentation must be generated. If your customer is the U.S. Department of Defense, documentation describing software requirements, preliminary design, and detailed design must typically be in accordance with DoD-STD 2167A. A careful review of the chapter headings and guidelines for chapter contents reveals that 2167A requires much of the same information generated by rigorous application of this methodology. Therefore, while the mechanics of document generation may be tedious, collecting necessary technical data is not difficult at all.

This methodical approach is emphasized in the traceability of requirements into code. User interface requirements are traced into an operations message scenario. Message scenario needs are correlated to control and data flow requirements. These requirements are assigned to architecture processes and allocated between hardware and software within each process. Software requirements within an architecture process are further subdivided among tasks and to sequential software components within each task. Requirements satisfied by each sequential software design construct are thus correlated to objects and types implemented by Ada packages and finally to pseudocode. Executable pseudocode is then employed to correlate detailed design back to operation message scenarios. Thus, the goal of requirements traceability is accomplished.

Several secondary effects are obtained by rigorous application of this methodical process. One is that Ada provides excellent support for implementing an architecture and design, significantly reducing code and unit test schedules. Another important effect is that integration and test difficulties are significantly reduced. Discovered errors are easily fixed, since methodical development combined with employment of Ada design constructs localizes the effect of code changes. Finally, incorporation of changing or newly discovered requirements is accomplished by continued rigorous application of this methodical approach.

For real-time systems, steps in the development process are typically followed in exactly the order indicated. Specifically, event response specification and concurrency and tasking determination usually precede object identification. Attempting to reverse this process is a sure formula for disaster during integration and test and during operations. Hiding event response specification under objects leads to programmers choosing event responses at code implementation time. Distributed response to events may cause systems to malfunction with no indication as to why a problem has occurred. In fact, distributed response at implementation often leads to Fortran-like designs in which one can not tell exactly how a system will respond or what events have not been anticipated in the design. Incorporation of tasks within objects as an afterthought leads to individual programmers making decisions regarding task usage and task interaction. Failure to elevate tasking architecture to a system level activity often leads to significant throughput degradation and potential disaster due to extensive internal blocking. Thus, to develop a real-time system methodically in Ada, one must develop in a manner that elevates system level issues to a more appropriate level. This philosophy—to treat software as a system that exhibits behavior—is the basic foundation for the steps employed in this methodology. Validity of this approach has been demonstrated by successful delivery of real-time Ada systems rigorously developed according to the methodology.

2.3 METHODOLOGY USAGE GUIDELINES

A real-time system, as envisioned here, possesses a number of important characteristics, all of which are important in driving the steps in the methodology. These characteristics are:

1. User interaction is limited. Typically, a user puts a system into some operational state or mode. Then the system performs autonomously from the user until a new state or mode is indicated;
2. Autonomous operation employs sensors and actuators. Sensors collect raw data that must be analyzed to effect regular operation. Actuators provide control of raw data collectors and usually cause physical activity to occur;
3. Sensors and actuators generate events that require responses. These events may occur synchronously (at regular intervals) or asynchronously (at random intervals);
4. Event responses are time constrained. For real-time systems, event response must occur within microseconds or milliseconds;
5. Events occur at interfaces that must be managed according to some specific operational protocol;
6. Event responses require extensive analysis of sensor data;
7. Event responses do not require extensively indexed and correlated data structures; and
8. Interfaces have been sufficiently specified to be represented as digital data.

These characteristics dictate elements employed within the detailed methodology as well as specific sequencing and ordering of steps. Specific event patterns must be formally characterized. Event responses must be clear, concise, and visible. Synchronous and asynchronous accommodation of multiple sensors and interfaces that provide incoming data in any form must reflect how concurrency is employed within the design. Simple data structures must be effectively encapsulated under objects.

No assertions or claims are made concerning applicability of this development methodology to data intensive systems. Development within this latter class of systems is dominated by an extensive data structure. A detailed indexing scheme is established above the data structure, which also happens to be distributed across a complex network. For the most part, minimal data management needs are associated with systems addressed using the described methodology. At best, encapsulation of data structures totally stored within memory must be accomplished.

Four major phases of methodical order are employed. These phases include the following:

1. **Operations model:** translate customer requirements into message flows and test input/output pattern;

2. **Requirements model:** generate control and data flows necessary to support message flows and test input/output pattern;
3. **Architecture model:** identify process flows and interconnections that satisfy control and data flows; and
4. **Design model:** determine detailed software components—tasks and packages—that perform control and data flows within each process.

These steps need to be performed in this order, with iteration and feedback, of course. Multiple projects have demonstrated the effectiveness of this sequence for real-time systems.

Any experienced developer knows that software developments do not occur within a perfect world. As concurrent hardware development proceeds, additional requirements are generated. Steps within software development activities also yield changes to requirements. For complex systems, an incremental development approach is often employed, leading to additional requirements facing the developer. Evolving requirements are a fact of life. To successfully develop within a changing requirements basis, *a rigorous development methodology must be employed.*

By establishing a rigorous framework with specific output products, evolving requirements can be readily factored into the developed system. Moreover, a methodological framework allows an incremental development strategy that controls the number of "development variables" currently affecting development activities. This reduces the risks associated with normal developments, increasing the likelihood of success.

Application of this methodology has been successfully applied in an iterative fashion, which reduces development risk. Initially, a complete iteration leads to implementation of a version of the system that performs end-to-end data flow under normal, routine operations for the simplest mode of operation. End-to-end data flow guarantees the behavioral integrity of the integrated system. All future iterations build on this integrity. The level of detail is maintained in such a way that one person can conceptually grasp software system behavior through operations, requirements, architecture, and design models.

Subsequent iterations add processing algorithms associated with the simplest mode, introduce error recovery mechanisms, and optimize performance. Finally, algorithms for complex modes of operation are integrated into the basic operational system.

Most developments make the mistake of targeting a fully functional deployment with the first increment. This strategy incorporates too many "development variables," which can not be effectively controlled and result in an integration and test grind. As a result, schedules are missed and cost overruns result. Intelligent iteration is the key to project success. Emphasis upon end-to-end data flow for routine operations is a basis for initial deployment, since this guarantees an operational system. Iteration can best be accomplished within the framework of a methodical development process. Additional requirements are easily incorporated into the system.

Many developers who use a methodology often still experience development problems. Typically, this results from improper emphasis upon sensor processing algorithms, to the exclusion of more critical system issues. Proper application of a methodology emphasizes issues that ease hardware and software integration. Details of sensor processing algorithms need not be incorporated until end-to-end control processing has been established and integrated into target hardware.

A word of caution is offered to the practitioner who intends to employ this methodology. While steps and heuristics described in later chapters have been successfully employed on multiple projects, *do not treat this methodology as a religion.* Performing the steps in the prescribed order while applying indicated heuristics improves the likelihood of development success. However, methodical development does not and should not be interpreted as the blind application of a set of memorized rules. Systems that have benefited from use of this methodology have done so because of two important constraints: the systems have fit within the class characteristics described earlier; and applications of heuristics to make important decisions are carefully evaluated with respect to performance, integration and test effort, etc. Please think your way through the use of this methodology.

An important implication of non-religious application is to acquire an ego-less approach to software system engineering. Recognize that initial versions of methodology formatted products serve to gain consensus, provide feedback, and focus discussions on critical issues. Do not be defensive. Accept constructive criticism. Listen to comments and reviews. Iterate, iterate, iterate. . .

While the methodology appears to be straightforward, its application to a specific problem requires a number of key decisions. Initially, software specification begins with an effective selection of system interfaces/boundaries. Characterization of data and control flows across these boundaries implies an ability to choose a correct level of abstraction. A software system is not concerned with thousands of physical nodes. From an abstract perspective, physical locations are best represented as sources and destinations within a control flow at the system interfaces.

Each of the steps in the methodology involves decisions regarding the appropriate application of concurrency. Failure to include concurrency during requirements generation may not be disastrous, if concurrency usage is accurately reflected in the architecture or detailed software design.

Generating a complete set of control specifications involves specification of at least one state machine. At the heart of state machine generation is identification of an appropriate set of states. Incorrect selection of states leads to incorrect specification of decision conditions and responses. Simply describing the number of concurrent elements is not sufficient.

Another important aspect of methodology application is the establishment of a control hierarchy in a manner that limits the complexity of interaction among concurrent components.

From a life-cycle perspective, adopting a view of software as a system that exhibits a specific behavior implies a number of important considerations. Approaches are adopted that support an incremental development approach consistent with the suggested iterative application of the methodology. All approaches and alternatives must consciously balance satisfaction of a user's operational requirements against the ultimate level of integration and test effort. Cost, effectiveness, and risk need to be employed when balancing the user's needs against integration efforts. Software system engineering requires the ability to step above the system and to focus upon the interactions of key elements from an operational perspective. This is a new perspective with very few experienced practitioners.

3

Operations Model Generation

A necessary first step in developing an effective real-time Ada system is to capture a users perspective when describing system operations. Two levels of user view are needed. First, an exact representation of user interfaces is made. Typically, however, a real-time system has hardware interfaces that are controlled through the user interfaces. These interfaces take the form of sensors and actuators. Both views (user and hardware interfaces) must be specified and integrated into a consistent picture. Ultimately, this integrated view (user interfaces and sensors/actuators) becomes the criteria against which all requirements and design are measured.

In Figure 3.1, a detailed representation that describes an operations model generation is provided. Some form of customer specification is employed as a basis for operations model determination. Unfortunately, customer specifications typically consist of a combination of requirements, design, constraints and limitations, and a long list of useless information. Extensive review and culling are necessary to sift information needed to initiate development of an operations model.

Initially, a user interface specification is generated in the form of an interface transition graph (ITG). By rapid prototyping or analysis, this interface specification is translated into an order of operations. Using the order of operations as a basis, a detailed operational scenario that employs all the interfaces managed by the real-time system is generated. An operational scenario describes a sequence of message flows that characterize the systemic behavior of the software.

Message flows, or event/response sequences, represent a precise time-ordered description of how the system is to work, based on commands by the user. This time ordered sequence of events is critical to development success and is used for several levels of testing—implementor requirements, top level design, detailed design, software unit testing, and subsystem operational testing.

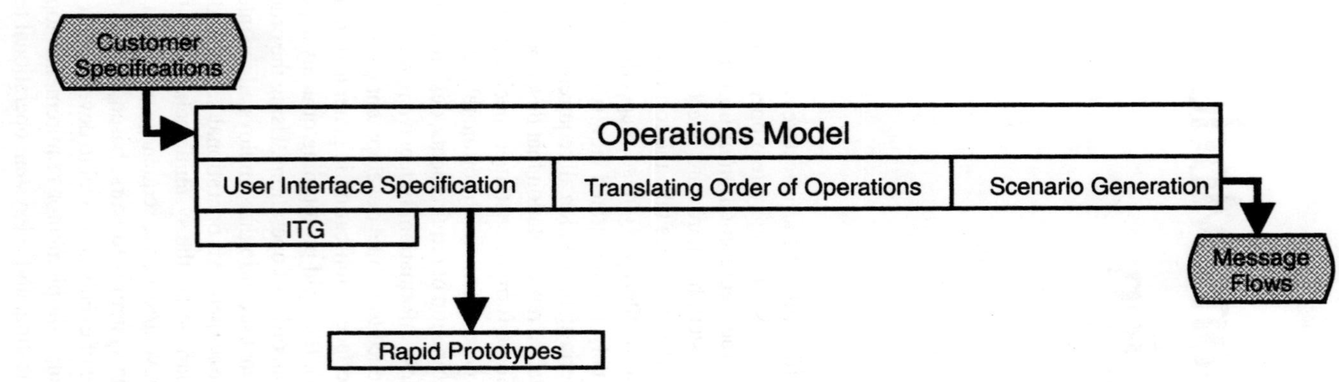

Figure 3.1 Operations Model Generation

Specifying a user's view of software system operations consists of the following steps:

1. Specify user interfaces and order of operation of user interaction;
2. Translate order of operation of user interaction into an initial message sequence;
3. Expand the message sequence into detailed operational scenarios involving sensors, actuators, and other interfaces; and
4. Divide the detailed message sequence into an event/response pattern indicating inputs and outputs.

Each of these steps involves specific products in specific formats. Of particular importance is the test input/output pattern of events/responses, which is the basis for evaluation of all subsequent development activities.

3.1 USER INTERFACE SPECIFICATION

Users feel most comfortable with a set of requirements if these can be demonstrated to start with their own interface to the real-time system. For this reason, specification of a detailed user interface is initially accomplished. Clear and unambiguous specification of the user interface obtains several important goals: Insures that a consistent and complete interface will be provided to the user of the real-time system; a framework that is employed to initially formulate a behavioral view of the software system is generated; and users can obtain a "look and feel" introduction to the system when the interface is rapidly prototyped.

Consistency of the user interface is accomplished by employing a specification approach which demonstrates that all components are used for the same purpose in any given context. This usually translates to insuring that specific mouse buttons (or keys) are used for the same purpose all the time. As an example, a user interface specification would identify that the left mouse button is used to allow a user to change his mind on one screen, while the right mouse button is being employed to accomplish the same purpose on a different screen. This condition represents an inconsistency in the user interface and needs to be corrected.

User interface completeness is obtained by demonstrating how the specification responds to a typical user's invocation of that interface during regular system operations. To accomplish this, one needs to formulate a set of user interactions within a typical operational session. Then, these interactions are traced through the user interface specification to assure that responses to the interaction sequence are adequate and complete.

Comparison of user interfaces over a large number of real-time systems demonstrates that several important components are typically employed. Menus allow users to select from among a set of predefined choices. Dialogs are necessary to provide a means whereby a user can specify one or more required pieces of data. During real-time operations, both graphics and textual displays are directly driven by incoming data or indirectly created by analysis results derived from incoming data. An appropriate set of graphical notations appears in Figure 3.2. This illustration provides symbols for menus, dialogs, display, and for labeling transitions among user interface components.

Dynamic effects resulting from specific user interaction are indicated with a transition labeling convention. Transition labels employ an element for indicating a specific user choice and an element for describing the response induced prior to transition to a new interface element. Effective specification of a user interface requires that both interface elements and responses to user interactions be clearly characterized with this notational scheme.

Application of these symbols to specify a user interface suggests a number of useful guidelines. When specifying a user interface, freely intermix menus, dialogs, and displays. Take care to specify appropriate transitions among user interface elements for every possible interaction with a single element. Label each transition with a choice/action specification. As this process is performed, you will usually generate a complex specification.

To avoid excessive complexity in a single user interface specification diagram, a decomposition approach is employed. Decomposition assumes a hierarchical concept in the evolution and use of a user interface. Most user friendly interfaces, in fact, exhibit this hierarchical structure. (Can you think of the last time a user friendly interface wasn't hierarchical in nature?) When decomposing a user interface specification to its lower level components, take care to assure that the decomposed specifications are appropriately balanced. Balancing means that all choice/action specifications in the parent interface transition specification must occur in the child decomposition specification.

Evaluation of this detailed specification is accomplished by deriving an implied order of operations. This operational order describes a set of selected interfaces and choices that demonstrate how a typical user would navigate through the interface, as specified. Each choice in the order of operations is directly applied to the user interface specification. Careful records are maintained indicating the transition that occurred and the response that was induced. Completeness is obtained if every interaction in the order of operations leads to an appropriate transition to a new interface element and leads to a response that makes sense to the user.

An extremely effective approach to evaluating the order of operations is to implement it within a rapid prototyping environment (such as HyperCard). In fact, the prototyped interface can be programmed to record choices made by the user as he navigates through the prototype. Recorded choices form the order of operations. Application of the steps in the order of operations to the specified interface quickly confirm or deny the completeness of the specified user interface. Failure to respond to each interaction in the order of operations identifies shortcomings in the interface specification. An iterative process consisting of updating the specification (and order of operations) and reevaluating for completeness is accomplished to refine the interface transition graph.

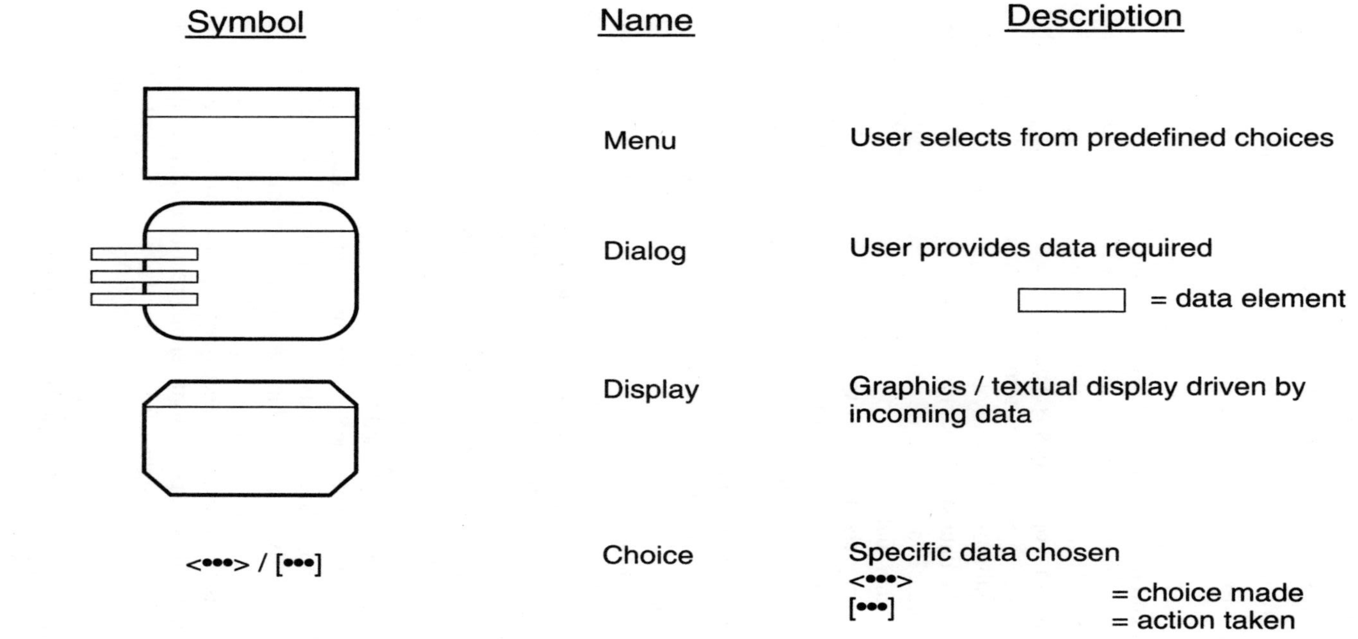

Symbol
Name
Description
Menu
User selects from predefined choices
Dialog
User provides data required
= data element
Display
Graphics / textual display driven by incoming data
<•••> / [•••]
Choice
Specific data chosen
<•••>
[•••]
= choice made
= action taken

Figure 3.2 User Interface Specification Notation

An example of a user interface specification for a typical real-time system appears in Figure 3.3. Initially, a user is presented with a menu (the user interface). Four choices are available at this level:

1. Parameter Database Access—another menu;
2. Initialize Real-Time Operations—a sequence of dialogs;
3. Control Real-Time Operations—a combined graphics/text display; and
4. Quit—exit the real-time application.

Selection of any of these choices has an associated action and a transition to some new component of the specified user interface.

If a user chooses to Initialize Real-Time Operations, then an action is performed that is characterized as Invoke Parameter Set Query. After an appropriate set of internal operations is performed, a dialog is displayed that requires a user to provide a specific data item named Parameter Set Name. Furthermore, a user may employ the <esc> key to change his mind and must indicate final acceptance of the data value provided by pressing the <F10> key. Depressing the <F10> key causes a response described as "Save and Continue" and causes transition to another dialog.

A consistency check against this portion of the specification reveals that the <esc> key is consistently employed to allow a user to change his mind. Additionally, <F10> always means that an input has been accepted and will be permanently stored until needed at a later time. Inconsistent use of <esc> and <F10> in the dialogs would be revealed now. Moreover, developers of subsequent interfaces now employ the same conventions, since specific usage roles for <esc> and <F10> have been specified.

As one can easily see, any more information than already included would only serve to confuse a reviewer. To include additional details, decompositions are appropriate. Only two candidates are available for decomposition within this typical user interface specification. One element entitled Parameter Database Access is indicated to consist of a menu. Thus, this element is a prime candidate for decomposition. Another candidate is the graphics/textual display indicated by the icon labeled Operations Display.

As an example of an appropriate decomposition, Figure 3.4 is included. Balancing is appropriately performed by inclusion of the transitions employed to enter into and exit from the interface. These entry and exit transitions are labeled <Control RT Ops> and <^S>, respectively. Corresponding choice/action transition labels appear exactly as specified in the parent diagram above.

Note the existence of feedback loops within this decomposition example. These feedback transitions occur as a necessary condition to indicate when and how displays are updated in response to incoming real-time data. In this example, as raw sensor data is provided at the hardware interfaces, a user interface must respond by insuring that raw data is displayed and that the combined graphic/textual operations display is updated to reflect both raw data and analytical results. A feedback loop indicates that these responses do, in fact, occur as described.

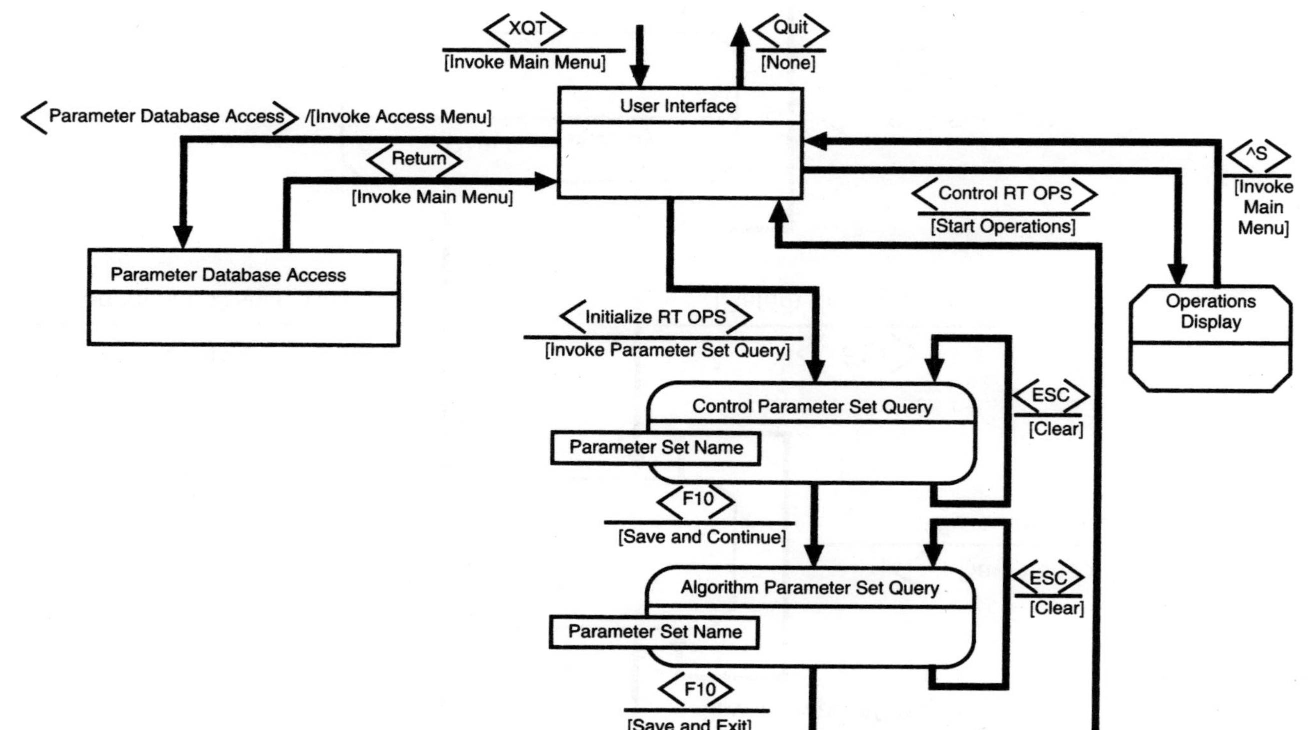

Figure 3.3 Typical User Interface Specification

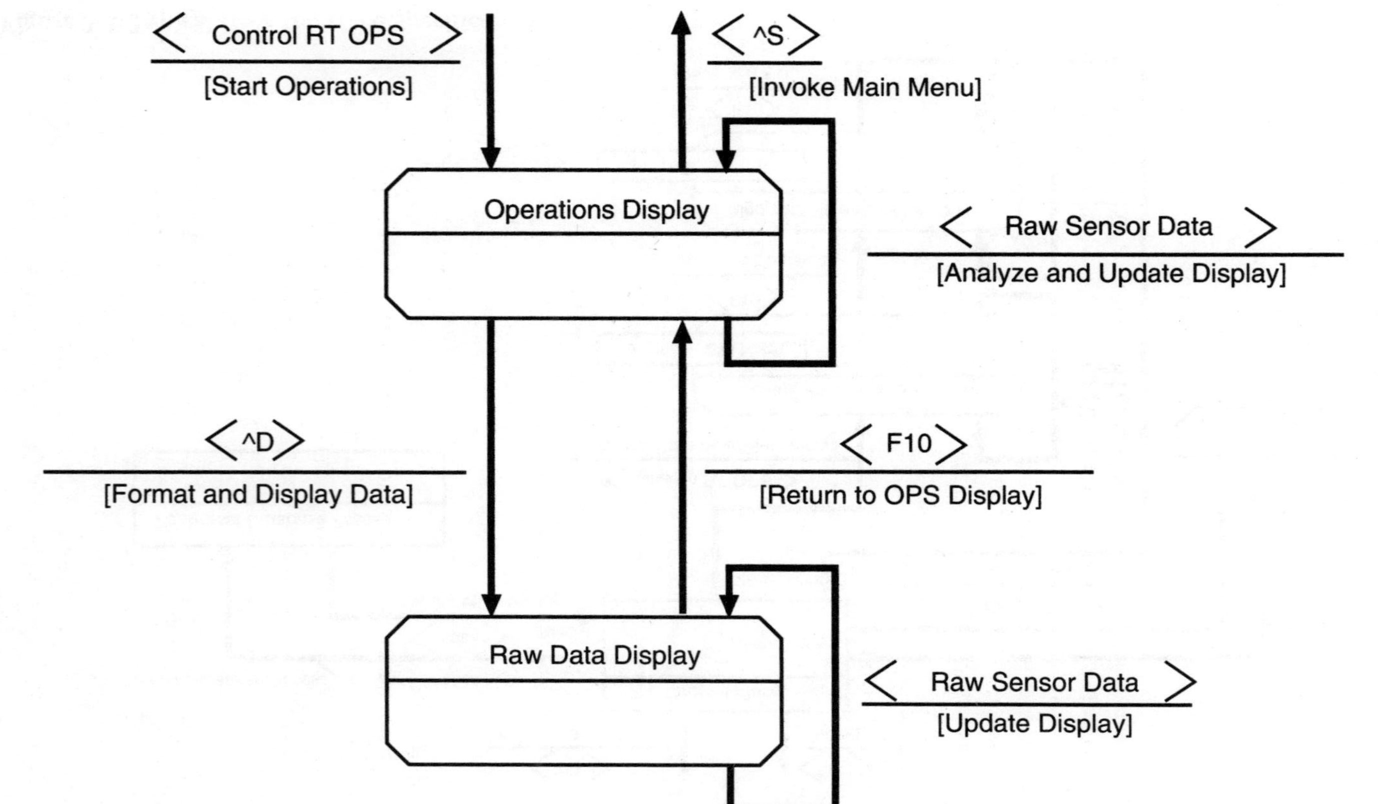

Figure 3.4 User Interface Specification Decomposition

Use of a hot key is also demonstrated in this decomposed specification. When the user presses <^D>, a response that formats and displays raw data occurs. Transition to a completely textual display, Raw Data Display, is specified. As new raw sensor data is introduced at the hardware interfaces, this new data must be employed to update the display. A feedback transition exists to assure that this response occurs.

A detailed screen layout is associated with each element in the user interface specification. Screen layouts normally include a precisely formatted picture of the actual screen contents. All features of the screen are carefully drawn in detail, along with textual descriptions of the contents of each screen. Use of colors and icons is highly recommended, as is review of screen descriptions by a human factors engineer. This helps eliminate busy screens and conflicting colors. All user interfaces should be designed to be aesthetically pleasing, easy to use, and understandable.

Once the user interfaces and transitions have been constructed, an implied order of operations is to be derived, which specifies a sequence of user interactions with the interfaces that have been characterized. Elements of an order of operations include menu selection choices, dialog data entries, and specific chosen values (demonstrating transition among interfaces). Once derived, this order of operations is applied to the user interface specification to assure that a complete specification has been accomplished. Moreover, verification of the order by a group of users is essential. Later steps in the methodology assume that the implied order of operations accurately reflects the manner in which a typical user employs the specified interface. If user verification has not been accomplished, later activities in the development process will be invalid.

An example of an implied order of operations for a typical real-time system appears in Figure 3.5. Two distinct and separate phases of user interaction are represented. During non real-time operations, a user employs the interface to build databases of control parameters or to generate sets of algorithm parameters. Control parameters are necessary to feed tables that represent distributed hardware configurations, event response logic, routing information, etc. Algorithm parameters are employed in the process of evaluating incoming sensor data. These parameters might include such elements as error bounds, statistical decision trees, iteration limits, etc.

The second phase is the entry into and exit from real-time operations. This involves selecting appropriate prestored control and algorithm set parameters, switching back and forth between analysis results displays and raw data displays, and employing hot keys to exit from real-time display updating.

Initiation of non real-time operations begins by user invocation of the user friendly interface (hence, the appearance of <XQT>). From the main menu, the user chooses to enter the parameter database access menu. Within this submenu, a user then opens the databases, chooses between control or algorithm parameter database accesses, and selects a database function (<Add>, <Delete>, or <Update>). Database activities require selections from among menu options. Choosing between control and algorithm parameter access requests the user provides data via a dialog. After a series of dialogs necessary to acquire data for the chosen database function, the database is closed via another appropriate menu choice. Verification of database contents is accomplished by selecting a menu option to dump the whole database (in a predefined textual report format). Finally, a menu choice allows return to the main menu.

Real-time operations are entered by choosing to initialize real-time operations from the main menu. According to the prototypical real-time user interface specification in Figure 3.3, this choice is the transition to a dialog that requires the user to provide a control parameter set name, followed by invocation of the function key <F10>. This results in transition to another dialog, which repeats the same actions for solicitation of an algorithm parameter set name. Final entry of the acceptance key (<F10>) returns the user to the main menu.

Entry into real-time display updating is accomplished by deciding to control real time operations from the main menu. This choice leads to a combined textual/graphics screen displaying combined raw sensor data and analysis results (for example, symbolic target boxes overlayed on infrared imagery). The real-time display is regularly updated as new sensor data and new analysis results are received by the underlying processing system (and, hence, the feedback loop described in the discussion of Figure 3.4). At any time, a user can display raw sensor data simply by employing a hot key (<^D>). Return to the analysis results display requires use of <F10>. After successful operation, use of the stop display hot key <^S> returns the user to the main menu. Selection of the quit item on the main menu leads the user to exit from the interface.

Users who review this analysis come to feel that the developer understands the user's needs. Since the order of operations is a primary step that influences the remainder of system specification and design, this analysis and subsequent review assures that the developer has a relevant and accurate starting point for further development. A careful review of the previous analysis indicates conditions under which problems can occur. For example, a user must initialize real-time operations by identifying parameter set names before going into operational display activities. Thus, an excellent candidate for error recovery has been identified. In fact, a hook has been provided for this error checking. In Figure 3.3, a transition labeled <Control RT Ops> has an associated event [Start Operations]. A careful definition of [Start Operations] indicates that a check needs to be made to assure that both control and algorithm parameter set names have been initialized.

Additionally, a characterizing order of operations helps to assure that integration and test activities will not be extremely painful exercises. This analysis is the first step in providing both development requirements and testing criteria. If requirements, design, and testing are accomplished in the same order, then integration and test activities will proceed quite smoothly. All activities are calibrated to the user's view. When a user finally does employ both the system and the user interface, surprises should not occur. User satisfaction is likely to result.

Nonreal Time	Real Time
<XQT>	<Initialize RT Ops>
<Parameter DB access>	<F10> (Control parameter set query)
<Open DB>	<F10> (Algorithm parameter set query)
<Choose control or agorithm parameters>	
<Access DB>	<Control RT Ops>
<Add>	<^D> (Display raw data)
<Update>	<F10> (Return to ops display)
<Delete>	
<Close DB>	<^S> (Stop displaying)
<Dump DB>	<Quit>
<Return>	

Figure 3.5 Implied Order of Operations

3.2 TRANSLATING ORDER OF OPERATIONS

As a first step in generating a message flow sequence, the implied order of operations must be converted to a sequence of events. Each action performed by the user is assessed for possible translation into a specific input event at the system interfaces. Not every user action in the derived order of operations translates to an event. Those user interactions that do translate into events are recorded; order of occurrence is maintained. This is necessary to establish a time-ordered basis for subsequent message flows.

Initially, four user events provided a basis for message flows. From the analysis in Section 3.1, recall that a user initializes real-time operations, controls real-time operations, stops the real-time display via a hot key, and exits the interface. Each of these events has been represented by an appropriate message flow in Figure 3.6. For example, an event to control real-time operations has been translated to a message flow named <user_commands> with an argument initialized to "operational." The order of the four <user_commands> messages is exactly the same order required by the implied order of operations example. Thus, the time-ordered basis of the event sequence is effectively established.

3.3 OPERATIONS SCENARIO GENERATION

Operations scenario generation consists of identifying system boundaries and generating a dynamic, behavioral picture of messages flowing across those boundaries. Messages can flow into the software system (incoming events) or out from the software system (outgoing responses or events). For precise characterization of user needs, a test input/output pattern is generated that describes a time ordered sequence of events and immediate responses.

During actual real-time operations, system activity occurs in response to specific events. These events represent the manner in which external interfaces interact with the real-time system to be developed. Some of the events are generated via user interactions (specified in the previous section). Other events result from continuous operation of a set of one or more data collectors (referred to as sensors), which provide raw data for the real-time system. Responses to each event may involve commanding one or more actuators to assure some specific physical activity. Events and precise responses are carefully and thoroughly characterized.

Event characterization describes the order in which events and responses happen. Thus, each event has a specific context of occurrence. This context consists of events which have occurred before, events which may occur after, and the status of analytical results which have been partially or fully determined. Specification of anticipated responses is also necessary. At this stage, contents of the messages (events/responses) are not of particular interest. Order and sequencing of events and corresponding responses is extremely important. Events/responses which occur during real-time operations are described in the form of message flows. Operational scenario generation is the process of generating a series of message flows. Message flows consist of a sequence of events, followed by appropriate responses representing information flow across the interfaces to the system being developed. Sequences/message flows are specified in a time-ordered sequence consistent with user interactions with the system. Both incoming events and outgoing responses are to be captured in the message flows. Message flows (time ordered, event/response patterns) are critical to the remaining development activities. They represent a concise formulation of the user's view of system operations and will be extensively employed to evaluate all future activities accomplished by the developer.

Message flow generation begins with the implied order of operation described for the user interface specification. Each user interaction has been translated into a message at the system interface. In response to user interaction events, other external interfaces are operated by the real-time system. Data collectors, activity effectors, and other interfaces provide both periodic and aperiodic data flows at the boundaries to the system. These flows are now incorporated into the initial set of message flows derived from the implied order of operation. Accuracy of time-ordered sequencing is of paramount importance when augmenting the initial flows. Augmentation of the initial message set generated by user interaction proceeds by determining events and responses associated with other interfaces which both precede and follow a user interaction event. Moreover, preceding and following events and responses must somehow be controlled by the user interaction events. Remember to include appropriate outgoing responses immediately after each incoming event.

User Interface Interaction	Control Event
<Initialize RT Ops>	<User_Commands> = Power Up
<Control RT Ops>	<User_Commands> = Operational Mode
<^S> (Stop Displaying)	<User_Commands> = Standby
<Quit>	<User_Commands> = Power Down

Figure 3.6 Translation of Implied Order of Operations into Events

For an actual real-time system, event sequences occur as parallel time-lines. Representation of parallel operations as a single, time-ordered event sequence is an artifice. This representation is conceptually easier for the customer/user to understand. If carefully constructed, no serious impacts upon integration and test or software integrity is usually experienced.

As one can easily imagine, this step can become very complex. For even a small real-time system, literally thousands of message flows can be appropriate. Some guidelines in accomplishing this process are helpful. Where appropriate, identify major subsequences of message flows. If hundreds of messages can be abstracted as a sequence of six or eight messages, then this abstracted sequence is employed (rather than the hundreds of messages). Focus on critical or important message sequences rather than all message sequences. Adding non-critical sequences later is easy. Specify as many variations of critical sequences as can be described. Again, emphasize critical variations only. Do *not* attempt at this stage to determine every possible sequence and all possible variations of sequences. In fact, components of message sequence generation are maintained consistent with the iterative application of the methodology. Initially, a time-ordered message sequence that represents end-to-end flow of data under routine operations for the simplest operational mode is generated. As other methodical iterations are performed, additional message flows reflect the specific goals of the iteration in progress. Appropriate selection of events and responses is a key leverage item easing the transition from concept to implementation. All future activities are to be correlated to these event sequences.

Scenario generation employs two specific diagrammatic notations. An external interface diagram shows all external devices employed by the real-time system. A user interface appears as one of the interfaces on this diagram. Now, however, data collectors and action effectors are incorporated into the diagram. Actual data flows need not be illustrated. Interfaces are simply being identified. Identification of interfaces must occur before data flows can be generated. This diagram is employed as a guide to evaluate message flows.

A second notational component of the scenario is the message flow table itself. Each message is characterized as to type, source and destination. Each message also has an attached description that justifies the appearance of the message in the message sequence. Justification places the message in its proper context from the user's perspective. Sources and destination appear on the external interface diagram so that an evaluator can physically trace the message flows while reading the message justification. Messages flowing into the system and responses moving out of the system are included in the message sequence. Messages appear in the table in a time-ordered sequence, consistent with user interaction events.

Generation of an external interface diagram begins with identification of the interfaces to the software system. Developers often complain about a significant lack of agreement as to the interfaces. In order to proceed, *interfaces must be identified.* Effective identification of interfaces is an essential component for assuring a smooth transition during integration and test activities. If system interfaces are not formalized, software architects are encouraged to take the initiative. Specify a set of interfaces. Record and publish your selected interfaces for review. Proceed with the methodical development process, assuming your published interfaces are appropriate. However, *do not proceed to implementation without a formally selected set of interfaces.*

Upon publication of formalized interfaces, compare the real interfaces with those you specified. If there are no difficulties, proceed with your development. However, if differences appear, some negotiation may be necessary to change the published interfaces. You may be able to convert data in the actual interfaces to data needed within your interfaces. Or, your interface definition might need to be modified. Any changes in assumed interfaces typically modify the external interface diagram and necessitate regeneration of message flows. All other methodology analyses must also be updated. If the methodology is being vigorously applied, reflecting modified interfaces is not particularly difficult to accomplish.

Once an external interface diagram is generated, the message flow table is initially populated with user interaction events. Resultant events preceding and following user interactions are then added to the event table, based on the external interface diagram. Time-ordered sequencing *must* be maintained. Repetition of an event/response pattern or a sequence of patterns is indicated by employing an ellipsis (. . .). Subsequences and combinations of subsequences are further incorporated into the table as detailed understanding of system operation evolves.

An operational scenario for a typical real-time system appears in Figure 3.7. After the operational mode message, two types of message flows can occur. Raw sensor data is provided by one or more data collectors which operate synchronously. These events occur at regular time intervals, totally under the control of each individual data collector in the system. In response to incoming raw sensor data, several outgoing responses occur. Sensor data is echoed to the user interface for live data display. Data analysis commands are packaged to the data analyzer for application of statistical algorithms to the raw sensor data. In this situation, two specific responses (sensor data echo, data analysis command) are generated for a single event_raw sensor data. Analysis results determined by processing algorithms are received as results are determined. Since the time to analyze raw data is usually dependent upon contents of the raw data, these analysis event results occur aperiodically. Based upon analysis results, actuator commands are generated and transmitted to physical devices which are being controlled (such as turrets). Additionally, a message is transmitted to the user interface to inform the user of the results. Again, multiple responses are suggested for a single event. Therefore, a typical subsequence during real-time operations is a raw sensor data event, with responses, followed by a position/velocity data event (results from analyzing raw data) and associated responses. An integrated representation of user event messages, data collector messages, analysis results messages and actuator commands is generated in accurate, time-ordered sequence in Figure 3.7. Ellipses are employed to indicate repeated occurrence of the major operational mode subsequences.

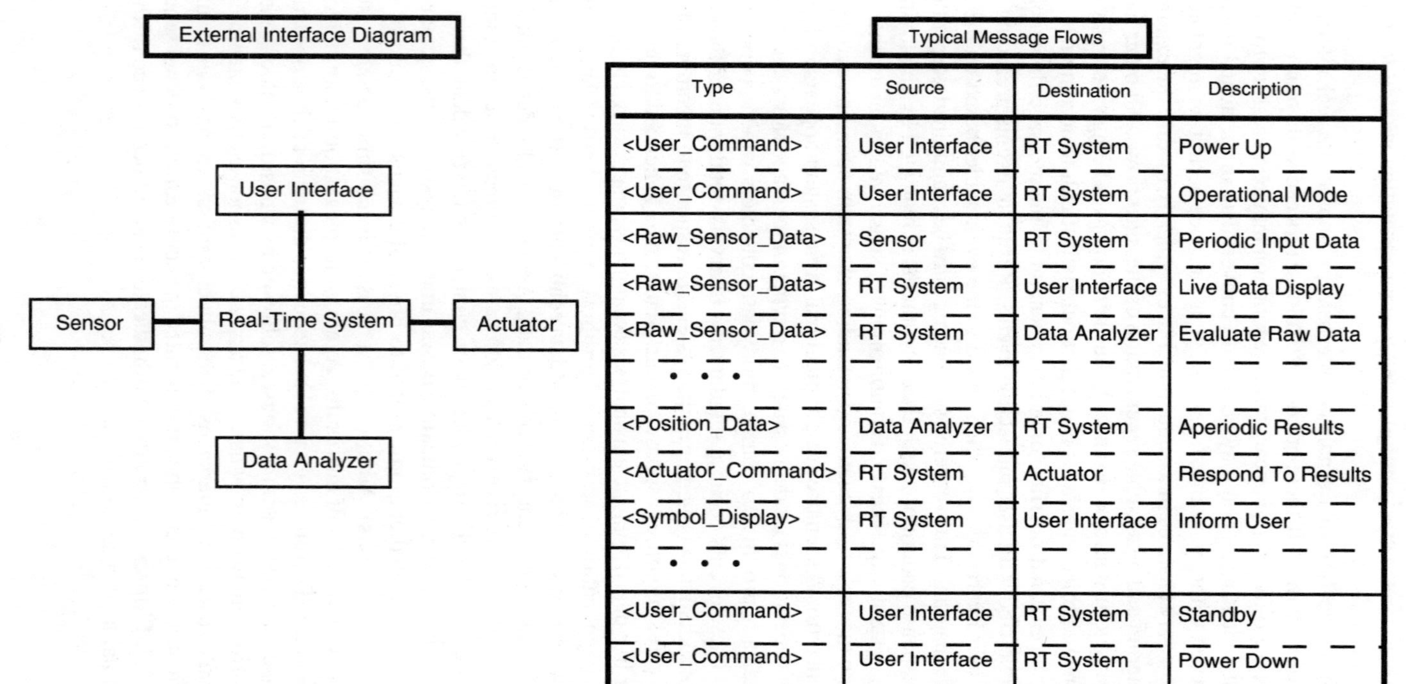

Type	Source	Destination	Description
<User_Command>	User Interface	RT System	Power Up
<User_Command>	User Interface	RT System	Operational Mode
<Raw_Sensor_Data>	Sensor	RT System	Periodic Input Data
<Raw_Sensor_Data>	RT System	User Interface	Live Data Display
<Raw_Sensor_Data>	RT System	Data Analyzer	Evaluate Raw Data
• • •			
<Position_Data>	Data Analyzer	RT System	Aperiodic Results
<Actuator_Command>	RT System	Actuator	Respond To Results
<Symbol_Display>	RT System	User Interface	Inform User
• • •			
<User_Command>	User Interface	RT System	Standby
<User_Command>	User Interface	RT System	Power Down

Figure 3.7 Typical Operational Scenario Generation

Identification of critical sequences and key leverage variations is difficult and is usually accomplished by senior and experienced system/software engineers. Accurate and time-ordered representation of message sequences, proper choice of critical sequences, and effective emphasis on critical variations can make for a highly successful development effort. Incorrect selections, of course, can make for painful integration and test phases. Failure to accomplish this step at all may lead to high frustration during integration and test as well as missed schedules and large cost overruns. These event/response sequences are the criteria against which subsequent steps are evaluated. Poor specification lends to ineffective results during later development activities.

To assure accuracy and correct selection, extensive review is suggested. Incorporate customers, system engineers, hardware engineers, project managers, thinkers, and anyone willing to listen in to this review process. More views increase the likelihood of ultimate success. Do not be defensive or resistant. Attempt to resolve any conflicts and contradictions among reviewers. Promote constructive criticism and employ the results. Strive for consensus, if possible. Do *not* attempt to accomplish this step in a vacuum. One individual is not capable of providing an accurate message sequence by himself, no matter how small or trivial the system seems to be. Insure that all data flowing across system interfaces is represented, including both events and responses. For instance, many system/software engineers do not include sensor data as events. If sensor data is not specified as an event with a specified response pattern, later stages in development cannot perform a correct response. In this case, individual programmers typically choose an event response at implementation time. An incorrect response is chosen and buried in the implemented code, often due to lack of experience and due to lack of system level understanding. This is the approach which causes integration and test headaches. So much difficulty can be eliminated simply by incorporating all data (including sensor data) flowing across system interfaces into the operational scenario generation process.

Initially, message/event flows contain both incoming events and corresponding outgoing response flows. For later evaluation purposes, message sequences are broken into two separate groups. A tabular format is suggested in Figure 3.8. In the first column, an incoming event is listed. The second column lists the corresponding and immediate outgoing responses to each event. Depending on the system under consideration, some events may have no outgoing responses. Typically, these events result in updating one or more data stores. Other events may invoke multiple, immediate outgoing responses. For clarity, multiple responses are listed in separate lines of the test input/output pattern.

In Figure 3.8, the typical event/message sequence illustrated in Figure 3.7 has been partitioned into a test input/output pattern. For the simplistic, real-time scenario, user commands elicit no formal outgoing data response. These typically update an internal state variable or modify one or more data stores. Incoming raw sensor data has two associated output responses—raw sensor data flows to two different destinations (user interface and data analyzer). Analysis results, in the form of position and velocity data associated with a specific object in the sensor's view also elicit two immediate responses. A command to move the sensor is trans-

Event	Response
<User Command>=Power Up	—
<User Command>=Operational	—
<Raw Sensor Data>	<Raw Sensor Data>
—	<Raw Sensor Data>
<Position Velocity Data	<Actuator Command>
—	<Symbol Display>
<User Command>=Standby	—
<User Command>=Power Down	—

Figure 3.8 Test Input/Output Pattern for a Typical Real-Time System

mitted to the actuator. Additionally, a symbol display pattern reflecting newly identified position and velocity passes to the user interface. Note that multiple immediate responses are listed as separate table entries in the test input/output pattern.

This test input/output pattern is the output of operations model generation. During later methodology steps, events listed in the incoming event list are employed to perform consistency and completeness checks, verifying that outgoing responses are generated. As a result, real-time performance and integration and test ease are achieved.

4

Requirements Model Generation

Message flows generated in the operations modeling phase of activities represent a user's view of what the system must do. Now a developer's view can be generated. This view should represent what the system/software must do based on the developer's experience with similar systems implemented in his previous experience. Rigorous discipline should be enforced to focus upon requirements and to avoid design. One can not specify design without a reasonable set of requirements which the design must satisfy.

Requirements model generation activities are characterized in Figure 4.1. Requirements specification begins with a precise event-response sequence/message flow specification and yields a combined control/data flow specification of implementors' requirements. Implementors' requirements are specified using notational schemes common to the real-time community. Specifically, data and control flows, combined with control specifications (CSPECs) and process specifications (PSPECs) are employed. Data flows identify the manner in which data is functionally transformed during system operation. Each transformation is either refined into a greater level of detail or is described in a pseudo-English format. Of equal importance to real-time systems are the control flows and specifications. Control flows and control specifications represent formal decision making required to effectively manage the message flows generated from the operations model analysis. Control flows identify the circumstances under which decisions must be made (i.e., events that require a decision and their context). Additionally specified are the alternatives for each decision and the effect of each decision upon the underlying data transformations. As part of the decision effect, both concurrency and sequencing of responding data transformations are addressed. Leveled and balanced implementors' requirements form a "requirements tree." Leaf node requirements contain PSPECs. CSPECs are composed of state transition diagrams (STDs)

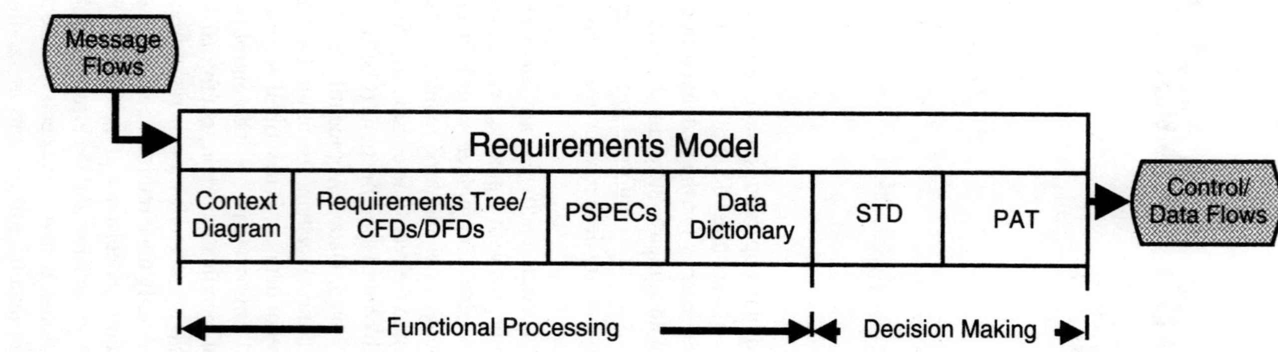

Figure 4.1 Requirements Model Generation

and process activation tables (PATs). For most real-time software systems, CSPECs span the requirements tree, characterizing use of PSPECs to respond to incoming events.

Control flow specification is extremely important for real-time systems. If decision making is not specified as a set of requirements to the implementor, programmers must implement a response based on their own experience and knowledge of system operations. Typically, programmers are not system aware (nor are they necessarily expected to be so). Therefore, actual response details implemented may not be appropriate. Moreover, event responses are distributed and hidden throughout the implementation. When submitted to actual operational testing, problems that appear to be and often are insoluble occur. No one knows where to start looking for problems because response mechanisms are hidden all over. These integration and test problems can be avoided if control flows are specified as part of the requirements.

The concept of decomposition is central to both functional and control flow modeling. Decomposing requirements begins with some simple representation, which is successively refined to greater and greater levels of detail. As refinement is accomplished, internal consistency is maintained between data flows at various levels of detail. Of course, this refinement process must eventually end.

After both control and data flows have been generated, these sets of requirements must be evaluated for consistency and completeness. Consistency/completeness evaluation can be achieved via a "simulation" of requirements. Each event/control flow in the test input/output pattern is employed to evaluate both control and functional specifications. Incomplete specifications are immediately apparent from the evaluation mechanism employed. Moreover, this evaluation validates the transition from a user's view to an implementor's view of requirements. An evaluation such as this can be significantly helpful in reducing customer uncertainty over requirements, as well as in increasing the likelihood of a timely and painless delivery of the developed system.

Requirements are specified using notational symbols common to the real-time community. The symbols used in data and control flow diagrams are pictured in Figure 4.2. A major element in specifying functional requirements is a process, indicated by a bubble. Each process bubble is labeled with a meaningful name indicating the data transformation that occurs within the process. Functional process interfaces involve two kinds of movement—control flows and data flows. Control flows, indicated by a dashed arrow, are any signal requiring a response by the system to be implemented. A data flow is any actual data that moves anywhere within the system and is specified by using a solid arrow. Each type of flow is labeled by a name that summarizes the contents of the data which is flowing. Decision making (specifications of control) employs a number of important symbols.

Any system condition is characterized as a state and is represented on a state transition diagram as a rectangle with a descriptive label inside the rectangle. Transitions among states occur in response to specific events and require precise actions. Transitions must be labeled by the event causing the transition (indicated by <...>) and the response (denoted [...]). Either a vertical or horizontal bar beginning or terminating a control flow indicates an underlying and more detailed control

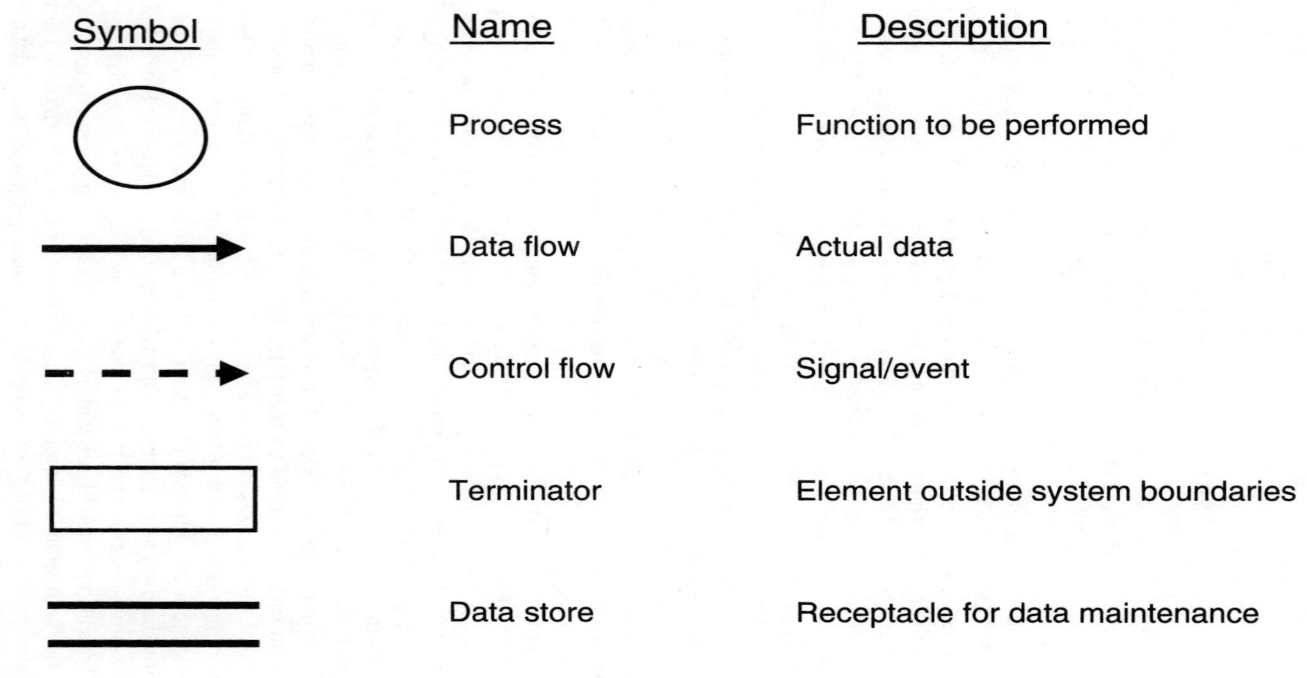

Symbol
Name
Description
Process
Function to be performed
Data flow
Actual data
Control flow
Signal/event
Terminator
Element outside system boundaries
Data store
Receptacle for data maintenance

Figure 4.2 Functional Specification Notation

specification. Permanent and temporary receptacles for data are represented by data stores. Symbolically, a data store is indicated by two parallel lines and a descriptive label between the two lines. Finally, elements outside the boundaries of a system are indicated as labeled squares called terminators.

Generation of an appropriate set of functional and control requirements is an iterative process. Initial interface requirements are generated according to data flowing at the external interfaces (as indicated in the test input/output patterns of the operations model). These are decomposed into an initial set of functional and control requirements. Each of these functional and control requirements is further decomposed to lower levels of detail. At the lowest level, primitive functional processes or primitive control processes are precisely specified. Decomposition requires that a number of important activities be accomplished. Each level of decomposition must be balanced relative to its parent requirements. Additionally, a stopping level must be determined.

Iterative decomposition of functional requirements leads to a requirements tree (Figure 4.3). Leaf node requirements need no further decomposition. Nonleaf node requirements simply serve as intermediate repositories to allow limited focus during further decompositions. Due to the limited knowledge of developers and due to the iterative application of the methodology, requirements encompass different levels of decomposition. As a result, the requirements tree is likely to be deeper in some areas of specification than other areas. In fact, leaf requirements, for which PSPECs are written, represent the real requirements faced by the implementor. PSPECs describe the actual data transformations and, thus, describe the real work being accomplished during software system operations.

Identification of the appropriate level at which decomposition ceases is an important decision. Too little decomposition of requirements fails to adequately build an initial framework for analysis. Too much detailed decomposition early in the requirements specification cycle tends to confuse and obfuscate the system's requirements. Several criteria for determining an appropriate stopping level are suggested. Cease the decomposition process at a level consistent with your knowledge and experience with systems of the type under development. Since specification of requirements is a framework for discussion, restricting decomposition of requirements to an understandable level serves to promote and to focus discussion. An even more important criterion is to cease decomposition at a level that provides requirements for implementing a minimal but complete processing chain of the system (i.e., end-to-end flow of data during routine operations). Excessive detailed decomposition within the functional specification of a system prohibits effective delivery within a constrained schedule. Attempting a complete implementation during the first iteration introduces uncontrollable complexity into integration and test activities. By assuring that a minimal but complete processing chain is specified, an initial build (with appropriate hooks for future enhancement) can be successfully accomplished within very narrow schedule constraints. Integration complexity is controlled. Both minimality and completeness of an initial specification are evaluated at a later step in this methodology.

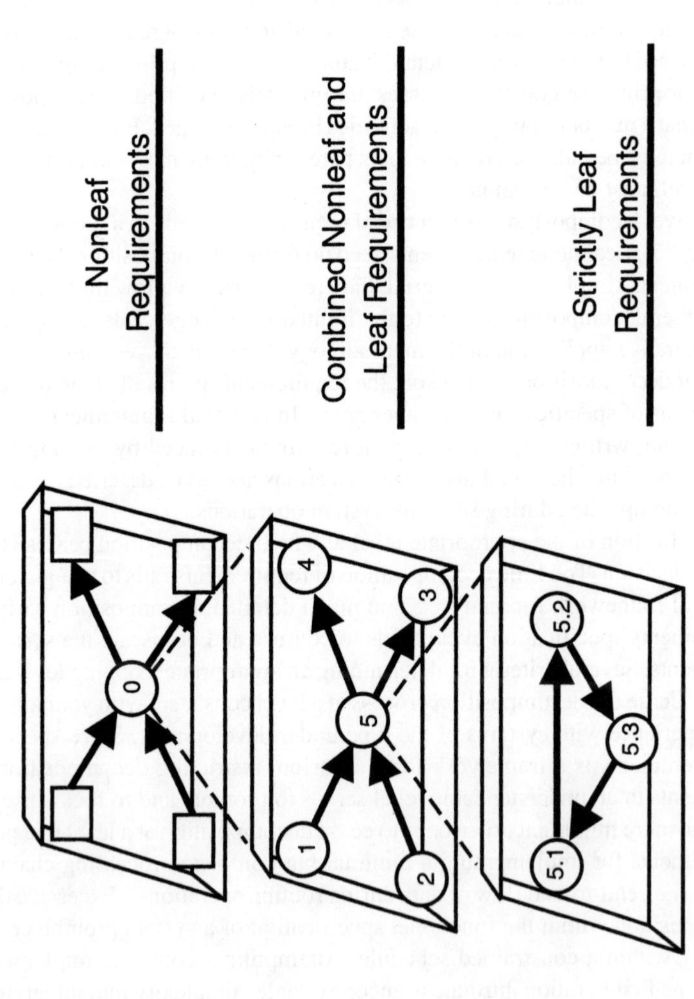

Figure 4.3 Requirements Tree Concept

Defining an implementor's view of software system requirements needed to satisfy the operational/user's view consists of the following steps:

1. Generate a software system context diagram using the detailed message sequence;
2. Construct functional requirements in the form of a requirements tree and PSPECs;
3. Describe event response logic for managing the PSPECs of the form of STDs and PATs;
4. Perform a consistency and completeness check for implementor requirements against operational requirements;
5. Use the data dictionary to determine an initial set of data abstractions and operations on abstractions; and
6. Allocate timing requirements to PSPECs.

Each of these steps involves specific products in specific formats. Of particular importance is the consistency/completeness check against operational requirements. Checking to see that operational requirements are met increases customer confidence and verifies that a working system can be delivered.

4.1 EXTERNAL INTERFACES/CONTEXT DIAGRAM

Transition from user requirements into implementor requirements is accomplished by generation of a software system context diagram. This diagram summarizes all external interfaces, both sources and targets of interaction. Control and data flows are combined on a single diagram. Typically, all external interfaces that provide incoming data are represented as control flows. Since incoming data from an external source either requires a response by the software system or engenders a response on the opposite side of the interface, treating sources of incoming events as control flows makes sense for real-time systems.

Message flows generated by the operational model specification provide the basis for a context diagram. One process bubble represents the system being specified. This bubble is labeled with a functional name, rather than an implementation name. Each external interface is represented by a terminator symbol and is appropriately labeled. Since terminators are specific other systems which are implemented, these terminators are labeled with an implementation type name, representing the specific system/subsystem on the other side of the interface.

Each unique message in the message flow appears on the context diagram. While a message may occur multiple times in a message flow, only one occurrence of the message is incorporated into a context diagram. Message flows represent the dynamic behavior of the software system. In contrast, a context diagram is a static description of the interface requirements. Summarization of the interface requirements is the primary goal of this step of requirements generation.

Context diagrams are best formatted in a manner which aids and enhances communications to the viewer. Randomly placed terminator symbols cause confusion to the viewer. Distribute terminators evenly and symmetrically around the process bubble. Place data collectors on the left of the process bubble, and data receivers on the right. This placement scheme supports a notion of organized data flowing through the system. Moreover, human perception tends to flow from left to right in viewing a picture or illustration. (Photographers have known and employed this concept for years.) By constructing drawings in a manner that supports understanding and is consistent with human physical perceptions, communications are greatly enhanced.

An external interface/context diagram for a typical real-time system appears in Figure 4.4. Typical categories of data that usually flow across boundaries of a real-time system are characterized. Data collectors (sensors and user input interfaces) appear on the left side of the diagram. Data receivers or emitters (actuators and displays) appear on the right. Collectors and emitters are evenly and symmetrically distributed on the sides of the process bubble. Both data and control flow from left to right, as does the human eye when interpreting the diagram.

All incoming and outgoing data must appear on this diagram. This diagram is the basis from which implementor requirements are to be generated. Failure to include any specific messages/flows in this initial specification results in non-specification of processing and control requirements for the system in the next phase of modeling. Using message flows from the operations model as a foundation assures that messages/flows are not omitted.

Implementors' requirements begin with an initial decomposition of the data/control context diagram. Two types of decompositions are employed. Data flows and corresponding PSPECs represent internal data transformation which the implementor employs. Characterization of event responses to control signals arriving at the interfaces appears as control flows and associated CSPECs. Descriptions of these elements of requirements specification appear in the following sections.

4.2 DATA PROCESSING FUNCTIONAL REQUIREMENTS

Data flow diagrams are employed to represent internal functional processing that must be performed by the implementor during normal processing of events. Generation of data flow diagrams employs functional processing bubbles, labeled data flows, and data stores. Each specific functional process shows data flowing into a process bubble and data flowing out of the same process bubble. Sources and destinations of data flows can be other processes, data stores, or higher level flow diagrams. As greater understanding of the target system is developed, functional processes are refined to further levels of detail, employing flow decomposition.

Generation of data flow/functional processing requirements is an easy concept to describe but a difficult approach to employ. Two major criteria are employed in generating data flow diagrams. Start with very simple representations at a fairly

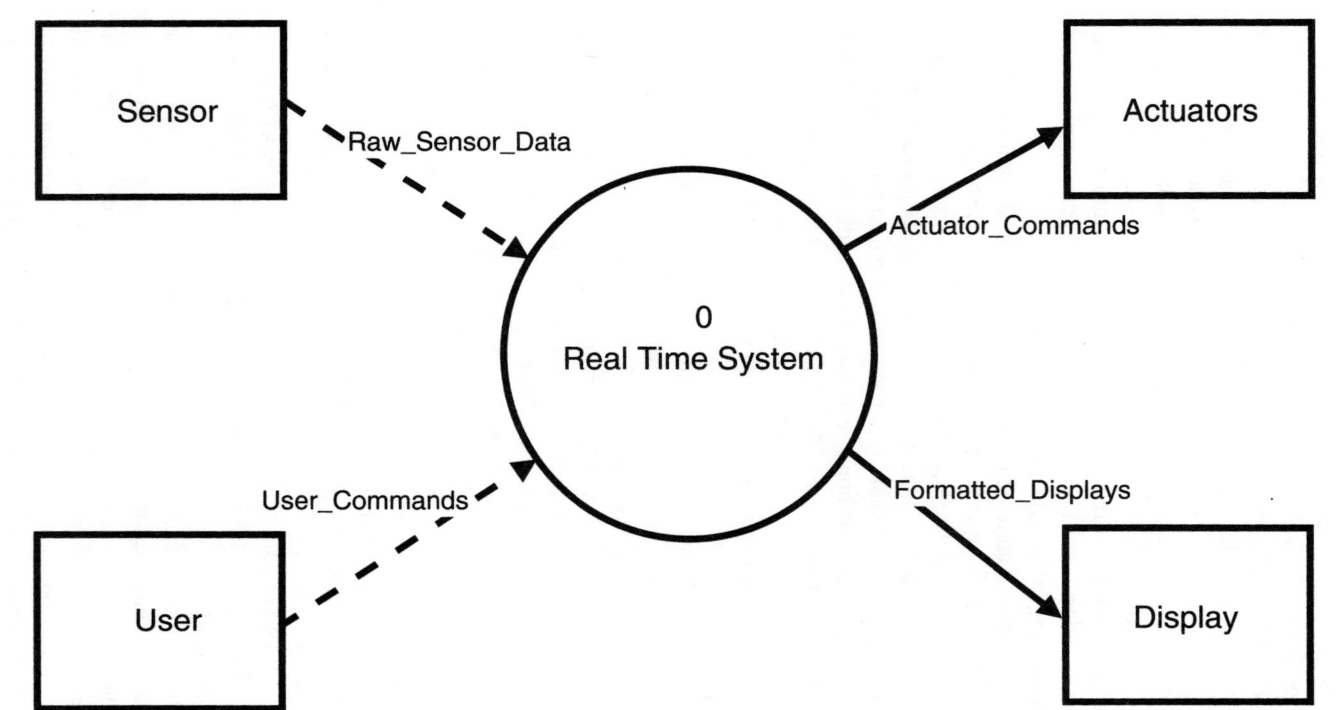

Figure 4.4 Typical Context Diagram

high level of functional abstraction. Focus on those requirements necessary to implement a minimal, end-to-end capability as an initial build. Employing these criteria and applying your own experience in the target system domain usually generates an effective set of functional requirements, assuring successful implementation and easing integration and test grind.

Many specifiers of real-time Ada systems fail to appreciate the need for a simplistic initial specification. Data flow diagrams are generated with extensive detail as a first pass. Excessive detail confuses customers, designers, and coders and usually emphasizes inappropriate requirements. Providing an initial simplified representation of implementors' requirements eliminates confusion in both understanding and interpretation of requirements. Moreover, an initial simple representation provides excellent focus upon key issues regarding system operations, which can ease future integration and test efforts.

Emphasis upon requirements necessary to implement an initial minimal capability is extremely important. Specifically, minimal capability is defined to be the necessary control, functional, and data requirements needed to move data through the software system. Elaborate details of algorithms are not particularly necessary at this point. Most implementors generate detailed data flow diagrams describing raw data processing algorithms in excessive detail to the exclusion of insuring end-to-end data flow in the system. As a result, detailed algorithms are implemented early in the process. This leads to bottom up implementation and omission of important control specifications leading to an implementation that is incredibly painful to integrate and test.

Of course, an extensive experience base with the target system domain is necessary to provide a solid foundation for generation of functional requirements. However, implementors must employ significant judgement and self-discipline to assure emphasis upon both simplicity and minimal end-to-end processing flow of data. Added detail is easily incorporated on later builds/increments, once an initial methodical framework and an initial build have been implemented.

An implementor's experience base is best employed to determine which specific process bubbles to include in the data flow diagram and in selection of process, data store, and data flow names. Inappropriate choices of either specific functional requirements or data stores demonstrate lack of experience and lack of judgement to reviewers and customers. Employing the end-to-end functionality criterion provides significant aid in choosing specific functions to employ in the generation of each data flow diagram.

Two factors are important to consider when applying experience in order to generate data flow diagrams: *Appropriate functions must be included. Inappropriate transformations need to be excluded.*

As an example, consider a system control function. Two functions need to be included in an initial decomposition: retrieve current event and respond to current event. Inclusion of any more details at this level of specification are confusing to a reviewer and thus are inappropriate. An initial specification for system control does not include any mention of specific mechanisms (such as buffering) by which event data is moved into the software system. Also, note that this is a minimal set of requirements for implementing end-to-end data flow for a system control function.

Data can be completely handled if retrieval and response functions are fully implemented at a later phase of development.

Use of names meaningful to the problem domain is critical. Function A is not as meaningful as a function named Retrieve Incoming Message. Additionally, implementation oriented names are to be avoided. System Controller (which implies a specific implementation component) is not appropriate. A more functional descriptor for this process would be "Control System." To effectively specify a requirement, an *action verb* is necessary. Nouns indicate design/implementation and do not play a role during requirements specification.

Another important aspect of data flow generation is to draw the flow diagram in a manner that effectively enhances communications. Emphasis is placed upon attempting to communicate important concurrent processing streams. Randomly placed process bubbles, data stores, and data flows on the diagram cause lack of clarity and precision, as well as subjective interpretation. Place inputs from and outputs to higher level data flows along the outer edges of the flow diagram where they will be visible and easily identified. Data stores typically are placed in central areas of the diagram, since these are "internal" to the flow diagram. Interpretation of data flow is aided by requiring a viewer to proceed from processes on the left sequentially across the diagram to processes on the right. Nonprimary transforms appear above or below a primary processing chain. Finally, left to right primary processing chains reside stacked from top to bottom of the flow diagram.

Indication of primary concurrent processing chains is an excellent means for providing guidelines to an implementor without dictating a specific design. Implementors may not understand intricacies of either the specific data or the target system domain. Emphasizing concurrent processing chains in a flow diagram gives an implementor/designer clues to requirements partitioning for architecture component generation. However, an architect can collect multiple concurrent chains together, if desired. Thus, a careful approach towards drawing diagrams serves as an effective design guideline. Typically, an implementor chooses to establish implemental builds according to a scheme that addresses one primary concurrent processing chain at a time.

Specification of functional requirements through flow diagrams is accomplished through an iterative process. Initially, a context diagram is decomposed into a first level of requirements employing criteria and guidelines described above. Each process in this diagram is further decomposed into a lower level diagram. This process is called leveling. A child flow diagram is generated from a requirement process bubble on a parent diagram. Decomposition continues, so that multiple levels of flow diagrams are generated for a given target system, subsystem, etc.

A numbering convention is employed for identification of process bubbles, which aids in traceability of requirements decomposition. Each process in a leveled diagram is labeled with a number consisting of the parent bubble number concatenated with a decimal point followed by a unique local number. A process bubble labeled with the number 2.4.6 indicates process bubble 6 at this level and derived from the parent bubble 2.4.

As requirements decomposition occurs, flow diagrams must be balanced. Balancing consists of insuring consistency of a given level diagram with the parent process. In practical terms, this simply means that all inputs into and all outputs from a parent bubble are represented on the child or leveled flow diagram. This is easier to verify if the suggested diagramming layout guidelines have been effectively utilized. Specifically, if all inputs into and outputs from a particular diagram appear around the outer edges of a diagram, verification against the parent is more easily accomplished.

During requirements decomposition, continuously employ the simplicity, minimality, and end-to-end data flow criteria described above while drawing more detailed flow diagrams. General studies on psychology and other methodology texts indicate that seven plus or minus two bubbles per flow diagram are effective simplicity criteria. Decomposition is constrained within the limits of known information about any aspect of the software system being specified. Admittedly, some elements of the requirements may be more fully specified than other areas. Since an iterative approach is being suggested, this is acceptable, since later iterations can generate more details. Again, completeness of end-to-end data flow is to be the dominating criterion for determining the level at which to stop decomposition, at least for the initial iteration.

Evaluation and review of data flow diagrams is necessary to initially assure their correctness. Data that must persist between any pair of events in the operations model must appear as a data store. Software engineers cannot assume that developers know to store data, since developers are typically not "system" aware. Failure to preserve needed data results in long hours of integration and test effort. Identification of missing data within several hundred thousand lines of code has a significant negative impact on integration schedules.

Additionally, at least one complete data flow path must be visible from inputs of the diagram to each output. Verification of input to output paths usually leads to high performance. Actually tracing data flow from inputs to outputs serves to initially eliminate unnecessary functionality. Expulsion of unneeded functionality is an important step towards achieving high software performance. Implementing the least amount of functionality to perform a user's job is a necessary prerequisite to the generation of tight, high performance software.

The typical context diagram of Figure 4.4 has been decomposed in Figure 4.5. Since this is the first real specification of implementor requirements, process bubbles at this level are labeled according to a single unique integer. Simplicity is obtained, since only five bubbles appear on this diagram. An end-to-end data flow has been accomplished and flows from left to right in the diagram. Raw Sensor Data is submitted to Preserve Raw Data. This transmits a Raw Data Location to Perform Real-time Operations. Analysis generated Position and Velocity Data is moved to Format Actuator Commands which generates actual Actuator Commands. A complete flow from data collector (input) to data receiver (output) has been represented. Moreover, this is a primary concurrent processing chain—an important clue to the eventual implementor. Note that all inputs and outputs typically appear near the edges of the flow diagram. Comparison of these easily identified inputs and outputs against the parent bubble (from the context diagram in Figure 4.4) indicates that this diagram has been properly balanced (all inputs/outputs represented). Process bubble names and data flow names are appropriate to

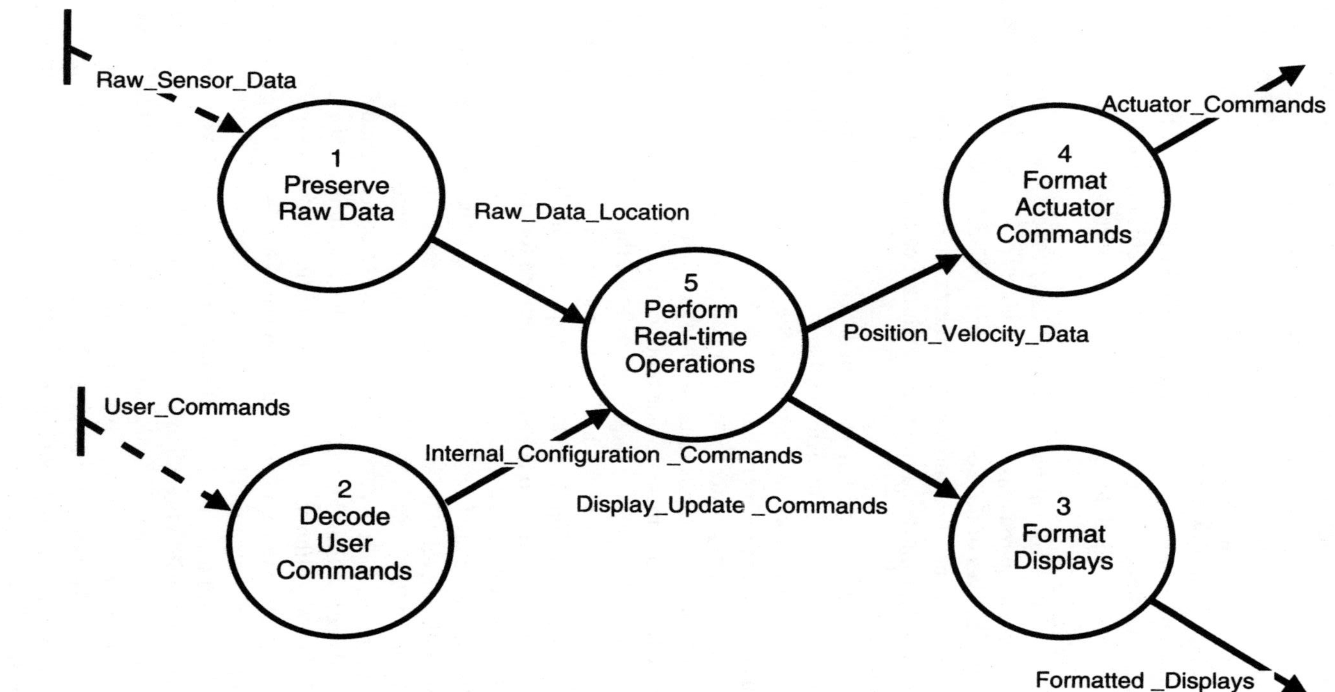

Figure 4.5 Typical Decomposition Diagram

the target system domain. This diagram is easy to understand, simple to interpret, and allows an implementor to focus on key/critical requirements for implementing an end-to-end processing chain in an initial system build.

Comparison of this decomposed diagram with the context diagram reveals an important interpretation of the control flow concept. Each incoming flow of data is treated as a control flow, not a data flow. Each of these control flows must appear on the first level data flow diagram. However, these flows contain both control information and associated raw data. To indicate this, control flows on the first child data flow diagram point to requirements in which the associated data is used and *simultaneously* include a bar at the base of the control flow to indicate the existence of an underlying CSPEC. This is radically different from a number of other methodological texts but has been employed repeatedly with this methodology.

A model of leveled and balanced functional processing requirements can be envisioned as a requirements tree. Internal nodes of the requirements tree are further leveled. Leaves of the tree need no further clarification for the current iteration on requirements. Leaf node requirements are often referred to as primitive requirements or primitives. Primitives are further explicated in the form of process specifications.

All typical real-time system requirements displayed until now form a requirements tree. This tree was depicted earlier in Figure 4.3. Requirement 0, Context Diagram, forms the root of the tree. Since this requirement is further decomposed, a non-leaf requirement is indicated. As illustrated previously, the Context Diagram is decomposed to a data flow diagram containing five requirements numbered 1 through 5. Four of these (1–4) are not further decomposed, and are considered leaf requirements. Since requirement 5 has a child data flow diagram, this requirement is a nonleaf requirement. Thus, the middle data flow diagram is composed of both nonleaf and leaf requirements. Finally, all requirements in the child diagram of requirement 5 are leaf requirements. Since PSPECs are created for each leaf requirement, one PSPEC is defined for each of requirements 1, 2, 3, 4, 5.1, 5.2, and 5.3.

PSPECs are structured English representations of the data transformed to occur at this primitive level. All flows into and from the primitive process must be included in the PSPECs. Each input is employed as a source of data in the structured English representation of data transformation. Moreover, generation of every output is explained within the PSPEC. Note also that functional transformation descriptions are algorithmic in content and not implementation specific.

Very few rules are employed in generation of a structured English representation of data transformation. Limited statement structures for incorporating selection and iteration aspects of transformation may be employed. Selection statements include constructs such as if-then, if-then-else, and case structures. Iteration may be represented via constructs such as "while—end while," "for—each," and "repeat—until" structures. Actual operations performed on inputs to generate outputs are best described using a limited vocabulary constrained to verbs, objects, conjunctions (but, and, either-or, etc.), relational operators (<=, etc.), and equations (:=).

Every effort is made to keep PSPECs at a high level of abstraction so that transformations are easy to read and to understand. A limit of one-half page per PSPEC is recommended. Clarity and concision are important goals to strive for in specifying transformations within primitive processes. Orientation is towards describing rules governing transformation of data while avoiding implementation procedure. Abstract specification of the steps in a sort algorithm is appropriate. Describing exact data structures and code mechanics of implementing that same sort is inappropriate.

Process 5, Perform Real-time Operations, from Figure 4.5, is further decomposed into primitive processes in Figure 4.6. Evaluation of this diagram for balance, location of inputs/outputs, identification of concurrent processing chains, and appropriate name selection remains to be accomplished by the reader. PSPECs for each of these primitive processes appear in Figures 4.7, 4.8, and 4.9. Each PSPEC shows how inputs are employed to generate outputs without describing implementation mechanics. For example, Evaluate Raw Data requires that elements of Control_Parameters are employed by algorithms to evaluate data at the Raw_Data_Location. Statistical results generated by this data evaluation are placed into Analysis_Results yielding a Results_Location. Each input is employed within the PSPEC. All outputs are explicitly generated. Remaining PSPECs accomplish the same purpose as described above.

An initial specification of functional processing requirements is an important first step in building a requirements model of a software system. However, this step is not sufficient to assure successful delivery and implementation. Event response specification detailing use of the PSPECs must also be accomplished. This portion of the requirements model is described below.

4.3 EVENT PROCESSING CONTROL REQUIREMENTS

A major capability in a real-time system is the ability to respond to events. Event response specification entails characterizing decision making required by the software system during actual operations. Specifically, event responses must describe the following components:

1. Conditions under which decisions must be made;
2. When a decision is made, alternatives that can be chosen; and
3. For each alternative, translation of that alternative into a combination of underlying functional processing primitives.

Failure to specify events and corresponding responses in these terms translates into a number of important and limiting effects on embedded system development.

With event responses unspecified, individual programmers are free to employ any response deemed appropriate. Typically, an incorrect response is employed.

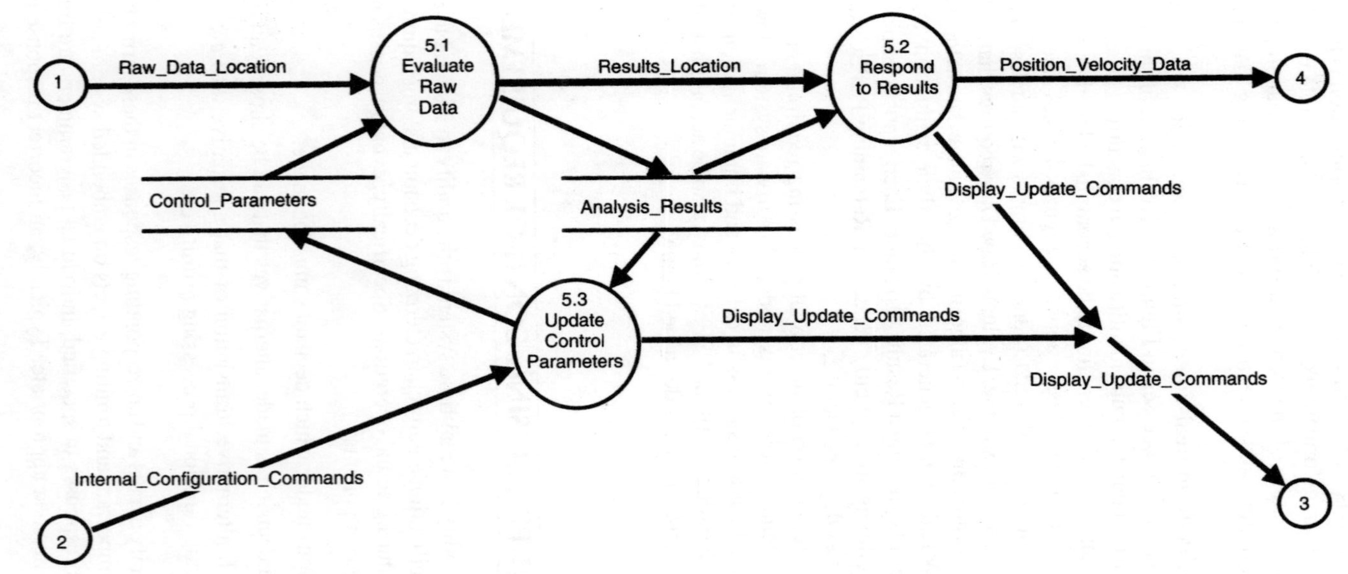

Figure 4.6 Typical Detailed Decomposition

```
Process 5.1:  Evaluate_Raw_Data:

input data flows
  Raw_Data_Location, Control_Parameters

output data flows
  Results_Location, Analysis_Results

description
  apply algorithms to data at Raw_Data_Location using
       1. algorithm parameters in Control_Parameters; and,
       2. resources indicated in Control_Parameters ;
  place statistical results into Analysis_Results returning
       Results_Location ;
end pspec
```

Figure 4.7 PSPECs for Typical Detailed Decomposition

```
Process 5.2:  Respond_To_Results:

input data flows
  Results_Location, Analysis_Results

output data flows
  Display_Update_Commands, Position_Velocity_Data, Display_Update_Commands

description
  using Results_Location, extract Analysis_Results ;
  using Analysis  Results,
       1. generate Display_Update_Commands ;
       2. determine Position_Velocity_Data for control of actuator ;
end pspec
```

Figure 4.8 PSPECs for Typical Detailed Decomposition

```
Process 5.3: Update_Control_Parameters:

input data flows
  Internal_Configuration_Commands, Analysis_Results

output data flows
  Display_Update_Commands, Control_Parameters

description
  acquire Internal_Configuration_Commands ;
  acquire Analysis_Results ;
  use Internal_Configuration_Commands and Analysis_Results to compute
      new Control_Parameters ;
  install Control_Parameters ;
  format resultant parameter descriptions into Display_Update_Commands ;
end pspec
```

Figure 4.9 PSPECs for Typical Detailed Decomposition

This results from both lack of experience and limited system level awareness for the particular target system domain. Moreover, decentralized event responses imply no central picture of event response mechanisms. In other words, no central picture describes conditions under which a system can effectively respond. Poor design usually results, since a nasty mess of nested "if" statements is employed to generate event response logic. All of these manifestations lead to significant integration and test headaches.

Ongoing integration testing suddenly comes to a screeching halt. Unplanned halting occurs because the software decides to "go south." Unfortunately, since no central picture of event responses exists, no one understands why the software system ceases to operate. Moreover, since unknown implementation decisions were made relative to event responses, an initial location for problem identification is difficult to ascertain. After a significant number of hours spent performing tedious debugging, the problem is usually isolated to some poor decision logic in a set of nested "if" statements. Now, interjecting new nested "if" statements becomes a major headache. A nested "if" approach does not readily allow an individual to determine event responses with any clarity. This tedious debugging scenario during integration and test can be easily avoided if event responses are specified as requirements to implementors. Additionally, event response requirements must be in a format that admits to more effective design approaches.

Control flow diagrams and corresponding control specifications (CSPECs) are the specific mechanism employed to avoid these problems. Control flow diagrams specify the manner in which control flows enter the system. A control flow is defined to be any data entering into a given system that *requires an explicit response.* Typically, a required response spans the requirements tree. By this interpretation, raw data provided by a sensor/data collector *must* be classed as a control flow. Although an incoming flow contains raw sensor data, a specific response must occur. Many real-time systems experience the symptoms described above, even though a modern methodology has been employed. Exhibition of these symptoms occurs chiefly because data from sensors/data collectors are not treated as events, an event response is not specified, and implementors are again left to their own prerogatives to choose an appropriate event response.

Every event which occurs at a software system interface must appear in a control flow diagram and must be appropriately accommodated in one or more CSPECs. Whereas, control flows show how events enter into the system, CSPECs detail specific event responses. Components of CSPECs are state transition diagrams and process activation tables. State transition diagrams show conditions under which decisions occur (a given event occurs in a specific state) and provide specific responses (a specific action is taken). State transition diagrams are often referred to as "state machines." Process activation tables translate action names into specific combinations of activity by underlying functional processes. Both sequential and concurrent responses are indicated. A synonym for process activation tables is the term "action machine."

Using these mechanisms—control flows, state transition diagrams, and process activation tables—serves to practically eliminate the integration and test problems described above. Event responses are assured to be optimal from a system point of view, if both architecture and design adequately satisfy the event responses. A centralized view of event response is provided. Both state machines and action machines are easily represented as tables, strongly suggesting a table-driven approach to software implementation. Table-driven software designs serve to increase the speed with which integration and test problems can be resolved. If conditions are such that no event response has been specified, table accesses return empty results. At this point, an effective software design dumps all internal data stores before conditions become confused by processing current data to create incorrect data. Usually, problems are easily resolved under these conditions. Moreover, event responses are easily and directly traceable into tables stored in the code. Implementing fixes is often a speedy process requiring additional table entries with little or no recompilation. For the class of event-intensive systems addressed by this methodology, maximum development leverage is obtained by placing emphasis upon control. Emphasis upon control aspects appears in subsequent methodological steps.

Generation of control flows requires symbols depicted in Figure 4.10. Some of the symbols are employed for data flow diagrams and need no further elaboration here. However, a few new symbols are introduced. Dashed arrows indicate an event which requires a response. Control flows into or from a bar symbol. Bar symbols indicate a further detailed CSPEC (consisting of a state transition diagram and

Name	Description	Symbol
Control Flow	Event requiring response	name
Bar	Detailed CSPEC exists	
State	Mode of system behavior	
Transition	<•••> = event requiring response [•••] = action (response)	<•••>/[•••]

Figure 4.10 Control Flow Specification Notation

process activation table). Multiple bars on the same control flow diagram indicate the same underlying CSPECs. A single CSPEC may also employ functional requirements that appear at different levels in the requirements tree. As a result, bar symbols in numerous flow diagrams may reference a single set of software system CSPECs.

Since control and data flow diagrams contain a number of symbols in common, many system and software engineers chose to combine control and data flow diagrams into a single diagram. This is an extremely effective approach. Fewer diagrams are necessary to specify a requirements model. As a result, less confusion is encountered. However, combined control and data flow diagrams cause a very interesting problem.

Since data flow diagrams are leveled, an explicit decision must be made as to the appropriate level at which to incorporate control flows. A guideline that has worked repeatedly in the past suggests that control flows appear at a diagram level close to the functions which process raw data. An example of a combined control and data flow that satisfies this criterion is presented in Figure 4.11. This flow diagram is a further decomposition of process 2, Decode User Commands, which appeared in Figure 4.5. At this level of requirements, raw data has been buffered temporarily away from a specific memory mapped hardware interface so that message decoding can be accomplished without destruction by a new incoming message. Since this is the closest level to actual message data manipulation, event responses to user commands appear at this level. A control flow labeled User_Commands appears on the diagram. Pointing to a bar symbol indicates that actual responses to user command events appear in an underlying control specification. Note, also, that this combined control and data flow diagram is drawn to employ the effective communications criteria described in the previous section.

Control specifications are composed of two important components. Decision conditions are modeled as state transition diagrams. Translation of decisions into functional specifics is represented in the form of process activation tables. Both elements (state transition and process activation) must be included for complete event response specification. Detailing event responses requires that the action machine (process activation) be employed specifically to translate responses into functional processing. Failure to include this translation leaves a significant component of the response mechanics to the discretion of the implementing programmer, yielding integration and test aggravations.

State transition diagrams consist of states and transitions among states. Each state represents the memory of the software system, characterizing the combination of conditions that prevail. States are indicated by rectangles, labeled with a descriptive name for the state. Transitions are characterized by an event that causes the transition to occur and by an action that is a descriptive term summarizing the response. State transition diagrams show states and transitions. Each transition is labeled according to the event/action combination associated with the transition.

Appropriate selection and definition of states is a key element in the successful specification of control requirements. Unfortunately, since state selection is unique to an application domain, state definition is a difficult task. However, a number of guidelines may be formulated as follows:

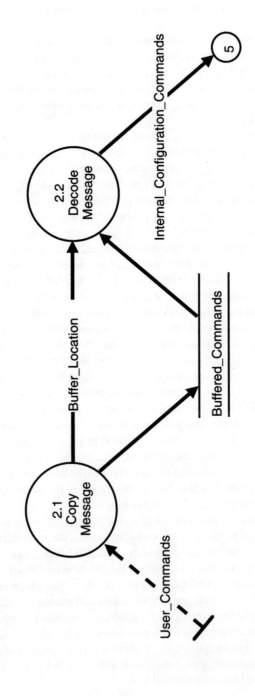

Figure 4.11 Typical Combined CFD/DFD

1. States represent the "memory" of the software system;
2. States reflect a set of conditions that has occurred during software system operations;
3. Most often, states reflect something that has occurred most recently; and
4. States reflect a user's view of software system operations.

Careful application of these guidelines help to reduce state identification difficulties. Examples of state selection appear in the case study chapters.

Two major categories of transitions are usually employed—state changing transitions and state preserving transitions. State changing transition cause transition to a unique and different state; i. e., conditions have changed. State preserving transitions allow maintenance of the same state; i.e., conditions are not changing. Typically, but not always, periodic events (such as raw sensor data inputs at a fixed rate), require state preserving transitions. This category of transitions manifests in the form of feedback transitions on a state diagram. Aperiodic events (occurring according to some probabilisticly distributed schedule) can result in either state changing or state preserving transitions, depending on the application domain.

Many specifiers fail to describe state preserving transitions, indicated by a lack of feedback transitions in the state transition diagram. Ignoring state preserving transitions leads to incomplete event response specification. As a result, software implementors are again free to respond as desired. Of course, all the frustrating integration and test conditions emerge from this freedom of implementation decision. In fact, treating all data flowing at system interfaces as control events assures that state preserving transitions are included in event response control specifications. Since all data at the interface is treated as control data, CSPECs include responses to the data/event. Enforcing treatment of incoming data as events and incorporating explicit event responses that are state preserving is a major factor in assuring easy integration and testing.

Unfortunately, many developers feel that simply writing an STD is sufficient. This is simply inaccurate. A transition diagram, as initially conceived, usually fails to incorporate all possible decision conditions. If an incomplete STD moves into implementation, integration and test activities can be quite time consuming. Events can enter the software system, causing failure conditions that can be difficult to diagnose. Therefore, transition diagrams *must* be evaluated for completeness prior to the next methodological step. Since an STD is a static representation of decision logic (given an event, describe the response), completeness checking requires a dynamic view of events as its basis. Using incoming events in the test input/output pattern (operations model) is an excellent foundation for completeness checking and is described later.

A general format for process activation tables appears in Figure 4.12. Along the left column of the table appears each of the unique actions from the corresponding STD. Although an action may be employed in more than one transition, only one definition is needed. Across the top row are leaf node process bubble numbers appearing in the combined control and data flow diagrams. Leaf node functional processes, which represent PSPECs, are to be specified as part of the event

Leaf Requirements / Actions	P_1	P_2	•••	P_m
A_1		0 (deactivated)		
A_2	1 (in parallel)		1 (in parallel)	
⋮				
A_n		1 (sequential)		2 (sequential)

Figure 4.12 Process Activation Table

response. Since PSPECs perform the real data transformation activities, only leaf node requirements appear in the process activation table.

Entries in the body of the table indicate precise event responses as related to functional processing bubbles with PSPECs. Deactivation of a process is indicated by a 0 entry in the table. Two processes must occur concurrently (in parallel) if the same number appears in their individual process columns. Sequencing of functional processes as an event response is indicated via sequential numbers below the required processes. Of course, combinations of concurrent and sequential processes can be incorporated into an event response. Actions that employ complex combinations of sequencing and concurrency are simplified by the introduction of additional states. Each state then employs action details, which separate the initial complex responses.

Entries in the process activation table reveal a detailed, precise, and unique response to every event in any given context. Non-unique responses in a process activation table indicate shortcomings in the state transition diagram. Fixing the state transition diagram generally requires introduction of intermediate states combined with creation of internal events to force proper state transitions.

As a general guideline for event-intensive systems, incorporate as much detail as possible into the state transition diagram/process activation table combination. Large state diagrams and activation tables all support a table driven implementation approach to be employed during software development. A table driven implementation tends to lead to centralized control in the architecture, aiding requirements traceability, maintainability, and performance. Some developers place details of event response logic into PSPECs for the leaf requirements. Hidden event response mechanisms within PSPECs are difficult to integrate and test because no central picture exists for determining how control works or fails in the software system. Another approach frequently employed by developers is to minimize control, simply translating data flow into architecture and letting the data flow through the architecture. This approach also leads to extensive integration and testing problems, since no system awareness of control is incorporated into this data driven architecture. While these other approaches can eventually lead to a working system (given enough time and effort), deployment of a real-time Ada system is most effectively accomplished by maximization of control specification and by minimization of data flow. This precept contradicts approaches and guidelines presented by other authors yet seems to work well in practice.

Figure 4.13 presents a typical CSPEC for the control flow which appeared in Figure 4.11. Both state transition diagram and process activation table are shown. Three states are employed—start, standby, and operational. Transitions among these states depend on a specific component of the user command control flow. If the system is in standby state and receives a user command, operational mode is desired, and a specific response is indicated. One component of the specified response—action name—indicates that an Awaken_Processing action is to be performed. Another component of the response—transition—says that transition to operational state occurs. By reviewing the process activation table, further explicit details of the required response are available. This response is quite complex. Processes 1.1, 3.1, 4.1, 5.1, 5.2, and 5.3 (these numbers predominantly refer to

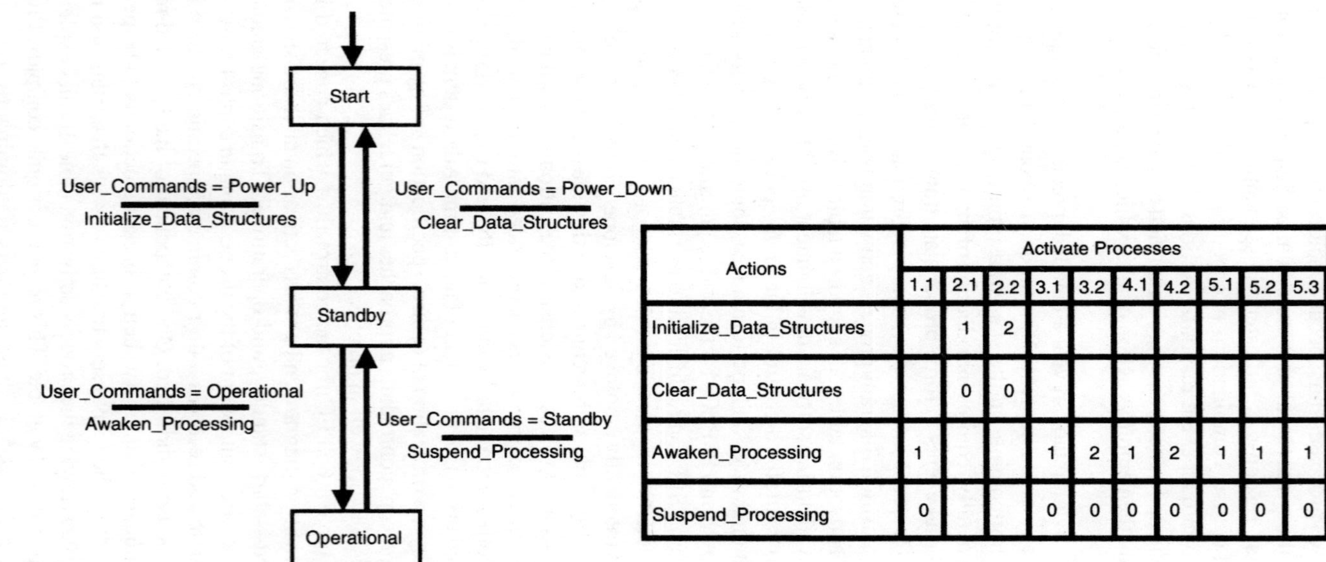

Actions	Activate Processes									
	1.1	2.1	2.2	3.1	3.2	4.1	4.2	5.1	5.2	5.3
Initialize_Data_Structures		1	2							
Clear_Data_Structures		0	0							
Awaken_Processing	1			1	2	1	2	1	1	1
Suspend_Processing	0			0	0	0	0	0	0	0

Figure 4.13 Typical CSPECs for Combined CFD/DFD

process bubbles appearing in both previous and forthcoming examples) must occur concurrently. All have the same number—1—in their individual process columns. Processes 3.2 and 4.2 must occur concurrently (same number—2—in their columns), but subsequent to concurrent occurrence of processes 1.1, 3.1, 4.1, 5.1, 5.2, and 5.3. No state preserving transitions were required in this CSPEC. By definition, only responses to the event labeled User_Commands are specified in this CSPEC. These are aperiodic events and specifically invoke only state changing transitions according to the specification.

As with any other form of specification, CSPECs can be decomposed into lower levels of detail. Several decomposition options are available. Multiple types of events can be represented by decomposed CSPECs within a single combined control/data flow diagram. Alternatively, events appearing on different combined control/data flow diagrams can have separate CSPEC representations. For many real-time system applications, one CSPEC spans all events/control flows in a requirements tree. Centralized CSPECs lead to architectures in which a maximum amount of information is embedded into tables that directly represent the CSPECs. Table-driven architectures yield a number of important benefits, to be described.

If Figure 4.6 is leveled and balanced (decomposed) to reflect combined control and data flows, a small number of specific events are represented—Raw Data Location, Position and Velocity Data, and User Commands (Operational and Standby variants). Details of a CSPEC to accommodate these events are provided in Figure 4.14. Notice the appearance of feedback (state preserving) transitions. Raw_Data_Location enter into this portion of the requirements periodically as new sensor data is provided at a hardware determined rate. Typically, sensor based systems must simultaneously manage multiple frames of sensor imagery, each in a different phase of processing. Responding to incoming raw data or to incoming analysis results requires that the Process_Pipeline state be maintained. An important implication here is that operational conditions have not changed; thus, the current set of responses are to be continuously applied. However, when a standby state message is received, conditions must change. Thus, a state changing transition occurs admitting differing responses to the same messages. Now, incoming raw data is registered but ignored—no analysis jobs are generated. Similarly, analysis results from sensor data currently in the pipeline are registered but ignored. This state of activity serves to clear the pipeline of partially processed sensor data, from which the state name is derived—same data, different responses due to different operational conditions. Implementors with little experience in pipelined systems and with no system awareness would have a difficult time attempting to invent this event response complexity.

As the control and functional processing requirements are constructed, application specific control and data flows are generated. Extensive confusion can arise over the definition of these application-specific flows. A disciplined effort must be accomplished to carefully define the internal structure of application specific control and data flows simultaneously.

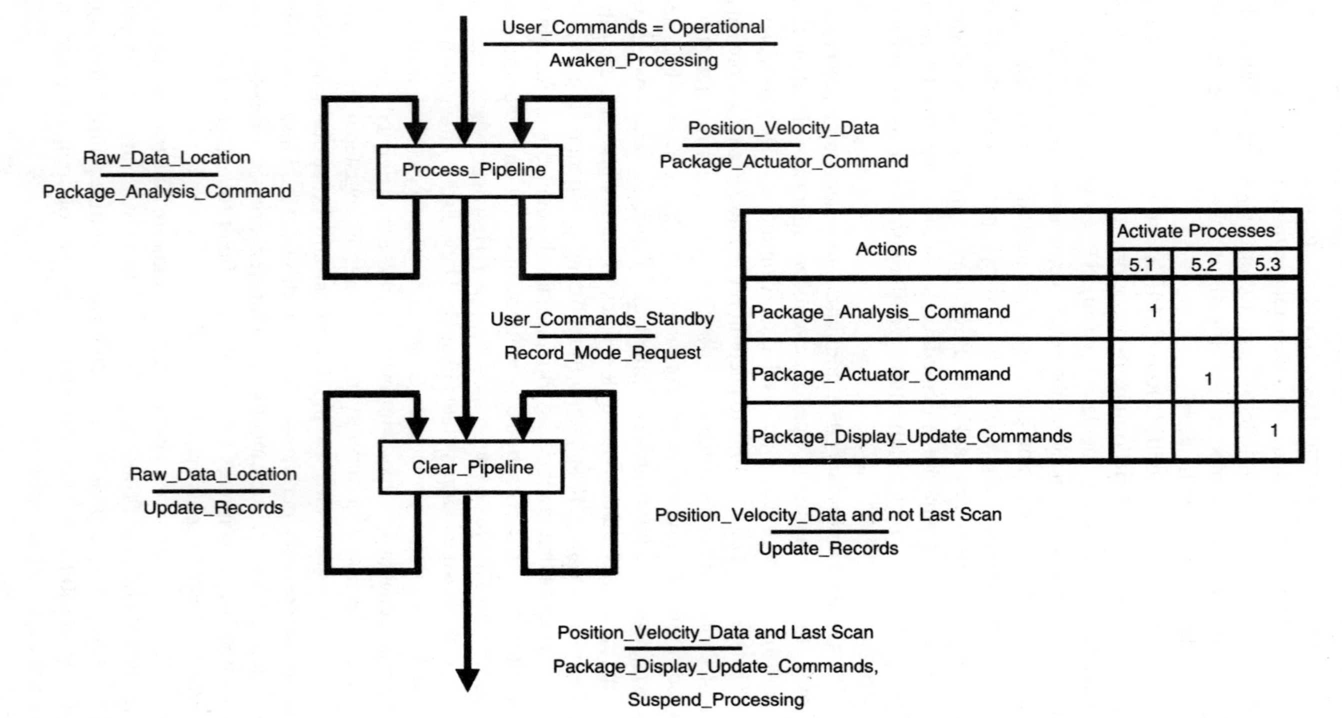

Actions	Activate Processes		
	5.1	5.2	5.3
Package_ Analysis_ Command	1		
Package_ Actuator_ Command		1	
Package_Display_Update_Commands			1

Figure 4.14 Typical CSPEC Decomposition for Operational Mode

4.4 DATA MODEL

Careful and detailed definition of specific data and control flows provides commonality across a project, serving to reduce confusion. Individuals working on different elements of a real-time system often use one name assuming different definitions. Additionally, several names are regularly employed for a fixed definition. Providing a common data dictionary eliminates this kind of confusion.

An additional benefit to providing common control and data flow definitions is agreement on criteria by which data is classified as to data or control. This is an important distinction. Control flows require event responses to be specified; data flows need functional transformations to be provided. Since this specific methodology employs a very precise criterion for identifying control flows, all members of the specification activity need to apply this same criterion.

Data dictionary formulation also serves to aid in the identification of potential objects. For event-intensive systems, objects are interpreted as data structures. Thus, any data dictionary component which possesses a complex structure is a likely candidate for an object. The detailed structure of the object is employed to identify an initial list of appropriate operations. Typically, complex structures require creation, destruction, and read/write access to the components. However, this is only a *preliminary* set of operations. Operations may be implied by the requirements specification. For example, a function to check that a message appears from a specific source location is an operationally derived requirement, not a structurally generated requirement. Therefore, final delineation of object operations can not occur until detailed software design.

No effort is made to include a specific methodology for entity-relationship diagrams with normalization of data structures. Most real-time systems within the realm of this methodology are not data-intensive. Typically, small amounts of data describing workloads and analytical results are all that is required for operation of the real-time systems within the domain of this methodology. Therefore, concepts such as normalization of relations and entity-relation models are simply not applicable.

Data Dictionary Usage

Detailed specification of a data or control flow elaborates component structure and component type as a minimum. Performing this kind of definition requires a metalanguage capable of describing component construction. Such a language is summarized in Figure 4.15. Decomposition into individual components is indicated by :=. A required specific combination of components can be constructed with a + operator. Alteration of components is simply achieved by enumerating alternatives, separating them with a "," symbol. Complex structures are characterized by composition of other complex structures, using combination (+) operators or alteration (,) operators. Several forms of commenting are allowed, using either a single asterisk or a double slash as both beginning and ending delimiters. String literals are delimited with single quotes.

Description	Symbol	Is	Comment
Is equivalent to	:: =	Composed of	Equal in math sense (Also, →, ⇒)
And (sequence)	+	Together with	Imply addition or ordered grouping
Iteration (repetition)	{ }	Iterations of	No index or 0 to
Either-or (selection)	[ ]	Select 1 of	At least (2) expressions
Optional	( )	Optional	Expression may/may not be included
	* *	Comment	
	' '	Literal	
	\ \	Description/comment	

- Hierarchical data structure combines some set of sequence, selection, and/or iteration [nested!]
- Avoid overly hierarchical/nested data structures

Figure 4.15 Data Dictionary Notation

Data Structure Definition

An example of data structure composition is diagrammatically portrayed in Figure 4.16. Raw Sensor Data usually consists of two components: Sensor_Parameters and Raw_Data itself. For instance, infrared imagery is accompanied by a map of ranges for various points in the raw imagery data. This is easily structured as an array of integers, each integer value representing a range in meters for a row in the corresponding raw pixel data. Raw pixel data, in this example, is a two-dimensional array of pulse code modulated (pcm) data (mapped into the range 0–255). Each pcm value represents an eight bit pixel describing the infrared or heat level at that range. These component and type declarations are pictured in Figure 4.15.

Using the data dictionary language described earlier, the pictorial representation is translated into three declarations, as follows:

Raw_Sensor_Data	:= Sensor_Parameters + Raw_Data
Sensor Parameters	:= vector of integers
Raw_Data	:= array of pcm data.

Along with other appropriate structured and type declarations, these declarations appear in Figure 4.17. Declarations listed form a more complete set for the example specifications provided in earlier sections. Little room for confusion exists when these definitions are made available for all project members. Moreover, redundant definitions are eliminated, since software system engineers tend to capitalize on previous definitions to build more complex definitions/structures.

Since Raw_Sensor_Data is defined by a complex structure, an abstract type or object is suggested. Multiple copies of data are in the processing pipeline during real-time operations, suggesting the need for an abstract data type (as opposed to an object manager). Proposed operations include the following:

1. Create an instance of Raw_Sensor_Data;
2. Destroy an instance of Raw_Sensor_Data;
3. Get sensor parameters;
4. Put sensor parameters;
5. Get raw data at logical location i, j in the sensor frame; and
6. Put raw data at logical location i, j in the sensor frame.

However, these need not be the only operations on this abstract data type. A specific functional requirement or PSPEC may indicate an operation such as "determine if sensor Parameter A is equal to a specific value." An operationally dictated abstract interface only becomes apparent during the layered virtual machine/object-oriented design activities conducted to generate a detailed software design model.

Control flows, CSPECs, data flows, PSPECs, and data dictionary definitions form an extensive and detailed requirements model from an implementor's perspective. Combined, they reflect an implementor's understanding of and experience with the target system domain. Lack of clarity, lack of precision, and lack of

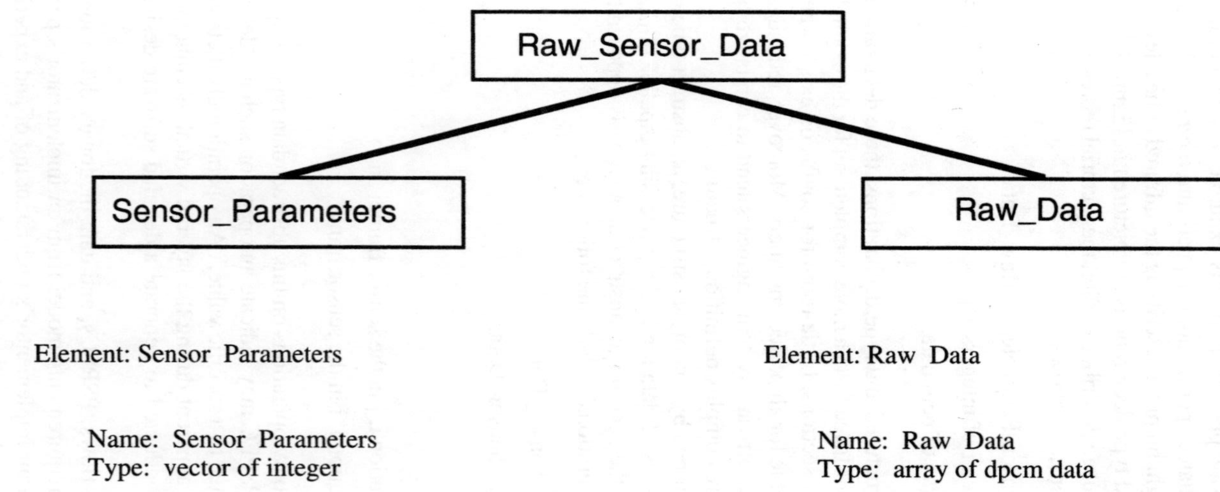

Figure 4.16 Typical Data Structure Declaration

Op_Code :: = integer
Argument_Data :: = integer
Actuator_Commands :: = Op_Code + Argument_Data
Analysis_Results :: = array (1..number_observations, 1..number_statistics) of float
Buffer_Location :: = address
Buffered_Op_Code :: = array (1..max_buffer_size) of integer
Buffered_Arguments :: = array (1..max_buffer_size) of integer
Buffered_Commands :: = Buffered_Op_Code + Buffered_Arguments
Algorithm_Parameters :: = array (1..x) of float
Configuration_Parameters :: = array (1..y) of integer
Control_Parameters :: = Algorithm_Parameters + Configuration_Parameters
Display_Operations :: = integer
Display_Arguments :: = array (1..2) of integer
Display_Update_Commands :: = Display_Operations + Display_Arguments
Pixel_Array :: = array of raster data
Formatted_Displays :: = Pixel_Array
Config_Ops :: = integer
Config_Arguments :: = integer
Internal_Configuration_Cmds :: = Config_Ops + Config_Arguments
Position_Vector :: = array (1..3) of float
Position_Vector :: = array (1..3) of float
Position_Velocity_Data :: = Position_Vector + Velocity_Vector
Raw_Data_Location :: = address
Sensor_Parameters :: = vector of integers
Raw_Data :: = array of pcm data
Raw_Sensor_Data :: = Sensor_Parameters + Raw_Data
Results_Location :: = key into database
Command_Data_Op_Code :: = integer
Command_Data_Argument :: = integer
User_Command_Data :: = Command_Data_Op_Code + Command_Data_Argument
User_Commands :: = (Power_Up, Power_Down, Operational, Standby)

Figure 4.17 Typical Data Dictionary Specification

focus when generating these implementor requirements suggests to a customer or reviewer both a lack of experience and a lack of engineering discipline. Final validation to a customer or reviewer is comprised of a consistency and completeness check against a user's view of software system operations.

4.5 REQUIREMENTS CONSISTENCY/COMPLETENESS CHECKING

Prior to continuing into architecting activities, requirements specified thus far are to be evaluated. Since delivery of a system to a user is a primary goal, implementor requirements are evaluated against a user's needs. Correlation of implementor requirements against user requirements is accomplished by a process which interrelates message flows from the operations model with control and data flows from the requirements model. As a by-product of this interrelating process, consistency and completeness of implementor requirements is thoroughly evaluated. Moreover, a framework is established for allocation of timing constraints to specific requirements.

Requirements Evaluation Approach

Evaluation of functional requirements employs a process that is in effect a "simulation" of requirements. Each incoming event in the test/output pattern of the operational model represents an event the requirements must accommodate. Requirements evaluation consists of determining the adequacy of the response to each message as indicated in both control and data flow specifications. A "message trace" or "signal flow" is the specific output product created by this evaluation. Contents of the message trace serve to verify that desired responses to each event (from the test input/output pattern) do, in fact, occur under the specified control and functional requirements.

Conceptually, each incoming event is evaluated by using a state transition diagram to assess both state and action details. Details of each action response are further evaluated by using the process activation table and appropriate PSPECs. Requirements evaluation or simulation is algorithmically described as follows:

1. Start with the system in its initial state;
2. For each incoming event (message) in the test input/output pattern of the operations model:
   a. Determine the control flow diagram which contains the CSPEC for the event;
   b. Retrieve the state transition diagram of the CSPEC;
   c. Transition to the "new" state indicated by the transition diagram using the event and the current state. Record the "new" state;

   d. Record the action indicated by the transition diagram using the event and the current state;
   e. Retrieve the process activation table of the CSPEC;
   f. Record the activated processes and their relationships (sequential and/or concurrent) indicated by the process activation table using the recorded action;
   g. Review the PSPECs of the activated processes to assure that the appropriate transformations have been invoked; and
   h. Record any responses generated by PSPEC invocation. A response can be either an outgoing data flow or an internal control event;

3. Compare all recorded data responses to anticipated responses indicated in the test input/out pattern of the operations model.

This activity is an important process to accomplish and should not be skipped. If any element of a response is missing (missing states, actions, or action components), tracing an event response through requirements quickly identifies the problem. Study of PSPEC transforms in the context of a specific message response determines if the transformation definition is consistent with conditions under which the PSPEC must operate. If any outgoing data responses are missing, both the process activation table and PSPECs are carefully evaluated for flaws. Other criteria for checking consistency and completeness can also be applied. Similar functional responses must accompany events within the same general category. For example, sensor data collection events are to engender very similar functional transformations. Differences in transformations for different classes of sensors are carefully evaluated in detail to assess appropriateness of differing responses. Completeness checking is most effectively performed by determining that a proper collection of functions is included in the response, that their mode is correct (sequential vs. concurrent), that appropriate outgoing responses do occur and that the terminal conditions obtained are appropriate.

Other important benefits derive from this process. Customer confidence and satisfaction usually results after a detailed walkthrough of both requirements and this consistency check. Satisfaction results because the implementor demonstrates detailed understanding of his own target system domain, because his requirements are demonstrated to meet the customer's specific operational needs, and because the customer comes to feel that a system implemented against these requirements will actually work. Lack of customer commitment usually disappears quite rapidly after a review of this evaluation process. Hidden operational assumptions on the part of the system engineers are revealed by virtue of performing this kind of analysis, saving significant integration and testing effort.

Requirements evaluation is thus necessary to achieve several important goals. Missing requirements are identified, unnecessary requirements are eliminated, and hidden operational assumptions are identified. This dynamic evaluation of user's view and implementor's view is the most effective mechanism for identification of these flaws. Proof is generated to assure that a workable software system can be delivered long before any code is written. Failure to perform this kind of evaluation allows undiscovered flaws to creep into the implementation. Identification and resolution of problems that are not eliminated by this form of evaluation is difficult to accomplish when problems/flaws are embedded into several hundred thousand lines of code distributed across multiple target platforms. Early identification and elimination saves significant integration and testing schedule and effort. Moreover, conditions for high performance levels are established since less code needs to be generated—only requirements needed to satisfy user operations are included in the implementation.

Requirements evaluation has been typified for the examples in this chapter and appears in Figure 4.18. An effective format for documenting a requirements trace is demonstrated in this figure. Six columns are employed: State Before, Real-Time Event, Action, Mode, Processing, and State After. Entries in the Real-Time Event column are the incoming events, in the exact order and context, as they appear in the operations model/test input/output pattern. State After and Action have been derived from the state transition diagram. Processing and Mode columns represent PSPEC process bubbles, sequencing, and relationship, as indicated in the corresponding process activation table using the action column value. Refer to Figures 4.12 and 4.13 to see how some of these entries are obtained. While not included here, a last column indicating outgoing data responses may be used to list flows generated by the invoked PSPECs.

Suppose the system is in operational state. When a Raw Sensor Data event occurs, a state preserving transition back to operational state results. An action entitled Process Raw Data occurs. Process Raw Data is defined in a process activation table as the following sequence of tránsformations: 1.1 Copy Raw Data; 5.1a Package Analysis Command. Reviewing the PSPECs for these transformations determines viability of this response under these conditions. (PSPECs are not included in this example but in reality are included in the table during informal or formal reviews.)/ Transformation sequencing appears in the "Processing" column of Figure 4.18.

At this point, several operational assumptions implicit in the overall requirements model surface as a result of the analysis. Copying raw sensor data implies the following:

1. Extensive memory must be available to store multiple copies of Raw_Sensor_Data;
2. A pipeline of sensor data is to be maintained, with each copy in different stages of algorithm analysis (under analysis, intermediate results received, all results completed, etc.); and
3. Raw sensor data is arriving at a rate which indicates that analysis performed on data stored in the sensor's memory mapped hardware interface will likely result in garbled analysis conclusions resulting from data across multiple raw sensor data frames.

While these operational assumptions may be intuitively obvious to a senior system engineer, a software engineer unfamiliar with sensor systems would fail to

State Before	Real-time Event	Action	Mode	Processing	State After
Start	<User_commands> =power-up	Initialize data structures	Seq	2.1 Copy Message 2.2 Decode Message	Standby
Standby	<User_commands> = operational	Awaken processing	Conc	1.1 Copy Raw Data 3.1 Construct Display 4.1 Construct Actuator Command 5.1 Evaluate Raw Data	Operational
Operational	<Raw_sensor_data>	Process raw data	Seq	1.1 Copy Raw Data 5.1a Package analysis Command	Operational
Operational	<Position_velocity_ data>	Process result data	Seq	5.2 Respond to results 4.1a Construct Actuator Command	Operational
Operational	<User_commands> = standby (^s)	Suspend processing	Conc	All Processes OFF Except Message Handling	Standby
Standby	<User_commands> = power down (quit)	Clear data structures	Seq	Message Handling Processes OFF	Start

Figure 4.18 Typical Requirements Evaluation

incorporate these assumptions into the software architecture and design. A thorough and detailed review of the message trace in Figure 4.18 serves to bring these kinds of assumptions to the forefront for discussion and inclusion in both requirements and ultimate design. Another interesting question arises as to the validity of these uncovered operational assumptions. By exposing these kinds of assumptions, their experiential basis can be questioned, discussed, and appropriate modifications can be accomplished.

In this very simple example, completeness of the response is almost trivially confirmed. Raw sensor data is quickly moved from the hardware interface to clear the interface for the next incoming sensor frame. Once this has been accomplished, generation of an analysis command is not only an appropriate next step (sequencing mode is correct) but is also the correct terminating condition for this response. Obviously, this response is complete.

An event analysis serves another important additional purpose. Event responses in real-time systems must be accomplished within a fixed time constraint. Event analyses serve as the basis for an initial allocation of event response time constraints.

Event Time-Line Allocation

Each table entry in the event analysis contains a detailed description of the functional transformations employed in the event response. Functional transformation sequencing is employed to generate an initial allocation of timing constraints to specific functions. For example, recall the table entry reviewed in the previous section. According to the event analysis, a Raw_Data_Location event resulted in process 1.1 Copy Raw Data followed by process 5.1 Package Analysis Command. If event responses must occur within 100 milliseconds, a typical allocation might look like the following:

Event:	Raw Data Location	Time Limit:	100 msec
Response:	1.1 Copy Raw Data	Allocation:	25 msec
	5.1 Package Analysis Command		60 msec
	SW Controller Overhead		15 msec

These allocations are usually justified on the basis of details contained in individual PSPECs, previous experience, and perhaps some benchmarking studies. Note the inclusion of time overhead for a software controller. Ideally, as will be described later, state transition diagrams and process activation tables are fed directly into a software controller. Thus, some computational overhead is engendered for performing state and action table lookups and for invoking procedures that implement corresponding PSPECs. However, this overhead is typically small by comparison with performance of an ill-specified, ill-designed piece of software to perform the same activity.

Time allocations can be added to Figure 4.18 as a separate column. Moreover, a unique list that summarizes the time allocated to each PSPEC/process is maintained. In this way, a consistent value is employed each time an event response requires the invocation of a given PSPEC. These process time allocations will also be employed later in evaluating a specific architecture for time-liness.

Now that requirements have been specified and checked for consistency, completeness, and time-liness, a full requirements model has been accomplished. Note again that a minimal, end-to-end set of requirements has been generated. Consistency and completeness checking assures that the simplicity and end-to-end criteria are satisfied. Verification of all event/response combinations in the test input/output pattern assures that end-to-end processing has been obtained. Activity can now proceed to the architecting process. Even if further requirements are added at a later date, inclusion of these new needs is easily accommodated within the analytical and modeling framework accomplished to this point.

5

Architecture Model Generation

Construction of an architecture model identifies system level processes that can be individually implemented in combinations of hardware and software. An important goal here is to partition the control and functional requirements in a manner that provides maximum leverage over remaining development activities. Partitioning of the requirements focuses on collections of requirements that must operate concurrently. Based on concurrency allocations, specific hardware/software design trades that have a limited scope of effect are accomplished. Effects of design decisions are restricted within boundaries of each specific architecture process. Moreover, faulty decisions are easier to fix when discovered, since changes are also limited by the partitioning of requirements into processes.

Architecture model generation consists of several discrete phases as depicted in Figure 5.1. Initially, control and functional requirements were generated with no concern for technological environment. A first step into architecture generation employs an explicit exercise to add requirements necessary to accommodate characteristics of external interfaces to be employed. Quite often, real-time systems successfully pass code and unit test but fail to integrate well. After long hours of debugging, symptoms observed are traced to incorrect assumptions regarding protocols and mechanics for managing specific hardware interfaces. These integration problems can be avoided if an explicit step that enhances initial requirements to reflect interface protocols and mechanics is accomplished.

Once interfaces have been incorporated into requirements, allocation of requirements into architecture modules can occur. An architecture module is defined to be a process that must operate in parallel during real-time processing activities of the system. Note carefully that each process is ultimately implemented as some combination of hardware and software. Of great importance is the manner in which enhanced requirements are mapped into architecture processes. In this chapter, a

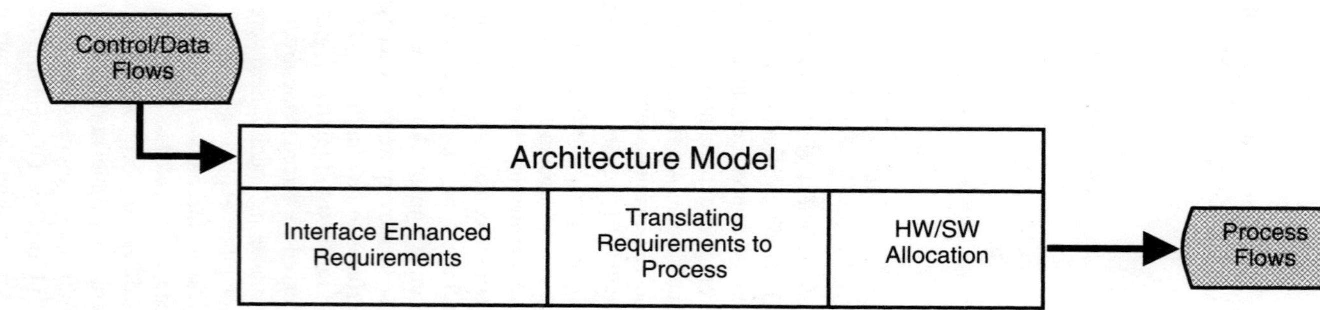

Figure 5.1 Architecture Model Generation

general set of heuristics is provided that are employed to translate requirements into architecture. These guidelines have been derived from an extensive review of a large number of real-time systems, most in Ada, the remainder in other languages. Heuristics employed in process determination play a critical role in assuring flexibility, performance and integration and test efforts during implementation and future methodology iterations.

Architecting a system is not a new concept. In the past, this activity was often referred to as top level design. An important difference here, however, is the guidelines for translating requirements into architecture processes. These translation guidelines reflect a need for software elements to operate concurrently and to reside within an integrated hardware environment. For these reasons, use of translation guidelines constrain system architects significantly more than in the past.

As with requirements generation, architecting is an iterative process. One form of iteration results from introduction of greater levels of detail in the architecture/design of a system. As additional architecture/design is introduced, additional requirements are derived. Derived requirements are incorporated into the requirements tree prior to introduction of additional architectural detail. An iterative architecture development activity reflecting incorporation of derived requirements is characterized in Figure 5.2. Initially, requirements are enhanced for interfaces using an architecture template concept. Enhanced requirements are then translated into architecture processes. Introduction of architecture processes implies a need to support process interaction (a derived requirement). Since these processes are likely to be accomplished in separate hardware elements, a physical architecture needs to be derived. Operating these processes within a system level, physical interconnection architecture introduces additional interface requirements. These interface requirements are incorporated into the requirements model. Within each architecture process, requirements are divided among hardware and software. Since software must operate/reside on implemented hardware within the architecture module/process, integration requirements must now be added to the requirements to be satisfied by software. Beginning with this significantly extended requirements tree, a software architecture is derived. If the derived software architecture satisfies these requirements, additional requirements are usually placed on the implemented hardware to accommodate the operational software architecture.

Architecture/design stages are not the only form of iteration between requirements and architecture. In addition to all of these derived requirements, performing a series of design decisions almost always results in discovery of requirements overlooked at a previous stage. Iteration is now necessary to introduce these missed requirements into the architecture/design. Introducing new requirements into a previously generated architecture/design requires tracing the effects of these new requirements through all the intervening requirements, architecture, and design stages.

Describing a top level design that effectively employs concurrent activity to satisfy both operational and implementor requirements consists of the following steps:

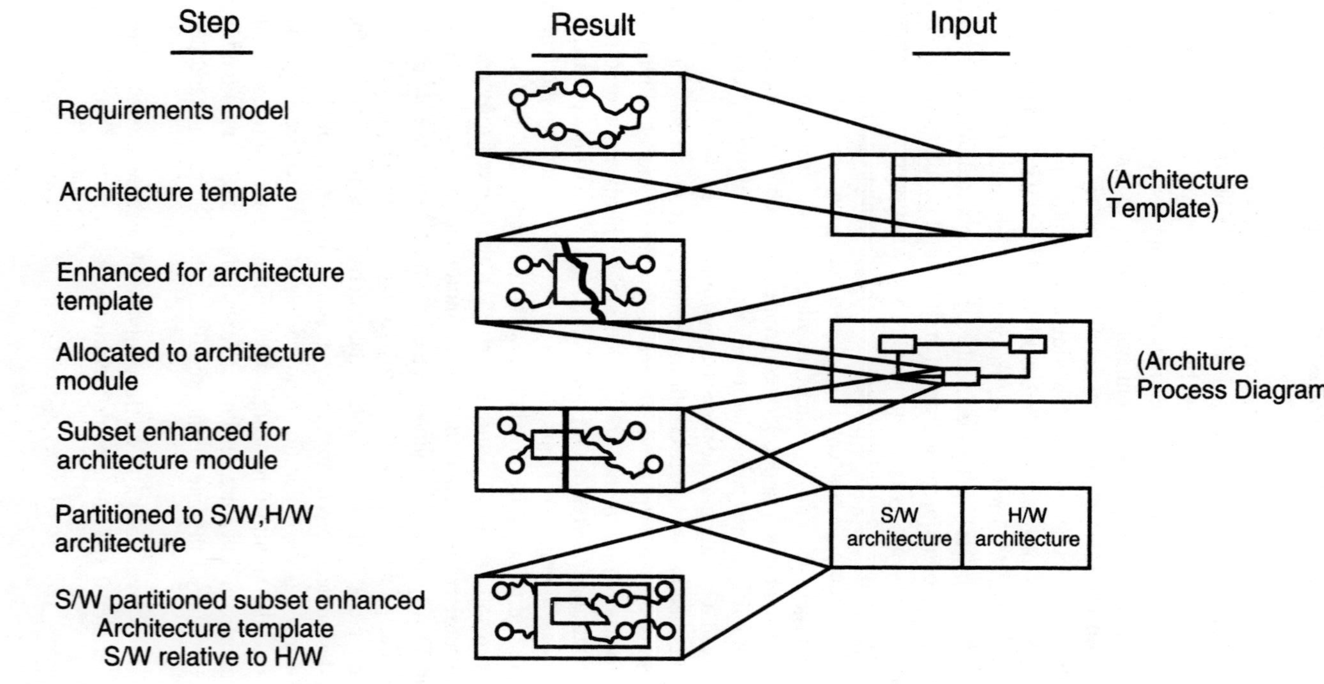

Figure 5.2 Architecture Development Guidelines

1. Enhance both functional and control requirements to accommodate specific hardware/technological interfaces;
2. Perform a consistency and completeness check of enhanced requirements against operational requirements;
3. Translate both functional and control requirements into a process architecture;
4. Perform a consistency and completeness check of the process architecture against operational requirements;
5. Evaluate architecture performance against timing constraints based on combining timing allocations for requirements mapped into each architecture process; and
6. Allocate requirements within each architecture process to hardware and to software.

Each of the steps involves specific products in specific formats. Two products are of particular importance. A process architecture flow diagram represents the concurrent organization of the top level design and divides development into manageable subproblems. An architecture evaluation table proves that the architecture is capable of performing the job desired by the user.

5.1 ENHANCING REQUIREMENTS FOR TECHNOLOGY/DESIGN

During integration and test activities, software and hardware are made to work together. Integrating software and hardware can often be a frustrating experience. Actual interfaces are hidden deep within software code structures. When integration testing goes awry, a typical symptom is for the system to simply stop working. Locating a problem cause can be difficult, since no one knows where to look for problems. Perhaps the major locations where integration and test problems occur are at the software/hardware interfaces. An extensive number of debugging hours are typically expended to trace problems to these interfaces. When a symptom is traced to an interface problem, fingers usually begin to point: hardware blames software, software blames hardware. In fact, both participants are guilty due to lack of communication.

In an effort to eliminate these kinds of problems, an explicit step is included in the architecting process which emphasizes hardware/software interfaces. Requirements for implementing interface protocols and mechanics are expressly incorporated into the requirements tree. Following of proper and assumed protocols is thus ensured. Moreover, hardware developers are placed on notice that software developers need to be informed when protocols or mechanics change. If application specific integrated circuits are being concurrently developed, hardware interface mechanics and protocols are guaranteed to change as hardware developers work through their own implementation process. Software design also changes during implementation.

Failure to include an explicit step incorporating interface requirements leads to an integration and testing nightmare. Finger pointing between software and hardware teams ensues. Software developers spend lots of hours debugging, only to conclude with "But, I thought you needed me to . . . !" To which hardware developers reply, "No, I assumed you would . . .!" Confrontations such as this can be avoided if interface requirements are addressed early in the architecture process.

Including interface mechanics helps assure the ability of a particular interface mechanism to achieve system operations. Consider, for example, a sensor that provides data into a hardwired, memory mapped area. If unspecified, a software implementor can choose to perform analysis on the data at the memory interface or can decide to copy the data to a temporary buffer for analysis at leisure. Performing in-place analysis affects the integrity of the software system. With in-place analysis, new data can intermix with older data if analysis is not accomplished in a timely manner. Intermixture of new and old data causes analysis results to become garbled. The results reflect both old and new data. Selection of an appropriate alternative is accomplished by a software system engineer aware of the performance/data integrity trade being performed. To assure integrity of software operations these kinds of decisions come as requirements to a software developer. Enhancing requirements to reflect interface mechanics and strategies prior to architecture process generation allows this kind of requirement to be generated and included. Waiting for spurious results during integration and test is not an effective approach. In a large system, identification of this kind of decision on the part of a software implementor after the fact is difficult to accomplish. Moreover, if a poor software design has been employed, an inappropriate policy may be spread across several software elements, making identification of the policy even more difficult.

As a guideline for requirements enhancement, an architecture template is employed. This template appears in Figure 5.3. Its purpose is to identify sources of interface requirements. User interface requirements are necessary to assure appropriate displays are updated. Ability to field keyboard, mouse, or lightpen signals are usually included here. Translation of vector data into raster data in a memory mapped frame buffer to feed display processing units is also an aspect of user interface requirements.

Another source of interface requirements is that of sensors or data collectors. These are indicated by the category "input processing" on the architecture template of Figure 5.3. Most data collectors are of the memory mapped type. These feed data into memory on a periodic or regular basis. Some interrupt the main processor; others do not interrupt the main processor. Protocols for handling interrupts or moving data to a temporary area for later processing are included for this category of interface requirements.

Data receivers or output processing requirements are a third category of interface requirements. These are usually physical mechanisms which orient or control other elements in a system, causing physical activities to occur. Typical of these actuators might be gimbals on a sensor turret. When commanded, a sensor is pointed in a different direction or oriented in a different manner. As with sensors,

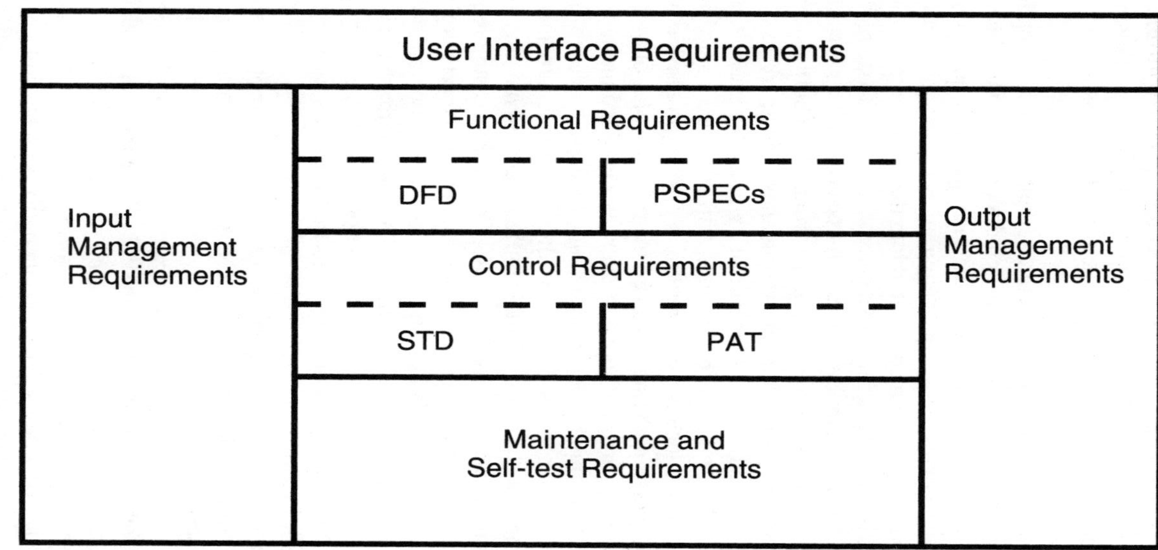

Figure 5.3 Notation for Requirements Enhancement

these interfaces are usually memory mapped. However, interfaces of this kind might poll memory rather than interrupt a main processor. Moreover, they may acknowledge commands in a manner that requires software on a main processor to maintain status data regarding the interface itself. Required mechanics and protocols for actuators are specified as part of the requirements enhancement process.

A final arena for representing interface requirements is that of maintenance and self test processing. Many systems require special protocols for system initialization—certain messages with specific data must pass back and forth to bring a system to an operational state. Other systems require specific built-in-test activities to be performed on a regular basis concurrent with actual processing of incoming sensor data. These requirements are explicitly stated to assure their correct implementation.

Figure 5.4 demonstrates an architecture template which is applied to a typical real-time system. This typical example includes only user interface, input processing, and output processing aspects of interface requirements. Inclusion of a specific template category suggests that requirements associated with each interface in the template category are incorporated into the current requirements tree. Keyboard input messages are copied into a command buffer. Control flows, indicated by User Commands, are employed with a message decoding function to assure an appropriate response to the message at the front of the buffer. Real-time system operations generate Display Update Commands, which are in a vector format. These are transformed into a raster format by a display generation function and stored in an internal buffer. This internal buffer is then copied into a memory mapped frame buffer location accessed by a display processing unit. Added requirements for accommodating keyboard input and display output, denoting user interface processing, are now added to the basic set of requirements.

In the category of input processing, a single function is needed. Transfer of raw data from a sensor's memory mapped hardware interface into a temporary buffer must be accomplished. Location of this buffered area in memory is passed to the real-time system for analysis and response. Output processing requirements, another category of interfaces, are necessary to translate an actuator's desired position and velocity (as provided by analysis during real-time operations) into a bit pattern which is acceptable to an actuator. Once an appropriate bit pattern is constructed into a formatted message in a temporary buffer, another function is required to copy the formatted message into the actuator's memory mapped hardware interface location.

Requirements representing interface mechanics and protocols must be either decomposed further or defined as PSPECs. A PSPEC for one of the enhanced requirements described in Figure 5.4 is provided in Figure 5.5. Explicitly defined in the PSPEC is a strategy requiring that incoming sensor data be copied into a temporary buffer for more leisurely processing. While this might seem obvious, remember that an individual with little or no real-time experience probably would not know to use this approach. Moreover, an experienced individual, who just happens to be a little overwhelmed, may accidentally forget to employ a strategy such as this. In fact, copying incoming data engenders some computational overhead. If this sensor provides raw data at a low periodic rate, in-place processing might be

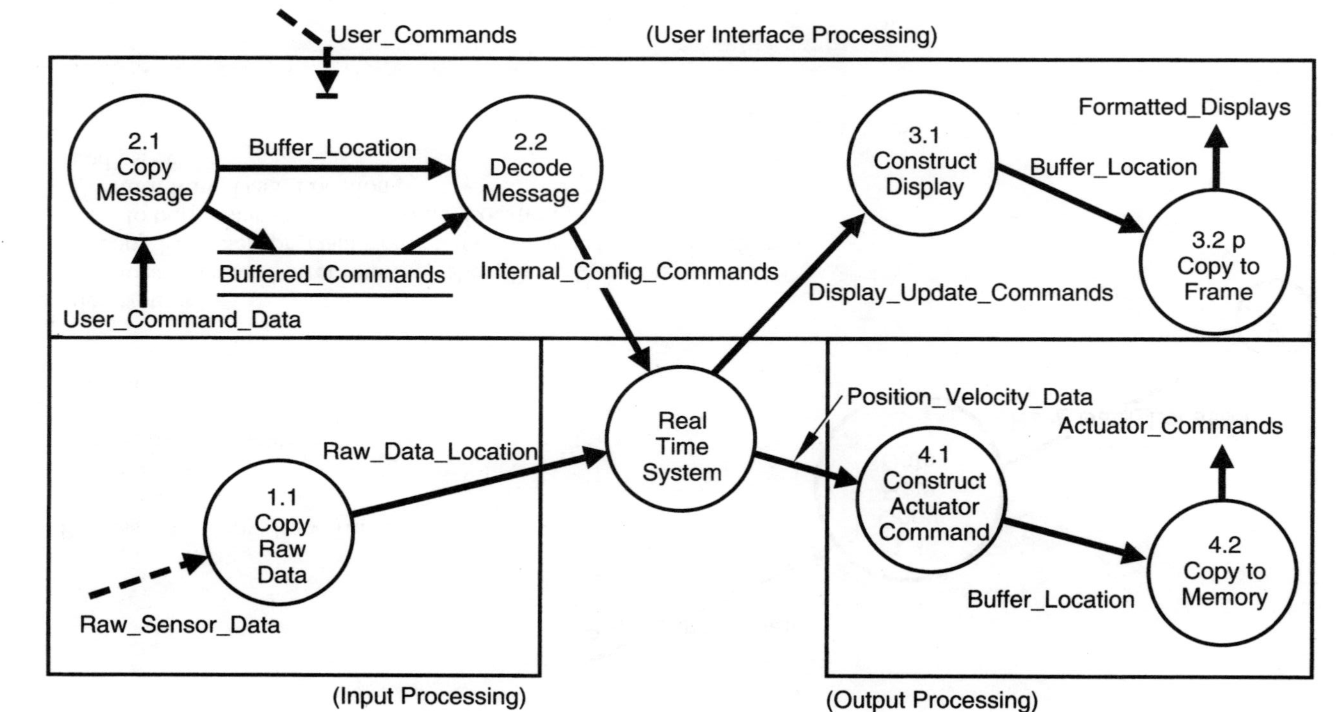

Figure 5.4 Typical Requirements Enhancement

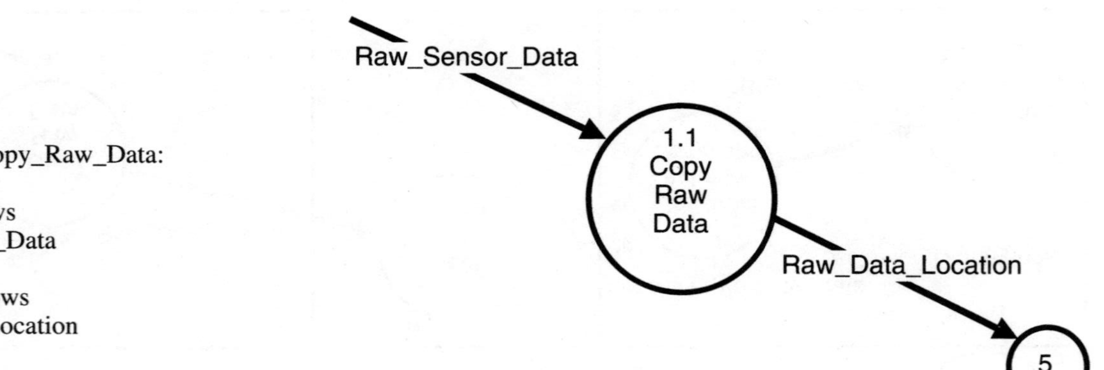

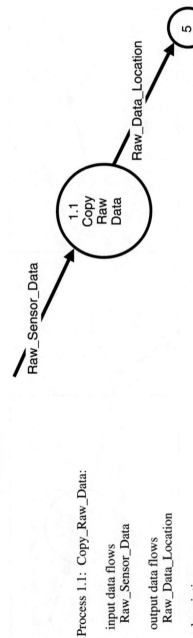

```
Process 1.1:  Copy_Raw_Data:

  input data flows
    Raw_Sensor_Data

  output data flows
    Raw_Data_Location

  description
      allocate scratch buffer returning Raw_Data_Location ;
      copy Raw_Sensor_Data from memory-mapped hardware interface
          to buffer starting at Raw_Data_Location ;
      return Raw_Data_Location ;
  end pspec
```

Figure 5.5 Typical Enhanced Requirements PSPEC

appropriate, since no overhead is incurred. By explicitly writing a PSPEC using the philosophy to move data away from the hardware interface for incoming sensor data, an intelligent discussion (and detailed performance analysis) can occur where all affected parties can evaluate the decision, its justification, and its inclusion in the final implementation. In this way, no hidden surprises surface during an infuriating integration and test debugging effort.

Of course, many of the interface requirements may have already been partially included during previous requirements specification efforts. Partial inclusion early in the specification of requirements is quite acceptable. Enhancing requirements through the architecture template serves as an explicit and formal sanity check to expand the incomplete earlier specifications and to assure all relevant interfaces are represented. Forming an explicit requirements enhancement assures that no interfaces or protocol are overlooked.

These enhanced requirements, along with the original control and functional processing requirements, are inputs into the architecture process generation activity that follows. Traceability of interface requirements into actual software is now assured, since interface requirements are formally stated and reviewed.

5.2 TOP LEVEL DESIGN

Performing top level design is the second aspect of architecture model generation. In this phase of activity, requirements are mapped into software system level processes. Process interactions are then captured as an architecture flow diagram. Each interaction between pairs of processes is labeled according to data flowing across the interactions. Consistency and completeness of the top level process architecture is evaluated against user requirements. Consistency/completeness checking translates the architecture into an operational framework to assure that the architecture can effectively respond to events dynamically appearing at the interfaces.

Most developers never accomplish this form of evaluation. Many do not even know that correlation to a user's view is an important process. Architecture consistency and completeness checking can indeed become an extremely tedious activity well worth the effort. This level of checking provides multiple benefits. Ability of the architecture to respond to all incoming events is verified. A trace of data flowing through the top level architecture in response to each event is generated. This data trace is successfully employed to reduce debugging difficulties during integration and test. When a problem occurs during integration, testers can dump data necessary to reconstruct the actual data flowing through the architecture prior to system failure. This actual response data can be compared to the design consistency trace to identify the cause of system failure. As a result, problem causes are easily and rapidly identified and fixed.

Process Abstraction

Basic components in the architecture are represented as processes or modules. As employed here, a process has a special definition. Each process represents a collection of requirements that must be accomplished concurrently with other requirements. Requirements collected into a single process are to be implemented in some appropriate combination of hardware and software.

Process definition requires that two important activities need to occur. Selection of specific architecture processes is accomplished by partitioning of control and functional requirements into concurrent units. Motivations for selection of each process and the corresponding requirements allocations are discussed and critiqued in an open forum. Reasons are provided to justify inclusion of each process and its allocations. Be quite wary of justifications as simple as "this is the way this has always been done." In many cases, using this justification propagates poor approaches that caused difficulty in the past and will cause even greater integration and test headaches when using Ada.

Associating a specific requirement with an architecture process requires an explicit decision. Again, the basis of each decision is rigorously and explicitly reviewed and justified. Poor mappings of requirements into architecture are quite difficult to identify and fix during later phases of development, such as integration and testing. Once an implementation is accomplished, visibility into the requirements allocation decisions is usually lost—hidden in hundreds of thousands of lines of code.

An overall architecture is best represented graphically. For this purpose, a process flow or architecture flow diagram is employed. A typical and simplistic process graph/architecture flow diagram is demonstrated in Figure 5.6. Each process or architecture module is represented as a rounded square. Inside the rounded square appears the process name. Process names are specified as nouns which accurately reflect capabilities of the process. Additionally, both control and data specifications allocated to the process are indicated by unique identification numbers within the process square. Interaction between two architecture processes is indicated by a straight line between the two processes. Interactions are further labeled by the data that flows between the processes during process interaction. If data flows between the interacting processes, this data appears as a smaller arrow above the process interaction arrow. This data must be identified as to name, direction of flow, and type of flow. A small circle at the base of the data flow indicates the data source process. An empty circle at the base of the data flow implies raw data flow while a filled circle suggests control flow, requiring an event response within the architecture process.

Identification of data flow between architecture processes is affected by specific requirements allocated to the individual interacting architecture processes (see Figure 5.6). For data to flow between two architecture processes (A and B), the following conditions must be satisfied:

1. A specific data flow must move between requirements R_1 and R_2 on a flow diagram; and

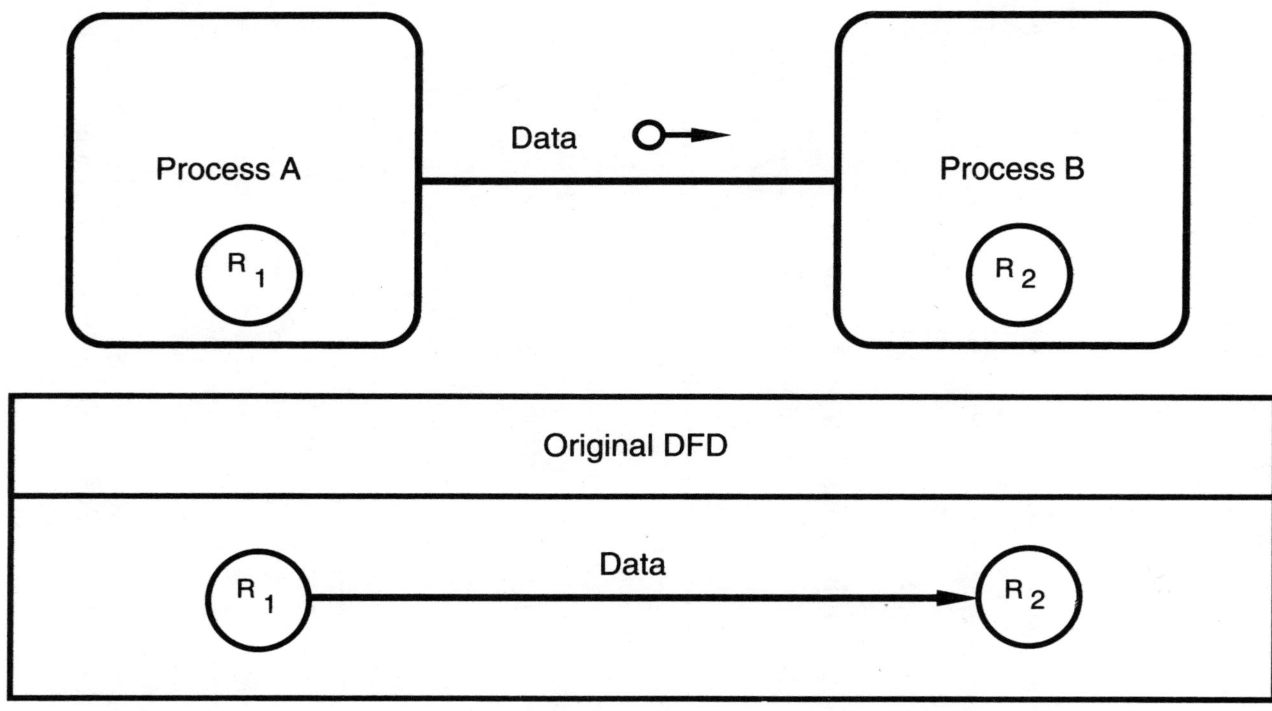

Figure 5.6 Typical Process Graph

2. Requirement R_1 must be allocated to process A while requirement R_2 is allocated to process B.

If these conditions hold, data flowing between R_1 and R_2 must flow along an interaction between Process A and Process B. These conditions assume that requirements are atomic and do not span processes. If a requirement needs to be allocated across processes, then requirements splitting needs to be accomplished. The original requirement is replaced by multiple requirements generated by the splitting activity.

A requirements data flow effects the direction of data flowing between two processes but does not determine the process initiating the interaction. *Interaction initiation decisions among concurrent processes must be made after an initial tasking architecture is generated.* One architecture process may result in multiple Ada tasks. Moreover, tasks that initiate interactions can experience blocking, which effects throughput. Thus, caller/callee decisions are deferred until an initial tasking architecture is generated, so that throughput impacts are properly considered.

Translating Requirements into Architecture

Examining a large number of successful and unsuccessful real-time systems suggests a number of guidelines or heuristics for translating requirements into architecture processes. These guidelines are based upon the explicit need to incorporate concurrency into process selection. As a start, a system controller process is employed. Use of a controller allows isolation of event response requirements into a centrally located portion of the architecture. An additional benefit of a centralized system controller process is to reduce the level of effort necessary to support integration and test activities. Isolation of problems caused by inadequate event response specification is easily accomplished when control requirements are centralized. In contrast, event response management distributed across architecture processes leads to poor design of event response software, difficulty in identification of conditions under which event response is inadequate, and extensive, frustrating debugging activities during integration and test. Moreover, centralized system control allows flexibility to be built into the design. To obtain centralized control, a large portion of the event response specifications (state transition diagrams and process activation tables) are allocated directly into this System Control architecture process. This encourages a table-driven approach to implementation, which allows easy modification. Modification of response management capabilities involves mostly changing of data in tables and involves very little coding effort.

Architecting a system that incorporates concurrency within the top level design requires great care. Minimal use of concurrency is adopted as an architectural goal to maximize throughput and to reduce integration and test efforts. Additionally, a hierarchical approach to control is more desirable. Control interactions should be carefully constrained to a discrete set of superior and subordinate processes. Each architectural process contains a "flat" control model, indicated by a state transition diagram and process activation table. These elements must include decision processes for managing internal computational requirements and interaction with subordinate and superior controls. A limited number of allocated requirements in the form of process specifications are associated with the allocated control specifications, hence, a "flat" control model.

Unfortunately, decentralized control approaches are often employed for real-time systems. As a result of improper emphasis upon processing algorithms, each data flow bubble is mapped to a separate architecture process. Unlimited control interaction occurs among all process elements in the architecture. No process is really in charge.

This architectural solution violates several important criteria for intelligent application of heuristics or guidelines suggested above. Flexibility is not obtained; simple changes in requirements involve major changes in the architecture requiring extensive new software development and incurring high levels of integration and test effort. Performance is usually degraded because data movement involves a significant number of process communications and extensive process synchronization. Decentralized architectures are usually characterized by maximal currency. An overly complex system that further exaggerates the integration and test grind results.

Since external interfaces provide data under their own control, and at their own rate, at least one architecture process or module is provided for each external interface. In this way, response to data generators (sensors) or driving of data receivers (actuators) occurs asynchronously with analysis operations and concurrently with event response processing. Providing at least one architecture process for each external interface is extremely important when data is provided by synchronously operating data collectors. Management of these interfaces requires explicit functionality to move the data away from the interface area for later processing. Data movement from the physical interface is not easily accomplished without an explicit process for each synchronous data collector. Actuator command construction and data positioning to a memory mapped interface is also typically implemented by a separate architecture process. Encapsulation of interface locations and protocols under abstraction by individual processes improves flexibility of design. Interfaces are easily replaced by removing access through the old interface and providing access through a new interface. Moreover, integration and test difficulties are reduced. Problems with interface management are isolated within specific architecture processes. Difficulties with successful integration to the hardware interface typically create symptomatic software behavior experienced totally within the specific architecture process managing the interface. Guidance as to problem location is immediately provided by the appearance of the symptomatic behavior within the architecture process.

Each specific hardware device is managed during software system operations. Typically, hardware devices provide data and receive commands. An important architectural trade relates to the number of processes employed to manage the hardware device interface. Two options are available. A single process can be utilized to manage both incoming data and outgoing commands. As an alternate, separate processes can be employed—one for incoming data, another for outgoing commands. Both throughput and flexibility are at issue. Fewer processes typically translate to greater flexibility. Modification is easier, since fewer potential integrations need to be accommodated. Reducing the number of processes to manage the device improves system throughput (less competition for available system resources) at a cost of reduced throughput for the device being managed.

Identification of concurrency centers to create modules/processes can be derived from data flow diagrams and process activation tables. A previous section describes an effective manner for representing parallel processing chains using the format and placement of processes in data flow diagrams. If this formatting approach is employed, each parallel requirements chain can be collected together into a unique architecture process. If processes have been "randomly" positioned on the flow diagram, an architect normally must redraw the data flow diagram in a format that emphasizes the primary processing chains. Potential architecture processes are then more easily identified.

As an example illustrating an application of the above guidelines, reconsider Figure 4.4. According to this diagram, two potential processing chains could be included as architecture processes. One process, potentially entitled Analysis Manager, represents the processing chain including functions 5.1, Evaluate Raw Data and 5.2, Respond To Results. A second process, entitled Feedback Manager, encompasses function 5.2, Update Control Parameters. However, other legal partitionings can be employed. As an alternative, a single architecture process named Application Manager could include functions 5.1, 5.2, and 5.3 into a single process. Selection of one architectural alternative over the other needs to be rigorously defended based on previous experience, evaluation criteria to be demonstrated shortly, and detailed simulation models evaluating performance effects.

Data contained in the body of a process activation table also indicates potential concurrency use during process generation. Recall that the body of the process activation table describes event response generation details in terms of the translation into underlying functional transformations. One aspect of this activation specification is to describe functional transformations that must be accomplished concurrently. Parallel response streams are excellent candidates for establishing architecture processes. If parallel streams are allocated to separate architecture processes, CSPECs (STD and PAT) controlling those functional streams must also be allocated. Of course, this may reduce traceability to the original control specifications through fractionation of the state transition diagram and process activation table.

Based on Figure 4.13, an example is provided of the usage of this guideline. According to this CSPEC and PAT, a User Command, indicating the onset of an operational state, requires invocation of a response with the action named Awaken Processing. In the body of the process activation table, Awaken Processing requires that functions 5.1, 5.2, and 5.3 be accomplished concurrently. Another architecture alternative—creating a unique architecture process for each individual function—can be generated by employing these concurrency requirements to justify a separate process for each function.

Application of any of the guidelines requires careful scrutinizing and evaluation. The selected architecture mapping must be justified and subjected to an extensive peer review. Moreover, iteration on requirements is performed to include support for specific inter-process communications implied by the selected architecture. This is an example of a step in methodical development identifying shortcomings in a previous step.

Capturing Process Flow

A complete architecture is specified by generation of an architecture flow diagram, sometimes referred to as process flows. All process interactions are collected together on a master diagram. Process interactions are explicitly labeled as to direction of data/control flow. Specific requirements are associated with modules/processes by placing identifiers of the bound requirements underneath the process name. All data/control flowing across the interfaces specified in the combined control/data context diagram appear on the architecture/process flow diagram.

Internal data/control flows among architecture modules also appear on the process flow. Identification of internal data/control movement within the architecture is accomplished by using the requirements mapping. If data or control moves between two requirements, and these requirements are in separate architecture processes, then an internal flow appears between the architecture processes. Flow between architecture processes consists of the data or control flowing between the two individual process requirements.

As with other diagramming techniques, an overly complex architecture/process flow diagram can result. To alleviate clutter, a leveled approach is suggested. Processes at one level can be decomposed into lower level architecture flow diagrams. Balancing rules are observed across the architecture levels. Flows into and out from a parent architecture process appear as inputs and outputs on the decomposed or leveled process flow diagram. Processes at the most primitive level no further decomposition are described according to a module specification. Contents of an architecture module specification include requirements bound to the module/process, data stores implemented within the process, preconditions and post conditions for module invocation, details of mechanics and protocols associated with process interaction, and any other appropriate information needed to characterize the module.

Control strategies implemented by an architecture have a major impact upon development activities. Some specific guidelines aid in architecture generation, as follows:

1. Severe limitations are placed upon control interactions of processes; and
2. A significant percentage of control specifications are allocated to a single controller process.

Limiting control interaction significantly reduces architectural complexity. As a result, performance is increased and integration efforts are decreased. Enforcing a hierarchical control concept limits control interactions sufficiently. Maximizing allocated control specifications in the form of large state transition diagrams and process activation tables leads to table-driven architectures. Resultant architectures are flexible, predominately constraining modification efforts to table changes. Minimal coding effort is typically involved. A "flat" control model employs a single large set of allocated control specifications, as opposed to multiple small allocations of control specifications.

Selection of an appropriate process architecture is performed through a set of trade studies. Alternative architectures (different translations from implementor requirements to processes) are formulated. From a software perspective, a number of criteria have proved useful in the comparative evaluation of architectures. An initial motivation is provided for each alternative. Experience has shown that trading concurrency complexity for control complexity usually proves to be the basic foundation for posing an alternative architecture. Evaluating an architectural alternative's impact on performance by assessing losses/gains in throughput is another criterion for comparative evaluation. Typically, architectures with excessive concurrency exhibit poor performance, even with strong hardware support. Level of effort needed to support integration and test of hardware/software is another important concern. Architectures that rely heavily upon extensive and/or special purpose hardware usually require high levels of integration and test effort. Reliability, defined as the ability of a process architecture to repetitively operate on a regular, stable basis, is another concern. In general, architectures that employ decentralized control fare poorly in this respect, compared to use of a hierarchical, flat control concept. Thus, control concept is another important criterion for evaluation. Level of effort required to maintain traceability is of particular interest to software developers. Again, strictly decentralized control fails in this regard. Due to evolving requirements and incremental build strategies, flexibility is an important attribute of a good architecture. For most customers, architectures which easily support portability across target platforms are highly preferred. Finally, both hardware and software dependence and their impacts are carefully evaluated.

In Figure 5.7, an architecture flow or process flow diagram for a typical real-time system is generated. These processes are derived according to the guidelines described in the previous sections. A central system controller process is employed along with processes for external interfaces—a sensor manager (data collector) and an actuator manager (data receiver). Of the three alternatives for requirements 5.1, 5.2, and 5.3 suggested in the last section, a single architecture process (Analysis Manager) is employed. Using a single architecture process for 5.1, 5.2, and 5.3 reduces concurrency complexity in the final design. Since each process is implemented in combinations of hardware and software, reducing the overall number of architecture processes reduces the overhead for interprocess communication (at the expense of reduced throughput resulting from less distributed hardware). This specific reduced concurrency approach is not the correct choice for every application. Comparing this figure to the original context diagram in Figure 4.2, all control/data flows appear (Raw Sensor Data, Actuator Commands, Formatted Displays, and User Commands/User Command Data). Internal process flows are generated by reviewing enhanced requirements, completed at the beginning of architecture model generation, to assure that all control and data flows appear in the architecture and flow from the correct source requirement to its desired destination requirement.

Evaluation of the typical process architecture of Figure 5.7 uses the criteria suggested previously. An evaluation summary appears in Figure 5.8. This process architecture is usually most effective for analysis functions that are computationally intensive and that require extensive hardware support to achieve high throughput. If a software intensive implementation approach is employed, moderate performance results from this separation of analysis and control processing, which

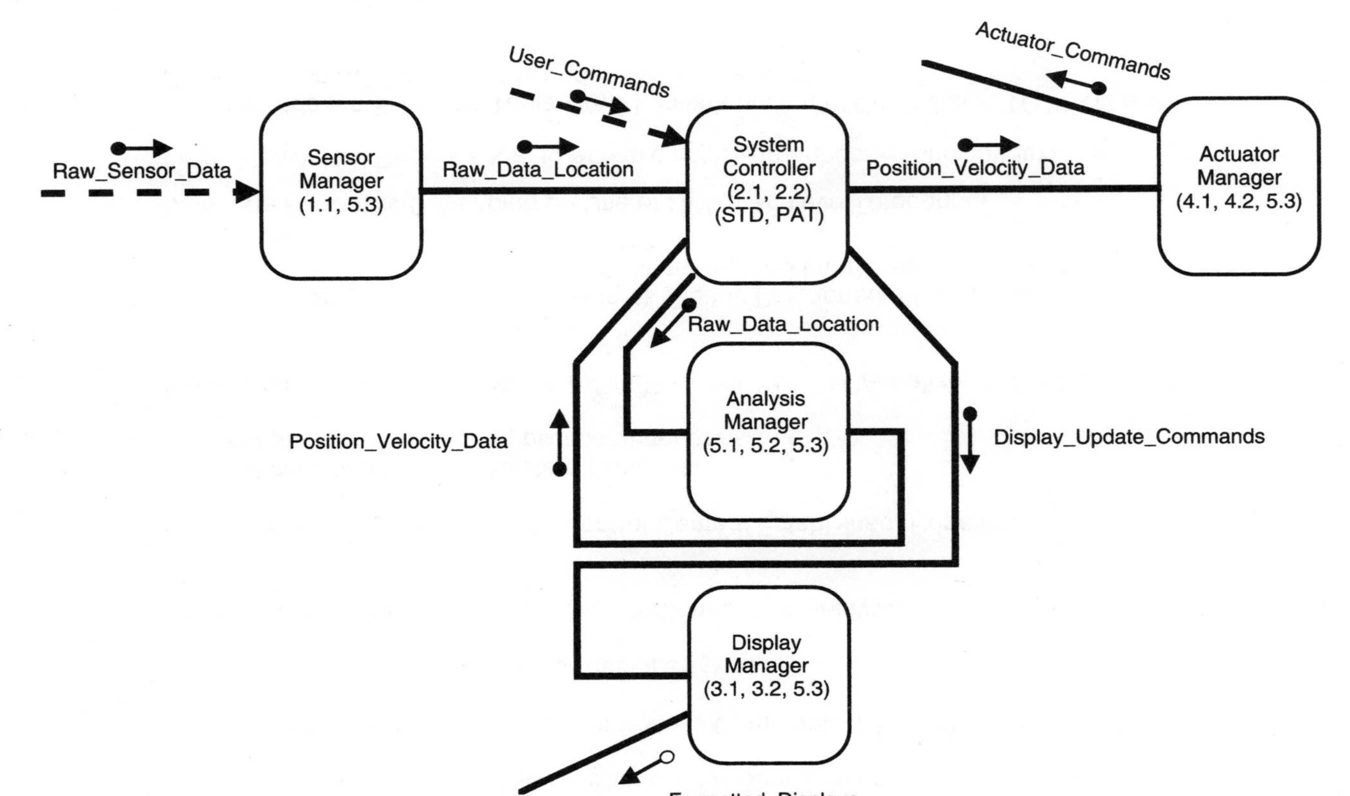

Figure 5.7 Typical Architecture Flow Diagram

General Justification:	Independent Handling of Interfaces, Control, and Analysis Can Be Effective for Computationally Intensive Analysis
Moderate Performance:	More Interprocess Communication vs. Concurrent Operations
Moderate Effort For Integration and Test:	Separation of Control and Analysis
High Reliability:	Once Control Centers Established, Repetitive Operations Stable
Hierarchical Control Concept:	System Controller Application/Interfaces
Moderate Flexibility:	Some Event Response Logic Centralized in System Controller
High Traceability:	Requirements Clearly Partitioned, Allocated Among Control, Analysis, and Interfaces

Moderate Portability Depending on Use of HW to Achieve Throughput

Likely Heavy HW Dependence to Achieve High Throughput Reducing Flexibility

SW Dependence Suggests Table Drive Implementation of Controller (STD, PAT) and Encapsulation of HW Interfaces under SW Abstractions

Figure 5.8 Evaluation of Typical Process Architecture

employs a medium amount of concurrency complexity. Medium concurrency complexity induces a moderate level of integration and test effort.

This event intensive architecture incorporates the hierarchical control concept described earlier. System Control interacts with subordinate controllers for managing interfaces (sensors, actuators, and displays) and for performing algorithm analysis. If algorithm analysis is further divided into separate architecture processes, their control interactions would be constrained to the Analysis Manager indicated in Figure 5.7. In this manner, process interaction complexity is significantly reduced.

Incorporation of a fairly large portion of the state transition diagram/process activation table into a system controller process supports reasonably high levels of traceability and flexibility. Abstraction of hardware interfaces (sensor and actuator) leads to an implementation that possesses a fair degree of portability, subject to use of hardware to improve performance. Implications to software design suggest a table-driven software controller with careful encapsulation of hardware interfaces. Both table-driven controllers and encapsulated interfaces are well supported by Ada.

Buffers and other intermediaries are not incorporated into the architecture in Figure 5.7. Inclusion of intermediaries is acceptable at this level of design specification. However, appearance of buffers within this architecture allows implementation of buffers to be in either hardware or software form. Speed is improved if hardware implementation is selected, but flexibility and integration and test effort are sacrificed. Hardware is difficult to change and necessitates extensive integrated efforts. From a software perspective, both flexibility and integration and test effort are extremely important. Integration of software into a hardware target platform requires an iterative development approach. Flexibility is necessary to assure success of this iterative approach. For this reason, incorporation of buffers (and other intermediaries) is best deferred to detailed software design. At this time, Ada's support for tasking allows software buffering to reduce integration and test effort and to allow architectural flexibility.

Design consistency and completeness checking is the next step in the architecture modeling activity. Each of the events in the test input/output pattern generated during operations modeling is traced through its response within the architecture flow diagram.

Architecture Consistency/Completeness Checking

Architecture completeness checking is performed in a manner similar to the approach employed to evaluate requirements. Each incoming event in the input/output pattern of the operations model is evaluated against the top level architecture. However, in the case of an architecture evaluation, significant complexity is introduced into the complete response evaluation. Events trigger movement of data through the architecture. Data flowing into an architecture process can cause multiple data elements to flow out of the process. Responses by the remainder of the architecture to each of the multiple output flows must be carefully evaluated. A direct result is that multiple paths of data can flow across the architecture in response to a single event. Tracing all these paths resulting from a single event at the software system's interfaces is an extremely important activity.

Engineering discipline needs to be exercised to perform the architecture evaluation for each event/response pair in the test input/output pattern. While some event/response pairs may appear to be repetitious, response paths leading from event to response may differ. Depending on the context in which the event occurs or the data embedded within the incoming event, radically differing architecture paths can lead to the same outgoing response. All these architecture paths need to be elaborated. Moreover, valuable insight is gained into the dynamic behavior of the architecture. Often, generation of a response desired or observed by the user requires processing a storage of a number of intermediate results. Representing this wave of intermediate results followed by a user observed response is easily accomplished through the architecture evaluation table.

Each path of data flowing through the architecture results in one of several possible terminal situations: Data is maintained in an internal data store, an output message results at an external interface, or an internal control event is emitted. Of course, combinations can occur. If every path resulting from an incoming event arrives at a combination of these destination results, then the architecture is classed as complete. Completeness of an architecture verifies that a working system can be delivered by the developer. Consistency is evaluated by examining each process visited along the process path to assure that invoking the process as part of the response path makes operational sense.

In addition to validating the architecture behavior, this response trace format is an invaluable aid that can be employed during integration and testing activities. Software needs to be designed and implemented in a manner that dumps all internal data stores and message buffers when a system abruptly ceases operating. From the dumped data, testers can construct a detailed representation of the "state" of the software system. State of a software system consists of the last event whose response was in process (message buffers are utilized to allow retrieval of the last event), the data in the data stores, and the history of emitted internal events and outgoing data flows. Details of an actual response have been constructed. By comparing this actual response with the anticipated response in the architecture flow evaluation, problem location can usually be identified. This is a simpler, faster, and much less frustrating approach than is normally employed. Typically, problem location is unknown, a symptom is observed and a random search is initiated. Problems are usually manifested by a symptom, such as the instantaneous termination of operations. Messages no longer flow. By knowing the required responses as stated in the CSPECs, by modeling data flowing through the architecture, by reconstructing the current data flow in the architecture during operations and by comparing these three elements, less effort is necessary to perform debugging on a system of any complexity. A precise problem location is determined, without wasting time to perform random search which is usually ineffective.

In Figure 5.9, examples of architecture evaluation are accomplished for the typical process flow diagram in Figure 5.7. Results of this analysis are presented in a tabular format. Each row in the table represents data flowing through a single architecture process or module. Data flow is characterized in the columns by

Data In	Architecture Module	Functionality	Data Out
Raw_Sensor_Data	Sensor_Manager	1.1 Copy_Raw_Data	Raw_Data_Location
Raw_Data_Location	System_Controller	2.1 Copy_Message	
		2.2 Decode_Message	Raw_Data_Location
Raw_Data_Location	Analysis_Manager	5.1 Evaluate raw data	
		5.2 Respond to results	Position_Velocity
Position_Velocity_Data	System_Controller	2.1 Copy message	
		2.2 Decode message	Position_Velocity_Data
Position_Velocity_Data	Actuator_Manager	4.1 Construct actuator_command	
		4.2 Copy to memory	Actuator_Commands
User_Commands, User_Command_Data	System_Controller	2.1 Copy message	Internal_Configuration_Commands
		2.2 Decode message	Display_Update_Commands
Internal Configuration_Commands	Sensor_Manager	5.3 Update_Control_Parameters	—
Internal Configuration_Commands	Actuator_Manager	5.3 Update_Control_Parameters	—
Internal Configuration_Commands	Analysis_Manager	5.3 Update_Control_Parameters	—
Display_Update_Commands	Display_Manager	3.1 Construct_Display	
		3.2 Copy to frame	Functional_Display

Figure 5.9 Architecture Evaluation

indicating data flowing into the process, name of the process invoked, functional transformations occurring (derived from the requirements traceability matrices), and data flowing out of the process. Process output data is either data moving to another process or data flowing across an external interface. As suggested earlier, multiple data outputs can result. Each of these multiple outputs must be subsequently evaluated. This table demonstrates architecture response to two specific events only, chosen to illustrate the basic concepts involved.

In the top portion of the table (above the dashed line), architecture responsiveness to a Raw Sensor Data Input is evaluated. Data flow begins when a sensor places data into a memory mapped hardware interface and signals the availability of the Raw Sensor Data. Initially, the Sensor Manager process copies the raw data into a buffer area. Raw Data Location is passed to the System Controller process. System Controller copies the message, decodes the message, and uses the state transition diagram and process activation table to determine that analysis is required. A message containing Raw Data Location is transmitted to the Application Manager process. Now, the latter evaluates the data according to an algorithm provided in a corresponding PSPEC, generates the results based on the analysis, and transmits Position and Velocity data needed to command the actuator back to the System Controller architecture process. System Controller again must copy the message into a scratch buffer and decode the message. Using its event response specification (STD, PAT), System Controller decides to transmit Position and Velocity Data to the Actuator Manager. On receipt of the message, Actuator Manager constructs an actuator command that is copied to a memory mapped hardware interface. This concludes a data path representing the complete response to the Raw Sensor Data Event. Comparison with a test input/output pattern reveals an event response pattern which begins with Raw Sensor Data and ends with an Actuator Command. Completeness of the architecture, relative to the event in this context is verified.

Now consider the bottom portion of the design evaluation table. In this part of the table, response to User Commands with embedded User Command Data is traced. Initially, User Commands come to the System Controller. Again, using event response logic, two process data flows result. Internal Configuration Commands are transmitted to all architecture process. Configuration Commands contain specific data necessary to allow each architecture processes to perform its intended function. A second output that System Controller generates is a Display Update Command to the Display Manager process. Response within the remainder of the architecture to each one of these output data transfers (Internal Configuration Command, Display Update) must be traced to its termination. Subsequent table entries show Internal Configuration Commands being received by other architecture processes and functions involved to update control parameters. Since all responses to configuration commands perform a similar update, terminating responses are consistent. Moreover, since each termination activity consists of an internal data store update, each response is complete. A final table entry demonstrates completeness of the response to the Display Update Command output flow. Response to the message includes transformations (represented by PSPECs) to construct the display and to copy the display into a memory mapped frame buffer.

Completeness is achieved since this sequence of functionality is logically correct and since termination results in data moving across an external interface (i.e., placed into the frame buffer).

Contribution of this kind of analysis to reduce integration and testing effort is apparent. If the current event and response details can be identified, an anticipated architecture response, extracted from this table, forms a basis for identifying problem location. Contents of actual data stores and message buffers represent an actual response by the combined hardware and software. Anticipated responses detailed in the analysis table can be compared with the actual response. Determination of the offending architecture element is usually immediate and obvious. In many cases, problem location can be precisely attributed to a specific hardware or software cause.

Comparison of actual vs. anticipated responses with this data typically results in one of several assessments. Within the actual responses, data enters a module but fails to exit the module. This typically indicates a software failure in the module and identifies a specific module for investigation. If data enters an interface but fails to surface on the receiver side of the interface, a hardware problem is indicated. Architecture evaluation data allows rapid identification and fixing of problems (two to three hours) embedded within hundreds of lines of distributed code.

Compare this with the normal approach used for problem resolution during integration and test activities. A "hit or miss" approach called random search is employed. Determining a start location is difficult. So, something is tried. If this random attempt fails, another random try is made. Eventually, the symptom may disappear. This is time consuming, further degrading integration and test schedules. Moreover, the symptom has disappeared with no guarantee that the problem has been treated. In reality, software behavior has been temporarily changed. Eventually, the same problem rears its ugly head later. Generation and proper use of architecture evaluation data eliminates this phenomenon, significantly improving integration and test schedules.

As a final benefit, this same architecture analysis/evaluation can be employed as a basis to predict time-liness of design responsiveness.

Timing Analysis

Subsequent to requirements evaluation, a specific time constraint is allocated to each functional transformation or PSPEC in the requirements model. This information can be combined with data in the architecture flow evaluation table to obtain estimates on event response time-liness.

Recall that a single table entry describes data flow across an architecture process and data transformations (PSPECs) invoked by the process. Time constraints allocated to each PSPEC are now combined to determine an estimated response attributed to this process invocation within the response path. Time consumed across an entire response path determines total time to update an internal data store, to generate an output message, or to emit an internal control event.

Unfortunately, complexity of response paths causes this approach to require careful thought. Since no hardware or software detailed design decisions have been made to this point, knowledge may be unavailable to indicate whether functional transformation times within an invoked architecture process are summed or computed in parallel and the minimum value employed. Certainly, summing the times provides a worst case estimate (sometimes referred to as an upper bound). Another solution to this dilemma is to defer the time-line analysis until after allocation of requirements between hardware and software. Since many software systems prefer not to employ Ada tasking, a summation approach for combining data transformation (PSPEC) times may be entirely appropriate. Decisions as to the application of functional timing allocations to the architecture evaluation table entries are made on an individual project basis according to the project conditions.

Another problem associated with predicting end-to-end event response times within this context is that of tracing multiple internal process flows in response to a single external event in the message flow. As demonstrated above, process response paths can be extremely complex. One process invocation can result in multiple output paths. Each output path can contain numerous others. Response times at any process in a path can be chosen as a criterion for the maximum response times from resulting multiple output paths. This suggests something like a dynamic programming algorithm to determine the total response time to each event in the test input/output pattern message.

One entry is employed from Figure 5.8 to illustrate response time prediction. For this example, the second entry of the typical architecture evaluation table is employed. Consider the following data:

Process Input: Raw Data Location	Process Flow: System Controller
Function	Allocated Time
Incoming Message Interrupt	1 millisecond
2.1 Copy Message	5 milliseconds
2.2 Decode Message	10 milliseconds
Outgoing Message Interrupt	1 millisecond
Total:	17 milliseconds

Overhead is included to represent mechanics associated with inter-process communication. These are important and necessary contributors to the individual process response time.

If this kind of evaluation is accomplished for every entry in the upper half of Figure 5.9, then a summation of the individual table entries yields a total predicted time to respond to Raw Sensor Data when provided by the operating sensor. Moreover, the total response time is given as performance criteria to the developers of the System Controller process. Unit testing of the System Controller process submits proof based on benchmarking measurements that both the total and individual allocations have been accomplished.

Traceability from user requirements (in the form of a test input/output pattern) to architecture is the goal of this last evaluation activity. A second and important form of traceability is between the implementor's requirements and the architecture.

5.3 REQUIREMENTS TRACEABILITY

To some extent this step has already been accomplished. Review the typical architecture/process flow diagram which appeared as Figure 5.7. Each process is labeled with the user requirements allocated to the architecture process. However, this representation is insufficient for performing an effective completeness evaluation. Requirements traceability matrices provide a more realistic and useful representation of the allocation of requirements to processes. A typical format for these matrices appears in Figure 5.10. Each row is labeled with a specific leaf requirement, PSPEC, or CSPEC element in the requirements model. Columns are labeled with an architecture process name. In the body of the table, a marker or symbol (X) is employed to record the allocation mapping of the requirement to the architecture process.

Evaluating the completeness of requirements satisfaction is easily accomplished in this format. At a glance, effectiveness of the mapping activity is assessed by reviewing exactly those requirements provided by each specific architecture process (data in a single column). Each row can be further inspected to assure that the requirement of the row is satisfied in at least one architecture process. Any requirement appearing in multiple architecture processes is reevaluated to assure its simplicity (further decomposition may be required) and to determine if multiple processes really need to employ this requirement. Software system level consistency checks are not easily accomplished by reviewing an architecture flow/process diagram in which allocated requirements are indicated underneath each process name.

Requirements traceability matrices serve as more than a counting artifice. Rationale supporting each specific allocation is attached to each marker entry in a requirements traceability matrix. Flaw assessment during later development activities is supported by recording of support rationales. Recording the rationale that underlies the allocation is as important as recording the allocation itself. Variations from architectures that employ a hierarchical, flat control need to be carefully justified.

An important point needs to be made here. Construction of requirements traceability matrices occurs concurrently with requirements mapping/process generation activities. Too many developers wait to record traceability after the system is already working (sort of working, at any rate). This delay is disastrous because the likelihood of error is quite high. When dealing with 500,000 lines of implemented Ada and an array of target platform processors, a high chance exists that reconstruction of a requirements traceability matrix under duress will fail to identify where many of the requirements are implemented. Allocation justifications are forgotten and cannot be reconstructed. Portions are usually generated but are insufficient for providing insight into architectural flaws.

A major symptom typically resulting from the failure to concurrently identify implementor requirements traceability is that a system works, sort of. After extensive debugging activity with attendant aggravation and miscommunication, hardware and software implementors come to determine that each assumes the incorporation of specific functional capabilities within a specific incremental build.

Architecture Module / Requirement	System Controller	Application Manager	Sensor Manager	Actuator Manager	Display Manager
1.1			X		
2.1	X				
2.2	X				
3.1					X
3.3					X
4.1				X	
4.2				X	
5.1		X			
5.2		X			
5.3		X	X	X	X
STD 2	X				
PAT 2	X				
STD 5	X				
PAT 5	X				

Figure 5.10 Requirements Traceability Matrix: Architecture Model

These integration and test problems tend to be eased or eliminated if requirements traceability is performed concurrently with process generation activities.

Now that architecture process flows, traceability to user requirements, and consistency with implementors' requirements have all been performed, an important framework has been established. Specifically, implementation has been converted into a set of small, bounded and integrated sub-problems called architecture processes. Each of the processes can be addressed as an implementation entity by a team of hardware and software engineers. System engineers interacting with architecture process development teams assure that subsequent detailed design decisions are consonant with identified process interfaces and acknowledge system level architecture/hardware decisions. Focus from this point shifts to an architecture process basis rather than a system perspective. Initially, each process is evaluated for hardware/software trade-offs.

5.4 ALLOCATING REQUIREMENTS TO HARDWARE AND SOFTWARE

A specific set of allocated control and functional implementation requirements must be satisfied within each architecture process. Allocated requirements are now partitioned to hardware or software or both. This is accomplished on a logical basis employing methods that evaluate the implications of a particular set of hardware/software allocation decisions. An iterative process is suggested here.

System engineers familiar with requirements to be implemented within a specific architecture process make an initial suggested partitioning of process requirements to hardware and to software. This initial partitioning is a suggested starting point for evaluation and not a decree. System engineers are usually not familiar with details of software or hardware implementation and can not fully understand the implications of a specific decision. Lead software and hardware engineers then evaluate this allocation from their own perspectives, employing simulation models, CAD/CAM systems, engineering experience, and reusable software component availability to assess the implications to the proposed allocation of requirements.

After an initial assessment, hardware, software, and system engineers meet to discuss the impacts of the allocation and to suggest more appropriate alternatives. Lead hardware and software engineers must be prepared to defend a specific objection and to suggest potential solutions. This process results in new suggested partitions that need further reevaluation by the individual hardware and software engineers. Multiple iterations might be necessary to accomplish a rational apportionment.

Hardware/software requirements allocation is a critical step in the development sequence and is not treated as a casual exercise. In many developments, system engineers assume that some requirement can be met by "a little clever and tricky code." This philosophy has a number of major detriments. Usually, "little" really turns out to be "big." As a result, software dependence in this form is neither cost effective nor performance effective from a system perspective. And, tricky code is a burden to integration and testing. Clever tricky code is difficult to associate with specific requirements, painful to debug, and impossible to maintain or to modify. These difficulties are avoided by employing an explicit development activity which systematically allocates requirements between hardware and software for each architecture process. The likelihood of meeting schedules and performance requirements is increased.

An additional benefit resulting from hardware/software requirements allocation is to form a team dynamic, which practically eliminates the hardware and software finger pointing which typically occurs during hardware and software integration and test. Assumptions regarding software and hardware interfaces are visible during design, rather than being painstakingly discovered during integration and test. Communications between hardware, software, and system engineering is established early in the development schedule. Dependencies are highlighted. This benefit alone makes performing a logical allocation priceless.

Software developers are significantly affected by hardware/software allocation decisions made in this phase. Contrary to popular belief by most software developers, a competent software interpreter must possess a fairly intimate knowledge of the hardware and its operational requirements. For instance, software developers must be quite proficient in assembly language programming for the target processor. Debugging during integration and test often requires that a software developer review intermixed Ada code and assembly code. This review is usually necessary to assess the validity of the code generated by the compiler. *Not all Ada compilers generate perfect code*. Even compilers with mature code generators (five years of application usage) can contain bugs for combinations of features that have never been heavily used by other developers. Moreover, many of the semantic requirements specified by the *Ada Language Reference Manual* are subject to extensive interpretation by the compiler vendor. Inconsistent interpretations often occur and must be identified. In most cases, resolution of inconsistent interpretations can only be determined by reading the assembly language produced by the code generator.

Interprocessor communications protocols associated with the hardware communications devices must be well understood by the software developer. Specific protocols are required to actually transmit data across communications devices. Software developers must either write and test their own software or must use commercially available software. In either case, integration and test is liable to be quite difficult. Communications software developed from scratch involves extensive testing. Integration of off-the-shelf software can be difficult due to lack of insight into the actual source code. Of course, if the incremental methodology strategy and the integration and testing approaches described in the text are employed, integration frustration can be significantly eased.

With many embedded applications, analysis algorithms are often implemented with hardware support. While this may appear to have no impact on the software developer, a significant problem is now faced by the software team. Concurrently developed application specific integration circuits (ASICs) lead to significant integration and test headaches. Software developers must resort to a carefully managed integration and test plan. At the foundation of this integration and test approach is a philosophy that assumes that much of the analysis and evaluation associated with this methodology has been employed. Software developers need to be aware of the mechanisms necessary to integrate with and manage this special purpose hardware to plan the development accordingly. Allocating requirements to hardware increases performance at the cost of flexibility and integration and test effort.

If the software developer disagrees with a specific hardware/software allocation (based on his knowledge of integration and testing implications and his understanding of Ada performance implications), he should attempt to have the configuration modified. Failure to identify the effects of these allocation decisions on both schedule and effort during integration and test often leads to the software receiving blame for the problems. The fault is really in the hardware/software partitioning process. If implications to integration and testing are not clarified by software architects, then they should rightfully receive the blame.

Each architecture process now has a specific set of requirements identified for implementation using software. Detailed software design generation is described next. Both concurrent and sequential software implementation methodologies are provided.

6

Software Design Model

Detailed software design consists of developing a software architecture that meets the requirements allocated to software within each specific architecture process. Maintaining traceability of the allocated requirements into the software design is an extremely important aspect of this activity. Traceability of requirements into software design is extremely difficult in most languages. Direct support for tasking and data abstraction, using private types and encapsulated objects, makes Ada an ideal language for maintaining traceability of requirements directly into implemented code. However, employing both tasking and data abstraction implies that the software engineer can capitalize on the strengths and avoid the weaknesses of each of these language paradigms. This chapter specifically addresses the manner in which Ada targeted software must be developed to effectively employ tasking and data abstraction while maintaining traceability to software allocated requirements.

Generation of a detailed software design consists of two distinct phases, as indicated in Figure 6.1. First, a software concurrency architecture is generated. Once a stable concurrent design is generated, individual sequential software designs are generated for task bodies. Sequential designs build upon the concept of layered abstractions employing encapsulated data objects or private types. With Ada, software concurrency must occur first. The Ada tasking model employs a blocking mechanism that engenders significant performance impacts if not managed appropriately. An object-first approach with a real-time Ada system typically results in tasks being hidden under objects. Blocking effects are thus overlooked, causing significant performance problems that are difficult to identify and resolve during a complex integration and test activity.

As with other elements of this methodology, a specific graphical notation is to be employed. Many notations have been suggested for representation of detailed

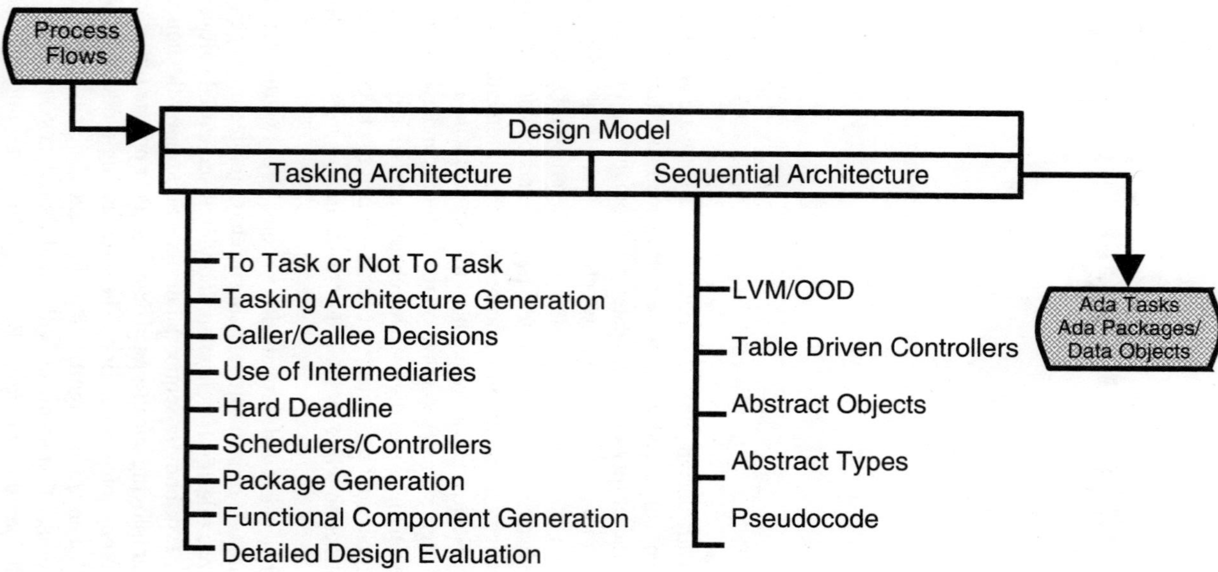

Figure 6.1 Design Model Generation

Ada software designs. Standard structure charts are not appropriate. Structure charts imply a single thread of control and do not effectively represent data abstraction. Other approaches tend to become overcrowded with details so that implications of decisions are hidden (this is an inappropriate use of "information hiding"). The approach employed here is the diagramming notation initially suggested by Grady Booch in *Software Engineering with Ada* (1987). Symbology proposed by Booch is illustrated in Figure 6.2. All major elements of program structure are represented—subprograms (procedures and functions), tasks, packages, and generics. Each element consists of a unique symbol. An identifier is provided in the top portion of each symbol as its unique symbolic reference. Specifications are distinguished from bodies by shading or crosshatching. Task entries or subprograms exported by normal or generic package specifications are indicated via a small but extended rectangle that exceeds the boundaries of the symbol body. Identifiers for each exported entry or subprogram appear within the extended rectangle. Exportation of an object or type is similarly indicated, except an extended oval is employed rather than a rectangle. Due to its simplicity, this symbolic notation has been particularly effective in illustrating Ada software designs.

Construction of a detailed software design diagram employs these symbols in a manner that describes interactions among software components to a much greater level of detail than process flows. Specific software interfaces are formulated. Interaction between two software elements is indicated by having an arrow proceed from one component or interface to another subprogram or to some visible task entry or package specification element, all of which are not precise interfaces. In this way, a detailed design diagram effectively portrays multiple threads of concurrent activity and dependence upon interfaces to data abstractions from any location in the design. These capabilities are directly supported by Ada and poorly supported or unsupported in other languages.

Generation of a detailed software design begins with a set of requirements that have been allocated to a specific architecture process. Allocated requirements are initially mapped to Ada tasks. Criteria for selection of Ada tasks and an overall tasking model design acknowledge and effectively employ an understanding of both strengths and weaknesses of tasking. Subsequently, a sequential design is generated within each task. An internal sequential design must satisfy requirements mapped to the specific Ada task and must effectively employ data abstraction capabilities of Ada, using private types or encapsulated objects to assure effective traceability of allocated requirements into actual code. In this regard, Ada shines over almost every other language.

Generation of a software design model that implements process requirements allocated to software is performed by the following steps:

1. Generate an initial tasking architecture;
2. Establish caller/callee relationships;
3. Employ (or do not employ) intermediaries;
4. Perform a consistency and completeness check of the tasking architecture against operational requirements;

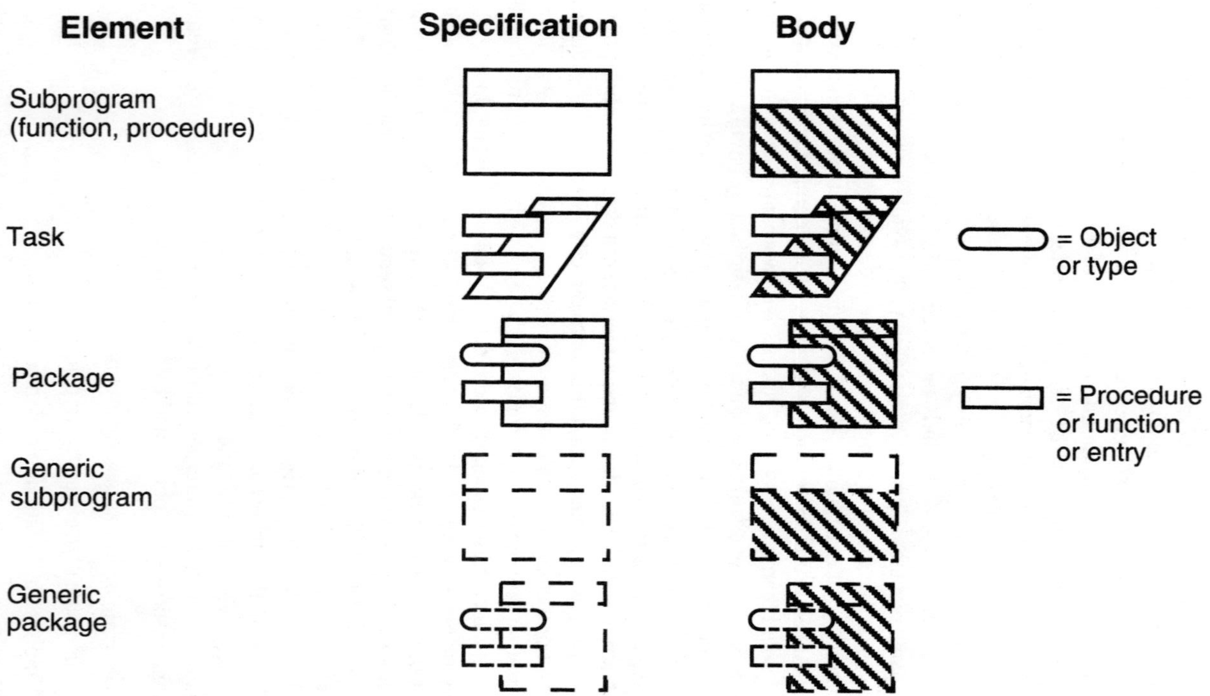

Figure 6.2 Design Model Notation

5. Allocate tasks to packages;
6. Generate functional components of the packages;
7. Use layered abstractions, table driven controllers, data objects, and data types to construct the sequential design of each task; and
8. Evaluate the detailed design to assess its quality.

Each of these steps involves specific products in specific formats. The tasking architecture and the tasking architecture evaluation table are of particular importance. Tasking architecture allows evaluation of the use of tasking to assure throughput and flexibility. The evaluation table verifies that the tasking architecture can perform the user's job and that a working software system can be delivered.

6.1 CONCURRENCY DESIGN DECISIONS

Tasking is perhaps the most misunderstood and maligned element of the Ada programming language. Contrary to popular belief, Ada tasking can be and has been employed with real-time systems. Many specific reasons support using the tasking paradigm. Machine independent interfaces are an important element of a tasking based implementation. Task rendezvous syntactically resembles a procedure call and does not require modification when a new compilation environment or target platform is utilized. Portability and reusability are obtained. Tasking applications execute regardless of either the host or target platform characteristics. Customers benefit from reduced costs and risks by reuse of complete tasking architectures. Implementors capitalize on previous developments by generating tasking architectures easily tailored to new instances of a general class of systems. Extensive flexibility is built into the tasking model, since practically any legal Ada code segment can be performed within a rendezvous. Access to encapsulated data structures is easily serialized, since accept clauses operate in the manner of critical sections, with access protocols being rigidly enforced by the run-time environment. Task rendezvous, through the accept clause, allows synchronization among separate and parallel software elements providing software reliability. Finally, data communications between tasks is strictly controlled by the run-time environment. Only tasks explicitly involved in a specific rendezvous can access the data at the interface between the tasks, in contrast to tasks that required access to global data. All of these benefits and real-time performance can be obtained by effective use of the tasking model in designing a tasking architecture.

Two major reasons cause the lack of tasking advocacy. From a maturity perspective, earlier implementations of the Ada run-time environment performed quite poorly when accomplishing task rendezvous. Criticism of these implementations, however, must be placed in proper perspective. These early implementations had the maturity of many older operating systems when performing multi-tasking. Just as more recent operating systems have delivered rapid and effective multi-tasking, so have many recent Ada run-time environments. Most real-time applications can effectively employ Ada tasking to achieve all the benefits described above and to exhibit high throughput. Ada tasking may not be appropriate in some cases.

Another reason for poor Ada tasking performance is the abuse of the tasking model by software engineers. This abuse occurs when software designs do not acknowledge limitations in the characteristics of the tasking model. Numerous benefits can be obtained when Ada tasking is effectively employed. To achieve these benefits, Ada uses a tasking model based upon the theory of cooperating sequential processes. An inherent component of this tasking model is that calling tasks can block. Task blocking, combined with vagaries in the specifications of task scheduling and with coding flexibility within an accept clause, can lead to significantly poor performance of a tasking based implementation. Do not blame Ada for poor tasking performance if blockage and accept clause contents are not properly engineered. Poor design is the problem here. Tasking performance problems can easily be eliminated through proper engineering. Do not allow individual programmers to make tasking implementation decisions. Use of tasking and tasking protocols by individual programmers is not usually determined by software system engineering activities. Code developers are allowed to make independent decisions regarding tasking. Do not allow individual programmers to make tasking design decisions. As a corollary to this, hiding tasks under objects is extremely dangerous in this class of real-time systems. Tasking implementations that hide tasks under objects are likely to perform quite poorly. Hidden tasks usually incur excessive blockage because subsequent requirements to employ tasking rendezvous are lost. Selection of task elements, management of task interaction, and design of code segments within accept clauses is best performed by a senior architecting team within the context of this methodical process. Moreover, tasking designs and associated interaction design decisions should be extensively and carefully reviewed by experienced Ada software engineers not directly connected with day-to-day design activities. By employing overview strategies, evaluating tasking usage to the system level, and carefully correlating task bodies to allocated requirements, tasking can be quite effectively employed on most real-time Ada systems.

To Task or Not to Task

Several important factors affect making the decision on the extent of Ada tasking usage. A primary determinant is the underlying hardware base. If all architecture processes are to be performed on a single processor (CPU), some form of software tasking must be employed to obtain concurrent operation of the architecture processes. If each architecture process receives its own CPU, then Ada tasking may not be as important, depending on the allocation of requirements to each process. In the absence of hardware support for concurrency within each software requirement being implemented, each architecture process needs to be reviewed to determine if software multi-tasking is necessary to meet throughput and other concurrency requirements. Allocated requirements that can be accommodated by a single control stream on a single CPU do not need to employ software tasking. A decision not to employ tasking is based upon requirements allocation and is not simply motivated by an arbitrary decision to "avoid software tasking."

Once an evaluation has determined the necessity to use software tasking, several approaches may be employed. One approach requires that the software implementor design and write his own scheduler. A second alternative suggests using operating system services. Finally, Ada tasking can be employed. Several implications are considered when selecting one of these alternatives. Each approach implies some form of computational overhead, affects development schedule, and limits reusability, security, etc. These effects must be compared when deciding on the appropriate form of software multi-tasking.

Writing a software scheduler gives a developer significant control over performance. However, this effort lengthens your schedule, since a scheduler must be designed, implemented, and integrated. Moreover, timer interrupts need to be employed, reducing the reusability of a scheduler-based software architecture. Operating systems services are often relatively easy to employ, initially easing stress on a schedule that is usually too short. However, computational overhead can be quite high when this approach is employed. Moreover, this approach is a throwback to non-portable software architectures. Using operating system services often requires access to global shared memory for inter-process communication. Integration and test headaches are guaranteed for an open data structure approach such as this. Moreover, interfaces to operating system services are both non-standard and non-portable. Ada tasking, when effectively employed, actually evaluates the best of the alternatives. Portability, reliability, reusability, and security of communications are all specific impacts designed into the Ada tasking model. Schedules are easier to meet—no laborious tweaking is necessary. Computational overhead in many tasking environments has been optimized to achieve significant performance time constraints. However, acquiring these benefits necessitates that a specific tasking architecture be carefully engineered.

Due to all these benefits, Ada tasking should not be eliminated because of a perception of poor performance. Impacts on schedules, reliability of inter-task communications, and maintainability are all carefully evaluated to assure that a software tasking usage decision is appropriate for the hardware and overall project constraints and goals.

Tasking Architecture Generation

Assuming Ada tasking has been chosen to satisfy a set of software requirements within a process architecture, several important decisions need to be made and carefully reviewed. Identification of specific tasks is an important decision. If a single CPU is to be employed for the whole process architecture, then the architecture flow diagram serves as the basis of the task architecture. Details of the task entry interfaces must then be refined into a Booch notational format. If multiple concurrent requirements need to be implemented on a single CPU within a specific architecture process, additional selection of Ada tasks is necessary to accomplish concurrent operations within the confines of a single CPU. At least two Ada tasks are necessary within an architecture process mapped to a single CPU. One is an interrupt handler that copies the input data into a buffer after any special formatting has been accomplished. A second task takes elements from the input buffer on a first-come, first-served basis and responds to the message/event retrieval. Employing this approach requires that task entries be mapped to interrupt registers via representation specification clauses.

Several guidelines may aid the developer in determining an initial Ada tasking architecture, assuming that each architecture process must include at least one Ada task. If each architecture process receives its own CPU, then the main program for that process is the "task." As indicated above, multiple tasks may be employed. If multiple tasks are needed, begin immediately to build a requirements traceability matrix that identifies the allocation of process requirements to individual Ada tasks. Strictly limit the number of tasks to a reasonable few. Placement of hundreds (or even tens) of Ada tasks on a single CPU is guaranteed to reduce performance and to result in extensive integration and test nightmares.

Due to the blocking characteristics of the Ada tasking model, all tasking decisions are usually elevated to a system level and carefully reviewed by Ada architects who understand the implications of a specific architecture. Initial generation of a tasking architecture is the first step in treating Ada tasking as a system level design. In no case are tasking decisions delegated to individual programmers/implementors. Delegated tasking decisions result in performance and integration problems, since all tasking interactions are now invisible and unknown. These problems can be avoided by treating use of Ada tasking at the software system level.

Caller/Callee Relations

Translating an architecture process diagram into a tasking diagram identifies required specific task interactions. Each of these interactions must be specified as to caller/callee relationships. A specific caller must be chosen to initiate an interaction. Selecting one task to be the caller between each pair of interacting tasks has significant implementation impacts. Calling tasks can block when a called task is busy, significantly increasing response times, reducing throughput and potentially leading to deadlocked software systems. Called tasks must export task entries and must contain accept clauses embedded within loop–select–end select–end loop constructs, dictating a specific internal design for the called task.

Several guidelines have been formulated for making effective caller/callee decisions regarding interaction between a pair of tasks. Tasks that interact with several other tasks are identified as called tasks or callees. Ability to respond to entry calls gives the called task the flexibility to respond to any task requesting its services. Algorithmically complex tasks are classified as callers. A task that consumes extensive CPU cycles to perform a complex algorithm is unavailable to respond rapidly to rendezvous entry calls. As a result, other calling tasks will block, causing potentially extensive backup blocking elsewhere in the tasking architecture. Tasks providing services such as control over a commonly accessed data structure are best implemented as called tasks. This role allows the called task to protect or monitor the commonly assessed data structure. Similarly, tasks needing service are best cast in the role of calling tasks.

After each task interaction has been characterized according to caller/callee relationship, additional tasking design is necessary. Called tasks (callers) block—unfortunately, duration of a task block can not be deterministically predicted. Extensive blocking during a single task interaction can have a cumulative effect, due to the complexity of interactions in the tasking architecture. As a result, tasking operations can deadlock all the way out to the tasks that manage external interfaces. Tasking architectures need to be modified to reduce or to eliminate blocking.

Use of Intermediaries

Task blockage time for a single task interaction can not be deterministically predicted within Ada. Unpredictable blockage time occurs because of the unpredictable duration of both queue wait times and rendezvous service times. A pending task rendezvous waits in an entry queue until the head of the queue is reached. Once the queue head is reached, two factors determine the rendezvous completion time. According to the *Ada Language Reference Manual*, an Ada implementation's task scheduler can choose from among the queue heads of multiple task entries in an "arbitrary manner." Once a rendezvous does begin, rendezvous service time depends on the nature of the code segment in an accept clause. Of course, this can be practically any legal Ada code segment. Picture an accept clause that performs an Ethernet call and suspends until a reply is received. Blockage time for a rendezvous entry call consists of the sum of the total service times of the queue entries in front of the specific call. Since each of these depends upon the factors above, blockage time is not deterministically predictable. However, decoupling paradigms do exist that can minimize or effectively eliminate task blocking.

A characterization of task decoupling paradigms is presented in Figure 6.3. Interacting tasks are represented as producers and consumers. A producer task generates data and serves as a caller, initiating interaction with a consumer. Initiation may also be accomplished by the consumer. However, symmetry allows consideration of a single direction of initiation for the purpose of discussing decouplers. Interaction involving non-usage of decouplers represents a baseline alternative and incurs maximum, nondeterministic blocking time. An extremely popular intermediary is the buffer task. Buffers are strictly called by both producer and consumer and are capable of storing multiple items. Use of this approach converts blocking time into a deterministic time with a finite upper bound. While the buffer task may be busy when called by either the producer or consumer, a specific time limit can be established for resulting blockage. During a rendezvous, only data copies into or out of the buffer are allowed. Since a fixed size element is always copied, copy time is deterministic and finite, providing a distinct and predictable upper bound on the amount of blockage that can be incurred.

Another form of decoupler is the transporter. A transporter is strictly a calling task capable of storing only a single entry. By using an intermediary which strictly calls both producer and consumer, neither producer nor consumer ever blocks. One or both may sit idle waiting for data but are always still available to respond to other rendezvous entry calls. This kind of intermediary completely eliminates blocking by either producer or consumer, since neither is a caller.

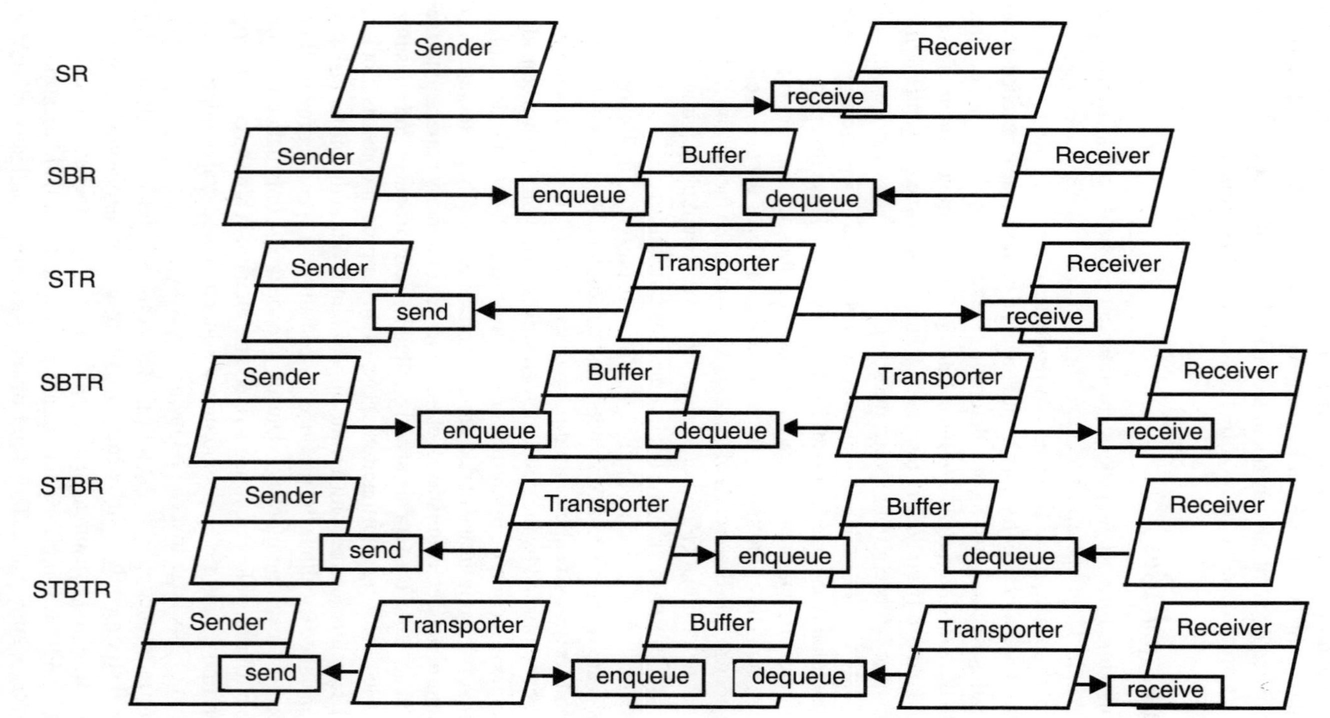

Figure 6.3 Tasking Intermediary Alternatives

Unfortunately, transporters store only a single item. To obtain complete elimination of blockage and to store multiple items, a decoupler entitled transporter-buffer-transporter (TBT) needs to be employed. Elimination of blocking is achieved by separate transporter interfaces to both producer and consumer. Incorporation of the hidden buffer provides the multiple object storage. A buffer task monitors writing into and reading from the same buffer location. Simultaneous reads and writes to the same buffer location would produce garbled results.

Relays eliminate blocking on a single side of the interaction between producer and consumer, and provide storage for multiple objects. Construction of a relay entails combining a transporter and a buffer. If the producer faces the transporter, then the producer experiences no blockage. Direct consumer interaction with the transporter eliminates consumer blockage. Transporters interacting with the buffer experience some blockage (with a finite, deterministic bound).

A decision as to decoupler employment must be made for every task interaction that can occur. Introduction of an intermediary can change the role of a consumer task from being a callee to that of being a caller. Changing a role may contradict caller/callee decision guidelines described in the previous section. Injection of decouplers is carefully evaluated to assure that system throughput is not adversely affected.

Perhaps the most often used intermediary is the buffer. Each buffer introduces only one extra task, and one additional rendezvous for data transfer. While some blocking may occur, blocking duration has a finite, maximum time limit—at most, the amount of time to transfer a single data object. Thus, blocking introduces only a slight degradation in performance. This usually yields the best system performance.

Excessive use of decouplers can also be hazardous to system response times and throughput. Each decoupler adds tasking management overhead to the CPU and requires additional rendezvous to transmit data, increasing response times and decreasing throughput. In the extreme, this can bring your tasking application to a screeching halt because the Ada run-time environment is spending so much time managing task context switches. For instance, suppose 20 task interactions are each decoupled using a TBT intermediary. This introduces 60 additional tasks (three per TBT intermediary) into the run-time environment for scheduling and management. Moreover, three additional task rendezvous are necessary to move data from one producer to its consumer. Additional rendezvous add communications overhead reducing throughput and increasing response times.

An expanded tasking architecture now exhibits caller/callee relationships and intermediaries introduced to limit or to eliminate task blocking. If some tasks must meet extremely hard scheduling deadlines, due to periodicity of inputs or outputs required by sensors and actuators, additional expansion of the tasking architecture is needed.

Hard Deadline Scheduling

Tasks that must meet hard scheduling deadlines are a fact of life in real-time system development. Periodic tasks occurring regularly at very short time epochs are one example. For example, sensors typically feed data into a memory mapped interface once every 1/30 of a second (30 frames per second). Any task that serves as a sensor interface manager has 33 milliseconds (1/30 second) to move the data away from the memory mapped hardware interface for later processing. As long as the data has been protected before the 33 millisecond duration expires, data integrity is maintained within a hard deadline schedule. Aperiodic tasks which can critically determine the fate of the system also require specific response time deadlines. Attitude corrections for satellite control do not occur with any particular frequency. However, when an attitude correction is received by an onboard controller, response must occur within a short time limit (10 milliseconds) to keep the spacecraft orbit from processing, causing the satellite to eventually tumble into space.

Assuring that schedule deadlines are met has been one of the burning research issues of the past several years. Significant progress has been made in this area. A theory of rate monotonic scheduling has been developed that allows one to schedule tasking execution to meet hard deadlines. Translating a hard deadline schedule into a specific tasking architecture requires the addition of scheduler tasks for controlling tasking execution. Additionally, internal code segments within tasks must be divided into code sequences executed according to the hard deadline schedule.

Incorporation of scheduler tasks is an activity accomplished subsequent to intermėdiary enhancement. Rate monotonic scheduling reflects the blocking effects when formulating a schedule. As a result, all other tasking interactions must be specified before the addition of scheduler or dispatcher tasks. The purpose of a scheduler or dispatcher is to assure proper scheduling of all other tasks under conditions computed by rate monotonic scheduling.

Hard deadline scheduling possesses an important limitation that can be problematic. Both theory and implementation approaches guarantee deadlines are met within a specific time duration. Note, however, that events are not guaranteed to occur at exact points in time. Failure to schedule at exact time epochs may not be a problem. In many situations, moving data from the critical hardware interface prior to the next precisely scheduled event is a satisfactory response. Achieving events at a specific time point is not required; rate monotonic scheduling is applicable and is extremely effective. Chiming of a clock represents a situation in which an event is required to occur at a specific point in time. Rate monotonic scheduling is marginally useful, since clock chiming needs to occur at specific time instants. However, no known scheduling solution exists that guarantees the scheduling of events at specific time instants when using Ada tasking or any other form of software concurrency.

Detailed architecting techniques using rate monotonic scheduling theory are not included at this time. Readers interested in using this approach are recommended to acquire the tutorial "An Analytical Approach to Real-Time Systems Design in Ada" by John Goodenough, Lui Sha, et al. of the Software Engineering Institute. Better yet, attend one of their frequent hands-on tutorials.

Solutions to tasking limitations always seem to involve additional tasks. Increased use of tasking requires extensive engineering at the software design level to assure that high performance is maintained.

Throughput Concerns

Several potentially significant performance implications result from application of the guidelines suggested above. Blocking time is reduced by adding decoupler tasks. Hard deadlines are met by performing a schedulability analysis and employing dispatcher tasks to assure correct execution sequencing. However, these solutions introduce additional tasks which consume computational overhead for task management.

Further complications result from extensive use of tasking. Calling tasks have multiple protocols that can be employed for controlling interaction with called tasks—unconditional, conditional, and timed entry calls. Inappropriate or indiscriminate use of these caller protocols can result in critical data loss (conditional entry call) or excessive delay (timed entry call with an extremely high time-out delay). Another factor affecting performance under tasking is the amount of work performed within each accept clause. Since practically any legal Ada code can appear within this clause, extensive throughput damage can occur by poor choice of included logic.

These factors lead to several important implications. The use of tasks, decouplers, and schedulers is accomplished as an engineering activity that balances throughput gains against overhead incurred for introducing new tasks into the tasking detailed design. Simple analytical approaches suggested in the Goodenough tutorial may suffice to allow effective analysis where appropriate. In reality, a complex tasking architecture is usually analyzed by accomplishing a detailed discrete event simulation that incorporates all of the competing factors described above. Treat use of Ada tasking as a serious engineering problem to be addressed with as much rigor as usually applied to hardware design. *Do not allow programmers to make tasking use, tasking interaction, or accept clause contents decisions.* Delegation of tasking usage decisions is inconsistent with treatment of tasking usage as a serious engineering issue. Integration and testing headaches are guaranteed to result. Performance degradation is exhibited and is not likely to be easily resolved. Determining the location and quality of poor tasking usage during integration to improve throughput performance is a time consuming and painful process. Moreover, changes are likely to entail significant architecture modifications requiring extensive reworking of large portions of the software system.

Tasking Architecture Evaluation

Comparative evaluation of a tasking architecture is accomplished next using two formats. A qualitative approach applies criteria to assess development ramifications. Performing an event/response evaluation provides more precise, formal insight into the operational impacts of the architecture.

Several criteria are employed to compare proposed tasking architectures. Performance is a key criterion. Another consideration is flexibility—the ability of the tasking architecture to accommodate evolving requirements. Finally, the level of integration and test effort needed to support implementation is a prime consideration. While many of these characteristics are determined by the dominating process architecture, significant impacts in these areas may result from the transition to a tasking architecture. Preferences for tasking architecture generation lean towards table-driven tasking architectures to achieve flexibility. Limited control interactions are emphasized to reduce integration and test efforts. Minimal but effective use of intermediaries serves to provide the highest throughput levels.

Several potential architectures are formulated according to the guidelines and heuristics presented earlier. Generation of other architectures needs to reflect the underlying process architecture and carefully balances the need to obtain flexibility, performance, reliability, and ease of integration testing. One specific architecture is selected as the implementation architecture of choice.

A selected tasking architecture must also be operationally viable. Evaluating the operational behavior of a tasking architecture employs a tabular format, similar to the process architecture evaluation table. This evaluation table also serves to verify individual event/response entries in the test input/output pattern.

A table consisting of five columns proves to be informative: Control Input, Internal Data Flow, Task Name, Internal Data Flow, Response. These column headings are the same as those in the process architecture evaluation table, with the exception of "Task Name," which replaces "Process Name." Entries in the response column can be outgoing data flows, internal control flows, or data store updates.

Tasking evaluation employs the time ordered message sequence described in the test input/output pattern of the operations model. Each incoming event is traced through the complete tasking architecture. Internal data flows and any external responses flowing across the output interfaces are recorded. If data entering a task emit multiple outgoing data flows, all the corresponding response paths must be traced to ultimate responses.

This evaluation primarily determines the consistency and completeness of the tasking architecture, establishes valuable integration and testing data, and proves that a working tasking application can be delivered. Flaws in the tasking architecture are easily identified by the data trace failing to result in the expected termination response. Anticipated tasking architecture behavior is characterized in great detail, providing valuable information for locating problems during integration. If the implemented tasking architecture fails to work properly, actual data can be employed to construct the actual response to the most recent event. Comparison of actual and anticipated response contained in the evaluation table indicates the uncooperative task, suggesting a starting location for problem resolution. Providing a behavioral description proves to the users that the tasking architecture works in a manner that satisfies his operational needs.

Requirements Traceability

As process allocated requirements are further allocated to Ada tasks, formal records of these tasking allocations are maintained. Moreover, justifications supporting each allocation are also recorded for future reference. A sample format for a tasking oriented requirements traceability matrix appears in Figure 6.4. Each functional requirement for which a PSPEC exists, and each STD and PAT appear in a single row of this matrix. Across the columns appear each of the architecture modules. Corresponding Ada tasks are associated with each module. An 'x' in any table entry indicates that the functional or control requirement allocated to the architecture module has been further allocated to the Ada task implemented within the architecture module. Note that both CSPECs and PSPECs are included in the traceability recording mechanism.

Every effort is made to record these allocation decisions during tasking architecture generation. Justification of allocation decisions is also recorded. Reconstructing allocation decisions and support justifications after a significant code implementation tends to fail miserably. Too much time is lost; detailed insights have evaporated from memory. As a result, significant duplication of unneeded requirements occurs within various parts of the tasking architecture and corresponding sequential designs. Ultimately, extremely poor performance results, tasks perform unneeded operations, and poor maintainability and modifiability are exhibited. Tasks are dependent upon unknown functions making change a difficult and tedious activity.

Package Generation Guidelines

Since every task must have a master, all application tasks included in the tasking architecture need to be assigned to specific Ada packages. Package generation is the activity that collects tasks into packages.

Packaging guidelines appear as a functional taxonomy in Figure 6.5. Specific application tasks can be collected into packages based upon a variety of criteria. Control cohesion is obtained by collecting tasks that support a software controller into a single package. Tasks that accomplish specific aspects of sensor data processing algorithms are often incorporated into a single package using a functional cohesion criterion.

Tasks supporting abstracted interfaces are often collected into packages. Isolation of machine dependencies and specific interface protocols is extremely important. During integration and test activities, a large number of problems are often traced to requirements for using external interfaces that changed prior to software implementation. Dynamically evolving interface usage requirements often occur when application specific hardware is being concurrently implemented with application software. Just as a software design often evolves during implementation, a hardware design iterates during implementation. Protocol or interface requirements that have changed are easily determined and modified if encapsulated and hidden under abstract interfaces. In this situation, execution typically fails in the area of memory associated with the abstracted interface/protocol. Identification of the offending code segment is accomplished using a compiler link map or a debugger. Code fixes are restricted to the source code under the abstracted interface.

Some concern is necessary when employing strictly functional guidelines to collect tasks into packages. Packaging incurs a computational overhead during runtime, since packages must be elaborated. If a compiler vendor chooses to statically elaborate package specifications and bodies once at first invocation, no computational burden is consumed. However, elaboration at first invocation involves static

SW-M / Reqmnt	System Controller		Application Manager		Sensor Manager	Actuator Manager	Display Manager
	Buffered Data	Action Manager	Buffered Data	Data Analysis			
1.1					X		
2.1		X					
2.2		X					
3.1							X
3.2							X
4.1						X	
4.2						X	
5.1				X			
5.2				X			
5.3				X	X	X	X
STD 2		X					
PAT 2		X					
STD 5		X					
PAT 5		X					
Derived	X		X				

Figure 6.4 Requirements Traceability Matrix: Detailed Design

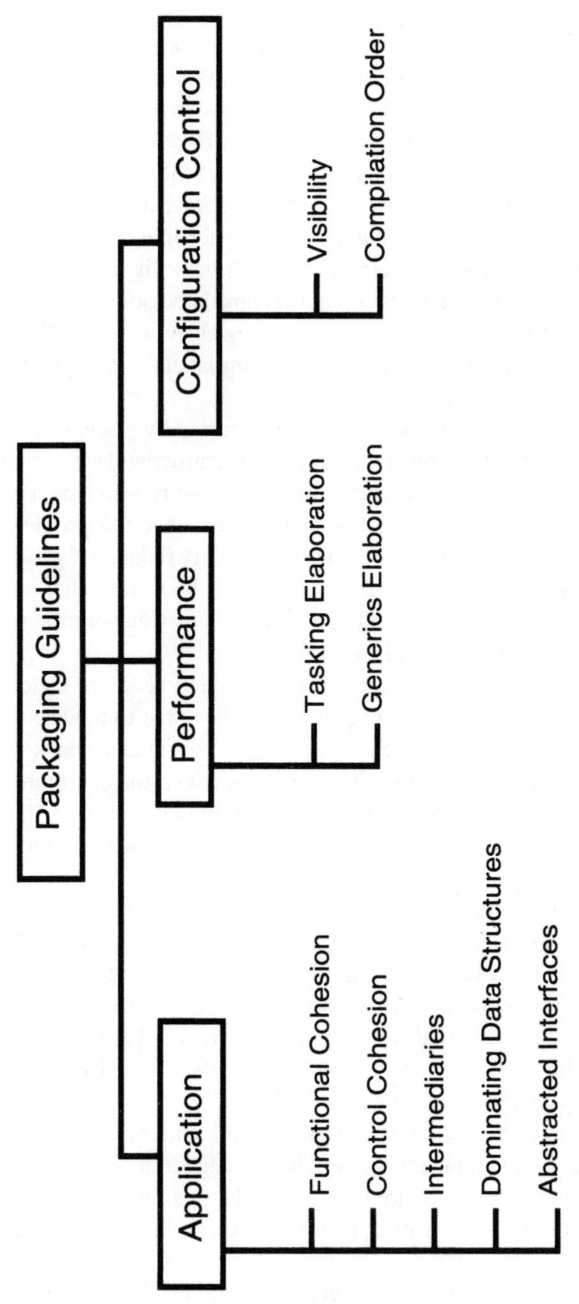

Figure 6.5 Package Generation Guidelines

allocation of memory that must be maintained for the execution life of the package. Permanent static allocation of memory can be a problem for memory-constrained memory target environments. In these particular environments, space must be reclaimed and reused. In these circumstances, package elaboration is dynamically accomplished upon entry to an appropriate context. De-allocation occurs subsequent to exit from the context, assuming no encapsulated objects appear in the local declarative sections. This strategy reclaims space, however, extensive overhead is incurred during execution, resulting in extremely poor performance. Extensive packaging can easily incur this form of performance overhead if strictly functional guidelines are employed. Again, careful engineering can control this problem. System architects must understand elaboration algorithms of the run-time environment. Extensive benchmarking and repackaging is accomplished to assure that packaging elaboration overhead does not have significant impact on system performance. If package bodies contain encapsulated objects, dynamic elaboration can not occur. By definition, encapsulated objects must persist through the execution life of the application. To achieve this, initial elaboration with static memory allocation must be employed.

Package elaboration overhead is further incurred by placement of tasks into generic packages. Instantiation of the generic can cause regular re-elaboration of both the instruction and of the task incurring significant run-time overhead every time generic elaboration occurs. A simple solution exists to this problem. Tasking and generic instantiation overhead can be significantly reduced if generics are instantiated as separate library units rather than inside bodies of other packages or subprograms. In this way, generic and encapsulated task elaboration typically occurs once—when the instantiation is initially invoked.

Another performance related criterion by which tasks are collected into packages is suggested by a need for some tasks to be able to rendezvous early in the initialization of the tasking application. These tasks must be packaged together. If placed into separate packages, a tasking error exception can more readily occur, depending upon the tasking elaboration algorithm employed by the Ada run-time environment. One task may be ready to rendezvous while the other task has not yet been elaborated.

Configuration control issues also provide valid criteria by which Ada tasks can be allocated to packages. Tasks that need to have visibility to other tasks are typically collected into a single package. Task visibility is often needed when an event response controller interacts with tasks employed to manage specific actions, such as table updating or internal control event generation. In this situation, all tasks—event controller and action management controllers—need visibility to each other and are encapsulated into a single package.

Visibility, in combination with packaging allocation, results in a specific compilation order for the total application. Knowledge of this implied compilation order must be employed to assure that no circular compilation conditions result in a non-compilable system. A poor packaging allocation scheme can result in this problem.

As with many other guidelines, conflicts may result when simultaneously applying these packaging allocation guidelines. No hard and fast answers are available to resolve application conflicts. Multiple package schemes are formulated. These alternatives are evaluated based on implications described above. Evaluation of implications is carefully recorded for later review, if needed. A specific packaging alternative is selected and forms the baseline implementation configuration.

Functional Component Generation

Once a specific packaging allocation has been selected, functional components of each package are identified. Each Ada package contains several components, including a specification and body for the package. Bodies for each of the Ada tasks allocated to the package are included as functional components. Additional Ada tasks/procedures necessary to support abstracted hardware interfaces are also incorporated as functional components within the package.

Specific interactions depicted in the packaging scheme provide a basis for functional component generation. Entrance procedures (as suggested in Nielsen and Shumate, 1988) provide a standardized and rigidly enforced caller protocol for each of the encapsulated task entries accessed across packages. In addition, specific functions or procedures exported by the packaging allocation must appear as functional components.

Dependence on support service packages or common definition packages is also indicated as part of the functional components. While support or definition packages do not require specific code to be generated for the package body, they do determine the context clause of the package. Thus, dependencies are included as part of the functional component generation.

Detailed Design and Evaluation

A detailed design diagram characterizes the combined tasking/packaging architecture generated so far. This diagram allows the developer to identify the path of data flow resulting from events at the software system interfaces. Every rendezvous entry call and entrance procedure invocation can be traced and evaluated to assure the integrity of data flowing through the detailed design, and to provide valuable data for problem isolation during integration and testing activities. Moreover, each output can be traced to its ultimate movement to an external recipient across the system interfaces.

Tracing inputs and outputs through the Ada architecture serves several important goals. Continuity of data flow is determined. Each input and output is determined to assure that data can actually start at its source, proceed through the tasking/packaging architecture, and end at its ultimate destination. Moreover, invaluable debugging information has been generated. If data disappears during integration and testing, an integrator can use this path information to isolate the module in which the data is lost. If data enters into one step in the path but fails to exit that step, then the developer knows to start looking for the problem in the piece of software associated with the offending step.

Assessing the detailed design also consists of providing a sanity check to assure that the integrity of the tasking architecture is not violated. Of special interest is the task creepage problem. In this situation, engineers responsible for detailed design may have allowed several new tasks to surreptitiously creep into the design during packaging and functional component generation.

Finally, a detailed design diagram is necessary to assess the validity of the overall design. A good Ada design exhibits a number of important characteristics. These characteristics can be evaluated through a careful review of the detailed design diagram. Central system control needs to be incorporated into the detailed design. Each hardware interface is accommodated by one or more separate Ada tasks. Use of concurrency to accommodate parallel processing chains is apparent. Each parallel activity in the detailed design exists for specific and justifiable reasons that have been identified and recorded earlier in the architecture generation and detailed design activities. An appropriate number of Ada tasks is employed—excessive software tasking is to be avoided. Assignment of caller/callee relationships is clear and justified. Use of intermediaries balances throughput gains against losses in throughput incurred by extra tasks and additional rendezvous entry calls. Entrance procedures are heavily employed throughout the architecture to hide the existence of encapsulated tasks and to enforce caller protocols in a uniform manner across all calling tasks. Specific details of hardware interfaces are encapsulated under abstract interfaces, either as Ada tasks or procedural abstractions, isolating problems of hardware and software integration.

6.2 SEQUENTIAL DESIGN DECISIONS

Generation of sequential software design consists of determining internal designs for each of the Ada tasks. Flexibility, reliability, and modifiability are achieved by extensive use of data abstraction. Ada provides more effective support for data abstraction than any other language. Data abstraction is supported via enforcement of private types and by persistence and invisibility of data objects within local declarative sections of package bodies. Many languages provide support for abstracted interfaces to hidden objects. However, unlike many other languages, Ada enhances the abstracted interfaces at compilation time. In this manner, errors associated with object access are restricted to a single code module, rather than being passed into a complex implementation causing extensive integration and debugging effort.

For instance, object-oriented versions of C provide excellent support for abstracted interfaces to objects. Data passed across an object interface must be appropriately type cast prior to transmission. This object-oriented model contains major flaws. As long as data is type cast, access across an interface is allowed. Moreover, in this model, declaring an object as a type creates a thinly disguised pointer. Object protection is easily subverted by employing an assignment statement (perhaps with an appropriate type cast) to assign an arbitrary integer to the data object. Of course, since type casting is invoked, this assignment statement compiles. During execution, this assigned integer is used as a pointer, causing system crashes. Implementors have no clue as to the problem cause or the problem source, since execution continues past the point at which the pointer is clobbered.

Approaches used in Ada avoid these problems. Extensive use of private types and encapsulated data objects allows access to be constrained to occur under abstract interfaces. Data needs to be exactly type consistent at the interfaces for an invocation to succeed, not temporarily type cast. Moreover, an assignment statement that attempts to assign an arbitrary integer to an encapsulated object is rejected at compilation time, not during execution. Awkward and difficult integration and test headaches are eliminated by refusing to accept this kind of code during compilation of the individual software component. Extensive use of data abstraction capabilities provided by Ada serves to ease the integration and testing process.

Effective sequential software design begins with a set of requirements allocated to a specific Ada task or to a specific architecture process, depending upon support by the underlying hardware architecture. An initial solution is formulated using the allocated requirements. A series of stepwise refinements then occurs. Identification of data abstractions is accomplished prior to each successive refinement. This methodical process is referred to as layered virtual machines/object-oriented design (LVM/OOD).

Significant benefits are derived from the proper application of LVM/OOD to sequential software design. By constructing software around a set of layered abstractions, greater flexibility is exhibited. Modifications to sequential software are restricted to software underneath abstracted interfaces when access to data structures is controlled. Moreover, significant performance is obtained. Forcing applications to access data through limited interfaces eliminates duplication of the data manipulation code, resulting in much tighter code. Giving direct implementation responsibility for an abstraction to a specific programmer allows a single individual to develop a high performance implementation. Reliability is also achieved, since control over encapsulated data structures is focused into a small, compact code segment that can manage all possible access problems. Layering of abstractions increases programmer productivity by encouraging reuse of previously developed abstractions.

Layered Virtual Machines/Object-Oriented Design

Attempts to employ data abstraction often meet with resistance and tend to fail. Failure is often caused by an attempt to convert to a data abstracted approach after a large amount of code has been deployed. Transformation to an approach based on data abstraction is not a function of simply replacing subprogram interfaces. Typically, sequential software design based on strict functional decomposition tends to employ globally visible data structures for inter-module communication. Global visibility of data structure was necessary in the past due to failure of previous languages to provide effective enforcement of abstraction at compilation time. Complex data structures are easily accessed without invocation of specified interfaces. Ada provides enforcement of access through interfaces at compilation time.

However, many developers performing sequential software design tend to carry a globally visible data structure approach into Ada designs.

Some subtle but insidious side effects result from global visibility. Functional decomposition using traditional standards of structural design actually encourages global visibility of data structure. As a result, one software module establishes a value in a specific component of the data structure. Another obscure part of the code employs the knowledge that the value was established elsewhere. Converting several hundred thousand lines of implemented Ada that used this kind of knowledge back into a data abstracted approach requires major redesign, not simple coding. In many cases, manipulation of a global data structure by one module is not known by developers of other modules. After-the-fact conversion to a data abstraction basis requires redesign and significant effort to locate and replace all manipulations of the global data structure. A different approach is needed to effectively employ data abstraction during generation of sequential software designs before, rather than after, code implementation is completed.

"Layered virtual machines/object-oriented design" is the name given to the resultant development methodology. A process of stepwise refinement is employed. As each refinement in the design solution is accomplished, explicit decisions are made as to the need for data abstraction. Use of data abstraction is a fundamental element in the design process rather than an after-the-fact attempt to convert to use of data abstraction.

A specific algorithm describing LVM/OOD is pictorially represented in Figure 6.6. An initial problem-oriented solution is invented. This initial solution is based on specific requirements to be satisfied within the task or architecture process. Each instruction in the current solution is then evaluated. If the instruction is of sufficient complexity, based upon engineering judgement, further decomposition is desired. Instructions needing further decomposition are called virtual machine instructions, representing operations at a lower-level, problem-oriented virtual machine.

If the instruction appears to be an operation on a single object or an operation on an instance of data type, then use of data abstraction is indicated. If no existing abstraction is available, one needs to be created. Creation of a new data abstraction requires a number of specific and important decisions. Since specific interfaces must be generated, a selection is made between interfaces to a single object (object manager) or accesses to multiple objects of an abstract type (type manager). Another important decision reflects the potential for a generic object or type manager. If concurrent access may occur during usage, an encapsulating monitor task is needed. If an appropriate data abstraction already exists, reuse of an existing interface needs to be considered. However, if the needed interface is unavailable, the data abstraction is updated to incorporate the new interface.

Decomposition is no longer necessary when every lower-level virtual machine is a simple machine. A machine is a simple machine (or module) when its components are combinations of sequencing instructions (loops, if-then-else constructs) and operations on abstract objects or types. An example of a simple machine is the following:

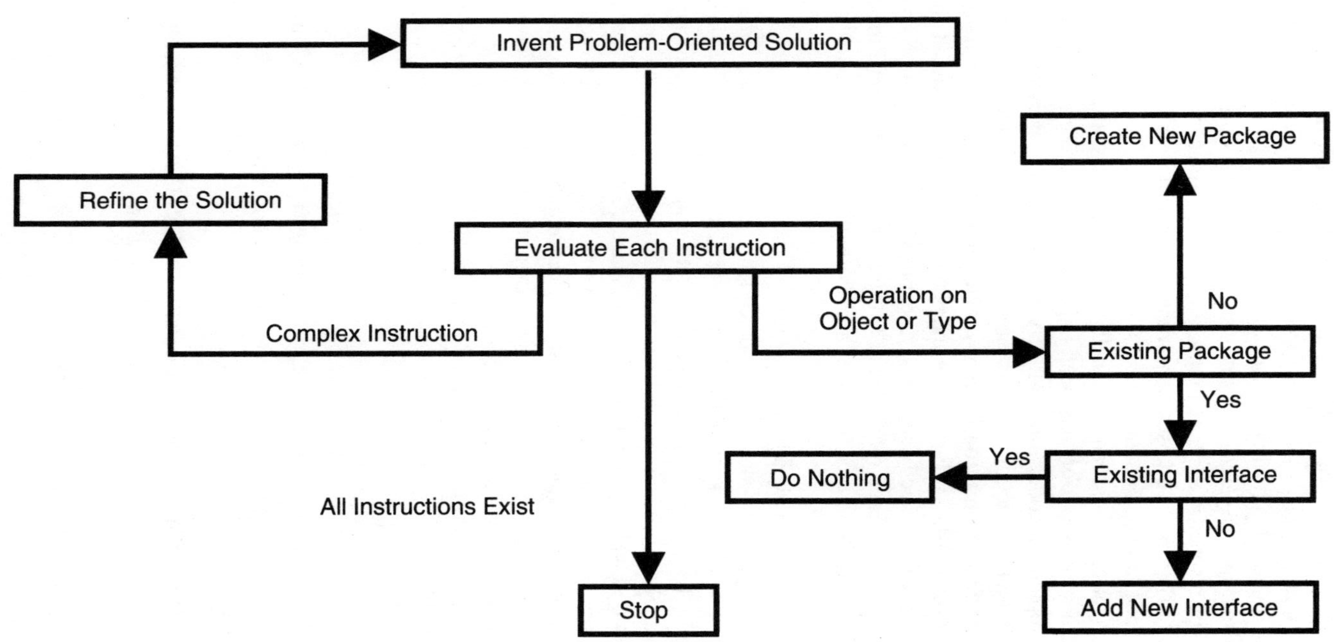

Figure 6.6 Layered Virtual Machines/Object-Oriented Design

```
loop
   stack_manager.pop( stack_name, x);    --  5.4
   flt_io.write( output_file_object, x); --  3.2
end loop;
```

This simple machine consists of a single sequencing construct (loop-end loop) and two operations on abstract objects (popping from stack object and writing to an output file object). No further decomposition is necessary to establish an effective design based upon layered abstractions. Each element in the example above is annotated by a specific implementor's requirement. Since each simple machine is usually a fairly small code segment, direct traceability of implementor requirements to code has been obtained.

With languages other than Ada, methodical developments tend to deteriorate at this point. Extensive effort has been expended to assure traceability of requirements to implement code. Unfortunately, most languages provide extremely poor support for data abstraction. While requirements are now traceable to specific abstracted interfaces, transition from abstracted interfaces into actual code is difficult. By virtue of Ada's private types and persistence of encapsulated objects, transition into code that directly supports traceability to an implementor's requirement is a simple process. Each requirement is traced into a virtual machine instruction or to an abstracted interface which is directly implemented in Ada with as little as a single line of code.

One important task which appears in most real-time architectures is a system controller or cyclic executive. Internal sequential software design of a cyclic executive task is easily generated by direct application of LVM/OOD principles. Three iterations are required. During the first iteration, initial allocated requirements are analyzed and an initial solution is constructed. A second iteration builds an abstraction level whose purpose is to manage control aspects of the allocated requirements. This abstraction level employs abstracted control structures, incorporating flexibility around hidden state and action tables. Beneath the control abstraction, a final iteration establishes abstractions for manipulation of raw data accessed by the control level abstraction.

A typical set of requirements allocated to a cyclic executive or system controller task is as follows:

1. Collect an event;
2. Respond to the event;
3. Provide event response control mechanisms in STD and PAT format; and
4. Implement PSPECs for leaf node requirements associated with action table entries.

An effective initial solution (first iteration of LVM/OOD) probably looks like:

```
loop
   collect an event;
   respond to the event;
end loop;
```

Event collection is treated as an operation on an abstract event queue, requiring no further decomposition.

Responding to the event can be further decomposed. Iterating to further refine "respond to the event" suggests a second level solution which is described by:

```
determine the action name from the state transition
                                              diagram;
retrieve an action list from the process activation
                                              table;
for i in 1.. action list loop
 perform action list (i);
end loop;
```

The first two steps in this iteration are justifiably treated as operations on abstract data objects. Appropriate abstractions and functional interfaces are constructed to accomplish these operations. Functional interfaces to access state and action tables represent the control abstraction. Underneath the interfaces, tabular structures of the control specification have been maintained, assuring flexibility to evolving requirements.

Performing individual actions that compose a specific response to an event requires manipulation of raw data utilized by application. A list of PSPECs is associated with an action in the action table. Execution of the list of PSPECs consists of operations upon data objects, which are implemented as a data layer of abstraction. Typical data management activities include decomposition of incoming events into components, collection of component data into an outgoing response, and management of tables for indicating status of work in progress and allocating of workload to resources.

As an example of an effective object-oriented design generated by LVM/OOD, consider Figure 6.7. A cyclic executive dequeues an event returning a Data_Type indicator or message code and a Data_Location indicator. A dequeue entrance procedure is employed to retrieve the next event. Data_Type and Current_State are passed to an abstract interface that manages specific implementation of a state transition diagram. Details of the actual transition diagram implementation are hidden or encapsulated in the local declarative section of the package body and within the code body of the Get_Next_State subprogram interface. A new state is returned. Next, Current_State and Data_Type indicators are passed across an abstract interface named Get_Action. Internal structure of the implemented process activation table is hidden beneath this interface. An indicator for This_Action to be completed is returned as a result of the process. This_Action indicator and the Data_Location indicator are then transmitted across another abstract interface, named Perform_Action. Perform_Action controls use of actual raw data to accomplish individual PSPECs listed by the This_Action indicator. Specific pre-programmed responses associated with individual PSPECs generate outgoing messages—Raw_Data_Location, Position_Velocity_Data, and Display_Update_Commands. Raw data is employed to generate these outgoing messages.

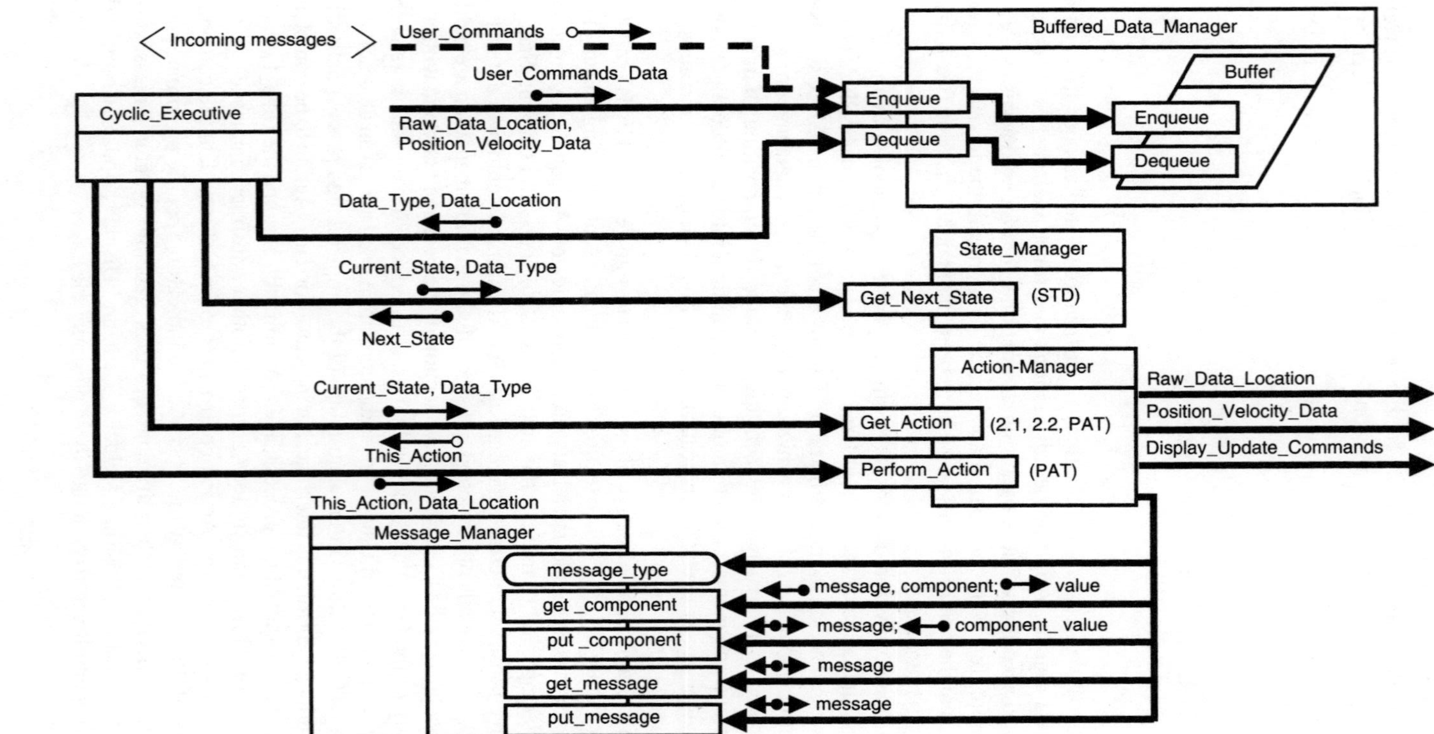

Figure 6.7 Typical Object-Oriented Detailed Design with Packages

Multiple levels of data abstraction are effectively employed by the PSPEC. Some implementations of the PSPEC actions maintain a pipeline of raw sensor data, each in various stages of the analysis processing chain. Pipeline management consists of tracking the status of each frame of sensor data in the pipeline. An abstracted object, the pipeline management table, is encapsulated or abstracted under the Pipeline Status Manager. Another example of raw data abstraction is encountered within the buffered data manager. Mechanics and protocols associated with receipt of incoming messages at hardware interfaces are encapsulated under an enqueue accept clause within an encapsulated buffer task. An explicit buffer task is needed because two asynchronous accesses to the buffer can occur—the actual hardware interrupt and the cyclic executive request for the next event. Serialization is accomplished via the rendezvous mechanism, since only one rendezvous can occur at any time. Furthermore, all buffer accesses are constrained to occur during task rendezvous.

Message, state, and action type indicators moving through the sequential software design are encoded as internal values. Internal coding is easily implemented using enumerated types. Allocation of requirements to sequential design components is indicated on the diagram itself. Specific PSPECs and CSPECs are associated with specific software components.

Individual design refinements generated through application of LVM/OOD methods form an initial basis for pseudocode generation. Detailed pseudocode is now produced for all levels of detail in both the tasking and sequential software architectures.

Ada Pseudocode Generation

Competing theories exist regarding the best approach for pseudocode generation during an Ada development. One approach employs a special pseudocode processor. Several of these are commercially available. When using a commercial processor, a special language is employed. Pseudocode and Ada statements are freely intermixed. Additional information is provided using English embedded within comments. During pseudocode processing, special language constructs are evaluated to assess code logic consistency and completeness. Some software engineers like this approach; others complain that extra effort is necessary to debug a pseudocode language, making this an untenable approach. Introducing an extra language also injects error into the traceability process, yielding additional integration and test headaches due to misplaced requirements.

A preferred approach is to simply generate pseudocode in the form of compilable Ada statements. An extra step is not required; no new language needs to be learned, and traceability is easier to achieve. This approach is an improvement, but is insufficient—a static representation of code logic results.

To obtain behavioral insight into code logic, pseudocode that is both compilable and executable is created. Compilable pseudocode preserves the essentials of the overall software code logic. Less abstract details are still incorporated into comments. Executable pseudocode translates logic and design into an action sequence, providing an operational representation of the code logic. Internal code logic is translated from an implementor's perspective back into a user's perspective, further demonstrating that a working system can be delivered.

One example of compilable pseudocode appears in Figure 6.8. This pseudocode represents the typical object-oriented design presented in Figure 6.7. Compilation demonstrates that the logic of the pseudocode is syntactically correct and that type consistency at interfaces is obtained. Semantic correctness is also of interest, both to the customer and to the implementor. Evaluating semantic correctness requires that this pseudocode be executable. Semantic correctness is verified if execution of the pseudocode represents a correct and complete response from the user's perspective.

```
procedure system  controller is
begin
   em. get_current_event (current_event);
   am. get_action (current_state, current_event,
                                    current_action);
   am. perform_action (current_action);
   while (current_state/= ctp. process_end) loop
      sm. get _state (current_state, current_event,
                                    next_state);
      current_state := next_state;
      em. get_current_event (current_event);
      am. get_action (current_state, current_event,
                                    current_action);
      am. perform_action (current_action);
   end loop;
end system_controller;
```

Figure 6.8 Typical System Controller Pseudocode

Design Verification Using Executable Pseudocode

Formulation of both compilable and executable pseudocode requires only slightly more effort than generation of compilable pseudocode. Subprogram interfaces are carefully specified to assure that relevant, type consistent data is passed across the interfaces during invocation. Loop controls are injected into the pseudocode to limit the number of passes through it. Finally, entry into each subprogram, task entry, etc., is signaled by printing a message to a file. Sequencing within pseudocode of each module is modified in a manner which allows each path through the pseudocode to be invoked at least once. Lowest pseudocode levels contain only stubs that place invocation messages into an output file.

After pseudocode execution, a file containing a list of messages exists. This list of messages represents an operational view of the pseudocoded logic. Semantic consistency and completeness is verified by evaluating message lists in the output file to assess if the listed responses are appropriate to the target application and are consistent with events and responses in the test input/output pattern.

An example of compilable, executable pseudocode, accompanied by copious comments, appears in Figure 6.9. Declaration and use of loop counters for pseudocode control are indicated. Examples of efforts to assure type consistency are highlighted. Comments are included that illustrate the effect of hidden dependencies upon control sequencing. Execution of this pseudocode requires one additional layer of subprograms which prints messages into a file in response to subprogram entry. A resulting message sequence appears in Figure 6.10. Completeness of the sequencing is almost obvious. In this case, inherent simplicity in the pseudocode makes this a trivial example. However, a more complex, detailed software design, with more complicated sequencing logic within each pseudocoded module would not possess such simplicity. Evaluating semantic consistency and completeness in those cases requires compilable and executable pseudocode to reveal inadequacies in the operational behavior of the pseudocoded logic.

```
procedure Exec is
    rec_State  : RDP. state_type ;
    rule_num : TBD.TBD_Int ;
    rule :            RDP.rule_type ;
    done :           boolean ;

--  pseudocode execution control
    max_loops : constant : = 1 ;
    loop_cntr :   integer ;
    max_cntr :   constant : = 1 ;
    rule_cntr :    integer ;
--  pseudocode execution control

    begin

--  pseudocode execution control
    loop_cntr : = 0 ;
--  pseudocode execution control

    remove_object ;
    Q_Head_Popped : = false ;
    done : = false ;
```

Same names as actual code; where possible, same types as actual code; possible if types identified, exported in another package

Pseudocode control for executable requirement delimited begin, end with comments, blank lines

Figure 6.9 Cyclic Executive—Compilable Executable Pseudocode

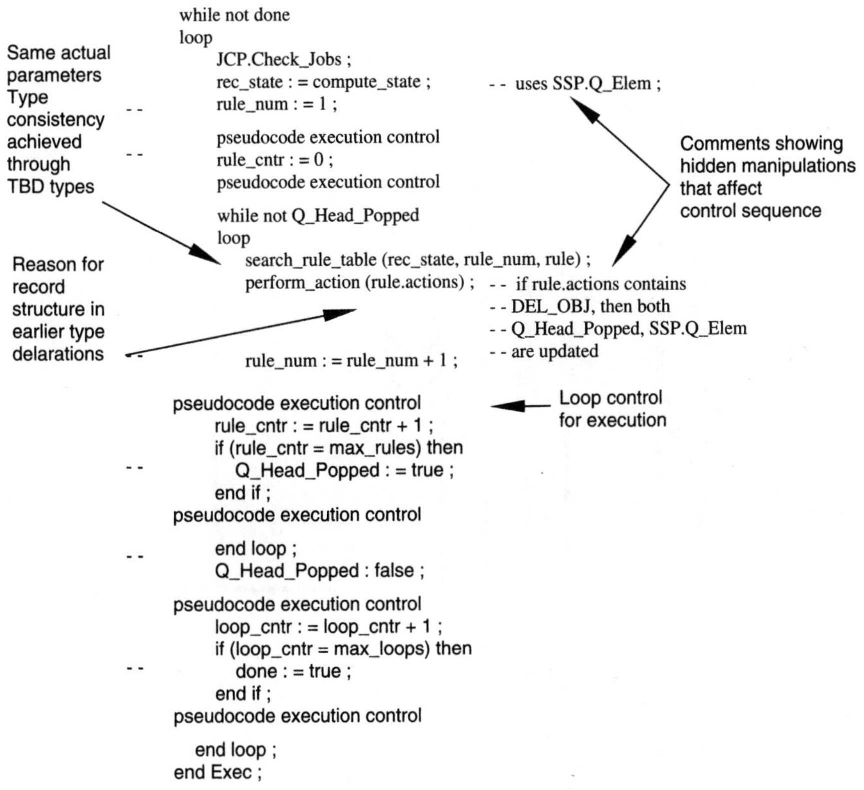


```
        while not done
        loop
            JCP.Check_Jobs ;
            rec_state : = compute_state ;         -- uses SSP.Q_Elem ;
  --        rule_num : = 1 ;
            pseudocode execution control
  --        rule_cntr : = 0 ;
            pseudocode execution control
            while not Q_Head_Popped
            loop
                search_rule_table (rec_state, rule_num, rule) ;
                perform_action (rule.actions) ;   -- if rule.actions contains
                                                  -- DEL_OBJ, then both
                                                  -- Q_Head_Popped, SSP.Q_Elem
  --            rule_num : = rule_num + 1 ;       -- are updated

        pseudocode execution control
            rule_cntr : = rule_cntr + 1 ;
            if (rule_cntr = max_rules) then
  --           Q_Head_Popped : = true ;
            end if ;
        pseudocode execution control
  --        end loop ;
            Q_Head_Popped : false ;
        pseudocode execution control
            loop_cntr : = loop_cntr + 1 ;
            if (loop_cntr = max_loops) then
  --           done : = true ;
            end if ;
        pseudocode execution control
          end loop ;
        end Exec ;
```

Figure 6.9, continued Cyclic Executive—Compilable Executable Pseudocode

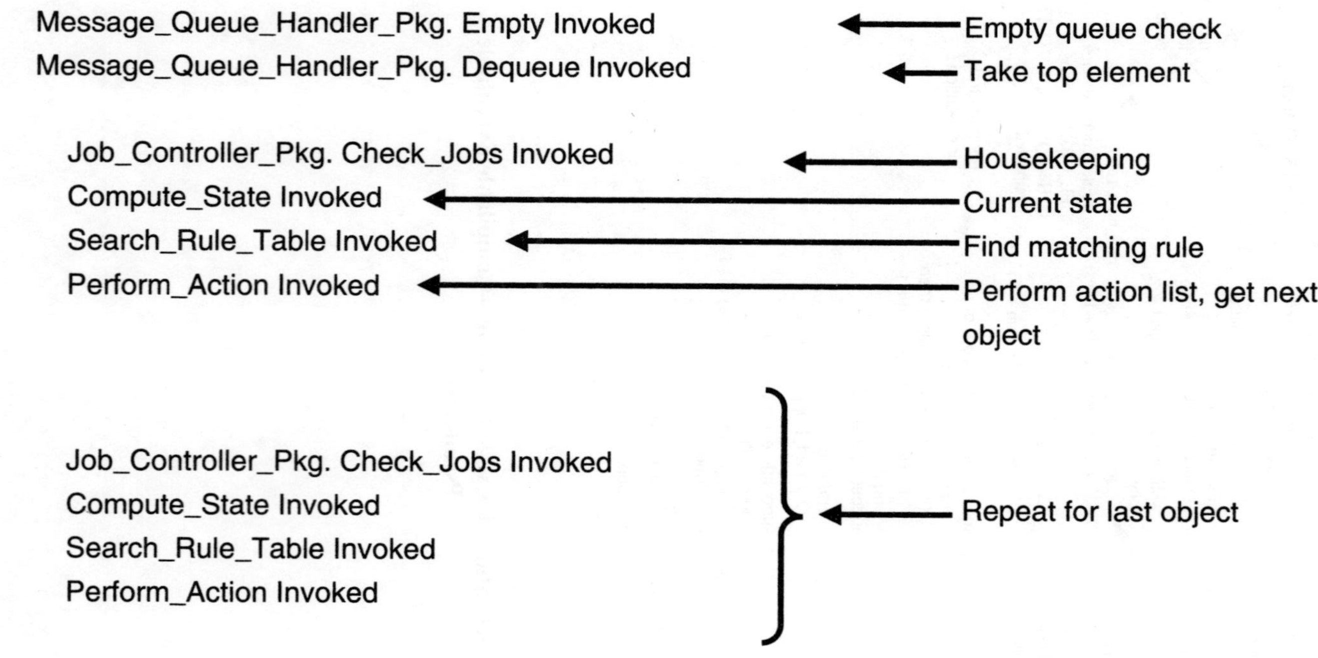

Figure 6.10 Cyclic Executive Pseudocode Execution Trace

7

Document Generation According to DoD Std 2167A

Documentation need not be the curse of a real-time system developer's existence, as most implementors seem to feel. Difficulties with document generation typically result from extra effort needed to translate technical results into required documentation format. Moreover, document generation is often accomplished after the detailed technical activity is completed. If extra effort is needed to transform implementation data into document consistent format, the implementation process is of questionable validity. Documentation standards are meant to reflect the commonly accepted methods by which implementation is achieved.

As a large customer for real-time systems, the U.S. Department of Defense (DoD) has played a major role in specification of documentation standards. DoD documentation standards are expressed in two major formats—Mil Std 490 and DoD Std 2167A.

In the framework provided by Mil Std 490, an A Specification describes system requirements. B0 and B5 Specifications describe software requirements and software preliminary design. Similar specifications are generated for hardware. This format jumps from system requirements directly to software and hardware requirements, ignoring system design issues. A more realistic approach is employed in DoD Std 2167A format. The documentation hierarchy is the following:

System Requirements Document

System Design Document

Software Requirements Specification

Software Design Document

Recognition of a system emphasis and inclusion of an explicit system design document are important attributes of the 2167A approach. Important information about system level designs significantly affects software requirements and design. This information is formalized and communicated through several levels of documentation. For this reason, DoD Std 2167A is a preferred approach. Documentation generation efforts in the sections below focus on those documents satisfying DoD Std 2167A.

Significant effort has been expended in the Ada community to assess the compatibility of DoD Std 2167A with Ada-oriented developments. Much of this hullabaloo has been totally unnecessary. In its current format, no major impediment exists to tailoring of DoD Std 2167A formats to accommodate real-time systems implemented in Ada. Document generation is a reasonable task, when employing the methodology described in this text.

7.1 SOFTWARE REQUIREMENTS SPECIFICATION

Required document components for DoD Std 2167A are provided in a series of Data Item Descriptions (DIDs), one for each specified document. Emphasis here is on those documents required for software development. Each DID specifies a Table of Contents and includes guidelines for tailoring each outline. Data generated by methodology steps are easily mapped into DID outlines for software documents.

A detailed outline, as specified by the 2167A DID for a Software Requirements Specification (SRS), is presented in Figure 7.1. Contents of these components are obtained by employing products generated during rigorous methodology application. Functional capabilities are represented in the form of data flows, PSPECs, control flows, and CSPECs. Both external and internal interface requirements are extracted from the data dictionary. Timing requirements include the timing allocations generated subsequent to the requirements evaluation.

7.2 SOFTWARE DESIGN DOCUMENTATION

An appropriate mapping of architecture and design products can be accomplished for Preliminary and Detailed Software Design Documents (SDDs) using the DID outline specified in Figure 7.2. Subsystem overview is composed of the external interfaces diagram, message flow, test input/output patterns, and requirements evaluation table to demonstrate operational concepts, which are explicitly required. Architecture process flow diagrams are the primary component of software system design. Similarly, tasking diagrams and Booch notated structure charts describing packaging schemes and layered abstractions are the basis for detailed design sections of the document. Requirements traceability contains both the architecture evaluation tables and the requirements traceability matrices in formats previously discussed.

- External Interface Requirements
  - Format
  - Content
- Capability Requirements
- Internal Interface Requirements
  - Format
  - Content
- Data Element Requirements
- Adaptation Requirements
- Sizing and Timing Requirements
- Qualification Requirements

Figure 7.1 SRS Contents

This suggested mapping approach has been employed on a significant number of real-time Ada projects. No resistance has been encountered on the part of customers. Applicability of both this mapping and of DoD Std 2167A to real-time systems implemented in Ada has been successfully demonstrated repeatedly.

- Subsystem Overview
  (Operations concept)
- Subsystem Design
  (Top level design)
- Detailed Design
- Global Data Elements
- Data Files
- Requirements Traceability

Figure 7.2 SDD Contents

8

Integration and Test Strategies

Perhaps the most feared aspect of real-time system development is the phase of testing and integration. Implementors envision long, frustrating hours of effort during which schedules are missed and budgets are exceeded. After an extensive heroic effort on the part of the programming and software engineering staff, performance is, at best, marginal. *This need not describe your experience*. More effective approaches can be employed that ease the transition from individual software and hardware components into a working system.

As a prelude to describing effective approaches to integration and testing, the reasons for painful integration and testing activities are evaluated. Complex real-time Ada systems are composed of an extensive number of software and hardware components. These components interact in a very dynamic manner during system operation. To complicate matters, several of the hardware elements are often application specific integrated circuits (ASICs) that are developed concurrently with the software components. Integration testing is likely to uncover problems/bugs with both software and hardware components.

Consider now a typical integration and test activity under these conditions. All the hardware, both off-the-shelf and ASICs, is individually tested. Concurrently, software components are submitted to unit testing. Once all hardware and software elements have passed unit level testing, integration testing begins. Integration testing is usually accomplished by a "big bang" approach. Hardware units are physically connected. Sometimes they are tested together as a system, but usually not. Software modules are loaded into this target platform. Real data is fed into the software at a real-time rate expected during normal operations and execution begins. Suddenly, the system simply stops. Execution goes south for the duration. Hardware and software engineers sit and look dumbly at their implementations. Hundreds of thousands of physical circuits and perhaps hundreds of thousands of lines of code are combined into a complex system possessing extremely dynamic behavior. Identifying the location of the problem based on this symptom, appears to be insurmountable. Everyone points fingers at each other. "This is a hardware problem." "No, this exhibits all the symptoms of a software bug." In reality, this is neither a hardware nor a software problem. Ultimately, responsibility for this symptom can be attributed to systems, hardware, and software engineers and their lack of a coherent integration and test strategy.

In fact, a simple but ineffective integration strategy has been employed. This strategy consists of pulling all the hardware and software pieces into a room and bringing them together. This form of instantaneous integration of all components is significantly flawed. Multiple conflicting factors are simultaneously incorporated into the integration environment; failure of the test is highly likely. Moreover, finding the problem tends to be even more frustrating due to the interaction complexity of the assembled collection of existing and new hardware and extremely complex software. This "go-for-broke" approach emphasizes making the system operational in a single fell swoop. Clearly, experience with this approach indicates its inadequacy and suggests that a more coherent approach needs to be employed.

First and foremost, testing tends to be more successful when tied to specific products generated during the specification and design of the system. Using the development methodology described in the preceding chapters, several specific products are available that can aid significantly in the testing and integration process. The test input/output pattern derived to represent the user's view of system operation is an excellent source for an initial set of test scenarios. Evaluating actual responses to incoming events to isolate and debug problems is accomplished by employing anticipated responses explicitly derived as the consistency and completeness check performed during architecture generation. Successful integration and test requires rigorous enforcement of a development methodology along the lines of the approach described in this text.

Since complete integration in a single step is inappropriate, a more rational approach employs selective introduction of technological complexity and risk in a phased manner. Incorporation of hardware is one area where phased introduction provides significant gains in easing the integration processing. Unit testing employs no target specific hardware. Subsequent integration steps include a single target CPU followed by multiple target CPUs sharing an internal communications bus. Inclusion of ASICs is allowed only after successful integration testing of all previous phases of hardware complexity.

Software subsystems also follow an incremental migration path similar to the approach employed for the hardware. Initially, individual computer program components are unit tested. Testing of multiple components in the form of an integrated subsystem follow as a second phase of testing. This integrated subsystem does not include any ASIC firmware. Adding firmware to the software test configuration is a final step in the integration process.

Operational complexity is also selectively introduced into the testing environment. Initial testing employs only the test input/output pattern with representative data. This step tests the end-to-end control flow of the software. Addition of a single raw data frame from each incoming sensor provides a first level of testing for the functional processing beneath the event response logic tested in the previous phase. Using these static sensor frames, cyclic testing is then accomplished. Cyclic testing on a single sensor frame allows dynamic behavior of interacting control and data processing to be evaluated with known analytical results. Finally, dynamic sensor data without orchestrated results is fed into the tested environment.

By contrast, the "big bang" or "go for broke" approach described earlier represents the last step characterized above when testing includes a completely integrated hardware and software environment. Dynamic behavior, resulting from real-time data interacting with fully implemented control and functional software elements combined with ASIC hardware and firmware in a full-up operational context, simply introduces too many complicating factors into the integration and test environment. Employing an approach that selectively introduces technological complexity (various mixtures of hardware, software, and operational conditions) into the testing and integration process effectively partitions these conflicting factors into manageable subsets. Each testing phase serves to eliminate errors by isolating the symptoms exhibited by a constrained combination of hardware, software and operational conditions. Thus, an observed symptom is directly related to the hardware and software components included in the testing "configuration." In this manner, finger pointing is reduced; integration and testing is orderly and controlled. Pain and stress are eliminated.

At work here is a very simple concept—control. This control is not achieved without cost, however. Extra hardware is required to support various testing configurations. Extensive and effective configuration management is needed. All this effort requires concerted planning. An important prerequisite is that development follow a rigorously employed methodology. A methodical development combined with a phased integration and testing approach is inconsistent with the approach characterized by, "Hit the keyboards now; we'll fix the problems later." Fixing the problems later never happens. Too much time and effort is wasted making the unplanned mess work. Rigorous methodology plus phased integration simply eliminates most integration problems in the first place.

Various aspects of hardware, software, and operational complexity are combined in a manner producing discrete phases of testing. Phased testing is necessary to contain costs as well as to recognize scheduled deadlines. Some integration and testing problems inevitably occur. However, a phased testing approach, combined with effective Ada design guidelines, results in far less effort to debug problems. Selective introduction of technological complexity assures that any problems can be easily traced to the hardware and/or software components most recently introduced into the tested environment. This incremental integration approach has been effectively employed on real-time systems numerous times, and has been demonstrated to significantly reduce technical staff frustration and to essentially eliminate schedule hits and cost overruns. Achieving these successes requires significant engineering discipline, investment in necessary hardware to support multiple testing configurations, and discipline to assure the test strategy is both planned and followed.

Remaining sections in this chapter characterize testing levels that combine significant aspects of hardware, software, and operational conditions. These testing levels are intended to serve as suggested guidelines and as examples of phased testing use. Adopting an approach peculiar to your own development needs is accomplished during initial planning phases of your development project.

8.1 SOURCES FOR SCENARIO TESTING

As testing occurs, data is employed to provide realistic scenarios for both software and integrated hardware and software. Several major sources of test data are available. Complexity and contents of test data need to reflect the type of testing in process. Potential data sources are characterized in this section.

For the simplest form of testing, appropriate test data is typically stored in stimulus test files. A stimulus test file consists of a series of messages that can be read from a file by a single computer software component (CSC). Messages in this file consist of the same sequence of incoming events in the test input/output pattern that were employed to generate requirements for the software. Message contents are artfully constructed to reflect an actual stream of data that would appear during actual operations. Typically, this data consists of a series of intermediate analytical results generated by processing a stream of raw sensor data. Care is to be taken to assure that message contents are consistent with an actual data stream. Consistency with actual data is necessary to assure that testing evaluates operations as it would actually occur in real-time. Successful processing of a stimulus test file verifies that control processing is accurate and complete.

More complex testing usually entails artificial sources of sensor input. One form of input provided by external devices consists of a vector of values at regular time intervals. Telemetry data from a vehicle under operation is usually presented in this format. Generation of a set of vectors over time results in a file containing time stamped vectors. A data generator is constructed and employed to generate this category of sensor data. Input into the data generator is described in the form of rise and fall patterns of the various vector elements. Pattern descriptions are composed in an English-like format, describing rise times, magnitude and duration of rises, and fall-times. Of course, generated data is in the form of a time-stamped set of vectors. By feeding these vectors into a single software component, combined control and data processing are validated for dynamic operations of the software component under test.

When sensor inputs require an array of test data, two forms of input data may be employed. Static sensor input consists of a single array of data with a known set of characteristics. By employing known characteristics, intermediate results and outgoing responses can be evaluated as to accuracy of contents. Employing this kind of test data requires either a stimulus test file containing historically captured data or a software tool that can stimulate repetitive processing of the static input data. Using combined static imagery and a small stimulus test file serves to validate combined control and data processing under dynamic conditions as do time-stamped vectors. Static imagery, combined with software for initiating repetitive processing, is extremely useful to assure accuracy of combined control and data processing activities of multiple, integrated CSCs in a subsystem.

Extensive dynamic testing of a complete subsystem constructed from multiple CSCs is typically accomplished using a sequence of raw data frames or vectors stored on a high speed storage device. Optical disks or wideband digital data tapes are the devices most often employed for storing test data in this form. A test environment is constructed that allows a sequence of raw data frames with unknown characteristics to be cycled through the complete software system. An extremely large number of frames are employed to assure a test duration sufficient to stress the subsystem to its performance envelope. This form of testing is accomplished just prior to final operational delivery and deployment.

Each of the test data formats described above suggests a series of goals compatible with the testing philosophy described. Simple patterns that formed the basis for original CSC implementor requirements are evaluated first. More complex data formats serve to test more complex operational characteristics. In this manner, systematic testing is obtained.

Unfortunately, many developments fail to follow this approach to test data generation. Typical projects move immediately to the complex dynamic form of test data utilized in the last phase of testing. This "go-for-broke" approach introduces too much complexity into the test and integration process. While justified on the surface as being necessary to meet short schedules, in fact, "going for broke" usually guarantees missed schedules, cost over-runs, and significantly painful effort. Easing into integration and test by utilizing carefully organized levels of testing around appropriate test data is the best, and perhaps only, manner in which short schedules can be met within limited cost constraints.

8.2 LEVELS OF TESTING

To accomplish an effective testing program, a large number of important factors need to be combined in a manner that accomplishes incrementally established testing goals. An intelligent incremental approach controls the extent of complexity introduced into the test environment, while simultaneously satisfying cost limitations and schedule constraints.

The following approaches combine hardware and software components in a manner that emphasizes control of complexity while striving to obtain a higher level of integration. Unit testing of individual CSCs is accomplished by employing stimulus test files. Evaluating operational behavior of a single CSC is the next step of testing. Operational CSC testing moves the CSC onto a specific target platform for the first time. Testing multiple CSCs as a subsystem on a target platform is the next phase of testing. Hardware/software integration on the target platform is the final phase of testing.

During the first three phases of testing, software complexity is introduced into the test environment and limited hardware is employed. Only stable hardware is allowed into the integration environment. Introducing stable hardware only provides the operational flavor of software module interaction without introducing potential hardware problems. These phases of software testing eliminate software bugs and assure that software is operationally conforming to performance and reliability requirements. Introduction of hardware during the last phase of testing limits introduction of problems to those problems caused by hardware faults or by miscommunication of protocols for hardware interface management. A deliverable system is incrementally constructed in each phase of testing. However, the introduction of problems is strictly controlled by isolating and limiting the factors that can contribute to problems.

Use of Stimulus Test Files and Cyclic Data Generators

Testing an individual CSC serves to test control and functional processing capabilities embedded in the CSC software architecture. To accomplish this kind of testing, a series of stimulus messages and associated raw data frames are submitted to the CSC. Responses to these events are recorded and evaluated for consistency with anticipated responses. Numerical results contained in outgoing responses are compared to simulations performed by algorithm developers to assure accuracy of numerical results generated by implemented functional processing.

Characterization of the unit test concept that employs stimulus test files appears in Figure 8.1. Since no target hardware is allowed into the test environment, all testing occurs within the host development environment. Usually, this environment contains a stable operating system with well-defined file interfaces. Effective utilization of this environment requires that hardware interfaces be encapsulated under functional abstractions. In this manner, interfaces can be simulated, using file inputs and outputs, by simply redirecting data flow into and from files underneath the abstracted interfaces.

Several forms of data are stored in the testing files. Static imagery or time stamped telemetry data may be stored in one input file. This data is necessary for evaluation of the functional processing capabilities of the CSC. Additional support for testing of functional processes also suggests that a file containing algorithm parameters is necessary. Another input file contains formatted messages in the same sequence as characterized in the test input/output pattern. However, actual message data is formatted exactly as the hardware interfaces would provide the data. Contents of message components reflect normal processing sequences in a consistent manner. This data, combined with state and action tables stored in yet another input file, are employed in testing control processing capabilities.

Evaluation of unit tests also employs the host environment's basic file services. A file of formatted output messages, containing data as actually formatted by the hardware interfaces, serves to assure that control responses observed are consistent with anticipated responses. Orderly logging of intermediate numerical results is necessary for comparison with independent algorithm simulations. Accuracy of results produced when the CSC evaluates raw input data in response to incoming events determines the functional validity of the CSC. Each CSC is required to log

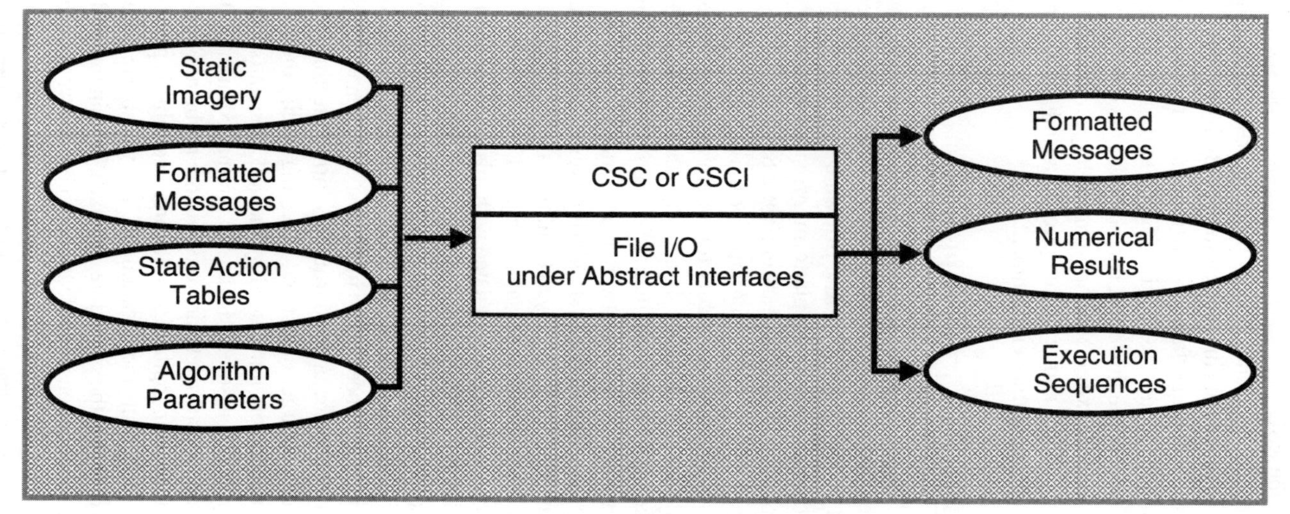

Figure 8.1 Unit Test Methodology

its entry into and exit from each procedure, recording actual subprogram parameters provided at invocation. Subprogram entry parameter data is employed to determine the integrity and effectiveness of the integrated control and processing capabilities within the CSC.

Adopting this approach depends heavily upon the abstraction of hardware interfaces and the redirection of data into and from files. Both discipline and effort must be expended to assure that interface abstraction is accomplished. Using files on complex data structures requires extensive coding to design and to employ overloaded file operations. While this effort can be both time consuming and tedious, performing this activity is extremely important. A large number of CSC software problems are easily isolated and remedied prior to introduction of additional software complexity into the testing environment.

Single Unit Testing on a Target Platform

Once control and data processing integrity are verified, unit testing of a single CSC within the target environment is accomplished. In this phase of testing, a single CPU is employed on the target platform. Software is integrated within a single, stable element of the target hardware platform. A representation of the interacting components of this environment appears in Figure 8.2.

With this mode of testing, file input/output primitives are replaced by software that manages communications protocols for an embedded communications bus. Replacement of file accesses is an easily accomplished process if hardware interfaces are abstracted under functional interfaces and if communications bus protocols are precisely stated. A single software configuration that contains both communications bus protocols and file system primitives is maintained. Compilation pragmas or software filters are employed to allow a switch control to dynamically determine which code segment is actually compiled.

Both input and output files are associated with this phase of testing. The important difference is that the CSC executes on the target platform. This testing phase assesses the control and data processing capabilities of the CSC while simultaneously evaluating embedded communications interfaces. While control and data processing capabilities have been tested in the host development environment, they may still exhibit erroneous behavior during this form of testing. A cross compiler is employed to generate target object code. Testing within the host environment will not eliminate new errors introduced by the code generator of the cross-compiler or protocol problems associated with the internal communications bus.

A simple example can suffice to demonstrate the problem of errors introduced by a cross compiler. In your application software, a variable is passed across a procedure interface as an "in out" mode parameter. The variable is not initialized prior to passing the value across the procedure interface. Within the host environment, lack of parameter initialization presented no problem. However, when cross compiled, random data may be in the area of memory allocated to the variable. This random data may cause constraint error exception to be raised during testing. Execution would then exhibit erroneous behavior not encountered during the prior phase of unit testing.

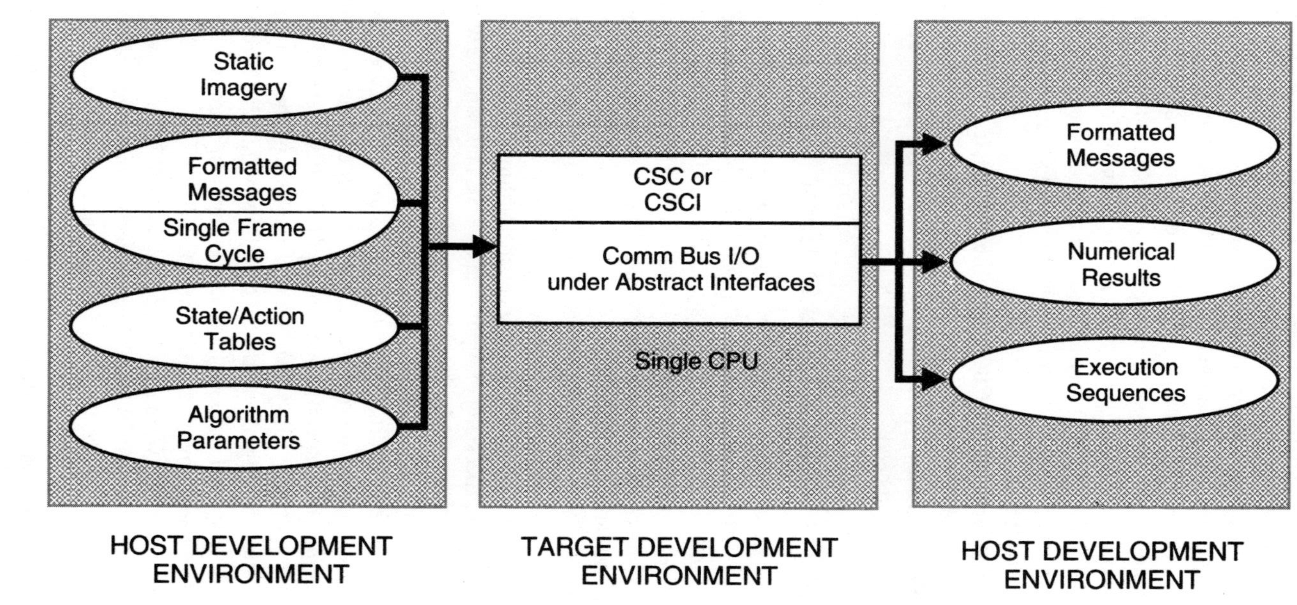

Figure 8.2 CSC Operational Testing Methodology

Evaluating cross compiler induced problems requires that the software tester be capable of reading and understanding intermixed Ada and machine language. When software is tested and operates within a single environment, lack of knowledge regarding code generation strategies may be acceptable. For real-time systems that operate within an embedded context, programmers must be capable of evaluating Ada code intermixed with generated machine code. Software developers of embedded systems are quite concerned with interactions between software and hardware. Code generation patterns that were employed for previous customers of the compiler vendor may have been acceptable for those customers. These same code generation strategies may be an impediment for your application and target domain. Without the ability to read and to understand intermixed Ada and machine code, even integration testing that employs stable hardware can be an extremely difficult task.

For a complex project, each CSC is submitted to unit test activities in parallel. A sufficient number of test components and test stations must be available to accommodate concurrent testing. Once individual CSCs have passed unit testing, subsystem testing can proceed.

Subsystem Testing on a Target Platform

As the next phase of integration, multiple software CSCs are concurrently operated to test the software subsystem as a whole. Data is input into the test environment in a manner that tests the cyclic and end-to-end data flow operations of the software subsystem. Hardware impacts are minimized within this environment through deployment of only stable hardware. Functional processing is limited to repetition of the same functionality.

In Figure 8.3, components of software subsystem testing are pictured. A combined host and target environment provides the basic environment. Data files that control the test and record test responses reside within the host development environment. All actual processing of input data by CSCs takes place within the target development environment. Multiple CPUs are employed, one for each CSC which has passed both unit test phases described in previous sections.

As with unit testing, internal communications interfaces are employed to allow software CSCs to reside on disparate CPUs and to communicate during actual operations. Application specific integrated circuits that were developed concurrently with the software subsystem are still not part of the system at this time. However, to allow testing of end-to-end data flow within the distributed software subsystem, these special purpose hardware components are represented by software simulators executing on an independent CPU.

Construction of a software simulator for an ASIC is a relatively easy task to accomplish. These simulators must simply accept a message and return a canned response consistent with the test data. For instance, assume that a special purpose hardware component analyzes a frame of static imagery and returns any potential candidate targets. A simulator for this ASIC receives a message to evaluate the static imagery. Its response is a message containing the known list of targets within the static image that drives the test. At most, this requires several hundred lines of

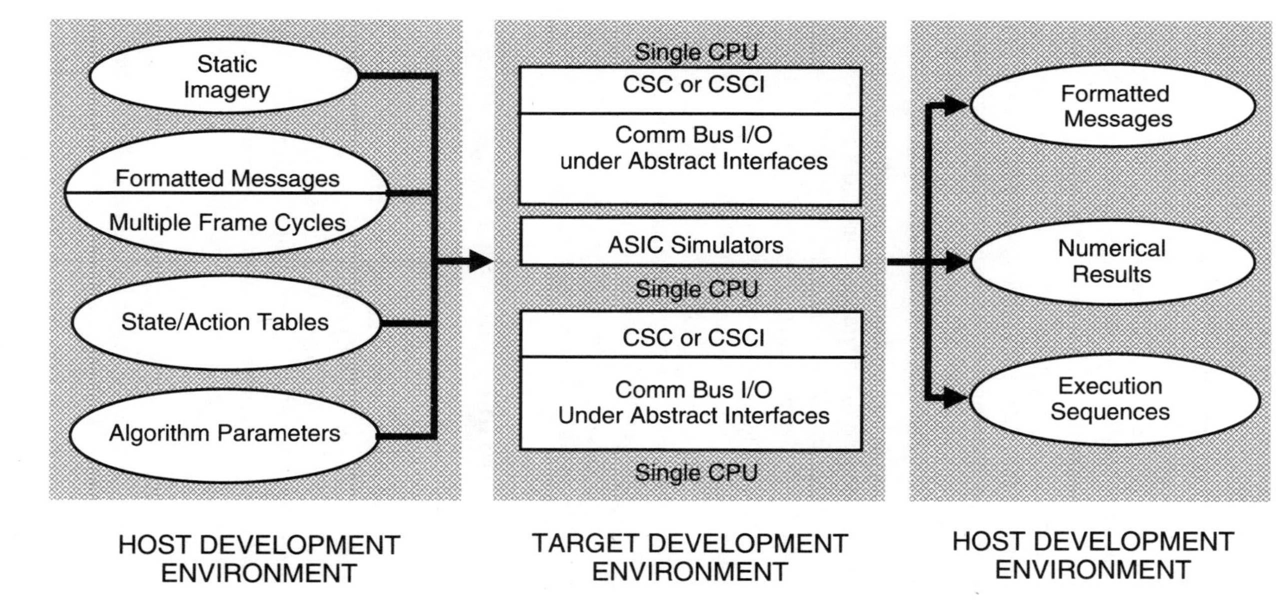

Figure 8.3 Subsystem Operational Testing Methodology

code and employs the reusable, functionally abstracted communications bus interfaces.

Input files employed by this testing phase are exactly the same as those of previous phases of testing, with one exception. Testing of the software subsystem requires a somewhat different list of formatted messages. In previous phases of testing, messages for other CSCs and for ASICs were incorporated into the stimulus message file. Now, however, actual CSCs or ASIC simulators reside in the target hardware test environment. Thus, messages representing operations of other CSCs can be deleted from the stimulus test file, as the actual component will generate them during subsystem operation. Only messages generated by other independent subsystems need be included in the stimulus input files.

Additional changes to the stimulus test file are necessary to achieve the goal of end-to-end operational testing. These changes consist of adding messages to assure that multiple data cycles are performed on the static sensor data. As a result of this testing strategy, a workload that represents a typical workload faced by the integrated software subsystem is generated. Assuring timely and reliable throughput of this workload is the purpose of this phase of testing.

Without doubt, this phase of integration is the most important phase of testing. A performance envelope is established for the integrated software components of the subsystem. Major software subsystem errors are identified, isolated, and fixed with no hardware interference and no potential confusion with hardware faults. All observed problems are software problems. Multiple data streams are created to test the software system. These are processed concurrently and followed from entry into until exit from the software subsystem. Queues managed by the software are allowed to fill to capacity so that problems with queue overflow are observed and eliminated. Experience has shown that software subsystems submitted to and passing this phase of testing are quite stable and reliable.

Hardware/Software Integration on a Target Platform

Stable, reliable, high-throughput software operating within a stable hardware platform has now been obtained. Two new factors are now entered into the test environment. Simulators for ASICs are replaced by the actual, concurrently developed hardware. Moreover, dynamic sensor data is now used to drive the test. Simultaneous incorporation of these two factors is no accident. Hardware problems do not seem to manifest themselves until placed under conditions of stress induced by management of a dynamic stream of sensor data. Dynamic sensor data causes software to push hardware to its performance envelope in ways not envisioned by the hardware testers.

Special purpose hardware is typically employed to provide rapid processing of raw sensor data, using a combination of unique hardware designs and proprietary software algorithms. Hardware provides the speed; algorithms are implemented in firmware incorporated into the hardware. Typically, hardware development and hardware/firmware integration occurs concurrently with development of software subsystems. While every attempt (such as employing a rigorous methodology) is made to communicate ongoing design changes, some aspects of change are not adequately communicated. Moreover, hardware testing is not exhaustive—every possible combination of circuit paths cannot be realistically tested. Hardware developers should not take umbrage at this comment. Software testing also fails to test every possible combination of logical paths through the software subsystem. As a result, hardware/software integration can produce quite a shock.

For these reasons, a separate phase of software subsystem integration is required to integrate an ASIC. Errors encountered during this phase of testing are almost always due to hardware faults (a wire was inappropriately wire wrapped to the wrong connections) or due to changes in hardware management or interface protocols. Most software integration errors were eliminated during the previous testing phase. ASIC integration errors occur when a simple hardware design change results in a different sequence of control messages or in a slightly different set of control bits. Neither hardware nor software receives fault in this situation. Fault occurrence is simply a manifestation of concurrent hardware/software engineering, even under the best attempts at communications and methodical support. If hardware interfaces have been encapsulated under abstract functional interfaces and if software subsystem integration has been performed, ASIC integration errors typically result in symptomatic errors occurring underneath the abstracted interfaces. Identification, isolation, and repair of the problems are easily accomplished. This conclusion is based upon actual experience of the author in the successful employment of these strategies.

A pictorial representation of the combined host/target environment is depicted in Figure 8.4. ASIC simulators are replaced by actual ASICs, each of which is a specially manufactured card containing integrated firmware. Formatted messages, state/action tables, and algorithm parameters that drive software subsystem testing are reused within this test environment. However, dynamic sensor data is now employed. Dynamic sensor data can take the form of a very large data file within the host development environment's file system. More typically, interfaces to digital cassette recorders, video cassette recorders, or optical disk readers are employed to provide a significant test base of raw data.

Testing within this environment accomplishes two major goals. Stress testing of ASIC hardware/firmware combined into a complete, working hardware/software subsystem demonstrates end-to-end total subsystem integrity. (Previous testing evaluated end-to-end integrity of the software subsystem.) Moreover, variety in the dynamic sensor data provides more complete evaluation of the functional processing capabilities of the subsystem. In this testing phase, detailed functional testing occurs after end-to-end integrity validation of the software subsystem. Breadth testing is accomplished before depth testing.

Most software developers attempt to test functional depth first or try to evaluate both functional depth and end-to-end total system integrity (breadth) simultaneously. Neither of these approaches is very effective in delivering integrated hardware/software subsystems within schedule and budget constraints. Evaluating software control before software functional processing (as suggested in this chapter) approaches the problem of integration and testing in a top-down manner. Verification of data flow from input to output establishes a stable software base from which incorporation of functional processing is a simple excursion. Testing the functional

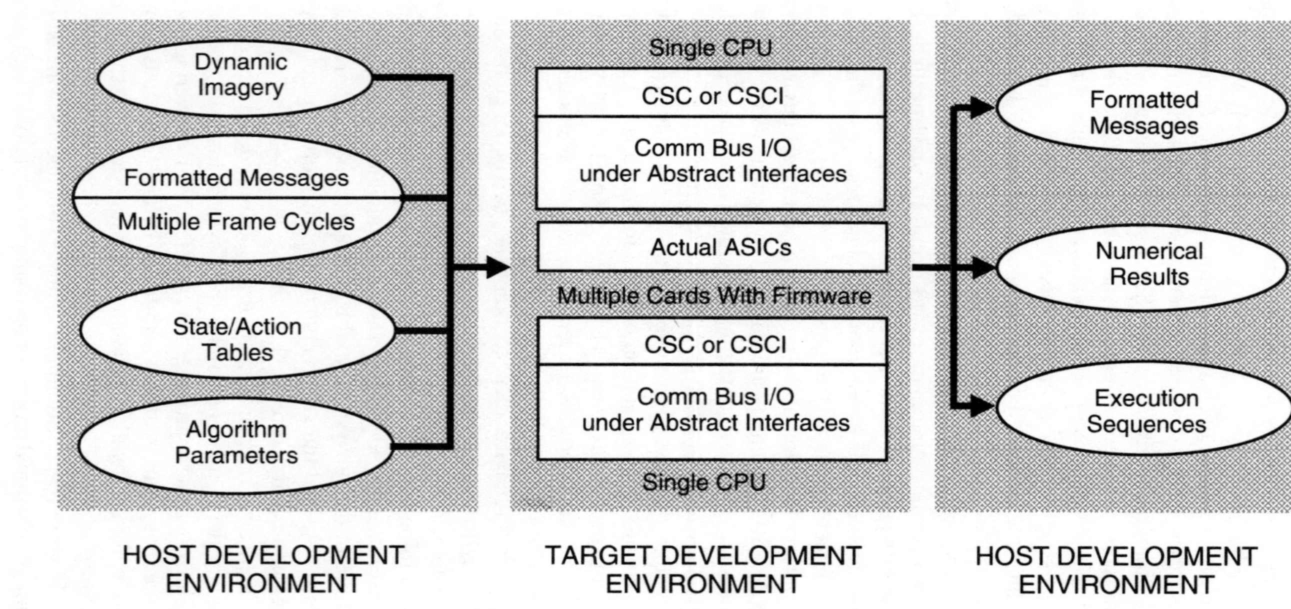

Figure 8.4 Subsystem HW/SW Testing Methodology

processing first and then assuring end-to-end data flow from input to output is simply another variant of the strategy that says get something working and make the system work later. Testing and integration establishes a working system first and then adds functional capability to improve the baselined system.

8.3 RETROTESTING FOR INCREMENTAL BUILDS

An integration and testing strategy such as the one described above strongly suggests and supports a concept of incremental builds. A first increment demonstrates that the control processing across each distributed CSC is sufficiently stable to guarantee end-to-end data flow through the system. Subsequent increments add more and more detailed layers of functional processing below the control layer of software. This concept has been successfully employed on many real-time projects. Using this approach in combination with a rigorously applied methodology significantly eases the integration and test nightmare typically experienced on embedded system projects.

New functional capabilities are best entered into the system using strict adherence to the rigorous development methodology, followed by retrotesting through the test and integration phases. Orderly introduction of carefully defined and limited functional capability is the most effective manner in which complex real-time systems can be delivered on schedule and within cost limits.

9

A Software Work Flow View of Real-Time Ada System Development

Methodologies are excellent tools for providing rigor, discipline, and focus to a real-time development in Ada. However, to be maximally effective, methodology usage must be tightly incorporated into daily development activities. This chapter describes how to integrate the methodology of previous chapters into daily development activities.

Only one aspect of the overall development process is dictated by a methodology. Other important contributors to the software-delivery process are activities, tools, and configurations. Activities are composed of those day-to-day endeavors that assure the overall quality of the software product. For example, both informal and formal reviews are activities regularly employed to allow a variety of viewpoints to critique a developer's view of the software system as expressed in the methodology-based output products. Another important factor that bears consideration is the use and availability of software development tools. Computer-aided software engineering (CASE) tools attempt to provide automated support for development methodologies. Document production tools are absolutely necessary to generate and to maintain quality documentation and test results. One final component of the software work flow equation is the configuration management process. Administering the incremental build policy described previously requires that a number of software configurations be maintained. All of these major components need to be managed as an integrated framework if a development is to be accomplished on schedule and within budget.

Previously, separate approaches were presented for software engineering, code and unit test, and integration and testing phases of development. Since the methodologies differ by development phase, interactions of the components also change with each development phase. Component interaction within each of the development phases is presented in a work flow format. For each phase, examples are given to demonstrate the integrated operation of the four basic components. For illustrative purposes, specific software tools and configurations are assumed. Neither quality nor sufficiency of these tools is to be assumed by their use in these examples.

9.1 SOFTWARE ENGINEERING, DEVELOPMENT ACTIVITIES, SEE TOOLS

Software engineering is the first phase of development. Examples of specific factors affecting the software engineering work flow appear in Figure 9.1. Methodical software engineering incorporates an operations model, an implementor's requirements model, an architecture model, and a detailed software design model. Each of these models results in a specific graphical product that describes precisely salient aspects of the software system under development. Test input/output patterns and message flows, control/data flows, process flows, and tasks/objects/packages in graphical format result from derivation of each of the models. Software work flows specifically address the manner in which other factors interact with these modeling activities to generate the graphical products.

Specific development process activities to be employed are informal/formal reviews and document generation. Reviews, whether informal or formal, are one of the greatest determinants of quality and accuracy and are conducted on a regular basis. A preferable scheme is to require each developer to present to an appropriate audience in an informal format at least once per week. Informal reviews focus on technical accuracy and provide constructive criticism. Presenters are encouraged not to be defensive and not to ignore significant technical criticism. Subsequent reviews must demonstrate responsiveness to criticisms levied at previous reviews. Using this iterative review process to generate methodology products results in crisp, clear, concise representations to which all participants subscribe. Ultimately, a much easier integration and test activity is achieved as a result of this iterative review approach.

Document generation is another factor that must be considered. Many projects employ documentation guidelines that are inconsistent with information content of reviews. This is simply a foolish approach. Twice as much work is required to produce documentation that differs in content from information presented during reviews. Translating from one frame of reference to another is likely to result in extensive technical errors and inconsistencies. Moreover, customers and reviewers tend to become greatly confused. A better approach is to use the informal review process to focus and formalize products already required by the software engineering methodology. Then, write documents around those pictorial representations. (Recall that an easy mapping exists between the methodology products and the data item descriptions incorporated into DoD Std 2167A.) Not only is the level of effort reduced, but customer and reviewer confusion is eliminated, since no differences exist between documented and review materials.

Software Engineering Methodology	TAS Subsystem Software Configurations	
Operations Model	TAS Controller CSC	Tracker CSC
Requirements Model	SPM Controller CSC	Ranger/Searcher CSC
Architecture Model	IPP Controller CSC	WAM Controller CSCI
Design Model	Image Processor CSC	Image Preprocessor CSCI
Development Process Activities	**Tools Employed**	
Informal/Formal Reviews	Teamwork	
Document Generation	InterLeaf	

Figure 9.1 Factors Affecting Software Engineering Work Flow

Two very important tools are necessary for automated support during the software engineering phase—a CASE tool and a document production tool. A number of CASE tools exist on the open market today. CASE tools primarily serve to provide automated support for a developer's methodology. Specific facilities for producing graphical outputs and performing requirements traceability are available to the user, all under the guise of a user-friendly interface. Document productions systems allow for easy intermixture of text and graphics and accept input from appropriate CASE tools. Due to the iterative and tedious nature of the products associated with the software engineering methodology, these tools are invaluable. For purposes of illustrating a software engineering work flow, two specific tools have been chosen as representative—Teamwork, a CASE tool, and InterLeaf, a document production system. Other tools of both types do exist. Proper choice of the tool set appropriate to your environment, application, and needs is an important decision.

Consonant with the incremental build approach described earlier, a set of CSCs is depicted in Figure 9.1. An exact definition of each CSC is not appropriate to this discussion. More importantly, these CSCs form a specific software subsystem under development. Thus, a work flow must describe the relationship among software engineering methodology as applied at both the software subsystem and at the CSC level. Clearly, subsystem models generated by the software engineering methodology must be consistent with CSC models subsequently generated, and vice-versa. Moreover, methodology derived results must feed forward as inputs to CSC methodical development. CSC model results must feed backward to update subsystem representation. Both subsystem and CSC methodology products feed the concurrent documentation process.

This discussion illustrates that significant interaction exists among software engineering methodology activities and the other factors contributing to software engineering work flow. Relationships among engineering activities and interacting factors are depicted in Figure 9.2. An important organizational assumption underlies the representation in this work flow. A lead software architect is assigned to generate the specific methodology products. He develops the methodology output products in a sequence, proceeding from operations model to requirements model to architecture model to software design model. Explicit focus is placed upon generating one model at a time in the prescribed order. The work flow represented in Figure 9.2 is from the perspective of generation of a single model within the methodological framework.

Initially, the subsystem software architect generates a specific model (operations, requirements, etc.) for the subsystem as a whole. This representation is reviewed informally via an oral presentation. Since these are subsystem level representations reviewers consist of appropriate members of hardware, systems, and project management teams whose responsibility is to assure quality and accuracy of methodology products. Multiple reviews are often necessary to achieve a consistent and complete view representing all criticisms and concerns. Obtaining rapid turnaround to criticisms levied during informal reviews requires significant support by a CASE tool (indicated by the appearance of TeamWork inside the box

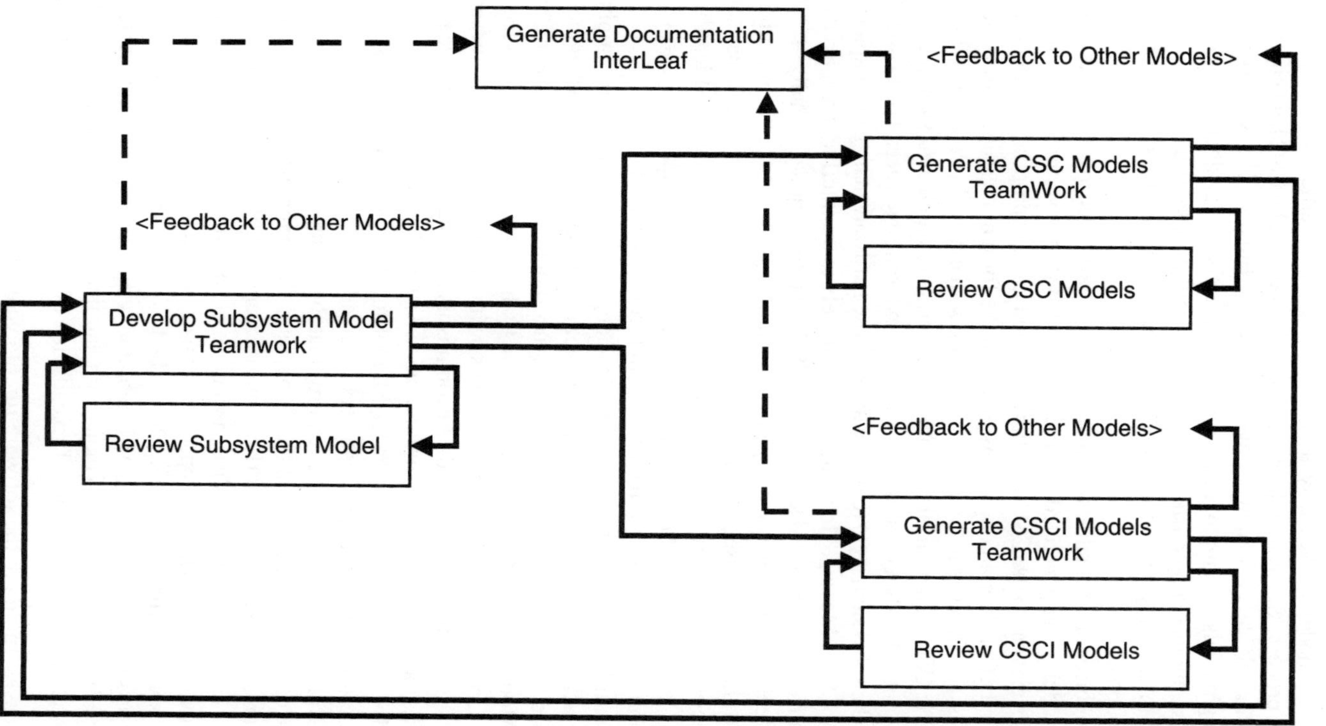

Figure 9.2 Integrating Software Engineering, Development Process, Software Configurations, and Tools

labeled "Develop Subsystem Model"). Results of this iterative process are transmitted to a number of other activities. Errors encountered in previous subsystem models (i.e., development of a subsystem requirements model pinpoints errors in the operations model for the subsystem) are fed back into earlier models in the development process. Subsystem level models are to be used by CSC lead engineers as a basis for CSC level versions of the same model. Finally, subsystem software engineering models are employed as inputs into the ubiquitous document generation process, indicated by dashed arrows in Figure 9.2. Use of dashed arrows is not meant to have any special meaning other than to emphasize the existence of the interactions.

Lead engineers responsible for each CSC now build their own variant of the specific model being generated. Initially, the subsystem level model is tailored. Elements irrelevant to the CSC are eliminated and more appropriate elements are incorporated. Consider an operations model in the form of message flows. Subsystem message flows may contain interactions with external interfaces not seen by a specific CSC. These irrelevant message flows are eliminated from the CSC operations model. Moreover, a CSC may see external interfaces not explicitly viewed at the subsystem level (e.g., special purpose hardware managed completely by a single CSC). Message flows attributed uniquely to the interfaces managed by the CSC must be incorporated to generate a CSC operations model. Finally, a CSC lead engineer may encounter message flows that are appropriate to his operations model and that were missed by the subsystem level operations model/message flows. These must also be incorporated into the CSC operations model. Identified subsystem level messages that have been overlooked by the subsystem software engineer must be fed back into the subsystem level operations model.

After significant informal review, CSC lead engineers are faced with a similar set of interactions as were faced by the subsystem architect. Flaws in earlier models identified by the current model need to be incorporated into those earlier CSC models. Model representations are transmitted to the subsystem architect as feedback to assure consistencies and completeness with the subsystem level representation. Documentation is generated. Accomplishing a dynamic and iterative process such as the one described requires automated support which is extremely well integrated. Data must move between CASE tool and document production system with little effort by the software engineers involved.

Successful software engineering requires that the document production system be capable of accepting input from the CASE tool. For the environment described in the figure, this means that InterLeaf must accept input from Teamwork databases. This is usually accomplished via a piece of software that filters the Teamwork database into InterLeaf compatible format. Most CASE tool vendors provide filter software for your usage. Do not be fooled into thinking that this is all that is necessary to integrate a CASE tool and a document production system. Existence of a filter is not synonymous with automatic use of the filter or correct format conversion of the raw data. Typically, use of a filter requires the following:

1. Extensive tuning of the software filter to your environment;
2. Detailed and tested instructions on invoking the tailored filter;

3. Processes and procedures describing the conditions under which the filter is to be used (how and when to update documents);
4. Significant training in both processes and procedures and detailed use instructions; and
5. Fine tuning of the filter output to meet your document formatting needs subsequent to each and every invocation of the filter.

These activities are not free and require a substantial number of iterations to finalize. Of course, failing to recognize the need to accomplish the above steps simply means that documents are not produced in a timely manner. Without integrated and automated support for software engineering, the desired software engineering work flow does not occur or takes significantly longer to achieve a repetitive, routine basis.

9.2 CODE AND UNIT TEST, DEVELOPMENT ACTIVITIES, SEE TOOLS

Code generation and unit test activities occur subsequent to software engineering. Basic elements associated with the previously described unit test methodology include code generation, compilation, linking, and testing of each CSC as an independent entity. Testing of each CSC employs test input/output patterns constructed during operations model generation. These methodology components appear with the remaining factors that effect the unit test work flow in Figure 9.3.

A detailed work flow characterizing code and unit test activities appears in Figure 9.4. Indicated development activities incorporate informal reviews dedicated to evaluation of actual code implementation and document generation. Configuration control describes the manner in which a tested software baseline for a single CSC is preserved. Any developer (Ada or not) has experienced the need to start again from a previously released software configuration. Moreover, if an incremental development strategy is to be employed, freezing each CSC configuration is absolutely necessary prior to establishment and testing of an integrated incremental build.

Many developers appear to employ a configuration management system, but seem to do so in a haphazard manner. Automatic installation procedures are generated for allowing easy installation of a CSC configuration and occasionally its associated test data. Unfortunately, review of the installation process is never really accomplished. An individual is usually assigned to "manage" the configuration control activity. However, he does not usually perform a review as envisioned in this context. Reviewing a CSC configuration established in a configuration management system consists of having the installer attempt to reconstruct and perform the unit tests from scratch, based on only the installed software and test data. Only in this manner can the accuracy of the baselined configuration be affirmed. Failure to perform this rigorous review is guaranteed to lead to integration

Code Generation/Test Methodology	TAS Subsystem Software Configurations	
Code Generation	TAS Controller CSC	Tracker CSC
Compilation	SPM Controller CSC	Ranger/Searcher CSC
Linking	IPP Controller CSC	WAM Controller CSCI
CSC Test	Image Processor CSC	Image Preprocessor CSCI
Development Process Activities	**Tools Employed**	
Code Review Test Plan Generation/Review Configuration Control/Review Document Generation	Editor Ada Compilation System Code Management System InterLeaf	

Figure 9.3 Factors Affecting Code Generation/Unit Test Work Flow

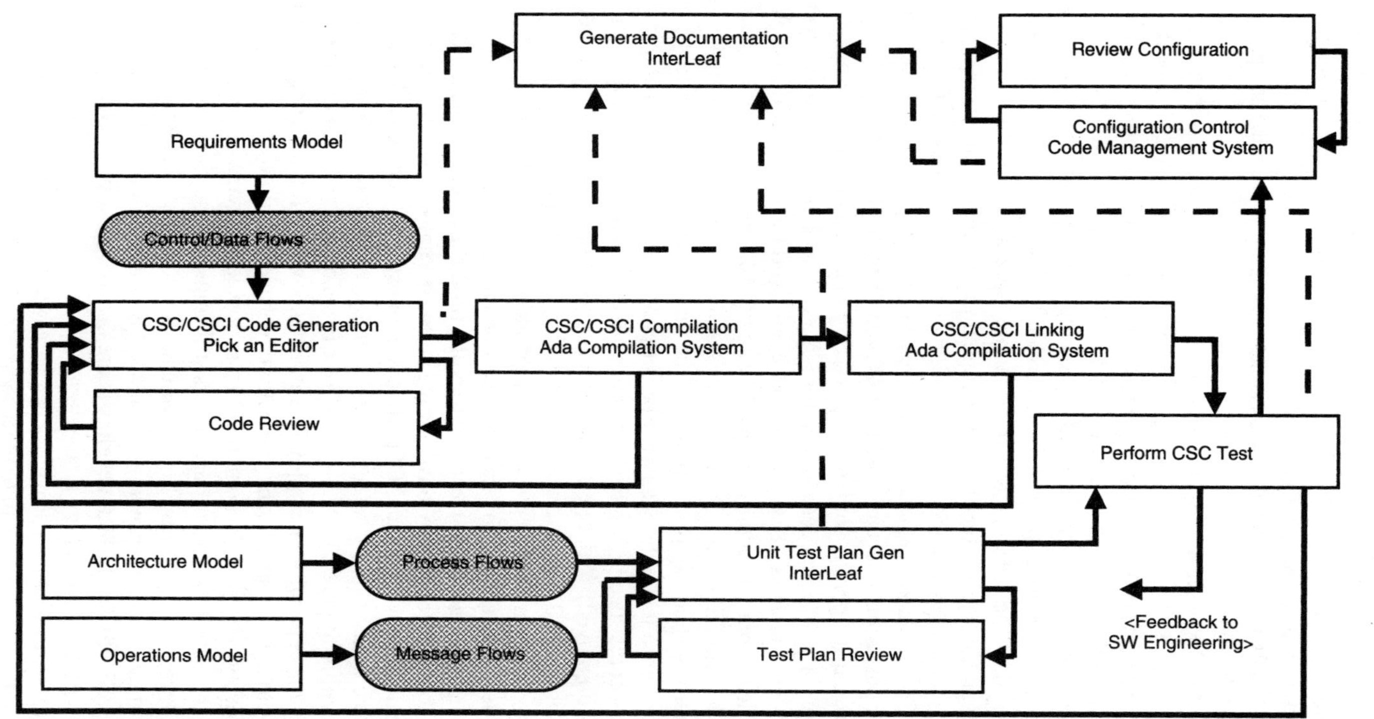

Figure 9.4 Integrating Code Generation, Development Process, Software Configuration, and Tools

and test headaches when changes need to occur and or when system failures require reconstruction of lost software. At this time, a nonverified configuration can not be accurately reconstructed. Do not adopt the attitude that developers do not have time to test their own configurations in the Configuration Management System. In fact, only the CSC developer is capable of rapidly testing the adequacy of his own installation.

Another development activity that bears on the unit test work flow is that of test plan generation. If the rigorous software engineering methodology has been followed, several sources of test planning data are available. Generation of an operations model results in a specific test input/output pattern. This pattern forms the basis for generation of a detailed set of test inputs. After architecture model generation, an architecture evaluation is performed to assess consistency and completeness against the same set test input/output pattern. From the architecture evaluation, an appropriate set of data structure updates and output message flows is derived, which represent the outputs resulting from the test inputs. Performing the actual CSC test consists of submitting the test inputs to the CSC and verifying that test outputs actually occur as a result of processing the test inputs.

Of course, if a rigorous software engineering methodology is not employed, construction of test inputs and outputs for CSC test is likely to result in several damaging consequences. Extensive effort is required to generate the test plan, causing at least some schedule slippage. More devastating is the high likelihood that the CSC will fail to pass its acceptance test, even after several attempts. An even greater schedule slip is incurred over the time necessary to generate the test plan. Acceptance test failure is likely because the CSC is not specified and designed to meet the specific test in the first place (no software engineering methodology was employed). Success in each development phase is highly dependent upon the content of the products generated during previous phases. Failure to perform methodically in any one phase endangers success in later phases, even if later phases of development employ their own distinctive methodologies.

Tools employed during unit test activities are, for the most part, radically different from those employed previously during software engineering with the exception of the document processor. Of particular interest is the choice of an editor to support code generation. Characteristics of an effective development editor include the ability to generate Ada syntax for expansion (i.e., a language-sensitive editor) and the capability to employ multiple windows. Windowing based environments prove to be significant productivity enhancers, allowing developers to simultaneously edit/modify, compile/link, and execute/review a single source module at the same time. Many developers still employ those vicious line editors, requiring developers to use multiple terminals to achieve a "windowing" effect. Using multiple physical terminals does not achieve any observable gains in programmer productivity. In fact, developers are generally less productive. Significant time is expended shuffling among terminals to view results of concurrent development activities. Do not provide developers with archaic and productivity constraining tools and expect them to meet short schedules.

Other important tools employed within this work flow include some type of code management system and, of course, an Ada compiler. By far and away, the latter is the most important and most often neglected tool in the developer's arsenal. Not all Ada compilers are alike. Yes, a compiler will accept and successfully compile the same source code, for the most part. However, behavior of the resultant object code and performance of the run-time environment often radically differ from compiler to compiler for the same target platform. Invest the time and effort to investigate and choose the compiler that meets cost, memory use, and performance constraints appropriate to your specific application domain. If possible, do not simply choose a compiler based strictly on cost. Cost dominated compiler selection almost always results in choice of an inappropriate compiler for your application.

9.3 INTEGRATION AND TEST, DEVELOPMENT ACTIVITIES, I&T TOOLS

Several phases of integration and testing are necessary to successfully merge software into a target platform with newly developed hardware components. Basic elements of integration testing include operational testing of individual CSCs, operational testing of a complete subsystem, and integrated hardware/software testing. Testing levels appear in Figure 9.5 as one of the factors affecting the integration and test work flow.

Development activities during integration and test include configuration control and review and document generation. A new wrinkle in the development activity sphere reflects the introduction of dynamic operations into integration and testing. To assure the ultimate behavioral integrity of the real-time software within its target environment, both static and dynamic sensor source data are employed. Static sensor source data with known characteristics are employed during CSC operational testing. Static sensor data provide a stable analytical basis for repetitive testing of a single CSC. With stable sensor input, which generates repeatable outputs, operational flaws are eliminated by elaborate testing of control and data structures within the CSC under test. Dynamic sensor source data is then employed against software whose control structures have been verified as to reliability and integrity. In this manner, dynamic behavior of analytic algorithm implementation is investigated to identify and to eliminate algorithm implementation shortcomings.

With this type of testing, both a code management system and document production system, such as InterLeaf, are employed. Integration testing typically uncovers and eliminates software operational flaws. Updated variants of software that are successfully integrated are then submitted to the configuration control process. Configuration control is directly supported by the code management system. Testing results are usually documented within a strictly specified customer format. Test documentation templates are created within the document production system and tailored as test results are collected.

Integration and Test Methodology	TAS Subsystem Software Configurations	
CSC Operational Testing	TAS Controller CSC	Tracker CSC
Subsystem Operational Testing	SPM Controller CSC	Ranger/Searcher CSC
Subsystem HW/SW Testing	IPP Controller CSC	WAM Controller CSCI
	Image Processor CSC	Image Preprocessor CSCI
Development Process Activities	**Tools Employed**	
Static Imagery Data Generation Dynamic Imagery Data Generation Configuration Control/Review Document Generation	Ripple Data ITE Code Management System InterLeaf	

Figure 9.5 Factors Affecting Integration and Test Work Flow

However, Figure 9.5 reveals two other tools that are often not immediately apparent—a sensor source data management system (indicated as Ripple Data) and an integration and test environment (ITE). Employing a large amount and variety of sensor source data requires that testers know what data are available, its characteristics, access methods (especially hardware platforms and formats), and any associated descriptive sensor parameters. Most developers manage a large amount of this data and correlate test results with sensor data characteristics using a manual accounting system. Manual management of algorithm tuning and development suffers from poor productivity and experiences a high error rate in the interpretation and management of results. An important aspect of the data management problem is to maintain the data in a standard format (hence, the term "ripple," a format once encountered by the author). Standard formats allow use of the raw sensor data in a variety of hardware environments. (The operative concept here is data reuse.) However, standard formats require documentation of the standard format and a library of filters allowing transforming into and out of standard format.

Perhaps the most maligned tool in the real-time developer's arsenal is the Integration and Test Environment (ITE). Transition of software from a host environment into an integrated hardware/software target environment is managed by this important and complex piece of software. Unfortunately, development of this tool usually occurs on an ad-hoc basis with managers convincing themselves that the tool is being effectively developed. Lack of an appropriate and integrated set of capabilities within an ITE is a major contributor to schedule hits and cost overruns for development of a real-time Ada system. Not surprisingly, development of an effective ITE is treated as a full-blown development project. A methodical approach that identifies an operational concept, functional capabilities implied by the concept, and a supporting hardware/software architecture are rigorously employed.

A detailed work-flow orientation characterizing the interactions among these contributing factors is represented in Figure 9.6. All phases of integration and testing are supported in various ways by the ITE. Operational testing of each CSC is accomplished by constructing a message stream from the host environment and capturing the resultant CSC response message streams. Contents of the incoming message stream are generated in a sequence consistent with the message flows and test input/output patterns generated by the operations modeling process. Usually, a static frame of sensor data with known characteristics and in a machine independent format provides a static basis for control and data structure testing. Input message flows test the control structures by building a workload in the presence of this static algorithm environment. Results are fed into the document generation process while tested software proceeds into subsystem operational testing.

Message flows, static sensor source data, tables generated by an architecture consistency and completeness check, and operationally tested software from all CSCs are employed to perform operational software subsystem test. A stable algorithm implementation base using static sensor data with known characteristics allows complete testing of subsystem control processes and structures. Message flows create a highly dynamic and thorough workload to assure that queues are appropriately sized and that specified event responses are accurately implemented

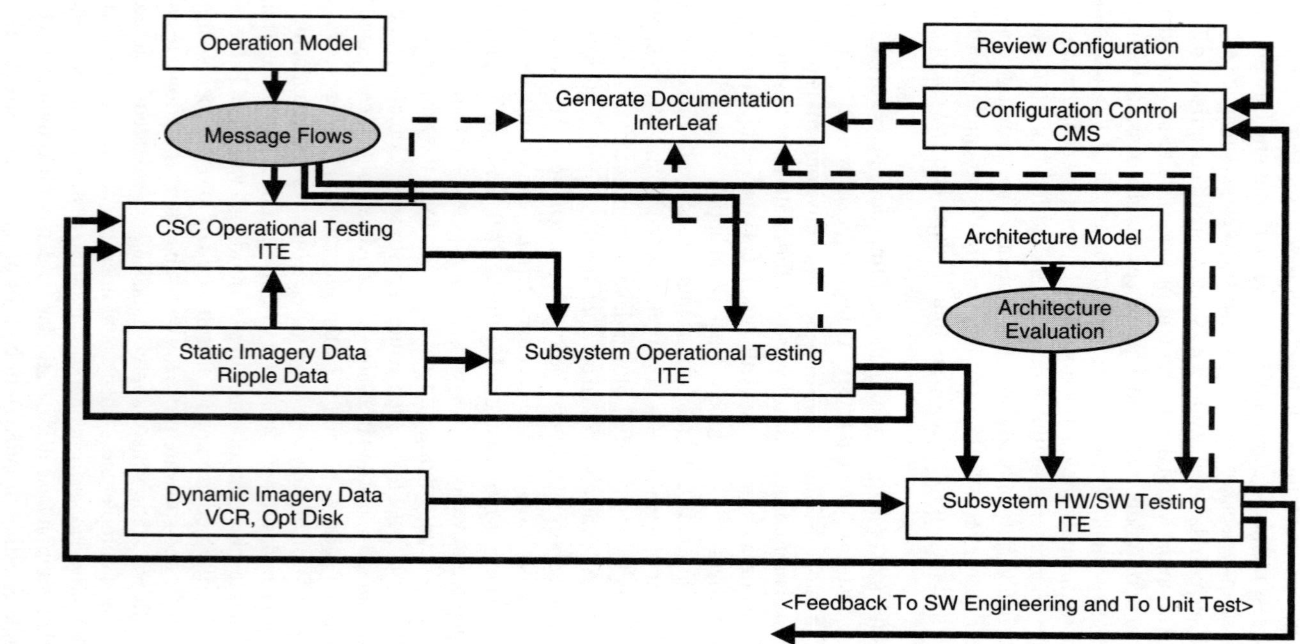

Figure 9.6 Integrating Integration and Test, Development Process, Software Configurations, and Tools

in the software. Architecture consistency and completeness evaluation data is used to identify problem areas in the system when operational performance is not obtained. Software that successfully passes this phase of testing independent of newly developed hardware is usually highly reliable. If hardware interfaces are adequately hidden under abstract interfaces, stability of the top level control processes and structures eases the process of integrating newly developed hardware. Any problems that occur after the incorporation of new hardware typically appear under the abstracted interfaces and are easily traced to specific hardware interfaces or to protocol problems. Subsystem operational testing feeds results in document generation. Code modifications are not immediately performed on the integrated subsystem software. Rather, required code modifications are implemented and tested for CSC operational integrity (hence, the feedback loop emanating from subsystem operational testing in Figure 9.6) prior to inclusion in subsystem operational testing. Developers often perform the code modification in the subsystem operational test. Modifying any code within a single CSC changes the operational integrity of that CSC. Identifying newly introduced errors is quite time consuming if accomplished within the context of an integrated software subsystem. Perhaps even more serious is the configuration management problem that is introduced. Developers working on subsequent enhanced versions of the CSC rapidly become out of synch with the integrated version, causing significant headaches during integration testing of the next version of the subsystem. For these reasons, code changes are introduced and tested for CSC operational integrity prior to injecting the changes into an integrated subsystem.

A software subsystem that is successfully integrated to perform with operational integrity becomes the basis for subsystem hardware/software testing. Message flows stored in disk files and emanating from the source platform assure the cyclic operation of the integrated hardware/software subsystem. Dynamic imagery sources provide an extensive range of conditions for evaluation of the new hardware that is introduced into the subsystem. Within this activity, an effective ITE is an important prerequisite to assure debugging ease and to insure that short delivery schedules are met. Effective encapsulation of hardware interfaces under Ada abstractions is also a key determinant in successful integrated testing of hardware and software. Once a successfully integrated hardware/software subsystem is obtained, configuration control is exerted to establish a baselined software configuration. As with unit test, configuration review consists of actual reconstruction of the installed configuration along with verification of the integrity of the de-installed version. Of course, the ubiquitous documents need to be generated. Finally, any introduced changes must be filtered back to ongoing software engineering and unit test activities for inclusion in subsequent versions of the software subsystem. At this point, a version of the subsystem is available for incorporation into a larger system or for delivery to the customer as a completely operational unit.

9.4 IMPLICATIONS FROM SOFTWARE WORK FLOWS

Implicit in the preceding discussion is an approach to software development which admits incremental builds. One build is in software engineering, another in code and unit test, while a third is undergoing integration and test. Different methodologies are operative. However, each methodology is significantly dependent upon specific products developed by methodologies at previous phases of development. Control/data flows form an integral basis from which code units are constructed. Test plans are generated by translating message flows, test input/output patterns and architecture process flow diagrams into formal test input data. Successful unit tested software is employed along with message flows to create realistic operational dynamics during integration testing activities. Architecture consistency/completeness checking results describe anticipated responses against which incorrect actual responses can be evaluated to identify implementation problems. To successfully meet cost limits and scheduled delivery dates, development must employ all methodological elements in this interrelated manner. This life-cycle orientation is the foundation approach of this text.

However, integrated methodologies are only a necessary condition for successful delivery of real-time Ada systems. High productivity rates are best achieved by software tool sets that strongly support these methodologies in an automated fashion and which are themselves integrated. CASE tools and ITEs currently available in the commercial market fail miserably in each of these categories. Usually, small and almost insignificant aspects of the methodologies are implemented. Filters that have been provided simply do not provide an integrated environment.

As a development language, Ada really shines if integrated methodologies and tools are employed. From a code generation perspective, tasking and data abstraction (as supported in the language) provide the easiest transition from requirements to design to code. In this manner, implemented Ada code looks more like the problem being solved, as opposed to looking like a spaghetti mess of data structure manipulation. Moreover, integration and test grind is eased by strong application of data abstraction to encapsulate hardware interface protocols and mechanics. Both of these results aid the debugging process by making error identification and resolution more manageable. Fixes and upgrades are constrained to code modifications within small code segments. Problems that used to occur at run-time within a complex system context are flagged by Ada during compilation of individual code units. While Ada as the target language eases the transition from requirements to working code, integrated tools with appropriate capability are necessary to mechanize the development process sufficiently to gain productivity levels necessary to meet cost limits and schedule goals. Successfully harnessing methods, tools and the Ada language requires that developers and managers adopt a strong life-cycle perspective and acknowledge the investment required to meet these goals. Only by significant investment in technology—integrated tools and methodically trained technical staff—can developers hope to successfully deliver real-time Ada systems that employ integrated hardware and software solutions within competitive cost and schedule constraints.

10

Lightweight Helicopter Target Acquisition Subsystem

Software engineering and testing approaches described in earlier chapters have been employed in a large number of projects over a wide range of application domains—target acquisition and tracking, sensor control, manufacturing control, gaming and real-time simulation, spacecraft control, and air traffic control. Initial formulation and application of the methodologies occurred on a prototype development for a target acquisition system. This system is intended to be the primary avionics package on a Lightweight Attack Helicopter (LH) to be built by the U.S. Army. In this chapter, an overview of the LH Target Acquisition System (TAS) is provided. Examples of methodology application to LH TAS are also discussed. Each illustration shows only a piece of the methodology application, in the interest of observing space limitations. Moreover, this chapter illustrates how methodology tailoring can be effectively accomplished based upon the characteristics of a problem and the implementation constraints. Incorporation of evolving requirements is also illustrated with this example application.

As envisioned by the system engineers, LH TAS employs an infrared (IR) imaging sensor to provide a live stream of infrared imagery over a specific field of view (FOV). Infrared imagery is chosen as the live data source to allow TAS to aid in battlefield assessment under very poor lighting conditions. Infrared sensors take heat pictures as opposed to light pictures. Heat data from engines, for example, is available even at night. However, actual infrared imagery possesses extremely poor visual acuity. For this reason, support for automated target recognition is included within TAS. Target acquisition/recognition consists of applying statistical algorithms to the incoming infrared imagery to determine the locations of targets. Target locations are then employed to display symbology and corresponding classification data over the identified targets. Since imagery is continually incoming and since potential targets are on the move, symbolic overlays must appear extremely quickly if they are to actually reside over the target image on the display. Real-time target identification and symbolic overlay generation are the primary operational goals of LH TAS.

To obtain these goals, a combined hardware/software/algorithm solution was adopted. From a hardware perspective, several ASICs were concurrently developed with the software. These ASICs provide extensive memory storage for imagery undergoing analysis and rapidly evaluate areas of an infrared imagery frame to identify potential targets. Actual ASIC designs are proprietary and are not discussed in detail in this chapter. Proprietary image processing algorithms that determine points of interest and then classify interest points as to target category were developed. Since algorithm details are of a proprietary nature, these are also not discussed in this chapter. Moreover, algorithm details are the primary focus of software systems engineering. Another important element of the solution was to employ a distributed processing platform. An array of general purpose processors provides a distributed processing platform to achieve high throughput. Hardware concurrence, as opposed to software concurrence, is the foundation for achieving real-time performance.

Of course, a distributed platform is only as useful as the software that manages the hardware platform. In this case, control functions and data processing functions (algorithm implementations) are operationally orchestrated to provide maximum CPU utilization. With TAS, an approach was employed whereby multiple IR frames would be concurrently undergoing analysis. Throughput is achieved by transmission of analytical results to and from processors, as opposed to moving lots of imagery around the system. Software mechanisms to manage a pipeline of multiple imagery frames under concurrent analysis are the emphasis of the remainder of this chapter.

10.1 PROFILING SENSOR MODES

Development of TAS was an incremental process based upon support for the operational modes of the IR sensor. These modes are characterized in Figure 10.1. While 11 modes are depicted, three of the modes form the basis for all other modes. When the operator places LH TAS and its IR sensor in a framing mode, the sensor is immobile, pointing straight ahead. A specific geographic area is covered. Subsequent frames include the same exact background. Only moving objects change from frame to frame. In step stare mode, LH TAS points the sensor at a specific geographic area for a fixed duration. At the expiration of this time period, the sensor turret moves the sensor slightly to the right. This process is repeated until the entire FOV allowed by the turret has been covered. After the final stare at the end of the FOV, a giant step back to the start of the FOV is performed.

As the final sensor derives operational mode, a scanning mode (referred to as gimbal scan mode in Figure 10.1) is available to the operator. In this mode, a turret is continually sweeping throughout the FOV. In fact, due to the accuracy of the IR sensor and due to storage limitations of the on-board memory, each scan is

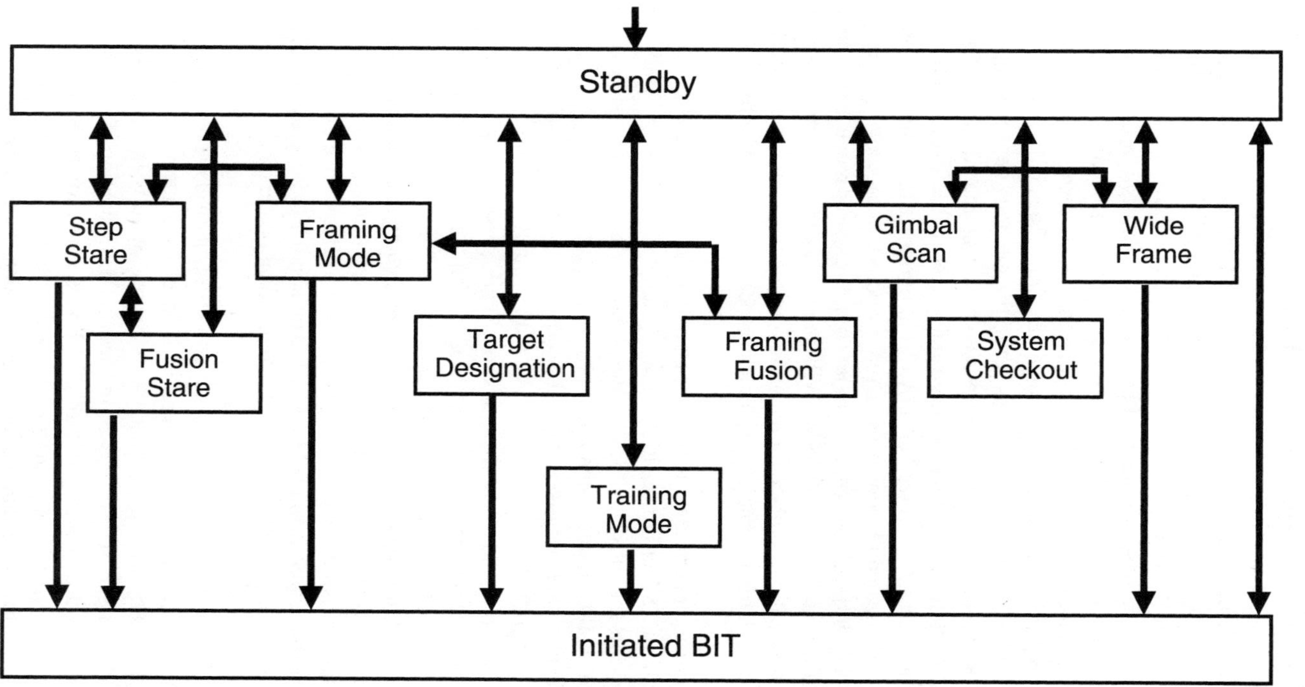

Figure 10.1 LH TAS State Transition

divided into three vertical swaths. At the end of each swath, a giant horizontal sweep followed by a vertical step is necessary to reposition the IR sensor for the next swath. After the last swath, a horizontal sweep, combined with a reverse vertical step accomplishes the reposition to start the next scan.

These three modes—framing, step stare and gimbal scan—appear here in order of increasing implementation complexity. Increased sensor movement requires more management work to be performed by TAS and results in more raw pixel data to be processed. Development of specific TAS capabilities was incrementally based on obtaining these sensor modes in order of increasing complexity. Due to the lack of a source level symbolic debugger and performance and memory constraints, the methodology described in previous chapters is absolutely necessary to "debug software" via analysis prior to implementation. Especially critical are the requirements and architecture evaluations using the methods described in Chapters 4 and 5. Requirements evaluation finds inconsistencies and incompleteness before design. Architecture evaluation determines inconsistencies and incompleteness before implementation as well as provides important data for integration and testing (recall anticipated responses vs. actual responses). Moreover, by providing a framework for development, each more complex sensor mode is treated as a special case of the basic framing mode. With the methodological framework and notational representations in place for the basic framing mode, incorporating a new sensor mode is a relatively simple and painless process—no heroic efforts need be employed.

Sensor dominated operational modes are characterized in Figure 10.1 as a state transition diagram. Specific transitions among states are to be supported. This diagram represents the subsystem level control requirements that must be accommodated by the software implementation.

Different displays are employed for each mode of sensor operation. Each basic display consists of raw IR imagery combined with symbolic overlays employed to indicate target location and target classification. While preserved imagery is being analyzed for target locations, new imagery appears on the display. Thus, analytical results used to obtain target locations and classifications have to be obtained rapidly. If target symbology generation is not rapid enough, an actual target will have moved significantly from its location in the stored imagery. This location difference results in symbolic indicators at locations different from the actual target locations in the newer displayed imagery. The number of imagery pixels to be processed for target classifications is highly dependent on the mode of sensor operation.

In Figure 10.2, raw IR data characteristics and resultant display are described for gimbal scan mode operations. Each scan is divided into three vertically stacked swaths. A single swath is composed of 20,944 horizontal by 960 vertical pixels (8 bits per pixel). Each swath must be processed in one second. Evaluation of each swath of pixels thus requires a processing rate of 20 Mbytes per second. Since physical memory in the on-board memory can store only a single swath, this rate is repetitively maintained so that incoming data will not overwrite data under analysis, destroying the integrity of the results. As a result of this required high throughput rate, gimbal scan mode of sensor operations is considered the most stressing case.

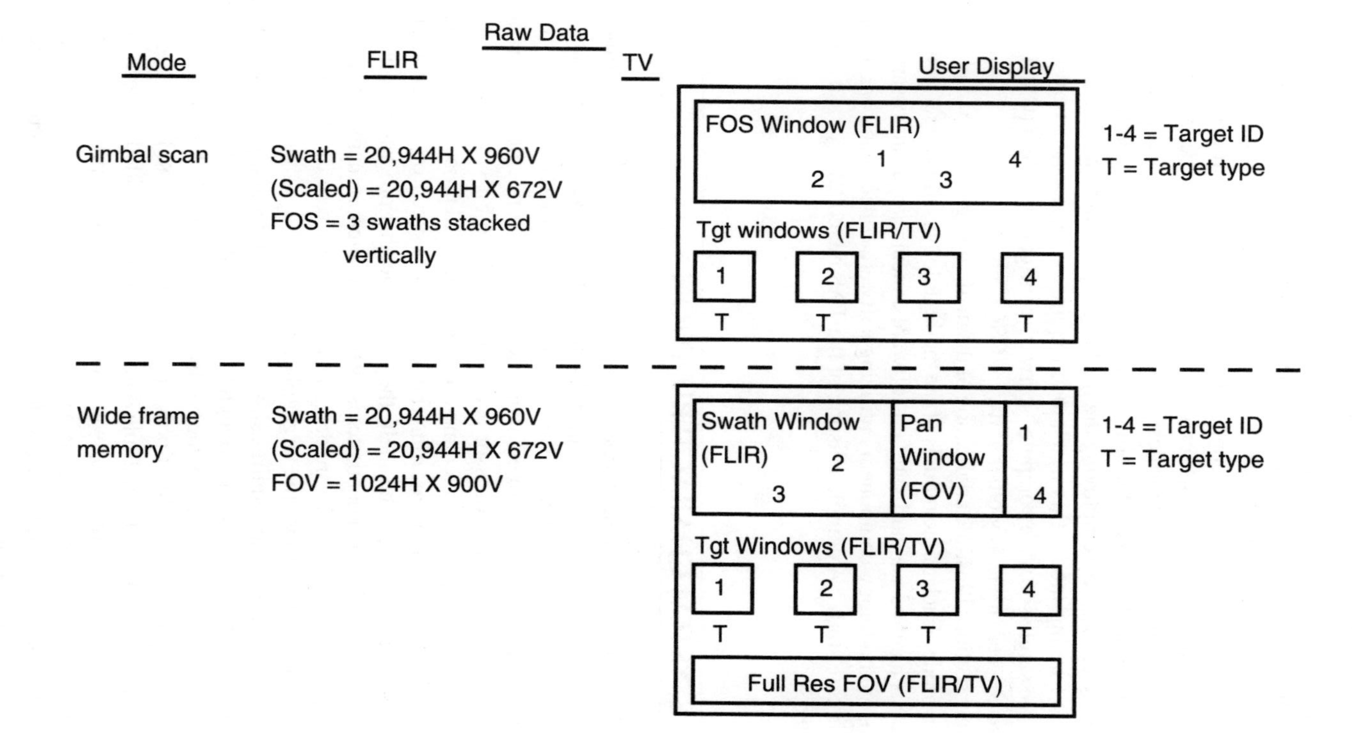

Figure 10.2 VISTA Raw Data to User Display

Gimbal scan mode's corresponding user display is also illustrated in Figure 10.2. In the top half of the screen, a single swath is displayed. This swath is the one currently under analysis. As targets are identified, their symbolic overlays and identifiers appear. Additional processing organizes identified targets into a prioritized list. Small windows containing the top four targets are displayed in the bottom half of the screen. Beneath each target window appears the classification information describing the target category of the target displayed within the window.

Due to its stressing nature, gimbal scan mode is the last mode to be implemented. Factoring new requirements into the design, updating the actual code, and integrating and testing within the target platform required only ten working days—no overtime, no heroic efforts. By employing the methodological framework established for the basic framing mode, this new mode requires very few and very simple changes to the single software computer software configuration item (CSCI). No changes were necessary to any other software CSCI.

Remaining sections illustrate application of the methodology steps to implement gimbal scan mode. Each of the models of the methodology is illustrated. Since all concurrency is handled via hardware, no software concurrency is necessary. For this reason, methodology components utilizing software concurrency are not applied in this case study. A complete listing of the TAS methodology case appears in Appendix A.

10.2 SUBSYSTEM CHARACTERIZATION

In developing LH TAS, system engineers employed past experience and simulation analyses to determine an appropriate hardware/software architecture to achieve required high throughput. This architecture is depicted in Figure 10.3. Hardware components consisted of eight off-the-shelf 1750A microprocessors and several ASICs. Each microprocessor accesses 64,000 16-bit words. Software written in Ada occupies these limited memory locations. All processors are interconnected by an internal communications bus capable of asynchronous operations. While these processors are off the shelf, they are somewhat programmer-hostile, since no symbolic source level debugger is available to support them. Lack of debugging support means that software design has to be relatively flawless and well tested before incorporation into the target platform.

Achieving high throughput requires simultaneous ongoing analysis of multiple frames of IR data. A memory large enough to hold about 17 frames of IR imagery was especially designed and built by the hardware developers. In Figure 10.3, this special memory appears as the Multiport Memory (MPM). In addition to extensive pixel storage, interfaces to multiple data sources are provided. These interfaces are necessary to allow both hardware and software testing prior to availability of an actual IR sensor, which was also under development. Access to IR data is necessary to perform both hardware and software testing during concurrent development and during integration.

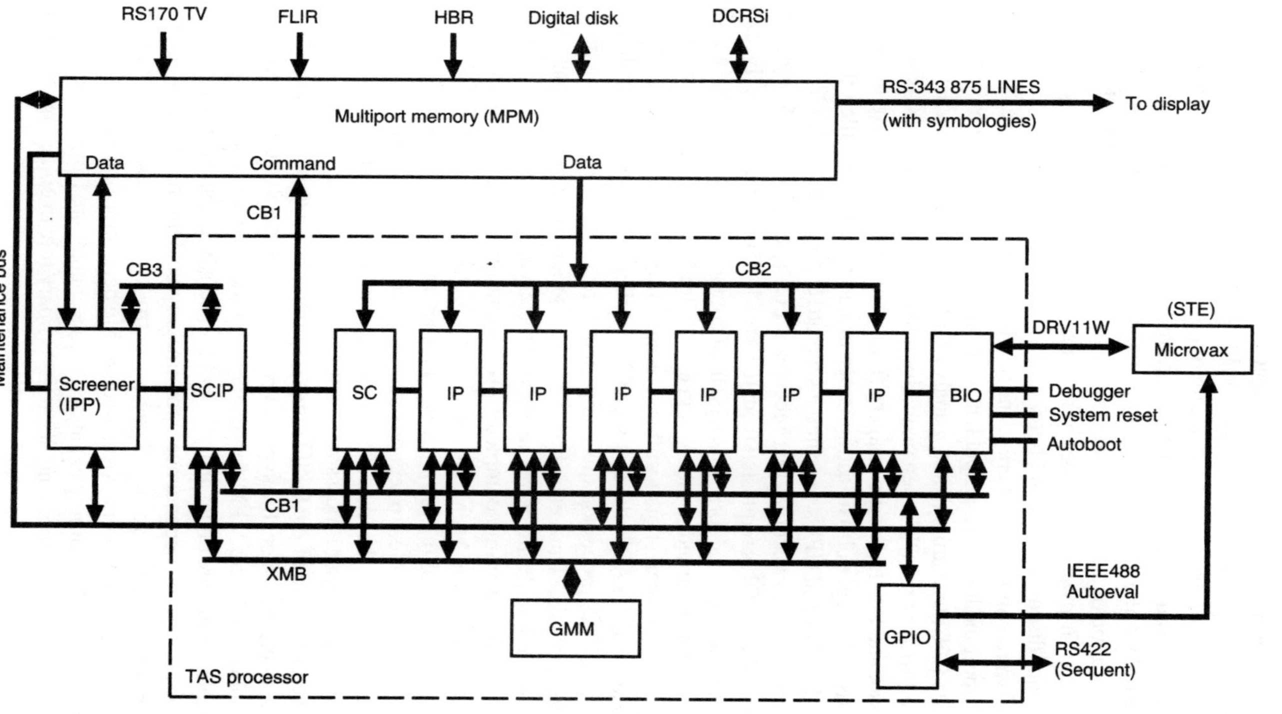

Figure 10.3 VISTA System Block Diagram

Another aspect of the architecture that enhances throughput is the development of an ASIC that rapidly identifies candidate targets—points of interest—eliminating insignificant areas of the imagery frame. Only data in close proximity to the identified point of interest needs to be employed in detailed classification activities. In Figure 10.3, this ASIC appears as the Image Preprocessor (IPP) or screener. Rapid processing of frame data is assured by not allowing interrupts to the Screener. Its firmware executive employs a simple loop that dequeues a request to evaluate a window of a specific imagery frame and returns either a negative indicator or the location of a potential target or point of interest (POI). Both hardware architecture and firmware embedded screening algorithms are proprietary in nature and are not discussed in detail here.

Three software components were identified by system engineers as being necessary to support the high throughput hardware architecture. To keep the screener busy, a single CPCI transmits window analysis jobs. This same Screener Controller Interface Processor (SCIP) then maintains a list of the identified POIs. A list of the POIs associated with a single imagery frame is then transmitted to the System Controller (SC). Target classification is performed by a CSCI called the Image Processor (IP). Several CPUs executed a separate copy of the IP CSCI. Again, a simple looping cyclic executive that receives a POI is employed. A window of imagery around the POI is requested from the MPM. This window is analyzed via proprietary classification algorithms (which, of course, are not detailed). A resultant classification is returned to the System Controller CPCI. If a non-target is registered as a point of interest, its resultant classification appears as clutter.

At the heart of LH TAS is the software CPCI called the System Controller. As the brains of the TAS processor, this component is required to manage multiple IR frames under analysis. Thus, each frame's status is monitored, work is parceled to other software and hardware components, and results are received, stored, and coordinated. When one frame completes processing, the System Controller must freeze a new frame in the MPM and then issue a low-level job to the SCIP. (This activity is defined as "rolling the pipeline.") When the SCIP returns a list of POIs, individual POIs are parceled to separate Image Processors for classification. Classified targets returned by the Image Processor are packaged and shipped to the General Purpose Input/Output Processor—GPIO (see Figure 10.3). As a result, a processor on the other side of the GPIO returns symbolic data to display target overlays in priority order. Once this symbology is received, the System Controller relays the symbology to the MPM for display, and then records frame completion. Since multiple frames are under analysis simultaneously and since processing time per job varies due to its dependence upon imagery content, results may return in any arbitrary order. Thus, for the System Controller to operate properly, a state machine–based approach is employed to carefully determine appropriate response to individual events. Remaining examples in this chapter are from the perspective of System Controller development, due to its primary role in obtaining operational reliability.

Detailed simulations and throughput calculations by the system engineering staff determined that under worst case conditions, all processing pertaining to a single frame of imagery must be performed within 150 msecs. A single frame typically requires a total of eight to ten events over the course of frame processing. Due to memory constraints, software on any CPU could occupy no more than 64K 16 bit words. Due to the effectiveness of the software engineering and testing methodologies described and thanks to the strong Ada support for abstract typing, these performance and occupancy constraints were never exceeded. Even after multiple modes of sensor operation were incrementally added, these constraints were not even close to being violated. No heroic effort was necessary to "push" the System Controller software to live within the performance and memory constraints. By developing System Controller software on a methodical basis, neither too few nor too many requirements are included the software implementation. Strong typing and effective abstraction as supported by Ada serve to allow very tight, very effective, high-performing code segments that are easy to debug and to integrate with the target hardware.

Several methodology steps are incorporated into Figure 10.3. In the abstract, each hardware/software combination represents an architecture process: MPM, IPP, SC/1750A, SCIP/1750A and IP/1750A. Inherent in the specific format employed in the diagram is a partitioning of requirements between hardware and software. For example, an image processing architecture process employs software to implement specific algorithms (IP CSCI), while using distributed hardware (multiple 1750A CPUs) to achieve throughput.

While not immediately apparent from Figure 10.3, a centralized hierarchical control strategy is adopted. Subsystem control resides in a TAS Controller (not shown), which appears on the other side of the GPIO interface. This controller interacts only with three other controllers—Run-Time Operator Interface (RTIO), System Controller (SC) and Turret Controller (TC). In response to commands from TAS Controller, System Controller manages operations and workload for three other processes: MPM, Image Processor and SCIP. Finally, SCIP interacts primarily with the Image Pre-Processor (IPP). Complexity of control is low as a result of limited interactions among controllers. Hierarchical control is established. Most of the event response requirements are embedded within the System Controller, yielding a centralized control strategy. Both flexibility and integration result from the adoption of a centralized, hierarchical control approach to process architecture generation.

10.3 GIMBAL SCAN MODE MESSAGE FLOWS

Development for gimbal scan operations begins with development of a set of message flows. Due to the complexity of this mode, two levels of message flows are necessary. At the mode mechanics level, specification of initialization, continuous operation, exit, and termination activities are represented. Within continuous operations, message flows experienced by the System Controller are represented as if a swath were nothing more than a large frame from framing mode operations. In this way, gimbal scan mode is represented simply as a special case of framing mode. Incorporating gimbal scan mode is quite easy, since a methodical framework already exists for framing mode. Injecting new gimbal scan mode requirements into the software system is a simple matter of updating the framing mode methodical analysis.

Mode mechanics message flows are characterized in Figure 10.4. Each of the conditions associated with managing gimbal scan mode operations (initialization, continuous operation, exit, and termination) is translated into corresponding message flows. A message flow is specified by naming the type of message (e.g., Freeze Swath), indicating in parentheses the number of messages that flow, and providing a source and a destination for the message. Of course, messages appear in exactly the sequence required to assure successful mode management.

On the surface, a developer might think that entry into the mode simply requires that a mode message be received. Another misconception is that when a standby mode message is received, processing simply stops. However, operation of the hardware causes these to be invalid assumptions. Analysis of IR imagery is performed on data stored in the Multiport Memory (MPM). Once a single swath in the scan is completely loaded, another swath needs to be loaded from the beginning of memory. In effect, a pipeline of at most two swaths is stored in the MPM at any point in time, since analysis typically lags loading of IR imagery. Thus, mode mechanics must assure the cycling of the pipeline to achieve maximum throughput.

In fact, message flows in Figure 10.4 exactly represent effective movement of imagery through the MPM by maintenance of two swaths in a pipeline. Entry into gimbal scan mode is accomplished by transmitting two Freeze Swath messages to the MPM. The first message causes the MPM to begin freezing the first swath for analysis. Placing a second message into the MPM's internal command queue assures that once the first swath is frozen, a second freezing operation immediately commences. Initiation of image processing against the first frozen swath is then begun by telling the SCIP to establish a workload for the IPP or screener.

Processing of a single swath in a scan is accomplished by treating the swath as if the swath were one extremely large scan. Message flows associated with processing a swath/scan appear in Figure 10.5. Signaling the end of a single swath is accomplished by receipt of another gimbal scan mode message. Response to this message consists of issuing another Freeze Swath message to the MPM. This message is necessary to roll the pipeline of imagery swaths. In effect, another freeze message is added to the internal queue of the MPM, so that at least one freeze message is always in the queue. A second aspect of rolling the pipeline requires signaling the SCIP (via an LL Job message) to begin processing of the most recently frozen swath. This swath begins loading in the MPM immediately after completion of the last swath freezing activity, since a Freeze Swath message is already queued to the MPM.

Appearance of a Gimbal Scan Mode message at the end of each swath to assure pipeline replenishment demonstrates the value of generating message flows. Initial versions of Interface Description Documents (IDD) specified a Gimbal Scan Mode message only at the end of each scan. By evaluating management of mode mechanics in a message flow format, an important shortcoming was discovered. Collection of each swath in the scan requires movement of the turret on which the

Entry	Gimbal Scan Mode: RTOI/Seq → SC
Initialization	Freeze Swath (2): SC → MPM (Load pipeline) LL — Job (1): SC → SCIP (1 swath lag)
Continuous	Frame Driven Processing { Swath = frame; No interaction with Sequent } Gimbal Scan Mode: RTOI/Seq → SC (Replenish pipeline) • (Repeat for 3 swaths) • Gimbal Scan Mode: RTOI/Seq → SC Trgt Rpt: SC → RTOI/Seq Trgt Prio: RTOI/Seq → SC Symb Disp: SC → MPM Freeze Swath: SC → MPM (Load pipeline) LL—Job: SC → SCIP • (Repeat for each scan) •
Exit	Standby Mode: RTOI/Seq → SC
Termination	Reset: SC → MPM Reset Status: MPM → SC Rest Status: SC → RTOI/Seg

Figure 10.4 Gimbal Scan Mode Message Sequence

Collecting (n + 1) (MPM)	
LLP (n) (SCIP/Screener)	Frame Freeze: SC → MPM LL Job: SC → SCIP LL FLIR/TV: SCIP → IPP Window Request: SCIP → MPM [FLIR/TV Data: MPM → IPP] LL FLIR/TV Res: IPP → SCIP ⋮ (No. windows)
Seg/Feat (n - 1) (IPA)	LL Results: SCIP → SC TR Job: SC → IP Video Request: IP → MPM Window FLIR/TV Data: MPM → IP TR Results: IPP → SC ⋮ (Repeat for each POI)
Trgt Rep (n - 2) (SC)	Trgt Report: SC → Seq Trgt Prio: Seq → SC Sym Disp: SC → MPM Unfreeze Frame: SC → MPM ⋮ (Per frame)

Figure 10.5 Frame Driven Processing/Message Sequence

IR sensor resides. Since physical sensor movement requires rolling of the software pipeline to assure proper attribution of target classification results to the appropriate swath, a signal is needed to indicate sensor movement. Initially, no such signal existed, as initial message flows (not pictured here) demonstrated. Thus, a requirement was added to the IDD to assure the appearance of this message at the end of each swath. While this may seem a trivial accomplishment, imagine attempting to determine the cause of missing target classifications overlays on a specific swath when integrating and testing 25,000 lines of Ada code spread across seven CPUs. This debugging effort would have taken weeks or more. Remember, no source level symbolic debugger was available.

At the end of each scan (in this case, processing of three swaths), a target report is constructed, consisting of all targets identified within the scan. This list is shipped to a controller processor residing on a Sequent computer. After prioritization, the same list of targets is returned to the System Controller as a Target Priority message. A set of symbolic overlays is established for the top priority messages. Resultant symbolic overlays are transmitted to the MPM for symbol generation on the physical display. At this point, pipeline replenishment is needed (queue a Freeze Swath with the MPM, start the SCIP working on a LL Job).

Upon receipt of a standby mode message, no immediate response is required. Due to the pipelining process, as many as two swaths are in process. Reliable operations require that all work in process be completed prior to actual transition into standby mode. Once the pipeline clears, termination actions are initiated. Forcing all hardware components to reset (by clearing queues, data structures, etc.) is accomplished via transmission of Reset messages. In Figure 10.4, only interaction with the MPM is illustrated. Reset Status messages are accepted until all components have responded. From individual component responses, a TAS Reset Status message is constructed and transmitted to the software controller residing on the Sequent computer.

A message flow view of single swath/frame processing appears in Figure 10.5. Processing of a single swath is initiated by transmission of an LL Job message from the System Controller to the SCIP. In response, the SCIP establishes a workload for the IPP. Each swath was broken into 16 logical frames. Logical frames are then carved into a set of windows. (Algorithms for this are proprietary, as indicated earlier.) An LL forward looking, infrared TV message is transmitted to the IPP to initiate processing of the FLIR imagery window. Transmission of the imagery window requires two messages: a Window Request to the MPM and FLIR Data Transfer from the MPM to the IPP. Identified POIs within the window are accumulated and returned to the SCIP. Continually feeding LL FLIR/TV messages to the IPP assures that the IPP is always busy. When all windows are analyzed by the IPP, resultant POIs for the logical frame are collected into an LL Results message and returned by the SCIP to the System Controller.

Each identified POI is packaged into a TR Job message and transmitted to an Image Processor according to a round-robin scheduling algorithm (to balance the workload across the Image Processors). Image classification is performed against a single POI by the Image Processor. A Video Request message is transmitted to the MPM to obtain a window of imagery around the POI. Of course, these requests are pipelined so that an imagery window for the next POI is always queued at the Image Processor upon completing analysis of the current POI. On receipt of the imagery window, target classification analysis is performed (again, algorithm details are proprietary). Resultant POI classification is packaged into a TR Results message and passed back to the System Controller. Classification results are returned in an asynchronous manner and in a random order. Random return order results from differing processing times associated with each POI. Processing of a single swath is not completed until all TR Result messages are returned for that swath.

Message flows presented in this section represent a conceptual view of TAS operations. This view is necessary to establish basic sequences for mode management mechanics, and to determine the exact relationship between gimbal scan operations and framing operations. However, these message sequences do not compose a formal operational model. Too many details are omitted. Special cases necessary to provide routine operations during gimbal scan mode are not included. For instance, the description above assumes that every swath had a least one POI. Exact message flows and responses during routine end-to-end gimbal scan operations are form.

10.4 OPERATIONS MODEL FOR GIMBAL SCAN MODE

Generating an operations model consists of two separate but interrelated activities: user interface specification and message scenario generation. In this example, specification of a user interface is unnecessary. Management of the actual user interface was accomplished by other hardware/software components not within the sphere of the Target Acquisition System (TAS). Thus, for this application, generating an operations model consists only of accurately detailing message flows to accomplish routine operations of gimbal scan mode.

Operations model generation begins with construction of an External Interface Diagram for the System Controller. This diagram appears as Figure 10.6. The System Controller is positioned in the center of the diagram emphasizing the central role played by System Controller for this analysis. Four external interfaces are visible to the System Controller—MPM, SCIP, IP, GPIO. While these interfaces are implemented by an internal communications bus which employs a specific communications protocol, these physical interface characteristics appear within the diagram. Roles and operation of the MPM, SCIP, and IP have previously been described. Interfacing to the Sequent computer and its attendant software controller process is accomplished through a special piece of hardware known as the General Purpose I/O (GPIO) adapter. During gimbal scan mode operations, only these interfaces are accommodated by the System Controller.

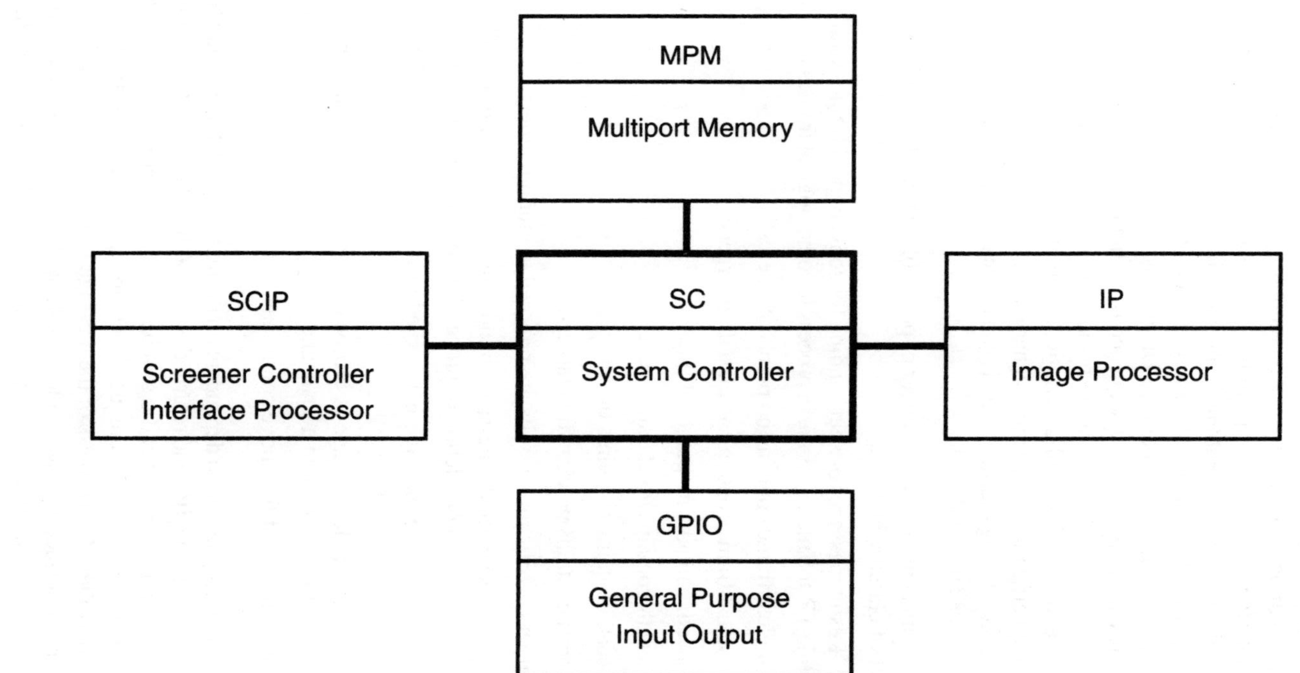

Figure 10.6 System Controller (SC) External Interface Diagram

While other hardware components were described in the conceptual message flows (e.g., IPP), these do not interact with the System Controller during normal gimbal scan operation and do not appear on the External Interface Diagram. This illustrates an important aspect of the methodology application—focus only on immediate interfaces to the exclusion of nonrelevant ones. Incorporation of interfaces not appropriate to the element under analysis simply confuses the developer.

Translation of the conceptual message flows into specific message flows within the context of the External Interface Diagram is illustrated in Figure 10.7. These flows represent a time-ordered sequence of actual events appearing at the interfaces as well as their corresponding responses. In addition to indicating message type, source, destination, and description, several columns are added to the message flow specification. An actual scenario reflects a number of special conditions that may occur during routine gimbal scan mode operations. Examples of the special conditions are as follows:

1. A swath contains some number of points of interest that result in some number of classified targets;
2. LL Result messages are outstanding for some logical frames within a swath, while TR Job messages are in process for other logical frames within a swath;
3. A logical frame contains no points of interest;
4. A logical frame contains no classified targets;
5. A swath contains no points of interest;
6. A swath contains no classified targets;
7. A scan contains no points of interest;
8. A scan contains no classified targets;
9. Target classification results are returned in random order;
10. A gimbal scan mode message to indicate a new swath or a new scan is received prior to completion of processing for the current swath;
11. A standby mode message is received prior to completion of processing of the last swath in a scan;
12. A standby mode message is received prior to completion of processing of the next to last swath in a scan; and
13. Combinations of the above conditions.

These conditions are often dependent on the number of POIs resulting from low-level processing by the IPP and returned by the SCIP. Columns at the extreme right of Figure 10.7 represent a specific swath in the test scenario, a specific POI identified within the swath, and a unique job number generated by software within the System Controller. Correctness of the message flows is best evaluated by placing the External Interface Diagram side-by-side with the message flow and actually tracing the movement of messages from component to component as the time ordered sequencing unfolds.

Type	Source	Destination	Description	Swath	POI	Job
Gimbal Scan	GPIO	SC	Start Gimbal Scan Mode	1	–	–
Freeze Swath	SC	MPM	Freeze Swath	1	–	–
Freeze Swath	SC	MPM	Queue Freeze Swath	2	–	–
LL Job	SC	SCIP	Identify POI	1	–	1
LL Results	SCIP	SC	2 POI Identified, Logical Frame 1	1	–	1
TR Job	SC	IP	Analyze POI	1	1	2
TR Job	SC	IP	Analyze POI	1	2	3
LL Results	SCIP	SC	0 POI Identified, Logical Frame 2	1	–	1
LL Results	SCIP	SC	2 POI Identified, Logical Frame 3	1	–	1
TR Job	SC	IP	Analyze POI	1	1	4
TR Job	SC	IP	Analyze POI	1	2	5
LL Results	SCIP	SC	2 POI Identified, Logical Frame 4	1	–	1
TR Job	SC	IP	Analyze POI	1	1	6
TR Job	SC	IP	Analyze POI	1	2	7
TR Results	IP	SC	Target Recognition Results	1	–	2
TR Results	IP	SC	Target Recognition Results	1	–	3
TR Results	IP	SC	Target Recognition Results	1	–	4
TR Results	IP	SC	Target Recognition Results	1	–	5

Figure 10.7 SC Gimbal Scan Mode Test Message Flow (I)

Mode entry management mechanics (two Freeze Swath messages and an LL Job message) are portrayed in Figure 10.7, followed by partial operations for four logical frames within a single swath. Two POIs are identified for logical frame one. These are translated into TR Job messages labeled with job numbers 2 and 3. TR Results messages for these jobs do not return until POIs for logical frames 2, 3, and 4 are received by the System Controller. At arrival time of the TR Results messages for job numbers 2 and 3, TR Jobs are outstanding for logical frames 2, 3, and 4. Moreover, LL Results messages are also pending for logical frames 5 through 16 of swath one in the current scan. In addition, logical frame number 2 contains no POIs. Message sequences on this page represent a combination of special conditions 1, 2, and 3 described above. Other message flows represent other possible combinations of normal gimbal scan mode operations but are not included here in the interest of space (see Appendix A).

For purposes of requirements evaluation, only those messages entering the System Controller are needed. A list containing only incoming message flows is generated, and is illustrated in Figure 10.8. This table contains exactly the same columns as the overall message flow but includes only messages flowing into the System Controller. Only the first nine entries in Figure 10.8 are extracted from the overall message flow illustrated in Figure 10.7. Remaining flows in Figure 10.8 appear in message flows, which are omitted due to space limits.

While only incoming message flows are employed for requirements evaluation, both incoming and outgoing flows need to be generated in the form of a test input/output pattern (not shown). Both incoming and corresponding outgoing message flows are employed later in architecture evaluation activities. Knowledge of outgoing flows that occur in response to incoming events is also necessary to support integration and testing activities.

Both Figures 10.7 and 10.8 comprise a detailed representation of the user's view of TAS necessary to achieve routine gimbal scan mode operations on a repetitive basis. Some experiential judgement is necessary to determine that routine operations included all the special conditions described above. Many developers fail to identify all of these possible conditions prior to actual coding, resulting in an insufficient code skeleton being implemented. This implementation is then submitted to raw IR data stored on video cassette recorder or some other device. Upon system failure, a "hit and miss" approach is applied to isolate the cause of failure. Some arbitrarily determined modification is accomplished. If the system continues to operate past the failure point, the change is usually deemed appropriate. In fact, the change usually modifies behavior of the software so that the same problematic conditions are not encountered after the change is accomplished. In other words, the fix does not really solve the problem as much as defer the problem until a later time. By analyzing potential operational conditions, reflecting these in the message flows, and developing requirements against the flows, many integration and testing problems are eliminated. Moreover, when symptoms that suggest problems are observed, a starting point for problem identification and resolution is available—these same message flows and architecture evaluation. No "hit and miss" approach is needed. "Hit and miss" approaches to problem resolution address the symptom, not the cause. Successful integration and test require that the

Type	Source	Destination	Description	Swath	POI	Job
Gimbal Scan	GPIO	SC	Start Gimbal Scan Mode	1	–	–
LL Results	SCIP	SC	2 POI Identified, Logical Frame 1	1	–	1
LL Results	SCIP	SC	0 POI Identified, Logical Frame 2	1	–	1
LL Results	SCIP	SC	2 POI Identified, Logical Frame 3	1	–	1
LL Results	SCIP	SC	2 POI Identified, Logical Frame 4	1	–	1
TR Results	IP	SC	Target Recognition Results	1	–	2
TR Results	IP	SC	Target Recognition Results	1	–	3
TR Results	IP	SC	Target Recognition Results	1	–	4
TR Results	IP	SC	Target Recognition Results	1	–	5
Gimbal Scan	GPIO	SC	Start Next Swath In Scan	2	–	–
TR Results	IP	SC	Target Recognition Results	1	–	6
TR Results	IP	SC	Target Recognition Results	1	–	7
LL Results	SCIP	SC	2 POI Identified, Logical Frame 1	2	–	8
LL Results	SCIP	SC	0 POI Identified, Logical Frame 2	2	–	8
LL Results	SCIP	SC	2 POI Identified, Logical Frame 3	2	–	8
TR Results	IP	SC	Target Recognition Results	2	–	9
TR Results	IP	SC	Target Recognition Results	2	–	12
Gimbal Scan	GPIO	SC	Start Next Swath In Scan	3	–	–

Figure 10.8 Gimbal Scan Mode Requirements Evaluation Test Set (I)

problem be addressed. Message flows and the corresponding methodical development activities allow problem identification, followed by immediate resolution, to occur.

10.5 REQUIREMENTS MODEL FOR GIMBAL SCAN MODE

Describing gimbal scan mode from an implementor's view is the next step of the development process. This step is accomplished by generating both functional and control requirements in support of gimbal scan operations. Simplicity is the main emphasis of this effort. Only those functional requirements necessary to assure end-to-end data flow under normal gimbal scan operations are specified. Event response logic in the form of a state transition diagram and a process activation table employ the same simplicity criterion and support all the cases described in the operations model determination. Finally, a detailed requirements evaluation is accomplished manually to assess the completeness of the combined functional and control requirements.

Functional requirements necessary to assure the smooth flow of gimbal scan mode operations appear in Figure 10.9 (again, a subset is used as an illustration). All functional requirements are organized around a specific set of data objects maintained by the System Controller. For coordination purposes, one data store maintains the current swath number under analysis. Intermediate results are stored in two data stores: one for LL Results contains points of interest; another for TR Results maintains a target list. Finally, individual data stores are necessary to hold the most recent event and to construct a specific response.

A number of simple but basic functions employ the data in the data stores. Swath freezing and unfreezing is performed by taking a swath number from an appropriate current event, possibly updating the swath number, and then modifying the value stored in the current swath data store. To package an LL Job message, the current swath is extracted from its data store and copied into the current response data store. Other actions are also necessary and are specified in the corresponding PSPEC. Updating a world model for LL Results occurs when points of interest are copied from the current event data store into the LL Results data store. Construction of a TR Job extracts a point of interest from the LL Results data store and places a copy into the current response data store. When a TR Results message is observed as the current event, any target identified within the message is entered into the TR Results data store. Packaging a Target Report message involves copying a target list in the TR Results data store into the current response data store.

While these requirements are presented as necessary to support gimbal scan mode, they are the same exact functional requirements necessary to operate in a simple framing mode. This is a strong indication that gimbal scan mode is simply a superset of framing mode. Accommodation of gimbal scan mode operations involves minor changes to the PSPECs, and significant changes to the CSPECs, easily implemented by changing tables. Understanding the reasons that gimbal scan mode was made operational in such a short time period (10 working days with

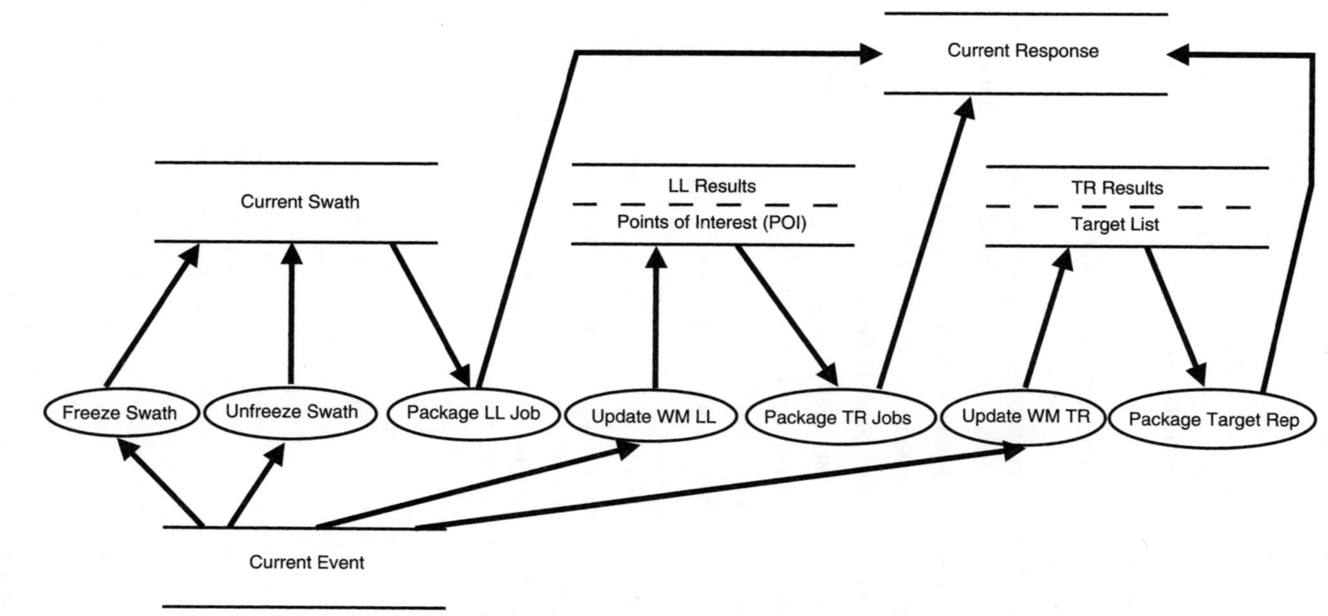

Figure 10.9 Gimbal Scan Mode Functional Requirements (I)

no overtime) is not difficult. Establishing the methodical framework during development of framing mode allowed easy incorporation of gimbal scan mode requirements. From a functional perspective, only a few PSPECs needed to be slightly modified to incorporate gimbal scan mode operations into the System Controller. This resulted in very few additional lines of code.

From a control requirements perspective, however, gimbal scan mode operations are significantly more complex and are derived from scratch. This occurs because of the number of conditions necessary to achieve gimbal scan operations. Gimbal scan mode operations require the ability to accommodate events occurring under the following conditions:

1. A swath contains some number of points of interest which result in some number of classified targets;
2. LL Result messages are outstanding for some logical frames within a swath while TR Job messages are in process for other logical frames within a swath;
3. A logical frame contains no points of interest;
4. A logical frame contains no classified targets;
5. A swath contains no points of interest;
6. A swath contains no classified targets;
7. A scan contains no points of interest;
8. A scan contains no classified targets;
9. Target classification results are returned in random order;
10. A gimbal scan mode message to indicate a new swath or a new scan is received prior to completion of processing for the current swath;
11. A standby mode message is received prior to completion of processing of the last swath in a scan;
12. A standby mode message is received prior to completion of processing of the next to last swath in a scan; and
13. Combinations of the above conditions.

Detailed control specifications for correct handling of each of these conditions are characterized in the form of a detailed state transition diagram (Figure 10.10) and an associated process activation table (Figure 10.11).

In Figure 10.10, the event response mechanisms for gimbal scan mode are presented as a state transition diagram. Six major states are required to accommodate the aforementioned conditions. A standby state is the initial state of TAS. Routine operations are performed in gimbal_scan state. Scan_pending state is necessary to assure correct event responses when an outstanding scan mode message is received. Similarly, wait-pipeline state assures smooth operations when a standby mode message is pending. Finally, an intermediate state that manages both a pending scan and a pending standby mode message is created, and is entitled scan_pending_wait_pipe. A preponderance of feedback loops is associated with each of these states. State preservation responses are so complex that had they been left to individual programmers, total disaster would result.

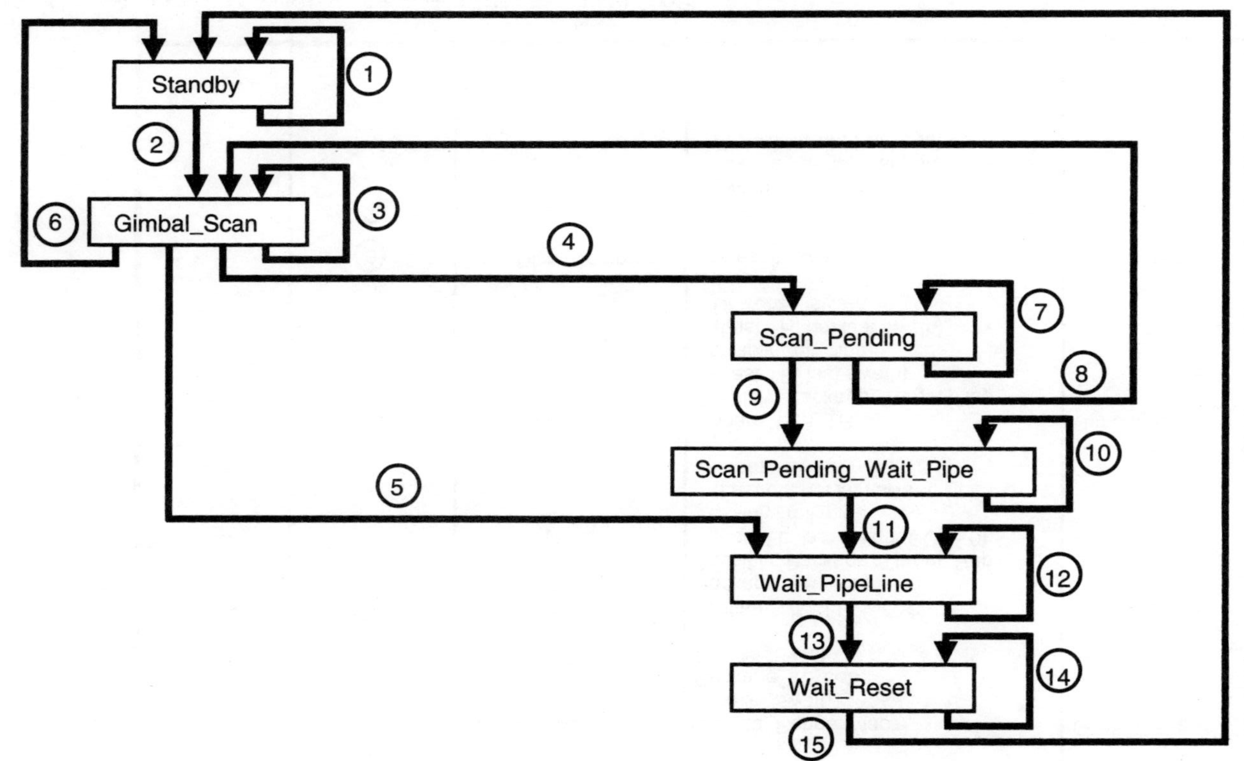

Figure 10.10 Gimbal Scan Operations State Transition Diagram

Start Mode	Transition No.	Event/Messages	Action List	End Mode
Standby	1	Standby_Mode	Trash_Obj	Standby
Standby	2	Gimbal_Scan_Mode	Update_Range_Map Freeze_Swath Package_LL_Job Freeze_Swath	Gimbal_Scan
Gimbal_Scan	3	LL_Results	Update_WM_LL Package_TR_Jobs Possibly: Package_Target_Rep (Last LL, last swath, POI = 0) Possibly: roll_pipe (Last LL, not last swath, POI = 0) Unfreeze swath	Gimbal_Scan
	3	TR_Results	Update_WM_TR Possibly: Package_Target_Rep (Last TR, last swath) Possibly: roll_pipe (Last TR, not last swath) Unfreeze_swath	Gimbal_Scan
	3	Sym_Disp_Command	Unfreeze_swath	Gimbal_Scan
	4	Gimbal_Scan	Possibly: roll_pipe (No jobs in swath) Update_range_map, dump range Freeze swath, Package LL Job	

Figure 10.11 Gimbal Scan Operations Process Activation Table (I)

Each transition is labeled by a number within a circle. This diagramming scheme is necessary because multiple events could cause each transition. For instance, maintaining basic gimbal_scan state is a response to receiving either an LL Results message, a TR Results message, or a Symbol Display message. While each of these messages comes from different sources and requires different detailed responses, they all require continued processing in the same state. Transition to a new state occurs only when a standby mode event or a new swath event, as evidenced by a gimbal_scan mode message, appears.

Specific state transitions are required to support the different ways in which responses vary, depending upon the conditions. For instance, detailed response to an LL Result message is different when a scan is pending than if no scan were pending. Differences in responses for a given event are captured in the PAT. One piece of the process activation table for gimbal scan mode appears in Figure 10.11. This table has a slightly different format than the format demonstrated earlier in the text. Each numbered transition represents potential responses to multiple and differing events. Entries in the PAT are thus keyed to numbered transitions and specific events. For example, three possible events are associated with the transition labeled 3. If an LL_Results message is received while in gimbal-scan state, the following response is taken:

```
Update_WM_LL;
Package_TR_Jobs; and,
if no POIs are reported, and if this is the last swath
in the scan,
   then Package_Tgt_Report.
```

Each of these steps corresponds to a specific function/PSPEC (see Figure 10.9). After the action list is performed in response to the LL_Results event, a state transition occurs. In this case, gimbal-scan state is preserved, as indicated in Figure 10.11.

Other events associated with transition 3 in the STD are a TR_Results message and a Symbol_Display_Command. Detailed responses to each of these events also appears in the PAT in Figure 10.11. The actual table is quite extensive and is included in Appendix A.

Incorporation of both the STD and PAT into the actual software without further evaluation could lead to major integration and test headaches. These tables are so complex that they are bound to contain extensive flaws in the actual decision logic. Debugging these tables with actual code is quite time consuming and prone to error. Some method is needed whereby flaws in these specifications are identified prior to injection into this code. Evaluating requirements against the message flows and test input/output pattern resolves this dilemma. Flaws and inconsistencies in event responses and functional processes are identified and eliminated. Problems are identified much more rapidly using paper and pencil than attempting to single step through code. Moreover, in this case, no source level debugger was available. Thus, the single step approach could not be employed. Either a "hit and miss" approach had to be employed or an analytical approach could be used. The analytical approach of tracing message flows through the requirements determines significant flaws in the specifications and saves hundreds of hours of intensive debugging.

A sample of the requirements evaluation for gimbal scan mode appears in Figure 10.12. This evaluation begins with the System Controller in the Standby mode. Each of the input events from the message flow in Figure 10.8 is applied to the requirements. First, the state transition is identified and recorded. Then, an appropriate response is determined from the PAT, using the event and the identified transition. Both response details and resultant state are recorded. Any PSPEC in a response that generates an output message is evaluated by recording the output message which results (see the last column in Figure 10.12). Completeness of the response is determined by assessing the response details for sufficiency and by evaluating the resultant state for appropriateness. Consistency is evaluated by comparing output messages generated by the PSPECs invoked. Obviously, if the detailed response generated the correct outgoing message flows, the response is deemed to be complete.

Consider for a moment the second entry in the requirements evaluation table. While in gimbal-scan state, an LL_Results message/event occurs next in the test input/output pattern. According to the state transition diagram (Figure 10.10), transition 3 occurs. Applying the LL_Results event and transition 3 to the process activation table in Figure 10.11 yields the following response:

```
Update WM LL; and
Package TR Jobs.
```

Again, consulting the STD, the new state is determined to be gimbal_scan. Finally, reading the PSPECs for the two responses above determines that the second function (Package TR_Jobs) emits two output messages, both of which are TR_Jobs (with appropriate data, of course). Comparing this response to Figure 10.7, one can see that the LL_Results message in line 5 (this is the event just evaluated) is followed by two TR_Job messages, exactly as determined in the above analysis. This demonstrates the completeness of this specified response to the LL_Results event.

While some messages appear more than once, evaluation of all the messages in the time-ordered sequence of message flows is critical to successful implementation. As demonstrated, a specific type of message can engender a different response depending on conditions. For example, an LL_Results event under the conditions described above simply results in two TR_Job messages flowing out of the System Controller. However, if the LL_Results message had contained no points of interest and if the swath had been the last swath in the scan, an additional message would be emitted. A Target_Report message flows to the operator interface residing on another machine. (See PAT in Figure 10.11.)

Since the complete message test input set described in Figure 10.8 represents all the possible variations described earlier, consistency and completeness are verified for all of these conditions. Incorporation of these new requirements into the actual software was smoothly and easily accomplished. In fact, gimbal_scan capability was operational on the target platform in 10 working days, with no over-

Type	Event	Transition	Response Details	State After	Output Message
Standby	Gimbal Scan	2	Update Range Map	Gimbal Scan	
			Freeze Swath		Freeze Swath
			Freeze Swath		Freeze Swath
			Package LL Job		LL Job
Gimbal Scan	LL Results	3	Update WM LL	Gimbal Scan	
			Package TR Jobs		TR Job (2)
Gimbal Scan	LL Results	3		Gimbal Scan	
Gimbal Scan	LL Results	3	Update WM LL	Gimbal Scan	
			Package TR Jobs		TR Job (2)
Gimbal Scan	LL Results	3	Update WM LL	Gimbal Scan	
			Package TR Jobs		TR Job (2)
Gimbal Scan	TR Results	3	Update WM TR	Gimbal Scan	
Gimbal Scan	TR Results	3	Update WM TR	Gimbal Scan	
Gimbal Scan	TR Results	3	Update WM TR	Gimbal Scan	
Gimbal Scan	TR Results	3	Update WM TR	Gimbal Scan	
Gimbal Scan	Gimbal Scan	4		Scan Pending	
Scan Pending	TR Results	7	Update WM TR	Scan Pending	

Figure 10.12 Gimbal Scan Mode Requirements Evaluation (I)

time. Incorporation of this capability mostly required changing internal tables representing the STD and the PAT. A few small code changes were also necessary to reflect small variations in the PSPECs to accommodate the handling of each swath as a "large frame." In all, these changes resulted in about 200 new lines of Ada code.

10.6 SYSTEM CONTROLLER SOFTWARE ARCHITECTURE AND DESIGN

Incorporation of the control requirements and functional requirements into the System Controller is accomplished using a table-driven, cyclic executive design. A table-driven approach is employed to allow ease in modification and ease in debugging during integration and test. Modification of event response logic simply requires changing the appropriate tables. Problems with event response logic that were not uncovered during requirements evaluation manifest themselves in the form of null entries returned from a state table or action table lookup. On the occurrence of a table lookup, returning empty results, execution is halted, internal data structures dumped, and logic problems resolved in a short period of time—usually two to three hours.

The top level detailed design of the System Controller software is depicted in Figure 10.13. Two packages are referenced. An initialization procedure (SC-Init) exported by the Init_SC_Pkg package is first invoked by the System Controller. This procedure performs several major functions. First, the interrupt handler address is mapped into an interrupt vector table. Written in Ada, the interrupt handler places messages into a central message queue. A second function downloads and initializes both state transition tables and process activation tables. Finally, a table that translates virtual communications bus locations into physical bus addresses is loaded. Once initialization is completed, an executive procedure (Exec), exported by the SC_Exec_Pkg package, is invoked. This package contains the cyclic executive.

Figure 10.14 describes the detailed design of the cyclic executive. Subprogram interfaces employed by the cyclic executive are those necessary to support event response management. The Dequeue procedure, exported by a Message_Queue_Handler_Pkg package, is invoked to retrieve a message from the event queue (if the central event queue is not empty, of course). Responses are determined by using both the current state and the current event. These arguments are passed to a local procedure to determine the desired response (indicated by the embedded procedure named Search-Rule). A desired response is submitted to a Perform_Action procedure, which determines the list of desired simple actions and invokes the simple actions. (Note: each simple action represents a PSPEC from the original requirements specification.) Finally, a new state is determined by passing both current state and current event to the Compute_State procedure.

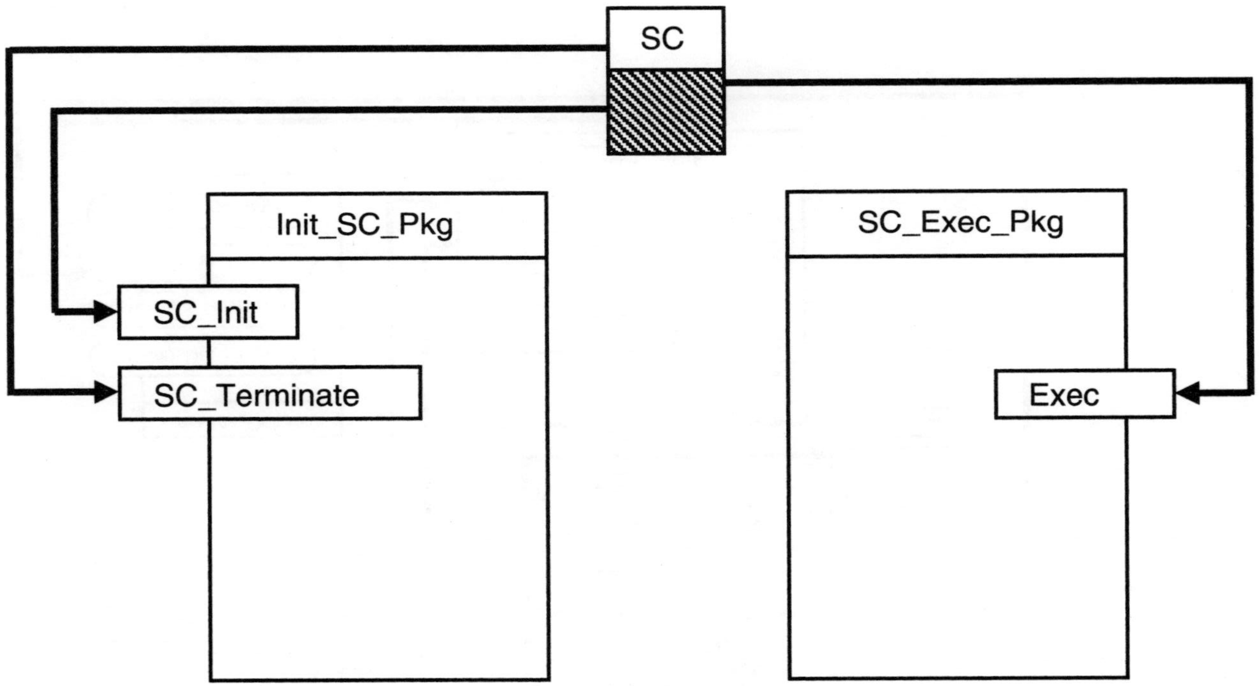

Figure 10.13 System Controller Software Architecture

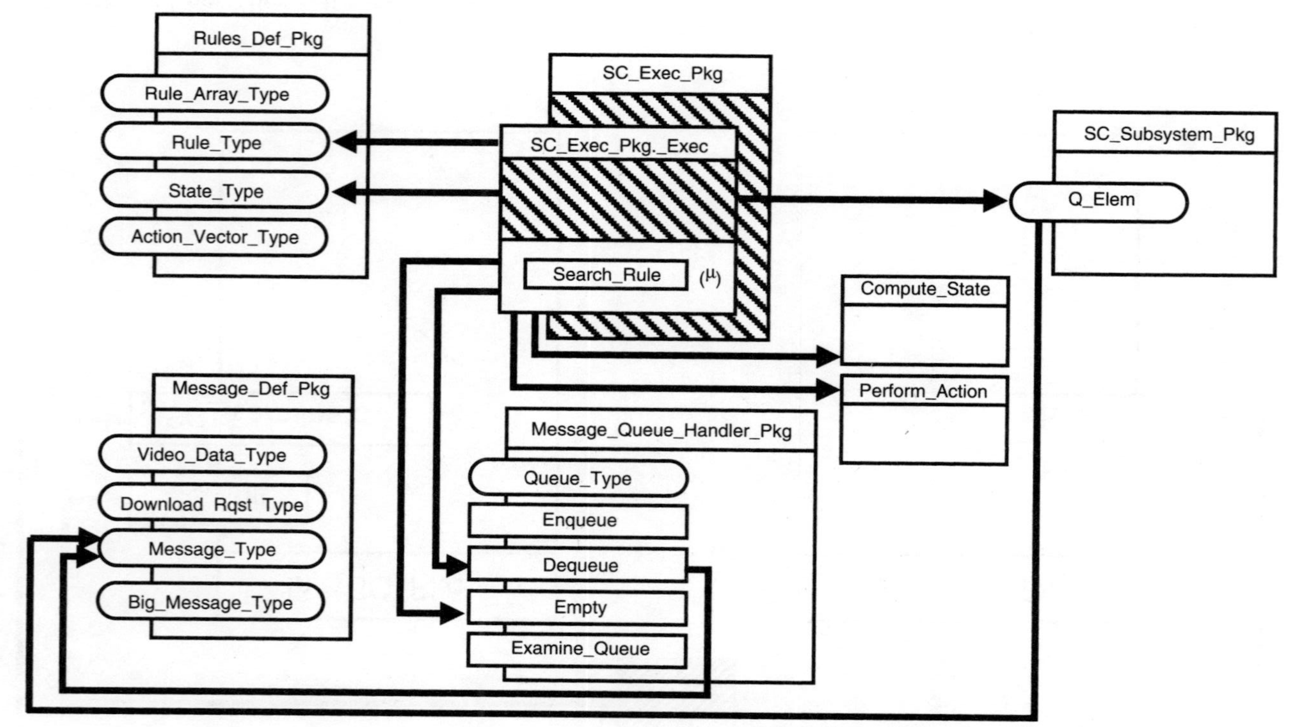

Figure 10.14 SC_Exec_Pkg. Exec Software Architecture

Several other packages are displayed in Figure 10.14. For the most part these contain type or object declarations necessary to support message processing. For instance, invocation of the Dequeue procedure exported by the Message_Queue_Handler_Pkg package returns the next event from the message queue. This event is stored in the Q_Elem object provided by the SC_Subsystem_Pkg package. Message_Type definitions, State_Type enumeration literals, and table component descriptions (Rule_Type) are all provided by other packages, as indicated in the figure.

10.7 CYCLIC EXECUTIVE EXECUTABLE PSEUDOCODE

A pseudocoded representation of the System Controller's cyclic executive appears in Figures 10.15a and 10.15b. The general logic is described in the previous section and is not repeated here. However, this pseudocode is both compilable and executable. To achieve compilation, all interfaces syntactically resemble the actual code interfaces. Moreover, data type consistency is achieved at each of the interfaces. In some situations, type consistency is obtained by using TBD (To Be Determined) types. In other cases, actual type consistency is obtained by using types whose details were exactly as in the final implementation. Selecting specific types to defer is dependent on the state of information about the data types at the time the pseudocode is written.

Obtaining executable pseudocode requires special handling. Special counters are created to control the number of times each loop is executed. By having each procedure call implemented as a stub that prints a message, an operational representation of module invocation order is generated. Invocation order linearizes the pseudocode, translating the code logic into an operational form that demonstrates that the code really works as needed to process events.

Extensive use of comments is employed within the executable pseudocode. Comments are necessary to highlight modifications used to achieve execution, to pinpoint hidden effects inside the code, and to demonstrate use of actual and TBD data types. Comments are extremely important for pseudocode generation. Since large amounts of actual coding details are omitted, comments describe which ones have been omitted or assumed by the pseudocode. In this way, compilation and execution are obtained with a minimum of coding effort. By translating the pseudocode logic into an invocation order description, operational validity is achieved.

```
procedure Exec is
    rec_State  : RDP. state_type ;
    rule  num : TBD.TBD_Int ;
    rule :          RDP.rule_type ;
    done :          boolean ;

- -  pseudocode execution control
    max_loops : constant : = 1 ;
    loop_cntr :   integer ;
    max_cntr :   constant : = 1 ;
    rule_cntr :   integer ;
- -  pseudocode execution control

    begin

- -  pseudocode execution control
    loop_cntr : = 0 ;
- -  pseudocode execution control

    remove object ;
    Q_Head_Popped : = false ;
    done : = false ;
```

Same names as actual code; where possible, same types as actual code; possible if types identified, exported in another package

Pseudocode control for executable requirement delimited begin, end with comments, blank lines

Figure 10.15a Cyclic Executive—Compilable Executable Pseudocode

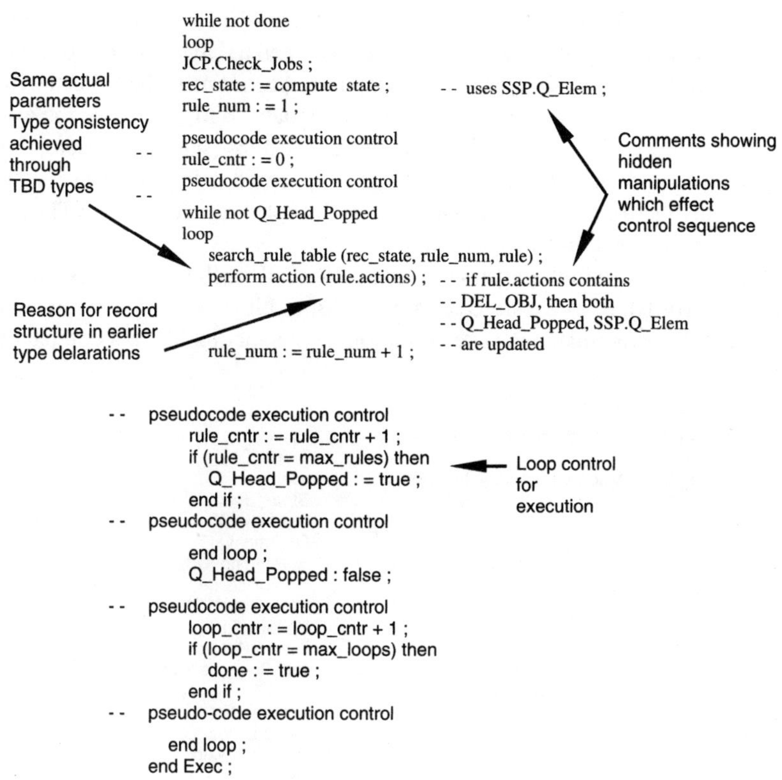

Figure 10.15b Cyclic Executive—Compilable Executable Pseudocode

10.8 RULE TABLE INPUT FOR SYSTEM CONTROLLER

Due to the complexity of the event response specifications, a shorthand notation is adopted. Both tables are combined into a set of rules. Each rule has the following format:

```
(Event Name) (State Condition) => (Action List).
```

An event consists of a specific message that can appear at the head of the central message queue. State conditions are composed of a state name followed by a boolean indicator (True or False). Each action list consists of a list of primitive action names.

A portion of the rule table for gimbal_scan operations appears in Figure 10.16. Consider the fourth entry in the figure. This is the same event and response (i.e., transition number 3) illustrated in previous examples. When an LL_Results message (event) appears at the head of the queue and when the System Controller is in gimbal_scan mode, a specific response is required. According to the indicated rule, two important elements of this response are to Update_WM_LL (save the event data into the world model database) and to Pkg_TR_Jobs (start target recognition jobs). Response details are exactly the same as appeared in Figure 10.11 for transition 3 under these conditions. In other words, this rule is the combined STD, PAT for one specific event under transition 3.

To save space within the System Controller (recall, each CPU possessed only 64K 16 bit words), rules are stored as a linear list of bit patterns. Each row in the list contains an event name, a state condition, and an action list in a compact bit

```
( Standby_Mode ) ( Standby_M True )                      =>
                                                         Trash_Obj ;
( Gimbal_Scan_Mode ) ( Standby_M True )                  =>
                                                         Store_Scan ,
                                                         Standby_Off ,
                                                         G_Scan_On ,
                                                         S_Pending_Off ,
                                                         Wait_Pipeline_Off ,
                                                         Wait_Reset_Off ,
                                                         Update_Range_Map ,
                                                         Dump_Range ,
                                                         Set_Scan_Parameters ;
( Gimbal_Scan_Mode ) ( Standby_M True )                  =>
                                                         Freeze_Swath ,
                                                         Pkg_LL_Job ,
                                                         Freeze_Swath ,
                                                         Del_Obj ;
( LL_Results ) ( Gimbal_Scan_M True )                    =>
                                                         Update_WM_LL ,
                                                         Dump_LL_Results ,
                                                         Pkg_TR_Jobs ,
                                                         Jobs_Out_Swath ,
                                                         Check_Swath ,
                                                         EOS_Off ,
                                                         Check_Scan ;
( LL_Results ) ( Gimbal_Scan_M True ) ( Jobs_Swath False ) ( EOS True )
                                                         =>
                                                         Pkg_Tgt_Report ;
( LL_Results ) ( Gimbal_Scan_M True ) ( Jobs_Swath False ) ( EOS False )
                                                         =>
                                                         Unfreeze_Swath ;
( LL_Results ) ( Gimbal_Scan_M True )                    =>
                                                         Jobs_Out_Swath ,
                                                         EOS_Off ,
                                                         Del_Obj ;
```

Figure 10.16 Gimbal Scan Mode Rule Table (I)

pattern notation. Determining a required response consists of searching the rule list for a bit combination (event name, state condition) that matches the presented arguments. While this approach does save space, execution time is sacrificed. Searching is linear—a simple table lookup with array references would have been much faster. Moreover, multiple rules could match a specific set of arguments. Therefore, a response is never complete until all rule firing conditions are compared with input arguments. Even with the extra time this consumed, time constraints were never a problem. Optimal performance from inception is a direct result of the methodical development of requirements combined with Ada's support for data abstraction.

Methodical development of mode management requirements with attendant consistency and completeness checking assures that only code necessary to meet requirements is actually implemented. Reliance upon data abstraction and typing to generate code that looks exactly like the PSPECs results in very tight code which executes quite rapidly. For these reasons, performance was never a problem within the System Controller. Other benefits also accrue to the combined rigorous methodology/data abstraction combination. Once debugged, the System Controller and attendant rules tend to be highly reliable, requiring very few changes. And debugging was simple. Employing the testing philosophies described earlier and abstracting hardware interfaces under functional abstractions assures that by the time hardware is integrated, software bugs are pretty much eliminated—another contributor to software reliability. Software quality is designed into the implementation, not obtained after the fact.

10.9 RETROTESTING CYCLE

Integration and testing strategies described earlier were actually employed in this development. In Figure 10.17, a retrotesting cycle that typifies the levels of integration and testing employed to incorporate new requirements into the implementation is illustrated. Initially, unit test is performed solely within a VAX environment. Files contain message test streams consistent with the test input/output pattern. A single CPU is involved in the host environment. Abstracted hardware interfaces are configured to allow access to the event data stored in the input files. No special test environment is necessary to perform unit testing in this environment, since no target platform bridge is needed.

A second level of testing consists of placing a collection of unit tested CSCs into a target platform. This platform is known as the Software Development Station (SDS). Special purpose hardware is replaced by simulators that return canned messages. A canned message contains data consistent with input test data used for cyclic operational testing. Multiple CPUs are employed to obtain end-to-end processing integrity, cycling over multiple infrared imagery frames.

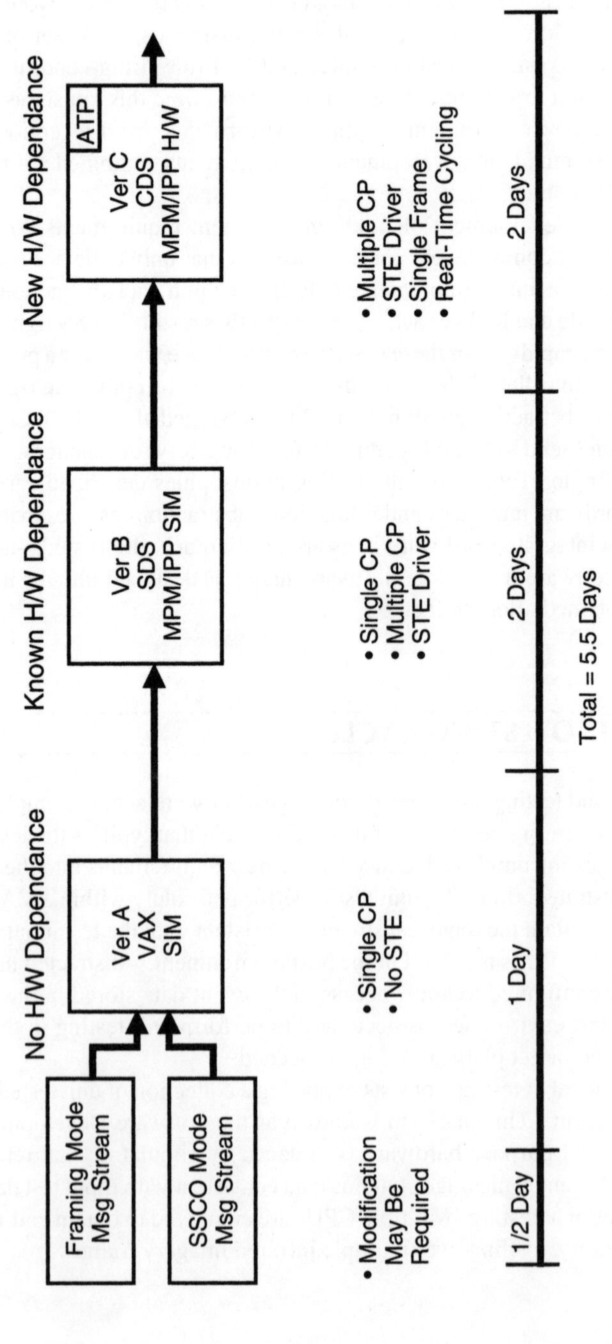

Figure 10.17 Retrotesting Cycle

Known hardware dependencies are included in the form of communications bus interfaces underneath functional abstractions. In the previous testing level these interfaces were configured to deal with data in files. (Ada supports this kind of abstraction control quite well.) Tests are controlled by stimulus commands provided by a Special Test Environment (STE) interface.

Upon successful completion of this testing process, hardware and software integration testing activities begin. This level of testing is accomplished in a platform named Code Development Station. Distributed CPUs are employed in this target platform. However, concurrently developed hardware is now introduced into the test environment. Prior to this testing, previous testing levels effectively removed an extremely large percentage of errors in the software. Since the only additional variable entered into this environment is newly developed hardware, problems during this testing level typically manifest underneath abstracted hardware interfaces which manage the newly developed hardware. As a result, these problems are easy to identify. They usually result from misinterpretations of protocols for managing the hardware, hardware design changes that occurred during hardware development but were not communicated, or hardware faults that had not been identified during concurrent hardware testing. Contrary to popular belief, hardware testing does not exhaustively test every circuit path combination (any more than software successfully tests every possible logic path). An occasional software problem does occur, but infrequently during this level of testing.

As indicated in Figure 10.16, retrotesting required approximately five and a half days to successfully incorporate a new requirement into the system. Simple code fixes typically require about two hours to resolve. By establishing a thorough methodical framework, changes stemming from new requirements are identified in about four and a half days. Combining the two statistics suggests that a new sensor mode can be reliably introduced into the actual target system within ten working days. In fact, this is exactly the duration required to incorporate the gimbal scan mode into the TAS. Four days were spent moving new mode requirements through the methodical framework to identify relevant changes. Roughly 200 lines of new code were generated. A significantly new and larger STD and PAT were generated. Five days were necessary to move the new changes through the retrotesting cycle indicated. No overtime hours were expended in this activity; a simple manufacturing process was involved. The combination of methodology and effective use of Ada characteristics produced this phenomenon.

10.10 CONCLUSIONS

Development of the LH Target Acquisition System presented an interesting and challenging set of constraints for implementation of a real-time Ada system. Severe memory and performance constraints were needed. A hostile programmer development environment was provided (no source level symbolic debugger was available). Schedules were optimistic, yet all constraints and schedules were satisfied with Ada as the development language.

These constraints resulted in several important implications to the developers. Proof of operational software integrity had to be obtained long before code was even developed. Detailed debugging information had to be generated. Care had to be taken to assure that only needed requirements were met and implemented in the code.

As a result of these implications, a detailed development methodology was created by significant enhancements to existing methodology texts. Moreover, products generated by this methodology were carried into both code and unit test and integration testing activities. This life-cycle emphasis, combined with Ada as the development language, assured performance and memory constraints satisfaction within the extremely short time schedule. In conclusion, the LH TAS and its gimbal_scan mode are positive proof that *Ada can be used in real-time system development, and Ada is the language of choice for real-time system development.*

11

Satellite Control System Case Study

In this case study, a prototype satellite control system is developed. Software emulators are constructed for both data sources and data sinks. Development begins with a set of "customer requirements," and proceeds through the methodological phases (operations, requirements, architecture, design). Traceability is maintained across the phases and to the user's view. Trade studies are performed within each phase. Complete, accurate and end-to-end methodology application is illustrated within this study. *This is not a toy problem.* While strictly limited in functionality, complexity of the real system is fully represented. Moreover, both process architecture and software design can be easily incorporated into an actual satellite control system.

Assume that hardware interfaces are transparently handled beneath vendor developed software interfaces. An all-software solution on is to be adopted, necessitating the use of Ada tasking to achieve concurrent operations. This case study has been implemented many times by students using the architectures and designs elaborated within the study. Students are divided into teams consisting of four to six individuals. Typically, teams perform the methodical analyses independently and receive immediate critique and feedback through oral presentations. In most cases, 90 percent of both schedule and effort is spent iterating on the analyses. Coding and integration of pieces implemented by separate team members consumes two to four days. These statistics have been observed over a reasonably healthy number of student teams indicating consistency of the observed performance.

A slightly different format is adopted for the case studies in this and succeeding chapters. Detailed discussion is associated with a specific illustration. Each discussion is preceded by the name and number of the relevant figure. Corresponding text follows the title and describes the contents of the illustration. Illustrations are discussed in terms of principles described in the text and in terms of understanding the target system under analysis. This format is employed to emphasize the value of the pictorial approach to obtain clear communications.

Several raw data sources are included in this development. Communications packets are relayed via the satellite control system. Periodically (plan to use a simple delay statement), a sender transmits a packet consisting of a source identifier, a destination identifier, and an 80 character message string. Maintenance is managed by the control system and is invoked via telemetry and command messages. Periodically (plan to use a drift compensating delay for this data source), a ground control station transmits a telemetry and command (T&C) message. This message consists of an operation code and two argument fields. For development purposes, assume the following data source characteristics:

Twenty communications packets are to be created:

two distinct data sources, each identified by a unique code;

two distinct destinations, each identified by a unique code;

same arbitrary message text for each message; and

a periodic delay parameter of 0.25 seconds.

Thirty T&C messages are to be generated:

fifty percent require thruster firings;
fifty percent require additions to a destination lookup table;
thruster firing takes 0.10 seconds;
additions to destination lookup table consist of
  an arbitrary destination code number and
  an arbitrary destination bandwidth.

Operationally, the spacecraft control system performs two distinct functions. On receipt of a communications packet, the control system relays the packet. Packet relay requires determining destination bandwidth (kbps) from a table, computing the transmission delay (dividing message length by bandwidth), adding 0.15 seconds for propagation delay, and delaying to simulate the transmission to the receiver.

Other functions are performed in response to a T&C message. If the message indicates an addition to the bandwidth lookup table, then the table update must be accomplished. An acknowledgement message is sent to the screen display device indicating successful table update. If a thruster firing is commanded by the message, thrusters are fired to re-orient or stabilize the spacecraft. Thruster firing requires determination of a firing duration. Firing duration time is the minimum of message specified time and the ratio of fuel remaining to fuel consumption rate.

Three important data objects are necessary to support these operations. An arbitrary destination/bandwidth table is initialize d consistent with characteristics of raw data sources. Both maximum fuel amount and fuel consumption rate are also input parameters to this prototype. Actual initial values are dependent on design characteristics of the thruster hardware.

Relayed messages are provided to ground nodes listed in the destination/bandwidth table. The receiving ground node copies the message into a local storage area on receipt. After transmission is completed, the received message is displayed on the computer screen along with an identification of the source and time tag.

On-board control must be capable of responding to messages received from the data sources. Once a message is received, its type is determined. Appropriate responses are as follows:

1. If a communications packet, then convey to the on-board message transmitter for relay to the ground;
2. If a T&C command, then respond to the message operation code according to the following:
   a. If operation code = 1, a thruster firing is commanded. Argument 1 contains the firing time. Argument 2 is ignored.
   b. If operation code = 2, an addition to the bandwidth table is required. Argument 1 is the destination identifier. Argument 2 is its bandwidth in kbps.

A review of the problem description to this point reveals a mixture of operations, implementor requirements, architecture, detailed design, and performance. This is quite typical of the format in which most real-time system developers receive instructions from customers. Do not be dismayed, however. By applying the methodology in a stepwise manner, order emerges from the apparent chaos.

11.1 GENERAL PROBLEM DESCRIPTION

Several important components and interfaces are assumed for the purpose of analyzing and solving this problem (see Figure 11.1). While this is to be a general purpose satellite control system, a single sender and receiver node are included in this case study. This assumption does not influence problem analysis or solution in any way. After all, additional sources and destinations are easily accommodated through a series of T&C messages to update the destination bandwidth table. A ground control node is also incorporated into the problem.

From an operational perspective, a sender aperiodically transmits a communications message, <Comm Msg> to the satellite. Since hardware interfaces are handled beneath abstract interfaces, no networking protocols are incorporated into this analysis. The satellite control system simply relays the message to the receiver on receipt of a communications message.

Ground control, which is responsible for maintaining the health of the satellite system, manages two categories of maintenance. Attitude management consists of issuing commands to fire thrusters on the spacecraft. Thruster firing causes satellite spin or de-spin to increase, reduce, or eliminate orbit precession. Commands

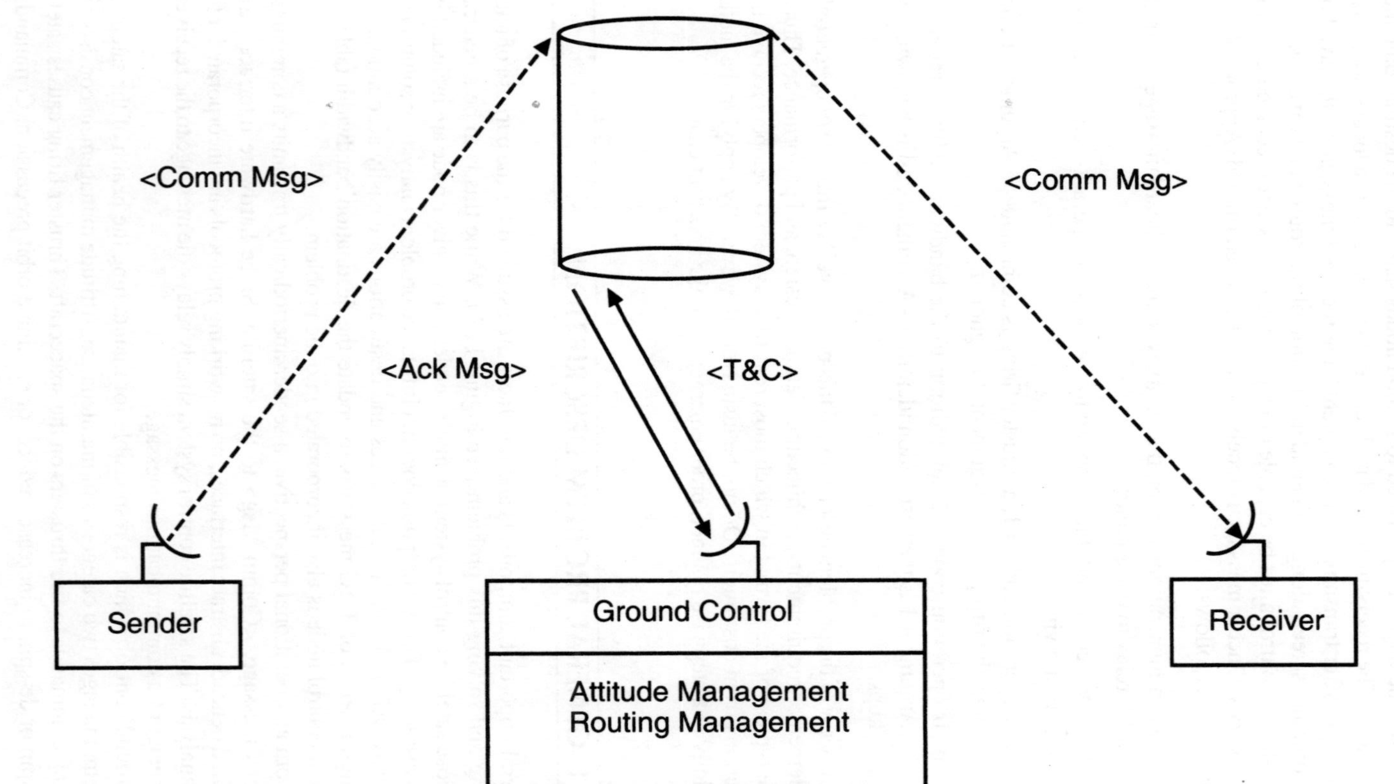

Figure 11.1 General Problem Description

that update the on-board routing table exercise routing management functions. This table, describing destinations and their bandwidths, is modified to allow more receiver nodes to be accessed by senders. Actual ground control activities are performed by periodic transmission of <T&C> messages to the satellite control system. Successful processing of T&C messages is followed by increased or decreased satellite rotational velocities or by acknowledgement messages to ground control indicating successful table update.

11.2 OPERATIONS MODEL GENERATION

Specifying a user's view of software system operations (see Figure 11.2) consists of the following steps:

1. Specify the user interfaces and order of operations of user interaction;
2. Translate order of operations of user interaction into an initial message sequence;
3. Expand the message sequence into detailed operational scenarios involving sensors, actuators, and other interfaces; and
4. Divide the detailed message sequence into a detailed event/response pattern, indicating inputs and outputs.

Since this system appears to include little or no sophisticated user interfaces, a slight variation of this sequence is to be employed. Operations model generation begins with a combination of steps 2 and 3. A detailed message sequence is generated that incorporates a time ordered sequence of events involving senders, receivers, and ground control.

11.3 EXTERNAL INTERFACE DIAGRAM

Major interfaces managed by the satellite control system are captured in Figure 11.3. Both communications message source (Msg Source) and communications message sink (Msg Destination) appear. For telemetry and command operations, specific interfaces include Ground Control, Computer Screen, and Thruster.

Ground Control represents the source of all telemetry and command messages. The destination (or sink) associated with these messages is the Computer Screen (for acknowledgement messages) or the Thruster (for firing messages). While Ground Control and Computer Screen could have been combined into a single interface, two separate interfaces are employed. With a view to ultimate implementation, using separate interfaces allows visibility to development efforts surrounding each interface. Software systems engineers are responsible for assuring that interfaces and interface management protocols are visible and are consistently applied across these parallel development activities.

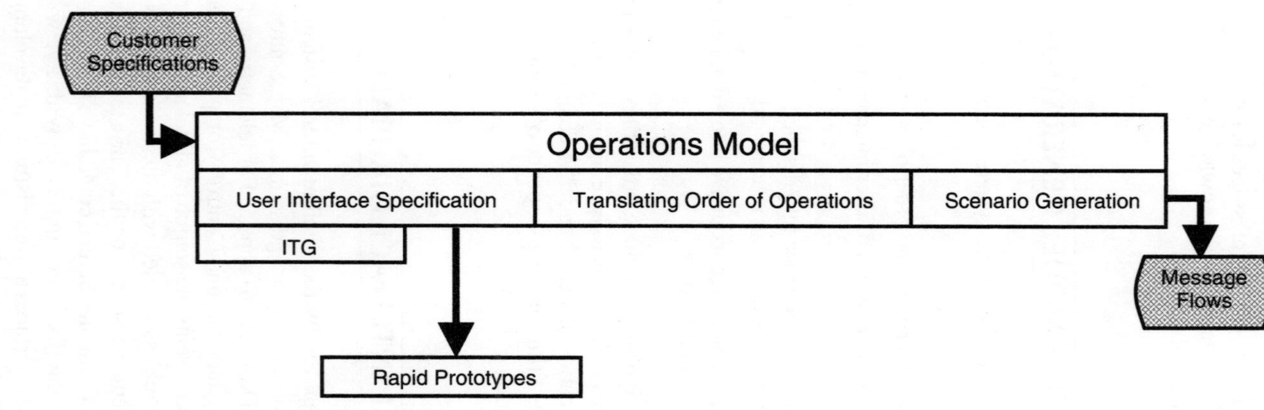

Figure 11.2 Operations Model Generation

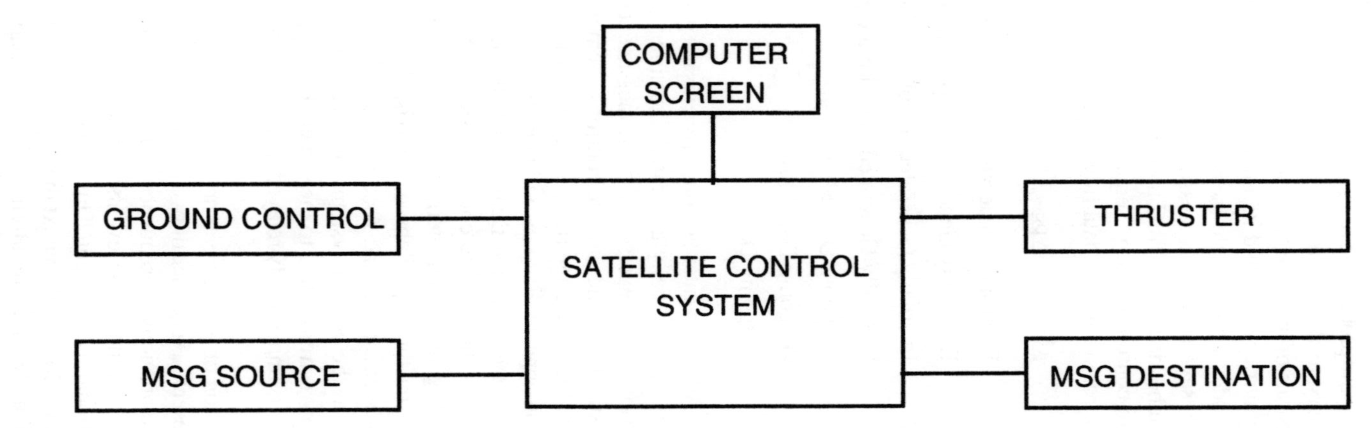

Figure 11.3 External Interface Diagram

11.4 TIME ORDERED EVENT SEQUENCE (I)

Message sequences provided in Figure 11.4 and the following figures were derived after an extensive review process. Several iterations covering a two to three week period were necessary to determine all the high leverage combinations of sequences. Initial versions of message sequences revealed an important characteristic of the satellite control system and its interfaces. A <T&C> message is really two messages embedded into a single message. To successfully employ a large state transition table, several internal messages are formulated, one for each category of message embedded in the T&C message.

To obtain satellite control, message sequences are composed of combinations of the following control events and data flows at system interfaces:

Event/Message	Message Type
<T&C >	Externally Generated, Incoming Control Flow
<Comm Msg >	Externally Generated, Incoming Control Flow
<Fire >	Internally Generated, Incoming Control Flow
<Add Loc >	Internally Generated, Incoming Control Flow
<Comm Msg >	Outgoing Data Flow
<Ack Msg >	Outgoing Data Flow
<Fire >	Outgoing Data Flow

Both <Fire> and <Add Loc> internal control events are generated in response to data embedded within an externally generated, incoming <T&C> control event. Internally generated events are represented in the message sequences as having the same source and destination—the satellite control system itself.

In the top portion of this message flow, a sequence of messages representing a nonstressing situation appears. Each incoming event is completely processed before another incoming event occurs. Beginning with the first incoming event, a <T&C> message enters the satellite control system. This attitude management command immediately generates an internal <Fire> event. A corresponding <Fire> command is issued to the thrusters. Subsequent to issuing a command to the thrusters, a second <T&C> event appears. As a result, an internally generated <Add Loc> event appears at the control system interfaces. After a short duration, the <Ack Msg> data flow is transmitted to the screen. Finally, a <Comm Msg> is received. This message is immediately relayed to its destination, with no intervening events.

In the middle portion of the figure, a new <Comm Msg> is then relayed. This <Comm Msg> represents a sequence of two immediate communications messages, one at the end of the previous subsequence, followed by this new one. Ability to handle back-to-back <Comm Msg> events with no intervening <T&C> events is an important operational requirement. This sequencing also illustrates the difference between message flows and context diagrams. Two <Comm Msg> events in sequence represent a dynamic requirement. In comparison, placing a single

Message	Source	Destination	Description
<T&C>	Ground Control	Sat Control	Attitude Management
<Fire>	Sat Control	Sat Control	Internal Event
<Fire>	Sat Control	Thruster	Fire Thrusters
<T&C>	Ground Control	Sat Control	Routing Management
<Add Loc>	Sat Control	Sat Control	Internal Event
<Ack Msg>	Sat Control	Screen	Acknowledgement
<Comm Msg>	Msg Source	Sat Control	Receive Raw Data Packet
<Comm Msg>	Sat Control	Msg Destination	Relay Raw Data Packet
<Comm Msg>	Msg Source	Sat Control	Receive Raw Data Packet
<Comm Msg>	Sat Control	Msg Destination	Relay Raw Data Packet
<T&C>	Ground Control	Sat Control	Routing Management
<Add Loc>	Sat Control	Sat Control	Internal Event
<Ack Msg>	Sat Control	Screen	Acknowledgement
<T&C>	Ground Control	Sat Control	Attitude Management
<Fire>	Sat Control	Sat Control	Internal Event
<Fire>	Sat Control	Thruster	Fire Thrusters
<Comm Msg>	Msg Source	Sat Control	Receive Raw Data Packet
<Comm Msg>	Sat Control	Msg Destination	Relay Raw Data Packet

Figure 11.4 Time Ordered Event Sequence (I)

<Comm Msg> in a context diagram implies a static requirement to manage a specific interface in a given data format. Dynamic requirements have different implications to an implementor from static requirements. Capability to accommodate dynamic requirements must appear within event response logic embedded in a combined state transition diagram/process activation table. Static requirements, appearing as interface flows in a context diagram, are satisfied via an appropriate data structure declaration in a data dictionary, and possibly some protocol logic in a PSPEC.

The above sequence of events is reversed in the bottom portion of the event sequencing. A routing management event (<T&C> mess age) and its internally generated <Add Loc> are completely processed through the control system prior to appearance of the next event. A subsequent <T&C> message and its corresponding internal attitude management control event and outgoing data flow are completely processed prior to receipt of the final event in the scenario. As the last event in the subsequence, a <Comm Msg> appears at the satellite control system interfaces, and is relayed to its destination.

11.5 TIME ORDERED EVENT SEQUENCE (II)

Previous event sequences assume that each incoming event completes its end-to-end response prior to arrival of a new incoming event. While this may be a preferable mode of operation since simple systems result, this is unrealistic since external devices provide data at their own rates. The time-ordered sequence in Figure 11.5 introduces more realistic variations of satellite control system operation, consistent with externally determined data arrival rate.

In the top half of the figure, an incoming <T&C> event containing an attitude management command appears at control system interfaces. As described previously, this event results in generation of an internal <Fire> event. However, prior to emission of this internal event, a new <Comm Msg> enters the control system. This intervening event can easily occur because the actual implementation is going to require processing of the <T&C> event. Event processing typically delays arrival of the internal event at the event management interfaces. During this delay, another external event can easily enter the system and begin processing. In this case, the intervening external event is a <Comm Msg>. At this point, the relayed <Comm Msg> emerges at the other side of the control system, exiting the system prior to arrival of the internal <Fire> event caused by the previous <T&C> message. Upon receipt and processing of the internal <Fire> event, an outgoing <Fire> response to the satellite thrusters occurs. The scenario in the top portion of the figure is completed by observing another <Comm Msg>, which is relayed to the ground.

A similar sequence is accomplished for a routing management event in the bottom half of the figure. A <T&C> event results in an <Add Loc> internal event. Prior to generation of the internal event, an intervening <Comm Msg> event arrives at the satellite control system interface. This event is completely processed,

Message	Source	Destination	Description
<T&C>	Ground Control	Sat Control	Attitude Management
<Comm Msg>	Msg Source	Sat Control	Receive Raw Data Packet
<Comm Msg>	Sat Control	Msg Destination	Relay Raw Data Packet
<Fire>	Sat Control	Sat Control	Internal Event
<Fire>	Sat Control	Thruster	Fire Thrusters
<Comm Msg>	Msg Source	Sat Control	Receive Raw Data Packet
<Comm Msg>	Sat Control	Msg Destination	Relay Raw Data Packet
<T&C>	Ground Control	Sat Control	Routing Management
<Comm Msg>	Msg Source	Sat Control	Receive Raw Data Packet
<Comm Msg>	Sat Control	Msg Destination	Relay Raw Data Packet
<Add Loc>	Sat Control	Sat Control	Internal Event
<Ack Msg>	Sat Control	Screen	Acknowledgement
<Comm Msg>	Msg Source	Sat Control	Receive Raw Data Packet
<Comm Msg>	Sat Control	Msg Destination	Relay Raw Data Packet

Figure 11.5 Time Ordered Event Sequence (II)

relaying the <Comm Msg> packet to the ground, prior to arrival of the internal <Add Loc> event. When the internal event is generated, an immediate <Ack Msg> response moves from satellite control to the screen. As before, this portion of the scenario ends with another <Comm Msg> event relayed to the Msg Destination.

While the two subsequences in this figure appear to have similar characteristics, they represent different operational requirements to the implementor. One sequence provides a context in which interference with processing the attitude management command is the primary focus. The second sequence emphasizes interrupted processing for a routing management command. Each of these requires different functional and control responses on the part of the implemented system; therefore, they are not the same dynamic requirement from a user's perspective.

11.6 TIME ORDERED EVENT SEQUENCE (III)

In the previous figure, <T&C> command processing is interlaced with <Comm Msg> packet processing. In Figure 11.6, processing of multiple kinds of <T&C> commands is intertwined. Two back-to-back attitude management commands enter the control system in the top portion of the figure. Before an internal <Fire> event for the first command is generated, a second <T&C> command, representing the second attitude management command, appears at system interfaces. After processing the second <T&C> event, the first internal <Fire> event arrives to be processed by the control system. This event is effectively processed, resulting in the outgoing <Fire> response to the thrusters. No sooner does the latter response occur than the second internal <Fire> event arrives. This is also immediately processed, resulting in another corresponding <Fire> response to the thrusters. This portion of the scenario is completed by arrival of a <Comm Msg> that is immediately relayed to the Msg Destination.

The scenario in the bottom portion of the figure begins with a <T&C> event representing an attitude management command. Immediately, a second <T&C> event arrives containing a routing management command. As the scenario unfolds, the internal <Fire> event generated by the first <T&C> event arrives and is dispatched. This is followed by the internal <Add Loc> event and its response, an <Ack Msg>. Again, completion of the scenario involves arrival and relay of a <Comm Msg> packet.

11.7 TIME ORDERED EVENT SEQUENCE (IV)

In the final phases of the time ordered event sequence, two other combinations of interleaved <T&C> command processing are represented. In the upper portion of Figure 11.7, a routing management <T&C> command is followed by an attitude management <T&C> command. Two immediate routing management <T&C> commands appear and are processed in the bottom portion of the figure. These two

Message	Source	Destination	Description
<T&C>	Ground Control	Sat Control	Attitude Management
<T&C>	Ground Control	Sat Control	Attitude Management
<Fire>	Sat Control	Sta Control	Internal Event
<Fire>	Sat Control	Thruster	Fire Thrusters
<Fire>	Sat Control	Sat Control	Internal Event
<Fire>	Sat Control	Thruster	Fire Thruters
<Comm Msg>	Msg Source	Sat Control	Receive Raw Data Packet
<Comm Msg>	Sat Control	Msg Destination	Relay Raw Data Packet
<T&C>	Ground Control	Sat Control	Attitude Management
<T&C>	Ground Control	Sat Control	Routing Management
<Fire>	Sat Control	Sat Control	Internal Event
<Fire>	Sat Control	Thruster	Fire Thrusters
<Add Loc>	Sat Control	Sat Control	Internal Event
<Ack Msg>	Sat Control	Screen	Acknowledgement
<Comm Msg>	Msg Source	Sat Control	Receive Raw Data Packet
<Comm Msg>	Sat Control	Msg Destination	Relay Raw Data Packet

Figure 11.6 Time Ordered Event Sequence (III)

Message	Source	Destination	Description
<T&C>	Ground Control	Sat Control	Routing Management
<T&C>	Ground Control	Sat Control	Attitude Management
<Add Loc>	Sat Control	Sat Control	Internal Event
<Ack Msg>	Sat Control	Screen	Acknowledgement
<Fire>	Sat Control	Sat Control	Internal Event
<Fire>	Sat Control	Thruster	Fire Thrusters
<Comm Msg>	Msg Source	Sat Control	Receive Raw Data Packet
<Comm Msg>	Sat Control	Msg Destination	Relay Raw Data Packet
<T&C>	Ground Control	Sat Control	Routing Management
<T&C>	Ground Control	Sat Control	Routing Management
<Add Loc>	Sat Control	Sat Control	Internal Event
<Ack Msg>	Sat Control	Screen	Acknowledgement
<Add Loc>	Sat Control	Sat Control	Internal Event
<Ack Msg>	Sat Control	Screen	Acknowledgement
<Comm Msg>	Msg Source	Sat Control	Receive Raw Data Packet
<Comm Msg>	Sat Control	Msg Destination	Relay Raw Data Packet

Figure 11.7 Time Ordered Event Sequence (IV)

sequences and the two sequences in the previous figure contain all possible combinations of intermixed <T&C> command processing scenarios.

No doubt a large number of other scenarios can be generated, each of which would appear to be important. However, the scenarios presented in this and the previous figures are the only scenarios necessary to successfully implement this control system. Any other scenario intended to achieve end-to-end processing under normal repetitive operations can ultimately be refined to one of the subsequences described in these figures. For this reason, these are often classified as "key leverage" scenarios. Scenarios are classified as "key leverage" if they are the shortest scenarios necessary to obtain a complete and consistent set of functional and control requirements (as will be demonstrated later in the case study). Ability to identify "key leverage" scenarios is dependent upon both the problem being analyzed and the experience of the software system engineer. Quite often, iteration between message flow generation and requirements consistency/completeness checking is necessary to hone the event sequences to represent "key leverage" conditions.

11.8 TEST INPUT/OUTPUT PATTERN (I, II)

For later use in evaluation of implementor requirements, process architectures, and tasking architectures, event sequences are grouped into two categories (input events and output responses). This categorization yields a test input/output pattern consisting of events, correlated with corresponding responses.

Consider the first time ordered event sequence table (Figure 11.4). In the first line of this table, a <T&C> event occurs. Line two of the table contains its response—an internal <Fire> event. This pair—<T&C> event, <Fire> response—appears as the first event/response pair in this figure. Subsequent event/response pairs appear as other table entries. Subsequences that were differentiated in the original message flows/event sequences are maintained as subsections of the input/output pattern by separation using dashed lines.

Each event in the scenarios has exactly one outgoing response. This is quite unusual. For other systems, some events will have no immediate response. Other events may have multiple responses. Later evaluations apply each event to one of the models (implementors' requirements, process architecture, or tasking architecture) to verify that the required outgoing responses do occur. For this reason, responses must be specifically attributed to the events which cause the responses.

Event	Response
<T&C> <Fire> <T&C> <Add Loc> <Comm Msg>	<Fire> <Fire> <Add Loc> <Ack Msg> <Comm Msg>
<Comm Msg>	<Comm Msg>
<T&C> <Add Loc> <T&C> <Fire> <Comm Msg>	<Add Loc> <Ack Msg> <Fire> <Fire> <Comm Msg>
<T&C> <Comm Msg> <Fire> <Comm Msg>	<Fire> <Comm Msg> <Fire> <Comm Msg>
<T&C> <Comm Msg> <Add Loc> <Comm Msg>	<Add Loc> <Comm Msg> <Ack Msg> <Comm Msg>

Figure 11.8 Test Input/Output Pattern (I)

Event	Response
<T&C> <T&C> <Fire> <Fire> <Comm Msg>	<Fire> <Fire> <Fire> <Fire> <Comm Msg>
<T&C> <T&C> <Fire> <Add Loc> <Comm Msg>	<Fire> <Add Loc> <Fire> <Ack Msg> <Comm Msg>
<T&C> <T&C> <Add Loc> <Fire> <Comm Msg>	<Add Loc> <Fire> <Ack Msg> <Fire> <Comm Msg>
<T&C> <T&C> <Add Loc> <Add Loc> <Comm Msg>	<Add Loc> <Add Loc> <Ack Msg> <Ack Msg> <Comm Msg>

Figure 11.9 Test Input/Output Pattern (II)

11.9 REQUIREMENTS MODEL GENERATION

Defining an implementor's view of software system requirements necessary to satisfy the operational/user's view consists of the following steps:

1. Generate a context diagram using the detailed message sequence;
2. Construct functional requirements in the form of a requirements tree and process specifications (PSPECs);
3. Describe event response logic for managing the PSPECs in the form of state transition diagrams (STD) and process activation tables (PAT);
4. Perform a consistency and completeness check of implementor requirements against operational requirements;
5. Use the data dictionary to determine an initial set of data abstractions and operations on abstractions; and
6. Allocate timing requirements to PSPECs.

11.10 CONTEXT DIAGRAM

Generation of the requirements tree begins with formulation of the context diagram. A context diagram describes the static interfaces to be managed by the satellite control system. Review of the preceding event sequences reveals the following unique flows at the interfaces:

Message	Source	Destination
<T&C>	Ground Control	Satellite Control
<Comm Msg>	Message Source	Satellite Control
<Ack Msg>	Satellite Control	Screen
<Fire>	Satellite Control	Thruster
<Comm Msg>	Satellite Control	Message Destination

These interfaces are summarized in the context diagram. All incoming events are characterized as control flows, since each is likely to require responses which span multiple requirements. This is demonstrated later in the case.

A context diagram is a static picture of interface requirements. Since each interface appears only once and is not expected to appear or disappear, its existence on this diagram is static or unchanging. Even detailed definitions of interfaces (as described in the forthcoming data dictionary) are assumed to be statically defined within this representation. By comparison, event sequences provide a dynamic view of data movement across these interfaces; as such, event sequences represent a dynamic set of requirements compared to those implied by interfaces statically characterized in the context diagram.

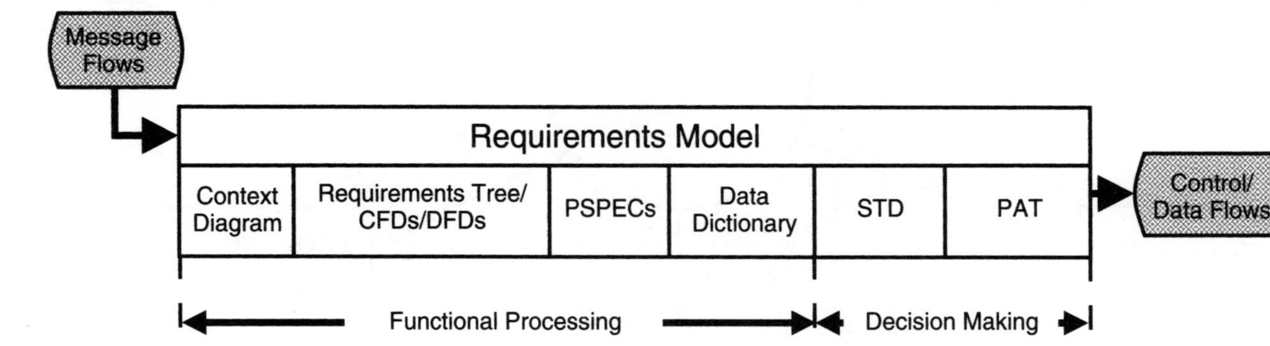

Figure 11.10 Requirements Model Generation

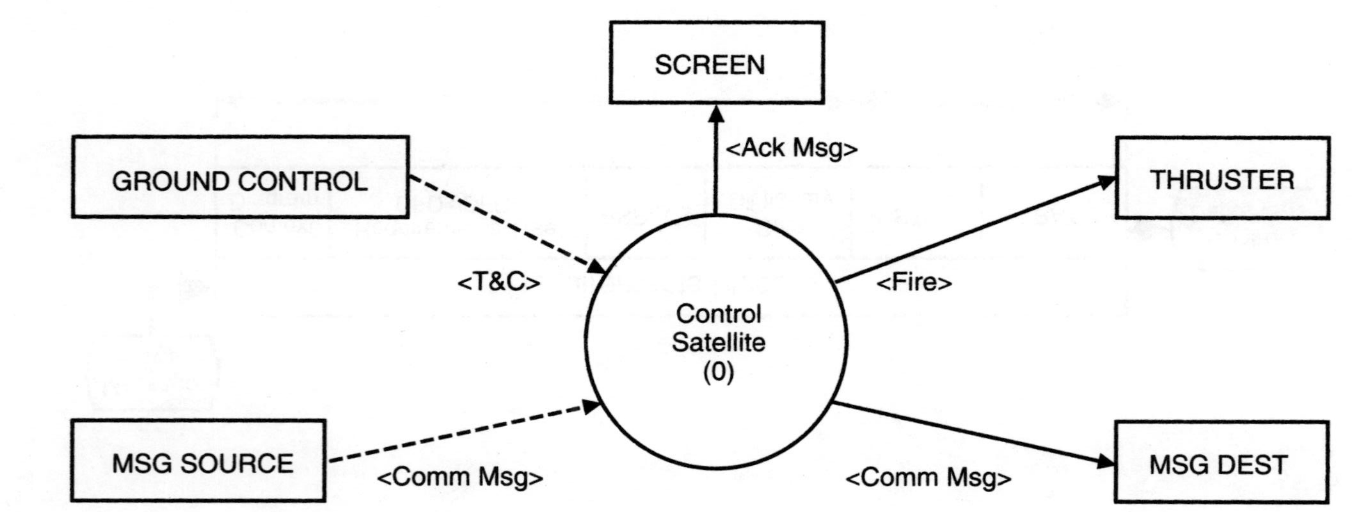

Figure 11.11 Context Diagram

11.11 FUNCTIONAL REQUIREMENTS

A fully balanced, initial decomposition of functional requirements is provided in Figure 11.12. Incoming messages are processed (process 1), transforming incoming events into internal data flows. Raw data associated with a <Comm Msg> is routed to packet data analysis (process 2). Performing management actions (process 3) receives the data associated with a <T&C> event.

Packet data analysis (process 2) uses data embedded within the <Comm Msg> data flow to key into a table containing destination locations and their bandwidths. Associated bandwidth is used to compute a transmission delay, after which the <Comm Msg> is transferred to the external interface represented in the context diagram.

Management function operations (process 3) employ <T&C> data to control thruster firing or to modify the destination/bandwidth table. If the bandwidth table is updated, an <Ack Msg> is generated at the interface specified in the parent context diagram. Thruster firings involve using and updating the remaining fuel level and issuing a <Fire> message at the thruster interface. Additionally, incoming <T&C> data flows are transformed into internal control events, <Fire> and <Add Loc>.

This data flow diagram, as well as the following diagrams, employs the guidelines suggested in the text. Data flows naturally from left to right. Input and output flows derived from the parent diagram typically appear around the outer edges of the child diagram. Concurrent processing chains are characterized by parallel sequences of requirements, placed from top to bottom in the diagram.

11.12 DECOMPOSED FUNCTIONAL REQUIREMENTS WITH PSPEC (I)

Parent requirement—Process Incoming Message (process 1)—is decomposed into its constituent details in the upper half of Figure 11.13. Raw data is accepted (process 1.1). This raw data is transformed into an internal data flow, and transmitted to determine the message type (process 1.2). As a result, incoming control event interfaces are routed to the appropriate satellite control system.

Requirement two, Analyze Packet Data, consists of two important functions. In function 2.1, destination of the <Comm Msg> is extracted and forwarded to function 2.2. In the latter, bandwidth is determined from the destination/bandwidth table (named Locations) and returned to function 2.1. Associated bandwidth is appended to the <Comm Msg>, which is emitted for further processing.

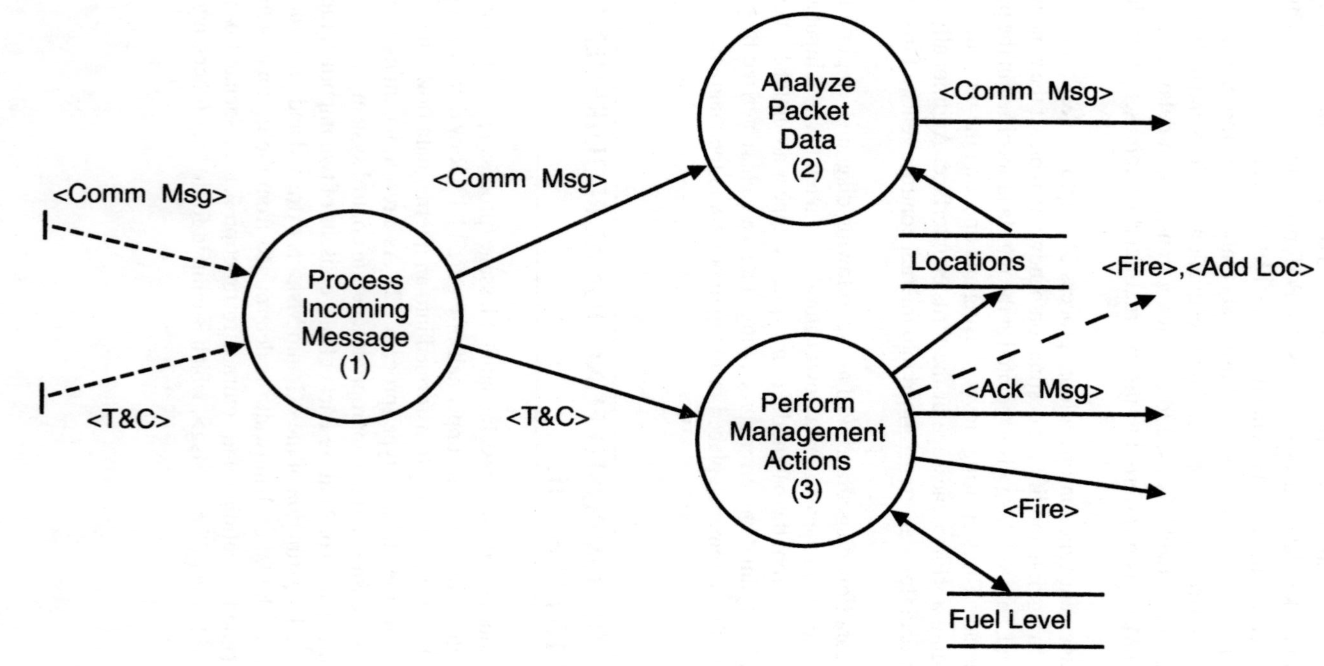

Figure 11.12 Functional Requirements

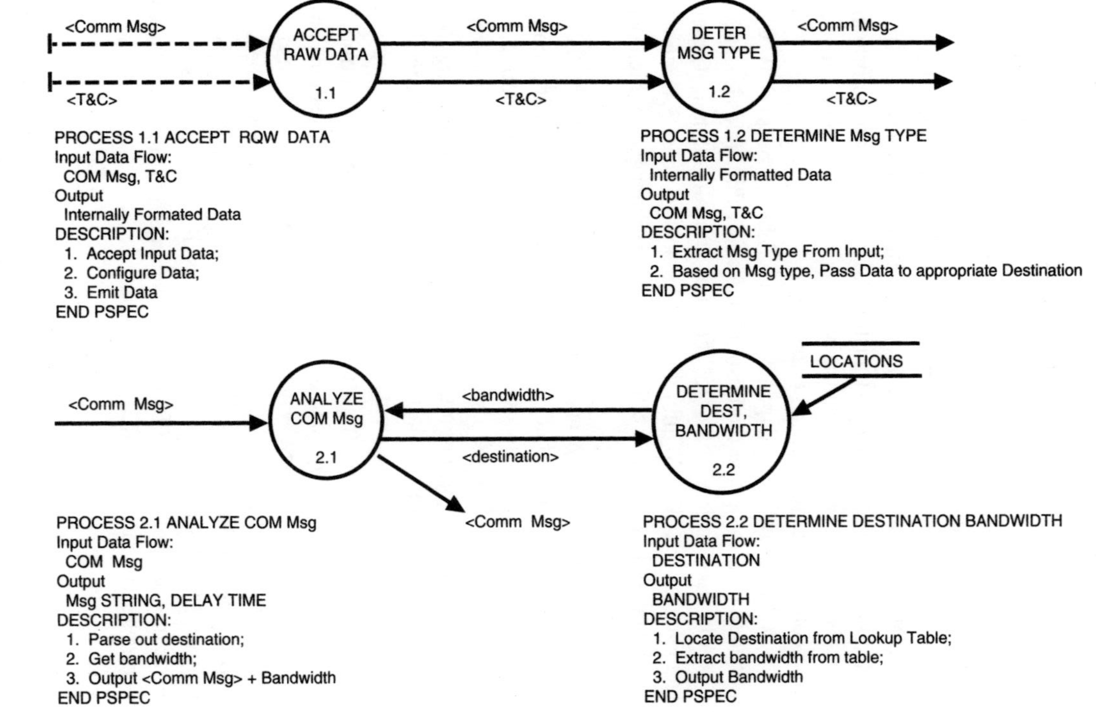

<Comm Msg>
<T&C>
ACCEPT
RAW DATA
1.1
<Comm Msg>
<T&C>
DETER
MSG TYPE
1.2
<Comm Msg>
<T&C>
PROCESS 1.1 ACCEPT RQW DATA
Input Data Flow:
COM Msg, T&C
Output
Internally Formated Data
DESCRIPTION:
1. Accept Input Data;
2. Configure Data;
3. Emit Data
END PSPEC
PROCESS 1.2 DETERMINE Msg TYPE
Input Data Flow:
Internally Formatted Data
Output
COM Msg, T&C
DESCRIPTION:
1. Extract Msg Type From Input;
2. Based on Msg type, Pass Data to appropriate Destination
END PSPEC
<Comm Msg>
ANALYZE
COM Msg
2.1
<bandwidth>
<destination>
<Comm Msg>
DETERMINE
DEST,
BANDWIDTH
2.2
LOCATIONS
PROCESS 2.1 ANALYZE COM Msg
Input Data Flow:
COM Msg
Output
Msg STRING, DELAY TIME
DESCRIPTION:
1. Parse out destination;
2. Get bandwidth;
3. Output <Comm Msg> + Bandwidth
END PSPEC
PROCESS 2.2 DETERMINE DESTINATION BANDWIDTH
Input Data Flow:
DESTINATION
Output
BANDWIDTH
DESCRIPTION:
1. Locate Destination from Lookup Table;
2. Extract bandwidth from table;
3. Output Bandwidth
END PSPEC

Figure 11.13 Decomposed Functional Requirements with PSPEC (I)

11.13 DECOMPOSED FUNCTIONAL REQUIREMENTS WITH PSPEC (II)

Perform Management Actions (process 3) is further decomposed in this figure. Individual <T&C> data flows enter transformation 3.1, to be converted into internal control events—<Fire> or <Add Loc>. Processing associated with these internal events is determined via access to a control specification, as indicated by the vertical bar attached to the internal control flow. Raw data associated with each internal event is forwarded to other requirements for additional processing in response to the internal control events.

<Fire> data flows move through requirement 3.2. Data stored within the <Fire> flow is compared with the current fuel level to assess fuel sufficiency. If sufficient fuel is available, the <Fire> data flows to transformation 3.5. This transformation, Update Fuel, reads current fuel level, adjusts by the amount consumed, and transmits the <Fire> command to the thruster interface.

An <Add Loc> data flow enters Update Lookup Table (process 3.3), which employs embedded data to update the destination/bandwidth table (Locations). From here, <Add Loc> flow exits to the next transformation, Generate Acknowledgement (process 3.4). Within this requirement (process 3.4), an <Ack Msg> is constructed and placed at the Screen interface managed by the control system.

Several important observations are appropriate at this point. A fairly realistic set of functional requirements is described, employing only three levels of decomposition. This is roughly the appropriate level of detail to obtain a set of requirements that aids successful hardware/software integration. Any further details regarding a specific sensor processing algorithm are both superfluous and confusing. Many developers make the mistake of emphasizing algorithm details to the exclusion of software system operational requirements.

With this simple formulation constrained by the original problem description, a well-balanced requirements tree is generated. All primitive specifications are at level three. In general, for a complex system, a well-balanced requirements tree is not the case. Some requirements may decompose to only two levels. Others may be described to four levels. Regardless of the level at which a requirement is classified as primitive, PSPECs are the real requirements that must be satisfied. An event response can span multiple PSPECs across the requirements tree, resulting in extensive complexity to accomplish the response.

11.14 CSPEC: STATE TRANSITION DIAGRAM

Event responses are managed through a state transition diagram given in this figure. Four basic states are necessary to adequately represent all possible decision conditions. Relay Com Pkts indicates that a communications message has been processed and relayed. Decode Operation suggests that a T&C message has been processed, generating an internal event. Reacting to specific internal events is

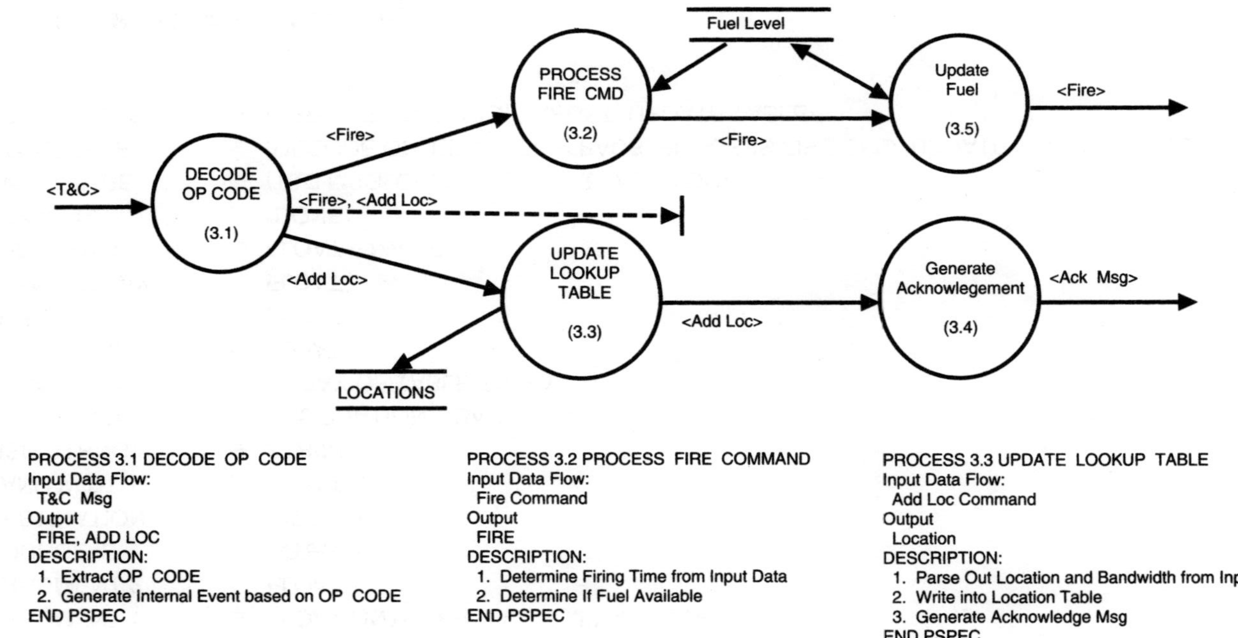

PROCESS 3.1 DECODE OP CODE
Input Data Flow:
T&C Msg
Output
FIRE, ADD LOC
DESCRIPTION:
1. Extract OP CODE
2. Generate Internal Event based on OP CODE
END PSPEC

PROCESS 3.2 PROCESS FIRE COMMAND
Input Data Flow:
Fire Command
Output
FIRE
DESCRIPTION:
1. Determine Firing Time from Input Data
2. Determine If Fuel Available
END PSPEC

PROCESS 3.3 UPDATE LOOKUP TABLE
Input Data Flow:
Add Loc Command
Output
Location
DESCRIPTION:
1. Parse Out Location and Bandwidth from Input Data
2. Write into Location Table
3. Generate Acknowledge Msg
END PSPEC

Figure 11.14 Decomposed Functional Requirements with PSPEC (II)

```
COMM MSG        ::=  SOURCE ID + DESTINATION ID + MSG STRING + BANDWIDTH
T&C             ::=  OP CODE ID + ARGUMENT 1 + ARGUMENT 2
FIRE MSG        ::=  OPCODE ID + FIRING TIME
ADD LOC         ::=  OPCODE ID + TABLE ENTRY
OP CODE ID      ::=  EVENT  TYPE
ARGUMENT 1      ::=  FLOAT | INTEGER (DISCRIMINANT TYPE)
ARGUMENT 2      ::=  FLOAT
SOURCE ID       ::=  INTEGER
DESTINATION     ::=  INTEGER
BAND WIDTH      ::=  FLOAT
MSG STRNG       ::=  STRING
TABLE ENTRY     ::=  DESTINATION + BAND WIDTH
LOCATIONS       ::=  ARRAY OF TABLE ENTRY
FIRING TIME     ::=  FLOAT
MAX FUEL        ::=  FLOAT
TRANS DELAY     ::=  FLOAT
FUEL LEVEL      ::=  FLOAT = MAX FUEL
ACK MSG         ::=  "DONE"
EVENT TYPE      ::=  (T&C MSG, COMM MSG, FIRE, ADD LOC)
STATE TYPE      ::=  (DECODE OP, RELAY COM PACS, PROCESS FIRE CMD, UPDATE LOOKUP TABLE)
ACTION TYPE     ::=  (PERF OP, XMT MSG, THRUST, UPDATE TABLE)
```

Figure 11.15 Requirements Data Dictionary

reflected in the remaining states. Process Fire Command represents a condition in which an internal <Fire> event has been processed. Responding to an internal <Add Loc> event is reflected in the state named Update Lookup Table. These state definitions are consistent with the guidelines described in the text. Appropriate selection of states is a key determinant of integration and operational success and varies from system to system.

Transitions among states are labeled according to the convention described earlier in the text. Each transition is labeled with an event causing the transition and the name of a corresponding action performed prior to actual transition. As an example, assume that the satellite control system is in a Relay Com Pkts state. If a <T&C> event occurs, then a Perf Op action is performed. Subsequent to performing this action, the control system transitions to the Decode Operation state.

An important view of the state transition diagram is to assess the total set of transitions into or out of a specific state. Transition assessment is accomplished to initially assure that the state transition diagram is complete, allowing for all possible transitions associated with a given state. Consider the state named Process Fire Command. Allowable transitions from this state are as follows:

Event	Action	Destination State
<T&C>	[Perf Op]	Decode Operation
<Add Loc>	[Update Table]	Update Lookup Table
<Comm Msg>	[Xmt Msg]	Relay Com Pkts
<Fire>	[Thrust]	Process Fire Command

A similar table can be constructed for all transitions into the state named Process Fire Command, as follows:

Source State	Event	Action
Decode Operation	<Fire>	[Thrust]
Update Lookup Table	<Fire>	[Thrust]
Relay Com Pkts	<Fire>	[Thrust]
Process Fire Command	<Fire>	[Thrust]

This last table clearly illustrates that the state Process Fire Command indicates the condition in which an internal <Fire> event has just been processed.

Notice the existence of feedback or state preserving transitions within the state transition diagram. By use of this specific characteristic, back-to-back messages of any type (<Comm Msg>, <T&C>, <Fire>, or <Add Loc>) are effectively and properly managed. Software architects often do not incorporate state preserving transitions into their control specifications. As a result, programmers chose to implement any response within their knowledge for back-to-back sequences of operations. Usually, programmed responses are incorrect and are hidden, causing significant integration and test effort.

For this very simple control system, responding to sequences of events requires an extremely complex set of transitions. According to problem definition, only three functions are performed by the satellite control system:

1. Relaying communications packets;
2. Maintaining the destination/bandwidth table; and
3. Firing thrusters to maintain on-orbit stability.

Yet, in spite of this simplistic functionally, the state transition diagram is extremely complex. Every transition included in this diagram is necessary if the operational model is to be achieved. Failure to incorporate any of these transitions can lead to extensive integration and test effort, since some elements of the operational model are not properly managed.

Several iterations are necessary to detail a state transition diagram of this complexity. In fact, simply writing a state transition diagram usually fails to provide an accurate transition specification. Evaluation of the diagram against the operational model determines flaws in the transition diagram. As a first approach, most software architects tend to define three states—Relay Com Pkts, Process Fire Command, and Update Lookup Table. While this set of states can work, decision logic must be embedded within PSPECs to handle special decision problems. Unfortunately, hiding decision logic within PSPECs has significant impact upon development effort. Integration and test effort is usually incurred, since decision logic hidden within PSPECs may be distributed throughout the implementation architecture. Resultant hidden decision logic is difficult to identify as the source of problems during integration and test. Moreover, hidden decision logic reduces flexibility. Accomplishing simple changes requires identification of all the hidden decision logic and replacing this logic with new logic. Achieving flexibility requires that state transition tables contain as much decision logic as possible. These tables are maximized in size. Adopting an approach that maximizes transition table size usually results in use of intermediate states (Decode Operation) with internally generated events (<Fire> and <Add Loc>). While this incurs some ultimate throughput degradation by increasing the workload on the architecture, gains in flexibility are usually worthwhile. After all, throughput can be obtained with a little tricky hardware.

11.15 CSPEC: PROCESS ACTIVATION TABLE

Translation of actions into sequences of functional processing data flows is accomplished in the process activation table. Reviewing the previous state transition diagram reveals that only four basic actions are employed throughout the event response logic. These appear in the leftmost column of the figure—[Xmt Msg], [Perf Op], [Thrust], and [Update Table]. Across the top of the table are listed the leaf requirements from the requirements tree. Recall that leaf requirements are those for which PSPECs have been written.

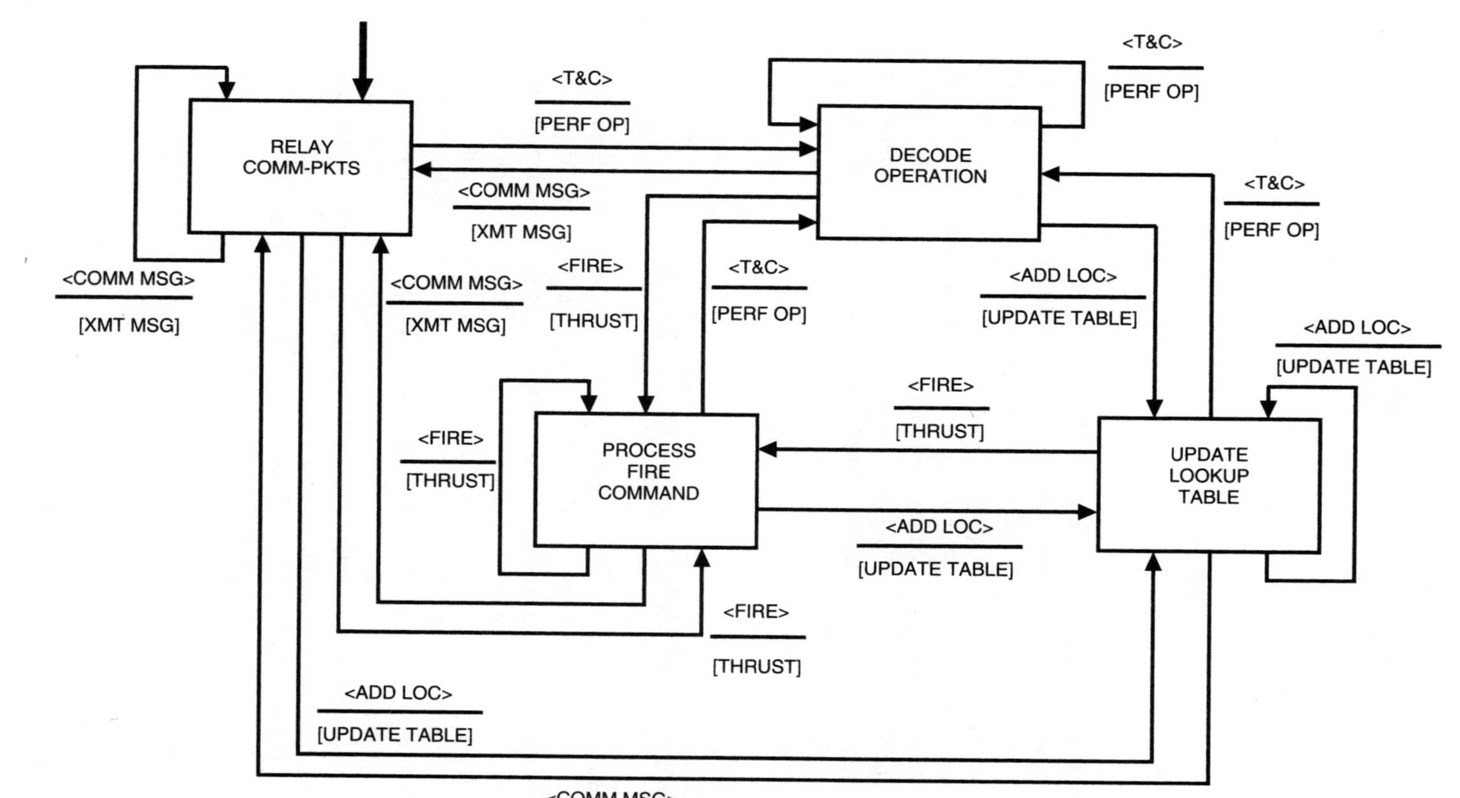

Figure 11.16 CSPEC: State Transition Diagram

Detailed responses associated with each action appear in the body of the table. All of the action details in this system employ sequential processing of data. For example, consider [Xmt Msg]. Detailed processing requirements associated with this action are as follows:

1. Accept Raw Data (1.1);
2. Deter Msg Type (1.2);
3. Analyze Comm Msg (2.1); and
4. Determine Dest (2.2).

These functions span various areas of the requirements tree. For most real-time systems, this is the case, suggesting that a "flattened" control model is necessary to respond to events managed by the system. Many methodology texts suggest that a control specification be restricted to a specific decomposition level of the requirements tree. Restriction control specifications would cause significant problems for the satellite control system. As illustrated above, response to <Comm Msg> events span both the 1.x and 2.x decompositions of the requirements. Restricting the response specification to either 1.x or 2.x would cause major integration and test headaches as well as lead to catastrophic system failure. A careful review of the table shows that another action, [Perf Op], also spans several decomposition levels.

11.16 REQUIREMENTS DATA DICTIONARY

All control and data flows through the satellite control system are defined in this data dictionary. Both structures and types are described. A <Comm Msg> consists of a source identification, a destination identification, a message string, and a place holder for the bandwidth (appended during one of the functional transformations). Each <T&C> message contains an operational code indicating <Fire> or <Add Loc> commands and storage for at most two arguments, depending on the event type. Two data stores are defined: Locations and Fuel Level. An assumption is made that Fuel Level is initialized to its maximum value. Primarily, this dictionary serves to provide project-wide, standard definitions for all data moving through the satellite control system, eliminating confusion by software implementors.

Since structure declarations are provided, this dictionary is also employed to begin the definition of data abstractions. For instance, a <T&C> data abstraction is suggested by the dictionary. Support for this abstraction is provided by the following operations:

Create_T&C_Object;

Get_Opcode_ID;

Put_Opcode_ID;

Get_Argument_1;

Leaf Reqmts / Action	ACCEPT RAW DATA 1.1	DETER MSG TYPE 1.2	ANALYZE COM MSG 2.1	DETERMINE DEST 2.2	DECODE OP CODE 3.1	PROCESS FIRE CMD 3.2	UPDATE LOOKUP TABLE 3.3	GENERATE ACKNOWLEDGEMENT 3.4	UPDATE FUEL 3.5
XMIT MSG	1	2	3	4					
PERF OP	1	2			3				
THRUST						1			2
UPDATE TABLE							1	2	

Figure 11.17 CSPEC: Process Activation Table

Put_Argument_1;

Get_Argument_2;

Put_Argument_2; and

Destroy_T&C_Object

While this is a primary set of operations, these operations are usually insufficient to complete the abstraction. Identification of the complete set of operations for the operation can not be fully determined until the layered virtual machine/object-oriented design methodology is applied during sequential software design. Application of LVM/OOD to specific PSPECs identifies any application required operations such as T&C_Operation_Code_Is_Fire or T&C_Operation_Code_Is_Add_Loc, which are not obvious from the structural definition given in the data dictionary.

11.17 REQUIREMENTS EVALUATION (I-VIII)

In this rather detailed set of figures, a full consistency/completeness evaluation is accomplished. Correlation to the user's view of the operations model occurs by employing the test input/output pattern to assure that each event results in the corresponding response. A single example illustrates the evaluation process.

Recall the first entry from the earlier test input/output pattern, as follows:

Event	Response
<T&C>	<Fire>

Evaluation of this element in the test input/output pattern begins with the system in the state named Relay Comm Pkts, since this is the initial state of the satellite control system. Next, the combination of current state (Relay Comm Pkts) and current event (<T&C>) is applied to the state transition diagram. Under these conditions, according to the transition diagram, a [Perf Op] action is performed. Referring to the process activation table, the following action sequence occurs:

1. Accept Raw Data (1.1);
2. Deter Msg Type (1.2); and
3. Decode Op Code (3.1).

A state transition is accomplished subsequent to this sequence of actions. Returning to the state transition diagram, the satellite control system transitions to the Decode Op state. Finally, using the data flow diagrams for requirements 1.1, 1.2, and 1.3, an internal <Fire> event is emitted from requirement 3.1. This sequence of evaluations is contained as the first entry in the figure and verifies that the above event/response pattern occurs.

Evaluation continues, employing the last observed state (Decode Op) and the next event in the test input/output pattern. For reader ease, original groupings of event subsequences are maintained by separation with solid lines. Dashed lines are employed to separate verification data for individual event/response entries.

As the reader verifies all the event/response entries in the test input/output pattern, each transition that is tested is carefully recorded. Incomplete control specifications are identified when a nonexistent transition is identified for a given (current state, current event) combination. Of course, this shortcoming must be remedied. Furthermore, some transitions may not be tested by the test input/output patterns. Transitions not tested by the event sequence typically indicate shortcomings in the event sequence and also need to be remedied by reevaluating the message sequence.

In fact, iteration from event sequences to requirements evaluation and back is usually necessary. An event sequence is hypothesized. This sequence is carried through to requirements evaluation, identifying incomplete and inconsistent control and requirements specifications. Of course, erroneous specifications are fixed. Untested transitions in the state transition diagram require enhancement of the event sequence, necessitating another pass through the steps. After several iterations, both satisfactory event sequences and consistent/complete specifications are identified.

This iterative process serves to eliminate problems in event response logic and functional processing long before coding is begun. Identifying flaws in event response logic during integration and test is a complex, time consuming, and frustrating process. Usually, a symptom such as catastrophic system failure is observed. Tracing the cause of the symptom to faulty event response logic typically requires a great amount of work. Generating a correct fix is the next step, usually accomplished by trial and error. A fix is tried, and if the problem disappears, is assumed to work. In fact, the problem usually reasserts itself later. (But, I fixed that problem earlier, you cry.) Disappearance of a symptom does not guarantee the correctness of the fix. Usually, a disappearing symptom indicates a change in code behavior when a "hit and miss" approach is utilized. Employing a technique such as the requirements evaluation process serves to eliminate potential problems analytically prior to implementation.

State Before	Event	Action	Action Details	State After	Response
Relay Comm Pkts	<T&C>	[Perf Op]	1.1 Accept Raw Data 1.2 Deter Msg Type 3.1 Decode Op code	Decode Optn	<Fire>
Decode Optn	<Fire>	[Thrust]	3.2 Process Fire Cmd 3.5 Update Fuel	Process Fire Cmd	<Fire>
Process Fire Cmd	<T&C>	[Perf Op]	1.1 Accept Raw Data 1.2 Deter Msg Type 3.1 Decode Op Code	Decode Optn	<Add Loc>
Decode Optn	<Add Loc>	[Update Table]	3.3 Update Lookup Table 3.4 Generate Ack	Update Lookup Table	<Ack Msg>
Update Lookup Table	<Comm Msg>	[Xmt Msg]	1.1 Accept Raw Data 1.2 Deter Msg Type 2.1 Analyze Comm Msg 2.2 Determine Dest	Relay Comm Pkts	<Comm Msg>
Relay Comm Pkts	<Comm Msg>	[Xmt Msg]	1.1 Accept Raw Data 1.2 Deter Msg Type 2.1 Analyze Comm Msg 2.2 Determine Dest	Relay Comm Pkts	<Comm Msg>

Figure 11.18 Requirements Evaluation (I)

State Before	Event	Action	Action Details	State After	Response
Relay Comm Pkts	<T&C>	[Perf Op]	1.1 Accept Raw Data 1.2 Deter Msg Type 3.1 Decode Op Code	Decode Optn	<Add Loc>
Decode Optn	<Add Loc>	[Update Table]	3.3 Update Lookup Table 3.4 Generate Ack	Update Lookup Table	<Ack Msg>
Update Lookup Table	<T&C>	[Perf Op]	1.1 Accept Raw Data 1.2 Deter Msg Type 3.1 Decode Op Code	Decode Optn	<Fire>
Decode Optn	<Fire>	[Thrust]	3.2 Process Fire Cmd 3.5 Update Fuel	Process Fire Cmd	<Fire>
Process Fire Cmd	<Comm Msg>	[Xmt Msg]	1.1 Accept Raw Data 1.2 Deter Msg Type 2.1 Analyze Comm Msg 2.2 Determine Dest	Relay Comm Pkts	<Comm Msg>

Figure 11.19 Requirements Evaluation (II)

State Before	Event	Action	Action Details	State After	Response
Relay Comm Pkts	<T&C>	[Perf Op]	1.1 Accept Raw Data 1.2 Deter Msg Type 3.1 Decode Op Code	Decode Optn	<Fire>
Decode Optn	<Comm Msg>	[Xmt Msg]	1.1 Accept Raw Data 1.2 Deter Msg Type 2.1 Analyze Comm Msg 2.2 Determine Dest	Relay Comm Pkts	<Comm Msg>
Relay Comm Pkts	<Fire>	[Thrust]	3.2 Process Fire Cmd 3.5 Update Fuel	Process Fire Cmd	<Fire>
Process Fire Cmd	<Comm Msg>	[Xmit Msg]	1.1 Accept Raw Data 1.2 Deter Msg Type 2.1 Analyze Comm Msg 2.2 Determine Dest	Relay Comm Pkts	<Comm Msg>

Figure 11.20 Requirements Evaluation (III)

State Before	Event	Action	Action Details	State After	Response
Relay Comm Pkts	<T&C>	[Perf Op]	1.1 Accept Raw Data 1.2 Deter Msg Type 3.1 Decode Op Code	Decode Optn	<Add Loc>
Decode Optn	<Comm Msg>	[Xmt Msg]	1.1 Accept Raw Data 1.2 Deter Msg Type 2.1 Analyze Comm Msg 2.2 Determine Dest	Relay Comm Pkts	<Comm Msg>
Relay Comm Pkts	<Add Loc>	[Update Table]	3.3 Update Lookup Table 3.4 Generate Ack	Update Lookup Table	<Ack Msg>
Update Lookup Table	<Comm Msg>	[Xmit Msg]	1.1 Accept Raw Data 1.2 Deter Msg Type 2.1 Analyze Comm Msg 2.2 Determine Dest	Relay Comm Pkts	<Comm Msg>

Figure 11.21 Requirements Evaluation (IV)

State Before	Event	Action	Action Details	State After	Response
Relay Comm Pkts	<T&C>	[Perf Op]	1.1 Accept Raw Data 1.2 Deter Msg Type 3.1 Decode Op Code	Decode Optn	<Fire>
Decode Optn	<T&C>	[Perf Op]	1.1 Accept Raw Data 1.2 Deter Msg Type 3.1 Decode Op Code	Decode Optn	<Fire>
Decode Optn	<Fire>	[Thrust]	3.2 Process Fire Cmd 3.5 Update Fuel	Process Fire Cmd	<Fire>
Process Fire Cmd	<Fire>	[Thrust]	3.2 Process Fire Cmd 3.5 Update Fuel	Process Fire Cmd	<Fire>
Process Fire Cmd	<Comm Msg>	[Xmt Msg]	1.1 Accept Raw Data 1.2 Deter Msg Type 2.1 Analyze Comm Msg 2.2 Determine Dest	Relay Comm Pkts	<Comm Msg>

Figure 11.22 Requirements Evaluation (V)

State Before	Event	Action	Action Details	State After	Response
Relay Comm Pkts	<T&C>	[Perf Op]	1.1 Accept Raw Data 1.2 Deter Msg Type 3.1 Decode Op Code	Decode Optn	<Fire>
Decode Optn	<T&C>	[Perf Op]	1.1 Accept Raw Data 1.2 Deter Msg Type 3.1 Decode Op Code	Decode Optn	<Add Loc>
Decode Optn	<Fire>	[Thrust]	3.2 Process Fire Cmd 3.5 Update Fuel	Process Fire Cmd	<Fire>
Process Fire Cmd	<Add Loc>	[Update Table]	3.3 Update Lookup Table 3.4 Generate Ack	Update Lookup Table	<Ack Msg>
Update Lookup Table	<Comm Msg>	[Xmt Msg]	1.1 Accept Raw Data 1.2 Deter Msg Data 2.1 Analyze Comm Msg 2.2 Determine test	Relay Comm Pkts	<Comm Msg>

Figure 11.23 Requirements Evaluation (VI)

State Before	Event	Action	Action Details	State After	Response
Relay Comm Pkts	<T&C>	[Perf Op]	1.1 Accept Raw Data 1.2 Deter Msg Type 3.1 Decode Op Code	Decode Optn	<Add Loc>
Decode Optn	<T&C>	[Perf Op]	1.1 Accept Raw Data 1.2 Deter Msg Type 3.1 Decode Op Code	Decode Optn	<Fire>
Decode Optn	<Add Loc>	[Update Table]	3.3 Update Lookup Table 3.4 Generate Ack	Update Lookup Table	<Ack Msg>
Update Lookup Table	<Fire>	[Thrust]	3.2 Process Fire Cmd 3.5 Update Final	Process Fire Cmd	<Fire>
Process Fire Cmd	<Comm Msg>	[Xmit Msg]	1.1 Accept Raw Data 1.2 Deter Msg Type 2.1 Analyze Comm Msg 2.2 Determine Test	Relay Comm Pkts	<Comm Msg>

Figure 11.24 Requirements Evaluation (VII)

State Before	Event	Action	Action Details	State After	Response
Relay Comm Pkts	<T&C>	[Perf Op]	1.1 Accept Raw Data 1.2 Deter Msg Type 3.1 Decode Op Code	Decode Optn	<Add Loc>
Decode Optn	<T&C>	[Perf Op]	1.1 Accept Raw Data 1.2 Deter Msg Type 3.1 Decode Op Code	Decode Optn	<Add Loc>
Decode Optn	<Add Loc>	[Update Table]	3.3 Update Lookup Table 3.4 Generate Ack	Update Lookup Table	<Ack Msg>
Update Lookup Table	<Add Loc>	[Update Table]	3.3 Update Lookup Table 3.4 Generate Ack	Update Lookup Table	<Ack Msg>
Update Lookup Table	<Comm Msg>	[Xmit Msg]	1.1 Accept Raw Data 1.2 Deter Msg Data 2.1 Analyze Comm Msg 2.2 Determine Dest	Relay Comm Pkts	<Comm Msg>

Figure 11.25 Requirements Evaluation (VIII)

11.18 ARCHITECTURE MODEL GENERATION

Describing a top level design (Figure 11.26) that effectively employs concurrent activity to satisfy both operational and implementor requirements consists of the following steps:

1. Enhance both functional and control requirements to accommodate specific hardware/technological interfaces;
2. Perform a consistency and completeness check of enhanced requirements against operational requirements;
3. Translate both functional and control requirements into a process architecture;
4. Perform a consistency and completeness check of the process architecture against operational requirements;
5. Evaluate architecture performance against timing constraints by combining timing allocations for requirements mapped into each architecture process; and
6. Allocate requirements within each architecture process to hardware and to software.

11.19 INTERFACE ENHANCED REQUIREMENTS

According to the problem specification, the solution to this problem is to include emulators for data sources and sinks (Figure 11.27). Moreover, implementation is to be completely software based within a stable file system. These constraints have been incorporated into the enhanced requirements specification in this figure.

Enhanced requirements are added to the first level of requirements, since this is the level at which the interface flows originally appeared. Input management requirements include generation of two sources of data—Generate Comm Msg (4) and Generate T&C Msg (5). Notice that the numbering scheme of the original requirements is maintained, sustaining traceability to the original requirements specification.

Output management requirements accommodate a single sink for the outgoing data. Each <Comm Msg> is transmitted to a new transformation which computes a transmission delay (6) and then suspends processing for the duration of the delay. A bandwidth is added to the <Comm Msg> within a child transformation of requirement 2, Analyze Packet Data. Message size is divided by this bandwidth to determine a required transmission delay. This description is incorporated into a PSPEC for the added requirement. After the transmission delay expires, the <Comm Msg> is emitted to the final output management requirement.

Subsequent to processing by child requirements of Perform Management Actions (3), response messages <Fire> and <Ack Msg> are also forwarded to the

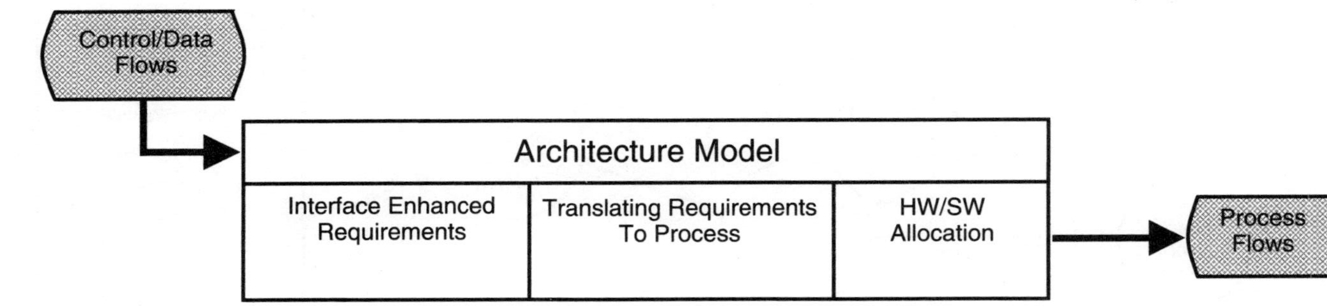

Figure 11.26 Architecture Model Generation

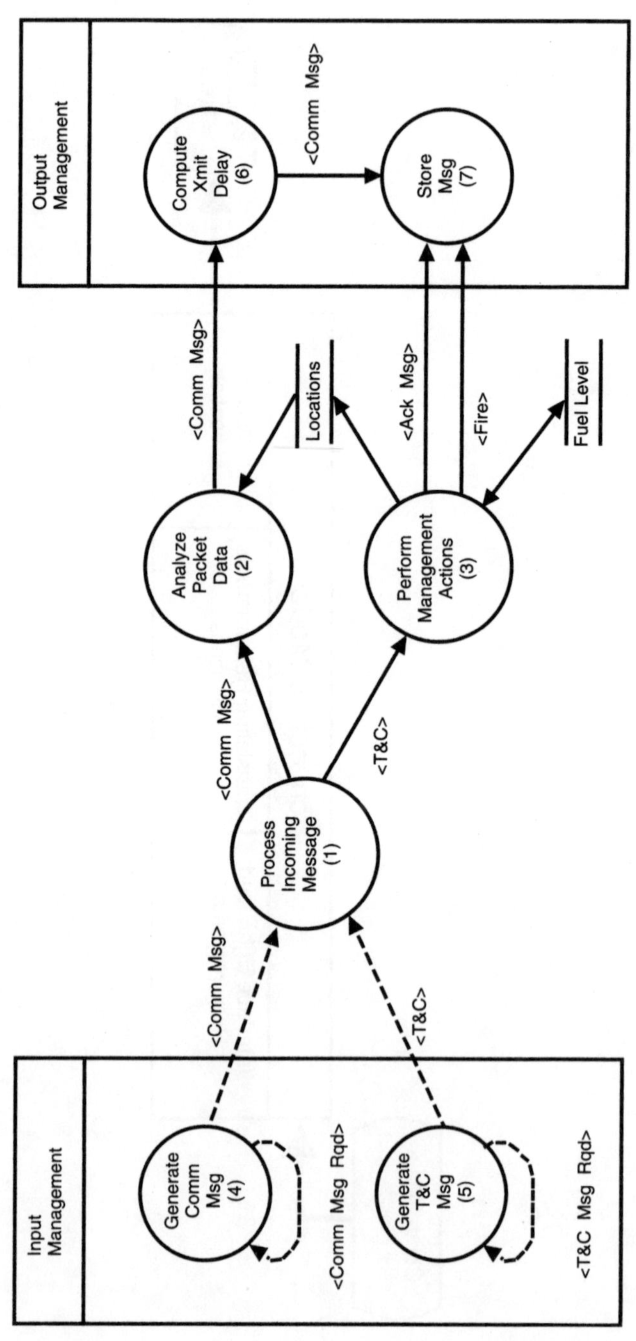

Figure 11.27 Interface Enhanced Requirements

same output management requirement. All outgoing messages enter the functional transformation named Store Msg (7). A PSPEC for this new requirement describes the manner in which all outgoing messages are stored into a sequential output file.

Requirements that describe mechanics of managing specific hardware interfaces are added here, if appropriate. However, constraints in this case do not require specific hardware interfaces. Reviewing the original problem description (these are customer specifications) indicates an all software solution. From this indication, a stable file environment is inferred. *Always refer to the original specification when in doubt or when taking the next methodological step.*

11.20 CSPEC: ENHANCED STATE TRANSITION DIAGRAM

If functional requirements change, control requirements which manage those functions must also be modified. Figure 11.28 contains the state transition diagram to manage the enhanced functional requirements. No new control flows/events have been added, so the state transition diagram does not change. However, to promote traceability, the original state transition diagram is incorporated into the enhanced requirements.

Often, the actual transition diagram is not carried forward. A "mental note" is registered to remember that the same transition diagram is to be employed. During integration and test activities, this "mental note" is likely to be overlooked, causing significant and unnecessary effort. One of the major goals of applying this methodology is to enforce a rigorous discipline in the recording of important decisions. Carrying forward a detailed specification such as the state transition diagram illustrates the importance of recording these "mental notes" to avoid later confusion.

11.21 CSPEC: ENHANCED PROCESS ACTIVATION TABLE

Adding functional requirements causes important changes in the process activation table portion of the CSPEC (Figure 11.29). Changes necessary to incorporate the new functional requirements appear in this figure. Rigorous requirements for concurrency appear in the table body. An explicit decision to require simultaneous operation of multiple functions places important constraints on future activities. By placing requirements for concurrent operations into the process activation table, system and software architects must insure that these concurrent operations are satisfied.

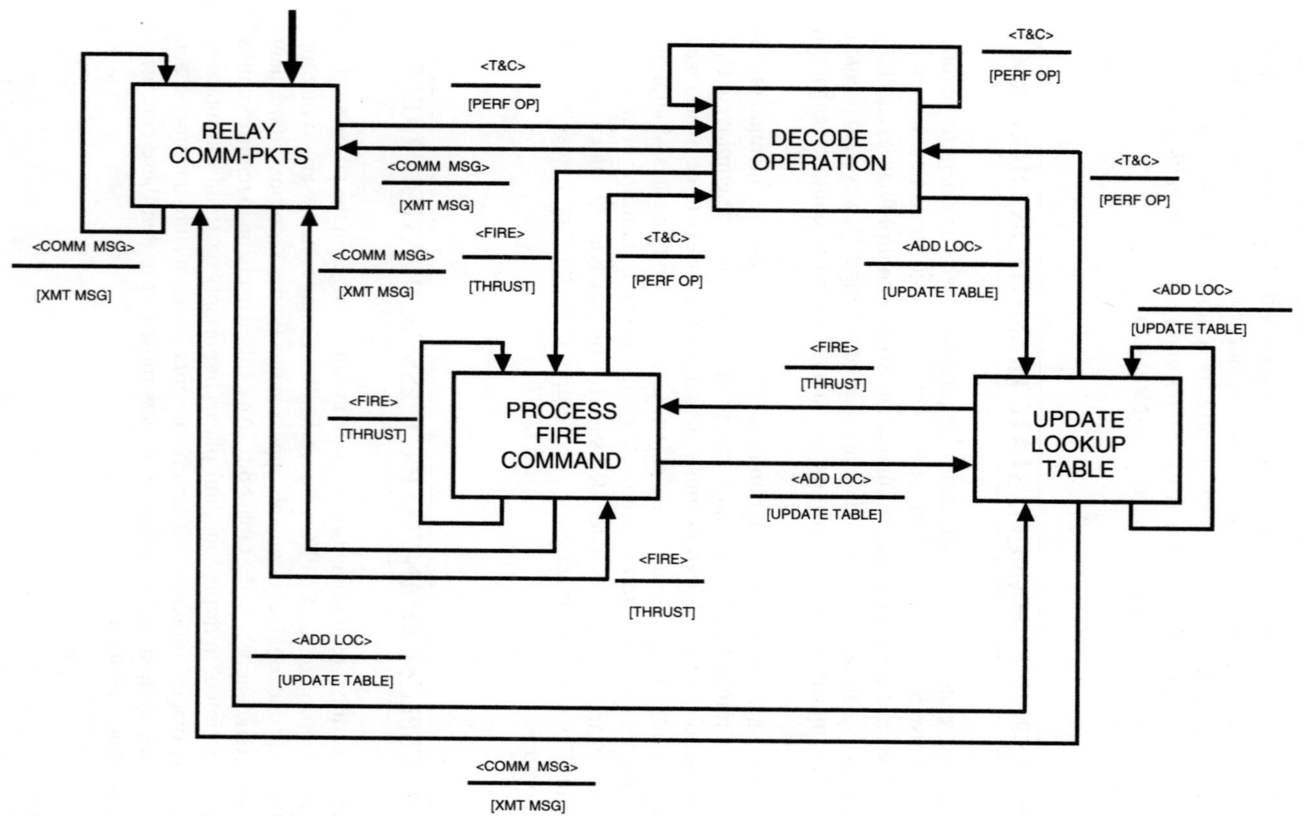

Figure 11.28 CSPEC: Enhanced State Transition Diagram

Leaf Rqmnt / Action	Generate Comm Msg 4	Generate T&C Msg 5	Accept Raw Data 1.1	Deter Msg Type 1.2	Analyze Comm Msg 2.1	Deter Dest 2.2	Decode Op Code 3.1	Process Fire Cmd 3.2	Update Lookup Table 3.3	Gen Ack 3.4	Update Fuel 3.5	Compute Xmit Delay 6	Store Msg 7
Xmt Msg	1		1	2	3	4						5	6
Perf OP		1	1	2			3						
Thrust								1			2		3
Update Table									1	2			3

Figure 11.29 CSPEC: Enhanced Process Activation Table

Consider the [Xmt Msg] action in the first row of the table. Performing this action requires that the following functions occur in parallel:

1. Generate Comm Msg (4) and
   Accept Raw Data (1.1);

In other words, the current <Comm Msg> event is accepted into the system while the next event is being generated. Once the current event is accepted, a sequence of transformations follows:

2. Deter Msg Type (1.2);
3. Analyze Comm Msg (2.1);
4. Deter Dest (2.2);
5. Compute Xmit Delay (6); and
6. Store Msg (7).

This response is significantly expanded over the original response to a <Comm Msg>. Such an expanded response is necessary to incorporate the functionality of the enhanced requirements. In the original process activation table, details of action [Xmt Msg] included only functions 1.1, 1.2, 2.1, and 2.2. Even more than the previous process activation table, this expanded table clearly illustrates how a response can span the requirements tree in a complex manner.

Responses to <T&C> events are incorporated into the action named [Perf Op]. As specified in the table, this requires concurrency as part of the detailed response. As with [Xmt Msg], the current response is accepted while regeneration of the <T&C> arrival process (5 and 1.1 both contain the entry 1 in the body of the PAT) is accomplished. Requiring that both transformations occur simultaneously is a judgement call based upon the experience of the architect in developing this class of systems. Certainly, these responses could be handled sequentially. However, according to the architect's understanding of the workings of satellite control systems, a sequential response is not likely to produce the operational performance normally desired for satellite control systems. Requiring simultaneous acceptance of a current event with regeneration of the event input stream is more likely to accurately capture operational behavior of satellite control systems and is incorporated into the process activation table. This decision is binding upon future architecture decisions. Somewhere in the remaining development process, specific design decisions must assure that these concurrency requirements are satisfied.

11.22 ENHANCED REQUIREMENTS EVALUATION (I–VIII)

Since requirements have changed, a new requirements evaluation must be performed. As before, the purpose is to identify and eliminate potentially incomplete and inconsistent specifications prior to subsequent decision making (Figure 11.30 to 11.37).

Incorporating concurrency into the evaluation of event responses requires a slight change in notational specification. Indication of simultaneous responses employs the conjunction "and," highlighted by an encapsulating circle. As did the previous requirements simulation, evaluation begins with the satellite control system in its initial state, Relay Comm Pkts, and proceeds to verify the first event/response combination contained in the test input/output pattern. Stepping through the evaluation, the first table entry contains exactly the same entries as the evaluation prior to requirements enhancement with the exception of the Action Details column. This column contains data associated with the expanded process activation table and incorporates the new PSPECs added to the action details characterizing event responses.

In the first figure, evaluation of the enhanced control and functional requirements to the first event—<T&C>—is accomplished. The following entries are contained in the Action Details column for this first event:

5 Generate T&C Msg *and*
1.1 Accept Raw Data
1.2 Deter Msg Type
3.1 Decode Op Code

Both 5 and 1.1 occur simultaneously, as indicated by the existence of the "and" connective. Message type is determined (1.2), and the internal <Fire> event is generated (3.1) subsequent to acceptance of the current event. All occurrences of <Comm Msg> events and <T&C> events within the original test input/output pattern exhibit this simultaneous response mechanism.

Completeness of the response specifications in the process activation table is verified since a state transition exists for each event in the test input/output pattern and all transitions are tested. Consistency is also confirmed. All event streams that require regeneration are refreshed as part of the response. Regeneration is consistently accomplished in parallel while processing the current event. All responses are stored in the same output file.

Since the Action Detail column is often the only column which changes (reflecting a modified process activation table), this evaluation is often not redone. This is a mistake. Recording the effects of changes is extremely important for complex systems, no matter how obvious the changes may appear to be to the software engineer. Again, enforcement of the recording discipline is an important part of the communications process, informing others of implications that may be obvious to one person but not obvious to another.

State Before	Event	Action	Action Details	State After	Response
Relay Comm Pkts	<T&C>	[Perf Op]	5 Generate T&C Msg (and) 1.1 Accept Raw Data 1.2 Deter Msg Type 3.1 Decode Op Code	Decode Optn	<Fire>
Decode Optn	<Fire>	[Thrust]	3.2 Process Fire Cmd 3.5 Update Fuel 7 Store Msg	Process Fire Cmd	<Fire>
Process Fire Cmd	<T&C>	[Perf Op]	5 Generate T&C Msg (and) 1.1 Accept Raw Data 1.2 Deter Msg Type 3.1 Decode Op Code	Decode Optn	<Add Loc>
Decode Optn	<Add Loc>	[Update Table]	3.3 Update Lookup Table 3.4 Generate Ack 7 Store Msg		<Ack Msg>
Update Lookup Table	<Comm Msg>	[Xmt Msg]	4 Generate Comm Msg (and) 1.1 Accept Raw Data 1.2 Deter Msg Type 2.1 Analyze Comm Msg 2.2 Determine Dest 6 Compute Xmit Delay 7 Store Msg	Relay Comm Pkts	<Comm Msg>

Figure 11.30 Enhanced Requirements Evaluation (I)

State Before	Event	Action	Action Details	State After	Response
Relay Comm Pkts	<Comm Msg>	[Xmt Msg]	4 Generate Comm Msg (and) 1.1 Accept Raw Data 1.2 Deter Msg Type 2.1 Analyze Comm Msg 2.2 Determine Dest	Relay Comm Pkts	<Comm Msg>
Relay Comm Pkts	<T&C>	[Perf Op]	5 Generate T&C Msg (and) 1.1 Accept Raw Data 1.2 Deter Msg Type 3.1 Decode Op Code	Decode Optn	<Add Loc>
Decode Optn	<Add Loc>	[Update Table]	3.3 Update Lookup Table 3.4 Generate Ack 7 Store Msg	Update Lookup Table	<Ack Msg>
Update Lookup Table	<T&C>	[Perf Op]	5 Generate T&C Msg (and) 1.1 Accept Raw Data 1.2 Deter Msg Type 3.1 Decode Op Code	Decode Optn	<Fire>
Decode Optn	<Fire>	[Thrust]	3.2 Process Fire Cmd 3.5 Update Fuel 7 Store Msg	Process Fire Cmd	<Fire>
Process Fire Cmd	<Comm Msg>	[Xmt Msg]	4 Generate Comm Msg (and) 1.1 Accept Raw Data 1.2 Deter Msg Type 2.1 Analyze Comm Msg 2.2 Determine Dest 6 Compute Xmit Delay 7 Store Msg	Relay Comm Pkts	<Comm Msg>

Figure 11.31 Enhanced Requirements Evaluation (II)

State Before	Event	Action	Action Details	State After	Response
Relay Comm Pkts	<T&C>	[Perf Op]	5 Generate T&C Msg (and) 1.1 Accept Raw Data 1.2 Deter Msg Type 3.1 Decode Op Code	Decode Optn	<Fire>
Decode Optn	<Comm Msg>	[Xmt Msg]	4 Generate Comm Msg (and) 1.1 Accept Raw Data 1.2 Deter Msg Type 2.1 Analyze Comm Msg 2.2 Deter Dest 6 Compute Xmit Delay 7 Store Msg	Relay Comm Pkts	<Comm Msg>
Relay Comm Pkts	<Fire>	[Thrust]	3.2 Process Fire Cmd 3.5 Update Fuel 7 Store Msg	Process Fire Cmd	<Fire>
Process Fire Cmd	<Comm Msg>	[Xmt Msg]	4 Generate Comm Msg (and) 1.1 Accept Raw Data 1.2 Deter Msg Type 2.1 Analyze Comm Msg 2.2 Deter Dest 6 Compute Xmit Delay 7 Store Msg	Relay Comm Pkts	<Comm Msg>

Figure 11.32 Enhanced Requirements Evaluation (III)

State Before	Event	Action	Action Details	State After	Response
Relay Comm Pkts	<T&C>	[Perf Op]	5 Generate T&C Msg (and) 1.1 Accept Raw Data 1.2 Deter Msg Type 3.1 Decode Op Code	Decode Optn	<Add Loc>
Decode Optn	<Comm Msg>	[Xmt Msg]	4 Generate Comm Msg (and) 1.1 Accept Raw Data 1.2 Deter Msg Type 2.1 Analyze Comm Msg 2.2 Deter Dest 6 Compute Xmt Delay 7 Store Msg	Relay Comm Pkts	<Comm Msg>
Relay Comm Pkts	<Add Loc>	[Update Table]	3.3 Update Lookup Table 3.4 Generate Ack 7 Store Msg	Update Loopup Table	<Ack Msg>
Update Lookup Table	<Comm Msg>	[Xmt Msg]	4 Generate Comm Msg (and) 1.1 Accept Raw Data 1.2 Deter Msg Type 2.1 Analyze Comm Msg 2.2 Deter Dest 6 Compute Xmt Delay 7 Store Msg	Relay Comm Pkts	<Comm Msg>

Figure 11.33 Enhanced Requirements Evaluation (IV)

State Before	Event	Action	Action Details	State After	Response
Relay Comm Pkts	<T&C>	[Perf Op]	5 Generate T&C Msg (and) 1.1 Accept Raw Data 1.2 Deter Msg Type 3.1 Decode Op Code	Decode Optn	<Fire>
Decode Optn	<T&C>	[Perf Op]	5 Generate T&C Msg (and) 1.1 Accept Raw Data 1.2 Deter Msg Type 3.1 Decode Op Code	Decode Optn	<Fire>
Decode Optn	<Fire>	[Thrust]	3.2 Process Fire Cmd 3.5 Update Fuel 7 Store Msg	Process Fire Cmd	<Fire>
Process Fire Cmd	<Fire>	[Thrust]	3.2 Process Fire Cmd 3.5 Update Fuel 7 Store Msg	Process Fire Cmd	<Fire>
Process Fire Cmd	<Comm Msg>	[Xmt Msg]	4 Generate Comm Msg (and) 1.1 Accept Raw Data 1.2 Deter Msg Type 2.1 Analyze Comm Msg 2.2 Determine Dest 6 Compute Xmit Delay 7 Store Msg	Relay Comm Pkts	<Comm Msg>

Figure 11.34 Enhanced Requirements Evaluation (V)

State Before	Event	Action	Action Details	State After	Response
Relay Comm Pkts	<T&C>	[Perf Op]	5 Generate T&C Msg (and) 1.1 Accept Raw Data 1.2 Deter Msg Type 3.1 Decode Op Code	Decode Optn	<Fire>
Decode Optn	<T&C>	[Perf Op]	5 Generate T&C Msg (and) 1.1 Accept Raw Data 1.2 Deter Msg Type 3.1 Decode Op Code	Decode Optn	<Add Loc>
Decode Optn	<Fire>	[Thrust]	3.2 Process Fire Cmd 3.5 Update Fuel 7 Store Msg	Process Fire Cmd	<Fire>
Process Fire Cmd	<Add Loc>	[Update Table]	3.3 Update Lookup Table 3.4 Generate Ack 7 Store Msg	Update Lookup Table	<Ack Msg>
Update Lookup Table	<Comm Msg>	[Xmt Msg]	4 Generate Comm Msg (and) 1.1 Accept Raw Data 1.2 Deter Msg Data 2.1 Analyze Comm Msg 2.2 Determine Dest 6 Compute Xmit Delay 7 Store Msg	Relay Comm Pkts	<Comm Msg>

Figure 11.35 Enhanced Requirements Evaluation (VI)

State Before	Event	Action	Action Details	State After	Response
Relay Comm Pkts	<T&C>	[Perf Op]	5 Generate T&C Msg (and) 1.1 Accept Raw Data 1.2 Deter Msg Type 3.1 Decode Op Code	Decode Optn	<Add Loc>
Decode Optn	<T&C>	[Perf Op]	5 Generate T&C Msg (and) 1.1 Accept Raw Data 1.2 Deter Msg Type 3.1 Decode Op Code	Decode Optn	<Fire>
Decode Optn	<Add Loc>	[Update Table]	3.3 Update Lookup Table 3.4 Generate Ack 7 Store Msg	Update Lookup Table	<Ack Msg>
Update Lookup Table	<Fire>	[Thrust]	3.2 Process Fire Cmd 3.5 Update Final 7 Store Msg	Process Fire Cmd	<Fire>
Process Fire Cmd	<Comm Msg>	[Xmt Msg]	4 Generate Comm Msg (and) 1.1 Accept Raw Data 1.2 Deter Msg Type 2.1 Analyze Comm Msg 2.2 Deter Dest 6 Compute Xmit Delay 7 Store Msg	Relay Comm Pkts	<Comm Msg>

Figure 11.36 Enhanced Requirements Evaluation (VII)

State Before	Event	Action	Action Details	State After	Response
Relay Comm Pkts	<T&C>	[Perf Op]	5 Generate T&C Msg (and) 1.1 Accept Raw Data 1.2 Deter Msg Type 3.1 Decode Op Code	Decode Optn	<Add Loc>
Decode Optn	<T&C>	[Perf Op]	5 Generate T&C Msg (and) 1.1 Accept Raw Data 1.2 Deter Msg Type 3.1 Decode Op Code	Decode Optn	<Add Loc>
Decode Optn	<Add Loc>	[Update Table]	3.3 Update Lookup Table 3.4 Generate Ack 7 Store Msg	Update Lookup Table	<Ack Msg>
Update Lookup Table	<Add Loc>	[Update Table]	3.3 Update Lookup Table 3.4 Generate Ack 7 Store Msg	Update Lookup Table	<Ack Msg>
Update Lookup Table	<Comm Msg>	[Xmt Msg]	4 Generate Comm Msg (and) 1.1 Accept Raw Data 1.2 Deter Msg Data 2.1 Analyze Comm Msg 2.2 Deter Dest 6 Compute Xmit Delay 7 Store Msg	Relay Comm Pkts	<Comm Msg>

Figure 11.37 Enhanced Requirements Evaluation (VIII)

11.23 SUMMARY OF ARCHITECTURAL APPROACHES

Four major architectural alternative approaches are presented and evaluated within this case (Figure 11.38). These specific alternatives are chosen to illustrate the potential range of solutions and to reflect the kinds of approaches observed on a large number of projects.

In general, each architecture adopts a specific strategy relative to the use of concurrency and the amount and level of control. Typically, the architectures tend to reduce the amount of physical concurrency by increasing the amount of logical control. Increasing the amount of logical control is accomplished by application of two specific heuristics involving hierarchical and centralized control. The first heuristic introduces a hierarchical control concept in which control interactions are strictly limited to precise parent and child control processes. Limited control interaction serves to reduce the operational or behavioral complexity of the architecture, decreasing the level of integration and test effort required. A second heuristic involves maximizing the size of state transition diagrams and process activation tables allocated to a single process controller. Adopting this heuristic improves the flexibility of the architecture by allowing table driven designs for control, which are easily modified. Additionally, this maximized table approach also aids in reducing integration and test effort by localizing the symptoms of erroneous behavior. Rather than allowing operations to continue so that symptoms emerge in an architectural location different from the problem location, localized symptoms are immediately spotted; processing is halted at the problem location.

Several control concepts are employed within the architectures. A decentralized approach implies that each architecture process determines the next recipient of the results. A distributed, hierarchical approach suggests strict limits on interaction of controls, but with some next recipient decisions embedded within specific architecture processes. A final approach, named centralized hierarchical, employs strict limits on control interaction with most processing and decision logic embedded within a dominant controller. Centralized, hierarchical architectures are preferred to obtain flexibility and to result in reduced levels of integration and test effort.

While at first glance excessive effort (at least for software) may seem to be devoted to analysis of architectures, this effort is quite justified. Decisions made during the determination of architectures have a major impact on development activities that follow. Architectural decisions can make the software developer's future efforts easy or difficult, depending on the flexibility and complexity of the chosen architecture. Each of these implications is discussed in detail for individual architectures.

Alternative	Concurrency Complexity	Control Complexity
#1	Extremely High	Decentralized
#2	Moderate	Distributed Hierarchical
#3	Low	Centralized Hierarchical
#4	Lowest	Centralized Hierarchical

Figure 11.38 Summary of Architectural Approaches

11.24 ARCHITECTURE ALTERNATIVE-1

In this alternative, each functional requirement is mapped to a single architecture process (Figure 11.39). Software logic within each process determines the next destination of any data flow. Movement of data through the architecture is complicated and difficult to trace. Process interactions are labeled by straight lines, indicating that initiation decisions are deferred until a tasking architecture is generated. This approach is often referred to as a data-driven architecture. Flow of data through the architecture controls operation of architectural entities.

Consider the architecture process named Comm Msg Analyzer. As indicated, this process simply performs the requirement numbered 2.1—Analyze Comm Msg. For this process to perform operationally, embedded software is implemented which has the following structure:

```
loop
 collect incoming message;
  case ( message ) is
   when <Comm Msg> =>
     extract destination, forward to Destination
                                      Determiner;
     temporarily store <Comm Msg>;
   when <Bandwidth> =>
     retrieve <Comm Msg> from temporary storage;
     concatenate to <Comm Msg>, forward to Delay
                                      Calculator;
  end case;
end loop;
```

The pseudocode for this approach raises a number of important issues. For instance, a strategy must be adopted to manage <Comm Msg> while waiting for its bandwidth to be returned. If bandwidth is lost, causing original <Comm Msg> entries to become out of synch with incoming bandwidths, a specific recovery strategy must be specified.

Determination of end-to-end data flow can be complex, if not impossible. As an example, consider the sequence of process interactions that represent end-to-end processing of <Comm Msg> events. Starting from its source, a <Comm Msg> event moves through the following processes:

Comm Msg Generator
Raw Data Acceptor
Msg Type Determiner
Comm Msg Analyzer
Destination Determiner
Comm Msg Analyzer
Delay Calculator
Message Storer

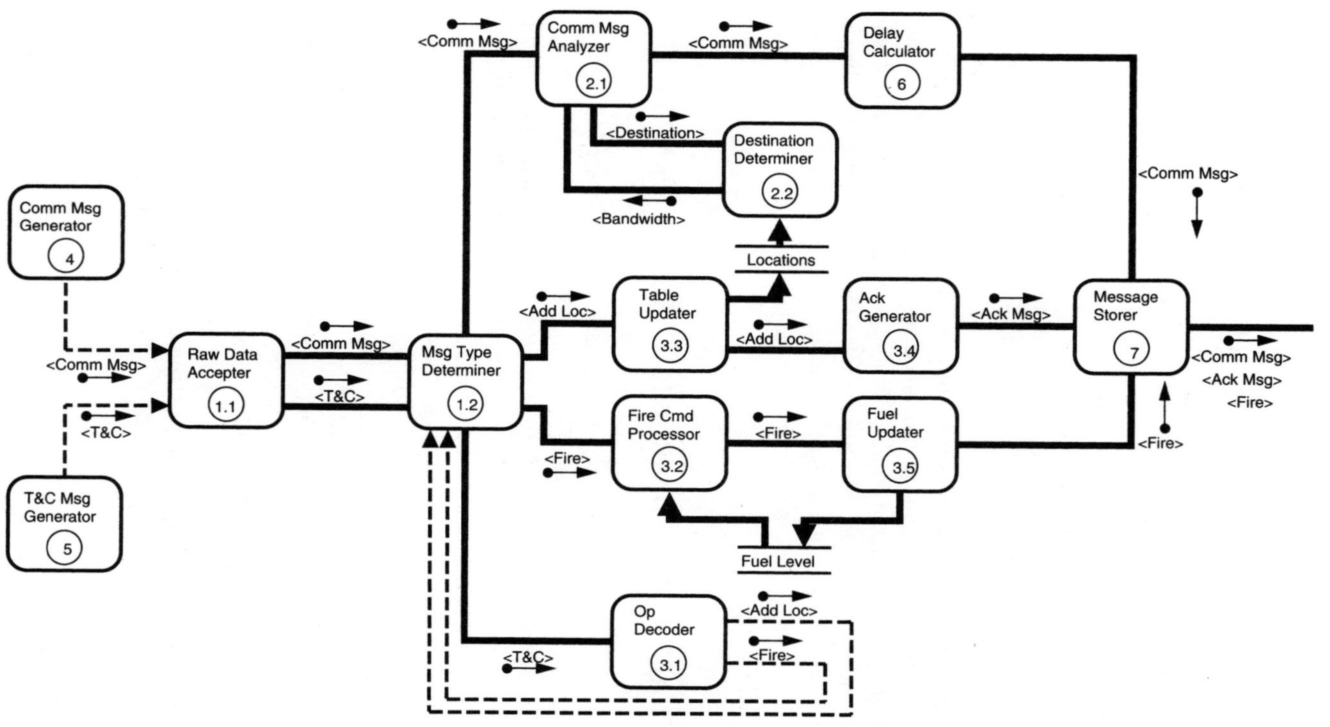

Figure 11.39 Process Architecture Alternative-1

Response to a <Comm Msg> event flows through Comm Msg Analyzer twice to complete its end-to-end response. Debugging is difficult under these circumstances as a result of this response complexity.

11.25 REQUIREMENTS TRACEABILITY (1)

As the size of this table indicates (Figure 11.40), each requirement is mapped to a single architecture process. This introduces significant concurrency complexity into the architecture, involving a large number of intermitting concurrent processes with significant synchronization problems.

Another aspect of this architecture is quite visible from the table. No entries appear for the elements of the state transition diagram and process activation table. In fact, control is broken into small pieces, completely spread across the set of architecture processes. No limits are placed on control complexity. Control interactions are not constrained to a few specific processes. Typically, when this architectural paradigm is employed, the number of process interactions is extreme. Moreover, decision logic is spread across and hidden throughout the processes. As a result, debugging errors during integration and test is a difficult and time consuming activity resulting in cost and schedule overruns.

11.26 EVALUATION OF ARCHITECTURE ALTERNATIVE-1

Application of the heuristic architecture evaluation criteria described in the text reveals some important implications affecting the acceptability of this architecture (Figure 11.41). Performance is likely to be quite poor. Movement of data through the architecture requires an extensive number of process interactions. Each interaction consumes resources that detract from actual work being performed in the satellite control system. As a result, a satellite control system (or any system, for that matter) that employs this architecture is likely to experience poor throughput.

Another area where this architecture tends to have high costs is in terms of integration and test effort. As illustrated above, end-to-end movement of data is likely to involve a significant number of interacting processes. As the number of process interactions increases, ability to detect and resolve problems during integration and test decreases. Typically, decreased problem resolution ability translates directly into greater effort and into schedule slips. More people have to work longer hours to identify and to resolve the problem, as more processes are integrated to obtain a working system. In other words, more complex systems are more difficult to integrate.

Requirements / Arch Process	Generate Comm Msg 4	Generate T&C Msg 5	Accept Raw Data 1.1	Deter Msg Type 1.2	Analyze Comm Msg 2.1	Deter Dest 2.2	Decode Op Code 3.1	Process Fire Cmd 3.2	Update Lookup Table 3.3	Gen Ack 3.4	Update Fuel 3.5	Compute Xmit Delay 6	Store Msg 7	STD, PAT
Comm Msg Generator	X													
T&C Msg Generator		X												
Raw Data Acceptor			X											
Msg Type Determiner				X										
Comm Msg Analyzer					X									
Delay Calculator												X		
Destination Determiner						X								
Table Updater									X					
Ack Generator										X				
Fire Cmd Processor								X			X			
Fuel Updater														
Op Decoder							X							
Message Storer													X	

Figure 11.40 Requirements Traceability (1)

General Justification:	Data Driven Processes Translate Each Function to a Single Process
Poor Performance:	Significant Interprocess Communications
Significant Integration and Test Effort:	Too Many Interacting Processes
Low Reliability:	No Control Established Synchronization of Data Flow a Significant Problem
Decentralized Control Concept:	No Coordination Anywhere in Architecture Data Flow Controlled by Logic Hidden in Each Process
Low Flexibility:	Incorporation of New Requirements Causes Major Architecture Changes
Low Traceability:	Control Aspects Completely Lost
Low Portability:	Excessive Concurrency Complexity Failure To Encapsulate HW Interfaces

Likely Very Heavy HW Dependence or OS Services Dependence To Achieve Throughput, Further Degrading Flexibility

SW Will Likely Be Required To Make the System Work and Will Likely Receive the Blame When System Does Not Work

Figure 11.41 Evaluation of Architecture Alternative-1

This architecture, when implemented, is quite likely to exhibit extremely poor reliability. With no limits on control complexity and due to distributed control/ decision making within each process, an architecture typically does not behave correctly. Distributed decision making in systems of this complexity usually results in faulty implementations based upon implementor assumptions or lack of system visibility. Implementors responsible for each process are usually unaware of the impacts of their individual decision logics upon system behavior. So, incorrect decisions are implemented. Improper decision logic (handling of synchronization requirements and data storage issues) leads to unreliable behavior by the system. Sometimes the satellite control system works; sometimes not. Unfortunately, an incorrect decision often leads to further integration and test effort. Incorrect decision logic within this architectural approach can cause improper or incorrect data to be forwarded, so that symptoms appear in an architecture at a location other than where the problem is caused. Identification of this situation, correlation to the actual process causing the problem, and problem resolution require excessive effort.

From a flexibility perspective, this architecture does fare well. Incorporation of new requirements is difficult and tedious. New processes must be added, old processes deleted. This usually translates into addition and elimination of hardware components. (Recall that an architecture process *must* operate in parallel in the final implementation.) In other words, changing requirements involves major architectural changes, requiring significant levels of integration and test effort. If changes involve control specifications as they often do when adding complex sensor modes, old decision logic must be deleted. New decision logic must be inserted. Since decision logic is spread throughout the architecture, these kinds of changes lead to insidious and often malicious behavior on the part of changes in the implementation. Changing event response logic under these circumstances is often a time-consuming, hit or miss activity. An architecture that employs this amount of concurrency complexity with no control interaction constraints is quite inflexible.

Traceability is poorly supported in this architecture. While traceability to functional requirements is maximized (one architecture process per functional requirement), no traceability is achieved for control requirements. For complex systems, maximum reduction of integration and test effort is obtained by tight traceability to control requirements. Reliability and flexibility are also obtained. Therefore, complete lack of traceability for control requirements is an important cause of all the shortcomings discussed so far.

With an architecture of this type, portability is quite difficult to obtain. Architectures such as the one envisioned here usually require global access to data structures to work at all. Excessive concurrency complexity is the cause. Without global access to data, all data must be moved during process interaction, further reducing throughput. Global access to data usually requires capabilities provided by hardware interface services or target environment services. Global access to services such as these means that these services are not encapsulated or hidden. As a result, visible knowledge is propagated throughout the architecture. Changing the target platform requires changing all these globally visible references. Sometimes, whole architectures have to be changed to port to a new target platform. All of this involves significant redesign and testing, suggesting that portability across target platforms is difficult to achieve.

Due to the high number of concurrent processes, significant dependence on hardware support or operating system support is usually necessary to achieve high throughput. Typically, one processor is necessary for each architecture process. Unfortunately, recent studies show that adding processors works only to a point. After this, overhead of interprocessor communications typically works to further reduce throughput, even with a larger number of processors. Greater dependence on hardware to achieve throughput also reduces flexibility within the architecture.

This is an extremely poor architectural alternative, which is best avoided at all costs. As a result of all the negative implications described above, significant amounts of intelligent software are necessary to make this architecture perform properly. Implementation of a little "tricky" software is not really likely to solve many of the problems. However, software usually receives the blame for missed schedules and budgets. In fact, the problem is the poor system architecture approach represented by alternative 1.

11.27 PROCESS ARCHITECTURE EVALUATION (1-I, 1-II)

As indicated in the body of the text, an architecture evaluation is performed to correlate the architecture to a user's view of system operation (Figure 11.42 to 11.43). Each event in the test input/output pattern is traced completely through the architecture to demonstrate that the corresponding responses are emitted. Individual event/response combinations are separated by dashed lines.

In the first row of the test input/output pattern, a <T&C> event arrives at the external interface to the satellite control system. As depicted in the architecture process flow diagram, this event enters the satellite control system from the Comm Msg Generator. From the latter emerges a <T&C> flow, which moves into the Raw Data Acceptor. This flow is then transferred to the Msg Type Determiner. Once received by the Msg Type Determiner, the <T&C> data is then transmitted to the Op Decoder. As a result of processing within the Op Decoder, an internal <Fire> event is emitted. Comparison with the test input/output pattern reveals that this is indeed the desired response.

Verification of the second event/response combination from the test input/output pattern appears in the next section of the table. When combined together, the two evaluations illustrate an important aspect of system behavior for real-time systems. Multiple events may be necessary for an external response to occur. This "wave" of multiple events causes internal events to be generated or internal data stores to be updated. Once the series of events has provided all the necessary data and information flow, an externally observed response is created and observed.Evaluation of this wave-like pattern is necessary to gain real insight into the dynamic behavior of the satellite control system (or any system), and is one of the key benefits obtained from generation of this kind of table.

Control Input	Internal Data Flow	Architecture Process	Internal Data Flow	Response
<T&C>	—	Comm Msg Generator	<T&C>	—
—	<T&C>	Raw Data Acceptor	<T&C>	—
—	<T&C>	Msg Type Determiner	<T&C>	—
—	<T&C>	Op Decoder	—	<Fire>
<Fire>	—	Msg Type Determiner	<Fire>	—
—	<Fire>	Fire Cmd Processor	<Fire>	—
—	<Fire>	Fuel Updater	<Fire>	Update Fuel Level
—	<Fire>	Message Storer	—	<Fire>
<T&C>	—	T&C Msg Generator	<T&C>	—
—	<T&C>	Raw Data Acceptor	<T&C>	—
—	<T&C>	Msg Type Determiner	<T&C>	—
—	<T&C>	Op Decoder	—	<Add Loc>
<Add Loc>	—	Msg Type Determiner	<Add Loc>	—
—	<Add Loc>	Table Updater	<Add Loc>	Update Locations
—	<Add Loc>	Ack Generator	<Ack Msg>	—
—	<Add Msg>	Message Storer	—	<Ack Msg>

Figure 11.42 Process Architecture Evaluation (1-I)

Control Input	Internal Data Flow	Architecture Process	Internal Data Flow	Response
<Comm Msg>	—	Comm Msg Generator	<Comm Msg>	—
—	<Comm Msg>	Raw Data Acceptor	<Comm Msg>	—
—	<Comm Msg>	Msg Type Determiner	<Comm Msg>	—
—	<Comm Msg>	Comm Msg Analyzer	<Destination>	—
—	<Destination>	Destination Determiner	<Bandwidth>	—
—	<Bandwidth>	Comm Msg Analyzer	<Comm Msg>	—
—	<Comm Msg>	Delay Calculator	<Comm Msg>	—
—	<Comm Msg>	Message Storer	—	<Comm Msg>

Note: For an actual system, remainder of test input/output pattern should be evaluated.

Figure 11.43 Process Architecture Evaluation (1-II)

Only a portion of the test input/output pattern has been evaluated in these figures. For the sequences described in the event scenario, all other evaluations would look exactly the same. However, in the case of a more realistic system, data embedded within the events is likely to cause different paths through the architecture to result. Therefore, with a more realistic system, the whole test input/output pattern is evaluated by this method.

11.28 ARCHITECTURE ALTERNATIVE-2

With this architecture, a more realistic attempt is made at managing complexity of control interactions (Figure 11.44). Consistent with the requirements in the enhanced process activation table, separate architecture processes are employed for message sources. Both Comm Msg and T&C Msg Generators appear as architectural processes. A Message Manager architecture process incorporates primary decision making and internal event generation activities. Specific processes oriented towards managing unique, problem-oriented entities are employed within this architecture. Each <Comm Msg> is handled by a Comm Msg Manager process. Adding entries to the Locations table is accomplished by a Table Update Manager process. Management of the Fuel Level data store and issuance of <Fire> commands to the thrusters are managed by the Fire Cmd Manager process.

Processes within this architecture use a mix of table-driven and cyclic, command-driven implementation approaches. Processes that manage problem oriented activities—Comm Msg Manager, Table Update Manager, and Fire Cmd Manager—use a cyclic, command-driven implementation, which directly employs the specific requirements mapped to the process. As an example, consider the Comm Msg Manager. According to the illustration, PSPECs 2.1, 2.2, and 6 are allocated to this process. Implementation of this process includes some kind of cyclic executive that incorporates the following logic:

```
loop
 collect next incoming <Comm Msg>;
 analyze comm msg;           --  2.1
 determine destination;      --  2.2
 compute xmit delay;         --  6
 forward <Comm Msg> to Msg Storer;
end loop;
```

This logic still incorporates some of the sequencing of the process activation table, implemented directly into the architecture process.

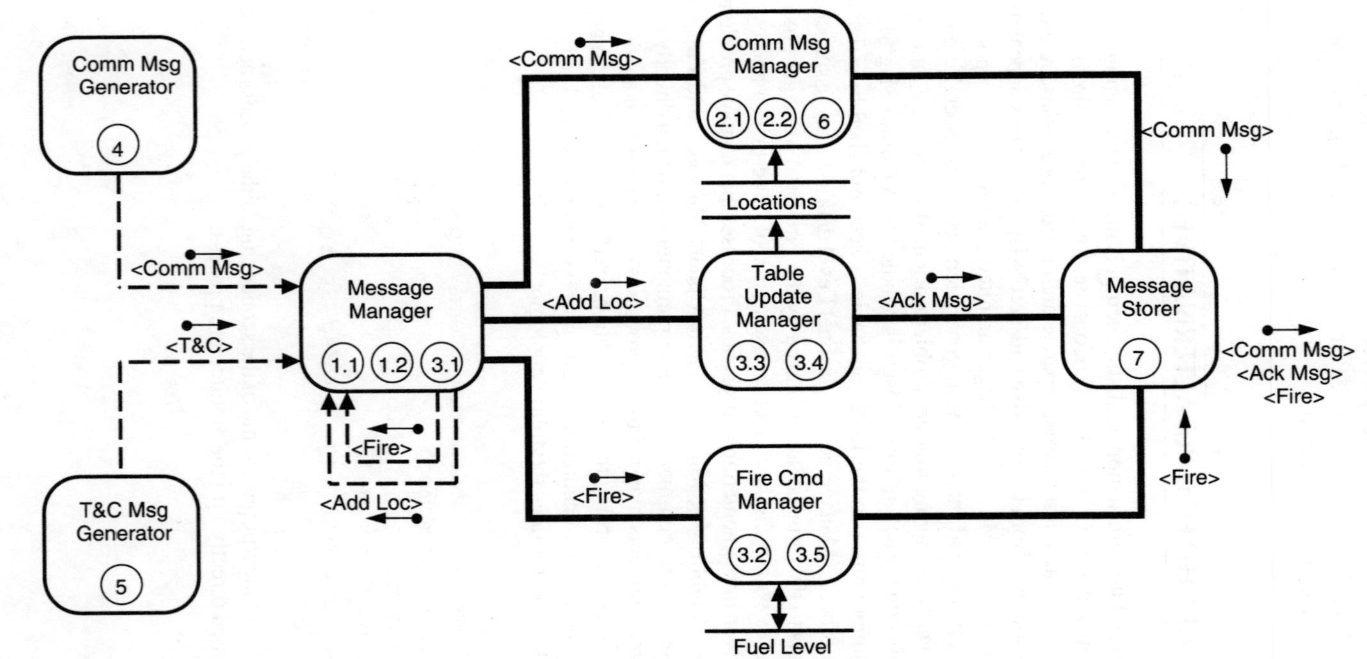

Figure 11.44 Process Architecture Alternative-2

11.29 MESSAGE MANAGER ALLOCATION OF CSPECS

By comparison, some portion of the CSPECs are directly allocated to the Message Manager process. Subsets of the CSPEC allocated to the Message Manager are indicated by the labels STD-1 and PAT-1 in Figure 11.45. Specifically, those decision-making requirements oriented towards converting external events into internal events are maintained as part of the logic of the requirements allocated to the Message Manager process.

Specific processing control logic implemented within Message Manager is easily implemented in a more table driven format, based on the allocation of the state transition diagram/process activation table. Specific logic employed is as follows:

```
loop
 collect incoming message;
 case ( message ) is
  when <Comm Msg> | <T&C> =>
   determine action name from STD-1;
   determine response from PAT-1 using action name;
   perform response using PSPECs listed as response;
    -- 1.1, 1.2, 3.1
   update state using STD-1;
   if <T&C> then
     forward internal event to Message Manager;
   end if;
   if <Comm Msg> then
     forward <Comm Msg> to Comm Msg Manager;
   end if;
  when <Fire> =>
   forward <Fire> to Fire Cmd Manager;
  when <Add Loc> =>
   forward <Add Loc> to Table Update Manager;
  end case;
end loop;
```

Any response returned from the process activation table, PAT-1, is in the form of a list of PSPECs. If [Xmt Msg] is the action name, then the PSPEC list is 1.1, 1.2. Similarly, the PSPEC list 1.1, 1.2, 3.1 is the response determined by PAT-1 for the action named [Perf Op]. Details of these PSPECs are actually executed in the order listed. No assumptions are made regarding software or hardware implementation at this point. Either all hardware circuitry, combined hardware/firmware, or all software solutions can be employed with varying impacts.

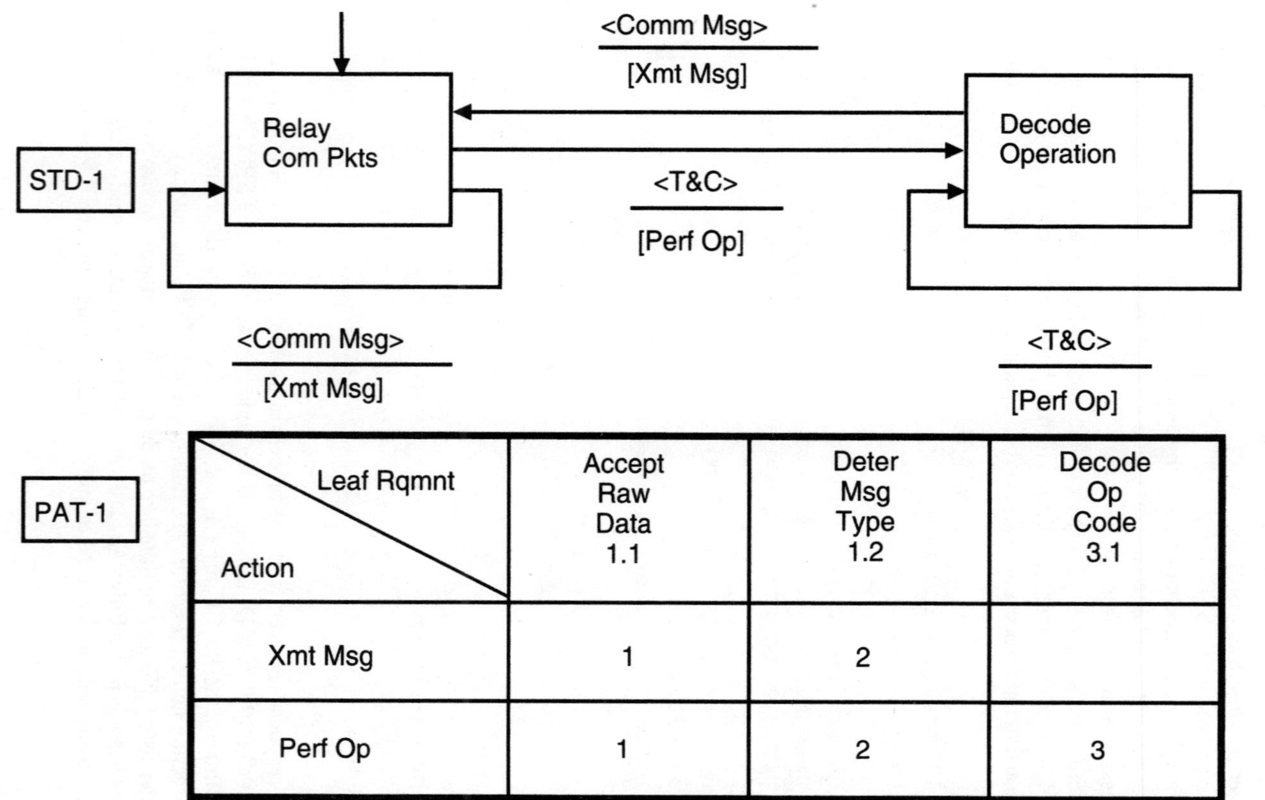

Action \ Leaf Rqmnt	Accept Raw Data 1.1	Deter Msg Type 1.2	Decode Op Code 3.1
Xmt Msg	1	2	
Perf Op	1	2	3

Figure 11.45 Message Manager: Allocation of CSPECs

11.30 REQUIREMENTS TRACEABILITY (2)

While the reduced complexity is obvious from the architecture process diagram, Figure 11.46 reinforces the reduction in complexity. A significantly smaller traceability matrix is obtained in comparison with the matrix for architecture alternative-1. Moreover, the column labeled "STD, PAT" now contains the entry "1," indicating the allocation of STD, PAT subset 1 to the Message Manager. Better traceability to control requirements is achieved, in addition to reduced concurrency and control complexity in the architecture.

11.31 EVALUATION OF ARCHITECTURE ALTERNATIVE-2

This architecture is typical of the kind offered when an "object-orientation" is assumed early in the development process (Figure 11.47). Specific architecture processes are employed for handling interfaces, control, and analysis. If fact, an approach such as this architecture can be effective if the analysis functions are computationally intensive. However, several negative aspects derived from evaluation of this architecture suggest that perhaps another approach might be more fruitful.

Performance under this architecture is likely to be moderate, at best. Some of the concurrency complexity is definitely reduced. For the small work level associated with the analysis functions (table updating, table lookups, reducing fuel levels), interprocess communication overhead is likely to swamp the computation time devoted to analysis functions. In simple terms, this architecture still carries too much interprocess communication overhead relative to the computational complexity of the algorithms.

Due to the reduced number of concurrent processes and as a result of the lesser complexity of control interactions, some relief is obtained in the level of integration and test effort. Fewer possible paths through the architecture indicate fewer potential problems in moving data through the architecture during routine operations, resulting in reduced integration and test effort.

As an architecture, a distinct improvement is obtained in the realm of control. Better utilization is made of the preferred hierarchical control concept. A Message Manager interacts with input interface managers and analysis/application managers. Analysis managers interact with either the Message Manager or the output interface manager (Message Storer). Thus, a hierarchy of control interactions is established, as follows:

Requirements / Arch Process	Generate Comm Msg 4	Generate T&C Msg 5	Accept Raw Data 1.1	Deter Msg Type 1.2	Analyze Comm Msg 2.1	Deter Dest 2.2	Decode Op Code 3.1	Process Fire Cmd 3.2	Update Lookup Table 3.3	Gen Ack 3.4	Update Fuel 3.5	Compute Xmit Delay 6	Store Msg 7	STD, PAT
Comm Msg Generator	X													
T&C Msg Generator		X												
Message Manager			X	X			X							1
Comm Msg Manager					X	X						X		
Table Update Manager									X	X				
Fire Cmd Manager								X			X			
Message Storer													X	

Figure 11.46 Requirements Traceability (2)

General Justification:	Independent Handling of Interfaces, Control, and Analysis Can Be Effective for Computationally Intensive Analysis Typical "Object-Oriented" Design
Moderate Performance:	More Interprocess Communication vs. Concurrent Operations
Moderate Effort For Int & Test:	Separation of Control and Analysis (Fire Cmds, etc)
High Reliability:	Once Control Centers Established, Repetitive Ops Stable
Hierarchical Control Concept:	Message Manager Application/Interfaces Some Tables in Message Manager, Some Sequencing of PSPECs
Moderate Flexibility:	Some Event Response Logic Centralized In Message Manager
High Traceability:	Requirements Clearly Partitioned, Allocated Among Control, Analysis, Interfaces

Moderate Portability Depending on Use of HW To Achieve Throughput

Likely Heavy HW Dependence To Achieve High Throughput Reducing Flexibility

SW Dependence Suggests Table Driven Implementation of Controller (STD, PAT) and Encapsulation of HW Interfaces Sender SW Abstractions

Figure 11.47 Evaluation of Architecture Alternative-2

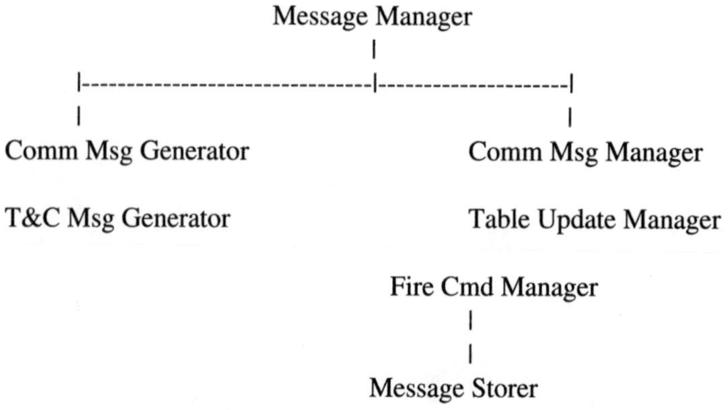

These are the only control interactions allowed. Limitations on control interactions, such as those exhibited by this architecture, are an important guideline for defining an architecture that eases the integration and test burden. However, this is not the only aspect of control management that must be observed.

Since some central logic is centralized within tables in the Message Manager, moderate flexibility is achieved by this architecture. Greater flexibility could be obtained if the control tables are made larger. Unfortunately, due to the spreading of the process activation table across the processes, more extensive architecture flexibility is unattainable.

Since an increased amount of the control logic is centralized, traceability is improved. Moreover, clearly partitioning architecture processes among control, analysis, and interfaces serves to alleviate some of the loss in clarity caused by the breakup of the process activation table. As a result, this architecture barely obtains slightly improved traceability.

An important gain for this architectural alternative is in the area of reliability. Once hierarchical control centers are implemented and center interactions are tested, routine operations are quite stable. Therefore, this architecture exhibits a high degree of reliability.

Depending on use of hardware, moderate portability can be attributed to this architecture. Clarity derived from partitioning requirements among interfaces, analysis, and control is a major contributor to portability. Isolation of interface management allows encapsulation of actual interface mechanics and protocols. This architecture can evolve to new target platforms with a small level of effort. Portability is accomplished by modifying the interface management activities strictly within the confines of specific processes allocated to interface management.

As a result of the continued high amount of interprocess communications and corresponding reduced throughput, significant use of hardware is likely to be necessary to assure reasonable response times. Extensive hardware use may not be a problem if analysis functions are so computationally complex that hardware support is needed anyhow. However, use of extra hardware to achieve high throughput levels results in lowered flexibility, poorer portability, and less reliability, since more hardware and software are typically integrated.

Isolation of control and interface management into separate processes suggests several important software design approaches. Flexibility is best obtained by using a table-driven software controller within the Message Manager process to incorporate both STDs and PATs. Actual implementation of interface managers encapsulates hardware interfaces beneath software abstractions to gain the moderate portability benefits suggested earlier.

On the whole, this architectural alternative is not optimal for a number of reasons. Flexibility is moderate due to small control tables. Integration and test effort are high due to the extensive concurrency complexity and hardware dependence. Low portability also results from hardware dependence. Perhaps this architecture is most appropriate when analysis functions are so computationally intensive that hardware support is necessary to achieve throughput.

11.32 PROCESS ARCHITECTURE EVALUATION (2)

Evaluation of the first portion of the test input/output pattern against the process architecture reveals the significant complexity reduction obtained by this architecture (Figure 11.48). Fewer interprocess interactions are needed to move data completely through the architecture. This table is significantly smaller than the table for the previous architecture.

The first event in the test input/output pattern consists of a <T&C> event. This event moves from the T&C Message Generator process into the Message Manager. After processing by the Message Manager, an internal <Fire> event emerges. Only two processes are necessary to verify the first complete entry in the test input/output pattern, compared to four architecture processes employed in architecture alternative-1. Evaluation of each of the remaining elements in the test input/output pattern generally indicates that fewer architectural processes are employed in generating the end-to-end response associated with a specific input event.

As in the evaluation of the previous architectural alternative, both data store updates and outgoing responses are indicated in this evaluation. Each appears next to the process in which the activity occurs. In this architecture, however, data stores are updated by processes whose primary motivation is to manage access to a specific data store. As a result, data store management activities are less likely to become lost or forgotten during implementation. Direct support is provided for an object-oriented approach that encapsulates data objects, easing the level of effort associated with maintenance and modification activities.

Control Input	Internal Data Flow	Architecture Process	Internal Data Flow	Response
<T&C>	—	T&C Message Generator	<T&C>	—
—	<T&C>	Message Manager	—	<Fire>
<Fire>	—	Message Manager	<Fire>	—
—	<Fire>	Fire Cmd Manager	<Fire>	Update Fuel Level
—	<Fire>	Message Storer	—	<Fire>
<T&C>	—	T&C Message Generator	<T&C>	—
—	<T&C>	Message Manager	—	<Add Loc>
<Add Loc>	—	Message Manager	<Add Loc>	—
—	<Add Loc>	Table Update Manager	<Ack Msg>	Update Locations
—	<Ack Msg>	Message Storer	—	<Ack Msg>
<Comm Msg>	—	Comm Msg Generator	<Comm Msg>	—
—	<Comm Msg>	Message Manager	<Comm Msg>	—
—	<Comm Msg>	Comm Msg Manager	<Comm Msg>	—
—	<Comm Msg>	Message Storer	—	<Comm Msg>

Note: For an actual system, remainder of test input/output pattern should be evaluated.

Figure 11.48 Process Architecture Evaluation (2)

11.33 ARCHITECTURE ALTERNATIVE-3

As a further aid to reduce the concurrency complexity, this architecture employs an event-intensive approach (Figure 11.49). Architectural processes are not derived from a direct correlation to specific entities within the requirements. Architecture processes that emphasize generic event management tend to be much more effective. A large majority of successfully implemented control systems employ an architecture that utilizes processes defined in this architecture. Thus, this is an experience based architecture rather than an object based architecture.

Primarily, most of the functionality associated with event processing is allocated to a specific architectural process—the System Controller process. Message source generation is also allocated to a single architectural process, named Message Storer. Response storage activity appears within the single process entitled Message Storer.

Two additional processes which do not directly correlate to specific functional requirements are included. For the most part, introducing additional processes not directly correlated to requirements leads to both poor performance and low reliability, and is to be discouraged. However, if addition of the architectural process is appropriate to the experience of the software engineer, then its inclusion is not prohibited but is carefully and clearly justified. In this situation, experience with concurrent processing systems indicates that obtaining true concurrency within separate architecture processes requires use of buffers. Buffers can be implemented in either software or hardware. No decisions are made yet in this regard.

Another important decision is the allocation of message generation functions to a single architectural process. The enhanced PAT indicated that message generation functions must operate concurrently with other functions. For concurrent operations of these functions to occur within a single architectural process, software tasking is employed. Architecture processes translate into a single CPU or into software tasks on a shared CPU. Employing multiple CPUs to implement a single architectural process usually results in a hardware architecture that is overly complex and extremely difficult to integrate and test.

As with the previous architecture, individual processes employ a mix of table-driven and cyclic executive controllers. However, the complexity of each of these controllers is changed dramatically. Within the SC process, a greater dependence upon the STD and the PATs is obtained. Larger tables in SC translate into simpler cyclic executives in the remaining processes. Detailed knowledge of sequences embedded within the PAT are not implemented within the cyclic executives.

Logic within the Message Generator consists of a simple cyclic executive, characterized by the following pseudocode:

```
loop
  delay until next message is to be emitted;
  emit next message;
end loop;
```

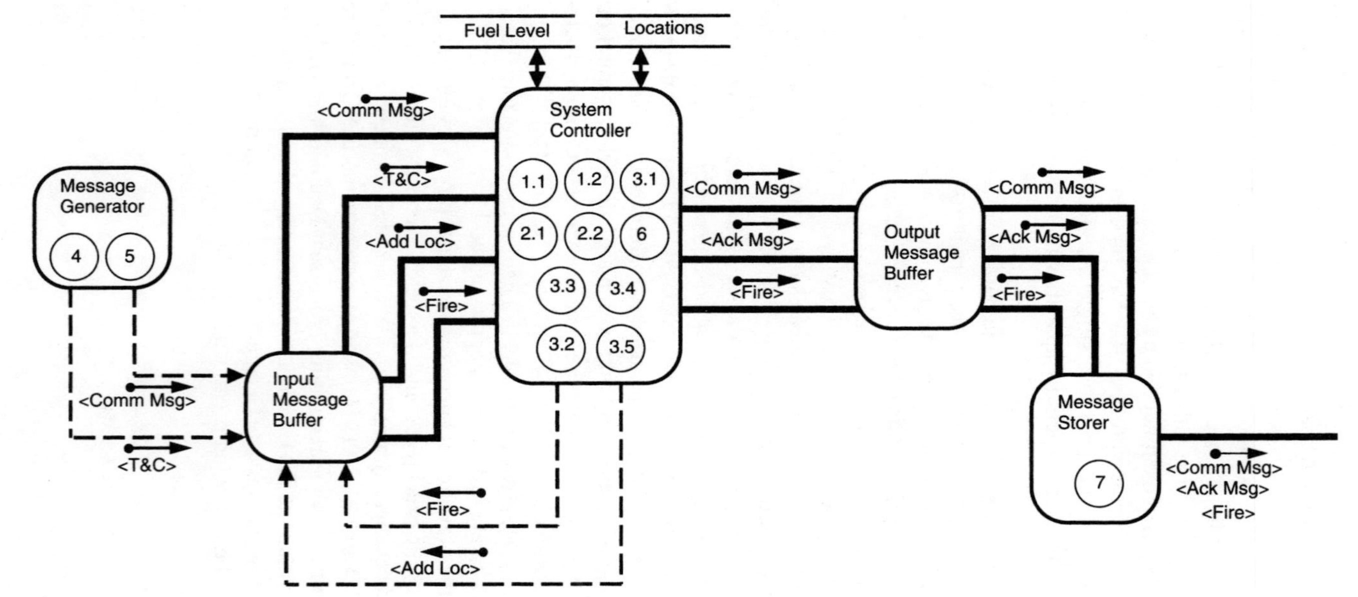

Figure 11.49 Process Architecture Alternative-3

This logic represents a single column extracted from the enhanced process activation table and translated into code. A similar internal logical structure is employed within the Message Storer, Input Message Buffer, and Output Message Buffer processes.

11.34 SYSTEM CONTROLLER: ALLOCATION OF CSPECS (1)

Figure 11.50 portrays the portion of the STD allocated to the SC process. This STD is labeled as STD-2, as denoted within the diagram, to distinguish between the original STD, the version allocated previously to Message Manager (STD-1), and this variation. A quick comparison with the enhanced CSPECs reveals that this is the entire STD. With so few architectural processes, most of which employ the simple internal control logic described above, maximum allocation of control requirements to a single process is easily accomplished.

By comparison with the Message Manager of Alternative-2, this is a much larger allocation of the state transition diagram to a single architectural process.

11.35 SYSTEM CONTROLLER: ALLOCATION OF CSPECS (2)

Since only three columns of the enhanced PAT are partitioned to architecture processes (requirements 4, 5, 7), a substantial portion of the PAT is allocated to the SC (Figure 11.51). This table is also assigned a different label—PAT-2—for purposes of distinction. An important benefit of this allocation is to maintain sequencing logic of event responses within a single large table—the process activation table—as opposed to hiding logic describing event response as hard wired code under architecture processes. Large tables allow sequencing logic to be treated as data rather than as implemented software or firmware in hundreds of "hidden" locations across the architecture. Centralized data tables are much easier to modify than distributed, hard-coded logic.

Specific processing control logic implemented within System Controller is easily implemented in a more table-driven format, based on this extensive STD/PAT allocation. Specific logic is employed as follows:

```
loop
  collect incoming message;
  determine response to message from STD-2;
  perform response to message using PAT-2;
  transition to state determined by message
                                    using STD-2;
end loop;
```

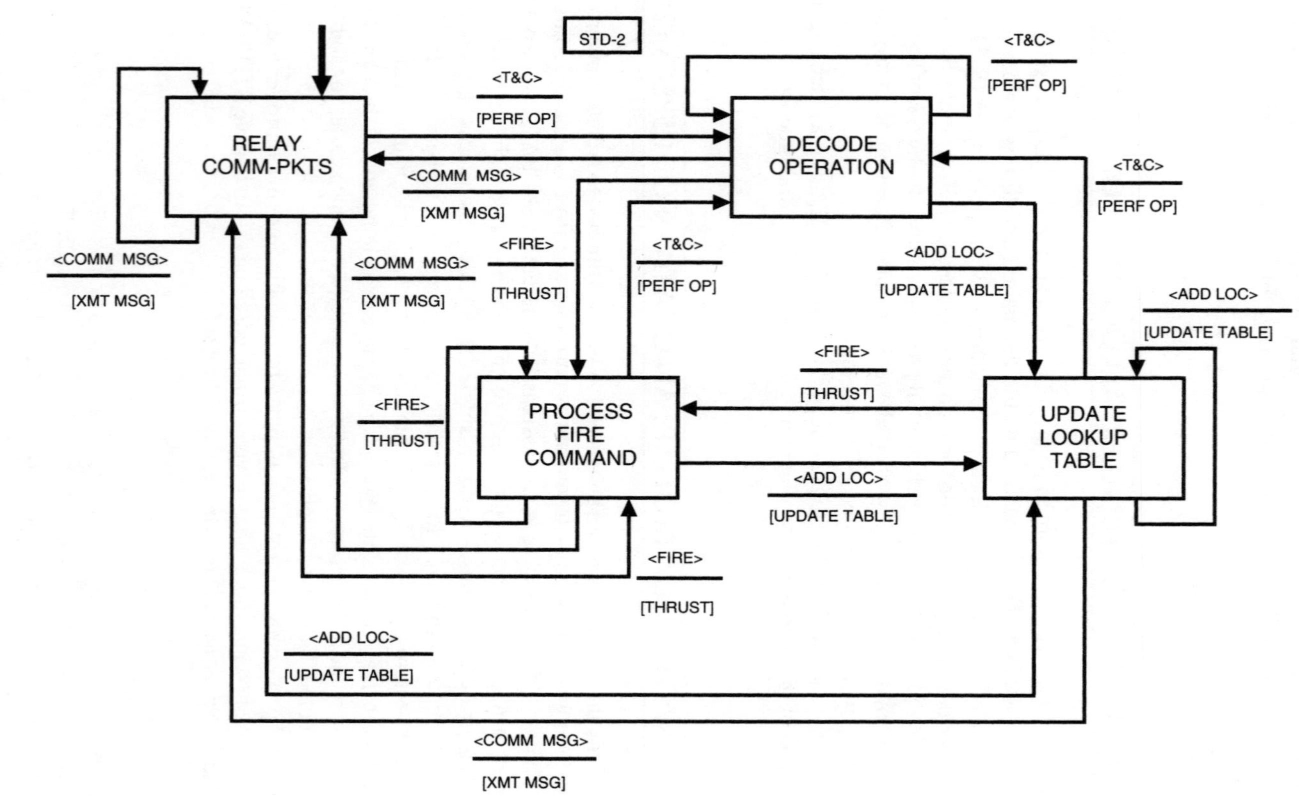

Figure 11.50 System Controller: Allocation of CSPECs (1)

PAT–2

Rqmnt / Action	Accept Raw Data 1.1	Deter Msg Type 1.2	Analyze Comm Msg 2.1	Deter Dest 2.2	Decode Op Code 3.1	Process Fire Cmd 3.2	Update Lookup Table 3.3	Gen Ack 3.4	Update Fuel 3.5	Compute Xmit Delay 6
Xmt Msg	1	2	3	4						5
Perf Op	1	2			3					
Thrust						1			2	
Update Table							1	2		

Figure 11.51 System Controller: Allocation of CSPECs (2)

Details of specific PSPECs listed as the response in the PAT employ incoming message/event contents to update data stores, to generate outgoing responses, or to generate internal events. Changes to the event response logic are easily incorporated into the architecture. Typically, incorporating changes requires changing STD and PAT contents and modifying some of the code that implements PSPECs. Major changes to operational requirements are isolated to a single architectural process and restricted primarily to updating data tables with minimal coding and integration and test effort.

11.36 REQUIREMENTS TRACEABILITY (3)

With fewer architecture processes, a much smaller, more easily evaluated requirements traceability table is generated (Figure 11.52). Most of the requirements are allocated to a single row of the matrix. Clearly, all requirements, including the control specifications, are satisfied within the architecture. Moreover, this clarity demonstrates that no requirements are too complex, since no requirement appears to be allocated to multiple architecture processes.

11.37 EVALUATION OF ARCHITECTURE ALTERNATIVE-3

In general, this architecture is motivated by two specific goals that dictate its specific processes and requirements allocation (Figure 11.53). Control interactions are minimized, while centralized control is maximized within the SC. This combination leads to significantly favorable evaluations using the suggested architecture evaluation criteria.

This particular architecture performs quite well, depending upon the computational complexity of the PSPECs implemented within the System Controller. With fewer concurrent processes, less interprocessor communication overhead is necessary to obtain end-to-end throughput of data. Thus, response times are high. For control-based systems, which primarily manage tables and generate messages, computational complexity of PSPECs is usually low, suggesting the appropriateness of this architecture. Moreover, including buffers accommodates concurrency, allowing work to be accomplished in parallel and further contributing to high throughput operations by this architecture.

Hierarchical control is definitely employed to the maximum possible extent within this architecture. SC interacts only with buffer processes. Buffer processes interact with interface management processes. Interface management processes interact solely with the devices managed and with buffer processes. This control hierarchy is depicted as follows:

Requirements / Arch Process	Generate Comm Msg 4	Generate T&C Msg 5	Accept Raw Data 1.1	Deter Msg Type 1.2	Analyze Comm Msg 2.1	Deter Dest 2.2	Decode Op Code 3.1	Process Fire Cmd 3.2	Update Lookup Table 3.3	Gen Ack 3.4	Update Fuel 3.5	Compute Xmit Delay 6	Store Msg 7	STD, PAT
Message Generator	X	X												
Input Message Buffer														
System Controller			X	X	X	X	X	X	X	X	X	X		2
Output Message Buffer														
Message Storer													X	

Figure 11.52 Requirements Traceability (3)

General Justification: Minimum Concurrency with Maximum Centralized Control

Moderate to High Performance Depending on Computational Intensity of PSPECs in System Control
Inclusion of Buffers Maximizes Effectiveness of Concurrency

Low to Moderate Int and Test Effort Depending On HW Dependence

Extremely High Reliability Once Control Implemented and Tested

Control Concept: Hierarchical Control—System/Buffers/Interfaces
Max Centralized Control—STD/PAT Allocated To System Controller

High Traceability Due to Separation Between Control (large tables) and I/F Management

High Flexibility if Table Driven SW Design Employed For System Controller

High Portability: Low Concurrency Complexity
Encapsulation of HW Interfaces

HW Dependence: Inclusion of Buffers at Arch Level Implies
Potential Allocation to HW To Achieve Higher Throughput

SW Dependence: Suggest Table Driven System Controller
Potential for High Usage of Tasking, Improving Portability

Figure 11-53 Evaluation of Architecture Alternative-3

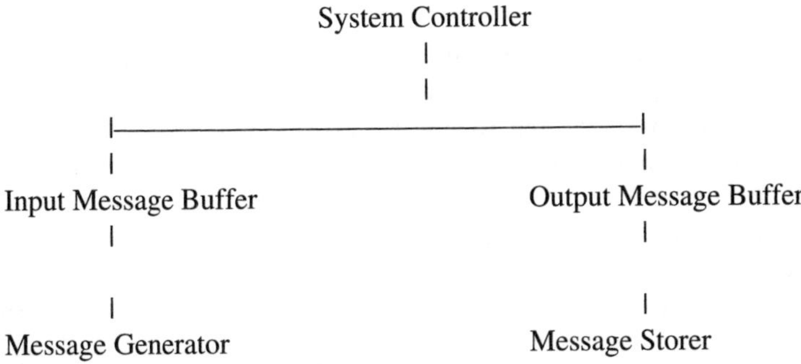

Significant restrictions are placed on the potential control interactions of individual processes. This restriction on control interactions is one of the highest leverage approaches to effectively manage subsequent development activities, allowing an incremental strategy to be described later.

Centralized control is also maximized with this architecture. Achieving centralized control is evidenced by the size of the STD and PAT tables allocated to the System Controller process. Incorporation of sequencing logic in the PAT allows sequencing logic to be treated as data within a table, rather than being hidden in code pockets all over the architecture. Distributed sequencing logic is difficult to debug and even more difficult to modify. Modification involves locating, modifying and testing changes to all the distribution software decision logic—a time consuming and frustrating task. Maximizing centralized control serves to reduce both debugging and modification effort.

As a result of limited control interactions combined with maximum centralized control, integration and test efforts are significantly reduced, further reducing both cost and schedule. Less hardware and software need to be integrated. Fewer potential process interactions eliminate a large number of potential operational problems. Centralized control removes those hidden "gotcha's" due to misinterpretation or lost sequencing of event response logic, phenomena which usually occur during implementation of distributed decision making. These benefits result in reduced integration and test effort.

An architecture such as this exhibits high reliability. Once controllers in each process are initially implemented and integrated (without functional details), repetitive operational behavior is extremely stable. Both limited complexity and the constrained number of control interactions contribute to stable, repetitive operations. Integrating control activities is accomplished by testing to assure that all the possible but limited interactions are accommodated by the implementation. No detailed functionality is necessary to test control structures. Stable control structures are obtained by testing the capability of interacting implementations to pass representative data across hardware interfaces. Control structure stability assures reliability during repetitive operations.

High traceability is obtained by this architecture. Most of the control requirements trace to specific tables in a single architectural process. Functional processing is also easily and explicitly traced to individual architectural processes. Most of the PSPECs managed by the tables are allocated to the System Controller process.

A table-driven approach to software design within the System Controller leads to easy modification of both event responses and functional details. Changes are accommodated by modifying data tables and by changing a few PSPEC implementations, all within a single architecture process. Other architectures typically require identifying appropriate changes in multiple processes, making the changes, and extensive and tedious integration and test activities to incorporate new capabilities.

Significant portability is obtained by this architecture. Typically, using fewer concurrent processes results in less explicit reliance on target platform capabilities. Reduced reliance on target hardware increases the portability of the implemented architecture. Moreover, by isolating interfaces to the target platform within explicit architecture processes (Message Generator, Message Storer), changes in target platform lead to isolated changes to the interface management processes. Changes induced by a modified target platform are restricted to specific, carefully isolated architecture processes.

An important aspect of hardware/software dependence is incorporated into the architecture by explicit inclusion of buffers. Representation of buffers at the process level allows the use of either hardware buffers to obtain speed or software buffers to allow more flexibility with somewhat reduced performance. Software concurrency always reduces performance but allows flexibility and portability, especially when Ada is the source language. In fact, this architecture can not be implemented without software concurrency, if the original requirements are to be met. Message Generator includes two requirements that must operate in parallel, according to the enhanced process activation table. Simultaneous operations of the two requirements, in combination with the desire to obtain architectural flexibility, strongly suggest that a software tasking based approach needs to be employed.

11.38 PROCESS ARCHITECTURE EVALUATION (3)

Evaluation of the first portion of the test input/output pattern against the architecture reveals even greater reduced complexity obtained by this architecture. Significantly fewer interprocess interactions are necessary to move data completely through the architecture. This table is also significantly smaller.

The first event in the test input/output pattern consists of a <T&C> event. This event moves from the T&C Message Generator process into the Input Message Buffer. When ready, the System Controller extracts the event from the Input Message Buffer and, in response, generates an internal <Fire> event. Three processes are involved in verifying the first complete entry in the test input/output pattern, compared to two architecture processes employed in architecture alternative-2. The extra process is the cost of flexibility and performance in the architecture. However, evaluation of each of the remaining elements in the test input/output pattern generally indicates that the exact same set of architectural processes are employed

Control Input	Internal Data Flow	Architecture Process	Internal Data Flow	Response
<T&C>	—	Message Generator	<T&C>	—
—	<T&C>	Input Message Buffer	<T&C>	—
—	<T&C>	System Controller	—	<Fire>
<Fire>	—	Input Message Buffer	<Fire>	—
—	<Fire>	System Controller	<Fire>	Update Fuel Level
—	<Fire>	Output Message Buffer	<Fire>	—
—	<Fire>	Message Storer	—	<Fire>
<T&C>	—	Message Generator	<T&C>	—
—	<T&C>	Input Message Buffer	<T&C>	—
—	<T&C>	System Controller	—	<Add Loc>
<Add Loc>	—	Input Message Buffer	<Add Loc>	—
—	<Add Loc>	System Controller	<Ack Msg>	Update Locations
—	<Ack Msg>	Output Message Buffer	<Ack Msg>	—
—	<Ack Msg>	Message Storer	—	<Ack Msg>
<Comm Msg>	—	Message Generator	<Comm Msg>	—
—	<Comm Msg>	Input Message Buffer	<Comm Msg>	—
—	<Comm Msg>	System Controller	<Comm Msg>	—
—	<Comm Msg>	Output Message Buffer	<Comm Msg>	—
—	<Comm Msg>	Message Storer	—	<Comm Msg>

Note: For an actual system, remainder of test input/output pattern should be evaluated.

Figure 11.54 Process Architecture Evaluation (3)

in generating the response associated with a specific input event, almost regardless of the type of event. This stability of response reflects the significantly greater constraints on control interactions and results in the greater reliability and reduced integration and test effort of this alternative architecture.

Both data store updates and outgoing responses are indicated next to the process in which the activity occurs. In this architecture, however, data stores are updated by processes whose primary motivation is to manage access to a specific data store. Thus, data store management activities are even less likely to become lost or forgotten during implementation. Using processes to manage data stores supports an object-oriented approach that emphasizes only encapsulation of data objects to limit visibility of internal data structures. Limited data structure visibility conforms to the best principles of information hiding, and is easily implemented in Ada using encapsulated objects or private types.

11.39 ARCHITECTURE ALTERNATIVE-4

In comparison, a final architecture alternative that is simpler than the previous architecture is presented (Figure 11.55). In this architecture, both input and output buffers are reduced to data stores. As a result, concurrency and control interaction complexity are significantly reduced. Fewer concurrent processes appear in the architecture. Access to the buffers occurs within specific functions internal to a single architecture process. Internally generated events are placed into the buffer by actions performed within the System Controller.

Representing the buffers as data stores rather than full-blown architecture processes significantly restricts the hardware options available during detailed design. According to the guidelines previously described, processes can be implemented with either hardware or software support. Data stores are managed strictly through software functionality.

11.40 REQUIREMENTS TRACEABILITY (4)

With fewer architecture processes, this matrix is even further reduced in size (Figure 11.56). Most of the functional requirements and all of the control requirements (STD-2, PAT-2) are allocated to the System Controller process, as in Alternative-3.

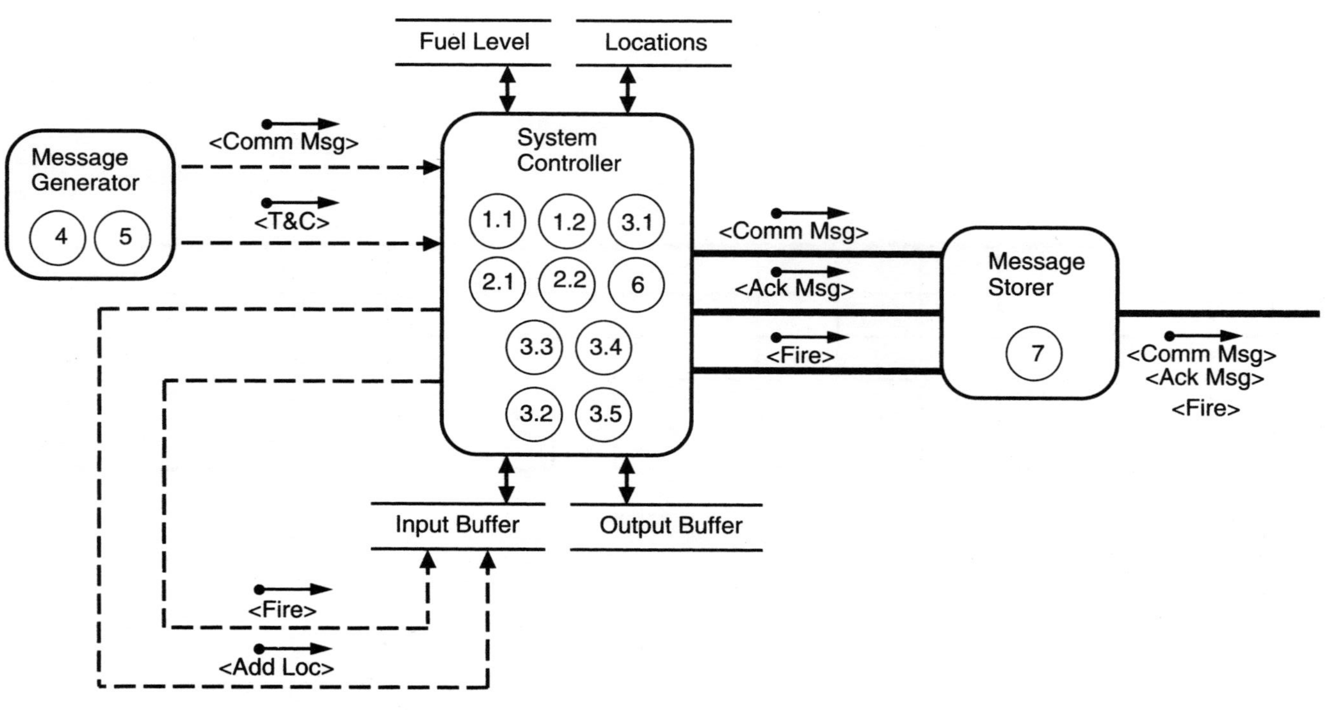

Figure 11.55 Process Architecture Alternative-4

Requirements / Architecture Process	Generate Comm Msg 4	Generate T&C Msg 5	Accept Raw Data 1.1	Deter Msg Type 1.2	Analyze Comm Msg 2.1	Deter Dest 2.2	Decode Op Code 3.1	Process Fire Cmd 3.2	Update Lookup Table 3.3	Gen Ack 3.4	Update Fuel 3.5	Compute Xmit Delay 6	Store Msg 7	STD, PAT
Message Generator	X	X												
System Controller			X	X	X	X	X	X	X	X	X	X		2
Message Storer													X	

Figure 11.56 Requirements Traceability (4)

11.41 EVALUATION OF ARCHITECTURE ALTERNATIVE-4

Almost all of the criteria evaluations described for Alternative-3 apply to alternative 4 and, thus, are not repeated here (Figure 11.57). However, as suggested above, both hardware and software dependency implications result. Inclusion of the buffers as data stores translates to less hardware dependence.

However, significant software dependency issues are raised by this approach, which represents the buffers as data stores. Portions of the System Controller attempt to respond to the top element of the input buffer while other portions of the Controller attempt to write incoming events into the tail end of the input buffer. Concurrent access to the buffer by different and simultaneous activities within the System Controller strongly necessitates usage of a software task to provide reliable, concurrent access to the buffer. Providing access control to the input buffer is usually accomplished by using software concurrency. Thus, heavy usage of Ada tasking is likely to be required. This dependency on software tasking to achieve access control illustrates the better applicability of Ada for this kind of system (as opposed to other programming languages which do not readily support software tasking).

11.42 PROCESS ARCHITECTURE EVALUATION (4)

Due to the reduced number of processes, this evaluation is even more simplified than previous evaluations (Figure 11.58). Verifying each event/response entry in the test input/output pattern requires movement through at most three processes and, in most cases, two processes. These responses are quite simple, revealing greater reliability and lowered integration and test effort.

Consider the first event in the test input/output pattern. This <T&C> event is emitted by the Message Generator and flows into System Controller. As a result of processing by the Controller, the internal <Fire> event then emerges as the response and is placed into the Input Buffer data store. Verification of the first event/response combination of the test input/output pattern involves only two architecture processes in a rather straightforward interaction.

11.43 SELECTION OF PROCESS ARCHITECTURE ALTERNATIVE

An important aspect of any methodical development is to record decisions and the justifications for those decisions (Figure 11.59). Specifically, Alternative-4 is the preferred architecture. In fact, this architecture has been successfully employed (at least by this author) on numerous real-time projects which require extensive control systems.

General Justification: Minimum Concurrency with Maximum Centralized Control

Moderate To High Performance Depending on Computational Intensity Of PSPECs in System Control
Inclusion Of Buffers Maximizes Effectiveness Of Concurrency

Low to Moderate Int and Test Effort Depending on HW Dependence

Extremely High Reliability Once Control Implemented And Tested

Control Concept: Hierarchical Control—System/Buffers/Interfaces
Max Centralized Control—STD/PAT Allocated to System Controller

High Traceability Due to Separation Between Control (Large Tables) And I/F Management

High Flexibility if Table Driven SW Design Employed for System Controller

High Portability: Low Concurrency Complexity
Encapsulation of HW Interfaces

HW Dependence: Less Potential for HW Support Due to Low Concurrency Complexity

SW Dependence: Suggest Table Driven System Controller
Potential for High Usage Of Tasking, Improving Portability
Inclusion of Buffers As Data Stores Implies
SW Support for Concurrent Access Control

Figure 11.57 Evaluation of Architecture Alternative-4

Control Input	Internal Data Flow	Architecture Process	Internal Data Flow	Response
<T&C>	—	Message Generator	<T&C>	—
—	<T&C>	System Controller	—	<Fire>
<Fire>	—	System Controller	<Fire>	Update Fuel Level
—	<Fire>	Message Storer	—	<Fire>
<T&C>	—	Message Generator	<T&C>	—
—	<T&C>	System Controller	—	<Add Loc>
<Add Loc>	—	System Controller	<Ack Msg>	Update Locations
—	<Ack Msg>	Message Storer	—	<Ack Msg>
<Comm Msg>	—	Message Generator	<Comm Msg>	—
—	<Comm Msg>	System Controller	<Comm Msg>	—
—	<Comm Msg>	Message Storer	—	<Comm Msg>

Note: For an actual system, remainder of test input/output pattern should be evaluated.

Figure 11.58 Process Architecture Evaluation (4)

- Implement Process Architecture Alternative – 4
- Minimizes Concurrency Complexity
- Effectively Uses Centralized Hierarchical Control Largest Tables
- Most Flexible
- Most Portable Approach for All SW Solution

Figure 11.59 Selection of Process Architecture Alternative

Several factors dictate selection of this architecture. Since this architecture minimizes complexity of control interactions while maximizing hierarchical centralized control, both flexibility and integration and test ease are obtained. Constantly changing requirements places both of these benefits high on the list of importance.

Moreover, this architecture is preferred because of its high reliance on software. Software reliance is desirable because software-intensive architectures that employ Ada tasking are machine portable, and are thus reusable across systems exhibiting similar characteristics. Beginning future developments with a reusable software architecture proves to be extremely effective. This architecture is easily adapted to a specific problem and usually reduces costs and results in obtainable schedules.

11.44 DESIGN MODEL GENERATION

Generation of a software design model (Figure 11.60) that implements the architecture model is performed by the following steps:

1. Generate an initial tasking architecture;
2. Establish caller/callee relationships;
3. Employ (or do not employ) intermediaries;
4. Perform a consistency and completeness check of the tasking architecture against operational requirements;
5. Allocate tasks to packages;

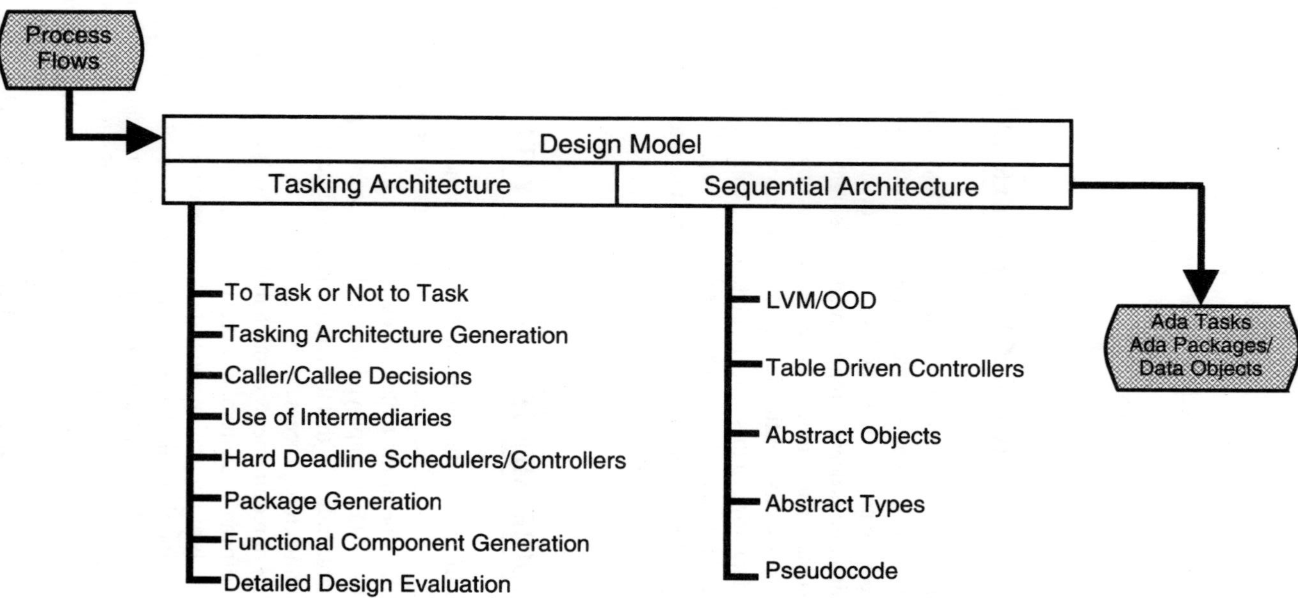

Figure 11.60 Design Model Generation

6. Generate functional components of the packages;
7. Use layered abstractions, table driven controllers, data objects, and data types to construct the sequential design of each task; and
8. Evaluate the detailed design to assess its quality.

Given a process architecture, multiple tasking architectures may be generated. As with process architectures, these alternatives are elaborated and then evaluated with the same criteria employed for architecture evaluation. Several tasking architectures are presented for the satellite control system and evaluated prior to selection of a specific tasking architecture.

11.45 TASKING ARCHITECTURE ALTERNATIVE-1

Process architecture Alternative-2 is the basis for this tasking architecture (Figure 11.61). All caller/callee decisions are made. Obviously, no intermediaries are employed, since none appear in the architecture diagram.

Each architecture process is represented by a single task. Caller/callee relationships are assigned in a manner that causes data to flow strictly in the direction of event source to response destination. Task entries are specified consistent with this direction of data flow. In this scheme, all tasks are called tasks, with the exception of the message generator tasks, which are caller tasks. As a result of this tasking architecture, <T&C> events are directly converted to internal data flows without the necessity of employing internal events.

11.46 REQUIREMENTS TRACEABILITY (T1)

This traceability matrix has an extended format to include correlation of requirements through architecture processes directly to the appropriate Ada task (Figure 11.62). Column one of the table lists each architecture process, immediately followed by a list of tasks employed within the architecture process. An entry in the traceability table indicates that the requirement is allocated to the specific Ada task within the architecture process.

Traceability of requirements through multiple levels of design is extremely important. For software systems of any complexity, multi-level traceability translates to reduced levels of integration and test effort. Determination of lost requirements is usually a major obstacle, causing extremely high levels of integration and test effort. Without multi-level traceability, determining implementation location of requirements within the software architecture is a difficult, if not impossible, job. Attempting to locate lost requirements during integration and test requires single stepping through multiple modules executing in parallel (a tedious process) and recognizing the point at which the requirement is missing. This simple multi-level format for the traceability matrix, combined with engineering discipline enforcing

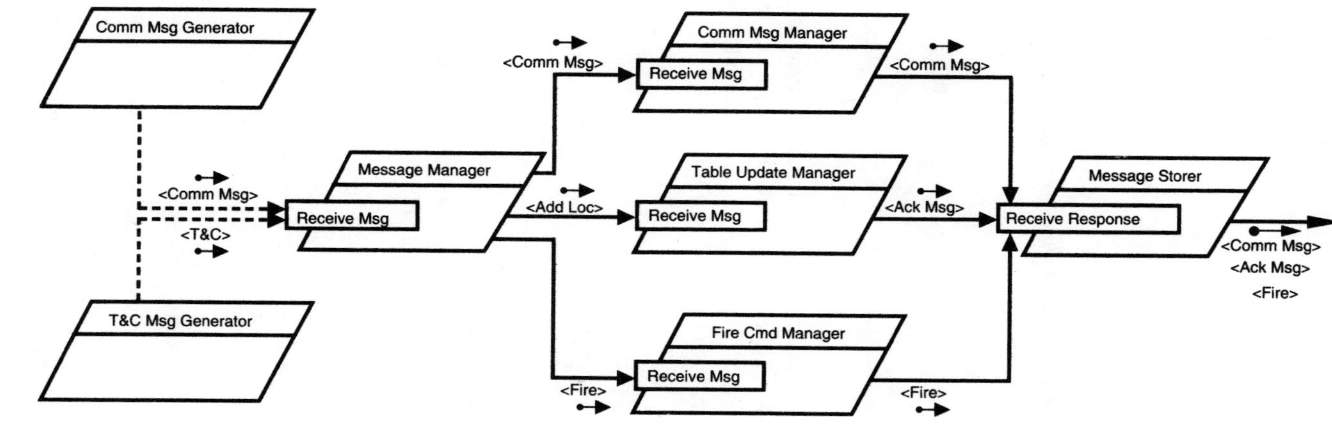

Figure 11.61 Tasking Architecture Alternative-1

its use, carefully identifies requirements allocated to each architecture process and its internal Ada tasks, eliminating much of the debugging effort. Requirements not allocated to a specific task are notably obvious (table entries are missing). Another important purpose is also served by multi-level traceability. A basis is established for the internal sequential design of each task. Those requirements specifically allocated to the software task must be satisfied by the internal sequential design. For instance, internal design of the Table Update Manager task must satisfy the following requirements:

1. Update Lookup Table (3.3); and
2. Generate Acknowledgement (3.4).

No other functionality needs to be incorporated into the body of this task. Therefore, a potential internal design for this task might be the following:

```
loop
 accept receive_message do
  extract destination and bandwidth;
  install into lookup table;
 end receive message;
end loop;
```

Elements inside the accept clause are implemented using layered abstractions and private types. Multi-level traceability leads to compact code which reads like the allocated requirements. Moreover, this code is extremely compact and efficient which, usually leads to high levels of performance.

11.47 EVALUATION OF TASKING ALTERNATIVE-1

Developers adopting an early "object-orientation" usually employ this architecture (Figure 11.63). Each task is mapped to an architecture process. Every architecture process is mapped to a "real world" entity in the problem space of the satellite control system. Unfortunately, this architecture usually leads to bad experiences with the use of tasking. A bad experience occurs because this architecture usually exhibits extremely poor performance.

Poor performance is likely to result because a set of caller/callee relationships is employed that ignores one of the important characteristics of the Ada tasking model—calling tasks can block. As an example, consider a single data path through the tasking architecture:

Comm Msg Generator emits a <Comm Msg>;

Comm Msg Generator performs a rendezvous entry call to Message Manager;

Message Manager performs a rendezvous entry call to Comm Msg Manager;

Comm Msg Manager performs a rendezvous entry call to Message Storer.

Requirements / Arch Module/Task	Generate Comm Msg 4	Generate T&C Msg 5	Accept Raw Data 1.1	Deter Msg Type 1.2	Analyze Comm Msg 2.1	Deter Dest 2.2	Decode Op Code 3.1	Process Fire Cmd 3.2	Update Lookup Table 3.3	Gen Ack 3.4	Update Fuel 3.5	Compute Xmit Delay 6	Store Msg 7	STD, PAT
Comm Msg Generator Comm Msg Generator	X													
T&C Msg Generator T&C Msg Generator		X												
Message Manager Message Manager			X	X			X							1
Comm Msg Manager Comm Msg Manager					X	X						X		
Table Update Manager Table Upate Manager									X	X				
Fire Cmd Manager Fire Cmd Manager								X			X			
Message Storer Message Storer													X	

Figure 11.62 Requirements Traceability (T1)

When considered independently, this data flow path appears to cause no particular problems. However, all data paths through the tasking architecture (as illustrated in Figure 11.63) include both Message Manager and File Storer in the same position in all data paths. Thus, each of these tasks is a potential bottleneck. If one or both of these tasks blocks for an extensive period of time, as they do when the callee task is busy, performance degrades significantly. This degradation potential results from the unidirectional caller/callee relationships and the absence of intermediary tasks such as buffers. When deployed during high traffic rates, extensive blocking is almost guaranteed. Of course, Ada tasking takes the blame. The real problem here is poor software system engineering, not Ada tasking.

Since each task is mapped to a real-world entity, adding functionality is likely to require added tasks. Adding a task is a major architectural change involving extensive integration and test effort. Both tables and routing logic within Message Manager must be updated. Additional tasks are added to the software configuration. Whole new task bodies need to be implemented. New task bodies must be unit tested, then integrated with the total satellite control system. Of course, existence of additional tasks within the context of a constant hardware platform usually results in even poorer performance. A constant number of CPU cycles are shared among more processes, reducing throughput. Ultimately, task proliferation results in a system consisting of an excessive number of tasks and one that performs poorly due to extensive blockage, high communications overhead, and significant task management overhead.

11.48 TASKING ARCHITECTURE EVALUATION (1)

Debugging this tasking architecture (Figure 11.64) requires insight into data flow through the architecture during real-time operations. Operational insight necessitates an evaluation using a format similar to the process architecture evaluation. All columns are the same, except the middle column. Rather than tracing flow through architecture processes, flow through tasks is relevant. Therefore, the middle column of the evaluation table is re-labeled from "Process" to "Task." Each element of the test input/output pattern needs to be verified in this tabular format.

The first entry in the test input/output pattern for the satellite control system contains the event/response pair: <T&C> and <Fire>. This pair is verified in the first two rows of this tasking architecture evaluation. A <T&C> event is emitted by the T&C Message Generator task. This event emerges as an internal data flow across a rendezvous entry call to the Message Manager. During the rendezvous, an internal <T&C> data flow exits T&C Message Generator and enters the Message Manager task. This entry appears in the Internal Data Flow column of the second row of the table. Message Manager operates on the data and emits an internal <Fire> control event through a rendezvous entry call to Message Manager. This emission appears in the Response column of the second row. Verification of the first test input/output pattern is accomplished. Remaining event/response pairs are validated according to the same mechanism.

- Based nn Process Architecture Alternative – 2
- Typical "Object-Oriented Design"
- Significant Potential For Blockage – Poor Performance
  - Comm Msg Generator → Message Manager → Comm Msg Manager → Message Storer
  - T&C Msg Generator → Message Manager → Table Update Manager → Message Storer
  - T&C Msg Generator → Message Manager → Fire Cmd Mgr → Message Storer

  If Message Manager Blocks, Satellite Control System Performance Degrades

  Unidirectional Caller/Callee Relations

  No Intermediaries
- Adding Functionality Can Require Excessive Int And Test Effort

  Update Tables In Message Manager

  Add Task

  Implement Task Body

  Integrate and Test New Task

  Performance Likely To Be Further Degraded

Figure 11.63 Evaluation of Tasking Alternative-1

Control Input	Internal Data Flow	Task	Internal Data Flow	Response
<T&C>	—	T&C Message Generator	<T&C>	—
—	<T&C>	Message Manager	—	<Fire>
<Fire>	—	Message Manager	<Fire>	—
—	<Fire>	Fire Cmd Manager	<Fire>	Update Fuel Level
—	<Fire>	Message Storer	—	<Fire>
<T&C>	—	T&C Message Generator	<T&C>	—
—	<T&C>	Message Manager	—	<Add Loc>
<Add Loc>	—	Message Manager	<Add Loc>	—
—	<Add Loc>	Table Update Manager	<Ack Msg>	Update Locations
—	<Ack Msg>	Message Storer	—	<Ack Msg>
<Comm Msg>	—	Comm Msg Generator	<Comm Msg>	—
—	<Comm Msg>	Message Manager	<Comm Msg>	—
—	<Comm Msg>	Comm Msg Manager	<Comm Msg>	—
—	<Comm Msg>	Message Storer	—	<Comm Msg>

Note: For an actual system, remainder of test input/output pattern should be evaluated.

Figure 11.64 Tasking Architecture Evaluation (1)

11.49 TASKING ARCHITECTURE ALTERNATIVE-2

Process architecture alternative-3 forms the basis for this tasking architecture (Figure 11.65). Each architecture processed is mapped into several Ada tasks, with the exception of Message Storer. Buffer processes are to be implemented in hardware and do not appear as tasks in the tasking architecture. Task interactions are adopted so that interaction flows from left to right, as in the previous tasking architecture. Incoming messages are emitted by the generator tasks (Comm Msg Generator and T&C Msg Generator) and are passed via rendezvous entry calls to the Message Manager task. Message Manager contains the state transition diagram allocated to this architecture. During processing, Message Manager attaches an action name to either the <Comm Msg> or the internal event generated by the <T&C> event. This combination of raw data and action name is passed to the Action Manager task. Of course, passage of data across tasks is accomplished via a rendezvous entry call. Action Manager contains the allocated action table and responds according to the data contained in the incoming data flow. In response to the rendezvous, appropriate simple actions in a corresponding action list are accomplished. Outgoing response messages are passed to the Message Storer through yet another rendezvous.

Traceability to the internal event flows is lost by this approach. Implementors are not allowed to simply disregard specified requirements such as internal events. The operational model, against which both designs and testing are evaluated includes these requirements. Acceptance testing requires verification that these internal events actually flow in the specified sequences. Thus, this loss of traceability causes tremendous difficulty during integration and test. Integrators waste a significant amount of effort attempting to determine the location of "missing" internal events. These internal events have been intentionally omitted in this tasking alternative. However, intentional omission is not recorded.

11.50 REQUIREMENTS TRACEABILITY (T2)

The multi-level format described earlier is employed here to simultaneously trace requirements through architecture processes to individual Ada tasks (Figure 11.66). Message Generator is split into two tasks—Comm Msg Generator and T&C Msg Generator. These two tasks implement requirements 4 and 5 concurrently in software and satisfy the original concurrency requirements specified in the enhanced process activation table. Two tasks are also employed to implement the System Controller process. While no requirements specify concurrency use relative to the implementation of System Controller, this form of concurrency is often necessary to obtain maximum throughput. Decisions and responses are performed in parallel tasks—Message Manager and Action Manager—decreasing the average response time and increasing average throughput. A single task is used to implement Message Storer.

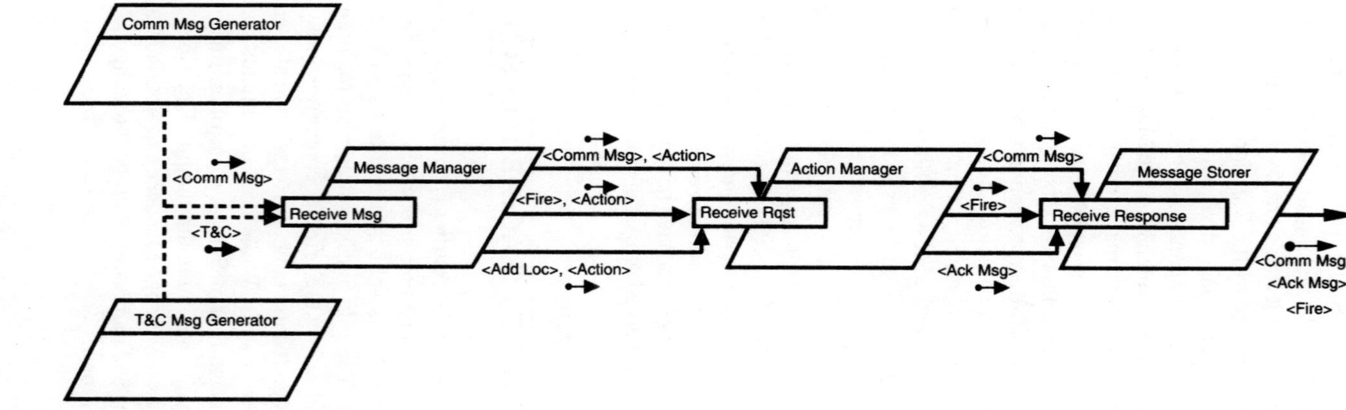

Figure 11.65 Tasking Architecture Alternative-2

Requirements / Arch Module/Tasks	Generate Comm Msg 4	Generate T&C Msg 5	Accept Raw Data 1.1	Deter Msg Type 1.2	Analyze Comm Msg 2.1	Deter Dest 2.2	Decode Op Code 3.1	Process Fire Cmd 3.2	Update Lookup Table 3.3	Gen Ack 3.4	Update Fuel 3.5	Compute Xmit Delay 6	Store Msg 7	STD, PAT
Message Generator														
Comm Msg Generator	X													
T&C Msg Generator		X												
System Controller														
Message Manager			X	X			X							STD 1
Action Manager					X	X		X	X	X	X	X		PAT 2
Message Storer														
Message Storer													X	

Figure 11.66 Requirements Traceability (T2)

Partitioning of the control requirements into two separate tasks is indicated by the entries in the STD, PAT column of the matrix. STD 1, described in figures detailing process architecture 2 is allocated to the task named Message Manager. Action Manager receives PAT 2 (formalized in the description of process architecture 3) as its allocation of control requirements. Operationally, this requires Message Manager to determine the required response in the STD and pass the action name to Action Manager. On receipt of an action name and event details, Action Manager determines the response through the allocated PAT. Details of the response are accomplished by access to the remaining PSPECs (2.1, 2.2, 3.2, 3.3, 3.4, 3.5, and 6), which are also allocated to the task Action Manager.

Internal sequential designs are now easily accomplished. Specific requirements must be implemented within each task. Significant effort is expended to apply layered virtual machines/object-oriented design to assure an internal design that meets the requirements, is flexible, and performs within constraints.

11.51 EVALUATION OF TASKING ALTERNATIVE-2

A key feature of this tasking architecture is the split of the System Controller architecture process into two separate Ada tasks (Figure 11.67). As described above, splitting a process into multiple tasks sometimes achieves better throughput, since context switching by the Ada scheduler if implemented or forced by the task implementor, encourages CPU sharing. As an architectural approach, this is most appropriate when the actions described by the PSPECs are computationally intensive. If some PSPECs perform operations such as Fast Fourier Transforms or hundreds of matrix multiplications, then this architecture provides an effective initial tasking structure. However, for this architecture to really work, tasking intermediaries must be added to avoid potential blockage that can degrade performance. Since the satellite control system does not require much computational intensity (PSPECs update simple data stores or copy data into outgoing response messages), computational intensity is not a sufficient justification for adopting this architecture for the satellite control system.

Based on the same criteria employed to evaluate process architectures, this tasking architecture rates only slightly better than tasking architecture 1. Control tables are divided into two separate Ada tasks. Thus, traceability of these control requirements into the tasking architecture is only slightly degraded. Unfortunately, significant potential for blockage is designed into this tasking architecture.

Tracing events from sources to destinations leads to identification of potential blockage points in the architecture. Consider a communications message. The end-to-end path of this message class is as follows:

Comm Msg Generator
Message Manager
Action Manager
Message Storer

- Based On Process Architecture Alternative – 3
- Splits System Controller Process into Two Ada Tasks
- Likely To Be Appropriate if Actions In PSPECs Computationally Intensive
  (Needs Some Merging with Tasking Alternative – 3)
- Splits Control Tables into Two Tasks Slightly Degrading Traceability
- Significant Potential for Blockage – Poor Performance
  Comm Msg Generator → Message Manager → Action Manager → Message Storer
  T&C Msg Generator → Message Manager → Action Manager → Message Storer
  Unidirectional Caller/Callee Relations
  No Intermediaries
- Adding Functionality Requires Minimal Int and Test Effort
  Update Tables in Message Manager, Action Manager
  Update PSPECs in Action Manager
  Integrate and test Same Tasks With Updated Tables
  Performance not as Likely To Be Further Degraded

Figure 11.67 Evaluation of Tasking Alternative-2

This path suffers from two important flaws. Unidirectional caller/callee relations are still the selected mode of tasking interaction for transmission of data from event source to response destination. Unidirectional caller/callee relations, combined with total disregard for the importance of intermediaries, lead to high blockage potential. As a result of these two flaws, both Message Manager and Action Manager become bottlenecks under conditions of high input event rates.

An important benefit derived from tasking architecture 2 when compared to tasking approach 1 is the significant reduction in integration and test effort needed to incorporate added functionality. With this tasking approach, adding functionality begins by updating appropriate elements in the tables in both Message Manager (STD) and Action Manager (PAT). A few PSPECs may have to be added to the body of Action Manager. With careful design, these PSPECs may use existing code in different ways or may require only small changes to existing software. Since no new tasks need to be added to the architecture, integration and testing is accomplished with the same tasks. Performance is not likely to be much further degraded by incorporation of the added functionality, since no new tasks are incorporated into the architecture.

11.52 TASKING ARCHITECTURE EVALUATION (2)

Each event in the test input/output pattern is applied to the tasking architecture to assure the consistency and completeness of the corresponding response (Figure 11.68). With this tasking architecture, an important problem is demonstrated by the tasking evaluation. To illustrate this problem, consider the first event in the original test input/output pattern.

This first event is a <T&C> event. During operations, this event moves as an internal data flow from the T&C Msg Generator to Message Manager. As a result of processing by Message Manager, an internal data flow named <Fire> moves to Action Manager. Processing by Action Manager results in another internal data flow of <Fire> to Message Storer. The final response—<Fire>—is then recorded by Message Storer.

Compare these first four entries to the original test input/output pattern. Something is missing. This missing entry is the internal control event named <Fire>. Since generation of this event is a key element that assures that the STD and PAT work properly and are as large as possible, elimination of this event is likely to cause the implementation to incorrectly operate. Attempting to resolve this kind of incorrect operation is extremely time consuming and frustrating, once a large number of lines of code are implemented and integrated with hardware. Correction of this problem requires changing of the architecture or modification of the original specification, either of which is liable to have significant impact upon the development effort. This is another indication of the inadequacy of this particular tasking architecture.

Control Input	Internal Data Flow	Task	Internal Data Flow	Response
<T&C>	—	T&C Msg Generator	<T&C>	—
—	<T&C>	Message Manager	<Fire>	—
—	<Fire>	Action Manager	<Fire>	Update Fuel Level
—	<Fire>	Message Storer	—	<Fire>
<T&C>	—	T&C Msg Generator	<T&C>	—
—	<T&C>	Message Manager	<Add Loc>	—
—	<Add Loc>	Action Manager	<Ack Msg>	Update Locations
—	<Ack Msg>	Message Storer	—	<Ack Msg>
<Comm Msg>	—	Comm Msg Generator	<Comm Msg>	—
—	<Comm Msg>	Message Manager	<Comm Msg>	—
—	<Comm Msg>	Action Manager	<Comm Msg>	—
—	<Comm Msg>	Message Storer	—	<Comm Msg>

Note: For an actual system, remainder of test input/output pattern should be evaluated.

Figure 11.68 Tasking Architecture Evaluation (2)

11.53 TASKING ARCHITECTURE ALTERNATIVE-3

Based on process architecture alternative-4, this tasking architecture (Figure 11.69) is constructed utilizing tasking intermediaries to significantly limit the amount of blockage. To satisfy the concurrency requirements of the enhanced PAT, two independent Ada tasks are employed as message emitters—Comm Msg Generator and T&C Msg Generator. Messages generated by these tasks are enqueued into an input buffer managed by the Input Buffer task for later processing. When ready to begin processing the next event, System Controller dequeues the event at the head of the input queue. System Controller operates on the event, generating an appropriate response, and transmitting that response to the appropriate buffer. Internal events are placed in the input buffer by rendezvous with Input Buffer task. Placement of an outgoing response into the output buffer requires a rendezvous entry call to the Output Buffer task, which manages the output buffer data store. Message Storer then simply dequeues responses from the output buffer to store the next response into an output file. This tasking architecture employs just the right number of tasks for an application. Moreover, this structure is a machine portable, reusable architecture easily tailored to any application, since its key components are centrally located tables—the STD and PAT in the System Controller task.

11.54 REQUIREMENTS TRACEABILITY (T3)

As with other tasking traceability matrices, both control and functional requirements are traced through architecture processes directly into specific tasks (Figure 11.70). With this architecture, most of the requirements are allocated specifically to System Controller. Both STD-2 and PAT-2, which were defined for process architecture alternative 3/4, appear in the System Controller task. Generator tasks—Comm Msg Generator and T&C Msg Generator—each perform a single function, emitting appropriate messages. Message Storer also performs a single function (requirement 7, Store Msg).

11.55 EVALUATION OF TASKING ALTERNATIVE-3

Since most of the functionality and control tables are allocated to a single Ada task, this approach (Figure 11.71) is most appropriate when the PSPECs are not computationally intensive. Low computational intensity is exhibited by PSPECs that simply update data stores, modify simple tables, or construct response messages by retrieving data from a variety of data stores. Simple computations such as addition, subtraction, multiplication, and division may by involved. A review of the PSPECs for the satellite control system indicates that the PSPECs for this system are not computationally intensive, suggesting that this is the ideal tasking architecture for the satellite control system.

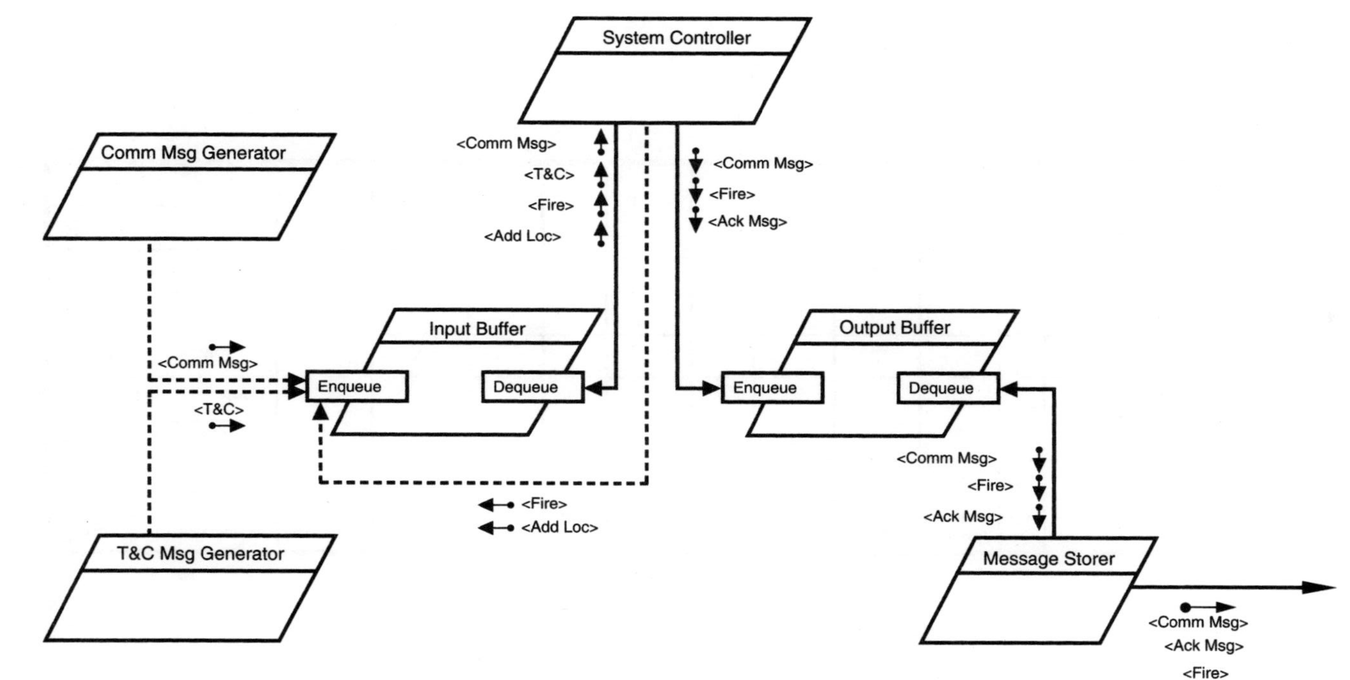

Figure 11.69 Tasking Architecture Alternative-3

Requirements / Arch Module/Task	Generate Comm Msg 4	Generate T&C Msg 5	Accept Raw Data 1.1	Deter Msg Type 1.2	Analyze Comm Msg 2.1	Deter Dest 2.2	Decode Op Code 3.1	Process Fire Cmd 3.2	Update Lookup Table 3.3	Gen Ack 3.4	Update Fuel 3.5	Compute Xmit Delay 6	Store Msg 7	STD, PAT
Message Generator														
Comm Msg Generator	X													
T&C Msg Generator		X												
System Controller														
System Controller			X	X	X	X	X	X	X	X	X	X		2
Message Storer														
Message Storer													X	

Figure 11.70 Requirements Traceability (T3)

- Based On Process Architecture Alternative – 4
- Maintains System Controller Process As a Single Ada Task
- Likely To Be Appropriate if Actions in PSPECs Not Computationally Intensive
- Leaves Control Tables in a Single Task Improving Traceability
- Almost No Potential for Blockage—High Performance

  (Also, Minimizes Number Ada Tasks)
  Comm Msg Generator → Input Buffer ← System Controller → Output Buffer ← Message Storer
  T&C Msg Generator → Input Buffer ← System Controller → Output Buffer ← Message Storer

  Bidirectional Caller/Callee Relations

  Appropriate Usage Of Intermediaries

  System Controller Always A Caller → High Throughput
- Adding Functionality Requires Even Less Int and Test Effort

  Update Tables, PSPECs in System Controller

  Integrate and Test Same Tasks with Updated Tables

  Performance Definitely Not Degraded

Figure 11.71 Evaluation of Tasking Alternative-3

In contrast to previous tasking alternatives, this architecture evaluates well according to the evaluation criteria. Traceability is extremely high, since both control tables are isolated within a single Ada task—System Controller. Moreover, performance is expected to be quite high for this architecture due to the low number of tasks and the proper use of buffers to manage throughput.

The number of tasks is minimized, assuring that tasking communications overhead does not significantly reduce end-to-end throughput. Further, almost no potential for task blockage appears within this architecture. With the introduction of buffer intermediaries, bidirectional caller/callee relations are introduced into the end-to-end data path from event source to response destination. These bidirectional interactions, combined with buffer intermediaries, serve to significantly reduce the blockage potential even in the presence of high data rate event sources. Since System Controller is always a calling task to a buffer task, its likelihood of blockage is extremely low. This low blockage translates into a reasonably high throughput rate, even during high traffic conditions.

Adding functionality to this architecture is the easiest of all the architectures presented. Most of the implementation effort is restricted to the internal body of System Controller. Within System Controller, implementation efforts are predominantly restricted to modification of the encapsulated control tables. Some small changes may be necessary to add or update a few PSPECs, but this effort is minimal if the software is appropriately designed to employ data objects and data types. In this context, adding PSPECs is usually accomplished by employing capabilities provided by existing software packages. No new tasks are added; internals of a single task are modified. Integration and test is accomplished using the same tasks, so new interactions need not be evaluated and debugged within a system operational context. In fact, integration is accomplished by using the same tasks with updated tables. As a result, integration and test effort is significantly reduced. Moreover, performance is definitely maintained at almost the same level obtained prior to addition of the new capability.

11.56 TASKING ARCHITECTURE EVALUATION (3)

End-to-end traceability of data flow through the tasking architecture is verified in Figure 11.72. This is accomplished, as usual, by application of each event in the test input/output pattern to the tasking architecture to verify generation of the indicated response. Evaluation of this tasking architecture illustrates the role played by the intermediaries to achieve high throughput.

Consider the first two entries in the test input/output pattern. A <T&C> event is the first event in the test pattern. This moves as an internal data flow from T&C Msg Generator directly into the Input Buffer task. Upon request, this same data flow is transmitted from Input Buffer to System Controller. Processing by System Controller results in generation of the internal event—<Fire>. Verification of the first row in the test input/output pattern is accomplished.

Control Input	Internal Data Flow	Task	Internal Data Flow	Response
<T&C>	—	T&C Msg Generator	<T&C>	—
—	<T&C>	Input Buffer	<T&C>	—
—	<T&C>	System Controller	—	<Fire>
<Fire>	—	Input Buffer	<Fire>	—
—	<Fire>	System Controller	<Fire>	Update Fuel Level
—	<Fire>	Output Buffer	<Fire>	—
—	<Fire>	Message Storer	—	<Fire>
<T&C>	—	T&C Msg Generator	<T&C>	—
—	<T&C>	Input Buffer	<T&C>	—
—	<T&C>	System Controller	—	<Add Loc>
<Add Loc>	—	Input Buffer	<Add Loc>	—
—	<Add Loc>	System Controller	<Ack Msg>	Update Locations
—	<Ack Msg>	Output Buffer	<Ack Msg>	—
—	<Ack Msg>	Message Storer	—	Ack Msg
<Comm Msg>	—	Comm Msg Generator	<Comm Msg>	—
—	<Comm Msg>	Input Buffer	<Comm Msg>	—
—	<Comm Msg>	System Controller	<Comm Msg>	—
—	<Comm Msg>	Output Buffer	<Comm Msg>	—
—	<Comm Msg>	Message Storer	—	<Comm Msg>

Note: For an actual system, remainder of test input/output pattern should be evaluated.

Figure 11.72 Tasking Architecture Evaluation (3)

This internal control event—<Fire>—begins the second row of the test input/output pattern. Again, at the request of System Controller, an internal data flow named <Fire> moves from Input Buffer to System Controller. System Controller employs the encapsulated control tables (STD, PAT and the allocated PSPECs to generate the outgoing <Fire> response. This outgoing response is transmitted into the buffer managed by Output Buffer. When Message Storer is ready for the next response message, this <Fire> message is extracted from Output Buffer and becomes an internal data flow to Message Storer. Finally, processing by Message Storer results in the emission of the <Fire> response. This evaluation verifies the second row (event/response pattern) of the test input/output pattern. Of course, the remainder of the pattern is similarly evaluated.

11.57 SELECTION OF A TASKING ARCHITECTURE ALTERNATIVE

Given the characteristics of the satellite control system and the high evaluation of tasking architecture 3, architecture 3 is selected for implementation. Specific reasons for selecting Figure 11.73 alternative relate to its support for both flexibility and performance.

Maximum throughput is obtained by architecture 3 through its minimal use of tasking and through its successful use of buffer tasks to decouple interaction of all the worker tasks. Flexibility is designed into the tasking architecture by incorporation of the largest tables into a single Ada task. Allocation of these tables to a single task reduces the effort to identify change locations. Further updating tables reduces the effort to actually make changes once change locations are identified. As a result, maximum flexibility is obtained with minimum effort.

Finally, since most of the PSPECs for this satellite control system are not computationally intensive, isolation of all PSPECs within a single task does not really impose a performance degradation upon this architecture. This architecture yields high performance with maximum flexibility and portability.

- Implement Tasking Architecture Alternative – 3
  (Or Alternative – 2 with Three Buffers : Input, Action, Output)
- Maximum Throughput by Using Buffers, Minimal Tasking
- Most Flexible Due to Largest Tables

Figure 11.73 Selection of Tasking Architecture Alternative

11.58 PACKAGING ALLOCATION ALTERNATIVE-1

Since all Ada tasks must have a parent, each task in the selected tasking architecture is mapped into a package (Figure 11.74). One approach employs three basic packages. A package named Msg Source Pkg contains the two message generator tasks. Another package, Resp Dest Pkg, serves as the parent to the Message Storer tasks. The final package—System Control Pkg—encapsulates the remaining Ada tasks.

System Control Pkg exports two interfaces to the remainder of the application. One interface provides an entrance procedure named Enqueue Input through which the message generators place events into the input buffer managed by Input Buffer task. A second interface, also an entrance procedure, presents a path through which responses are extracted from the output buffer encapsulated by Output Buffer. Interaction among System Controller and the buffer tasks—Input Buffer and Output Buffer—is totally contained within System Control Pkg. Therefore, no external interfaces need to be exported by System Control Pkg to assure the continuity of these data flows.

11.59 EVALUATION OF PACKAGING ALTERNATIVE-1

This packaging scheme (Figure 11.75) emphasizes the critical importance of System Controller. By encapsulation within the same package as the buffer tasks Input Buffer and Output Buffer, System Controller is given highest priority (easiest and clearest) visibility to the buffer tasks. As a result, integration of the interactions among these tasks is likely to require significantly less effort, since all interactions are encapsulated under the same package body.

However, from a system perspective, this scheme is likely to result in a much higher level of integration and test effort. During system integration, a new set of problems can emerge that are not apparent during package testing. Unfortunately, these problems are now hidden under the package body. Isolation, identification, and resolution of encapsulated task interactions is usually an extremely difficult and frustrating process. In this packaging scheme, effects of encapsulated task interactions are likely to be further exacerbated by the hidden flow of the internal control events. Hiding the flow of control events in this way creates a barrier behind which control flow failure is likely to occur. Since the failure of control events to occur is hidden, identification of the resulting problems requires elimination of the barrier.

Encapsulation of the buffer tasks in this manner usually causes significant performance problems, if generic tasks are employed. This degradation occurs because many compilers tend to re-elaborate the generic declared in this manner every time a rendezvous entry call occurs to the instantiation. Re-elaboration at runtime in response to every rendezvous entry call is a high overhead activity which significantly reduces throughput of the system.

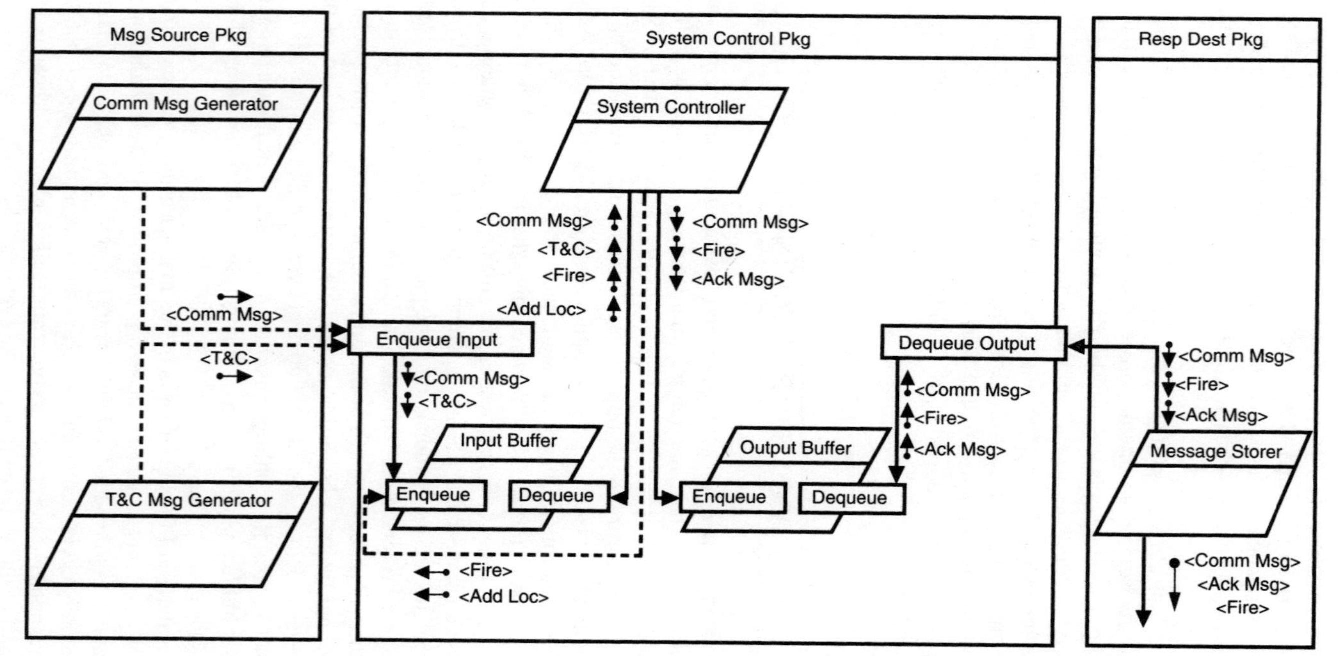

Figure 11.74 Packaging Allocation Alternative-1

- Collect Data Sources Together
- Collect Data Destinations Together
- Allocate System Controller, Buffers to Same Package
- System Controller Most Critical Tasks
- System Controller Given Highest Priority Visibility to Buffers
- Leads to Relatively High Level of Implementation, Int and Test Effort
  Separate, Independent Development of Buffer Tasks
  Hidden Interfaces Difficult to Identify, Debug
  (Internally Generated Control Events a Problem Since not Visible)
- Poor Performance if Generic Buffers Employed
  Re-elaboration at Every Rendezvous Entry Call

Figure 11.75 Evaluation of Packaging Alternative-1

11.60 PACKAGING ALLOCATION ALTERNATIVE-2

A second approach (Figure 11.76) differs in the manner in which buffer tasks are packaged. The same scheme is employed to manage message sources and destinations. Both generator tasks (Comm Msg Generator, T&C Msg Generator) are encapsulated into a single package named Msg Source Pkg. The destination task manager, Message Storer, is allocated to the same package, Resp Dest Pkg. With this packaging alternative, however, the remaining tasks are each given a single encapsulating package. System Controller is placed into the System Control Pkg. Each of the buffer tasks receives a parent package. Input Buffer is placed into Incoming Msg Pkg. Similarly, Outgoing Resp Pkg contains Output Buffer tasks. Each of the buffer packages exports entrance procedures that encapsulate the rendezvous entry calls to allow data to be entered into (e.g., Incoming Msg Pkg. En-

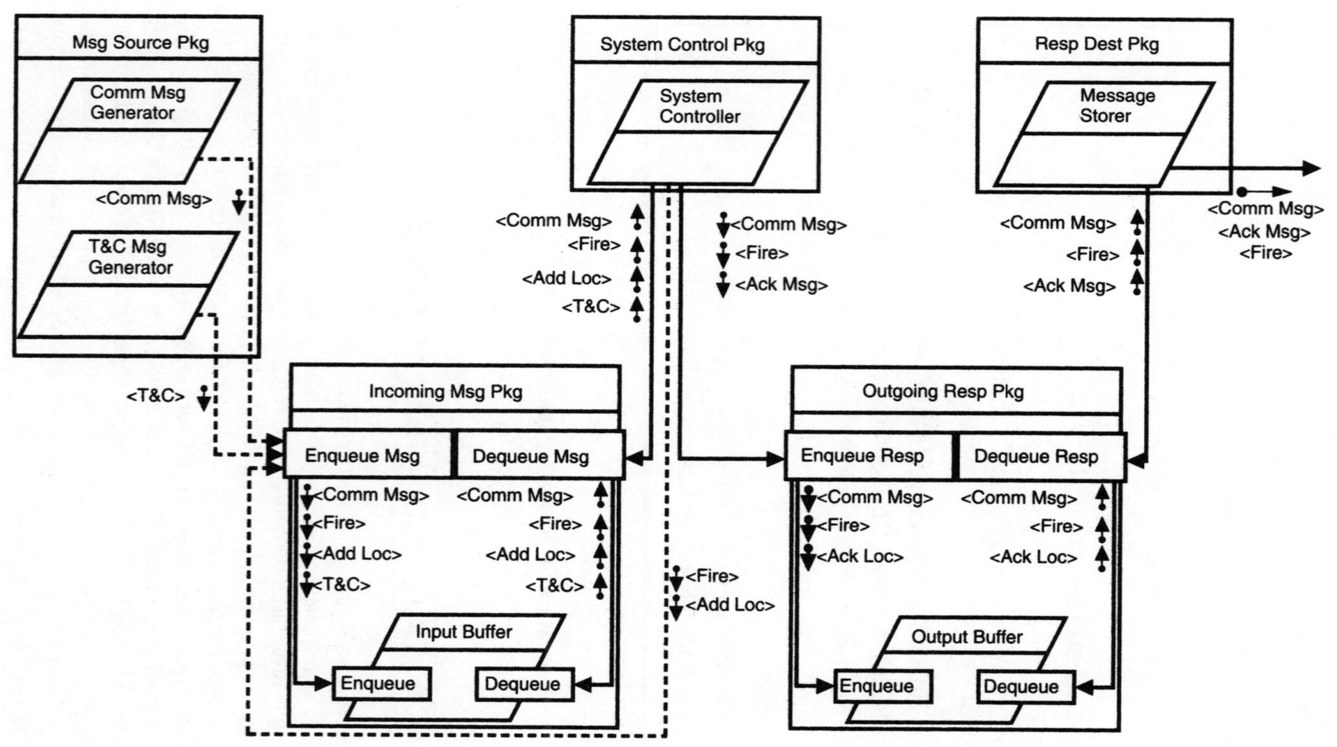

Figure 11.76 Packaging Allocation Alternative-2

queue Msg) or retrieved from (e.g., Incoming Msg Pkg. Dequeue Msg) the encapsulated buffer task. Typically, these buffer packages are instantiations of the same generic buffer package, each of which is independently and separately instantiated into the application library.

11.61 EVALUATION OF PACKAGING ALTERNATIVE

With this scheme (Figure 11.77), emphasis is placed on collection of tasks into packages based on both functional and performance criteria. Functionality is employed to allocate event generators to a single package and to allocate the response storer to its own package. Elaboration performance and visibility are the factors motivating independent and separate buffer packages.

Reduced integration and test effort is experienced as a result of the additional packages. Reduced levels of integration effort are predominantly due to the visibility of the internally generated control events. While some interaction complexity is introduced as a result of additional visible interfaces thus somewhat increasing integration and test effort, overall efforts are eased. No longer do hidden and missing control events plague the integration and test efforts. Failure of control events to occur during integration and testing is both visible and obvious.

Significantly better performance is also experienced. By independently and separately compiling the buffer instantiations into the library, the instantiations become globally visible. As a result, these instantiations are almost always elaborated once at initial program elaboration. Thus, the elaboration overhead is consumed only once, not every time a hidden task is re-elaborated.

- Collect Data Sources Together
- Collect Data Destinations Together
- Separate Packages for System Controller, Buffers
- Leads to Reduced Implementation, Int and Test Effort
  - Reuse Generic Buffer Packages
  - All Interfaces Visible
    - (Internally Generated Control Events More Accessible)
- Better Performance With Generic Buffers
  - Global Visibility of Generic Instantiations ➡
    - Elaboration Once In Response to First Rendezvous Entry Call

Figure 11.77 Evaluation of Packaging Alternative-2

- Implement Packaging Allocation Alternative – 2
- Best Performance
- Lowest Level of Int And Test Effort

Figure 11.78 Selection of Packaging Allocation Alternative

11.62 SELECTION OF PACKAGING ALLOCATION ALTERNATIVE

Based on the preceding evaluations, implementation of the second packaging alternative is a clearly superior approach (Figure 11.78). Visibility of the interfaces and internal control events reduces a potentially high level of integration and test effort. A high throughput level is assured, at least from a tasking overhead perspective.

11.63 GENERATION OF FUNCTIONAL ADA COMPONENTS

Having chosen a specific packaging scheme, functional Ada components are now described for each package. Each of the six packages has its functional components listed in Figure 11.79. Specific packages and desired interfaces are determined by reviewing the selected packaging scheme. Where appropriate, syntax of each of the interfaces is defined at this point.

As an example, consider one of the buffer packages, Incoming Msg Pkg. First, a specification for the package is needed:

```
package Incoming Msg Pkg is
 procedure Enqueue Msg( Incoming Event:
                             in event type );
 procedure Dequeue Msg( Current Event:
                             in out event type );
end Incoming Msg Pkg;
```

Exact syntax of each interface is specified. Additionally, arguments with modes and data types are also specified. Exported subprograms are derived from and consistent with interactions specified in the packaging diagram. Of course, a specification needs to be followed by a body for the package.

I. Msg Source Pkg

- Msg Source Pkg (Spec)
- Msg Source Pkg (Body)
- Comm Msg Generator (Task Body)
- T&C Msg Generator (Task Body)

II. System Control Pkg

- System Control Pkg (Spec)
- System Control Pkg (Body)
- System Controller (Task Body)

III. Resp Dest Pkg

- Resp Dest Pkg (Spec)
- Resp Dest Pkg (Body)
- Message Storer (Task Body)

IV. Incoming Msg Pkg

- Incoming Msg Pkg (Spec)
- Incoming Msg Pkg (Body)
- Input Buffer (Task Body)
- Enqueue Msg (Entrance Procedure)
- Dequeue Msg (Entrance Procedure)

V. Outgoing Resp Pkg

- Outgoing Resp Pkg (Spec)
- Outgoing Resp Pkg (Body)
- Output Buffer (Task Body)
- Enqueue Resp (Entrance Procedure)
- Dequeue Resp (Entrance Procedure)

Figure 11.79 Generation of Functional Ada Components

```
package body Incoming Msg Pkg is
 task Input Buffer is separate;
 procedure Enqueue Msg (Incoming Event:
                        in    event type) is separate;
 procedure Dequeue Msg (Current Event:
                        in out event type) is separate;
end Incoming Msg Pkg;
```

Details of components internal to the package body are deferred for later definition by use of the "is separate" clause. Similar declarations are generated for each package in the selected packaging scheme.

Comparison of the specified Ada functional components for both Incoming Msg Pkg and Outgoing Resp Pkg suggests the use of a generic buffer package. To employ such a package in this situation, a number of conditions need to be satisfied:

1. A generic buffer package exists and is available in a reuse library;
2. The buffered type is accepted as a generic formal parameter of the package; and
3. Internal design of the package employs an encapsulated buffer task to manage a physical buffer specified in the local declarative section of the hidden task body.

These conditions illustrate the importance of a reuse library and its attendant documentation. If a library is unavailable, separate programmers usually develop their own buffer packages, wasting valuable time and effort. If a library exists but documentation is poorly maintained, a generic buffer may not contain an encapsulating task. As a result, integration and test efforts are significantly hampered. Message generator tasks Comm Msg Generator and T&C Msg Generator may write into the same location of the unprotected buffer. Data lost or mangled in this manner cause significant integration and test headaches. Detection, isolation and elimination of a small data overwrite problem is tedious when embedded within a large number of lines of implemented Ada code.

11.64 SEQUENTIAL SOFTWARE DESIGN OF SYSTEM CONTROLLER

Detailed design of the Ada tasks within each package is now possible because the previous step precisely defined the syntax of each of the package interfaces. Requirements allocated in the multi-level requirements traceability matrix form the basis for the detailed sequential design of each task (Figure 11.80). Application of the layered virtual machine/object-oriented design methodology to these requirements is illustrated by this next series of figures.

Layered virtual machines/object-oriented design (LVM/OOD) is applied to the requirements for the internal design of the System Controller task. Referring to the

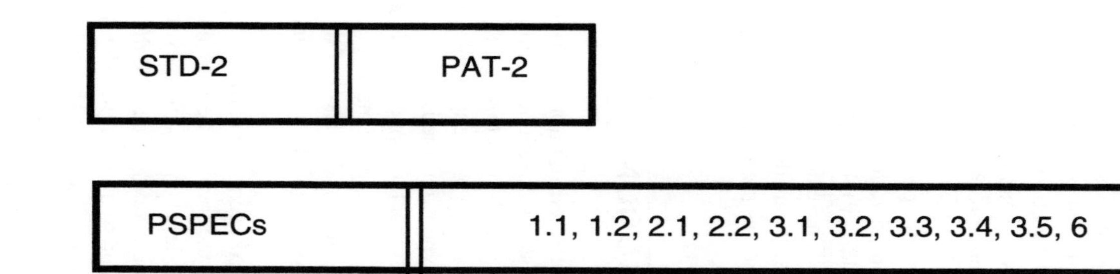

Figure 11.80 Sequential Software Design of System Controller

requirements traceability matrix labeled T3, a number of control and data flow requirements need to be satisfied within the task body of System Controller. Control requirements to be accommodated within System Controller are composed of a state transition diagram (STD-2, described in process architecture 3) and a process activation table (PAT-2, also specified in process architecture 3). A long list of PSPECs managed by the PAT is also implemented within the task body.

Moreover, all control and functional requirements must be implemented in a manner which promotes easy traceability and easy modification. Maintaining the control specifications in a tabular format while coding PSPECs using abstractions satisfies both of these goals. Tables form a centralized, compact, easily traceable implementation for the control specifications. Moreover, tables are easier to modify than actual code. Centralization and attendant traceability for PSPECs is accomplished by encapsulation of the PSPECs into a single procedure, accessed through an abstract interface. These design goals are best obtained by application of an LVM/OOD sequential software design methodology. In this way, knowledge of these design goals is applied as the solution is iteratively derived.

11.65 INVENT A SOLUTION

Initially, a simple problem oriented solution is formulated (Figure 11.81). In this case, a System Controller task, as envisioned within this architecture, conceptually loops in a regular cycle. Each pass through the cycle performs two simple operations. First, an input message or event is collected. As a result of acquiring this event, a specific event_type is returned.

An important assumption is that the input event is stored or encapsulated somewhere. Details of the internal structure are managed by the encapsulating software artifact and are hidden from view at this level of detailed design. Assumption of encapsulation of details works quite well in Ada, since Ada supports encapsulated objects and private types.

After acquisition of the next event, the extracted event_type is then passed to a procedure which responds to the specific message/event type. Again, details of the response are encapsulated at levels below this level of design specification. According to the LVM/OOD methodology, each of these procedural interfaces (collect an input message, respond to an input message) is now further detailed or is treated as operations on abstract objects or abstract types. Both of the procedures employed here need further decomposition and thus are considered machine instructions for a lower level virtual machine.

11.66 REFINEMENT: COLLECT AN INPUT MESSAGE

Collection of the next input message is further decomposed into more detailed, problem-oriented statements in Figure 11.82. Incoming input event collection

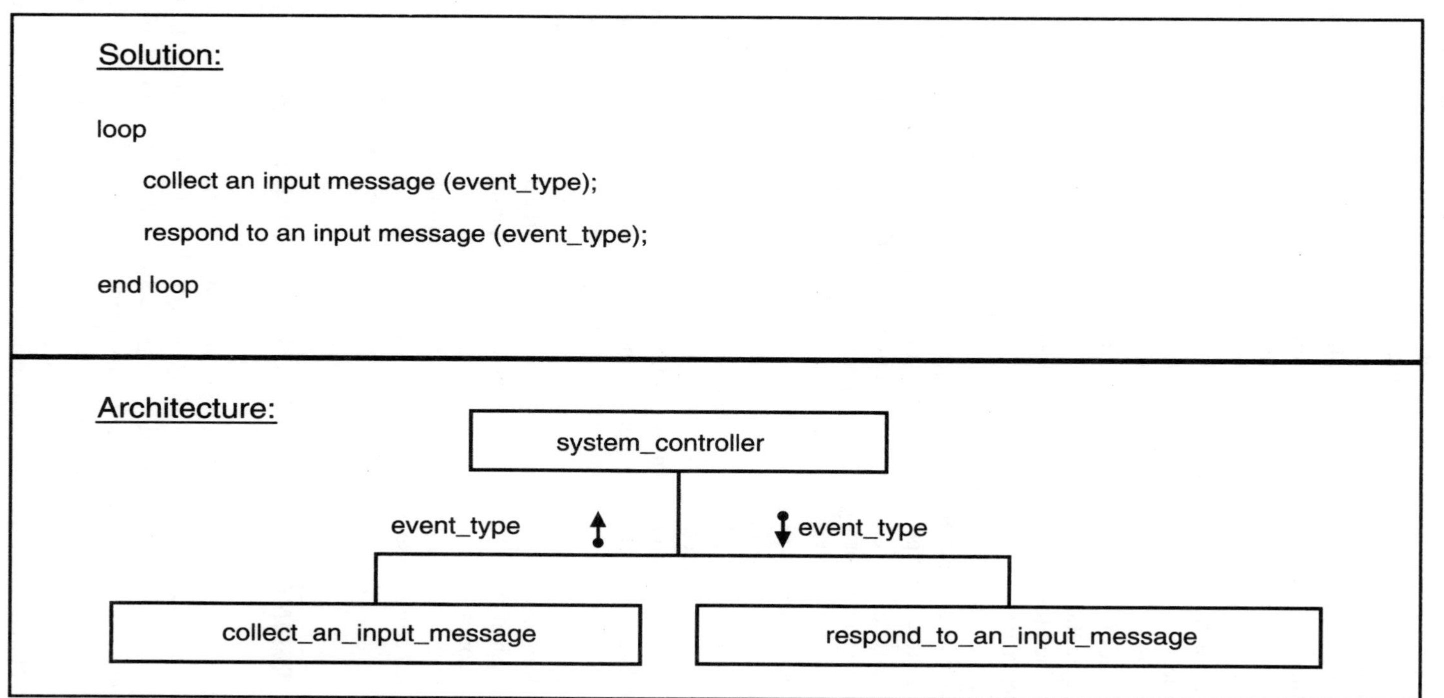
Solution:
loop
collect an input message (event_type);
respond to an input message (event_type);
end loop
Architecture:
system_controller
event_type
event_type
collect_an_input_message
respond_to_an_input_message

Figure 11.81 Invent a Solution

consists of a sequence of specific activities. A message is retrieved for the current event queue. This retrieval returns a current_event. Once retrieved, procedure extracts and returns the specific event_type. Event_type is extracted by access to the event through a logical component number. Physical knowledge of the internal event structure is not employed. Invocation ends by returning the event_type.

Both of these procedures are operations on data abstractions. Message retrieval operates on a current_event object of data type event. Of course, an event data type has components, one of which is the event_type component. Successful use of the object-oriented capabilities of Ada requires that a type manager be created here, since one does not currently exist. Creation of a type manager occurs via generation of a package specification that exports a private type named "event" an d an abstract operation entitled retrieve_message. Storing a message may also be required. Therefore, an abstract interface is also added, which is named store_message.

Similarly, controlling access to individual event or response components is managed in an abstract manner. Message_manager is declared to accomplish just such an abstraction. Specifically, applications typically need to either store or retrieve specific event components. Arguments include a message object of an abstract or private type, a logical component indicator, and an appropriate repository for the provided or retrieved value. *All details of the message data structure must be hidden under the interfaces*. In this way, changes to the message structure, which usually occur on a regular basis during an ongoing development, have no effect on the code which employs the needed event abstraction. Coding changes are limited in scope, reducing the amount of effort needed to reflect the evolving message structure. Compare this with placement of open data structures into package specifications. Simple changes in message structures exported by package specifications usually result in extensive and frustrating efforts. The tremendous effort to identify all the occurrences of access to the globally visible data structures is eliminated by adoption of this abstracted approach.

Since each of these procedural components is an operation on abstract types, no further decomposition is necessary here. This portion of the detailed design of System Controller is completed. However, further effort is necessary to complete the detailed design associated with message response.

11.67 REFINEMENT: RESPOND TO AN INPUT MESSAGE

Fairly straight forward sequential logic, in problem oriented terms, describes the details of responding to an input message (Figure 11.83). Input into this particular procedure is the event_type. First, event_type and current_state are employed to determine a name for the response. This is defined as an action_required. Determination of action_required is easily accomplished via a simple access to the PAT employing event_type and current_state as arguments. Once determined, action_required is transmitted to a procedure that performs the details of the event

Solution:

retrieve message from current event queue (current_event);

extract message type (current_event, field indicator, event_type);

Architecture:

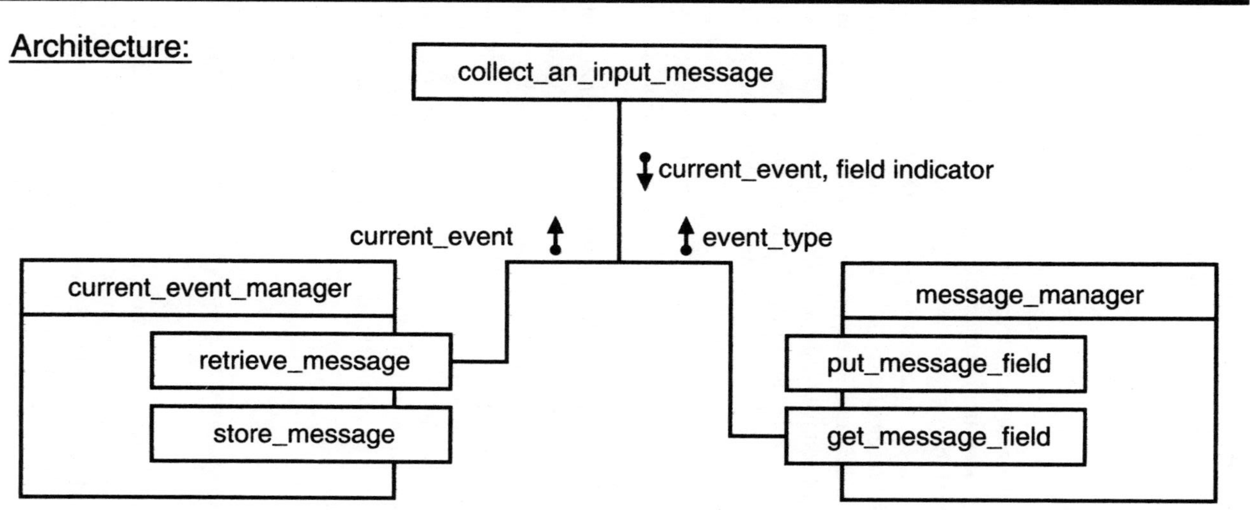

Figure 11.82 Refinement: Collect an Input Message

response. Of course, detailed mechanics of implementing the action_required are encapsulated under this interface. Finally, a new state needs to be determined. New state determination is accomplished by using the event_type and the current_state to update the current_state. Updating current_state is accomplished by fairly simple access to the STD or its tabular representation.

Each of these procedures is evaluated for further decomposition. Determination of action_required entails access to the tabular representation of the STD. In keeping with the stated design goals to maintain the state table in a compact form, this table is treated as an abstract object to be encapsulated within a package body. Since this table is likely to be a rather sparse matrix, encapsulation of the state table also allows a variety of table representations to be employed with no effect on the remainder of the code or the remainder of the design effort. This benefit simply reinforces the encapsulation approach, which maintains the state table in a centralized, compacted format to obtain both traceability and flexibility.

As described in the specification of an STD, action_required is a single name that summarizes the required response. Translation of this summary name into all the details to generate the required response involves a sequence of actions, entailing potentially significant computations and movement of data. Therefore, this instruction is treated as a virtual machine instruction to be further decomposed. Management of response details is likely to involve the PAT. Therefore, to obtain functional cohesion, perform_response and another procedure, retrieve_action_list, are provided as abstract interfaces to an encapsulated PAT. While perform_response may not itself directly access the PAT, its inclusion in the action_table_manager makes sense for configuration control purposes.

State determination is simply another abstract operation on the already encapsulated STD in tabular format. Thus, an additional interface named determine_next_state is included in the list exported by the state_table_manager package. Both provide access to the encapsulated table using event_type and current_state as input arguments. One interface—determinate_next_state—accesses the state transition portion. The remaining interface, determine_response, determines the action_required. Details of the "table lookup" are dependent upon the data structure employed to implement the table and are hidden under the abstract interfaces.

11.68 REFINEMENT: PERFORM RESPONSE

Given an action_required, further processing is necessary to effect the details of the action. Initially, action_required is converted to a list of PSPECs that need to be performed. Each listed PSPEC performed. A problem-oriented description of this sequencing appears in the Figure 11.84.

Action_required is passed as an argument to a procedure named retrieve_action_list. This argument is employed as a logical into the process activation table. As a result, an action_list is returned. A simple loop across the PSPECs appearing in action_list assures that each PSPEC is performed. Logical

Solution:

determine response to event (event type, current state, action required);

perform event response (action required);

determine next state (event type, current state);

Architecture:

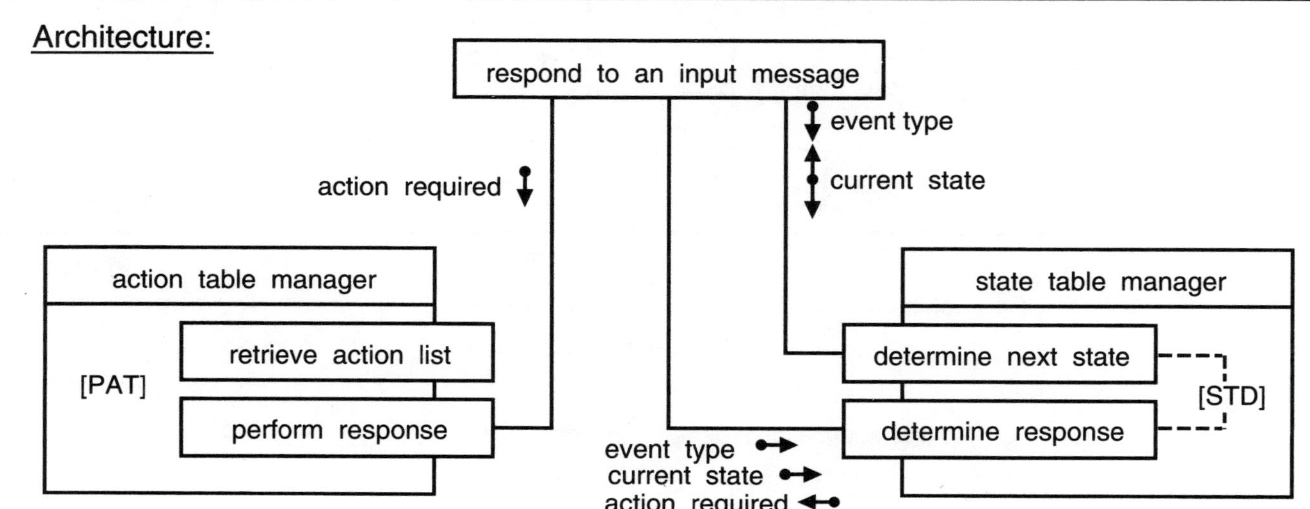

Figure 11.83 Refinement: Respond to an Input Message

Solution:

```
case action_list(i) is
  when action_type_1 ⇒          – when appropriate, specific actions will:
    . . .  [PSPEC 1.1]          – construct messages by field and
  when action_type_n ⇒          – store message into a file
    . . .  [PSPEC 6]            – code segment for each case alternative
end case;                       – exactly matches PSPECs
```

Architecture:

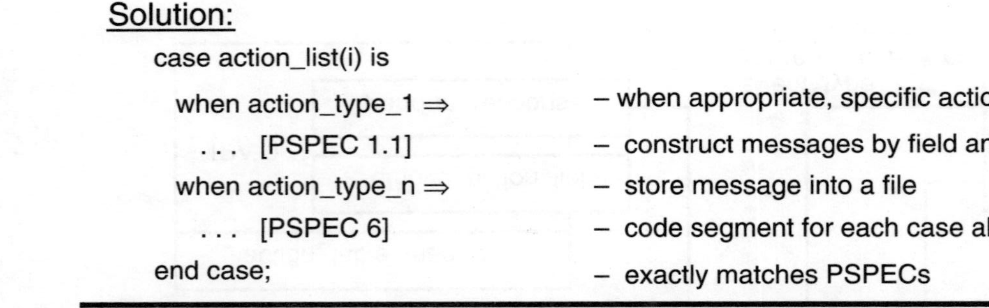
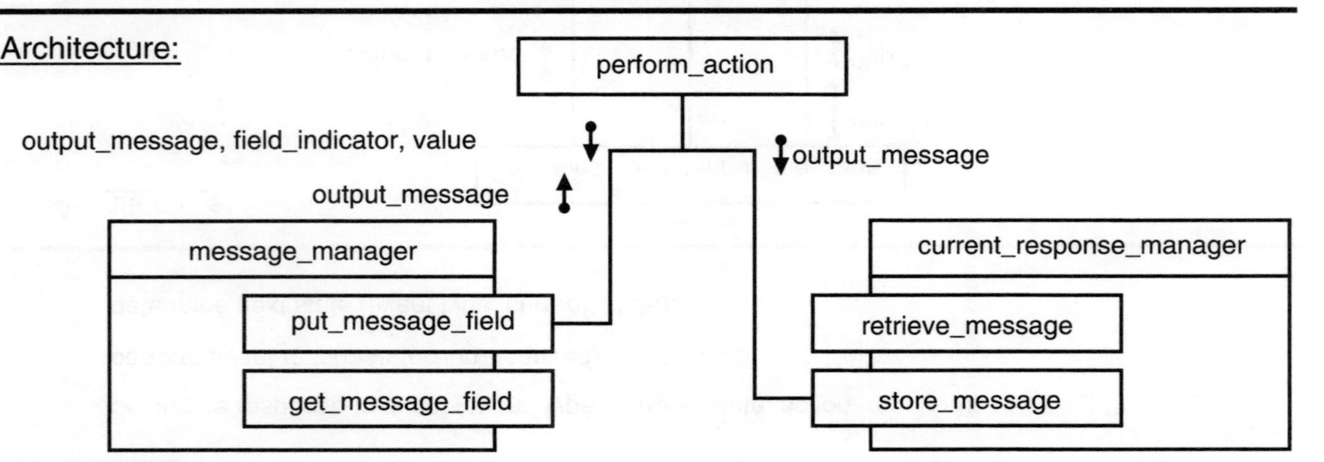

Figure 11.84 Refinement: Perform Action

component i of the action_list is passed as an argument to the procedure perform_action for processing according to its detailed specification.

Previously, retrieve_action_list was created as an interface encapsulating access to the PAT. Thus, this procedure is an operation on an abstract object that needs no further detailed decomposition. Since PSPEC details are hidden under perform_action, this component does require further detailing.

11.69 REFINEMENT: PERFORM ACTION

Perform_action receives the name of an individual PSPEC upon invocation (Figure 11.85). In response, an appropriate sequence of Ada code that clearly looks like the original PSPEC to the casual observer is executed. A problem oriented specification for the sequential software design to control response to a single PSPEC takes the form of a giant "case" statement. An incoming PSPEC name is compared to all of the case alternatives. The matching case alternative indicates the selected PSPEC and the appropriate code is executed. Each case alternative includes a single code segment representing a single PSPEC from the original requirements model. For the System Controller task of the satellite control system, perform_action is composed as follows:

```
procedure perform_action
     (pspec_desired: in process_specification)
is begin

case pspec_desired is
 when accept_raw_data      =>
  PSPEC 1.1;
 when deter_msg_type =>
  PSPEC 1.2;
 when analyze_comm_msg =>
  PSPEC 2.1;
 when determine_dest =>
  PSPEC 2.2;
 when decode_op_code =>
  PSPEC 3.1;
 when process_fire_cmd =>
  PSPEC 3.2;
 when update_lookup_table =>
  PSPEC 3.3;
 when generate_ack =>
  PSPEC 3.4;
 when update_fuel =>
  PSPEC 3.5;
 when comp_xmt_delay =>
```

```
    PSPEC 6;
   when others =>
    null;
   end case;
 end perform_action;
```

These PSPECs represent the complete set of PSPECs that appear in the body of the PAT allocated to System Controller. Moreover, they also compose the complete set of PSPECs allocated to System Controller.

Each PSPEC in the case statement above is replaced by actual code which performs the PSPEC. As an example, PSPEC 3.2 is replaced by the following code segment:

```
determine_firing_time( fire_event );
generate_firing_command_to_thruster( fire_event );
update_fuel_level( fire_event );
```

This code exactly mirrors PSPEC 3.2, as described in an earlier figure. Ada guarantees that this code can be implemented in exactly this form. By usage of encapsulated objects and private types, an appropriate set of abstractions and operations is generated to assure this.

Typically, PSPECs perform combinations of the following activities:

1. Simple to complex calculations;
2. Reading and writing of data stores and tables; and
3. Construction of response messages.

Different PSPECs associated with System Controller perform exactly these functions. Fuel level is updated (1, 2). A routing table is either read or updated (2). Both internal control events and outgoing response messages are constructed (3). All of these are implemented by proper selection of abstract objects and types.

Design of this small procedure centralizes the location of all the allocated PSPECs. Traceability to functional requirements is obtained by utilizing a centralized approach such as the one described here. Moreover, flexibility is enhanced because addition of PSPECs consists of adding PSPECs under the guise of more case alternatives. Extensive effort is not needed to determine all the necessary locations that require change to incorporate a new capability. New capabilities are usually added by updating the encapsulated control tables and by adding case alternatives. If sufficient object and type abstractions have been developed, addition of PSPECs is often accomplished by using already defined software. Use of existing software further reduces the level of effort needed to incorporate additional functionality into the satellite control system.

A final benefit to the approach of encapsulating PSPECs in a single procedure that builds upon abstractions is to create "lean and mean" code. "Lean and mean" code occupies a small amount of memory space and executes within very narrow time constraints. Careful allocation of specific PSPECs to the internals of a single task and further encapsulation of the PSPECs into a single procedure like

Solution:

determine response to event (event type, current state, action required);

perform event response (action required);

determine next state (current state);

Architecture:

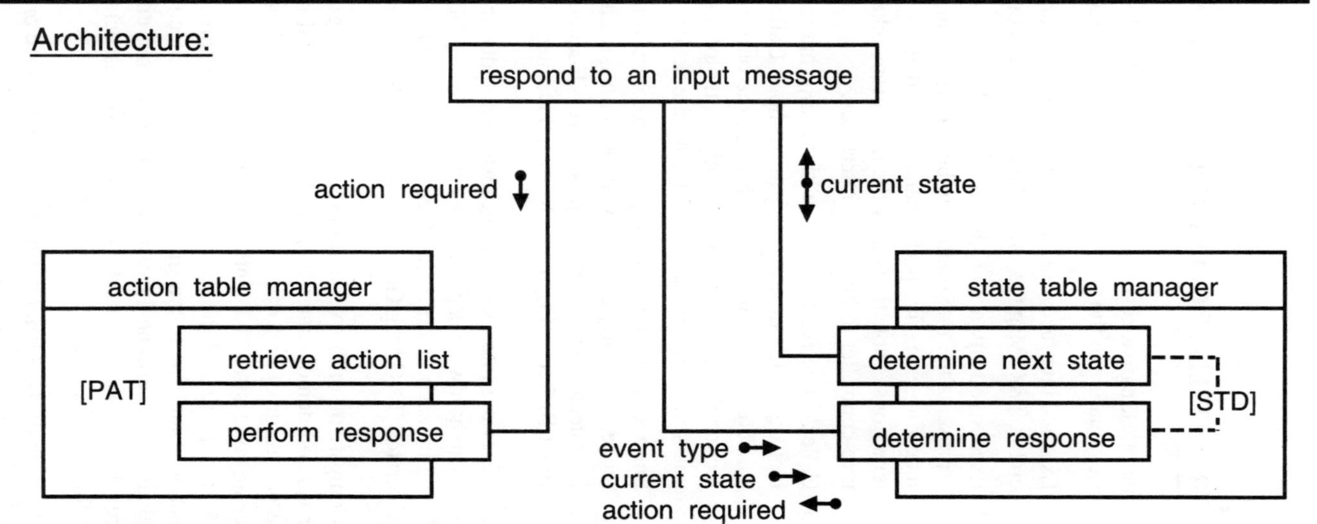

Figure 11.85 Refinement: Respond to an Input Message

perform_action assures that only code necessary to meet the user's needs actually gets implemented. No sloppy code is produced. This formulation typically leads to performance within severe constraints the first time an integrated system becomes operational.

11.70 SATELLITE CONTROL SYSTEM DETAILED DESIGN

The final tasking/packaging design is recapitulated in Figure 11.86 to perform a quality evaluation of the tasking design. Specific qualities are assessed as follows:

1. External interfaces are accommodated by separate tasks—Comm Msg Generator, T&C Msg Generator, and Message Storer.
2. Excessive software tasking is avoided—only six tasks are employed. This represents the maximum number of tasks which can be employed without incurring extensive performance degradations. The number of potential interactions is constrained by the limitations inherent in the original architecture-controller to buffers to interfaces.
3. Caller/callee relationships with tasking intermediaries effectively control blockage without restricting throughput. Caller/callee relations for this architecture are bidirectional through the buffer intermediaries. These bidirectional interactions significantly limit blockage without reducing throughput, since only two additional tasks are needed.
4. Entrance procedures are employed to control rendezvous caller protocols. All rendezvous entry calls are with buffer tasks. Each of the buffer tasks entries is protected by an entrance procedure—Enqueue Msg and Dequeue Msg for Input Buffer and Enqueue Resp and Dequeue Resp for Output Buffer.
5. Hardware interfaces are encapsulated under abstractions restricting visibility to hardware dependencies. Restricted visibility is accomplished by managing each external interface through a dedicated task—Comm Msg Generator, T&C Msg Generator, and Message Storer.

Comparison of this version of the tasking/packaging architecture with the earlier version demonstrates that "task creepage" did not occur. Generation of the internal design of each of the tasks, especially the System Controller, did not introduce any undesired tasks into the architecture.

A clear picture of the data path of all events through the architecture is easily generated, attesting to the simplicity of the architecture. Each input and output is evaluated to determine the exact use of rendezvous entry calls and entrance procedures. For instance, consider the interactions associated with a Comm Msg proceeding from source to destination:

1. Comm Msg Generator performs an entrance procedure call to

   Incoming Msg Pkg.Enqueue Msg;

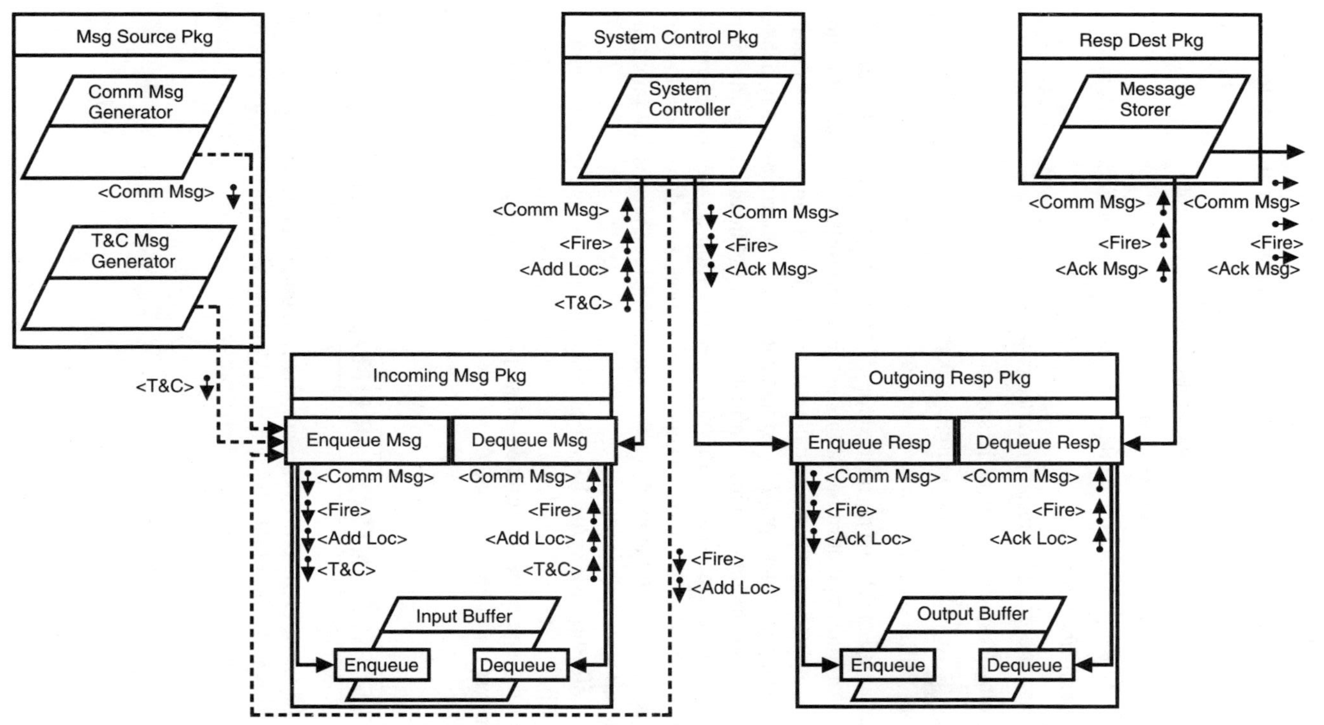

Figure 11.86 Satellite Control System Detailed Design

2. Incoming Msg Pkg.Enqueue Msg makes a rendezvous entry call to Input Buffer.Enqueue;
3. System Controller performs an entrance procedure call to Incoming Msg Pkg.Dequeue Msg;
4. Incoming Msg Pkg.Dequeue Msg makes a rendezvous entry call to Input Buffer.Dequeue;
5. System Controller performs an entrance procedure call to Outgoing Resp Pkg.Enqueue Resp;
6. Outgoing Resp Pkg.Enqueue Resp makes a rendezvous entry call to Output Buffer.Enqueue;
7. Message Storer performs an entrance procedure call to Outgoing Resp Pkg.Dequeue Resp; and
8. Outgoing Resp Pkg.Dequeue Resp makes a rendezvous entry call to Output Buffer.Dequeue.

Similar evaluations can be performed for <T&C>, <Fire>, and <Add Loc> control events. An important attribute of this architecture is that its simplicity allows these evaluations to be easily and visually performed. Performing these evaluations is a preliminary assessment prior to implementation to determine if any data can become lost during operation. This information is also an invaluable guide for isolation of problems during testing. Problem identification and resolution requires that the location of the offending module be identified. This data allows the tester to begin tracing through the modules to determine where processing failed, thus identifying the offending module.

On the whole, this tasking/packaging architecture rates very highly. Its simplicity and flexibility are commendable. Each of the heuristics for effective tasking design are fully and correctly utilized. High performance and low-levels of integration and test effort are anticipated.

11.71 SYSTEM CONTROLLER DETAILED DESIGN

Results of the LVM/OOD process are summarized into a single description in Figure 11.87. Several important characteristics of the sequential design are now readily apparent. The role of layered abstractions is revealed. Abstraction layers are employed to manage the details of responding to each event. Layering of abstractions is accomplished in the following manner:

1. respond_to_an_input_message;
2. state_table_manager, action_table_manager, perform_action; and
3. current_event_manager, message_manager, current_response_manager.

Each abstraction layer hides important details regarding data structures and mechanics from immediate, higher layers. Management of event, response, and message internals is hidden at the lowest level. Details associated with states, actions, and PSPECs are encapsulated at the second level. PSPECs in particular employ the lower level event/response/message abstractions. At the top level, overall response management is accomplished using table and action abstractions in a manner hidden from the main cyclic executive.

Incorporation of both traceability and flexibility into this detailed design is visually obvious. Tables are used extensively—STD and PAT locations are obvious and are recorded. A quick glance at this detailed design informs the developer or reviewer as to the exact modules containing the control specifications. The diagram also reveals the exact and centralized locations of the PSPECs in perform_action. Both verification and modification of PSPECs are easily realized.

Since this is a decomposition of a single element in the tasking architecture, care is taken to balance this diagram with the parent diagram. Reviewing the previous Satellite Control System Detailed Design reveals three interactions between System Controller task and the remainder of the tasking architecture. These appear at the bottom of this detailed design diagram for System Controller. To retrieve a current_event, current_event_manager.retrieve_manager performs an entrance procedure call to Incoming Msg Pkg. Dequeue Msg. Two categories of responses can occur—internal control events and outgoing response messages. These responses are appropriately queued by current_response_manager.store_message. Internal control events—<Fire> and <Add Loc>—are placed into the input buffer by an entrance procedure call to Incoming Msg Pkg.Enqueue Msg. Similarly, outgoing response messages to external devices, <Comm Msg>, <Fire>, and <Ack Msg> are transferred to the output buffer via an entrance procedure call to Outgoing Resp Pkg. Enqueue Resp.

In general, this detailed design exhibits high quality. Its use of layered data abstractions yields a flexible, traceable, high performance sequential software design within the System Controller task. Direct and successful application of the LVM/OOD methodology produces this design.

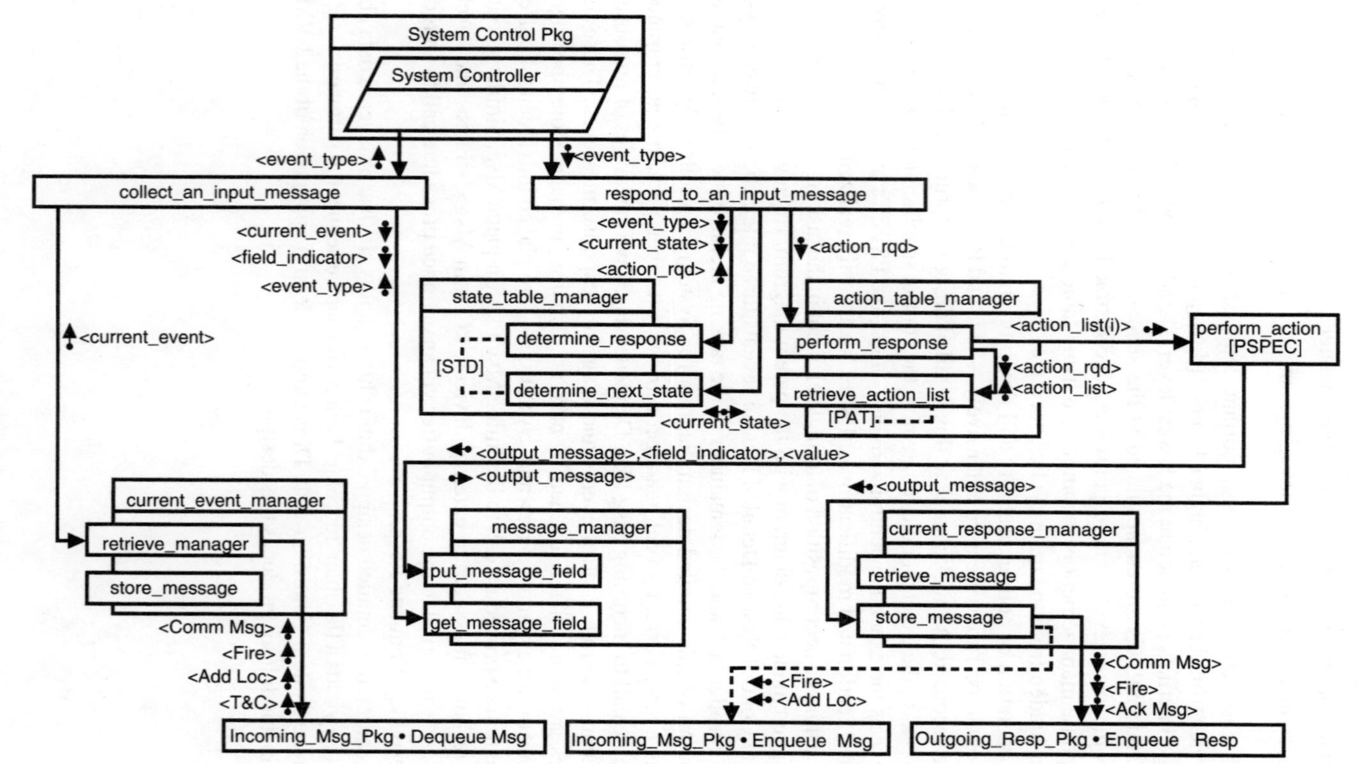

Figure 11.87 System Controller Detailed Design

12

Robot Controller Case Study

This chapter is the second case study illustrating application of the software engineering methodology to a prototypical real-time system. As an aid to understanding the value of methodical development, some of the steps illustrate flaws in the specification and design of the system under consideration. Flaws may or may not be corrected as encountered. Some disagreement may occur with some of the decisions made throughout the case study. This disagreement does not mean that the case study is flawed. Indeed, disagreement with decisions made throughout the analysis is not only natural but is also a fundamental reason for enforcing the methodical development. Employing an open forum to highlight and to justify all decisions made during the development ensures communication and obtains consensus on critical development decisions. Consensus and communications are important goals that significantly improve the likelihood of project success.

A Robot Controller represents another application of the development methodology to a typical embedded system. Embedded systems are characterized by a dedicated set of resources that fit into a small physical space and involve little or infrequent interaction with a user. These systems are typically placed into an operational mode by a user command. Repetitive operations ensue without significant interaction by the user for a lengthy period of time. After an extensive operational period, another user command causes the system to cease operation. This particular case study was adapted from *Ada in Distributed Real-Time Systems*, by Kjell Nielsen (McGraw-Hill, 1990). Significant extensions have been made to this case to illustrate application of the described methodology.

Industrial robots have become the focus of study in recent years to automate the manufacturing process. For the simplified robot envisioned in this study, several major components are assumed. A motorized base with its own smart controller allows mobility. For the robot to move, a command is issued to the motor controller. Once the move is completed, the smart motor controller returns an acknowledgment. Operation in this manner implies that the controller for the motor is capable of sensing its own internal operation and location and determining the successful completion of a move operation. As a result, inputs from the motor controller arrives aperiodically only in response to a specific motion command by the robot controller. Complete control over this interface is asserted by the robot controller.

In addition to moving its location, the robot can move the location of another object. To accomplish the move, the robot controller must participate actively. Moving another object is performed by direct control of another component of the robot—its arm. The controller commands the arm to move, senses the current location of the arm, assesses move completion conditions, and commands the arm to stop moving. Once the arm is activated, sensors on the arm feed location data directly to the robot controller at regular periods. Successful arm movement requires both management and utilization of sensor arm location data. In contrast to motor operations, the arm sensor is an interface over which the controller has no control. Once an arm movement is initiated, arm location data is provided by the arm sensor at regular intervals based on sensor hardware design.

Finally, this robot supports a predefined set of manufacturing operations. Six specific product operations are supported by the controller. Product support consists of a repeatable series of motor operations and arm activities. Repeatable sequences are written as a program and are pre-stored in read-only memory accessed by the robot controller. To support an actual production run, the operator of the robot controller chooses one of the pre-stored programs.

This case study captures many of the major characteristics of a typical real-time embedded system. Both aperiodic (totally under controlled) and periodic (independently controlled) interfaces are processed. Once production support is initiated, routine operations are accomplished without significant human intervention. A simple, severely limited user interface is needed. Finally, performance constraints are critical requirements—failure to respond within a time constraint results in extensive ruined raw product, which can be quite expensive.

12.1 OPERATIONS MODEL GENERATION

Specifying a user's view of software system operations Figure 12.1 consists of the following steps:

1. Specify user interfaces and the order of operations of user interaction;
2. Translate the order of operations of user interaction into an initial message sequence;
3. Expand the message sequence into detailed operational scenarios involving sensors, actuators, and other interfaces; and
4. Divide the detailed message sequence into a detailed event/response pattern indicating inputs and outputs.

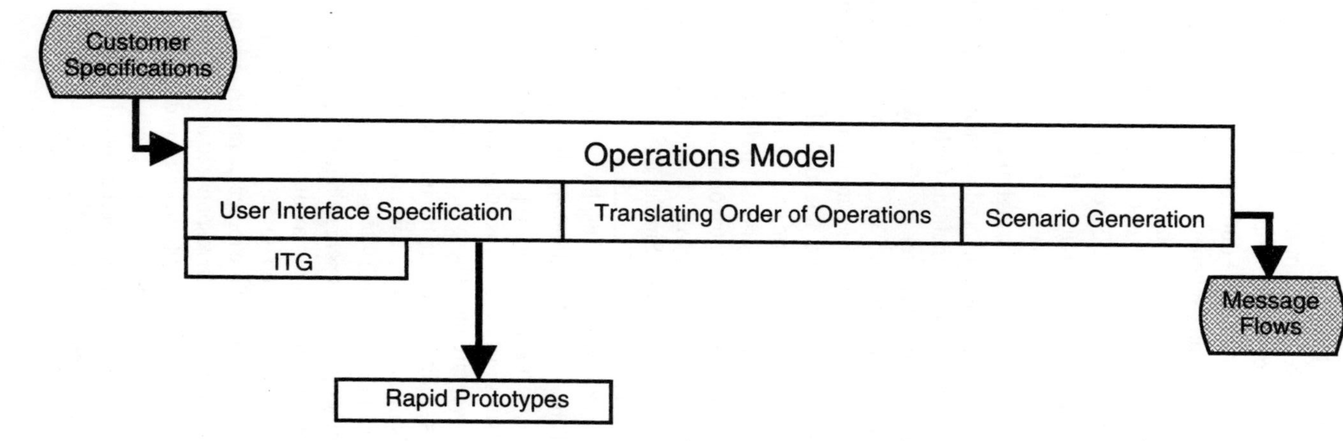

Figure 12.1 Operations Model Generation

12.2 USER INTERFACE SPECIFICATION (I)

A modern computerized front end Figure 12.2 is provided for operator management of the robot controller system. Potential operators are somewhat computer sophisticated and prefer a more sophisticated interface. Menus and queries are the primary form of interface. A point-and-click approach employing a mouse is highly desirable. Consistent use of mouse buttons is necessary to avoid confusion in the operator's mind. At any time during use of the interface, an operator needs the ability to change his mind. Whenever an operator inputs data or selects from a menu, rapid feedback is given as to the immediate effect of his decision. These criteria are employed to specify details of a user interface for the robot controller.

The user interface consists of a number of important components. A Main Menu provides top level control to the operator. Management of the power subsystem is accommodated via a Power Management Menu. Selection of one of the pre-stored control programs is accomplished through the dialog named Prestored Program Query. During real-time operations to produce manufactured items, an Operational Display serves to provide control functions to the operator.

An operator initially enters the user interface by choosing to execute the interface, indicated by a transition labeled Xqt. In response, Main Menu is displayed. According to the figure, four transitions are available from this interface—power management (Power Mgt), program selection (Program Selection), operations management (Program Execution), and exiting the main interface (Quit). Each of these transitions has an associated response, indicated within the transition label. If the user points to the Power Mgt entry on Main Menu and clicks the left mouse button, an action named Generate Power Menu occurs. This action is followed by transition to the Power Mgt Menu. Similar transitions are specified for selection of Program Selection and Program Execution menu entries. Choosing Quit from Main Menu results in clearing of the display screen.

Upon display of the Power Management Menu, several alternatives are available to the operator. Choosing specific power management operations—Power On, Power Off—results in an action to cause connection of controller components with the physical power circuits. These selections result in return to the Power Mgt Menu and appear as feedback loops in the interface transition graph. Selecting the Return entry in this menu causes transition to Main Menu.

When a Prestored Program Query is generated, the controller is asked to provide a program number (perhaps a name would be better). Once the user has typed the desired number, two options are available. Pushing the right mouse button causes a typed number to be cleared, giving the operator a second chance. Acceptance and permanent recording of the indicated program number occurs in response to pushing the left mouse button. In response to depressing the left button, the user interface returns to Main Menu. Automatic recording of a program number does not occur. Operators are forced to take an explicit action to record program number. An explicit action gives an operator the opportunity to change his mind, if the incorrect number is accidentally entered.

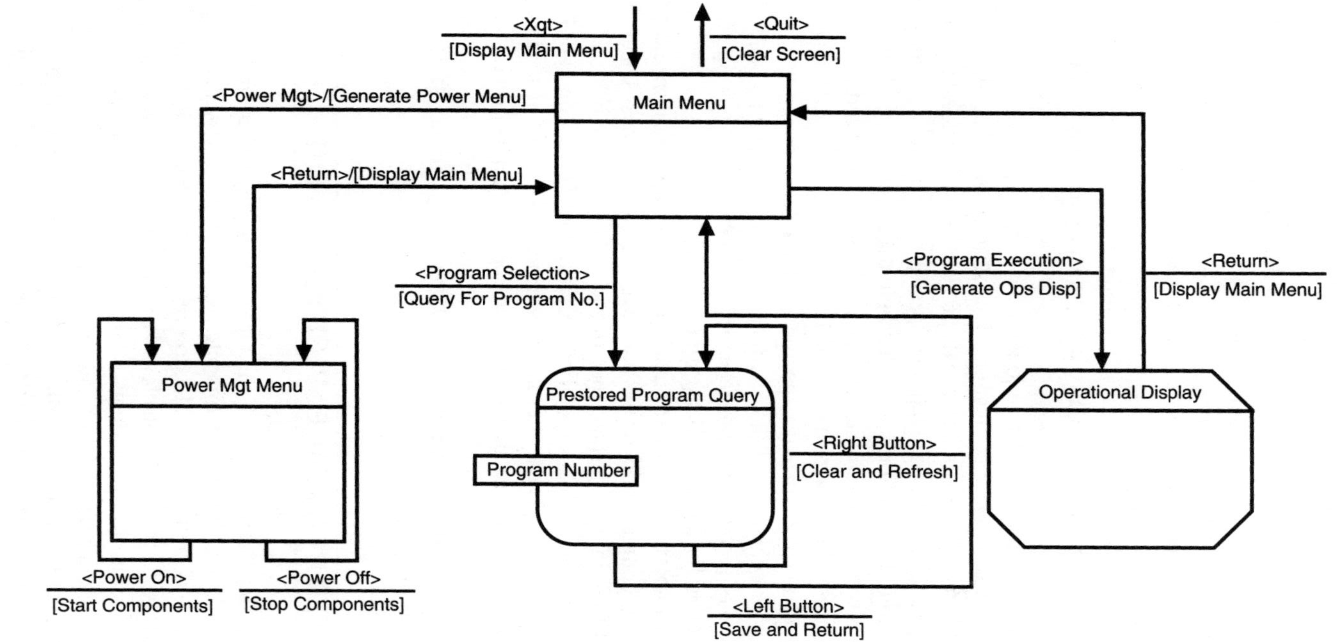

Figure 12.2 User Interface Specification (I)

Entry to and exit from Operational Display are characterized within this interface transition graph. Inclusion of further details of Operational Display would clutter this diagram, significantly reducing its readability and information content. For this reason, the next figure provides a detailed decomposition of the Operational Display portion of the new interface.

Extensive feedback transitions appear in the interface transition graph. Power Mgt Menu and Prestored Program Query both include specific feedback transitions. Feedback transitions are of great importance in the specification of a complete response to user interaction. Unfortunately, these transitions are often omitted. If omitted, an implementor is free to choose his own response, resulting in an inconsistent and flawed user interface. Eliminating flaws within the context of several thousand lines of implemented code typically requires significant debugging hours.

An important strategy relative to the user's interaction with these interfaces is also highlighted in this specification. This strategy is embedded in the Prestored Program Query. Once this query is displayed, a user provides data for the fields. According to the transition graph, two specific choices are available—right or left mouse button. Left Button means that field data is accepted. Right Button indicates that a second opportunity is desired. This strategy needs to be consistently employed throughout the remainder of the interface. Thus, an interface transition graph serves to standardize the specific mechanics of interaction, allowing future developers or enhancers of the interface to employ exactly the same mechanics. Elimination of inconsistent interface mechanics eases both learning curve and usage frustration for the controller operator.

Another important benefit of a detailed interface transition specification is consistency and completeness of the interface. A completeness check indicates an important flaw in the interface specification. Only two transitions are available from the query interface, as specified—Left Button (accept data) or Right Button (clear and try again). These alternatives are incomplete, failing to allow the user to exit without specifying a value. Perhaps an operator prefers to enter no value at all, simply returning to Main Menu. Maybe another button, such as Middle Button, could be utilized to simply transition to Main Menu with no effect.

12.3 USER INTERFACE SPECIFICATION (II)

Details of user interaction with the Operational Display are indicated in Figure 12.3. Entry into and exit from this interface are consistent with the parent display in the previous figure. The selection of Program Execution from Main Menu causes entry to Operational Display. Pointing to Return and clicking Left Button results in a return to Main Menu. This specification is leveled from the parent specification and balanced with indicated entry and exit conditions.

In addition to selecting Return, three other options are available to an operator. Choosing Run initiates robot controller and associated manufacturing operations. Transition returns directly to Operational Display. Remaining options allow an operator to either temporarily suspend execution (End) or to permanently cease operations (Stop). If End is selected, execution is temporarily suspended. Choosing Run again starts execution at the suspended location with the prestored program. Automated manufacturing operations often require temporary suspension to manually adjust raw input location that may have been displaced earlier during the production sequence. Once Stop is selected, return to Main Menu occurs. According to design of this interface, End is to be chosen before Stop can be selected. All of these rules are embedded within interface transitions specified in this figure.

Significant potential for confusion is incorporated into this interface component. Stop and End are too similar for most people. Renaming End to Suspend or to Pause would improve the clarity of the interface. An embedded rule requiring selection of End prior to choosing Stop is another potential problem. Special use protocols such as this rule are almost guaranteed to cause confusion, especially if a large number of rules must be learned. These shortcomings need to be remedied now rather than after implementation, when significant modification effort is required.

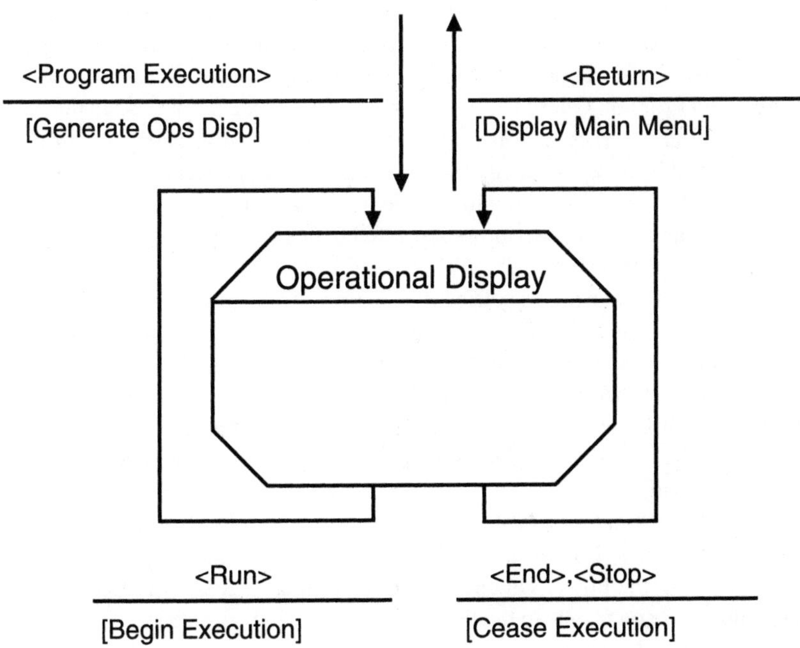

Figure 12.3 User Interface Specification (II)

12.4 USER INTERFACE SPECIFICATION (III)

While interface transition graphs are useful in providing a dynamic representation, explicit formats of each interface represent a set of static specifications (Figure 12.4). Formats for each of the interfaces above are characterized in this figure. Consistent with the requirement to provide immediate feedback describing effects of user selections, each of the interface formats includes three major subsections. Along the top of each interface appears its name. Menu selection options or data entry requirements, highlighted with a colored background, are displayed in the middle section of each interface. A bottom section provides status information in a graphical form—circles filled with colors. When a circle is green, status is normal. Red circles indicate problems with the most recent user specified input.

Some important assumptions are made in deciding which status indicators are appropriate to a given interface. Since all options in Main Menu lead to another menu, an operator can not make an inappropriate selection. Thus, only Power On and Running indicators are provided as status indicators for Main Menu. Extensive damages can be incurred if Operational Display is exited with the robot controller running. If robot controller remains running, Running is indicated by a red circle at Main Menu. Other interfaces also represent specific status display decisions. Each display needs an Invalid Input indicator. Since an operator may desire to change the selected prestored program number throughout the day, he needs the status of power. All other interfaces indicate Power On with a green circle. All interfaces employ status indicators appropriate to available selections or important to indicating global conditions of the robot controller.

Prestored Program Query employs some useful format variations. In the middle section of this interface, an operator is provided with information regarding his options for data entry. A specific query (Your Choice:) appears in a central position of the interface. Finally, allowable exit mechanisms appear below the input data area. Placing exit descriptors last reflects that they are not used until a program number is provided.

Review of these format specifications is important. Both strengths and weaknesses need to be identified. All of these interfaces have a common layout—top, middle, bottom. Information appears from top to bottom in the order in which an operator interacts with the interface. Operators receive immediate feedback regarding selections at the bottom of the interface consistent with top-middle-bottom order. Status is color coded to indicate appropriateness of a choice—green is good, red is bad.

Several flaws/limitations can be identified. Use of colors relative to Power On is a little confusing. For instance, after turning power on through the Power Management menu, the Power On circle is colored green. Exit from Operations Display with power on results in the Power On circle being colored red. This coloring scheme needs to be more thoroughly evaluated. Additionally, forcing operators to type a specific program number is a bit archaic. Most interface implementation environments (X-Windows, etc.) allow a point-and-click approach to be applied to a list such as the one that appears in Prestored Program Query. Selecting from

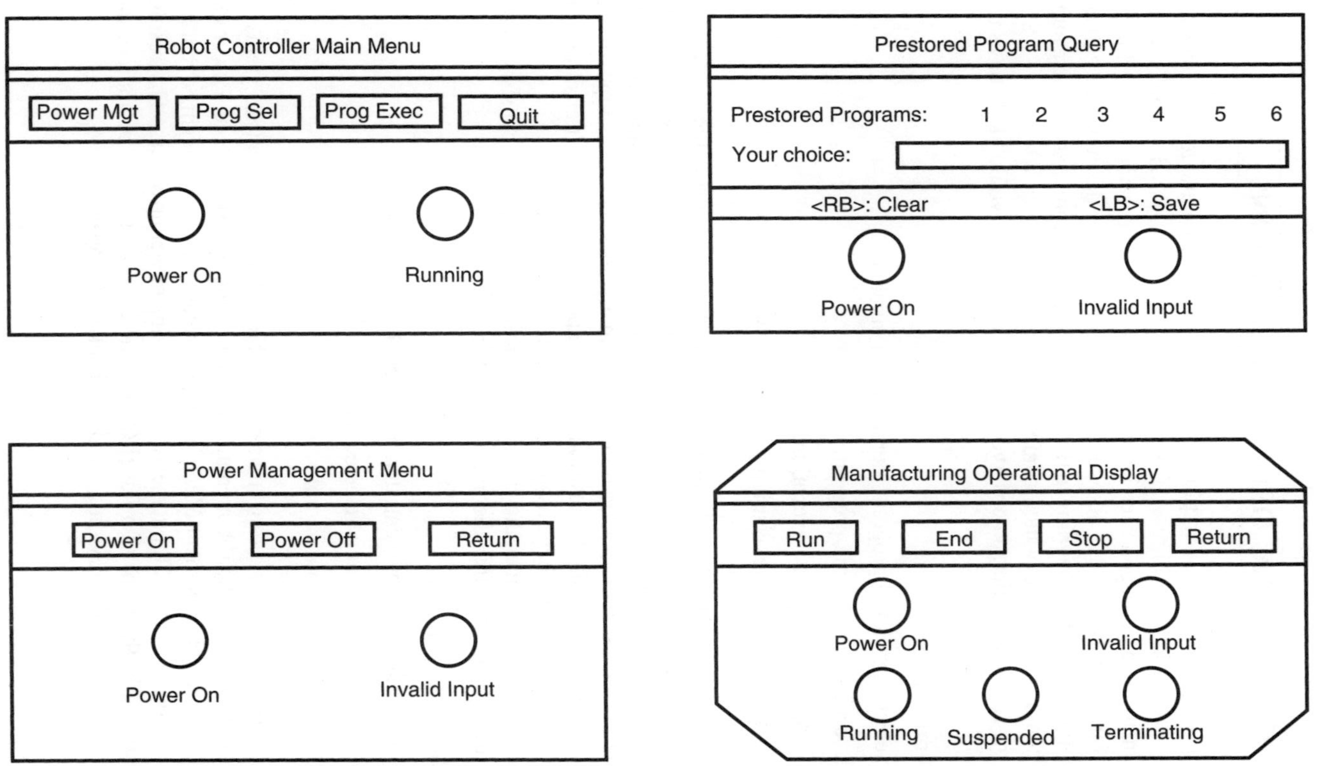

Figure 12.4 User Interface Specification (III)

a list allows an operator to manage robot control activities without typing. Point-and-click operations are utilized, a much easier and less error-prone approach.

12.5 TRANSLATING ORDER OF OPERATIONS

A rapid prototyping tool is employed to actually implement and test the interface transition specification (Figure 12.5). Each display is hardwired. Legally specified transitions based upon user input are allowed. An operator is placed at the helm of the prototype and is allowed to interact in any way desired. His choices are recorded. Rapid prototyping in this manner is easily accomplished with a number of commercial, off-the-shelf computer programs.

For the robot controller, an observed order of operations would likely be as follows:

1. Turn the power on;
2. Select a prestored program identification number;
3. Execute the prestored program;
4. Temporarily suspend execution; and
5. Permanently cease execution at the end of the shift.

In Figure 12.5, a sequence of user interactions is associated with the above order of operations. Each step above is described in the form of transitions through the interface transition graph (first column). In column two, specific interface selections are associated with detailed transitions. Finally, message flows/input events are associated with detailed transitions, where appropriate. Some transitions/interface selections do not have associated input control events.

As an example, consider the first step. Turning on the power consists of the following transitions within the interface transition graph:

1. Interface is started;
2. Power management menu item is selected;
3. Power on menu item is selected; and
4. Return to main menu item is selected.

These appear as the first four rows of the table. One of these entries yields an input control event to the robot controller. When the operator selects Power On from the Power Management Menu, an input event is generated. This event assumes the form of a Panel Input message, indicating power up occurs. This results in a response in the form of a Panel Output message to assure that appropriate circles are color-filled, providing rapid feedback to the operator.

Usage	User Input	Message Flow Generated
User Starts Interface	<Xqt>	–
User Needs to Manage Power	<Power Mgt>	–
User Turns Power On	<Power On>	<Panel Input> = (Power On)
User Returns to Main Menu	<Return>	–
User Needs to Select Program	<Program Selection>	<Panel Input> = (Manual Mode)
User Inputs Program Number	<Left Button>	<Panel Input> = (Program Select, Program Number)
User Needs to Begin Ops	<Program Execution>	–
User Chooses to Begin Xqt	<Run>	<Panel Input> = (Run)
[Operations Proceed]	–	–
User Chooses to End Xqt	<End>	<Panel Input> = (End)
User Chooses to Shut Down	<Stop>	<Panel Input> = (Stop)
User Returns to Main Menu	<Return>	–
User Needs to Manage Power	<Power Mgt>	–
User Turns Power Off	<Power Off>	<Panel Input> = (Power Off)
User Returns to Main Menu	<Return>	–
User Quits for Shift	<Quit>	–

Figure 12.5 Translating Order of Operations

12.6 OPERATIONAL SCENARIO GENERATION

Operations scenario generation (Figure 12.6) requires that the initial time-ordered message sequence be expanded to reflect the interaction of the robot controller with other interfaces. This other interaction results from the basic control exerted by the user commands and starts with the event sequence generated by the user interaction.

An external interface diagram that shows the interfaces managed by the robot controller is drawn. This diagram formally identifies robot controller interfaces. On the left side of the diagram, input interfaces are characterized. Input interfaces consist of the motor axis and the arm sensor. Actuators controlled during real-time operations are provided on the right side of the diagram—robot motor and arm turret.

A detailed message flow table or time-ordered event sequence table is generated, using the external interface diagram and beginning with the order of operations described above. A specific format is employed for the table. Each message in the sequence is characterized by its message type, its source and its destination. Of course, sources and destinations appear on the external interface diagram. Moreover, a short description is provided, justifying the appearance of the message in the time-ordered sequence. This description is absolutely critical for validation of the message sequencing by the customer and other reviewers.

Each of the Panel_Input messages and corresponding Panel_Output messages from the order of operations appears within the table. Note that these messages appear exactly in the desired order. Moreover, in the center of the table, real-time messages from and to the other interfaces are now included. These messages are incorporated into the message flow or event sequence between pushing the Run button and selecting the End button. From the user's perspective, this location is exactly where these messages appear in the time-ordered sequencing. Successful implementation of the robot controller requires that these events be accurately processed in exactly this context and this order.

Periodic inputs from the arm sensor appear as Sensor_Input messages. In response to these messages, either a motor command (Axis _Output) or an arm turret command (Sensor_Output) is generated. One of these outgoing responses occurs because the selected pre-stored program is being executed concurrently. Multiple occurrences of Sensor_Input messages on a repetitive basis are indicated in the message sequencing by an ellipsis.

In addition to inputs from the arm sensor, aperiodic inputs from the motor controller indicate the successful completion of motor commands. These acknowledgements appear in the message sequencing as Axis_Input messages. Sensor_Output or Axis_Output messages also follow these incoming events, indicating the concurrent processing of the selected pre-stored production management program. As before, repetitive occurrences are indicated by an ellipsis.

Messages in the time-ordered sequence that succeed the Run button message and precede the End button message are consistent with the order of operations deter-

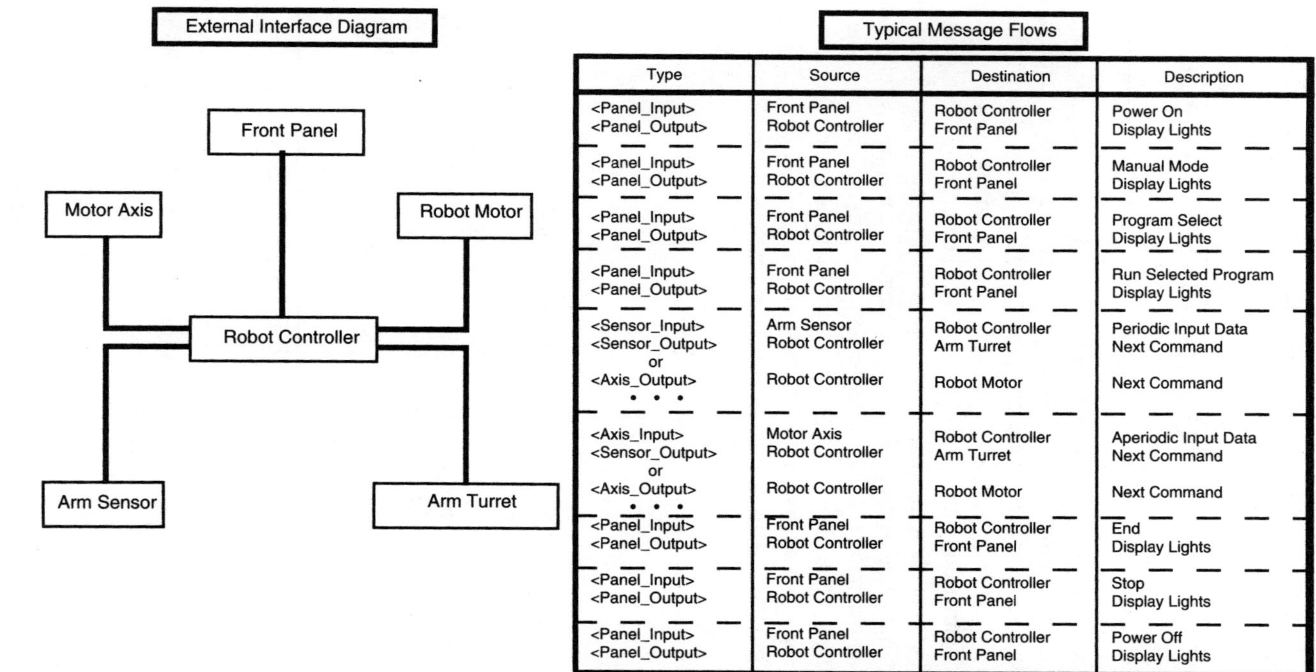

Type	Source	Destination	Description
<Panel_Input> <Panel_Output>	Front Panel Robot Controller	Robot Controller Front Panel	Power On Display Lights
<Panel_Input> <Panel_Output>	Front Panel Robot Controller	Robot Controller Front Panel	Manual Mode Display Lights
<Panel_Input> <Panel_Output>	Front Panel Robot Controller	Robot Controller Front Panel	Program Select Display Lights
<Panel_Input> <Panel_Output>	Front Panel Robot Controller	Robot Controller Front Panel	Run Selected Program Display Lights
<Sensor_Input> <Sensor_Output> or <Axis_Output> • • •	Arm Sensor Robot Controller Robot Controller	Robot Controller Arm Turret Robot Motor	Periodic Input Data Next Command Next Command
<Axis_Input> <Sensor_Output> or <Axis_Output> • • •	Motor Axis Robot Controller Robot Controller	Robot Controller Arm Turret Robot Motor	Aperiodic Input Data Next Command Next Command
<Panel_Input> <Panel_Output>	Front Panel Robot Controller	Robot Controller Front Panel	End Display Lights
<Panel_Input> <Panel_Output>	Front Panel Robot Controller	Robot Controller Front Panel	Stop Display Lights
<Panel_Input> <Panel_Output>	Front Panel Robot Controller	Robot Controller Front Panel	Power Off Display Lights

Figure 12.6 Robot Controller Operational Scenario Generation

mined in the previous illustration. The combined message sequences (user interface and other interfaces) in the exact time-order shown provide a concise description of the user's requirements for the system. By carefully evaluating the message/event sequencing justifications indicated in the descriptions column, the user validates his view of robot controller operations.

12.7 ROBOT CONTROLLER TEST INPUT/OUTPUT PATTERN

To support subsequent evaluation activities, the detailed message control flow/event sequence is converted to an input/output (stimulus/response) format (Figure 12.7). All flows into robot controller appear in the column labeled "Event." In this scenario, each input event results in one or more output responses. Responses associated with each input event appear in the column labeled "Response."

Several events elicit multiple responses, which appear in several rows of the table, each receiving a new row. All response rows immediately follow the event row. As an example, consider a Sensor Input event. According to the message scenario, two potential responses may occur. Either a Sensor Output or an Axis Output results, depending on execution of the current instruction in the selected prestored program. This conditional response appears as the following table entries:

< Sensor Input >	< Sensor Output >
--	or
--	< Axis Output >

Additional responses have empty event entries, indicating association with the most recent event.

Subsequent evaluations (requirements consistency/completeness checking, process architecture evaluation, and tasking architecture evaluation) employ this test input/output pattern. Each event is applied to individual models to verify that desired response(s) occur.

12.8 REQUIREMENTS MODEL GENERATION

Defining an implementor's view of software system requirements needed to satisfy the operational/user's view (Figure 12.8) consists of the following steps:

1. Generate a context diagram using the detailed message sequence;
2. Construct functional requirements in the form of a requirements tree and process specifications;
3. Describe event response logic for managing the PSPECs in the form of state transition diagrams and process activation tables;

Event	Response
<Panel_Input> = Power On	<Panel Output>
<Panel_Input> = Manual Mode	<Panel Output>
<Panel_Input>=Program Select	<Panel Output>
<Panel_Input>=Run	<Panel Output>
<Sensor Input>	<Sensor Output>
—	or
—	<Axis Output>
<Axis Input>	<Sensor Output>
—	or
—	<Axis Output>
<Panel Input>=End	<Panel Output>
<Panel Input>=Stop	<Panel Output>
<Panel Input>=Power Off	<Panel Output>

Figure 12.7 Robot Controller Test Input/Output Pattern

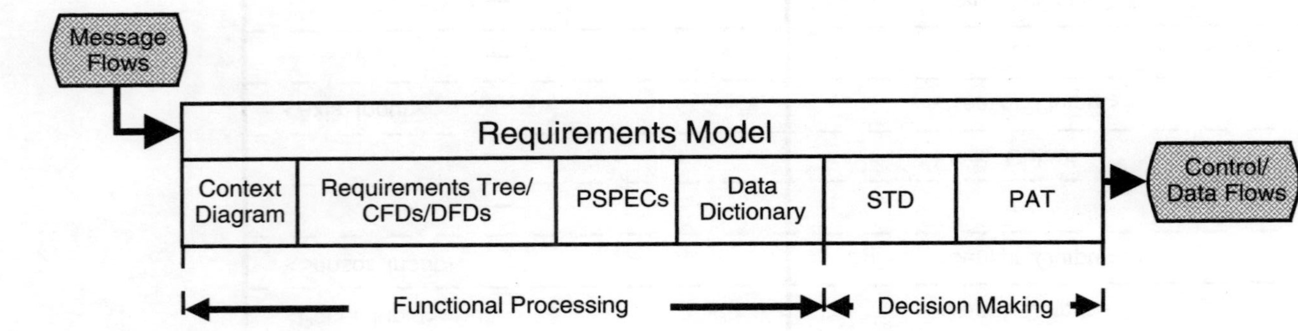

Figure 12.8 Requirements Model Generation

4. Perform a consistency and completeness check of implementor requirements against operational requirements;
5. Use the data dictionary to determine an initial set of data abstractions and operations on abstractions; and
6. Allocate timing requirements to PSPECs.

12.9 EXTERNAL INTERFACES/CONTEXT DIAGRAM

Review of the message sequencing indicates that six unique interfaces (Figure 12.9) are to be functionally managed. These interfaces are represented by message types: Panel_Input, Panel_Output, Axis_Input, Axis_Output, Sensor_Input, and Sensor_Output. The implementor's requirements accommodate these specific interfaces.

An initial specification of the implementor's requirements is captured in this context diagram. Each of the physical external interfaces (Control Panel, Motor, and Arm) is included. Specific and unique messages flowing across the interfaces represent functional interfaces. Notice that incoming messages appear as dashed arrows regardless of content. Indicating inputs as dashed arrows requires that specific responses are to be specified within a CSPEC.

12.10 COMBINED CONTROL FLOW AND DATA FLOW

A first level decomposition of the implementor's requirements for the Robot Controller is provided in Figure 12.10. Each of the external control and data flows is accommodated. Balancing with the context diagram is achieved. Bubbles or processes included within the diagram represent a functional requirement to be satisfied by the implementor. Each function is named by a verb—interpret, process, receive. Data is received by the function, transformed within the function, and results transmitted.

One of the most difficult steps to accomplish is determination of specific functions for inclusion within this first decomposition. A developer's experience bears heavily upon the proper choice. To start, input, processing, and output functions are usually included. For this diagram, input, processing and output include the following:

Input:	Interpret Panel Input	(0.2)
	Process I/O Command	(0.4)
	Receive Axis Acknowledgment	(0.5)

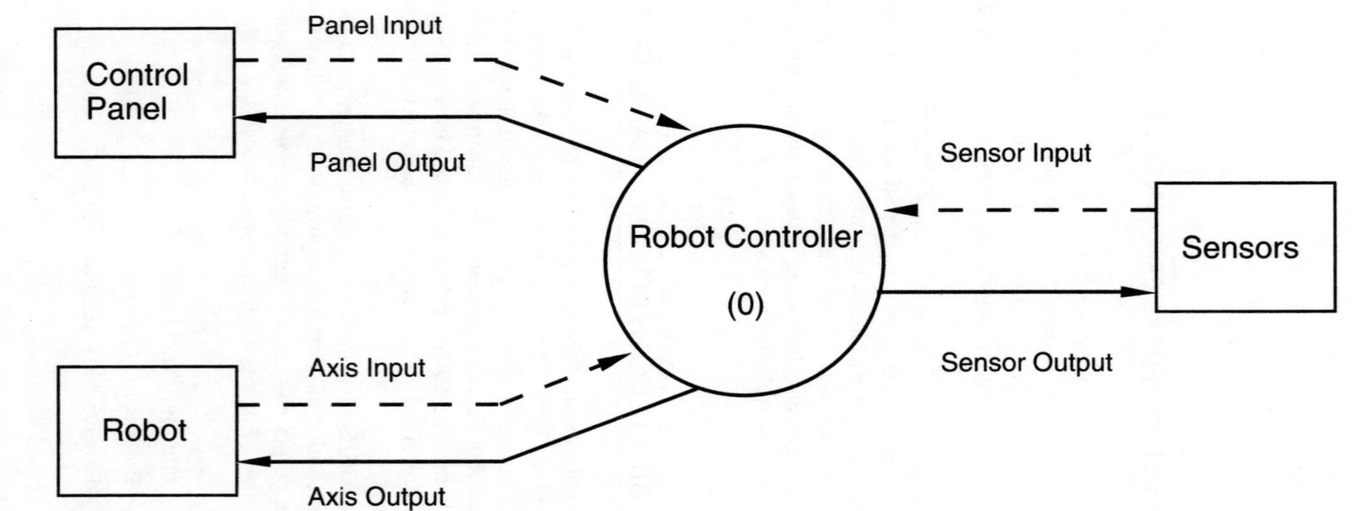

Figure 12.9 External Interfaces/Context Diagram

Processing:	Interpret Program Statement	(0.1)
Output:	Process Motion Command	(0.3)
	Process I/O Command	(0.4)

Specific functions are accompanied by a PSPEC indicating how the actual transformation occurs. For instance, Interpret Panel Input (0.2) acquires a Panel_Input message. Data within the message are used to generate an appropriate Panel_Output message. Moreover, if the Panel_Input message contains Program_Select data, selected program identifier is transmitted to the Interpret Program Statement function. A PSPEC representing this transformation might be as follows:

```
determine button_type of Panel_Input;
set appropriate components of Panel_Output;
check validity of button_type ;
if button-type not valid,
                set invalid_input in Panel_Output;
transmit Panel_Output;
if button_type is Program Select
                and button_type is valid,
   then extract program_id from Panel_Input;
     transmit program_id
                to Interpret Program Statement.
```

This description contains a general statement of the transformation that occurs. Use of each input is described, and all outputs are explicitly generated. Knowledge of Panel_Input and Panel_Output contents is employed; however, specific data structures are not assumed. Record component selection references do not appear within the PSPEC, since data structure details are disallowed at this stage.

Interpret_Program_Statement requires a specific Program_ID and a current location number. As a result of interpreting a pre-stored program statement, either a motion command or an I/O command to the arm turret occurs. Typically, processing an I/O command to move the robot arm turret requires knowledge of the current location of the arm. Thus, Interpret Program Statement shows a Sensor Value input data flow. Similarly, a motion command needs the status of the most recent motion, necessitating a Motion Acknowledge input data flow.

A number of important and potential flaws appear in this specification. Program_ID must be permanently stored somewhere to be used as a basis for calculations during execution. Therefore, Interpret Panel Input (0.2) probably stores the result into a data store, which Interpret Program Statement (0.1) always accesses. Similarly, the latest arm location, indicated as the data flow Sensor Value, and the Motion Acknowledge data flow need to flow into permanent data stores immediately accessible by either function.

Another important data store is also missing. Interpret Program Statement (0.1) needs the current instruction being executed. A data store entitled Current Instruction Counter is conspicuously absent. Successful execution of a program statement in the selected pre-stored program needs the Program ID, the Program, the Current Instruction Counter, Current Sensor Value, and the Motion Acknowledge Status. An appropriate PSPEC for Interpret Program Statement looks like the following:

```
loop
    Fetch current_instruction from Program area in ROM
        using Program ID
                  and Current Instruction Counter;
    If current_instruction is a motor command then
        generate Motion Command
                  using Motion Acknowledge;
    If current_instruction is arm turret command then
        generate I/O Command using Sensor Value;
     Increment Current Instruction Counter;
end loop;
```

Potential confusion can result from reading this diagram. Input and output processing for the motor are split into two separate functional requirements. Similar arm turret processing, however, is combined into a single functional requirement. This combination tends to hide the uniquely distinct differences between input and output processing and may cause extensive confusion at implementation. Moreover, traceability of requirements is hindered, due to the lack of clarification of the different requirements. Breaking arm input and output into two separate processing requirements is likely to save hours of confused debugging during integration and test activities.

Naming conventions employed in this specification are subject to criticism. Selection of names for data flows is both poor and confusing. I/O Command is more clearly named Turret Arm Command. Switching from Axis Output to Motion Block reduces traceability of requirements throughout future development efforts. Although indicated on this specification, the name switch is not likely to be carried through further development. As a result, actual meanings are lost or misconstrued later in the process.

A final criticism against this particular representation is that its format does not aid the implementor. Functional requirement bubbles are randomly located on the page, reflecting a lack of primary focus for the developer. Greater clarity is provided by using the representation suggested by the next illustration.

At the base of each control flow (dashed arrow) is a solid crossbar. This solid bar indicates that underlying event responses (i.e., a control specification or CSPEC) further detail the manner in which functional processing occurs. By convention, all of the CSPEC bars on this diagram refer to the same CSPEC (a combined STD and PAT for the whole robot control system).

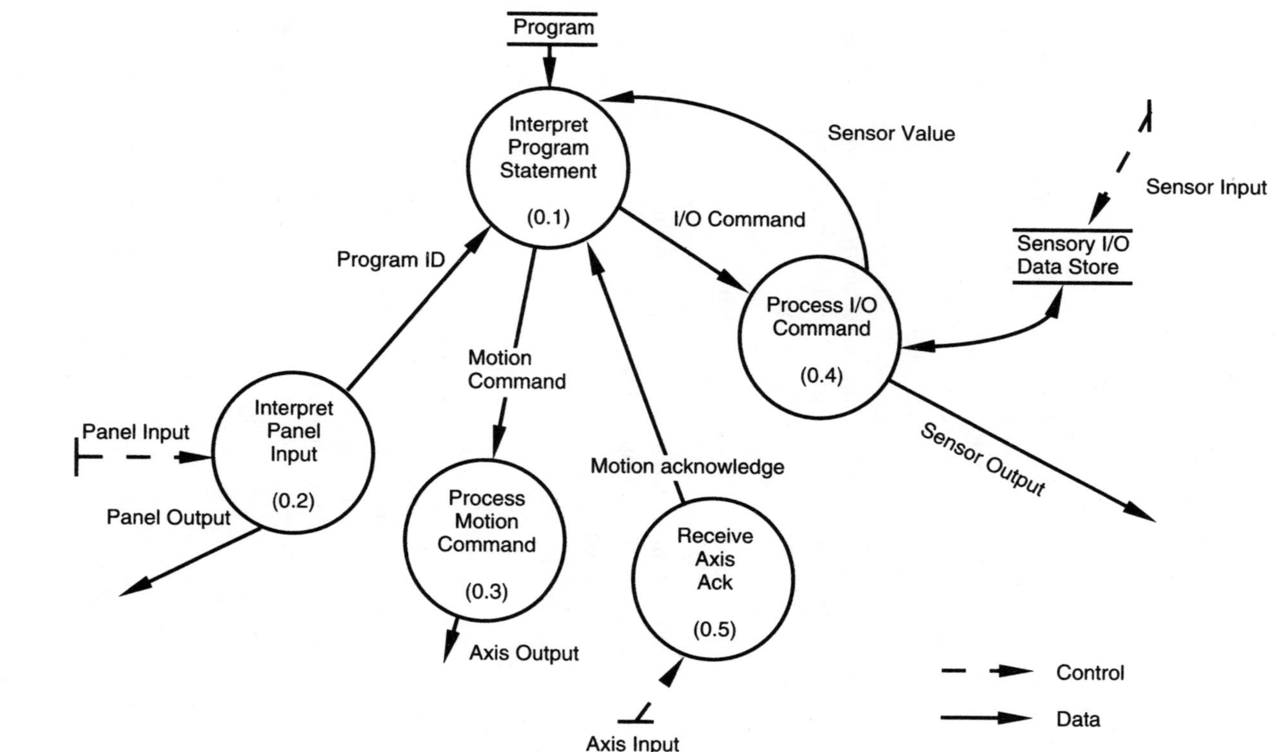

Figure 12.10 Combined Control Flow and Data Flow Technology Independent

12.11 AN IMPROVED CONTROL FLOW/DATA FLOW DIAGRAM

While emphasis upon diagramming technique may seem pedantic, a properly formatted diagram provides significant implementation suggestion and guidelines (Figure 12.11). Requirements traceability is also enhanced by proper formatting.

In this improved representation of implementors' requirements for the robot controller, all inputs and outputs from the parent requirement appear on the outer edges of the diagram. When a reviewer compares the parent to the child, extensive searching to verify proper balancing is necessary. Many who diagram tend to locate parent inputs and outputs haphazardly within the diagram making searching necessary to corroborate balancing. This searching can be tedious, aggravating, and prone to error. Errors in validating leveled and balanced flow diagrams result in requirements being lost during the decomposition process. Lost requirements lead to significant integration and test headaches.

Notice the flow of data within the diagram. In general, data flows (in a operational sense) from the left side of the diagram to the right side of the diagram. Representing flow of data from left to right is utilized because the human eye tends to perceive most readily in this way. (Photographers have known and used this characteristic for years.) For most readers, the requirements are more easily assimilated and understood when this format is employed.

By placement of processes on this diagram, some of the implementation experience of the specifier is transmitted to the developer. An initial working system that focuses upon routine, end-to-end data flow would naturally focus on the following sequence of functions:

Interpret Panel Input (0.2);

Interpret Program Statement (0.1);

Process Motion Command (0.3) or Process I/O Command (0.4).

Receiving Axis Acknowledgments (0.5) and Processing I/O Commands (0.4) for incoming Sensor_Input data are accomplished at a later date. Processing Sensor_Output data first also suggests the separation of turret arm sensor input/output handling into two unique requirements. Tracking partially satisfied requirements during incremental development is difficult and usually results in some requirements being missed. As a result, significant time is wasted during integration and test attempting to identify these missing requirements. Identifing and resolving partially satisfied requirements in the midst of several hundred thousand lines of Ada software integrated with attendant hardware is difficult. Significant effort is expended, resulting in budget overruns and missed schedules.

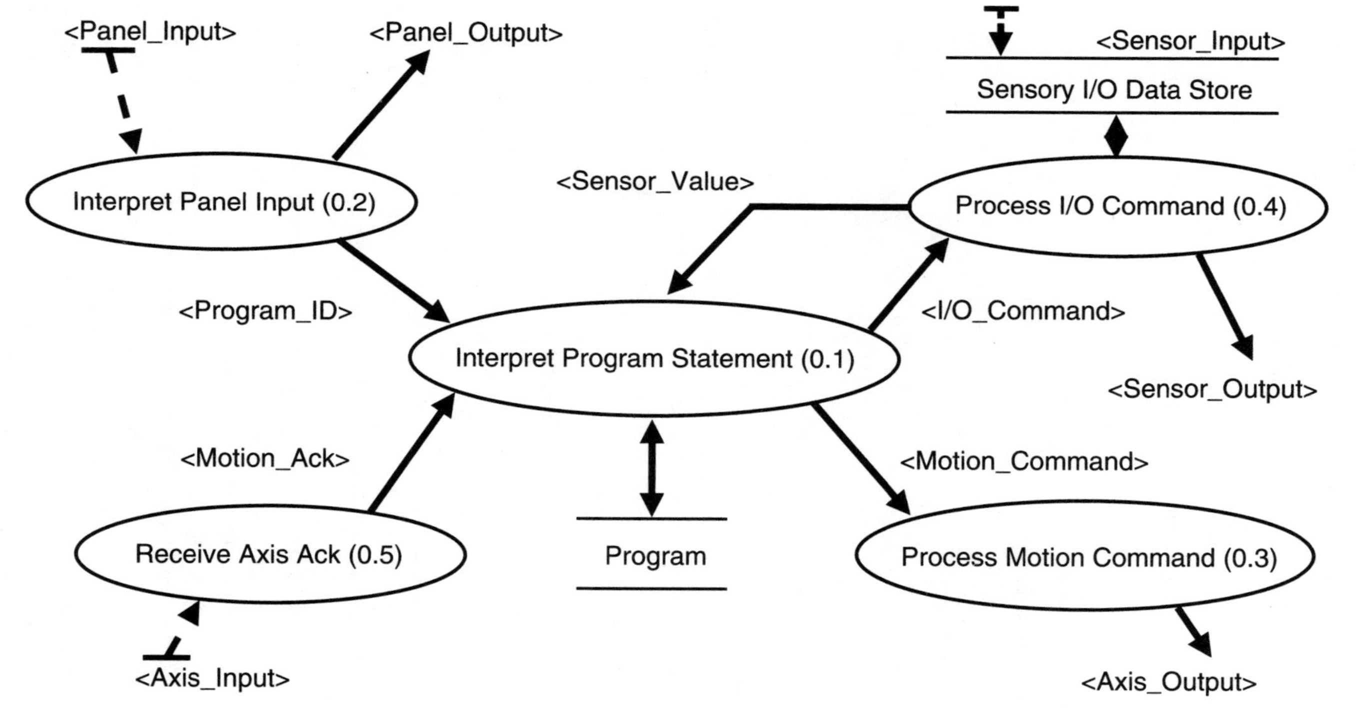

Figure 12.11 An Improved Control Flow/Data Flow Diagram

12.12 STATE TRANSITION DIAGRAM

A control specification or CSPEC describes the translation of events into underlying processing, i.e., decision making powers invested in the robot controller (Figure 12.12). Complete event response specification requires two components—the STD and the PAT. In the case of the robot controller, specific responses are dependent on the button-type component of the Panel_Input message. Since the specific event response is the same for any event regardless of its context, no summary action name is employed in this specification. Each event is employed as an action name.

Specific states for the robot controller are as follows:

1. System Inactive: no power is available
2. System Initialization: power has just been activated
3. Manual Mode: user is selecting a program
4. Executing Program: user selected program is being executed
5. Suspended: execution stopped at current location
6. Terminating: execution is no longer being repeated.

Legal transitions among the states depend on data necessary to assure the smooth operation of the robot. All the transitions indicated in the diagram are consistent with the implied order of operations.

Of primary importance are the feedback or state preserving transitions indicated on the diagram. As indicated in the user interface specification, an explicit Run button is pushed to start execution of the chosen program. Thus, a Program Select button keeps the robot controller in the Manual Mode state. If this is not specified as a requirement to the implementor, the implementor is free to respond as he chooses. Since the actual software implementor might not even see the system requirement description (this is likely to be the case in a large program development), he might choose transition to the Executing state with an appropriate response. As a result, significant manufacturing processing is performed before the surprised operator can halt operations if he has accidentally selected the wrong program. Raw materials might be ruined and significant financial losses incurred. Therefore, this state preserving transition is critical to the correct operation of the robot system.

Another example of a state preserving transition appears in the Executing state. Both incoming Sensor_Input and incoming Axis_Input maintain the Executing state. While this may be obvious for a small system such as the robot controller, large developments are so complex that details associated with processing incoming data are easily overlooked. Exact details of responding to these incoming events need to be described to the implementor, regardless of the size and complexity of the system under development. If response details are unspecified, software developers are free to choose their own implementations. An incorrectly implemented response can cause critical data to be lost. If the implementor does not know to save the data in some commonly accessed data store, he is not likely

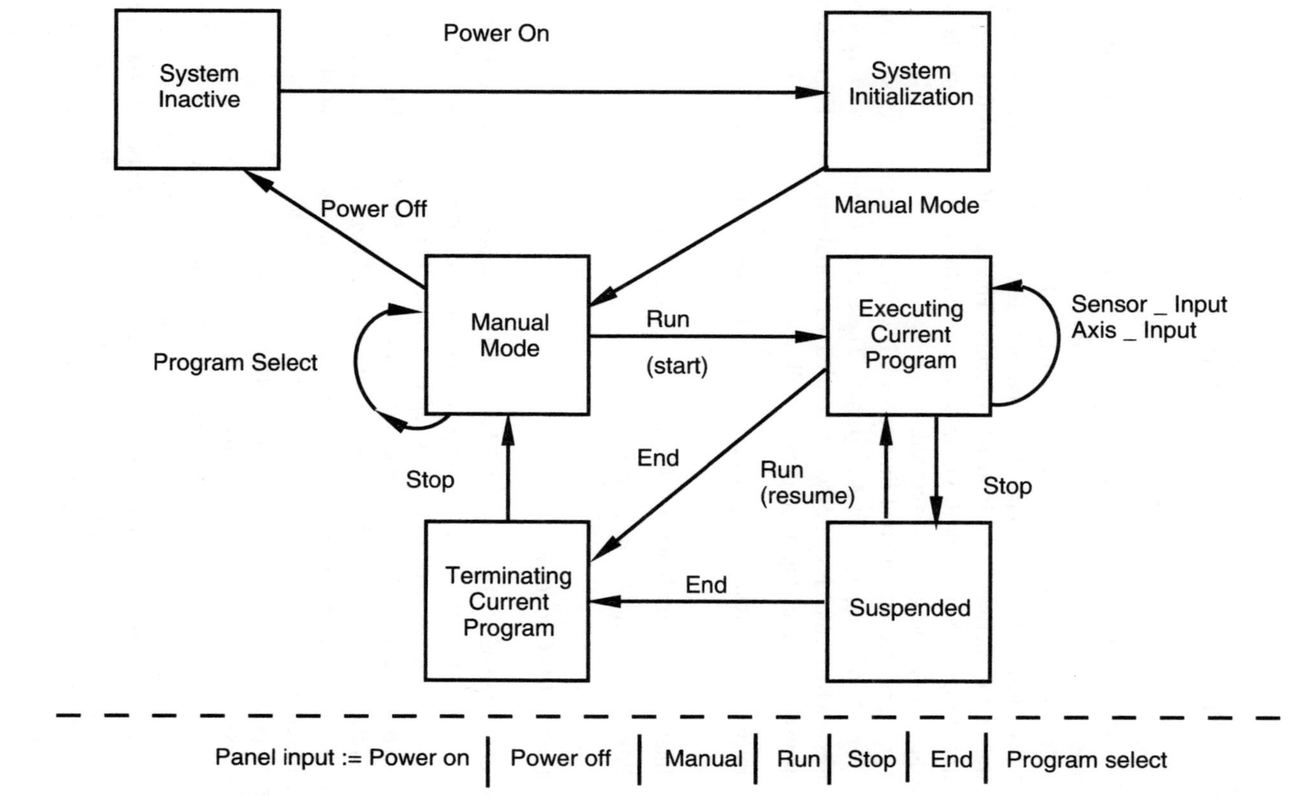

Figure 12.12 State Transition Diagram

to do so. Identification and resolution of inappropriate event responses is a problem when hidden within a large number of lines of Ada code integrated with complex hardware.

12.13 PROCESS ACTIVATION TABLE

Translation of events and responses into underlying functional requirements is the purpose of this PAT (Figure 12.13). Each event or action is correlated to a specific sequencing of functions or to combinations of functions that occur in parallel. For example, consider a Run button event. From the STD, this event causes the controller to transition from Manual Mode state into Executing state. In response to this transition, Interpret Panel Input (0.2) occurs. This is sequentially followed by Interpret Program Statement (0.1). In other words, the first statement of the selected pre-stored program is executed.

Of greater interest from a real-time perspective is the robot controller's response to either a Sensor_Input or an Axis_Input. These events require concurrent responses, each of which is composed of detailed sequential responses. For instance, a response to an Axis_Input requires the following:

```
Receive Axis Acknowledgment (0.5);   -- Parallel Sequence 1
    AND
Interpret Program Statement (0.1);   -- Parallel Sequence 2
Process Motion Command (0.3);
    OR
Process I/O Command (0.4).
```

This combined parallel and sequential response is indicated with a two letter combination and additional notation along the bottom of the process activation table.

In fact, using this overly complex representation (two letters and notes at the bottom of the table) indicates a poor state transition specification. This representation format is not to be utilized. Introduction of additional states usually eliminates this awkward response specification. Typically, an intermediate state with internal control events is necessary. For an example of intermediate state usage, see the previous case study (a satellite control system).

In this example, the event name is used as the action name. Using the same name for both event and action is acceptable if response to a specific event is the same, regardless of conditions. For most real-time systems, this condition is not usually the situation. Therefore, separate event and action names need to be employed. Also, using the same name for both event and action tends to cause proliferation of states in the STD, as more states are necessary to distinguish the variety of conditions faced by the system.

Input \ Process	0.1 Interpret Program Statement	0.2 Interpret Panel Input	0.3 Process Motion Command	0.4 Process I/O Command	0.5 Receive Axis Acknowledgment
Power On		1			
Power Off		1			
Manual		1			
Run	2	1			
Stop		1			
End		1			
Program Select		1			
Sensor Input	A1		A2	A2	
Axis Input	B1		B2	B2	C1

Parallel activity chains:
Sensor input: A1; A2 or A2 (.2; .3; or .4)
Axis input: B1; B2 or B2 (.1; .3; or .4)
and
C1 (.5)

Figure 12.13 Process Activation Table

12.14 DATA DICTIONARY

A data dictionary (Figure 12.14) provides common and useful names for all data elements in the requirements. Moreover, the detailed structure of data elements is identified. These data elements are to be represented by abstractions in the final software development. In the example dictionary for the robot controller, Sensor_Input, Sensor_Output, Axis_Input, and Axis_Output all employ some internal structure. For this reason, each must be implemented as abstract types with functional operations provided on those types.

For example, consider the Sensor_Input. According to the dictionary, this data element consists of two components—position and detection level. Abstract operations to be performed on an object of this type include the following:

1. create_sensor_input;
2. put_position_x;
3. get_position_x;
4. put_position_y;
5. get_position_y;
6. put_detection_level;
7. get_detection_level; and
8. destroy_sensor_input.

Once the data dictionary is defined, implementation as data abstractions can be accomplished in parallel to the remainder of the development of the robot controller. Other operations may be defined (if necessary) to support implementor requirements. These operations are identified during sequential software design by application of the LVM/OOD methodology

12.15 REQUIREMENTS EVALUATION

Events, control requirements, functional requirements, and responses are integrated in Figure 12.15. Robot controller operations are initialized in the System Inactive state. Each incoming event in the test input/output pattern is presented to the robot controller. A new state is determined from the STD. Then, the PAT is consulted to obtain the functional response. *Events are evaluated in the exact same order as they appear in the test input/output pattern.* Each Panel_Input message flow is replaced by its specific message type for clarity.

Two major and important flaws in the event response specification are revealed by this evaluation. An inconsistency appears in the response to a Sensor_Input in comparison with an Axis_Input. Each Axis_Input invokes two activities in parallel — Receive Axis Acknowledgment (0.5) and processing the next program statement (0.1, 0.3, 0.4). By comparison, Sensor_Input responses are restricted to

```
Panel_Input   : = Power On | Power Off | Manual | Run | Stop | End | Program Select
        Program_Select: = 1 | 2 | 3 | 4 | 5 | 6;
Panel_Output: = Power On | Invalid  Input | Manual | Running | Suspended | Termination

Sensor_Input: = Position + Detection_Level;
        Position: = (X, Y);
        Detection_Level: = 0 | 1;

Sensor_Output: = Pointing_Error | Motion_Block
        Pointing_Error: = (delta_x, delta_y);

Axis_Input: = Position;
        Position: = (x, y);

Axis_Output: = Location_Error;
        Location_Error: = (delta_x, delta_y);
```

Figure 12.14 Data Dictionary

State Before	Control Input	State After	Processing Performed
System inactive	Power On	System initialization	0.2 Interpret panel input
System initialization	Manual Mode	Manual mode	0.2 Interpret panel input
Manual mode	Program Select	Manual mode	0.2 Interpret panel input
Manual mode	Run	Executing	0.2 Interpret panel input then 0.1 Interpret prog statement
Executing	Sensor Input	Executing	0.1 Interpret prog statement then 0.4 Process I/O command or 0.3 Process motion command
Executing	Axis Input	Executing	0.5 Receive axis acknowledgment and 0.1 Interpret program statement then 0.4 Process I/O command or 0.3 Process motion command
Executing	End	Terminating	0.2 Interpret panel input
Terminating	Stop	Manual mode	0.2 Interpret Panel input
Manual mode	Power Off	System Inactive	0.2 Interpret panel input

Figure 12.15 Requirements Evaluation

processing the next program statement. This response is inconsistent with the Axis_Input response details, and reflects a major flaw within the requirements. No mechanism exists for assuring the flow of Sensor_Input data into the robot controller system.

An additional flaw in the event response mechanism is also revealed by this evaluation. While this system indeed works with these specifications, throughput (and corresponding response times) is likely to be quite poor. Execution of the next pre-stored program instruction is tied to either a Sensor_Input or to an Axis_Input event. During the time between these events, no pre-stored program instructions are executed. Constraining pre-stored program execution in this way poses a significant performance problem, resulting in wasted CPU time. Moreover, inadequate cycling on the selected pre-stored program might cause significant damage to the raw materials. If the arm keeps moving too long, its pressure can literally crush some fragile metal being used. A better approach is to specify that execution of the next instruction occurs independently and concurrent with processing of incoming events. Another alternative is to employ an internal control signal/event to signal execution of the next statement in the pre-stored program. Utilization of an internal control event results in a larger state table, enhancing flexibility of the ultimate implementation.

According to the major texts on specification of real-time systems, delineating data flows, PSPECs, STDs, and PATs is sufficient to assure complete specification of a real-time system. However, without the time-ordered event sequence to evaluate requirements, these major flaws are not identified, and are transmitted into the actual code implementation. Once incorporated into several hundred thousand lines of integrated Ada code, isolating these faults requires significant and highly frustrating efforts. In fact, identification of the cause of poor performance might be impossible.

12.16 ARCHITECTURE MODEL GENERATION

Describing a top level design (Figure 12.16) that effectively employs concurrent activity to satisfy both operational and implementor requirements consists of the following steps:

1. Enhance both functional and control requirements to accommodate specific hardware/technological interfaces;
2. Perform a consistency and completeness check of enhanced requirements against operational requirements;
3. Translate both functional and control requirements into a process architecture;
4. Perform a consistency and completeness check of the process architecture against operational requirements;

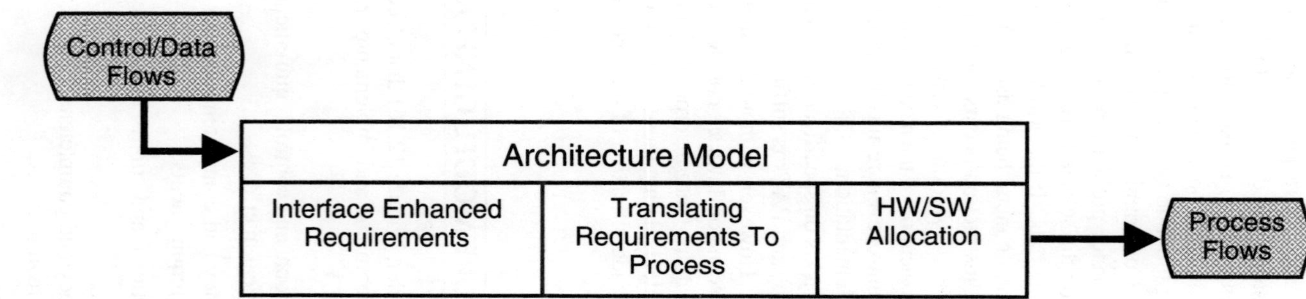

Figure 12.16 Architecture Model Generation

5. Evaluate architecture performance against timing constraints based on combining timing allocations for requirements mapped into each architecture process; and
6. Allocate requirements within each architecture process to hardware and to software.

12.17 ARCHITECTURE TEMPLATE ENHANCED CONTROL/ DATA FLOW DIAGRAM

As the design process begins, additional requirements are added to allow the robot controller operation within a specific hardware environment. According to the architecture template (Figure 12.17), four influences are important: input, output, user, and maintenance. Three of these are addressed in the illustration. From the user perspective, specific requirements are necessary to assure the movement of data to/from the user panel. Three new requirements are added to guarantee this integrity of data movement, as follows:

Read Panel Input (1)

This requirement, according to the PSPEC, assures that data is copied from the memory mapped hardware interface into a temporary storage;

Validate Panel Input (2)

Evaluating the preserved panel input for correctness is the purpose of this requirement. Each user command is evaluated using the STD to assure that the specific button pushed is valid under the current conditions;

Output To Panel (8)

Inputs to this requirement consist of either an error indicator or a Panel_Output command. In either case, a properly formatted Panel_Output message is constructed and copied into the memory mapped hardware interface for setting the hardware panel switches.

Additional requirements to manage turret arm interfaces are attributed (for purposes of this analysis) to the input category of interfaces described in the architecture template. Two additional requirements are added to manage the turret arm:

Read Sensors (11)

Managing the details of the memory mapped sensor input interface is the primary concern here. In the PSPEC for this requirement, some strategy for copying the arm sensor data into the Sensory I/O data store is specified. In this way, critical sensor arm location data is saved to avoid the danger of being overwritten by newer incoming data.

Output To Sensors (12)

Since commands to the turret arm of the robot move through a memory mapped area and are in a specific format, this requirement is explicitly added. Incorporating this new requirement eliminates one of the shortcomings of the specification identified earlier. A response is now specified, which assures the consistent management of incoming Sensor_Input events and incoming Axis_Input events.

Proper management of Axis_Input and Axis_Output data flows that move across memory mapped hardware interfaces is incorporated in two new requirements in the output component of the template. These new requirements are labeled Output Axis Data (8) and Control Axes (10). As with the other added requirements, new PSPECs are generated to describe the protocols employed for managing these specific hardware interfaces.

Several shortcomings in this specification are apparent. The numbering scheme is changed from the non-enhanced control/data flow diagram. These changed numbers are bound to cause significant confusion in accurately tracing requirements to design and implementation. Although a visual inspection reveals the relationship between the non-enhanced and enhanced requirements, visual representation is not an effective approach for requirements configuration management. Visual comparisons may work well for small systems but are guaranteed to be error prone when developing large systems.

Some inconsistency appears to exist in the way interfaces are managed according to this specification. Panel_Input and Panel_Output events are independently managed. Turret arm sensors (Sensor_Input) and turret arm commands (Sensor_Output) are also independently processed. For some unexplained reason, Axis_Input and Axis_Output are managed by a single functional requirement. Careful justification of this approach is needed. Perhaps Axis_Input and Axis_Output data move through the same memory mapped hardware interface, use exactly the same data format, and require a special protocol for managing the interface. These conditions are typically necessary when a "smart" controller resides on the other side of the interface, as is the situation with the motor axis interface. At any rate, this decision needs careful evaluation.

12.18 TECHNOLOGY DEPENDENT COMBINED CONTROL/ DATA FLOW

This diagram (Figure 12.18) is simply a version of the previous diagram with the architecture template influences/indicators eliminated.

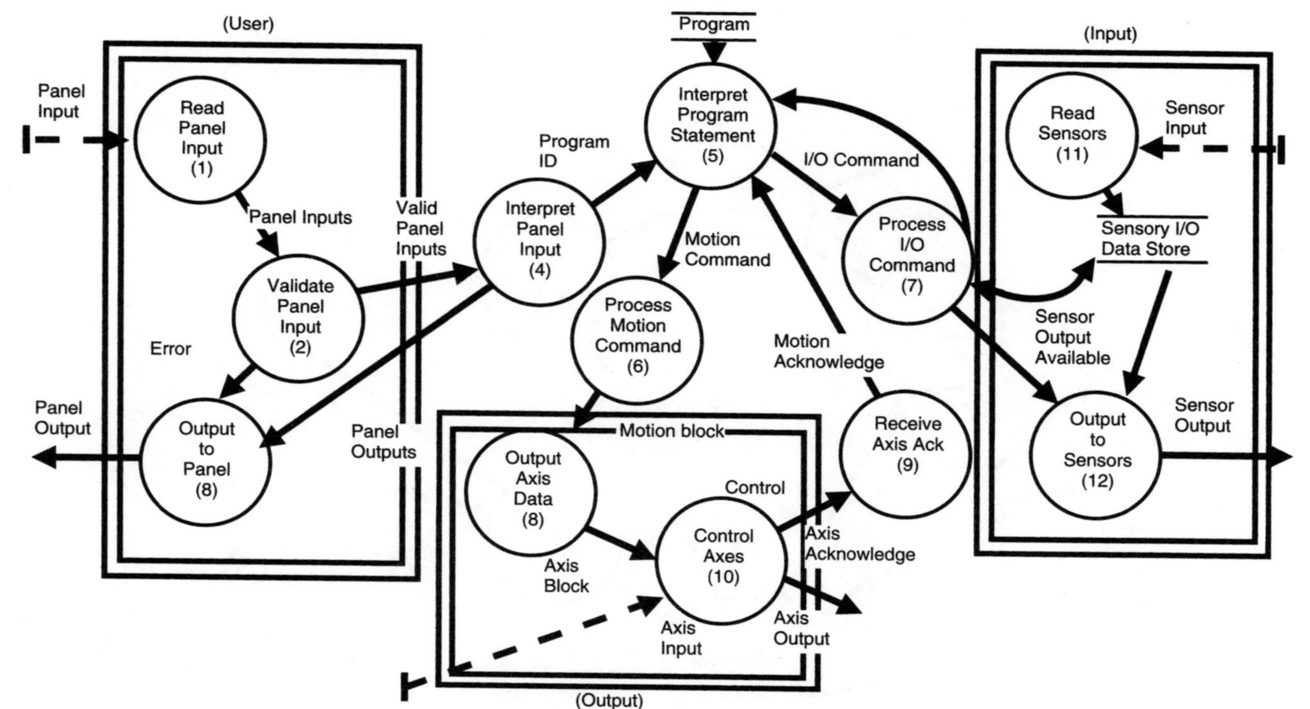

Figure 12.17 Combined Control Flow and Data Flow Diagram Enhanced for Architecture Template

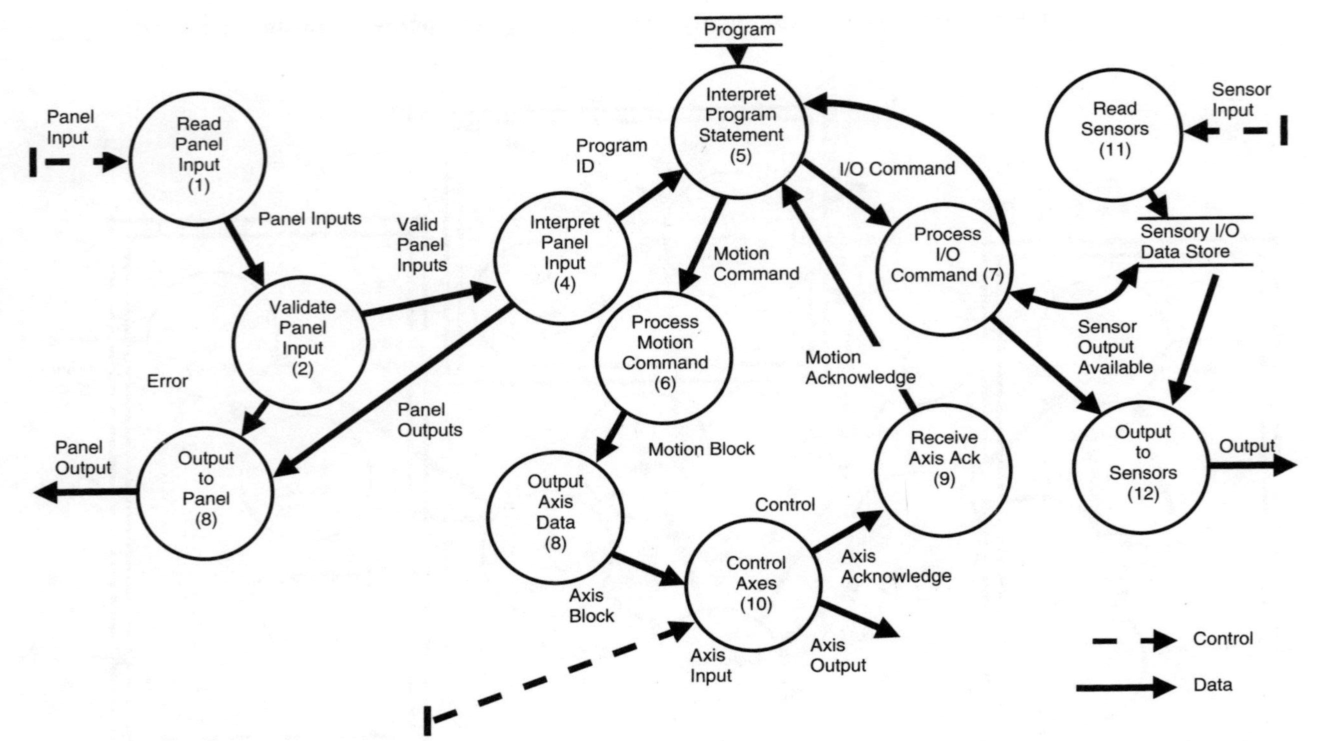

Figure 12.18 Combined Control Flow and Data Flow Technology Dependent

12.19 REVISED PROCESS ACTIVATION TABLE

Since functional requirements have changed, control requirements are updated to reflect these changes. No changes are indicated in the STD portion of the CSPEC. However, added functional requirements imply an extended process activation table, which is described in Figure 12.19. Functional transformations or processes are indicated across the top. Both the old and new requirements appear, along with a new numbering scheme. No new events are added, so the event column on the left side of the table remains unchanged.

Due to the increased functional specification, more detail is incorporated into the specific event responses. For example, consider the event associated with pushing the Run button. According to the new table, the response now consists of the following activities:

Read Panel Input (1)

Validate Panel Input (2) and Output To Panel (3)

Interpret Panel Input (4)

Comparing this to the actual data flow diagram, an immediate problem is discovered. Output To Panel (3) receives its input from Interpret Input (4). So, Interpret Panel Input cannot follow Output To Panel. To operate correctly, the appropriate response needs to be structured as follows:

Read Panel Input (1)

Validate Panel Input (2)

Interpret Panel Input (4)

Output To Panel (3)

This is an example of how an unspecified or poorly specified response can easily cause problems that are difficult to isolate after implementation.

At this point, a new requirements evaluation that employs the redefined PAT needs to be performed. A new requirements evaluation would reveal that one of the two identified deficiencies is eliminated. Consistent responses are now employed for both Sensor_Input and Axis_Input. Response to each of these events consists of handling data at the hardware interface and simultaneously interpreting the next statement of the selected pre-stored program. Unfortunately, coupling pre-stored program execution to real-time events (Sensor_Input and Axis_Input) still results in the degraded performance identified in the previous requirements evaluation.

Moreover, the problem of parallel activity chains is still unresolved. The same ambiguous, confusing functional sequencing notation appears in the revised PAT. An ineffective STD that needs correction badly is employed.

Input \ Process	(1) Read Panel Input	(2) Validate Panel Input	(4) Interpret Panel Input	(3) Output to Panel	(5) Interpret Program Statement	(6) Process Motion Command	(7) Process I/O Command	(8) Output Axis Data	(9) Receive Axis Data	(10) Control Axes	(11) Read Sensors	(12) Output to Sensor
Power On	1	2	3	4								
Power Off	1	2	3	4								
Manual	1	2	3	4								
Run	1	2	3	4	5							
Stop	1	2	3	4								
End	1	2	3	4								
Program Select	1	2	3	4								
Sensor Input					B1	B2	C2	B3		B4	A1	C3
Axis Input					E1	E2	F2	E3	D1	E4		F3

Parallel operation chains:

sensor input: (11) Read sensors
(5) Interpret program statement; (6), (8), (10), or (7), (12)

axis input: (9) Receive axis acknowledgment
(5) Interpret program statement; (6), (8), (10), or (7), (12)

Figure 12.19 Revised Process Activation Table

12.20 TRANSLATING REQUIREMENTS INTO ARCHITECTURE

Each architecture module is identified in the diagram (Figure 12.20) by surrounding the requirements allocated to the module within a rounded rectangle. A unique name is attached to each module, clearly identifying its role in the operation of the robot controller system. Specific guidelines suggested in the text are employed to map the requirements into architecture modules, as follows:

CP Command Interpreter: centralized control using a state transition diagram and a subset of the process activation table;

Program Interpreter: main application process which employs real-time data to perform the work of the robot controller;

CP Input Handler, CP Output Handler, Sensor Input Handler, Sensor Output Handler, Axis Manager, Robot Handler: at least one process for input interfaces, one process for output interfaces.

Employ a sufficient number of processes to assure high throughput operation of all external interfaces. In this case, all interfaces need to operate independently to achieve high throughput.

This solution is partially flawed by the inclusion of the requirement to Control Axes (10). As a result, a single architecture process manages both inputs from and outputs to the motor axis. If this seemingly questionable requirement were replaced by separate requirements, a slightly different architecture results. One architecture process, Motor Handler, could satisfy the requirement Output Axis Data (8). Another process entitled Axis Manager could contain the requirement Receive Axis Ack (9). In this way, input and output operations to the robot motor are independently managed by separate architecture processes, consistent with the way other interfaces are handled.

Even if two separate requirements described motor interface management, a single architecture process might still be employed. Using two processes, as proposed above, introduces extra communications and processing overhead into the architecture, ultimately requiring additional hardware to maintain throughput. Otherwise, poorer throughput results. If Axis_Input events and Axis_Output flows occur significantly infrequently, a single architecture process might be an effective architecture solution. However, software tasking is probably required to achieve concurrent operations across inputs and outputs. Performance evaluations and trade studies need to be accomplished to determine the best architectural design solution.

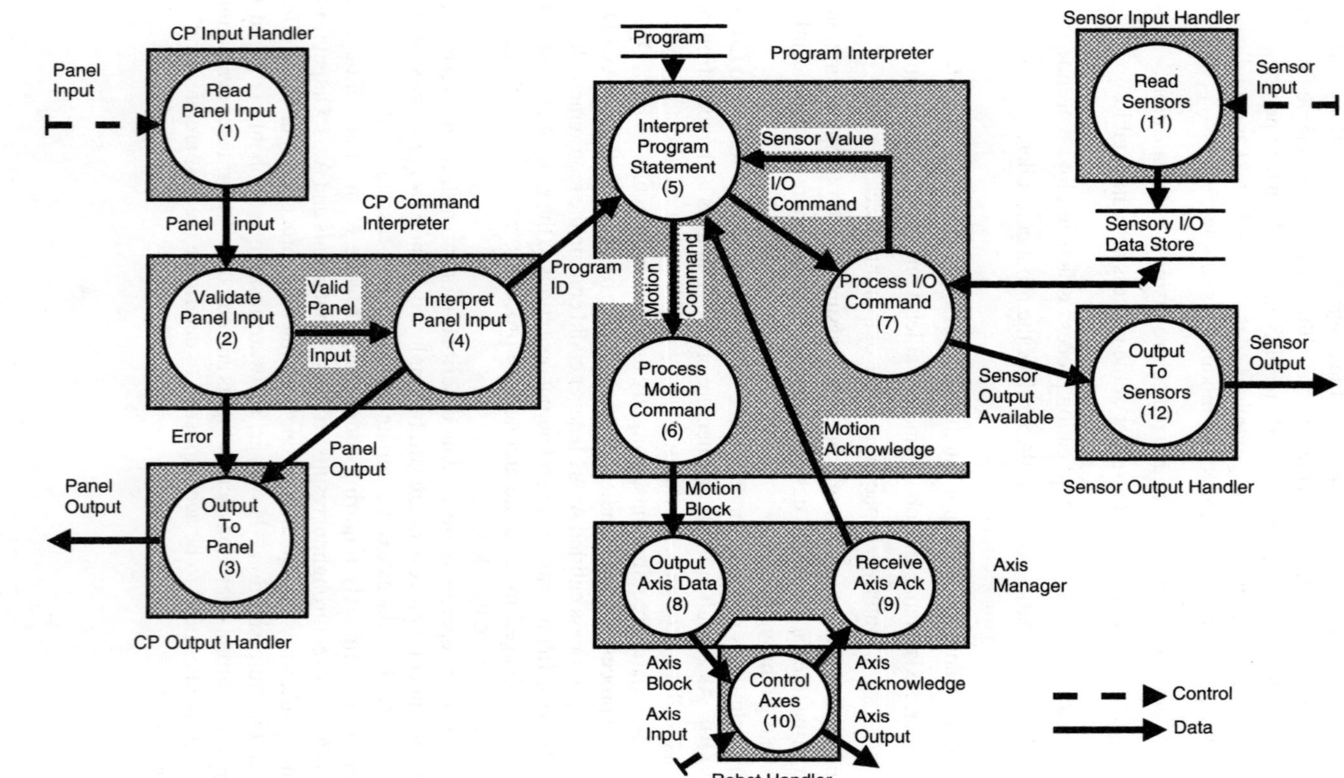

Figure 12.20 Translating Requirements into Architecture

12.21 ARCHITECTURE FLOW DIAGRAM

A summary representation of the architecture and data flowing among the processes appears in Figure 12.21. When a requirement allocated to one process transfers data to a requirement allocated to another, this data is added to the data flow list between the architecture processes.

As an example, consider the data that flows between the modules CP Command Interpreter and CP Output Handler. CP Command Interpreter contains two requirements. Validate Panel Input (2) transmits an Error data flow to requirement Output To Panel (3). Similarly, Interpret Panel Input (4) transmits a Panel_Output data flow to Output To Panel (3). Now, the requirement Output To Panel (3) is contained within the CP Output Handler Process. Therefore, the data flows—Error and Panel_Output—move from requirements in CP Command Interpreter to a requirement allocated to CP Output Handler. These two data flows appear on the data flow list between the two architecture processes. All other data flows between pairs of architecture processes/modules are quite easily justified, since only a single data flow moves between the processes.

With the exception of data moving across the robot controller boundaries, none of the architecture flows contains arrowheads. Placement of arrowheads implies a specific caller/callee relationship. Caller/callee decisions are inappropriate at this stage. Architecture processes require Ada tasks if all software solutions are employed. Ada tasking carries severe throughput implications associated with caller/callee relationships. For this reason, caller/callee decisions are explicitly accomplished with these throughput implications in mind during detailed software design.

This architecture does not follow the hierarchical, limited control interaction guideline indicated within the text. However, some restraint is exercised so that this architecture is not a maximal concurrence architecture. Performance is likely to be moderate. However, flexibility to changing requirements is not well managed by this architecture. With this many processes, and almost unlimited interaction complexity, integration and test are likely to exhibit extensive levels of frustration. Lack of restraint on control interactions also introduces integration and testing complexity, further delaying schedule and raising costs.

12.22 REQUIREMENTS TRACEABILITY MATRIX

While the architecture diagram proves one mechanism for tracing requirements into architecture, a more traditional approach is employed here. A mapping is provided, showing the manner in which requirements are translated into architecture processes/modules. For a normal development, justifications for the allocation decisions are attached to Figure 12.22.

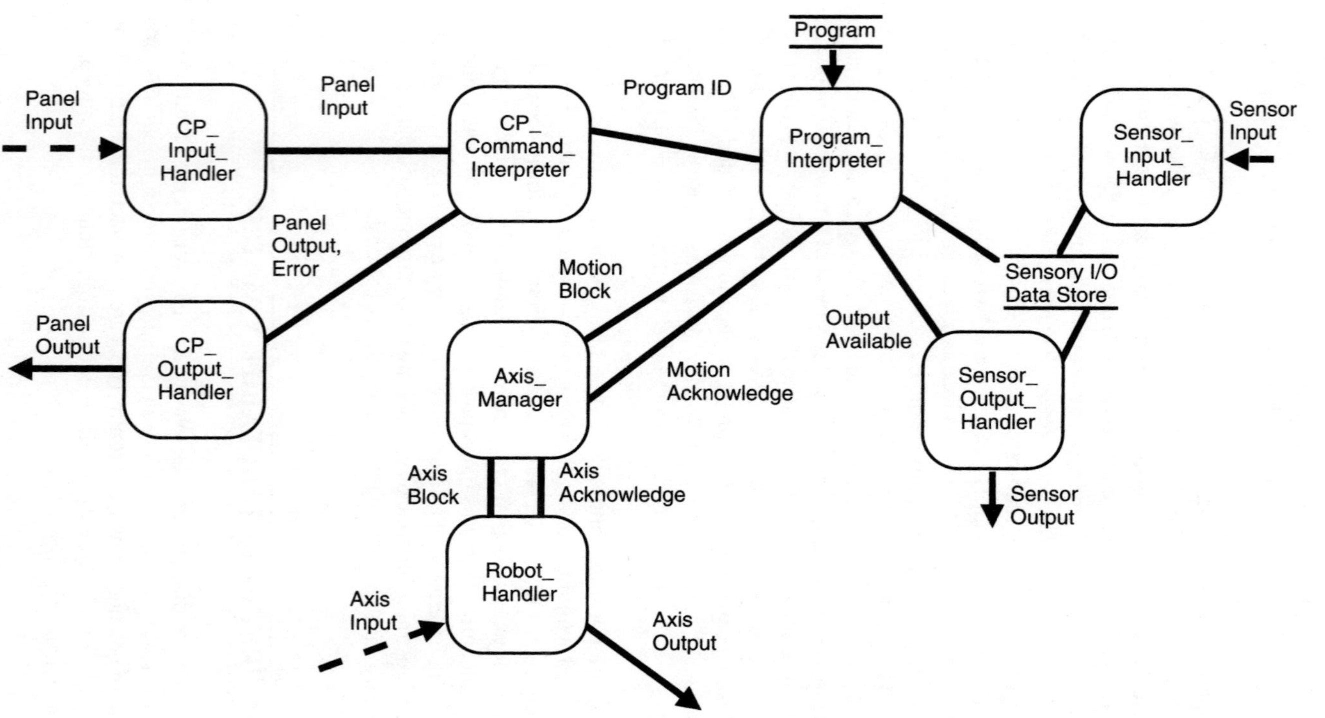

Figure 12.21 Architecture Flow Diagram

Process / Architecture Module	(1) Read Panel Input	(2) Validate Panel Input	(4) Interpret Panel Input	(3) Output to Panel	(5) Interpret Program Statement	(6) Process Motion Command	(7) Process I/O Command	(8) Output Axis Data	(9) Receive Axis Data	(10) Control Axes	(11) Read Sensors	(12) Output to Sensor	STD	PAT
CP input handler	x													
CP output handler				x		x								
CP command interpreter		x	x										x	
Axis manager								x	x					
Robot controller					x					x				
Program interpreter						x	x							x
Sensor input handler											x			
Sensor output handler												x		

Figure 12.22 Requirements Traceability Matrix

12.23 ARCHITECTURE EVALUATION (I-IV)

In this series of tables (Figures 12.23-12.26), an evaluation of the architecture is performed to assess the anticipated response of each event in the test input/output pattern. Proof demonstrating that the robot controller architecture works for its intended operational scenario is obtained. Each event is traced to its ultimate conclusions. Significant response complexities often result because a single event can result in multiple parallel response paths in the architecture.

Consider a simple example. When the Program Select event occurs, the CP Input Handler module is first invoked. As a result of the functions mapped into this process, an internal data flow named Panel_Input is generated. This flow moves to the CP_Command_Interpreter. Based on the functional requirements performed by this module, two response components occur. First, Program ID is permanently stored. (Recall that the exact location of Program ID is not known, due to flawed requirements.) Then, an internal data flow, named Panel_Output, is transmitted to the CP_Output_Handler process. Invocation of the functions in this process results in the Panel_Output message transmitted at the system interfaces.

This simple example illustrates several important concepts. Multiple observed responses result from a specific event in the test input/output pattern. Responses to a given event consist of some combination of data store updates and outgoing response message transmissions. Determination of all the anticipated responses is an important aspect of architecture validation. This validation information is also extremely useful as a debugging aid during integration and testing. Actual output messages are compared with the test input/output pattern of the operations model to assure that the actual response matches the anticipated response. For the Program Select event (embedded within a Panel_Input incoming event), the operations model requires generation of a Panel_Output message. This response is exactly the result determined by this analysis.

As an example of a more complex response that generates complex data flow paths through the architecture, consider the response when an operator pushes the Run button (again, embedded within a Panel_Input incoming event). This event enters the CP Input Handler. A Panel_Input internal data flow results and is transmitted to CP Command Interpreter. From this point, two independent and parallel responses are transmitted to the remainder of the architecture. An internal data flow named Panel_Output moves to the CP_Output_Handler. At the same time, a Program ID data flow moves to the Program Interpreter process. Each of these responses is now evaluated to its ultimate resolution.

Evaluating the remainder of the Panel_Output data flow is simple. This flow is transmitted to the CP Output Handler, where the appropriately formatted

Panel_Output message is created and copied into the memory mapped hardware interface. Following the path of the Program ID data flow involves even greater complexity. Transmission of Program ID to the Program Interpreter module begins execution of the selected pre-stored program. A single program instruction consists of either a Motion Block command to the motor or a Sensor_Output command to the turret arm. Each of these is further traced to its ultimate resolution.

Details of these two potential response components begins at the top of Architecture Evaluation (II). If a Motion Block command is generated, this data flows to the Axis Manager. Based on the functions in the Axis Manager, an Axis Block is passed to the Robot Handler process. This module formats the Axis Block data flow as an Axis Output message, placing the message at the memory mapped hardware interface to the motor axis. In contrast, a Sensor Output command proceeds directly to the Sensor Output Handler for appropriate formatting. As a result, a Sensor_Output message appears at the memory mapped hardware interface to the turret arm.

The anticipated response to a Run button event by the architecture is quite complex. At one point in the response, two separate paths occur. One of these separate paths later splits again into two response paths. Multiple response paths for a single incoming event explain why debugging an integrated system is a difficult process if this kind of information is not available. Responses for larger systems are even more complicated, making evaluation both tedious and time consuming. However, resolving integration and test problems without this data is next to impossible. By reconstructing the last event and the actual response in terms of data that has actually moved through the architecture, this information about the anticipated response is employed to quickly identify the faulty process/module. Without this data, a "hit and miss" approach is employed. Unfortunately, many tries are required in this approach. Moreover, the fix typically changes system behavior, hiding the problem rather than fixing the problem. Generation of this data during architecture model generation allows rapid identification and resolution of problems.

Comparing this last architecture response evaluation with the test input/output pattern shows that the architecture does result in the proper event sequencing. According to the test input/output pattern for the robot controller, a Run button event is followed either by a Sensor_Output command to the turret arm or by an Axis Output command to the motor, depending on the current instruction of the selected pre-stored program. As the response evaluation demonstrates, these outputs are exactly the response anticipated by the architecture. For this event, the architecture is validated. All of the events in the test input/output pattern are validated in this same fashion.

Control Input	Internal Data Flow	Architecture Module	Internal Data Flow	Response
Power On	– Panel Input Panel Output	CP_ Input_ Handler CP_ Command_ Interpreter CP_ Output_ Handler	Panel Input Panel Output –	– – Panel Output
Manual Mode	– Panel Input Panel Output	CP_ Input_ Handler CP_ Command_ Interpreter CP_ Output_ Handler	Panel Input Panel Output –	– – Panel Output
Program Select	– Panel Input Panel Output	CP_ Input_ Handler CP_ Command_ Interpreter CP_ Output_ Handler	Panel Input Panel Output –	– Save Program ID Panel Output
Run	– Panel Input Panel Output Program ID	CP_ Input_ Handler CP_ Command_ Interpreter { CP_ Output_ Handler and Program_ Interpreter	Panel Input Panel Output Program ID – Motion Block or Sensor Output and Output Available	– – – Panel Output – –

Figure 12.23 Architecture Evaluation (I)

Control Input	Internal Data Flow	Architecture Module	Internal Data Flow	Response
	Motion Block	Axis_Manager	Axis Block	–
	Axis Block	Robot_Handler	–	Axis Output
		or		
	Output Available	Sensor_Output_Handler	–	Sensor Output
<No Control Input>	–	Program_Interpreter	Motion Block	–
			Sensor Output and Output Available	–
	Motion Block	Axis_Manager	Axis Block	–
	Axis Block	Robot_Handler	–	Axis Output
		or		
	Output Available	Sensor_Output_Handler	–	Sensor Output

Figure 12.24 Architecture Evaluation (II)

Control Input	Internal Data Flow	Architecture Module	Internal Data Flow	Response
Sensor Input	– Sensor Data –	Sensor_Input _Handler Program_Interpreter and {Same Sequence as <No Control Input>}	Sensor Input –	– Save Latest Sensor Location/Status Axis Output or Sensor Output
Axis Input	– Axis Acknowledge Motion Acknowledge –	Robot_Handler Axis_Manager Program_Interpreter and {Same Sequence as <No Control Input>}	Axis Acknowledge Motion Acknowledge –	– – Save Latest Axis Location/Status Axis Output or Sensor Output

Figure 12.25 Architecture Evaluation (III)

Control Input	Internal Data Flow	Architecture Module	Internal Data Flow	Response
End	– Panel Input Panel Output Program ID	CP_Input_Handler CP_Command_Interpreter CP_Output_Handler and Program_Interpreter	Panel Input Panel Output and Program_ID=0 – –	– – – Panel Output Stops Program XQT
Stop	– Panel Input Panel Output	CP_Input_Handler CP_Command_Interpreter CP_Output_Handler	Panel Input Panel Output –	– – Panel Output
Power Off	– Panel Input Panel Output	CP_Input_Handler CP_Command_Interpreter CP_Output_Handler	Panel Input Panel Output –	– – Panel Output

Figure 12.26 Architecture Evaluation (IV)

12.24 DESIGN MODEL GENERATION

Generating a detailed software design (Figure 12.27) consistent with the process architecture involves two separate but interrelated steps: tasking architecture generation and sequential software design.

Detailed software design consists of the following steps:

1. Generate an initial tasking architecture;
2. Establish caller/callee relationships;
3. Employ (or do not employ) intermediaries;
4. Perform a consistency and completeness check of the tasking architecture against operational requirements;
5. Allocate tasks to packages;
6. Generate functional components of the packages;
7. Use layered abstractions, table driven controllers, data objects, and data types to construct the sequential design of each task; and
8. Evaluate the detailed design to assess its quality.

12.25 TASKING ARCHITECTURE WITH INTERMEDIARIES

Each of the software architecture processes in Figure 12.28 is implemented as a single Ada task. This assumption is an important assumption. Conceivably, some of the architecture processes could be implemented in hardware. Choosing to employ an all software solution that employs tasking increases the flexibility, portability, and reusability of the robot controller. If the underlying hardware base changes due to unavailability of specific hardware or customer preference for a different hardware platform, software tasking allows the robot controller to transition to the new platform unmodified for the most part. Only specific hardware interfaces need to be updated. These interfaces are normally encapsulated under abstractions.

However, blocking semantics associated with the Ada tasking model cause significant performance problems if not properly accommodated in the detailed design. Two important tasking decisions affect performance and are documented in Figure 12.28. Caller/callee relationships are established for each of the software tasks. Since caller tasks can block indefinitely, assigning a caller role to a task is an important and crucial decision. Again, heuristics described in the text are employed to make the caller/callee decisions. Since the CP Command Interpreter typically needs something from other tasks, a caller role is assigned to this task. This assignment contradicts the guideline that a task with multiple interactions is assigned a callee role. As described in the text, these guidelines often contradict

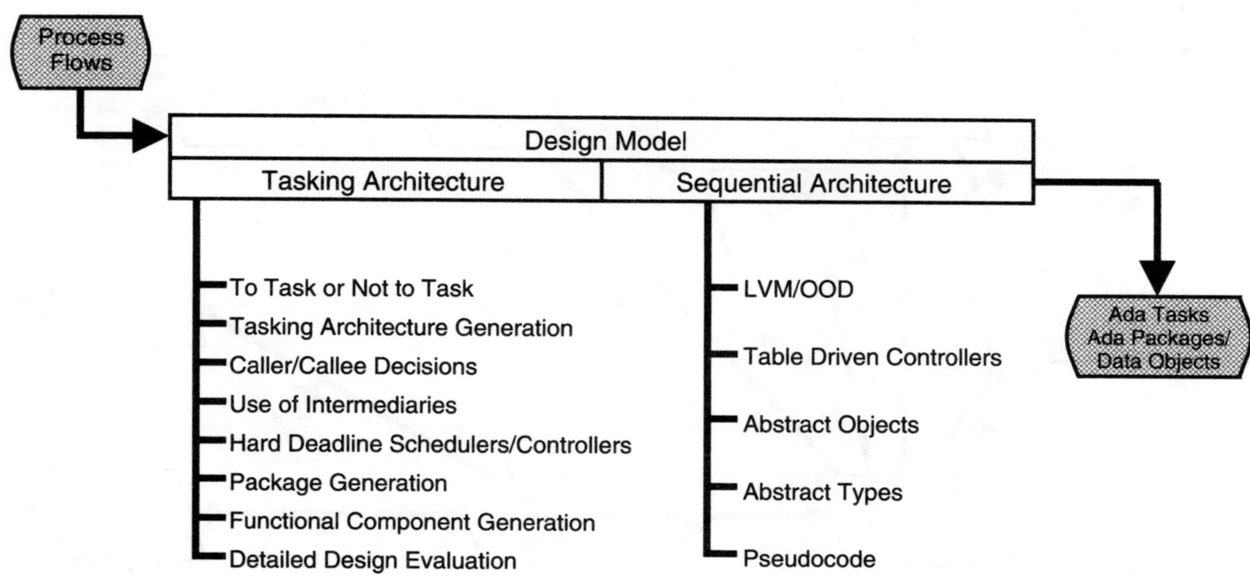

Figure 12.27 Design Model Generation

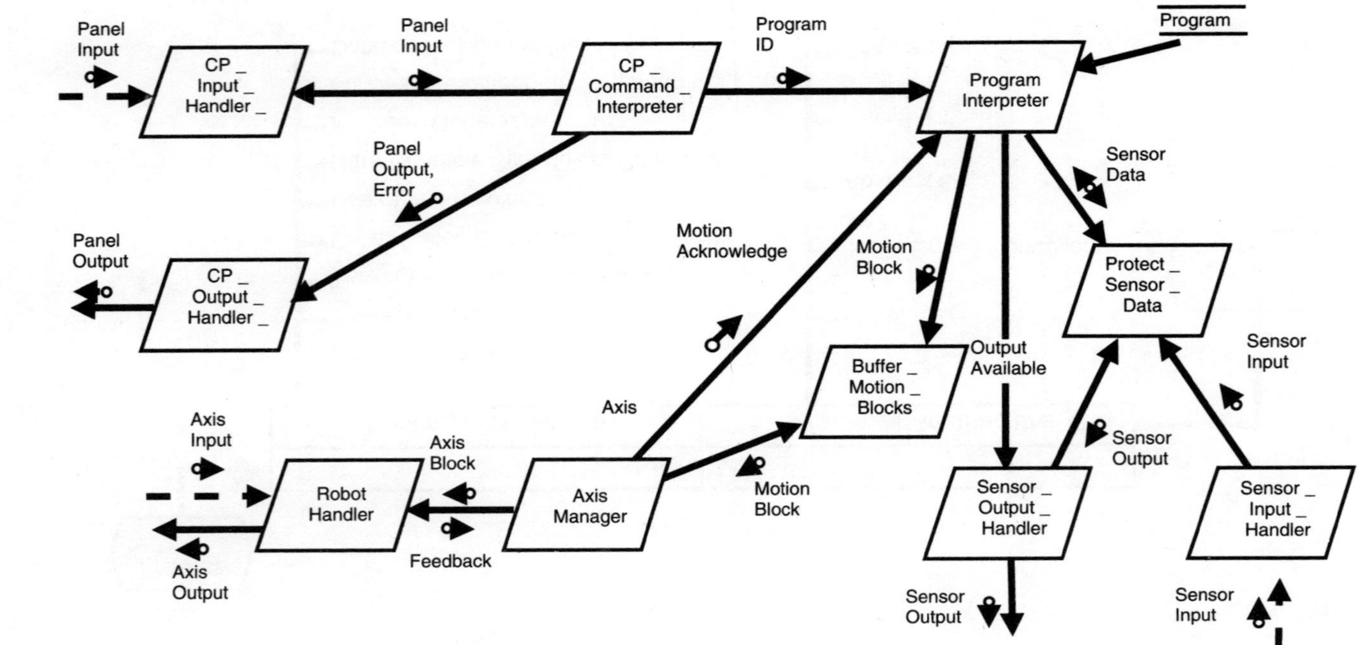

Figure 12.28 Tasking Architecture with Intermediaries and Caller/Callee Relations

each other. In this situation, such a contradiction occurred. Since the CP Command Interpreter serves as the central control for the robot controller, its caller role makes sense. After all, a task can only be in control if the task itself initiates interactions with all other tasks. An important assumption here is that tasks invoked by the CP Command Interpreter are not likely to cause the interpreter to be blocked for very long. In fact, CP Input Handler and CP Output Handler do not cause excessive blocking, since the jobs they perform are quite simple and since they interact with only a few other tasks. Moreover, the Program Interpreter is usually not busy when signaled by the CP Command Interpreter. A signal by the CP Command Interpreter initiates program interpretation. Prior to receipt of this rendezvous, the Program Interpreter is idle.

Once Program Interpreter begins executing the operator selected pre-stored program, its interaction role with other tasks is both caller and callee. When the Axis Manager acquires Feedback from the Robot Handler, a rendezvous is initiated with the Program Interpreter to transmit the generated Motion Acknowledge signal. For this interaction, Program Interpreter serves as a callee. However, for transmission of Motion Blocks and for sending and receiving data to the turret arm, the Program Interpreter serves as a caller. Allowing Program Interpreter to initiate interaction to transmit Motion Block commands to the motor and to transmit Sensor_Output commands to the turret arms is logical. After all, these commands are generated by execution of the current pre-stored program instruction.

As the diagram depicts, Axis Manager is a strictly calling task, relative to all its tasking interactions. This task needs specific data from all the tasks with which interaction is required. A task that needs services is usually assigned a role as a caller task, according to the guidelines presented in the text. Unfortunately, using this guideline contradicts the guideline that a task with multiple interactions is to be cast as a callee. An explicit decision is made to prefer one guideline over the other. Extensive justification needs to be provided for this decision. Preferably, detailed performance predictions are employed to demonstrate that this preference does not cause significant degradation in performance at the software system level.

Management of all incoming interfaces (Panel_Input, Axis_Input, and Sensor_Input) are implemented as strictly called tasks. These interfaces are to be implemented as interrupt handlers. By comparison, all output data flows (Panel_Output, Axis_Output, and Sensor_Output) are initiated by specific tasks managing the output interface. An important assumption here is that interfaces for outgoing data operate as polling interfaces, rather than being interrupt-driven as the input interfaces. These two assumptions have major implications to hardware developers for the robot controller and are communicated to the hardware development team.

The use of tasking intermediaries to reduce blocking is also indicated by this diagram. Each potential interaction is evaluated for blockage and subsequent effects on throughput. In this case, intermediaries are introduced in only two locations. Outgoing Motion Block commands to the motor are buffered in Buffer Motion Blocks until the Axis Manager can process them. Both incoming Sensor_Input events and outgoing Sensor_Output commands to the turret arm are buffered in the same intermediary, named Protect Sensor Data. Once Program Interpreter buffers a Sensor_Output command to the turret arm, a rendezvous signal to the Sensor Output Handler is necessary to assure that a Sensor_Output command is removed from the buffer.

Buffering the outgoing commands from the Program Interpreter effectively achieves a reasonable level of throughput. Buffers incur a deterministic, finite limit on blockage time, allowing Program Interpreter to quickly continue its job of executing program statements. Moreover, buffering of incoming Sensor_Input events seems an effective way to achieve throughput. Program Interpreter has no control over Sensor_Input events—they occur periodically at a rate determined by the hardware characteristics of the sensor. Buffering Sensor_Input events preserves the sensor data until Program Interpreter can acquire the data for processing and data store update.

However, placing Sensor_Output commands and incoming Sensor_Input data into the same buffer defeats the purpose of introducing the decoupler. A better approach is to place an additional dedicated buffer between Program Interpreter and Sensor Output Handler. In this way, blockage associated with Sensor_Output transmission is truly limited to a deterministic, finite amount. Unfortunately, modifying the tasking architecture to work in this manner introduces an extra task into the architecture. Addition of this task improves the clarity and consistency of the tasking architecture at the cost of potentially reducing throughput. Again, detailed performance analyses need to be performed to determine throughput impacts of these changes relative to the gains obtained.

All other interactions do not employ intermediaries. If justified, this is certainly an acceptable approach, since fewer tasks are employed (improving throughput). For this approach to work effectively, traffic through the remainder of the architecture must be at relatively low rates. In fact, low data rates are probably the situation for areas of the robot controller architecture in which no intermediaries are employed. Panel_Input events occur quite infrequently during real-time operations, as demonstrated by the message flows in the operational model. Axis_Input events only occur subsequent to Axis_Output commands. Since Axis_Output commands are generated during selected program execution, corresponding Axis_Input loading is likely to be at a low data rate. In the area of heaviest activity (periodic input from the sensor on the robot arm), a buffering intermediary is employed. Buffers achieve throughput. Additionally, loss of data is disastrous to reliable operation of the robot controller, so buffers further preserve the integrity of the hardware interface.

12.26 TASKING ARCHITECTURE EVALUATION (I-IV)

Since each architecture process is mapped to an Ada task, this evaluation (Figure 12.29 to Figure 12.32) closely follows the architecture evaluation. However, tasking intermediaries are now incorporated into the evaluation. For debugging purposes, following the flow of data through intermediaries is extremely important. Data can become lost within a queue, depending on the mechanism by which an empty queue query is handled. Knowing intermediary locations allows identification of an improper strategy employed to recover from empty queue queries.

Control Input	Internal Data Flow	Task	Internal Data Flow	Response
Power On	– Panel Input Panel Output	CP_ Input_ Handler CP_ Command_ Interpreter CP_ Output_ Handler	Panel Input Panel Output –	– – Panel Output
Manual Mode	– Panel Input Panel Output	CP_ Input_ Handler CP_ Command_ Interpreter CP_ Output_ Handler	Panel Input Panel Output –	– – Panel Output
Program Select	– Panel Input Panel Output	CP_ Input_ Handler CP_ Command_ Interpreter CP_ Output_ Handler	Panel Input Panel Output –	– Save Program ID Panel Output
Run	– Panel Input Panel Output Program ID	CP_ Input_ Handler CP_ Command_ Interpreter { CP_ Output_ Handler and Program_ Interpreter }	Panel Input Panel Output Program ID – Motion Block or Sensor Output and Output Available	– – – Panel Output – –

Figure 12.29 Tasking Architecture Evaluation (I)

Control Input	Internal Data Flow	Task	Internal Data Flow	Response
	Motion Block Motion Block Axis Block Sensor Output Sensor Output	{ Buffer_Motion_Block Axis_Manager Robot_Handler } or { Protect_Sensor_Data Sensor_Output_Handler }	Motion Block Axis Block – Sensor Output –	– – Axis Output – Sensor Output
<No Control Input>	– Motion Block Motion Block Axis Block Sensor Output Sensor Output	Program_Interpreter { Buffer_Motion_Block Axis_Manager Robot_Handler } or Protect_Sensor_Data Sensor_Output_Handler	Motion Block or Sensor Output Output Available and Motion Block Axis Block – Sensor Output –	– – – – Axis Output – Sensor Output

Figure 12.30 Tasking Architecture Evaluation (II)

Control Input	Internal Data Flow	Task	Internal Data Flow	Response
Sensor Input	– Sensor Input Sensor Data –	Sensor_Input _Handler Protect_Sensor_Data Program_Interpreter and {Same Sequence as <No Control Input>}	Sensor Input Sensor Data –	– – Save Latest Sensor Location/Status Axis Output or Sensor Output
Axis Input	– Axis Acknowledge Motion Acknowledge –	Robot_Handler Axis_Manager Program_Interpreter and {Same Sequence as <No Control Input>}	Axis Acknowledge Motion Acknowledge –	– – Save Latest Axis Location/Status Axis Output or Sensor Output

Figure 12.31 Tasking Architecture Evaluation (III)

Control Input	Internal Data Flow	Task	Internal Data Flow	Response
End	– Panel Input Panel Output Program ID	CP_Input_Handler CP_Command_Interpreter CP_Output_Handler and Program_Interpreter	Panel Input Panel Output and Program_ID=0 – –	– – – Panel Output Stops Program XQT
Stop	– Panel Input Panel Output	CP_Input_Handler CP_Command_Interpreter CP_Output_Handler	Panel Input Panel Output –	– – Panel Output
Power Off	– Panel Input Panel Output	CP_Input_Handler CP_Command_Interpreter CP_Output_Handler	Panel Input Panel Output –	– – Panel Output

Figure 12.32 Tasking Architecture Evaluation (IV)

12.27 ADA PACKAGING ALLOCATIONS

All tasks are assigned to specific Ada packages (Figure 12.33). For the most part, an application oriented guideline is employed in the assignment process. Tasks performing specific functions are collected together into packages. Typically, all tasks managing a specific hardware interface are packaged together. For instance, a package named Control Panel becomes the master or parent of two tasks: CP Input Handler and CP Output Handler. Centralized control is usually a functional area that receives its own package; hence, CP Command Interpreter is encapsulated in the package named CP Processing.

A second guideline presented in the text is to allocate tasks to packages based on visibility needs. This criterion is extensively employed to determine the ultimate location of the intermediary tasks. Tasks that are strictly called must be visible to both callers. Several alternatives are available for the packaging intermediaries. All called intermediary tasks can be collected into a common package, individually packaged, or combined in a package with the dominant caller. In this example, the last alternative has been employed for both intermediaries. This approach is employed so that fewer exported interfaces are required, significantly reducing integration and test efforts. Buffer Motion Blocks is allocated to the Motion package in which Program Interpreter resides. Protect Sensor Data is combined with Sensor Input Handler and Sensor Output Handler within a package simply named Sensors.

These choices also eliminate the potential for tasking elaboration problems, another visibility issue. Since Program Interpreter begins executing the chosen prestored program as soon as its elaboration is completed, a motion block data flow may be generated quite rapidly. If Buffer Motion Blocks were in another package, its elaboration may not be completed. In this case, tasking_error exception is raised. This justification, however, indicates a potential flaw in the packaging allocation decision for Protect Sensor Data. Using a similar justification suggests that Protect Sensor Data needs to be allocated to Package Motion, in combination with Buffer Motion Blocks.

Another questionable decision is the allocation of both input and output managing tasks for a hardware interface to a single package. An alternative scheme might be applicable. All input managing tasks could be packaged together. All output managing tasks could be integrated into another single parent package. This proposed approach is probably best employed when all input interface management tasks need to be elaborated at roughly the same time and when a single processor is employed. If the target platform is to be a distributed system, a single processor is often dedicated to handling both input and output for a single hardware interface. If this is the hardware architecture, collecting all the input managing tasks into a single package causes a viability problem. With the exception of a small number of vendors, very few Ada run-time environments support distributed tasking (and distributed parent packages).

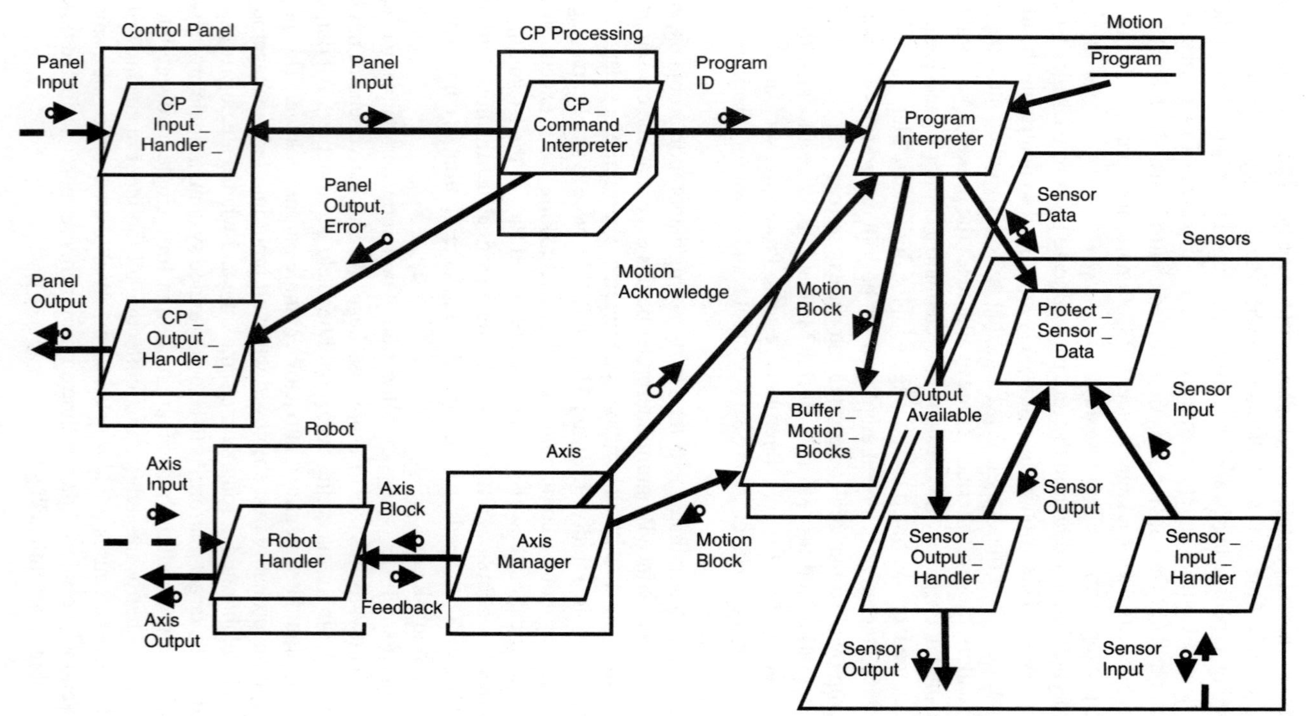

Figure 12.33 Ada Packaging Allocations

12.28 ADA PACKAGES-FUNCTIONAL COMPONENTS (PAGES 1 AND 2)

A functional component description is generated for each package (Figure 12.34 to Figure 12.35) defined above. Functional components include the following:

1. A specification and body for the package;
2. A specification and body for any Ada tasks included in the initial package generation;
3. Any additional Ada tasks necessary to support hardware interfaces or other architectural characteristics;
4. One subprogram to support each external access into the package;
5. Preliminary identification of support packages necessary to accommodate functional requirements allocated to the package; and
6. References to any common definitions packages or support services packages referenced within the body of the package.

Consider the Motion package as characterized on the Ada packaging allocation diagram. This package contains two tasks: Program Interpreter and Buffer Motion Blocks. Moreover, other packages reference the Motion package through three distinct interfaces. CP Processing passes the Program ID to initiate program interpretation. Motion Acknowledge flows enter the Motion package when initiated by Axis. Finally, Axis needs to dequeue Motion Blocks, necessitating an additional interface.

Now, consider the characterization of the Motion package on the second functional components diagram. A package specification and body for Motion are indicated. Both Program Interpreter and Buffer Motion Block tasks are included. Procedures for each of the three interfaces identified above also appear as functional components—start Program, Motion Ack, and Dequeue Motion Block. In addition, global constants are accessed through a Definitions package. All other components (labeled LVM/OOD) are generated to support requirements mapped to these packages. These components are generated through the sequential design process known as LVM/OOD.

1. Control _ Panel
   a. Control Panel (package spec and body)
   b. CP Input Handler (task body)
   c. CP Output Handler (task body)
   d. Provide Panel Input (procedure body)
   e. Take Panel Output (procedure body)
   f. Definitions (package spec)
   g. Robot HW Dependencies (package spec)

2. Robot
   a. Robot (package spec and body)
   b. Robot Handler (task body)
   c. Take Block (procedure body)
   d. Definitions (package body)
   e. Robot HW Dependencies

3. Axis
   a. Axis (package spec and body)
   b. Axis Manager (task body)
   c. Prepare Axis Block (procedure body)
   d. Stop (procedure body
   e. Resume (procedure body)
   f. Definitions (package body)

4. Sensors
   a. Sensors (package spec and body)
   b. Sensor Input Handler (task body)
   c. Sensor Output Handler (task body)
   d. Protect Sensor Data (task body)
   e. Update Data (procedure body)
   f. Output Available (procedure body)
   g. Provide Sensor Data (procedure body)
   h. Definitions (package spec)
   i. Robot HW Dependencies (package spec)

Figure 12.34 Ada Packages—Functional Components (Page 1)

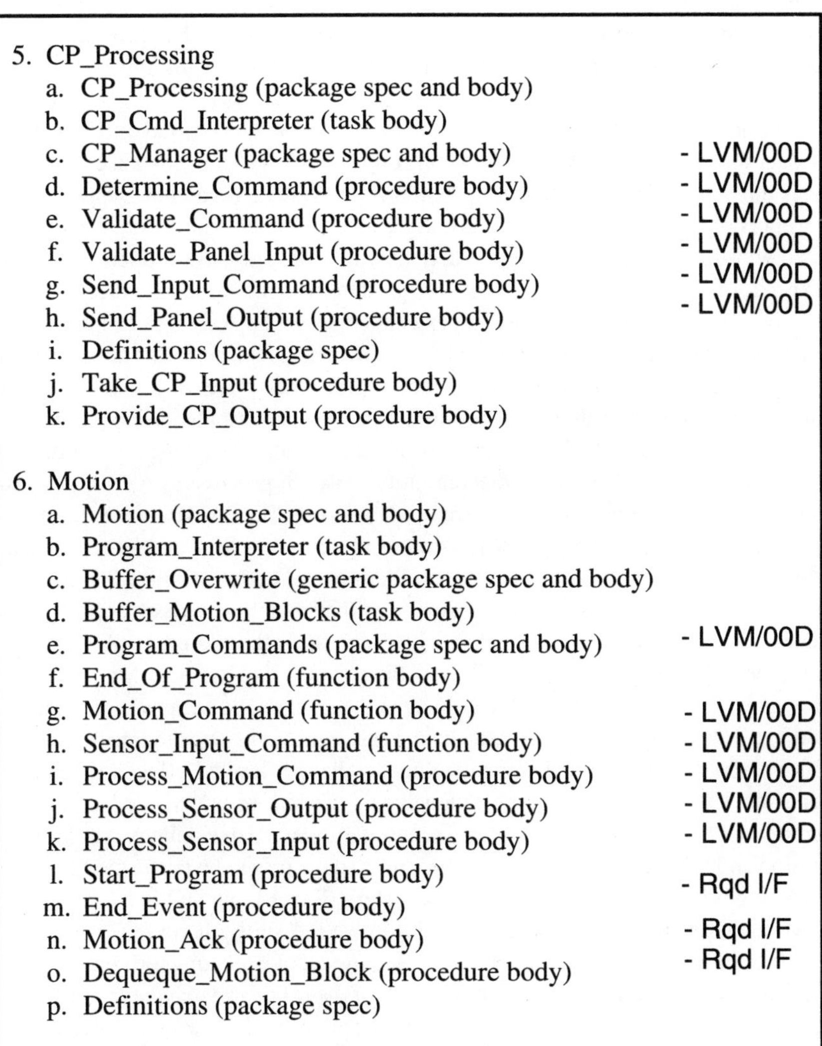

5. CP_Processing
   a. CP_Processing (package spec and body)
   b. CP_Cmd_Interpreter (task body)
   c. CP_Manager (package spec and body) - LVM/OOD
   d. Determine_Command (procedure body) - LVM/OOD
   e. Validate_Command (procedure body) - LVM/OOD
   f. Validate_Panel_Input (procedure body) - LVM/OOD
   g. Send_Input_Command (procedure body) - LVM/OOD
   h. Send_Panel_Output (procedure body) - LVM/OOD
   i. Definitions (package spec)
   j. Take_CP_Input (procedure body)
   k. Provide_CP_Output (procedure body)

6. Motion
   a. Motion (package spec and body)
   b. Program_Interpreter (task body)
   c. Buffer_Overwrite (generic package spec and body)
   d. Buffer_Motion_Blocks (task body)
   e. Program_Commands (package spec and body) - LVM/OOD
   f. End_Of_Program (function body)
   g. Motion_Command (function body) - LVM/OOD
   h. Sensor_Input_Command (function body) - LVM/OOD
   i. Process_Motion_Command (procedure body) - LVM/OOD
   j. Process_Sensor_Output (procedure body) - LVM/OOD
   k. Process_Sensor_Input (procedure body) - LVM/OOD
   l. Start_Program (procedure body) - Rqd I/F
   m. End_Event (procedure body)
   n. Motion_Ack (procedure body) - Rqd I/F
   o. Dequeque_Motion_Block (procedure body) - Rqd I/F
   p. Definitions (package spec)

Figure 12.35 Ada Packages—Functional Components (Page 2)

12.29 DETAILED DESIGN OF ADA PACKAGES/INTERFACES

This graphic (Figure 12.36) shows all Ada structural components, gives each component a name, and shows interaction of all components through appropriate interfaces. All Ada tasks are shown. Each task is encapsulated within its parent construct.

An important use for this diagram is to allow the developer to identify the flow of data that comes across the robot controller interfaces. For instance, consider Axis Input. This data enters the robot controller system via an interrupt. The interrupt is scheduled as a rendezvous entry call to the Robot Handler task encapsulated within the Robot package. When the Axis Manager task hidden within the Axis package is ready, the Axis Ack is requested from the Robot Handler task. On receipt of the Axis Ack, Axis Manager then conveys the Axis Ack to the Motion package through the Motion Ack interface. This interface performs a rendezvous entry call to the Motion Ack entry of the Program Interpreter task. At this point, Program Interpreter responds to the Motion Ack by performing its specified internal response. This is the final resolution of the Axis Input response. According to the detailed design diagram, a discontinuity exists in processing Axis Input data through the robot controller. As currently labeled, no flow of Motion Ack can occur from Robot into Axis. Identification of this missing flow and interface is an extremely difficult process when the problem is embedded within the bowels of several hundred thousand lines of Ada code distributed across several physical nodes. A simple solution is to add an interface that allows an Axis Ack to flow from the Take Block entry of the Robot Handler task into the Axis Manager task. However, this additional interface changes the syntax and semantics associated with the Take Block entry interface. In this case, since only one other task accesses this interface, syntactic and semantic changes have a limited effect. If multiple tasks move through this interface, extensive modifications would need to be made throughout the software architecture, necessitating extensive debugging and integration and test activity. A similar continuity analysis is to be performed for each incoming input into the robot controller system (Panel Input and Sensor Input).

Moreover, each output is traced to its ultimate movement across the robot controller interfaces to an external recipient. As a result of executing the current statement in the pre-stored program, a movement of the robot arm may be commanded. This command is transmitted by Program Interpreter to the Sensors package via a procedure call to Provide Sensor Data. Inside this procedure, a rendezvous entry call occurs to the Provide Output entry of the encapsulated Protect Sensor Data task. In this manner, robot arm movement commands are buffered. In response to the previously described Axis Ack, Program Interpreter signals that output is available. Only one robot arm movement is to be in progress at any time. This signal indicates completion of one movement and beginning of the next movement. Invocation of the Output Available procedure results in a rendezvous entry call to the Output Available entry of a hidden Sensor Output Handler task. In response, Sensor Output Handler performs an entry call to the Provide Output entry of the Protect Sensor Data task also encapsulated within the Sensors package. A suc-

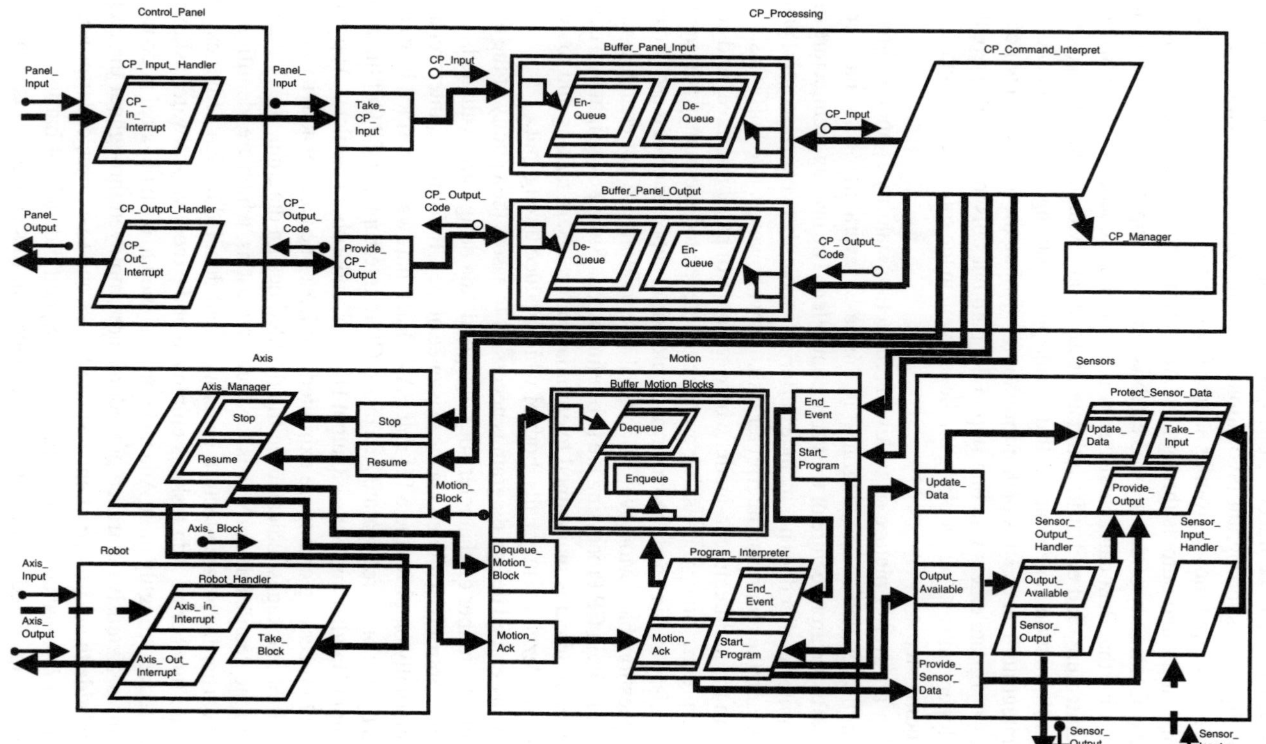

Figure 12.36 Detailed Design of Ada Packages/Interfaces

cessful rendezvous here results in the next robot arm command moving from Protect Sensor Data to Sensor Output Handler. This task then formats the robot arm command as a Sensor Output message and transmits the message across the appropriate hardware interface. To assure continuity of all output flows, each of the other outputs needs to be traced through the architecture (Panel Output and Axis Output). Specific subprogram invocations and rendezvous entry calls are to be listed, as each output moves from its source to its destination: an output interface.

Tracing inputs and outputs through the Ada architecture serves several important goals. Continuity of data flow is established. Each input and output is evaluated to assure that data can actually start at its source, proceed through the software architecture, and end at its ultimate destination. Moreover, invaluable debugging information is generated. If data disappears during integration and testing, an integrator can use this path information to isolate the location in which the data is lost. If data enters into one step in the path but fails to exit that step, then the developer knows to start looking for the problem in the software associated with the offending step.

Gaining an overall picture of tasking architecture stability is another goal of assessing the detailed design diagram. In this case, several new tasks have crept into the software architecture of the robot controller. The tasking architecture diagram exhibited earlier does not include buffering for data between the control panel interfaces and the command interpreter task. Now, however, two buffer tasks are included in the architecture to mediate between control panel interfaces and command interpreter. Since the tasking architecture generated previously was appropriate to satisfy traffic levels and to arrange blocking, appearance of these two new tasks is questionable. Moreover, if original assumptions are not changed, these two buffer tasks in CP Processing are to be eliminated. Strong oversight by a qualified system architect is maintained to eliminate unnecessary tasking and to avoid unneeded rendezvous entry calls, both of which reduce throughput.

Finally, a detailed design diagram is necessary to assess the validity of the overall design. A number of characteristics of a good Ada design are evaluated. Central system control is exhibited via the existence of the CP Command Interpret task, which internally employs the STD and PAT. Each hardware interface is accommodated by one or more separate Ada tasks (CP In Interrupt and CP Out Interrupt, Sensor Input Handler and Sensor Output Handler, and Robot Handler). Appropriate parallel processing chains are exhibited. At least one parallel activity appears in each of the packages indicated on the detailed design diagram. Each parallel activity in the detailed design exists for specific reasons, which are identified and recorded earlier in the architecture generation and detailed design activities. An appropriate number of Ada tasks is employed and excessive software tasking is avoided. In fact, roughly three Ada tasks are assigned to each physical node in the architecture. Extensive entrance procedures are employed throughout the architecture to hide the existence of encapsulated tasks and to enforce caller protocols in a uniform manner across all calling tasks. Specific details of hardware interfaces are encapsulated under abstract interfaces (in this situation, tasks are employed to abstract the interfaces), isolating the effect of problems during hardware and software integration.

12.30 HARDWARE ARCHITECTURE BLOCK DIAGRAM

A hardware target platform is developed concurrently with the development of a software design. An awareness of the evolving software design is usually employed in the development of the hardware architecture. At this step of the methodology, preliminary planning for hardware/software integration begins.

As the diagram (Figure 12.37) depicts, a distributed processing platform is envisioned. Several microprocessors of the 68000 family are being employed. Two of the processors are connected by VMEbus, an internal communications bus. A third processor is interconnected via an Ethernet. Since the VMEbus is an internal bus, interprocessor communication is faster in comparison to the Ethernet managed bus. While this architecture appears to be simple, significant complexity is inherent in this configuration, causing integration and testing headaches for the software developer.

Based on the system architecture, specific functionality is assigned to each node in this network. Individual network nodes are employed to manage the Control Panel, to Process Motion activities, and to manage the Robot and the Sensor. If the software developer disagrees with this allocation (based on knowledge of the software design and understanding of Ada performance implications), *Attempts to have the configuration modified.* In this architecture, using a dedicated processor for the Control Panel is a bit of overkill. This approach is typically necessary when extensive graphics are employed. No graphics are evident in the user interface. Status is indicated by colored circles. Moreover, user interaction, as evidenced by the event sequences, is relatively infrequent. This overall hardware solution requires extensive integration and testing effort by software developers. This hardware design is totally inappropriate and is questionable based on these justifications and its cost to software developers.

12.31 ALLOCATION OF ADA PACKAGES

Six Ada packages are identified in a previous illustration. In this case, each of these packages is allocated to a specific hardware architecture node. Since system and hardware engineers have identified the functionality of each processing node, allocation of packages to physical nodes is relatively easy. An appropriate mapping of packages to nodes appears in Figure 12.38.

With the inclusion of high level software tasking in Ada, the need for extensive hardware concurrency as employed by the architecture presented is less apparent. Employing excessive hardware concurrency leads to system architectures that are not reusable and are quite expensive to integrate and test. A careful evaluation of a total software solution using Ada tasking within a single CPU would reveal potentially sufficient performance to eliminate much of the hardware, reducing system complexity. Less hardware dependence certainly results in a cheaper solution for the purchaser of this system. Recent studies also show that hardware con-

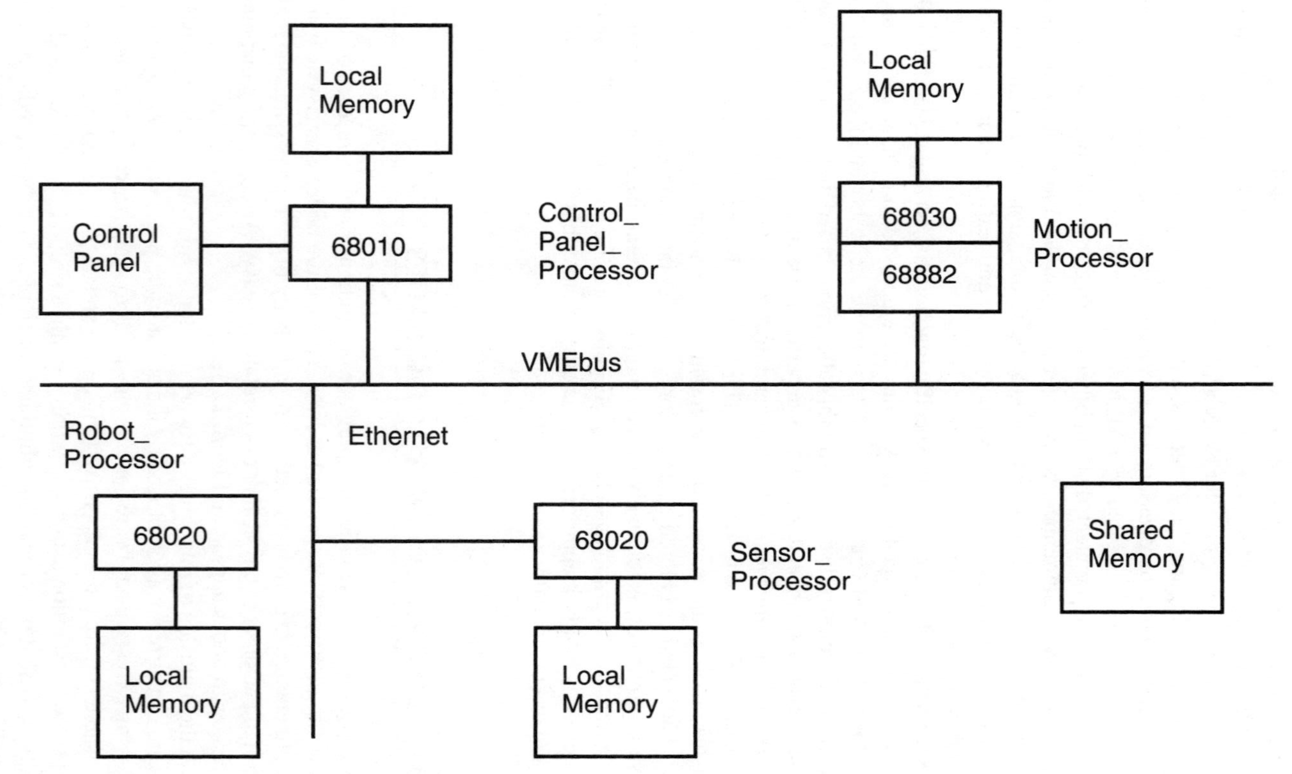

Figure 12.37 Hardware Architecture Block Diagram

1. Control_Panel_Processor
    a. Control_Panel
    b. CP_Processing
2. Robot_Processor
    a. Robot
3. Motion_Processor
    a. Axis
    b. Motion
4. Sensor_Processor
    a. Sensor

Figure 12.38 Allocation of Ada Packages to Hardware Architecture

currency is not necessarily a higher throughput solution. In fact, executing Ada packages on individual nodes requires that these packages reside above a software layer responsible for interprocessor communications. Resultant communications overhead is often more time consuming (reducing throughput) than an exclusively software solution.

An important point needs emphasis here. Software developers are justified in rejecting system architectures

1. *If they have not participated in the architecture generation process; or*
2. *If the architecture is not justified through a rigorous, believable analysis.*

If these assertions sound a bit aggressive, this is exactly as intended. A software developer's ability to deliver a software architecture integrated into a target platform within cost and schedule constraints is highly affected by this architectural complexity. Participation in the architecting process is of paramount importance to the software developer and to ultimate project success.

12.32 LVM/OOD FOR COMMAND INTERPRETER TASK

One of the tasks in the detailed design diagram, CP Command Interpret, is filled with white space. This white space is meant to indicate that a further detailed design effort is necessary. Several important requirements are allocated to the internal structure of this task via architecture generation. These requirements (Figure 12.39) are extracted from the requirements traceability matrix illustrated earlier. All control requirements, as evidenced by the STD and the PAT, are to be implemented within the body of this task. Moreover, validation and interpretation of panel input also occurs within the task body. Effective implementation of these requirements necessitates that a more methodical development be applied to the internal design of this task.

Experience with real-time developments and the representation of control requirements as a set of tables suggests that a table-driven approach is appropriate. However, hiding the data structure implementation of the "tables" indicates that a layered virtual machine/object-oriented design methodology is applicable.

Many developers tend to ignore the table-oriented specification of control requirements. Ignoring table-driven approaches results in software designs that hard code the event response. Modification and debugging of hard coded event responses is a difficult and tedious task. A table-driven software controller approach is much more effective in easing both modification and debugging headaches.

- Requirements to be satisfied
    - (2) Validate panel input
    - (4) Interpret panel input
    - State transition diagram
    - Process Activation Table
- Source—Requirements Traceability Matrix

Figure 12.39 LVM/OOD for Command Interpreter Task

12.33 STEP ONE—INVENT A SOLUTION

In accordance with the LVM/OOD methodology, an initial problem-oriented solution is invented. Each step in this solution (Figure 12.40) is categorized as either an operation on an abstract object or data type, or as a virtual machine instruction. Since a buffer is an abstract data object, the first line of the solution is an operation through a packaged interface. The second element of the solution is classed as a virtual machine instruction, requiring further analysis and detailing.

Classifying Respond To Input as a virtual instruction requires very little intellectual effort. Details of the response incorporate all of the allocated requirements that need to be accommodated. This complexity dictates further decomposition.

As the solution is identified in pseudocode format, an architecture diagram is generated for this step of the solution. Since this is a sequential software design, standard structure chart notation is employed.

12.34 STEP TWO—REFINE THE SOLUTION

Each virtual machine instruction in the initial solution is further refined (Figure 12.41). In this case, only one virtual instruction is defined: Respond To Input. This instruction is decomposed by using the same set of steps. A problem-oriented solution is generated. Two major components contribute to the solution at this level. Validate Input employs a State Variable, the Current Input, and the STD specified by the requirements allocation process. Moreover, Validate Input is one of the functional requirements to be satisfied by this sequential software design.

A second component is to Generate A Response. Generate A Response is interpreted as the requirement to Interpret Panel Input. This interpretation is accomplished by reading the PSPEC for the functional requirement Interpret Panel Input. According to the PSPEC interpretation of the panel, input is accomplished by utilizing the process activation table to determine a response.

Again, each component is categorized. Since Validate Input operates upon two data structures—a State Variable and an STD, this component is characterized as an operation on abstract objects, requiring immediate encapsulation. Since a package does not exist that abstracts the STD, a new package, CP Manager, is created to house the state table. Validate Input is one of the external interfaces exported by this package. Generate A Response requires further decomposition since no specific data object or type is employed.

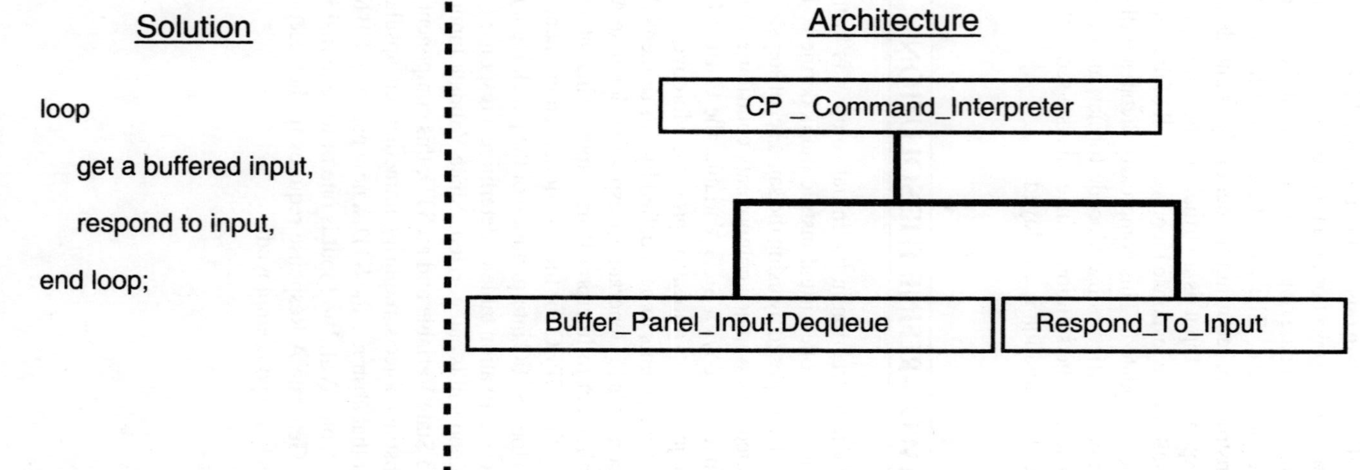

Figure 12.40 Step 1—Invent Solution

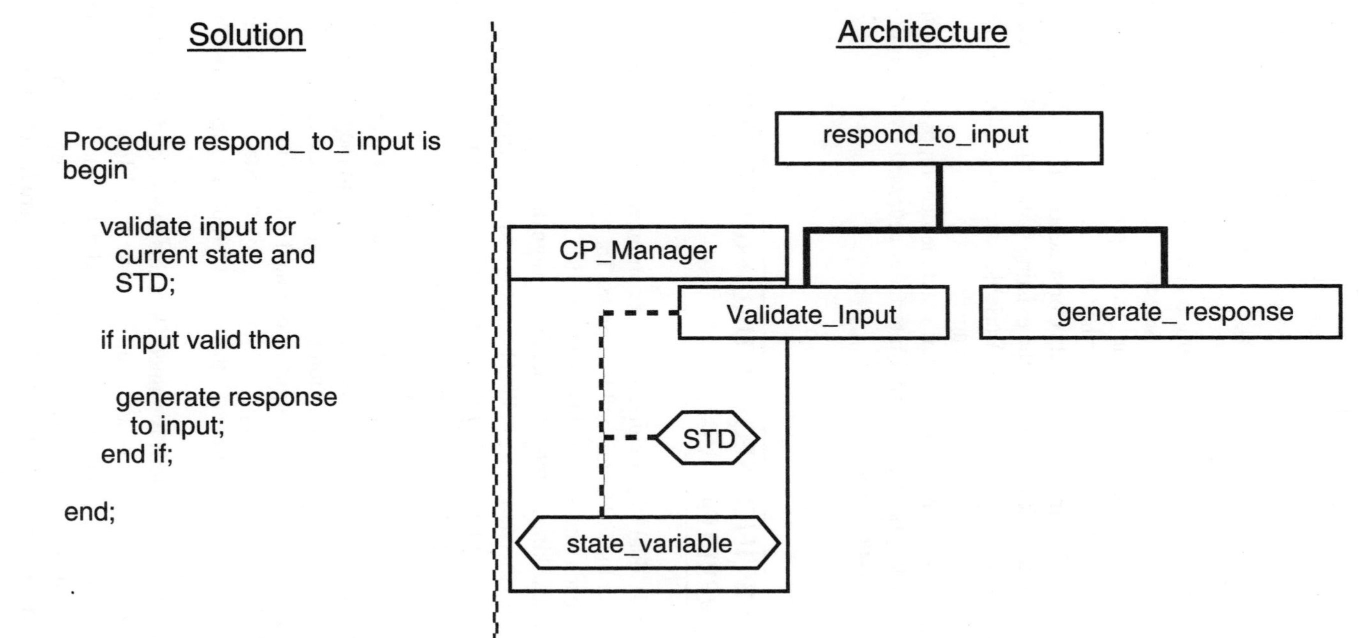

Figure 12.41 Step 2—Refine Solution

12.35 STEP THREE—REFINE THE SOLUTION AGAIN

As with the previous steps, an initial problem-oriented solution is generated (Figure 12.42). Three important components are employed and need evaluation. Determine A Response references a data structure—the PAT. Since use of the activation table requires knowledge of the state variable, Determine Response is added as an abstract interface to the CP Manager package. A hidden activation table is placed within the CP Manager package.

Another component within the solution is to send the Program ID to Program Interpreter to initiate execution of the selected pre-stored robot control program. This component is an access of an interface exported by another package in the software architecture and needs no further analysis.

Finally, a Panel Output is generated. Construction of an appropriate Panel Output message requires knowledge of the existing state. Since State Variable is encapsulated within CP Manager, State Variable access is implemented as one more abstract function exported by CP Manager.

Since all components of this virtual machine decomposition are traceable to operations on objects or to external interfaces accessed by this task, no further decomposition is necessary.

12.36 SIMPLIFIED SEQUENTIAL ARCHITECTURE FOR CP INTERPRETER TASK

All of the individual step architectures are combined into a single detailed design architecture for the CP Command Interpreter Task (Figure 12.43). Data flows are attributed to each interface in this representation.

As with the tasking architecture detailed design diagram, data flow continuity is evaluated with this diagram. A Panel Input is dequeued from Buffer Panel Input. This input is passed across Validate Panel Input, which is exported by CP Manager. Within this procedure, a specific user command is extracted. Data within the command is validated against the state diagram yielding a Valid indicator. Both command type and valid indicator are returned to the main body of CP Command Interpreter. If valid, the specific command is passed to the interface name Determine Response. Using the activation table, an appropriate response is performed (data structures updated, output signals generated, etc.). Finally, the command type is transferred to Send Panel Output, which employs the State Variable and the command type to construct and transmit the Panel Output message across the hardware interface.

Another important benefit is gained from this diagram. Complete traceability from requirements to code is assured. Validate Panel Input is the coded implementation of the functional requirement to Validate Panel Input. Determine Response, also exported by CP Manager, is the embodiment of the requirement to Interpret Panel Input. Both the STD and the PAT are traced to specific locations

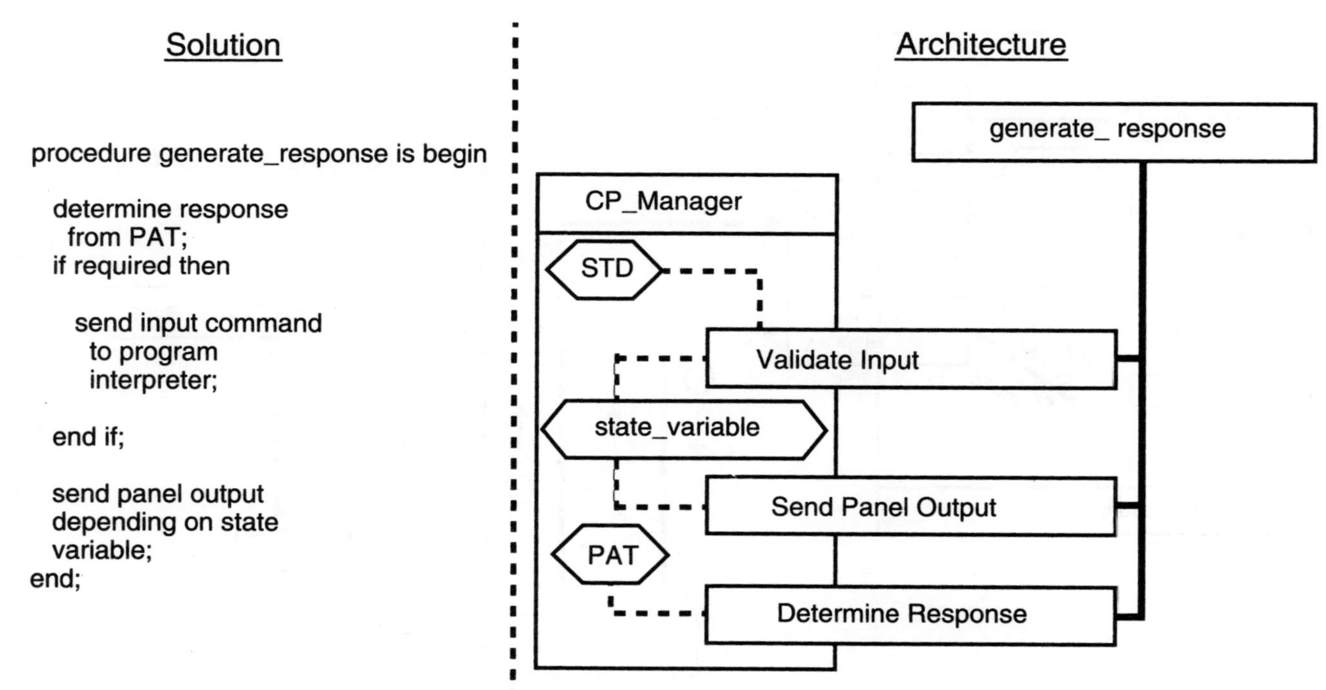

Figure 12.42 Step 3—Refine Solution Again

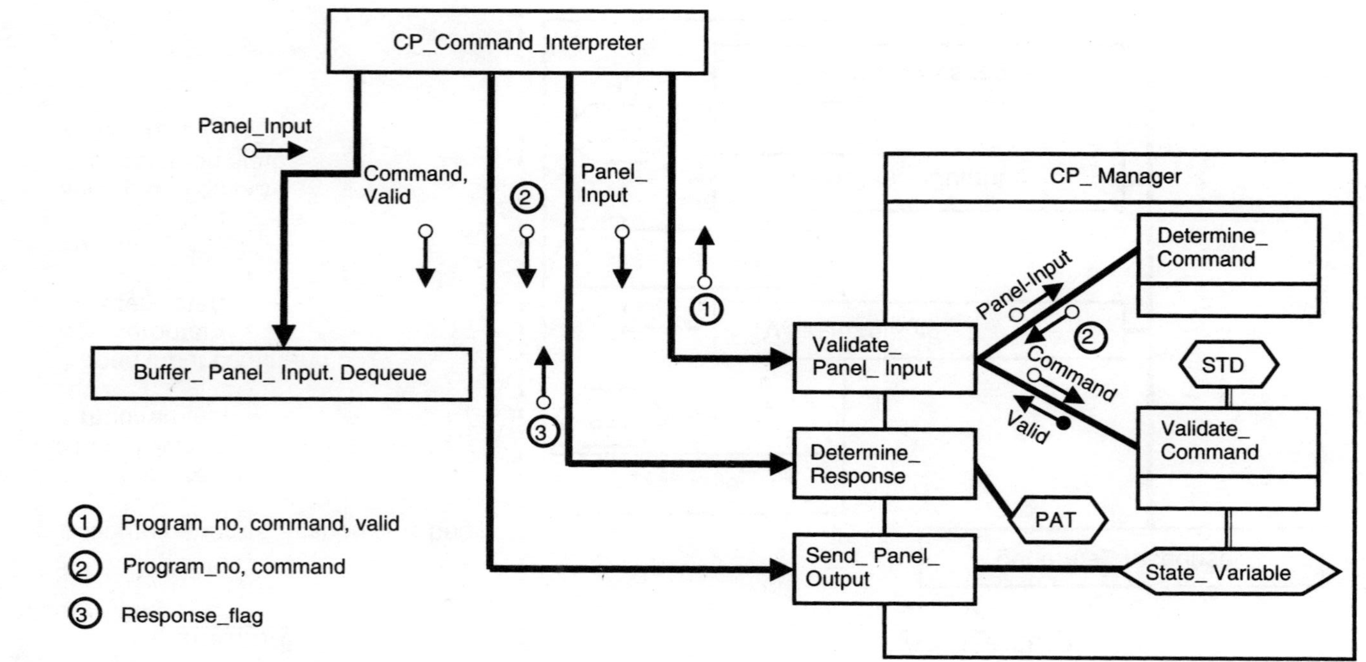

Figure 12.43 Simplified Sequential Architecture for CP Command Interpreter Task

within the detailed design—the body of CP Manager.

Effective use of information hiding is also demonstrated by this diagram. All data structures and objects are successfully encapsulated under abstract interfaces. Specifically, a State Variable, STD, and PAT are hidden within the package body of CP Manager.

12.37 CP COMMAND INTERPRETER TASK SEQUENTIAL DETAILED DESIGN

In Figure 12.44, the sequential design of the CP Command Interpreter task is provided in a standard structure chart format. Its value lies in the manner in which the diagram indicates the potential for a design that fails to employ information hiding. In a detailed sequential design accomplished by normal structured methods, internal structures of both STD and PAT are visible at every location in which CP Manager is referenced. This visibility may seem to exist in a small number of locations. For a system the size of the robot controller, these locations are indeed few in number. However, for larger systems, proliferation of data structure details causes problems with integration and testing and makes the modification process extremely difficult.

Even within this limited scope, proliferation of data structure details causes both testing and modification problems. Allowing visibility into data structure details results in pseudocode that no longer looks like the problem addressed by the code. Detailed array references with many nested loops cause the reviewer of the code to lose insight into the algorithm being implemented. As a result, accomplishing changes or isolating problem code becomes a difficult process.

12.38 PSEUDOCODE FOR SIMPLIFIED SEQUENTIAL ARCHITECTURE

Combining all intermediate solutions into one pseudocode representation and applying data flow interfaces from the previous diagram yields a task body for CP Command Interpreter. This pseudocode looks suspiciously like actual code. All interfaces appear as in the actual code (Figure 12.45).

Of great interest is the appearance of the pseudocode itself. This pseudocode is in problem oriented terms, not in the form of data structure details. By evaluating the pseudocode, a customer/project manager understands the logic and/or algorithms employed. In this manner, the data abstracting capabilities supported by Ada really shine. Ada allows direct translation of this pseudocode into actual Ada code, with no data structuring obfuscation. Other languages do not effectively support this transition from design to code.

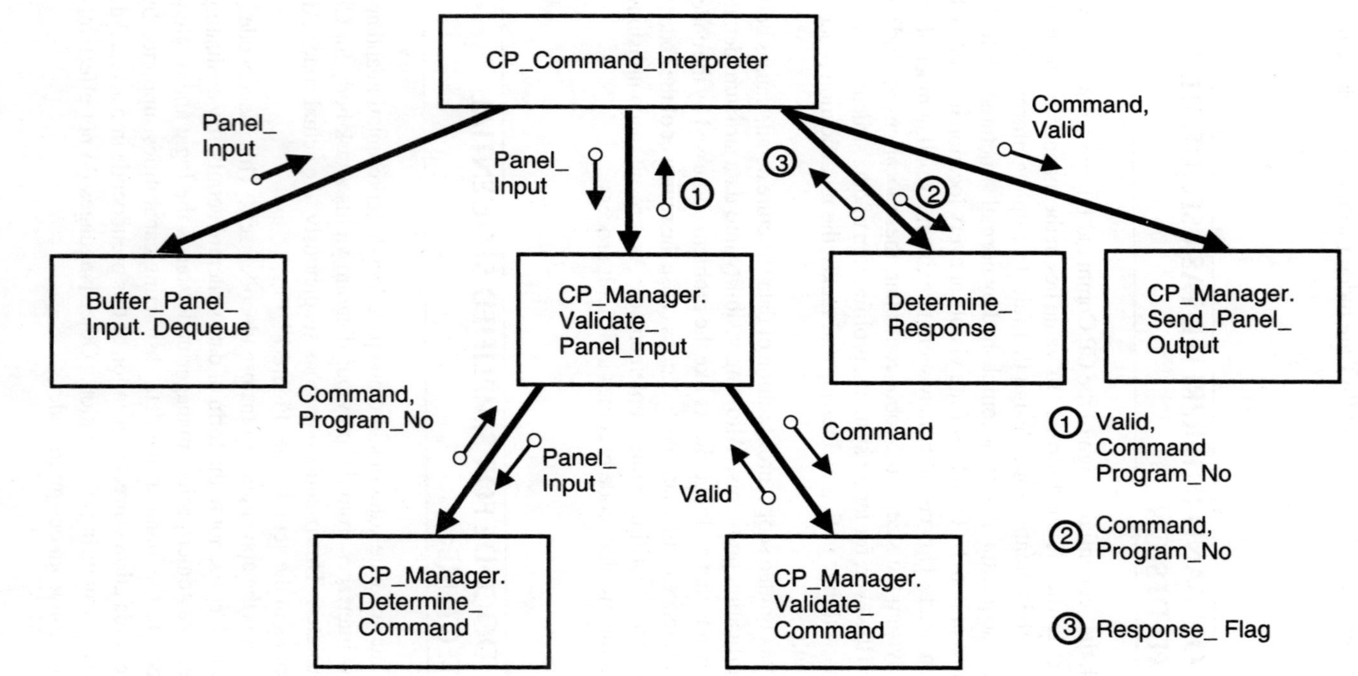

Figure 12.44 CP Command Interpreter Task Sequential Detailed Design

```
task body CP_Command_Interpreter is

    loop

        Buffer_Panel_Input. Dequeue (CP_Input);
        CP_Manager. Validate_Input (CP_Input, valid_flag);
        if valid_ flag then

                CP_Manager. Determine_ Response (command, Response_ flag);
                 if Response_ flag then
                          Motion. Start_ program;
        end if;
        end if;

        CP Manager. Send_Panel_Output (CP_Input, valid_flag);

    end loop;
                              =>
    exception
        when end_error
          text_io. put_line ("Pseudocode Executed")

end CP_Command_Interpreter;
```

Figure 12.45 Pseudocode for Simplified Sequential Architecture

13

Message Passing Operating System Case Study

Everyone who uses computers interacts with an operating system on a regular basis. Unfortunately, operating systems are the most poorly developed software systems in use. Despite the plethora of textbooks describing theory and implementation of operating systems, constructing an actual operating system is often difficult, tedious, and frustrating. As a result, operating systems are usually constructed by the tried and true "rush to the keyboards," resulting in bug infested delivered software. Moreover, actual implementations result in untold megabytes of object code. No wonder that users and application software developers cringe at the introduction of either a new system or an upgraded system.

Operating systems do not need to be developed in this haphazard manner. In fact, a message passing operating system is easily developed according to the principles in this text. Most implementations of operating systems occur within hardware architectures controlled by a series of interrupts. These interrupts are the "events" driving the operations of the operating system. With this perspective, development methods described within this text can be applied to yield high performance, minimal memory size operating systems. This case study illustrates application of the development methodology to specify and design a message passing operating system.

This study is not adapted from any other source. Steps in the development methodology are followed, as indicated in the text. Comparison of methodology results with a real operating system is difficult, since no operating systems are developed in a methodical manner. At least, no documentation exists to demonstrate application of a rigorous methodology.

13.1 OPERATION MODEL GENERATION

Simplifying a user's view of software system operations (Figure 13.1) consists of the following steps:

1. Specify user interfaces and the order of operations of user interaction;
2. Translate order of operations of user interaction into an initial message sequence;
3. Expand the message sequence into detailed operational scenarios involving sensors, actuators and other interfaces; and
4. Divide the detailed message sequence into a detailed event/response pattern indicating inputs and outputs.

Since a command language is employed as the user interface, operations model generation begins with step 3. An external interface diagram is employed to specify a message sequence that reflects typical multi-tasking use of operating system services and interfaces.

13.2 EXTERNAL INTERFACE DIAGRAM

An operating system manages a constrained set of resources available to multiple users. Interfaces accommodated by the operating system are characterized in Figure 13.2.

Individual users of the operating system are represented as application programs. For purposes of development, a single application program is employed to represent the class of users. User commands are accepted through a terminal, consisting of a keyboard with a display device consisting of a monitor. A printer is available for hard copy output. To be upward compatible with older systems, a card reader allows for entry of programs and data. Mass storage is provided in the form of a block structured disk.

Two important interfaces necessary for successful operation are included. These interfaces—clock and memory address translator—are usually hidden from the user. Clocks are necessary to assure context switching of application programs. Implementation of virtual memory requires hardware that can rapidly translate virtual addresses to physical addresses and can page fault if the logical address is not loaded into memory. Modern operating systems cannot realistically perform without this hardware support. Therefore, these components are included as part of the required external interfaces.

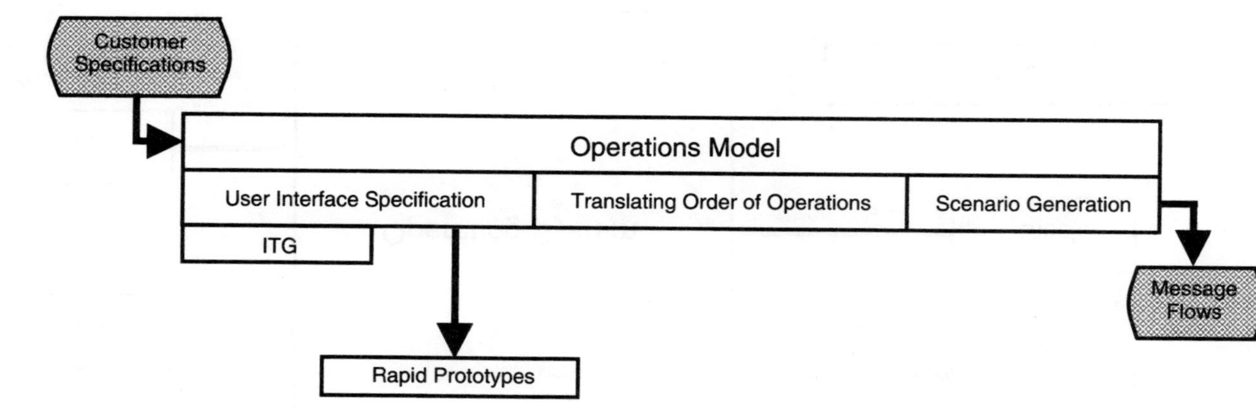

Figure 13.1 Operations Model Generation

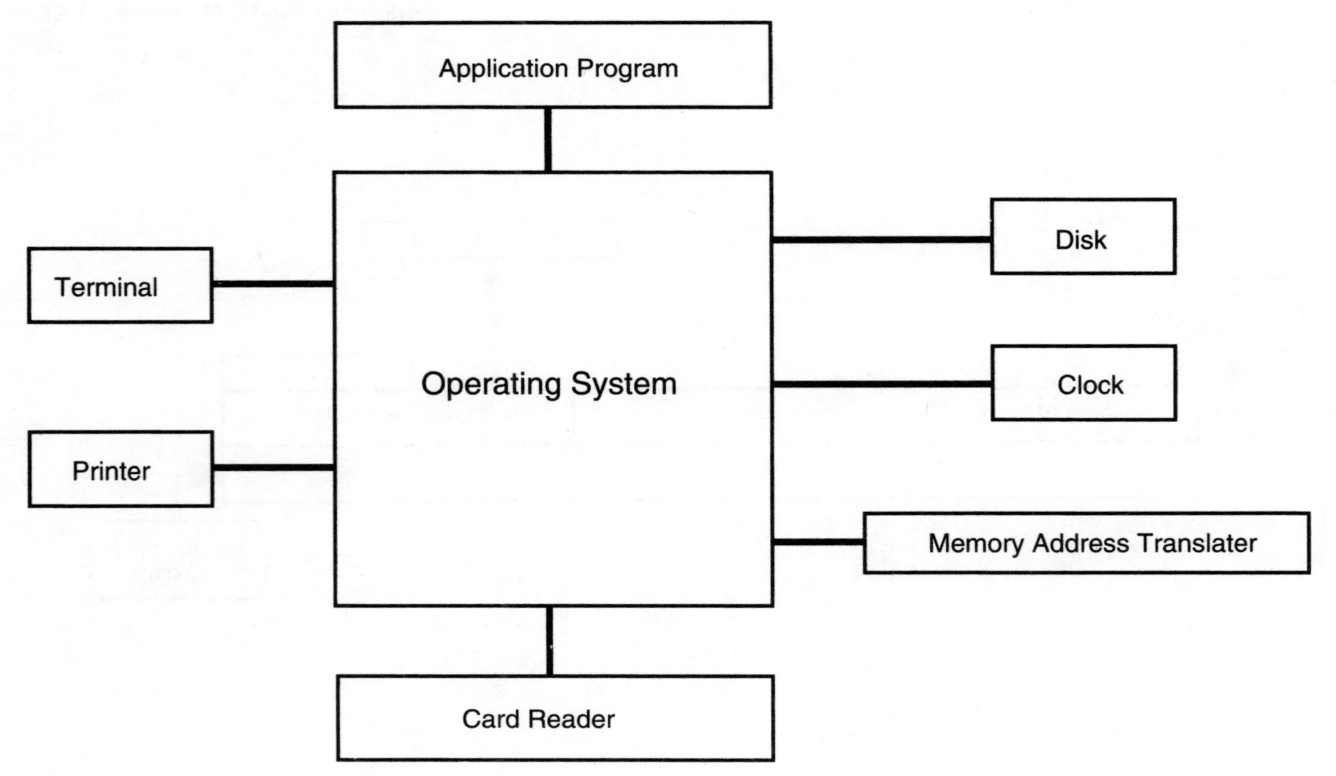

Figure 13.2 External Interface Diagram

13.3 TYPICAL OPERATIONS SCENARIO (I, II)

Development of an operating system requires a clear understanding of the manner in which events occur, from a user's perspective. An event/response scenario for a typical user session is provided in Figures 13.3 to 13.4.

First, a user logs into the operating system, then chooses to execute a program. These actions result in two user command events containing arguments indicating the command type. At the next timer interrupt, this application begins execution. Execution of the application program continues until the application program decides to request data from the mass storage device. An internal event, named input/output request, is generated to the operating system by the application program. In turn, a data block is requested from the disk controller. Eventually the data block appears at the memory mapped hardware interface by the disk controller. At the next timer interrupt, the application program requesting the data block continues execution.

This same application program continues execution until a virtual address is referenced for which no physical counterpart exists in memory. This access causes a page fault event to be generated by the memory management unit hardware. A resultant data block request is issued by the operating system to the disk controller to load the missing program page into physical memory. After the appropriate delays for track and sector positioning and data transfer, the data block arrives. Page tables are updated. Another timer interrupt is necessary before the application program begins execution. Execution is continued at the statement that references the formerly missing virtual address.

Meanwhile, other application programs begin execution under operating system control. Each timer interrupt leads to a context switch allowing a different application program to utilize the CPU. As a minimum, two timer interrupts/context switches are necessary to allow a specific application program to be suspended and then to continue execution. Due to the high priority of the currently executing task, execution continues until the application program completes processing its input data. At this point, the application program generates an input/output request event to signal completion of execution.

In response, the operating system transmits a user display response to the terminal. This informs the user that execution is successfully completed. Now the user terminates access and operating system control via a user command event signaling that logout is desired.

Other variations of this sequence are easily envisioned. However, this sequence represents the minimal end-to-end data flow necessary to characterize a typical user's interaction with and his application program's demand on resources managed by the operating system. From this perspective, an operating system is indeed a typical real-time system as characterized in this text. A collection of interrupts and internal service requests form a set of "events" resulting in specific responses.

Description	From	To	Message
User LogOn	Terminal	OS	<user_cmd> = login
User Executes Program	Terminal	OS	<user_cmd> = XQT program
Multitasking - Start Execution	Clock	OS	<timer>
Application Rqsts Data	Application Program	OS	<io_rqst>
OS Rqsts Data	OS	Disk	<data_block>
Data Returned	Disk	OS	<data_block>
Multitasking—Resume Execution	Clock	OS	<timer>
Application Page Faults	Memory Mgt Unit	OS	<page_fault>
Page Requested	OS	Disk	<data_block>
Page Returned	Disk	OS	<data_block>
Multitasking—Resume Execution	Clock	OS	<timer>

Figure 13.3 Typical Operations Scenario (I)

Description	From	To	Message
PreEmptive Multitasking-	Clock	OS	<timer>
2 Different Tasks	Clock	OS	<timer>
Application Completes XQT	Application Program	OS	<io_rqst>
User Informed	OS	Terminal	<user_display>
User Logout	Terminal	OS	<user_cmd> = logout

Figure 13.4 Typical Operations Scenario (II)

13.4 REQUIREMENTS MODEL GENERATION

Defining an implementor's view of software system requirements (Figure 13.5) needed to satisfy the operational/user's view consists of the following steps:

1. Generate a context diagram using the detailed message sequence;
2. Construct functional requirements in the form of a requirements tree and PSPECs;
3. Describe event response logic for managing the PSPECs in the form of STDs and PATs;
4. Perform a consistency and completeness check of implementor requirements against operational requirements;
5. Use the data dictionary to determine an initial set of data abstractions and operations on abstractions; and
6. Allocate timing requirements to PSPECs.

13.5 OPERATING SYSTEM CONTEXT DIAGRAM

Flows across external interfaces are extracted from the operations scenario above and are characterized in Figure 13.6. All incoming flows are marked as control events, requiring that event responses be formally specified. Outgoing response flows are labeled as simple data flows.

User commands enter the operating system from the terminal. When requested, data blocks are provided from the disk. At periodic intervals, timer events occur. Aperiodically, depending on program execution, page faults are generated by memory address translator hardware.

In a typical target environment, these interfaces are memory mapped. Data is placed into a special area of memory unique to each hardware interface. Underlying circuitry directly connects the external interface to this reserved memory area. When an external device provides data, the data is placed into the memory mapped area. Then, an interrupt is triggered via additional circuitry connected to the interrupt generation system of the CPU.

13.6 COMBINED CONTROL/DATA FLOW DIAGRAM

Basic functions performed by an operating system are captured in Figure 13.7. When an interrupt enters the system, the interrupt type is determined. Depending on the interrupt type, data embedded in the interrupt flows to the next function. The PSPEC for Handle Device Interrupt (2) describes interrupt type determination

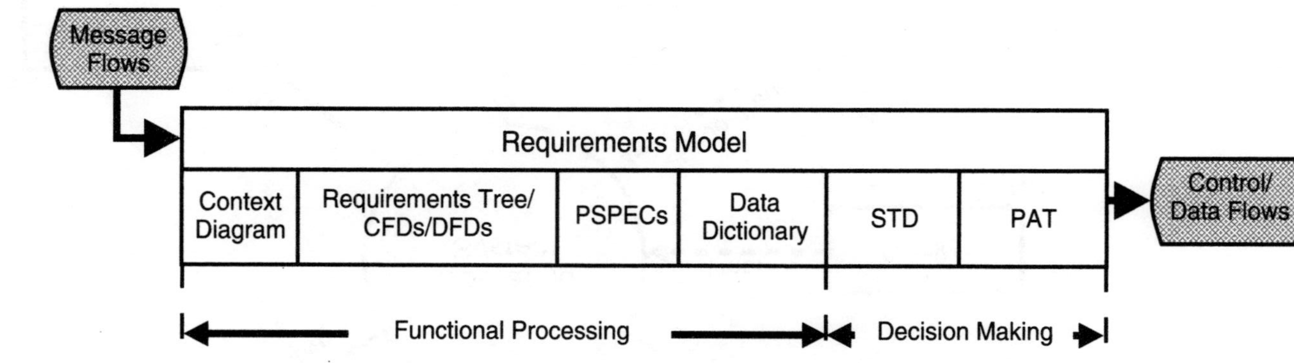

Figure 13.5 Requirements Model Generation

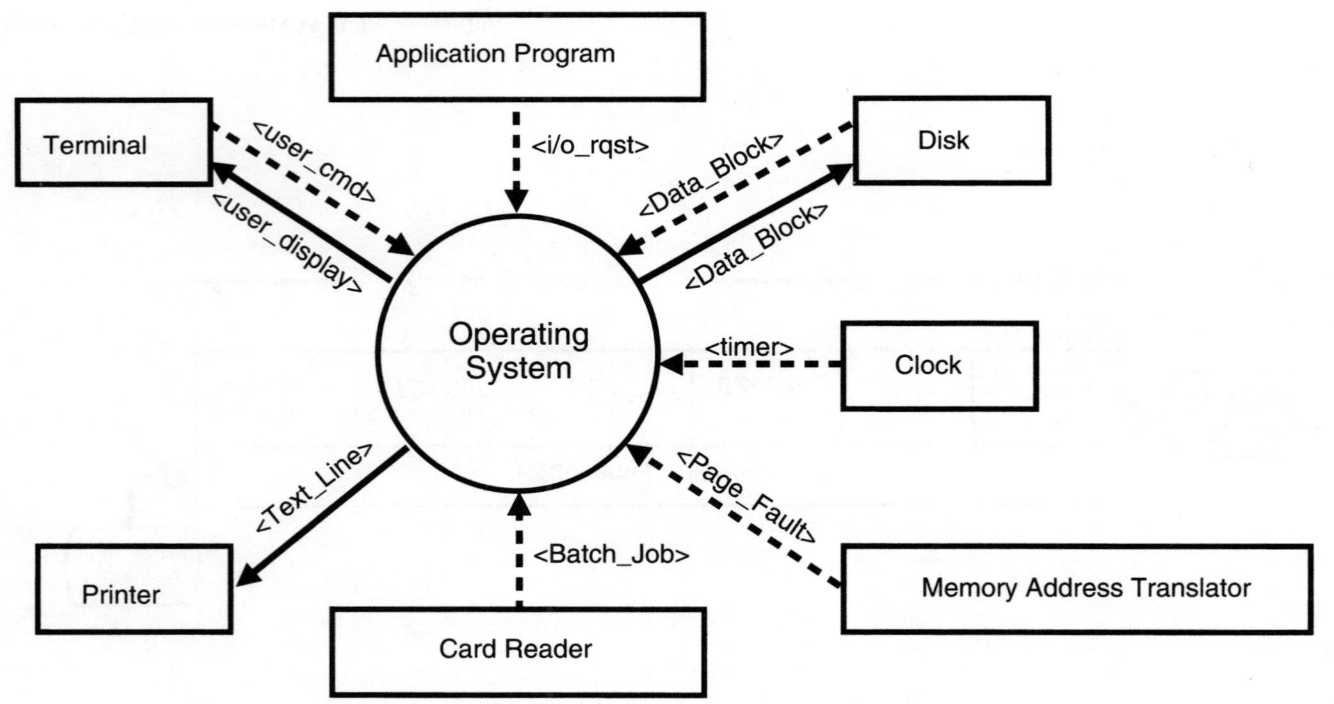

Figure 13.6 Operating System Context Diagram

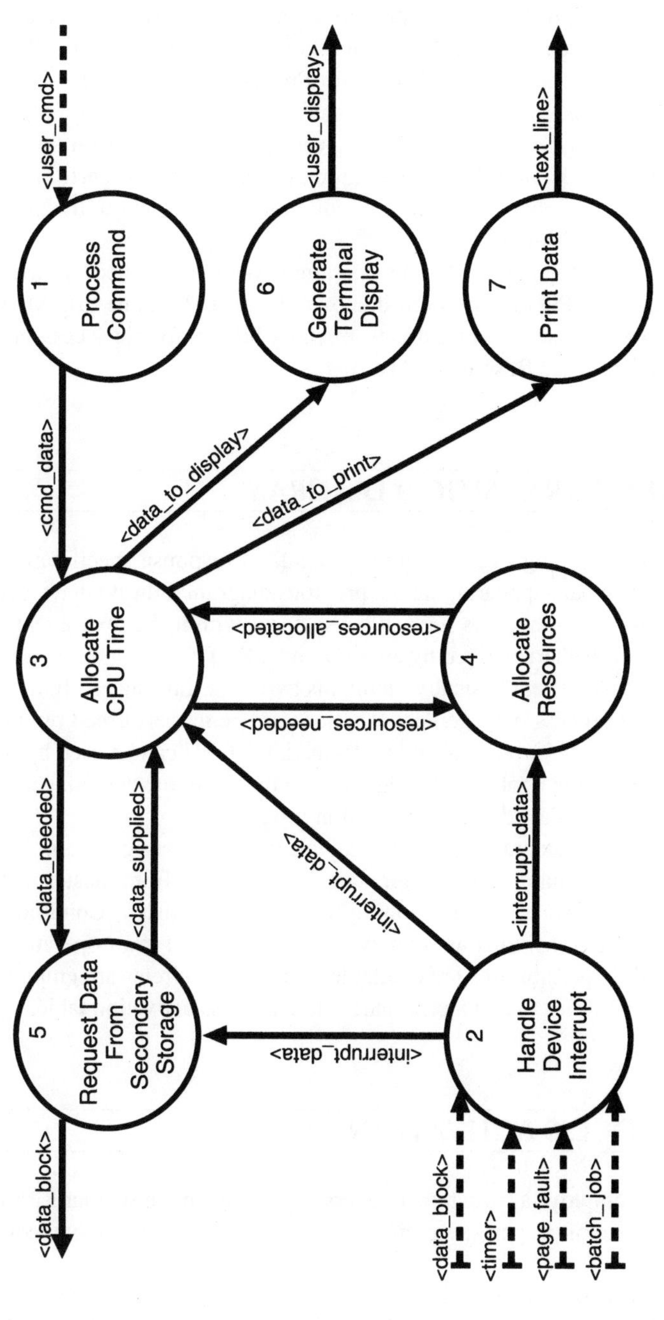

Figure 13.7 Operating System Combined Control Data/Flow Diagram

for a given interrupt event. If a data block arrives, identifying information is passed to the function requesting the data block. Both timer signals and batch jobs require a decision regarding CPU use. A page fault results in a request for data from secondary storage to load a missing virtual page. Each user command requires a specific processing response. Mechanics and decisions associated with user command processing appear in the PSPEC for Process Command (1).

Other functions serve to manage the formatting and control of outgoing data. Request Data from Secondary Storage (5) is responsible for transmitting data block requests to the disk controller. Generation of a user display is performed by Generate Terminal Display (6). Emitting individual lines of text to the printer is the responsibility of Print Data (7).

Resource management within the operating system is handled by the remaining two functions. CPU time is controlled by Allocate CPU Time (3). Management of other resources, such as tape drives, memory buffers for file access, etc., are the province of Allocate Resources (4).

13.7 STATE TRANSITION DIAGRAM

Each of the incoming events requires a detailed response specification (Figure 13.8). Control bars appearing on the previous diagram indicate that a detailed response is forthcoming. As with other systems within the text, event response mechanisms are characterized by an STD and a PAT.

An operating system basically maintains two important states. In master state, resource and process management functions are being performed by the system. When these functions need not be performed, the CPU can be used by one of the currently executing application programs. In this case, the operating system is in a slave state (i.e., slaved to the application program).

Four possible state transitions are available to the operating system. These transitions include remaining in master state, transitioning from master to slave, remaining in slave state, or transitioning from slave to master. Conditions associated with state transitions are somewhat complicated for an operating system. Since multiple possibilities are available, numbers in circles are employed to allow the possibilities to be incorporated into a process activation table.

13.8 PROCESS ACTIVATION TABLE

Figure 13.9 employs a format that differs slightly from the standard PAT format. As an example of proper interpretation of the contents of this table, consider the first row.

If the operating system is in master state and a timer event occurs, a specific response is required. This response is indicated in the section of the table labeled "Process List," and is composed of the following functions:

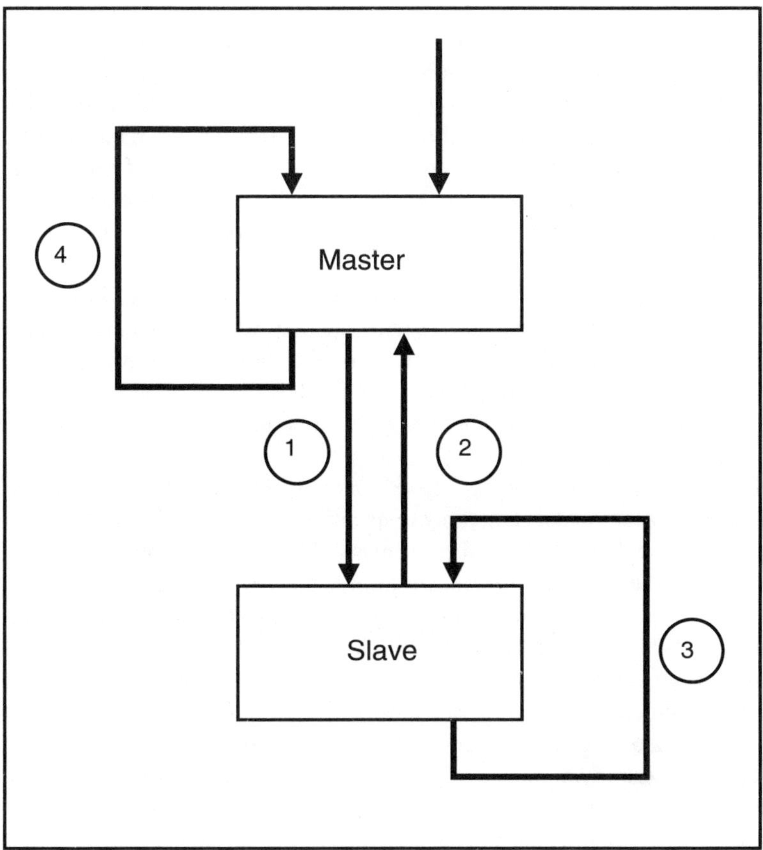

Figure 13.8 O.S. State Transition Diagram

1. Handle Interrupt (2);
2. Allocate CPU Time (3).

Continuing across the first row of the table, this condition is associated with transition labeled (4) on the STD, requiring that the system remain in master state.

Other response specifications involve some amount of parallelism, at least specified within this PAT. An input/output request, whether in master or slave state, involves the following functional requirements:

1. Handle Interrupt (2);
2. Request Data (5) and

Generate Display (6) and

Print Data (7).

Functions 5, 6, and 7 are performed concurrently, according to the table. The last two parts of the response result in status indicators and are dependent on the data contained within the input/output request interrupt. These components are highly questionable. Informing the user of every input/output request occurrence results in extensive loss of throughput. CPU cycles are wasted generating irrelevant status information. If an application program performs an extensive amount of input and output, a user is swamped by interrupt level details. This information is of marginal use to a user.

Any event can cause the operating system to maintain its state. If the system is in master state, each interrupt causes the system to stay in master state. State preservation for slave state is also associated with each possible interrupt. Only a timer interrupt results in a transition from master to slave or from slave to master. However, if none of the master functions need to be performed, even a timer event maintains the current state.

Two important shortcomings are exhibited by this CSPEC. Some ambiguities exist in the transition decision process specified in the table. For instance, a timer event causes either a transition from master to master or from master to slave. Contents of the table are insufficient to indicate which of the choices are made. The actual state transition decision is embedded within the PSPEC of Allocate CPU Time (3). While embedding decision logic within a PSPEC is acceptable, a better approach is to expand the STD, creating more states. Additional states allow the control specification to incorporate more decision logic into the state table and to eliminate this ambiguity of response hidden within the PSPEC.

Another weakness in this specification is the requirement that transitions from master to slave or slave to master occur in response to a timer interrupt. This transition restraint could result in extensive dead time, reducing system throughput. For instance, if an input/output request occurs and the system is in master mode, master mode is maintained. If no events requiring a master mode response are outstanding, this time is idle time. Application programs waiting to use the CPU are suspended until the next timer event, when the invocation of Allocate CPU Time (3) decides the next mode—master or slave. Moreover, depending on the decision algorithm embedded in the PSPEC of Allocate CPU Time, master state may be maintained, resulting potentially in more dead time.

Both of these shortcomings are relieved with further rework of the control specifications. However, with an appropriate PSPEC for Allocate CPU time, an implementation using this CSPEC would indeed work correctly, albeit slowly.

State Before	Control Signal	Process List ① Proc_Cmd	② Handle_Int	③ Alloc_CPU_Time	④ Alloc_Res	⑤ Rqst_Data	⑥ Gen_Disp	⑦ Print_Data	Transition Label	State After
Master	<timer>		1	2					④	Master
	<user_cmd>	1		2					④	Master
	<data_block>		1			2			④	Master
	<page_fault>		1		2	3			④	Master
	<batch_job>		1	2					④	Master
	<io_rqst>		1			2	2	2	④	Master
Slave	<timer>		1	2					②	Master
	<user_cmd>	1		2					②	Master
	<data_block>		1			2			②	Master
	<page_fault>		1		2	3			②	Master
	<batch_job>		1	2					②	Master
	<io_rqst>		1			2	2	2	②	Master
Master	<timer>		1	2					①	Slave
Slave	<timer>		1	2					③	Master

Figure 13.9 O.S. Process Activation Table

13.9 DATA DICTIONARY

Each of the data and control flows is defined in the data dictionary (Figure 13.10). In some cases, enumerated types are employed. In other cases, detailed component structures are provided.

Events require two specific data entries: a pending interrupt register and an interrupt data area. Actual data is placed in the interrupt data area (IDA) and is structured in the format of the incoming data. Once the IDA is filled, the external device generates an interrupt through the CPU circuitry. This constructs an appropriate bit pattern in the pending interrupt register (PIR) to specify the interrupt type. The PIR is described in the data dictionary as an enumerated type. Detailed structure definitions are given for each variant of the IDA.

Eventual implementation of these interfaces employs a representation specification clause. Enumerated literals are transformed into required bit patterns. A specific pending interrupt register and multiple interrupt data areas are mapped to specific locations in memory, as actually implemented.

A number of potential abstract types are identified from the data dictionary—user command, data block, timer, page fault, batch job, and input/output request. Moreover, several specific abstract objects are needed—a pending interrupt register and one interrupt data area for each interface. Of course, abstract operations such as create, destroy, get_component, and put_component need to be created. As the development proceeds, other operations may be identified (object_is_empty, component _is_empty, etc.).

13.10 REQUIREMENTS EVALUATION (I-II)

Using the operational scenario and control specifications (STD and PAT), a complete requirements evaluation is performed in Figures 13.11 to 13.12. This evaluation presents a precise, dynamic view of the way an operating system really works.

For the most part, state transitions are easy to determine. When one of the ambiguous conditions (as described above) occurs, an assumption is made as to the decision logic embedded in the PSPEC for Allocate CPU Time (3) to assure that an appropriate transition is chosen.

This requirements evaluation serves to highlight the loss in throughput associated with the limits on the transition from master to slave state. Master slave transitions are currently allowed only in response to a timer event. In the second line of the evaluation, a user command event occurs, indicating the name of a program to be executed. In response, Allocate CPU Time (3) determines that this application program is to be executed. However, the context switch does not occur until the next timer event. An idle CPU wastes potential execution time until the timer interrupt appears. While this wasted time may be only 100 msecs, this waste accumulates over time, significantly reducing operating system throughput. Most

```
<user_cmd>       : =  (Login, Logout, OS_Command, XQT_Proq, XQT_Prog_Cmd); - - ida
<user_display>   : =  (ASCII_String, Frame_Buffer);
<data_block>     : =  block_descriptor + block_data;                      - - ida
<timer>          : =  clock_name;                                         - - ida
<page_fault>     : =  process_id + virtual_page_number;                   - - ida
<batch_job>      : =  accnt_data + program + data;                        - - ida
<Text_Line>      : =  ASCII_string;
<io_data>        : =  (Data_Needed, Data_To_Display, Data_To_Print);      - - ida
<pir>            : = (user_cmd, data_block, timer, page_fault, batch_ job, io_rqst);
```

Figure 13.10 O.S. Data Dictionary

State Before	Control Event	State After	Action Details
Master	<user_cmd>	Master	(1) Process Command (3) Alloc CPU Time
Master	<user_cmd>	Master	(1) Process Command (3) Alloc CPU Time
Master	<timer>	Slave	(2) Handle Interrupt (3) Alloc CPU Time
Slave	<i/o_rqst>	Master	(2) Handle Interrupt (5) Rqst_Data (6) Gen_Disp
Master	<data_block>	Master	(2) Handle_Interrupt (5) Rqst_Data
Master	<timer>	Slave	(2) Handle Interrupt (3) Alloc CPU Time
Master	<page_fault>	Master	(2) Handle Interrupt (4) Alloc_Res (5) Rqst Data
Master	<data_block>	Master	(2) Handle Interrupt (5) Rqst Data
Master	<timer>	Slave	(2) Handle Interrupt (3) Alloc CPU Time

Figure 13.11 Requirements Evaluation (I)

State Before	Control Event	State After	Action Details
Slave	<timer>	Slave	(2) Handle Interrupt (3) Alloc CPU Time
Slave	<timer>	Slave	(2) Handle Interrupt (3) Alloc CPU Time
Slave	<i/o_rqst>	Master	(3) Handle Interrupt (5) Rqst_Data (6) Gen_Disp
Master	<user_cmd>	Master	(1) Process Command (3) Alloc CPU Time

Figure 13.12 Requirements Evaluation (II)

initial specifications do not find this flaw. Without the detailed requirements evaluation, an implementation includes this important limitation. Finding the problem amidst several hundred thousand lines of code is extremely difficult.

13.11 ARCHITECTURE MODEL GENERATION

Describing a top level design (Figure 13.13) that effectively employs concurrent activity to satisfy both operational and implementor requirements consists of the following steps:

1. Enhance both functional and control requirements to accommodate specific hardware/technological interfaces;
2. Perform a consistency and completeness check of enhanced requirements against operational requirements;
3. Translate both functional and control requirements into a process architecture;
4. Perform a consistency and completeness check of the process architecture against operational requirements;
5. Evaluate architecture performance against timing constraints based on combining timing allocations for requirements mapped into each architecture process; and
6. Allocate requirements within each architecture process to hardware and to software.

13.12 TRANSLATING REQUIREMENTS INTO ARCHITECTURE PROCESSES

Top level architecture processes are identified in a manner consistent with design approaches employed on most operating systems (Figure 13.14). Interfaces are managed by one process—device managers (4). Application programs are managed within the scope of the process controller (3). Files are managed by the file controller (1). Resource allocation is the province of the resource controller (2).

Below each architecture process a list of original requirements appears in parentheses. A requirement from the data flow diagram is indicated by the label Px, which indicates Process x on the original data flow diagram. Determination of data flowing among these processes is accomplished using the analysis approach described within the text.

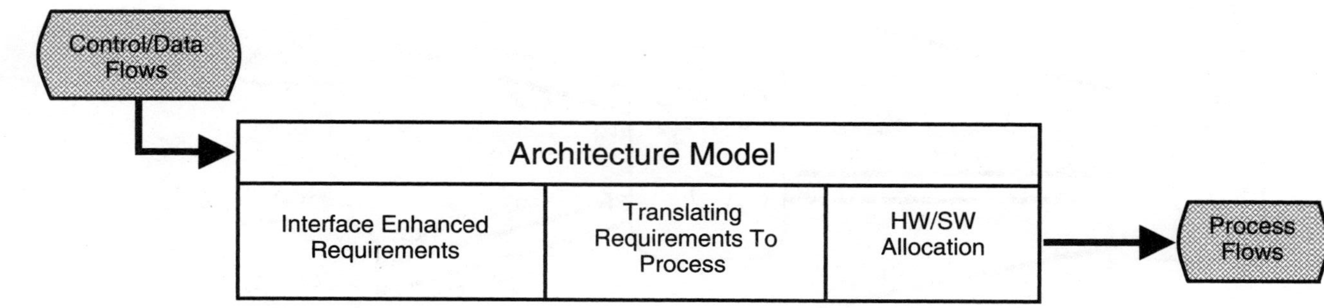

Figure 13.13 Architecture Model Generation

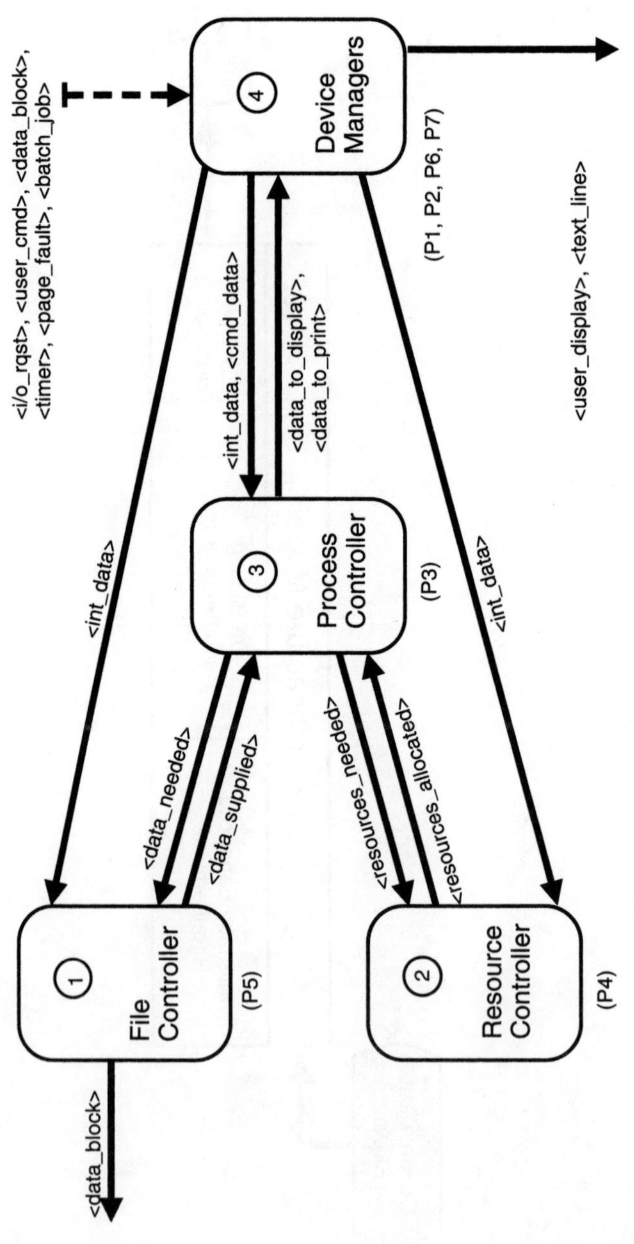

Figure 13.14 Translating Requirements into Architecture Processes

13.13 REQUIREMENTS TRACEABILITY MATRIX

Two levels of traceability are incorporated into Figure 13.15. Individual architecture processes are divided into one or more Ada software tasks. Original functional requirements are then traced into both architecture processes and corresponding Ada tasks.

As a representative example, consider the resource controller process. This process is divided into three Ada tasks—Allocator, Memory Manager, and Print Server. The original functional requirement named Allocate Resources (4) is divided among these three Ada tasks. Each task manages a specific resource category.

13.14 DESIGN MODEL GENERATION

Generating a detailed software design consistent with the process architecture involves two separate, but interrelated steps: tasking architecture generation and sequential software design (Figure 13.16).

Detailed software design consists of the following steps:

1. Generate an initial tasking architecture;
2. Establish caller/callee relationships;
3. Employ (or do not employ) intermediaries;
4. Perform a consistency and completeness check of the tasking architecture against operational requirements;
5. Allocate tasks to be packages;
6. Generate functional components of Ada packages;
7. Use layered abstractions, table division controllers, data objects and data types to construct sequential design of each task; and
8. Evaluate the detailed design to assess its quality.

13.15 TASK ARCHITECTURE DIAGRAM

Each architecture module is divided into one or more Ada tasks, as described above. Having identified individual Ada tasks, the previous process flow diagram is translated into a tasking architecture diagram. External interfaces are maintained in Figure 13.17.

Each interface typically (but not always) requires two levels of management—one for the actual interface, a second for higher level management activities. As an example, consider the disk interface. A file server tracks the open files

Requirement		1	2	3	4	5	6	7
Module/Process	SW Process/Task	Process Cmd	Handle Device Int	Alloc CPU Time	Alloc Resources	Rqst Data	Generate Term Display	Print Data
File Controller	File Server					X		
Resource Controller	Allocator							
	Memory Manager				X			
	Print Server							
Process Controller	Scheduler			X				
Device Managers	Terminal Driver	X	X				X	X
	Terminal Int Handler							
	Clock Int Handler							
	Printer Driver							
	Card Reader Handler							
	Memory Fault Handler							
	Disk Int Handler							
	Disk Driver							

Figure 13.15 Requirements Traceability Matrix

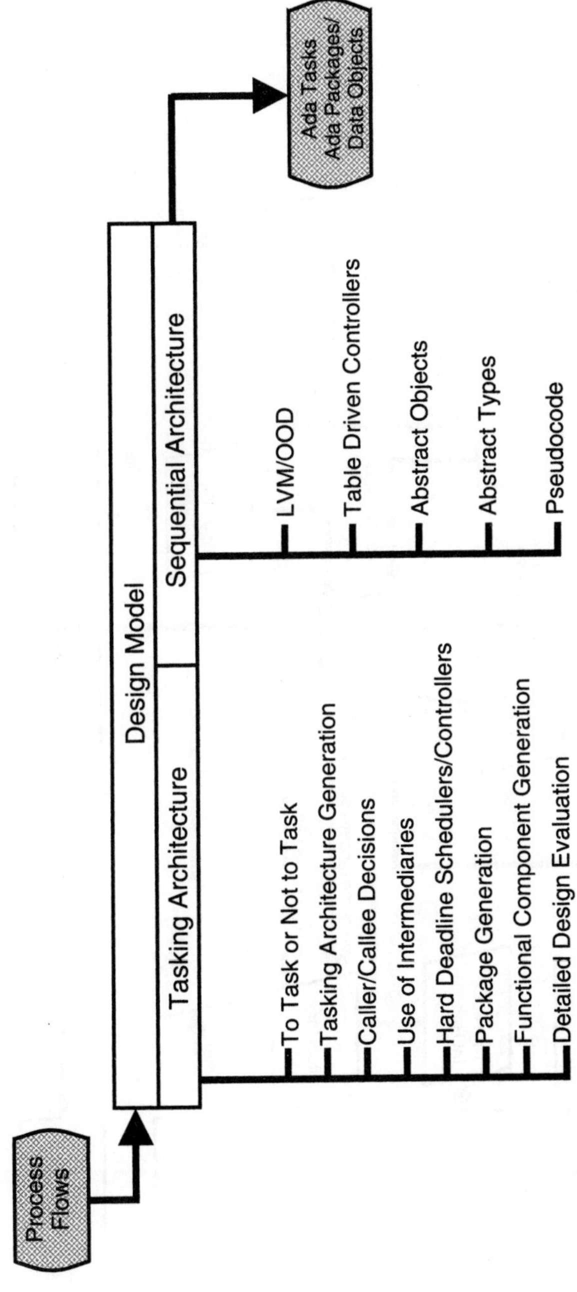

Figure 13.16 Design Model Generation

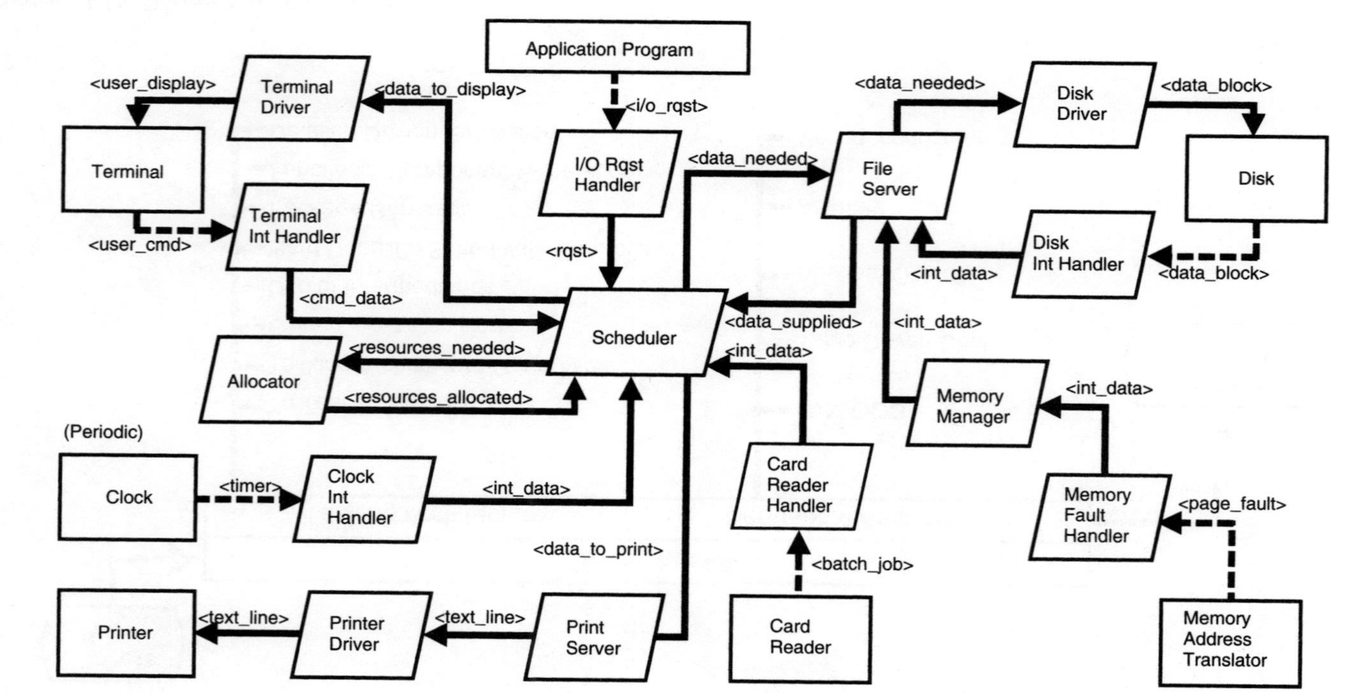

Figure 13.17 Task Architecture Diagram

managed by the system and controls issuing and management of read and write requests. Two separate tasks are employed to manage actual data moving across the memory mapped interface to the disk drive. For incoming blocks, an interrupt handler task named Disk Interrupt Handler serves to copy data from the actual IDA when signaled by the disk controller at the hardware interface. Writing a block to a file requires that a status register be checked to indicate the availability of the outgoing memory mapped interface. When available, the outgoing block of data is transferred to the data area and the disk controller is signaled by setting appropriate bits in the status register. Thus, two levels of tasking are required—file server and disk driver/disk interrupt handler. Both the printer and memory management require a similarly layered combination of Ada tasks.

Determination of caller/callee relations is a somewhat complex process. In general, two criteria are employed—tasks needing services are classed as callers and tasks providing services are categorized as callees. As a result, many tasks become both a caller and a callee, depending on the specific task interaction. For example, consider the file server task. When either the scheduler task or the disk interrupt handler task needs services of the file manager task, they initiate the interaction. File server is a callee, since services are provided to scheduler and disk interrupt handler. However, file server sometimes needs services from scheduler and disk driver. The file server is responsible for initiating the task rendezvous relative to these interactions. Depending on the interaction involved, file server is both a caller and a callee.

Other tasks also serve multiple roles as caller and callee. A detailed simulation or analytical model is used to determine if the set of caller/callee decisions provide realistic throughput rates. Moreover, detailed simulations also identify potential deadlock or significant side effects from task blockage. An important question is determination of blockage or deadlock in the tasking interactions. Blockage reduces operating system throughput. Operating system reliability is limited by potential for deadlock.

13.16 TASKING ARCHITECTURE EVALUATION (I-III)

Each event in the operations scenario/message sequence is traced through the detailed tasking architecture (Figure 13.18 to Figure 13.20). Due to the simplicity of this architecture, only one multiple response path appears. For the most part, each response sequence consists of a linear path through the tasking architecture. As with other evaluations, event reactions result in updates of data stores and/or output messages.

The scenario begins with a user command. This event/interrupt enters the tasking architecture as a rendezvous entry call to the terminal interrupt handler task. From here, command data flows to the scheduler. Inside the scheduler, a process table is updated to register the application program. Resources needed by the application during execution are identified and transmitted to the allocator.

Control Input	Internal Data Flow	Architecture Module	Internal Data Flow	Response
<user_cmd>	—	Terminal Int Handler	<cmd_data>	—
—	<cmd_data>	Scheduler	<resources_needed>	Process Table Updated
—	<resources_needed>	Allocator	<resources_allocated>	Resource Table Updated
—	<resources_allocated>	Scheduler	—	Process Table Updated
<user_cmd>	—	Terminal Int Handler	<cmd_data>	—
—	<cmd_data>	Scheduler	—	Ready Queue Updated
<timer>	—	Clock Int Handler	<int_data>	—
—	<int_data>	Scheduler	—	Running Queue Updated
<i_o/rqst>	—	I/O Rqst Handler	<rqst>	—
—	<rqst>	Scheduler	<data_needed>	Blocked Queue Updated
—	<data_needed>	File Server	<data_needed>	Rqst Table Updated
—	<data_needed>	Disk Driver	—	<data_block>

Figure 13.18 Tasking Architecture Evaluation (I)

Control Input	Internal Data Flow	Architecture Module	Internal Data Flow	Response
<data_block>	—	Disk Int Handler	<int_data>	—
—	<int_data>	File Server	<data_supplied>	Rqst Table Updated
—	<data_supplied>	Scheduler	—	Ready Queue Updated
<timer>	—	Clock Int Handler	<int_data>	—
—	<int_data>	Scheduler	—	Running Queue Updated
<page_fault>	—	Memory Fault Handler	<int—data>	—
—	<int_data>	Memory Manager	<int_data>	—
—	<int_data>	File Server	[<data_needed> (A) and <data_supplied> (B)]	Rqst Table Updated
(A) —	<data_needed>	Disk Driver	—	<data_block>
(B) —	<data_supplied>	Scheduler	—	Blocked Queue Updated

Figure 13.19 Tasking Architecture Evaluation (II)

Control Input	Internal Data Flow	Architecture Module	Internal Data Flow	Response
<data_block>	—	Disk Int Handler	<int_data>	—
—	<int_data>	File Server	<data_supplied>	Rqst Table Updated
—	<data_supplied>	Scheduler	—	Ready Queue Updated
<timer>	—	Clock Int Handler	<int_data>	—
—	<int_data>	Scheduler	—	Running Queue Updated
<timer> (2)	—	Clock Int Handler	<int—data>	—
—	<int_data>	Scheduler	—	Running Queue Updated
<i/o_rqst>	—	Scheduler	<data_to_display>	Running Queue Updated
—	<data_to_display>	Terminal Driver	—	<user_display>
<user_cmd>	—	Terminal Int Handler	<cmd_data>	—
—	<cmd_data>	Scheduler	<resources_needed>	Process Table Updated
—	<resources_needed>	Allocator	<resources_allocated>	Resource Table Updated
—	<resources_allocated>	Scheduler	—	Process Table Updated

Figure 13.20 Tasking Architecture Evaluation (III)

Resources are allocated and recorded in an internal resource management table. A list of allocated resources is returned to the scheduler which updates the process table to reflect the availability of needed resources. Finally, execution of the application program can begin. This response path results in updates of three internal data stores prior to its ultimate resolution.

In comparison, consider the input/output request generated by an executing application program. Initially, this event appears as a rendezvous entry call to input/output request handler. Details of the request are constructed and passed to the scheduler. In response, the scheduler adds the requesting application program to the queue of blocked processes. A data request is then transmitted to the file server. File server constructs the request to transmit a specific block. This description of requested data moves to the disk driver via a rendezvous entry call. When the rendezvous occurs, a data block appears at the interface to the disk controller. A complete response path for the input/output request results in two data store updates, followed by a specific response at an outgoing system interface.

An important shortcoming in the functional requirements specification is identified by this evaluation. Several data stores are assumed to exist in the developer's head. These are conspicuous by their absence from the combined control flow/data flow diagram. Initial introduction of new requirements as important as these data stores is not allowed during the design (first mention appears in the tasking architecture evaluation). Yet, in most developments, new functional and data requirements typically appear in this hidden manner. Since these data stores are needed and are critical to the end-to-end data integrity of the operating system, the combined control/data flow diagram is the logical location for their appearance. Their existence is then carried through the remainder of the methodical development. As illustrated with Target Acquisition System, iterating to include these discovered requirements is not difficult.

13.17 TASKING ARCHITECTURE DIAGRAM WITH INTERMEDIARIES

Only the buffer intermediary is employed throughout the tasking architecture (Figure 13.21). This option is chosen to minimize the number of additional tasks in the architecture, recognizing that limited blocking is incurred. Since the amount of blocking time is finite and deterministic, detailed analysis demonstrates that throughput is not particularly hampered.

Not every tasking interaction receives a buffer intermediary. Moreover, buffers are shared by multiple tasks. Assignment of buffer intermediaries is determined according to anticipated traffic patterns and disparity between response times on different sides of a task rendezvous. One buffer is employed for data provided by the terminal driver to the scheduler. Users typically desire to have immediate response to keystrokes; therefore, blockage needs to be minimized at the terminal input interface. Print jobs need buffering since the print server task is limited by

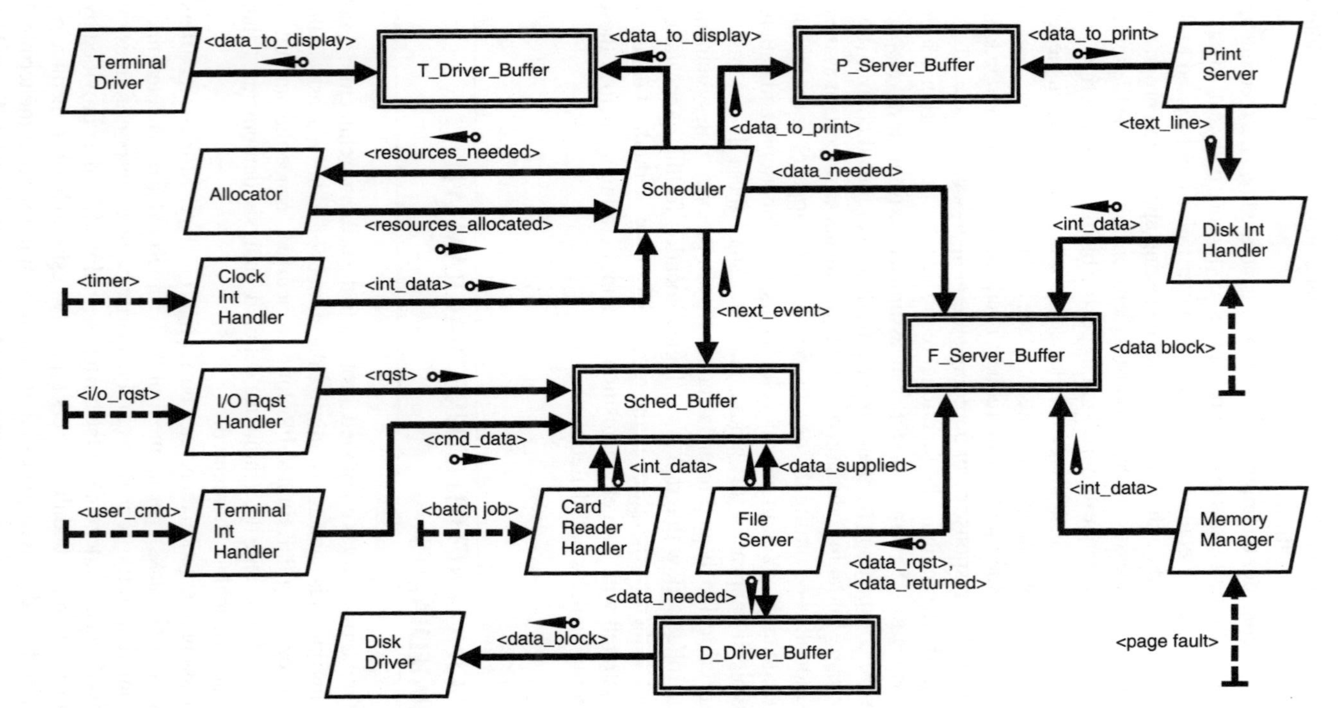

Figure 13.21 Tasking Architecture Diagram with Intermediaries

the speed to the printer hardware interface. Multiple tasks (scheduler, disk interrupt handler, and memory manager) need to interact with the file server. As a result, file server's traffic pattern is potentially quite large. These tasks share one buffer into the file server task. Finally, a buffer is inserted to improve throughput observed by the disk driver. Response time of the disk driver task is constrained by the speed of the disk controller, which is accessed one block at a time. Since the file server is likely to generate a high data rate request stream, data block write requests to the disk driver are buffered.

13.18 OPERATING SYSTEM PACKAGING DECISIONS

Three specific packages are employed in Figure 13.22. All interrupt handler tasks are contained in one package. Device driver tasks are collected into an appropriately named package. Management level tasks (file server, allocator, printer spooler, memory manager, and scheduler) are incorporated into a package named controllers.

Other packaging alternatives are easily envisioned. Both disk interrupt handler and disk driver tasks may be encapsulated into a single package named disk management. Other interfaces may be similarly allocated into functionally cohesive packages. The packaging scheme employed possesses important development implications. Fewer packages means less configuration management complexity. Moreover, this reduced complexity restrains the number of parallel development teams—one per package—potentially shortening integration and test activities.

A potential integration and configuration management problem is introduced into the development process by this packaging diagram. All buffers are excluded from the diagram. Loss of traceability to these buffers results in integration and test problems. Configurations may be created without including the buffers, since they are omitted at this step. As a result, an integrated software implementation tends to lose requests and data flowing through the architecture. Identifying causes of lost data and determining missing software elements is a tedious process when attempted in the context of a large amount of actual code.

13.19 CONCLUDING REMARKS

Notwithstanding some of the shortcomings included in this analysis, this specification and design eventually leads to an actual implementation of an operating system. By using operations scenarios to fully develop the requirements, architecture, and detailed design of the operating system, systems with high throughput and low memory occupancy are implemented. Moreover, fewer bugs are encountered by the users of the operating system.

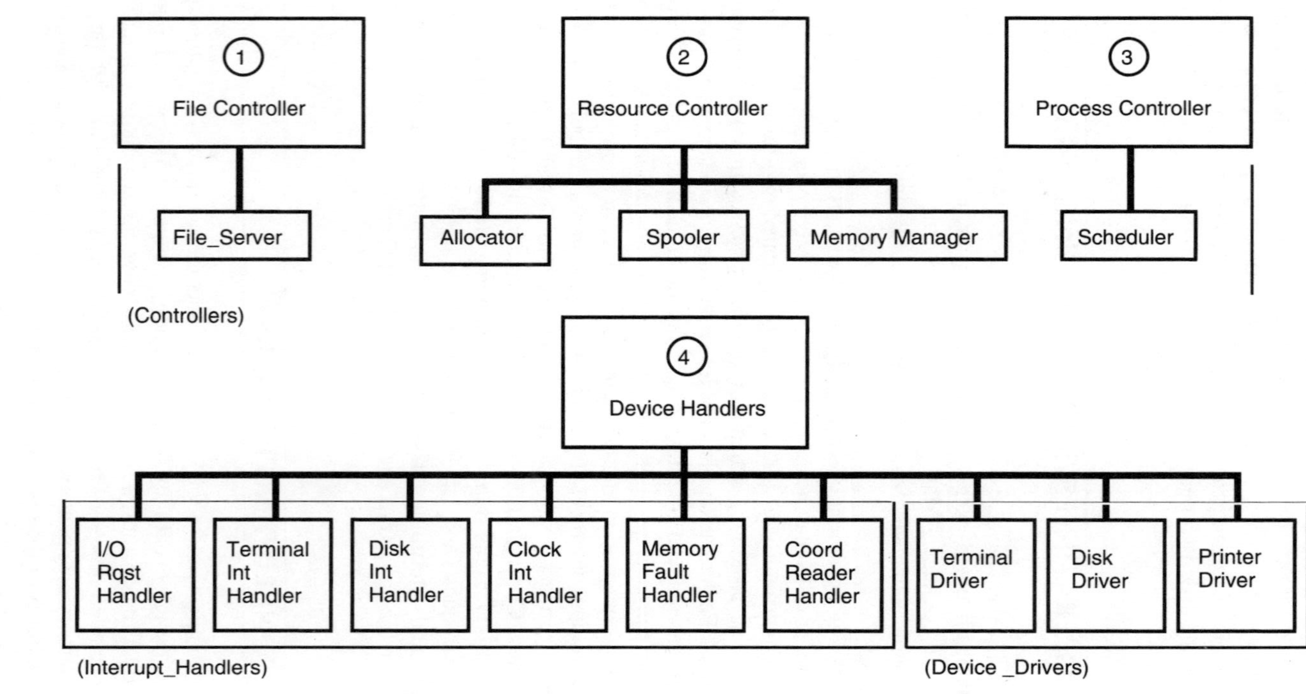

Figure 13.22 Operating System Packaging Decisions

14

Projects

Two problems are included in this chapter. These exercises are simplified versions of real world systems. As such, they represent a portion of the total system that would be developed. Essential characteristics of the system have been maintained. Each problem is formulated in a manner which eliminates the need to have detailed knowledge of sophisticated algorithms. Solutions do not require inclusion of statistical analysis or differential equation models.

Attempt to carry development through the complete methodology, performing every step in order, generating every product in the correct format. Students may defer implementation. However, both cases have been carried to complete implementation by students who have utilized process and tasking architectures described in this text.

If any assumptions are necessary, feel free to make those assumptions as long as they are meaningful and as long as they are documented. When making assumptions, choose to be as simplistic as possible. Simplicity keeps complexity low so that the basic problem does not become distorted beyond reasonable bounds.

14.1 AUTO BRAKE MANUFACTURING CONTROL SYSTEM

A manufacturing control system is to be implemented which allows automated production of brake rotors. Producing a brake rotor involves a precise sequence of operations utilizing a number of key hardware components. Precision is required so that raw product is not wasted or extensively damaged. Allowable tolerances for brake rotors, which must fit into brake drums, also requires production using precise operations. An automated controller is employed to allow a continuous high rate of production and to assure precision of produced rotors.

Production of a single rotor is composed of several important activities. These activities manipulate the raw input factors initially using a variety of hardware devices to produce the actual brake rotor. First, raw material is loaded onto a cutter jib. The raw material is clamped in place so that slippage does not destroy the precision of the cut. An actual cut is accomplished in three separate phases. First, outside diameter of the rotor is established by a cut that trims the excess flash from the raw material. Next, a face is cut into the raw material, yielding a rim on the inside and outside edges of the rotor. Finally, a finishing cut is performed to obtain the tolerance specified by the brake design engineers. Then the finished rotor is removed from the cutter jib. Once removed from the jib, this completed rotor is passed to the polishing machine.

Since a large number of these rotors are produced, a pipeline is established. Pipeline maintenance consists of always having raw material in the loader, one rotor being cut, and another rotor being polished. Manufacturing control operations are established to assure that all components in the pipeline are always busy.

Several specific hardware devices play key roles in manufacturing brake rotors—loaders, clamps, lathes, and polishers. In recent years, loaders are being designed with smart controllers. As with all smart controllers, any controller attached to a loader is issued a command to position the next load of raw material. All mechanics of this operation are managed by the loader's controller. On completion, an acknowledgement is returned to the command source. Polishers also employ smart controllers, which are commanded and acknowledge successful operations when completed.

A clamper is used to avoid slippage during cutting. This clamper is commanded by physically tripping a solenoid. Clamping or unclamping of the solenoid is accomplished by physically changing the solenoid's position. Only two positions can be adopted—clamp and unclamp. A motor on the clamp is commanded to tighten the clamp. Once commanded to start, the motor continues tightening until commanded to stop. Motor position is regularly reported by a sensor attached to the flywheel of the motor. This position is typically reported periodically at a rate of thirty position reports every second.

Actual cuts are performed by a lathe. First, lathe motors are commanded to start. Actual cuts are directed along three axes—x, y, and z. However, a cut is performed in discrete steps, commanded one step at a time. Each step command to the lathe consists of a delta amount to move in each of the three coordinate dimensions. Servo position sensors for each axis report the physical position in each coordinate frame. Manufacturing control observes these positions, decides if an additional step is necessary, calculates step size up to a maximum allowable limit, and issues the step command. Once the cut is completed, the lathe motor is commanded to stop. All servo position sensors in the reference frames report position data at the rate of sixty samples per second. Moreover, as a result of careful design by the lathe manufacturers, all position reports are in a standard frame of reference, requiring no special coordinate transformations prior to using the position data.

To allow operator control, a number of operational modes are envisioned for the brake manufacturing control system. During initialization mode, status of all components is assessed. Upon successful initialization, the control system is suspended until commanded into operational mode by the operator. Manufacturing operations can be either continuous, single step, or temporarily suspended. Temporary suspension is useful to allow the operator to reposition materials that have become nonaligned, avoiding potential damage due to miscuts or over-polishing. Completion of a production shift is also signaled at the discretion of an operator. Upon receipt of this signal, the pipeline is allowed to clear prior to actual shutdown of the manufacturing system.

Status information is continuously displayed to the operator. Each time a rotor completes passage through the pipeline after polishing, an updated manufacturing count is displayed. Moreover, a count of completed operations for each of the phases (loading, clamping, cutting, and polishing) is continuously updated on the operator display. Finally, current state, state initiation time, and current time are displayed on the operator console and regularly updated.

14.2 TARGET ACQUISITION SYSTEM

In this exercise, the goal is to develop a prototype target acquisition system, such as would be embedded in a radar or electro-optical platform. An emulator for the infrared sensor is also to be implemented. For the moment, assume that hardware interfaces are transparently handled underneath vendor developed software interfaces.

Several data sources must be represented in this implementation. An IR sensor provides a sequence of imagery frames. Each frame consists of a 10 by 10 array of pixels. Frames arrive periodically according to a constant rate. During implementation, a drift correcting delay is to be employed. An aperiodic data source is also interacting with the acquisition system. This is the Run-Time Operator Interface. Commands from this source represent a pilot's reaction to events unfolding on his display. For development purposes, assume the following data source characteristics:

Twenty frames of IR data are to be created:

pixels in a frame are arbitrary values in the range 0–255 ;
periodic inter-arrival time is 0.1 seconds.

Thirty operator commands are to be generated:

50 percent are armament firing commands;
50 percent are target destruction signals;
firing commands indicate number of missiles to fire (1–2);

target kills identify an arbitrary target number;

aperiodic delay is 0.2 seconds.

Target kill messages are to be forwarded to the Air Battle Controller on the ground. Unfortunately, this requires translation from the on-board target identification number to a target code recognized by the Battle Controller. A translation table is to be employed for this purpose. Incoming IR data is analyzed by an algorithm which returns a target location with a probability of correctness. These are recorded for use by the firing system. This data is then displayed to the pilot on a Heads Up Display System. Each frame is displayed with an identifying time stamp printed directly beneath the frame. In this way, the pilot can judge the freshness of the data. Armament firing commands also require special processing. Upon receipt, an assessment is performed to determine if sufficient missiles are available to satisfy the commanded number of missile firings. Individual firing commands are issued to the firing system, constrained by the number of missiles available. Firing commands are issued only if target correctness probability is greater than 80 percent. Number of missiles available is reduced each time a firing command is issued.

Some important parameters are implied by the above descriptions. A translation table that correlates on-board target identifiers to ground target identifiers must be maintained. This table is initialized to be consistent with data generated by the raw data sources. An arbitrary maximum number of missiles is an input into the acquisition system. Minimum threshold for probability of correctness is an additional parameter that needs to be established for the system.

As target kill messages are being received by the Air Battle Controller on the ground, they are permanently recorded into a local storage area. After transmission is completed, the message is echoed on the computer screen with accompanying target identification code and a time tag.

For purposes of this analysis, imagery analysis consists of sampling a random number of the range (0, 1). This value is returned as probability of correctness. Target location not being currently used by the firing algorithm, can be emitted as the same value for every imagery frame. Future versions of fire control anticipate use of this prediction; therefore, the position vector must be maintained in this implementation.

Successful target acquisition consists of correctly responding to raw data received from each of the data sources. Upon receipt of a message, its type is determined. Required responses are as follows:

1. If an IR imagery frame, the IR data is first analyzed for location and probability of correctness. Subsequently, the IR data is time stamped and passed to the Heads Up Display;
2. If a Run-Time Operator Interface Command, then the operation code is extracted from the message. Legal responses to the operation code are as follows:

a. If operation code = 1, an armament firing command is indicated. Argument 1 is the number of missiles to fire. If the current value for probability of correctness is less than 80 percent, no missiles are fired (the pilot is informed). Individual firing commands are issued for each missile fire;

b. If operation code = 2, a target kill has been signaled. A unique aircraft identification code is added to the message. Argument 1 contains the on-board identification number. This is translated to the number recognized by the Air Battle Controller. The updated message is passed to the on-board message transmitter for emission to the Controller.

Appendix A

LH Target Acquisition System Detailed Methodology Examples

In Chapter 10, examples are provided which illustrate application of methodology steps to the LH Target Acquisition System. These illustrations are presented as representative examples. Presenting a subset of a specific step is often confusing and frustrating to a reader. Complete details of the TAS examples are provided here as reference material for the reader desiring greater insight.

These complete details are in pictorial form only. No textual explanation is attached to each detailed example. The reader is encouraged to review the appropriate sections of Chapter 10 to properly interpret the detailed examples.

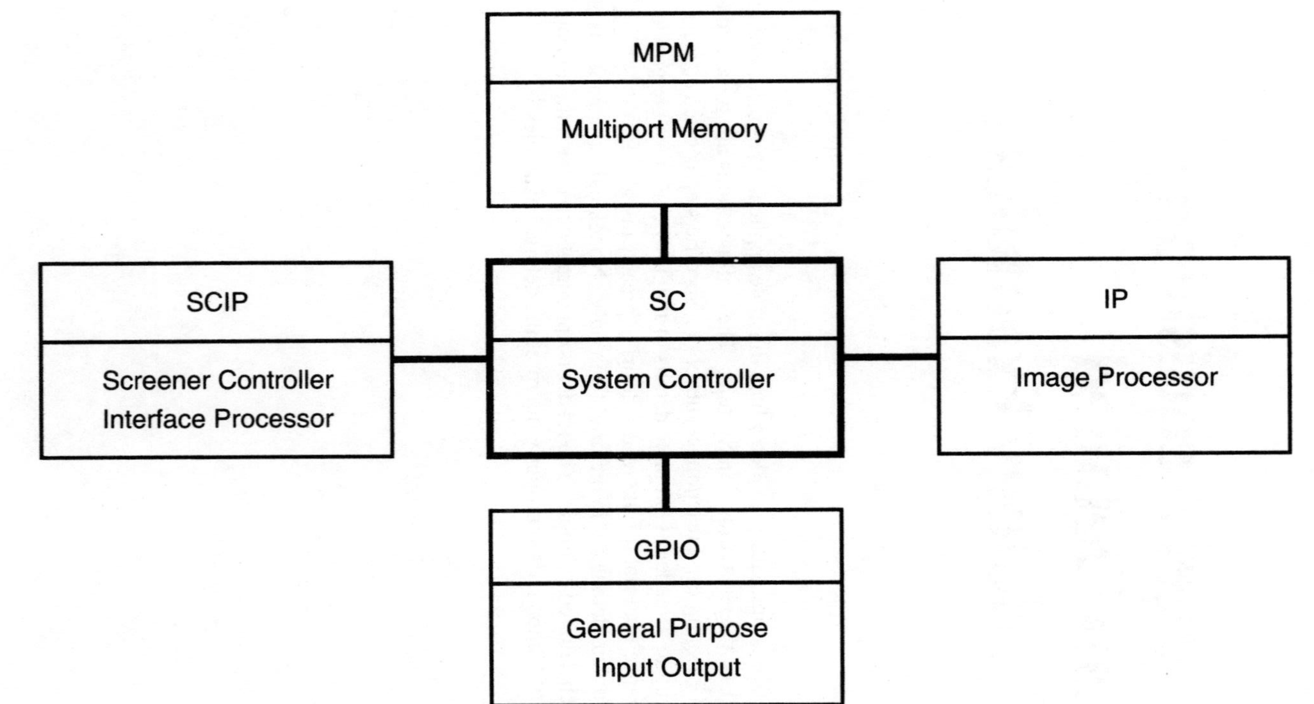

Figure A.1 System Controller (SC) External Interface Diagram

- A swath contains some number of POIs resulting in some number of targets
- LL_Jobs are outstanding for some logical frames within a swath; TR_Jobs are in process for other logical frames within a swath
- A logical frame contains no points of interest (POIs)
- A logical frame contains no classifications of targets
- A swath contains no POIs
- A swath contains no classifications of targets

Figure A.2 Gimbal Scan Mode Message Sequence Variation (I)

- A scan contains no POIs
- A scan contains no classifications of targets
- Target classification results are returned in random order
- A new swath or scan indication is received prior to completion of the current swath
- A standby mode command is received prior to completion of the last swath in a scan
- A standby mode command is received prior to completion of the next to last swath in a scan

Figure A.3 Gimbal Scan Mode Message Sequence Variation (II)

Type	Source	Destination	Description	Swath	POI	Job
Gimbal Scan	GPIO	SC	Start Gimbal Scan Mode	1	–	–
Freeze Swath	SC	MPM	Freeze Swath	1	–	–
Freeze Swath	SC	MPM	Queue Freeze Swath	2	–	–
LL Job	SC	SCIP	Identify POI	1	–	1
LL Results	SCIP	SC	2 POI Identified, Logical Frame 1	1	–	1
TR Job	SC	IP	Analyze POI	1	1	2
TR Job	SC	IP	Analyze POI	1	2	3
LL Results	SCIP	SC	0 POI Identified, Logical Frame 2	1	–	1
LL Results	SCIP	SC	2 POI Identified, Logical Frame 3	1	–	1
TR Job	SC	IP	Analyze POI	1	1	4
TR Job	SC	IP	Analyze POI	1	2	5
LL Results	SCIP	SC	2 POI Identified, Logical Frame 4	1	–	1
TR Job	SC	IP	Analyze POI	1	1	6
TR Job	SC	IP	Analyze POI	1	2	7
TR Results	IP	SC	Target Recognition Results	1	–	2
TR Results	IP	SC	Target Recognition Results	1	–	3
TR Results	IP	SC	Target Recognition Results	1	–	4
TR Results	IP	SC	Target Recognition Results	1	–	5

Figure A.4 SC Gimbal Scan Mode Test Message Flow (I)

Type	Source	Destination	Description	Swath	POI	Job
Gimbal Scan	GPIO	SC	Start Next Swath In Scan	2	–	–
TR Results	IP	SC	Target Recognition Results	1	–	6
TR Results	IP	SC	Target Recognition Results	1	–	7
Freeze Swath	SC	MPM	Queue Freeze Swath	3	–	–
LL Job	SC	SCIP	Identify POI	2	–	8
LL Results	SCIP	SC	2 POI Identified, Logical Frame 1	2	–	8
TR Job	SC	IP	Analyze POI	2	1	9
TR Job	SC	IP	Analyze POI	2	2	10
LL Results	SCIP	SC	0 POI Identified, Logical Frame 2	2	–	8
LL Results	SCIP	SC	2 POI Identified, Logical Frame 3	2	–	8
TR Job	SC	IP	Analyze POI	2	1	11
TR Job	SC	IP	Analyze POI	2	2	12
TR Results	IP	SC	Target Recognition Results	2	–	9
TR Results	IP	SC	Target Recognition Results	2	–	12
Gimbal Scan	GPIO	SC	Start Next Swath In Scan	3	–	–
TR Results	IP	SC	Target Recognition Results	2	–	11
TR Results	IP	SC	Target Recognition Results	2	–	10
Freeze Swath	SC	MPM	Queue Freeze Swath	4	–	–
LL Job	SC	SCIP	Identify POI	3	–	13

Figure A.5 SC Gimbal Scan Mode Test Message Flow (II)

Type	Source	Destination	Description	Swath	POI	Job
LL Results	SCIP	SC	2 POI Identified, Logical Frame 1	3	–	13
TR Job	SC	IP	Analyze POI	3	1	14
TR Job	SC	IP	Analyze POI	3	2	15
TR Results	IP	SC	Target Recognition Results	3	–	14
Gimbal Scan	GPIO	SC	Start New Scan	4	–	
TR Results	IP	SC	Target Recognition Results	3	–	15
Target Report	SC	GPIO	Report Results	–	–	–
Symbol Display Cmd	GPIO	SC	Receive Symbol Overlay Data	–	–	–
Freeze Swath	SC	MPM	Queue Freeze Swath	5	–	–
LL Job	SC	SCIP	Identify POI	4	–	16
LL Results	SCIP	SC	0 POI Identified, Logical Frame 1	4	–	16
Gimbal Scan	GPIO	SC	Start Next Swath In Scan	5	–	
Freeze Swath	SC	MPM	Queue Freeze Swath	6	–	–
LL Job	SC	SCIP	Identify POI	5	–	17
LL Results	SCIP	SC	0 POI Identified, Logical Frame 1	5	–	17
Gimbal Scan	GPIO	SC	Start Next Swath In Scan	6	–	
Freeze Swath	SC	MPM	Queue Freeze Swath	7	–	–
LL Job	SC	SCIP	Identify POI	6	–	18

Figure A.6 SC Gimbal Scan Mode Test Message Flow (III)

Type	Source	Destination	Description	Swath	POI	Job
LL Results	SCIP	SC	1 POI Identified, Logical Frame 1	6	–	18
TR Job	SC	IP	Analyze POI	6	1	19
Standby Mode	GPIO	SC	Clear Queues, Cease Processing	–	–	–
TR Results	IP	SC	Target Recognition Results	6	–	19
Target Report	SC	GPIO	Report Results	–	–	–
Symbol Display Cmd	GPIO	SC	Receive Symbol Overlay Data	–	–	–
Reset	SC	SCIP	Reset Sequence Begins	–	–	–
Reset	SC	MPM	–	–	–	–
Reset	SC	IP	–	–	–	–
Reset Status	IP	SC	Response Sequence Begins	–	–	–
Reset Status	MPM	SC	–	–	–	–
Reset Status	SCIP	SC	–	–	–	–
System Reset Status	SC	GPIO	All Clear Indicated	–	–	–

Figure A.7 SC Gimbal Scan Mode Test Message Flow (IV)

Type	Source	Destination	Description	Swath	POI	Job
Gimbal Scan	GPIO	SC	Start Gimbal Scan Mode	1	–	–
LL Results	SCIP	SC	2 POI Identified, Logical Frame 1	1	–	1
LL Results	SCIP	SC	0 POI Identified, Logical Frame 2	1	–	1
LL Results	SCIP	SC	2 POI Identified, Logical Frame 3	1	–	1
LL Results	SCIP	SC	2 POI Identified, Logical Frame 4	1	–	1
TR Results	IP	SC	Target Recognition Results	1	–	2
TR Results	IP	SC	Target Recognition Results	1	–	3
TR Results	IP	SC	Target Recognition Results	1	–	4
TR Results	IP	SC	Target Recognition Results	1	–	5
Gimbal Scan	GPIO	SC	Start Next Swath In Scan	2	–	–
TR Results	IP	SC	Target Recognition Results	1	–	6
TR Results	IP	SC	Target Recognition Results	1	–	7
LL Results	SCIP	SC	2 POI Identified, Logical Frame 1	2	–	8
LL Results	SCIP	SC	0 POI Identified, Logical Frame 2	2	–	8
LL Results	SCIP	SC	2 POI Identified, Logical Frame 3	2	–	8
TR Results	IP	SC	Target Recognition Results	2	–	9
TR Results	IP	SC	Target Recognition Results	2	–	12
Gimbal Scan	GPIO	SC	Start Next Swath In Scan	3	–	–

Figure A.8 Gimbal Scan Mode Requirements Evaluation Test Set (I)

Type	Source	Destination	Description	Swath	POI	Job
TR Results	IP	SC	Target Recognition Results	2	–	11
TR Results	IP	SC	Target Recognition Results	2	–	10
LL Results	SCIP	SC	2 POI Identified, Logical Frame 1	3	–	13
TR Results	IP	SC	Target Recognition Results	3	–	14
Gimbal Scan	GPIO	SC	Start New Scan	4	–	
TR Results	IP	SC	Target Recognition Results	3	–	15
Symbol Display Cmd	GPIO	SC	Receive Symbol Overlay Data	–	–	–
LL Results	SCIP	SC	0 POI Identified, Logical Frame 1	4	–	16
Gimbal Scan	GPIO	SC	Start Next Swath In Scan	5	–	
LL Results	SCIP	SC	0 POI Identified, Logical Frame 1	5	–	17
Gimbal Scan	GPIO	SC	Start Next Swath In Scan	6	–	
LL Results	SCIP	SC	1 POI Identified, Logical Frame 1	6	–	18
Standby Mode	GPIO	SC	Clear Queues, Cease Processing	–	–	–
TR Results	IP	SC	Target Recognition Results	6	–	19
Symbol Display Cmd	GPIO	SC	Receive Symbol Overlay Data	–	–	–
Reset Status	IP	SC	Response Sequence Begins	–	–	–
Reset Status	MPM	SC	–	–	–	–
Reset Status	SCIP	SC	–	–	–	–

Figure A.9 Gimbal Scan Mode Requirements Evaluation Test Set (II)

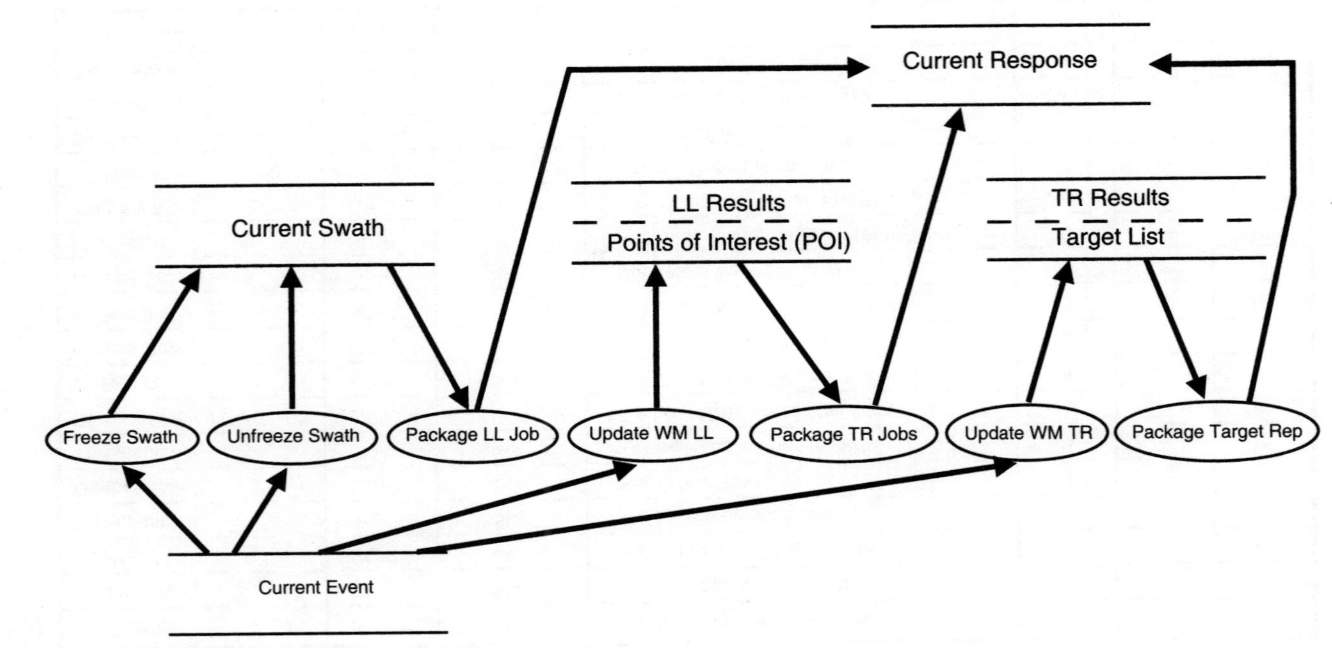

Figure A.10 Gimbal Scan Mode Functional Requirements (I)

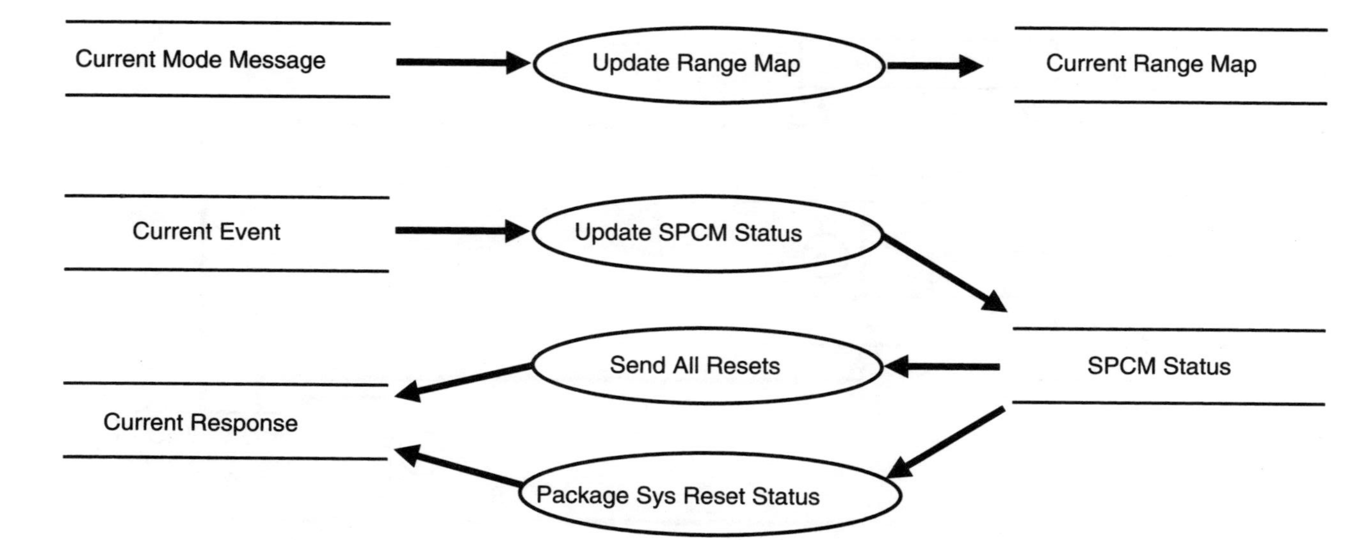

Figure A.11 Gimbal Scan Mode Functional Requirements (II)

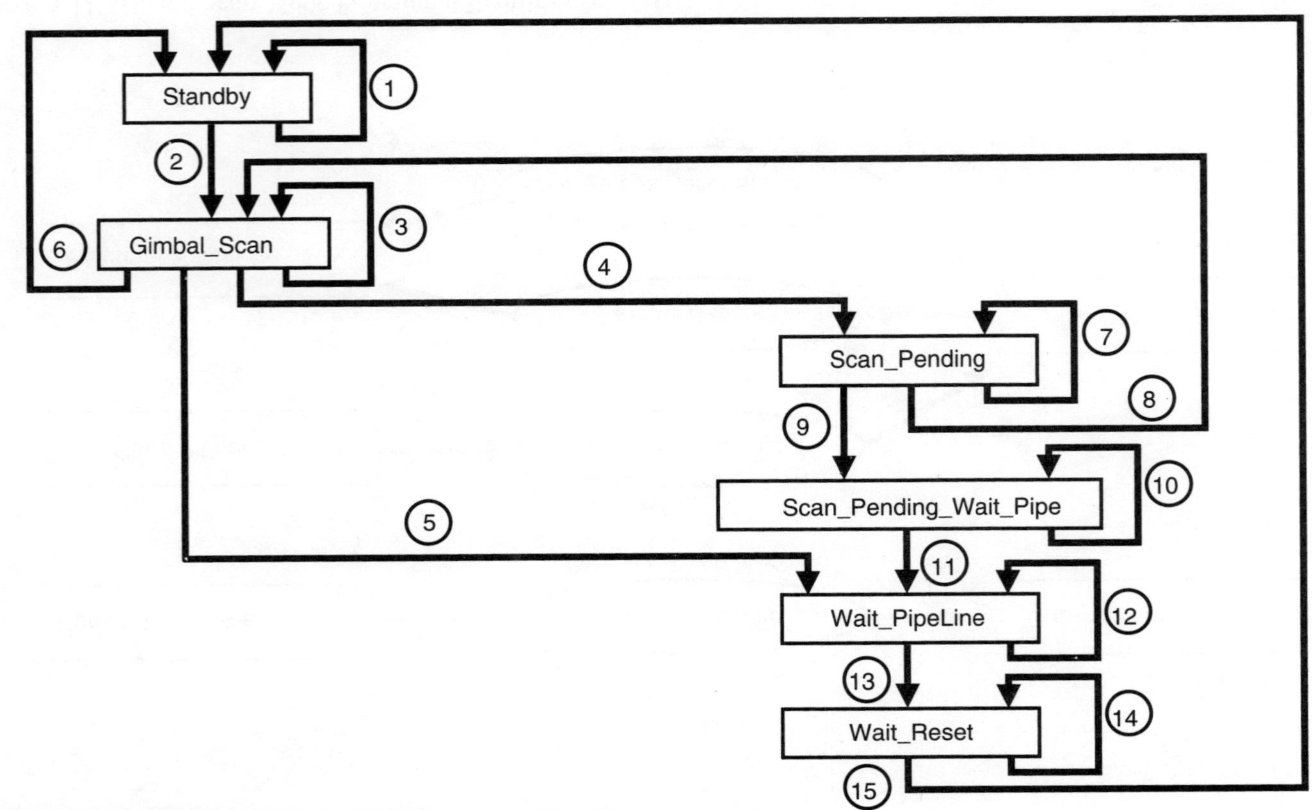

Figure A.12 Gimbal Scan Operations State Transition Diagram

Start Mode	Transition No.	Event/Messages	Action List	End Mode
Standby	(1)	Standby_Mode	Trash_Obj	Standby
Standby	(2)	Gimbal_Scan_Mode	Update_Range_Map Freeze_Swath Package_LL_Job Freeze_Swath	Gimbal_Scan
Gimbal_Scan	(3)	LL_Results	Update_WM_LL Package_TR_Jobs Possibly: Package_Target_Rep (Last LL, last swath, POI = 0) Possibly: roll_pipe (Last LL, not last swath, POI = 0) Unfreeze swath	Gimbal_Scan
	(3)	TR_Results	Update_WM_TR Possibly: Package_Target_Rep (Last TR, last swath) Possibly: roll_pipe (Last TR, not last swath) Unfreeze_swath	Gimbal_Scan
	(3)	Sym_Disp_Command	Unfreeze_swath	Gimbal_Scan
	(4)	Gimbal_Scan	Possibly: roll_pipe (No jobs in swath) Update_range_map, dump range Freeze swath, Package LL Job	

Figure A.13 Gimbal Scan Operations Process Activation Table (1)

Start Mode	Transition No.	Event/Messages	Action List	End Mode
Gimbal_Scan	4	Gimbal_Scan_Mode	Possibly: enter scan pending (LL or TR jobs out in swath)	Scan_Pending
Gimbal_Scan	5	Standby_Mode	Possibly: enter wait pipeline (LL or TR jobs out in swath)	Wait_Pipeline
Gimbal_Scan	6	Standy_Mode	Possibly: enter standby (No LL or TR jobs out in swath)	Standby
Scan_Pending	7	LL_Results	Update_WM_LL Package TR jobs Possibly: package_target_report (Last LL, last swath, POI = 0) Possibly: update range map unfreeze swath freeze swath package LL job (Last LL, not last swath, POI = 0) Possibly: shift state (gimbal scan) (Last LL, not last swath, POI = 0)	Scan_Pending
	7	TR_Results	Update_WM_TR Possibly: package_target_report (Last TR, last swath) Possibly: update_range_map unfreeze_swath freeze_swath package_LL job (Last TR, not last swath) Possibly: shift state (Gimbal Scan) (Last TR, not last swath)	Scan_Pending

Figure A.14 Gimbal Scan Operations Process Activation Table (2)

Start Mode	Transition No.	Event/Messages	Action List	End Mode
Scan_Pending	8	Sym_Disp_Command	Update_Range_Map Unfreeze_Swath Freeze_Swath Package_LL_Job	Gimbal_Scan
Scan_Pending	9	Standby	Enter Scan_Pending_Wait_Pipe	Scan_pending_Wait_pipe
Scan_Pending_Wait_Pipe	10	LL_Results	Update_WM_LL Package_TR_Jobs Possibly: package_target_report (Last LL, last swath, POI = 0) Possibly: update_range_map unfreeze_swath freeze_swath package LL job (Last LL, not last swath, POI = 0) Possibly: shift state (wait pipeline) (Last LL, not last swath, POI = 0)	Scan_Pending_Wait_Pipe
	10	TR_Results	Update WM TR Possibly: package target report (Last TR, last swath) Possibly: update range map unfreeze swath freeze swath package_LL_job (Last TR, not last swath) Possibly: shift state (wait pipeline) (Last TR, not last swath)	Scan_Pending_Wait_Pipe

Figure A.15 Gimbal Scan Operations Process Activation Table (3)

Start Mode	Transition No.	Event/Messages	Action List	End Mode
Scan_Pending_Wait_Pipe	11	Sym_Disp_Command	Update_range_map Unfreeze_swath Freeze_swath Package_LL_job	Wait_Pipeline
Wait_Pipeline	12	LL_Results	Update_WM_LL Package_TR_Jobs Possibly: package_target_report (Last LL, last swath, POI = 0) Possibly: update_range_map unfreeze_swath freeze_swath package_LL_job (Last LL, not last swath, POI = 0)	Wait_Pipeline
	12	TR_Results	Update_WM_TR Possibly: package target report (Last TR, last swath) Possibly: update_range_map unfreeze swath freeze_swath Package_LL_job (Last TR, not last swath)	Wait_Pipeline
	12	Sym_Disp_Command	Unfreeze_swath	Wait_Pipeline

Figure A.16 Gimbal Scan Operations Process Activation Table (4)

Start Mode	Transition No.	Event/Messages	Action List	End Mode
Wait_Pipeline	13	Sym_Display_Command	Possibly: Enter Wait_Reset (No LL, TR jobs out)	Wait_Reset
Wait_Reset	14	Reset_Status	Update SPCM_Status	Wait_Reset
Wait_Reset	15	Reset_Status	Update SPCM_Status Possibly: Package_Sys_Reset_Status Enter Standby Mode (No reset_status jobs out)	Standby

Figure A.17 Gimbal Scan Operations Process Activation Table (5)

Type	Event	Transition	Response Details	State After	Output Message
Standby	Gimbal Scan	2	Update Range Map	Gimbal Scan	
			Freeze Swath		Freeze Swath
			Freeze Swath		Freeze Swath
			Package LL Job		LL Job
Gimbal Scan	LL Results	3	Update WM LL	Gimbal Scan	
			Package TR Jobs		TR Job (2)
Gimbal Scan	LL Results	3		Gimbal Scan	
Gimbal Scan	LL Results	3	Update WM LL	Gimbal Scan	
			Package TR Jobs		TR Job (2)
Gimbal Scan	LL Results	3	Update WM LL	Gimbal Scan	
			Package TR Jobs		TR Job (2)
Gimbal Scan	TR Results	3	Update WM TR	Gimbal Scan	
Gimbal Scan	TR Results	3	Update WM TR	Gimbal Scan	
Gimbal Scan	TR Results	3	Update WM TR	Gimbal Scan	
Gimbal Scan	TR Results	3	Update WM TR	Gimbal Scan	
Gimbal Scan	Gimbal Scan	4		Scan Pending	
Scan Pending	TR Results	7	Update WM TR	Scan Pending	

Figure A.18 Gimbal Scan Mode Requirements Evaluation (I)

State Before	Event	Transition	Response Details	State After	Output Message
Scan Pending	TR Results	7	Update WM TR	Gimbal Scan	
			Update Range Map		
			Unfreeze Swath		
			Freeze Swath		Freeze Swath
			Package LL Job		LL Job
Gimbal Scan	LL Results	3	Update WM LL	Gimbal Scan	
			Package TR Jobs		TR Job (2)
Gimbal Scan	LL Results	3		Gimbal Scan	
Gimbal Scan	LL Results	3	Update WM LL	Gimbal Scan	
			Package TR Jobs		TR Job (2)
Gimbal Scan	TR Results	3	Update WM TR	Gimbal Scan	
Gimbal Scan	TR Results	3	Update WM TR	Gimbal Scan	
Gimbal Scan	Gimbal Scan	4		Scan Pending	
Scan Pending	TR Results	7	Update WM TR	Scan Pending	
Scan Pending	TR Results	7	Update WM TR	Gimbal Scan	
			Update Range Map		
			Unfreeze Swath		
			Freeze Swath		Freeze Swath
			Package LL Job		LL Job

Figure A.19 Gimbal Scan Mode Requirements Evaluation (II)

State Before	Event	Transition	Response Details	State After	Output Message
Gimbal Scan	LL Results	3	Update WM TR	Gimbal Scan	
			Package TR Jobs		TR Job (2)
Gimbal Scan	TR Results	3	Update WM TR	Gimbal Scan	
Gimbal Scan	Gimbal Scan	4		Scan Pending	
Scan Pending	TR Results	7	Update WM TR	Scan Pending	
			Package Target Rep		Target Report
Scan Pending	Sym Disp Cmd	8	Update Range Map	Gimbal Scan	
			Unfreeze Swath		
			Freeze Swath		Freeze Swath
			Package LL Job		LL Job
Gimbal Scan	LL Results	3	Unfreeze Swath	Gimbal Scan	
Gimbal Scan	Gimbal Scan	4	Update Range Map	Gimbal Scan	
			Freeze Swath		Freeze Swath
			Package LL Job		LL Job
Gimbal Scan	LL Results	3	Unfreeze Swath	Gimbal Scan	
Gimbal Scan	Gimbal Scan	4	Update Range Map	Gimbal Scan	
			Freeze Swath		Freeze Swath
			Pkg LL Job		LL Job

Figure A.20 Gimbal Scan Mode Requirements Evaluation (III)

State Before	Event	Transition	Response Details	State After	Output Message
Gimbal Scan	LL Results	3	Update WM LL	Gimbal Scan	
			Package TR Jobs	Gimbal Scan	TR Job
Gimbal Scan	Standby	5		Wait Pipeline	
Wait Pipeline	TR Results	12	Update WM TR	Wait Pipeline	
			Package Target Rep		Target Report
Wait Pipeline	Sym Disp Cmd	13	Unfreeze Swath	Wait Reset	
			Send All Resets		Reset (4)
Wait Reset	Reset Status	14	Update SPCM Status	Wait Reset	
Wait Reset	Reset Status	14	Update SPCM Status	Wait Reset	
Wait Reset	Reset Status	15	Update SPCM Status	Standby	
			Pkg Sys Reset Status		System Reset Status

Figure A.21 Gimbal Scan Mode Requirements Evaluation (IV)

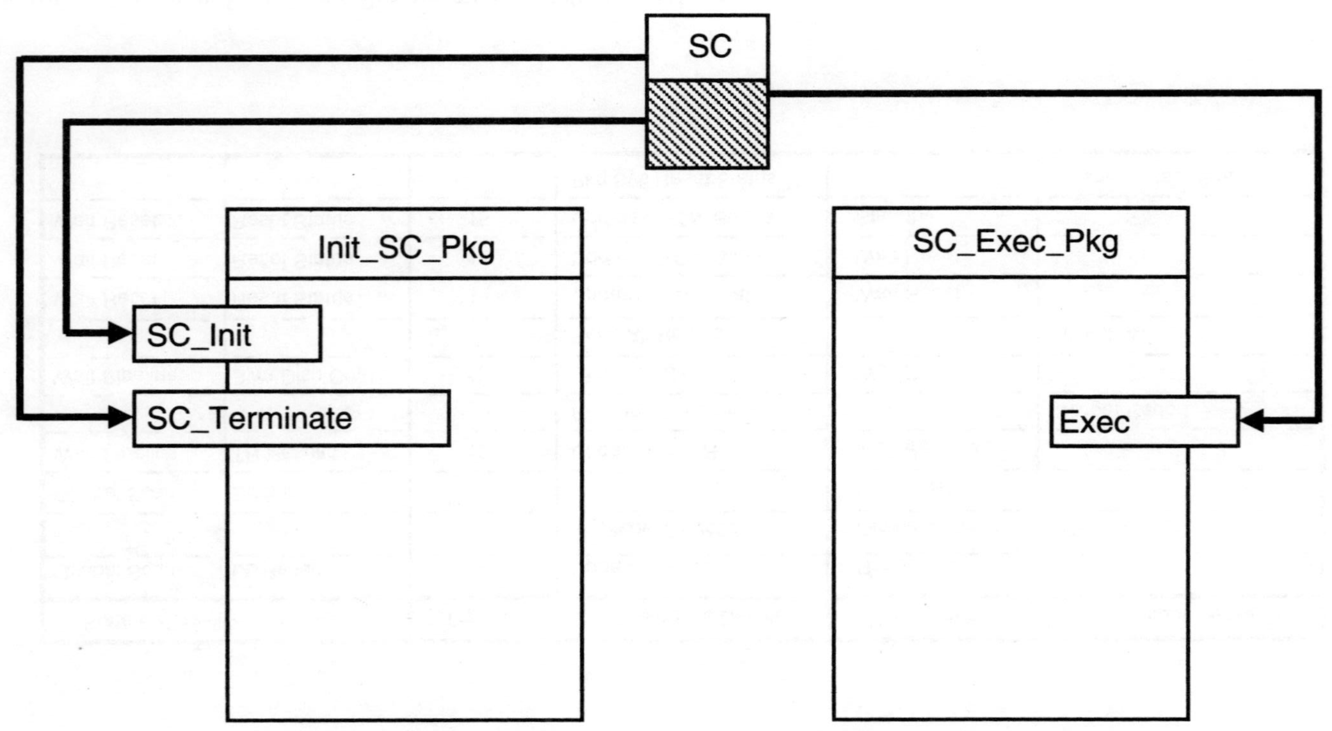

Figure A.22 System Controller Software Architecture

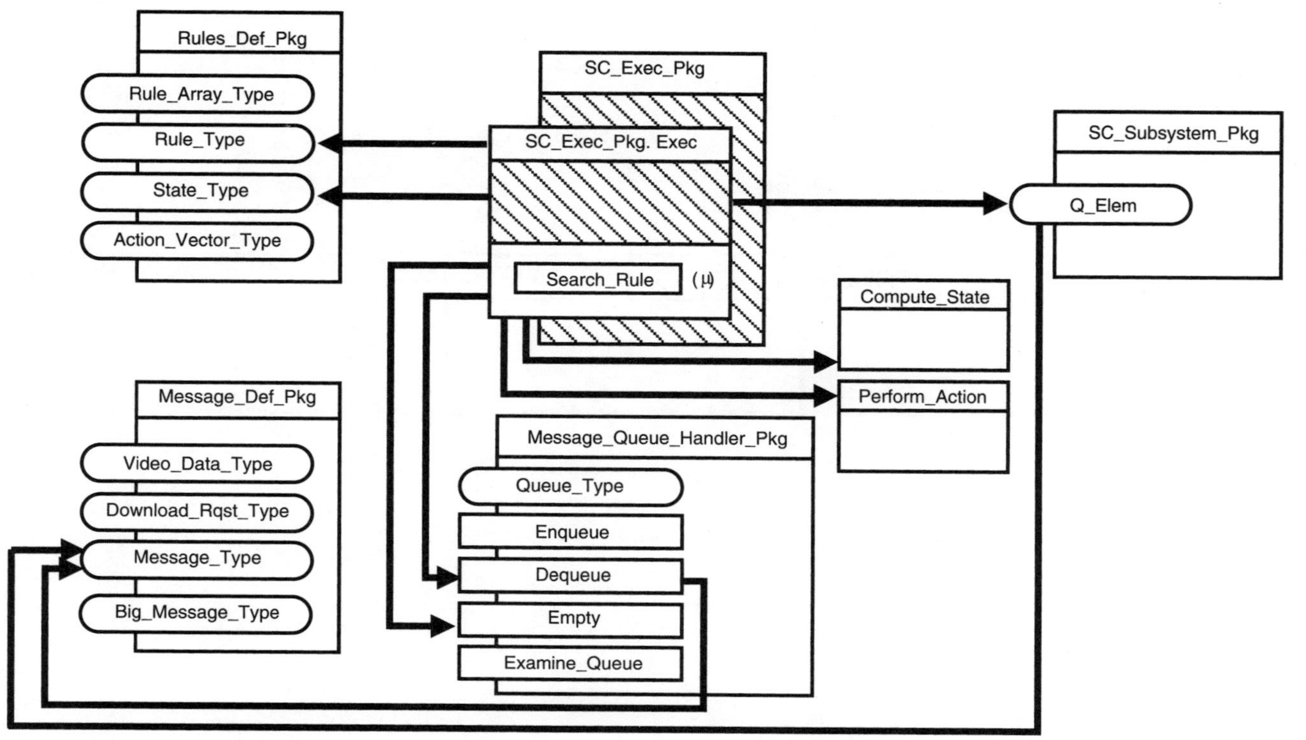

Figure A.23 SC_Exec_Pkg. Exec Software Architecture

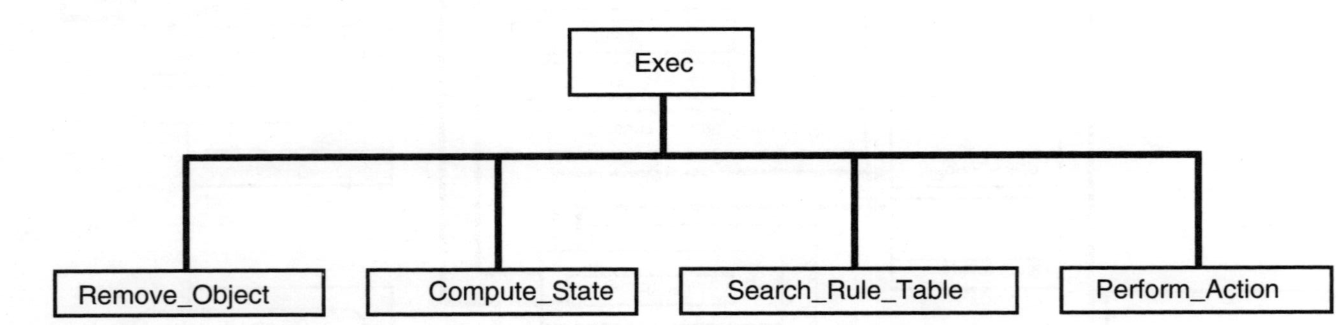

Figure A.24 SC_Exec_Pkg. Exec Internal Structure Chart

```
procedure Exec is
   rec_State  : RDP. state_type ;
   rule  num : TBD.TBD_Int ;
   rule :          RDP.rule_type ;
   done :          boolean ;

- -   pseudocode execution control
      max_loops : constant : = 1 ;
      loop_cntr :   integer ;
      max_cntr :    constant : = 1 ;
      rule_cntr :   integer ;
- -   pseudocode execution control

      begin

- -   pseudocode execution control
      loop_cntr : = 0 ;
- -   pseudocode execution control

      remove object ;
      Q_Head_Popped : = false ;
      done : = false ;
```

Same names as actual code; where possible, same types as actual code; possible if types identified, exported in another package

Pseudocode control for executable requirement delimited begin, end with comments, blank lines

Figure A.25a Cyclic Executive—Compilable Executable Pseudocode

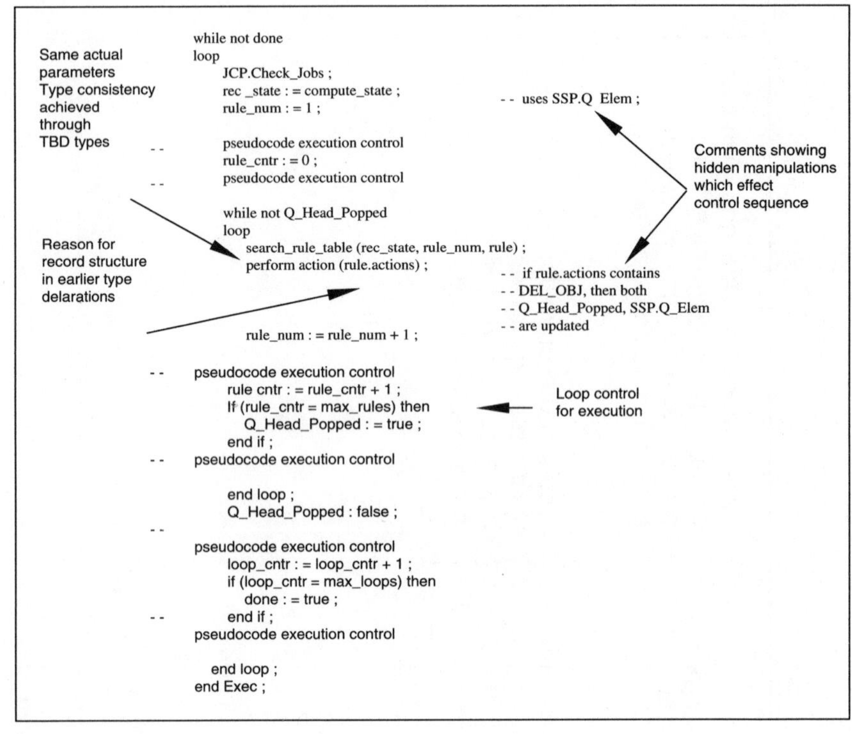

Figure A.25b Cyclic Executive—Compilable Executable Pseudocode

```
( Standby_Mode ) ( Standby_M True )                        =>
                                                           Trash_Obj ;

( Gimbal_Scan_Mode ) ( Standby_M True )                    =>
                                                           Store_Scan ,
                                                           Standby_Off ,
                                                           G_Scan_On ,
                                                           S_Pending_Off ,
                                                           Wait_Pipeline_Off ,
                                                           Wait_Reset_Off ,
                                                           Update_Range_Map ,
                                                           Dump_Range ,
                                                           Set_Scan_Parameters ;

( Gimbal_Scan_Mode ) ( Standby_M True )                    =>
                                                           Freeze_Swath ,
                                                           Pkg_LL_Job ,
                                                           Freeze_Swath ,
                                                           Del_Obj ;

( LL_Results ) ( Gimbal_Scan_M True )                      =>
                                                           Update_WM_LL ,
                                                           Dump_LL_Results ,
                                                           Pkg_TR_Jobs ,
                                                           Jobs_Out_Swath ,
                                                           Check_Swath ,
                                                           EOS_Off ,
                                                           Check_Scan ;

( LL_Results ) ( Gimbal_Scan_M True ) ( Jobs_Swath False ) ( EOS True )
                                                           =>
                                                           Pkg_Tgt_Report ;

( LL_Results ) ( Gimbal_Scan_M True ) ( Jobs_Swath False ) ( EOS False )
                                                           =>
                                                           Unfreeze_Swath ;

( LL_Results ) ( Gimbal_Scan_M True )                      =>
                                                           Jobs_Out_Swath ,
                                                           EOS_Off ,
                                                           Del_Obj ;
```

Figure A.26 Gimbal Scan Mode Rule Table (1)

```
( TR_Results ) ( Gimbal_Scan_M True )                              =>
                                                                   Update_WM_TR ,
                                                                   Dump_TR_Results ,
                                                                   Jobs_Out_Swath ,
                                                                   Check_Swath ,
                                                                   EOS_Off ,
                                                                   Check_Scan ;

( TR_Results ) ( Gimbal_Scan_M True ) ( Jobs_Swath False ) ( EOS True )
                                                                   =>
                                                                   Pkg_Tgt_Report ;

( TR_Results ) ( Gimbal_Scan_M True ) ( Jobs_Swath False ) ( EOS False )
                                                                   =>
                                                                   Unfreeze_Swath ;

( TR_Results ) ( Gimbal_Scan_M True )                              =>
                                                                   Jobs_Out_Swath ,
                                                                   EOS_Off ,
                                                                   Del_Obj ;

(Symbol_Display_Cmd ) ( Gimbal_Scan_M True )                       =>
                                                                   Unfreeze_Swath ,
                                                                   Del_Obj ;

( Gimbal_Scan_Mode ) ( Gimbal_Scan_M True )                        =>
                                                                   Store_Scan ,
                                                                   Jobs_Out_Swath ,
                                                                   Check_Swath ;

( Gimbal_Scan_Mode ) ( Gimbal_Scan_M True ) ( Jobs_Swath True )
                                                                   =>
                                                                   G_Scan_Off ,
                                                                   S_Pending_On ;
```

Figure A.27 Gimbal Scan Mode Rule Table (2)

```
( Gimbal_Scan_Mode ) ( Gimbal_Scan_M True ) ( Jobs_Swath
False )                                        =>
                                               Update_Range_Map ,
                                               Dump_Range ,
                                               Set_Scan_Parameters
                                               ,
                                               Freeze_Swath ,
                                               Pkg_LL_Job ;

( Gimbal_Scan_Mode ) ( Gimbal_Scan_M True )=>
                                               Jobs_Out_Swath ,
                                               Del_Obj ;

( Standby_Mode ) ( Gimbal_Scan_M True )        =>
                                               Jobs_Out_Swath ,
                                               Check_Swath ;

( Standby_Mode ) ( Gimbal_Scan_M True ) ( Jobs_Swath True )
                                               =>
                                               G_Scan_Off ,
                                               Wait_Pipeline_On ;

( Standby_Mode ) ( Gimbal_Scan_M True ) ( Jobs_Swath False )
                                               =>
                                               G_Scan_Off ,
                                               Standby_On ;

( Standby_Mode ) ( Gimbal_Scan_M True )        =>
                                               Jobs_Out_Swath ,
                                               Del_Obj ;

( LL_Results ) ( Scan_Pending_M True )         =>
                                               Update_WM_LL ,
                                               Dump_LL_Results ,
                                               Pkg_TR_Jobs ,
                                               Jobs_Out_Swath,

                                               Check_Swath ,
                                               EOS_Off ,
                                               Check_Scan ;
```

Figure A.28 Gimbal Scan Mode Rule Table (3)

```
( LL_Results ) ( Scan_Pending_M True ) ( Jobs_Swath False ) ( EOS True )
                                              =>
                                              Pkg_Tgt_Report ;
( LL_Results ) ( Scan_Pending_M True ) ( Jobs_Swath False ) ( EOS False )
                                              =>
                                              S_Pending_Off ,
                                              G_Scan_On ,
                                              Update_Range_Map ,
                                              Dump_Range ,
                                              Set_Scan_Parameters ,
                                              Unfreeze_Swath ,
                                              Freeze_Swath ,
                                              Pkg_LL_Job ;
( LL_Results ) ( Scan_Pending_M True )        =>
                                              Jobs_Out_Swath ,
                                              EOS_Off ,
                                              Del_Obj ;
( TR_Results ) ( Scan_Pending_M True )        =>
                                              Update_WM_TR ,
                                              Dump_TR_Results ,
                                              Jobs_Out_Swath ,
                                              Check_Swath ,
                                              EOS_Off ,
                                              Check_Scan ;
( TR_Results ) ( Scan_Pending_M True ) ( Jobs_Swath False ) ( EOS True )
                                              =>
                                              Pkg_Tgt_Report ;
( TR_Results ) ( Scan_Pending_M True ) ( Jobs_Swath False ) ( EOS False )
                                              =>
                                              S_Pending_Off ,
                                              G_Scan_On ,
                                              Update_Range_Map ,
                                              Dump_Range ,
                                              Set_Scan_Parameters ,
                                              Unfreeze_Swath ,
                                              Freeze_Swath ,
                                              Pkg_LL_Job ;
```

Figure A.29 Gimbal Scan Mode Rule Table (4)

```
( TR_Results )  ( Scan_Pending_M True )                 =>
                                                        Jobs_Out_Swath ,
                                                        EOS_Off ,
                                                        Del_Obj ;

( Symbol_Display_Cmd )  ( Scan_Pending_M True )         =>
                                                        S_Pending_Off ,
                                                        G_Scan_On ,
                                                        Update_Range_Map ,
                                                        Dump_Range ,
                                                        Set_Scan_Parameters ,
                                                        Unfreeze_Swath ,
                                                        Freeze_Swath ,
                                                        Pkg_LL_Job ,
                                                        Del_Obj ;

( Standby_Mode )  ( Scan_Pending_M True )               =>
                                                        S_Pending_Off ,
                                                        S_Pend_W_Pipe_On ,
                                                        Del_Obj ;

( LL_Results )  ( Scan_Pending_Wait_Pipe_M True)        =>
                                                        Update_WM_LL ,
                                                        Dump_LL_Results ,
                                                        Pkg_TR_Jobs ,
                                                        Jobs_Out_Swath ,
                                                        Check_Swath ,
                                                        EOS_Off ,
                                                        Check_Scan ;

( LL_Results )  ( Scan_Pending_Wait_Pipe_M True )  ( Jobs_Swath False )
( EOS True )                                            =>
                                                        Pkg_Tgt_Report ;
```

Figure A.30 Gimbal Scan Mode Rule Table (5)

```
( LL_Results ) ( Scan_Pending_Wait_Pipe_M True ) ( Jobs_Swath False ) ( EOS False )
                                                    =>
                                                    Update_Range_Map ,
                                                    Dump_Range ,
                                                    Unfreeze_Swath ,
                                                    Freeze_Swath ,
                                                    Pkg_LL_Job ,
                                                    S_Pend_W_Pipe_Off ,
                                                    Wait_Pipeline_On ;

( LL_Results ) ( Scan_Pending_Wait_Pipe_M True )
                                                    =>
                                                    Jobs_Out_Swath ,
                                                    EOS_Off ,
                                                    Del_Obj ;

( TR_Results ) ( Scan_Pending_Wait_Pipe_M True )
                                                    =>
                                                    Update_WM_TR ,
                                                    Dump_TR_Results ,
                                                    Jobs_Out_Swath ,
                                                    Check_Swath ,
                                                    EOS_Off ,
                                                    Check_Scan ;

( TR_Results ) ( Scan_Pending_Wait_Pipe_M True ) ( Jobs_Swath False ) ( EOS True )
                                                    =>
                                                    Pkg_Tgt_Report ;
```

Figure A.31 Gimbal Scan Mode Rule Table (6)

```
( TR_Results ) ( Scan_Pending_Wait_Pipe_M True ) ( Jobs_Swath False ) ( EOS False )
                                                        =>
                                                        Update_Range_Map ,
                                                        Dump_Range ,
                                                        Unfreeze_Swath ,
                                                        Freeze_Swath ,
                                                        Pkg_LL_Job ,
                                                        S_Pend_W_Pipe_Off ,
                                                        Wait_Pipeline_On ;

( TR_Results ) ( Scan_Pending_Wait_Pipe_M True )        =>
                                                        Jobs_Out_Swath ,
                                                        EOS_Off ,
                                                        Del_Obj ;

( Symbol_Display_Cmd ) ( Scan_Pending_Wait_Pipe_M True ) =>
                                                        Unfreeze_Swath ,
                                                        Jobs_Out_Swath ,
                                                        Check_Swath ;

( Symbol_Display_Cmd ) ( Scan_Pending_Wait_Pipe_M True ) ( Jobs_Swath False )
                                                        =>
                                                        Update_Range_Map ,
                                                        Dump_Range ,
                                                        Unfreeze_Swath ,
                                                        Freeze_Swath ,
                                                        Pkg_LL_Job ,
                                                        S_Pend_W_Pipe_Off ,
                                                        Wait_Pipeline_On ;

( Symbol_Display_Cmd ) ( Scan_Pending_Wait_Pipe_M True ) =>
                                                        Jobs_Out_Swath ,
                                                        Del_Obj ;
```

Figure A.32 Gimbal Scan Mode Rule Table (7)

```
( LL_Results )  ( Wait_Pipeline_M True)                                                =>
                                                                                       Update_WM_LL ,
                                                                                       Dump_LL_Results ,
                                                                                       Pkg_TR_Jobs ,
                                                                                       Jobs_Out_Swath ,
                                                                                       Check_Swath ,
                                                                                       EOS_Off ,
                                                                                       Check_Scan ;

( LL_Results )  ( Wait_Pipeline_M True )  ( Jobs_Swath False )  ( EOS True )           =>
                                                                                       Pkg_Tgt_Report ;

( LL_Results )  ( Wait_Pipeline_M True )  ( Jobs_Swath False )  ( EOS False )          =>
                                                                                       Unfreeze_Swath ,

                                                                                       Freeze_Swath ,
                                                                                       Pkg_LL_Job ;

( LL_Results )  ( Wait_Pipeline_M True )                                               =>
                                                                                       Jobs_Out_Swath ,
                                                                                       EOS_Off ,
                                                                                       Del_Obj ;

( TR_Results )  ( Wait_Pipeline_M True )                                               =>
                                                                                       Update_WM_TR ,
                                                                                       Dump_TR_Results ,
                                                                                       Jobs_Out_Swath ,
                                                                                       Check_Swath ,
                                                                                       EOS_Off ,
                                                                                       Check_Scan ;
```

Figure A.33 Gimbal Scan Mode Rule Table (8)

```
( TR_Results ) ( Wait_Pipeline_M True ) ( Jobs_Swath False ) ( EOS True )
                                              =>
                                              Pkg_Tgt_Report ;

( TR_Results ) ( Wait_Pipeline_M True ) ( Jobs_Swath False ) ( EOS False )
                                              =>
                                              Unfreeze_Swath ,
                                              Freeze_Swath ,
                                              Pkg_LL_Job ;

( TR_Results ) ( Wait_Pipeline_M True )       =>
                                              Jobs_Out_Swath
                                              EOS_Off ,
                                              Del_Obj ;

( Symbol_Display _Cmd ) ( Wait_Pipeline_M True )
                                              =>
                                              Unfreeze_Swath ,
                                              Jobs_Out_Swath ,
                                              Check_Swath ;

( Symbol_Display_Cmd ) ( Wait _Pipeline_M True ) ( Jobs_Swath False )
                                              =>
                                              Wait_Pipeline_Off ,
                                              Wait_Reset_On ,
                                              Clear_MPM ,
                                              Reset_Subsystems ,
                                              Wait_Reset_Off ,
                                              Standby_On ;

( Symbol_Display_Cmd ) ( Wait_Pipeline_M True )
                                              =>
                                              Del_Obj ;
```

Figure A.34 Gimbal Scan Mode Rule Table (9)

Appendix B

Methodology and Notation Summary

A centralized and convenient summary of the software engineering methodology is provided here for the potential practitioner. Each of the models (operations, requirements, architecture, and detailed design) is represented. This summary includes the following information for each model:

1. A list of the activities accomplished for each step;
2. Specific notation employed while accomplishing these activities;
3. Evaluation criteria to be applied, if appropriate; and
4. Design options available, if appropriate.

Together, these materials provide a handbook for practicing software engineers. For detailed explanations, refer to the appropriate sections of the text.

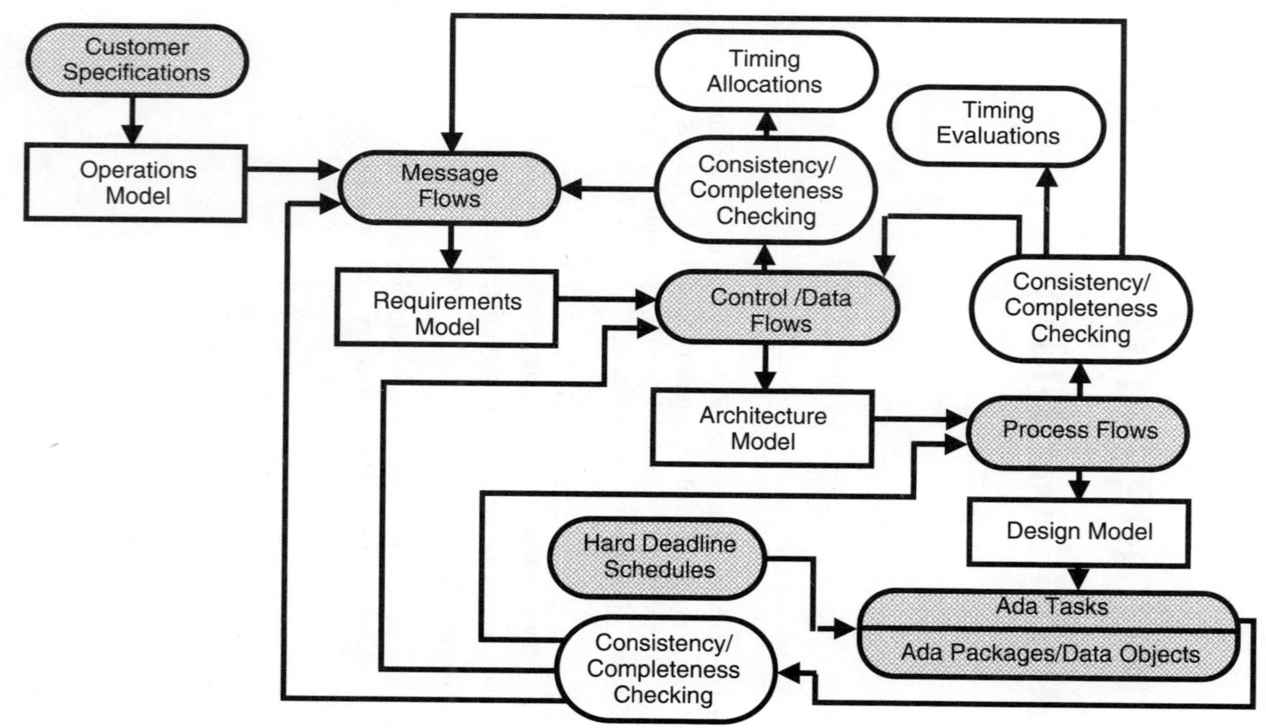

Figure B.1 Software Engineering Methodology

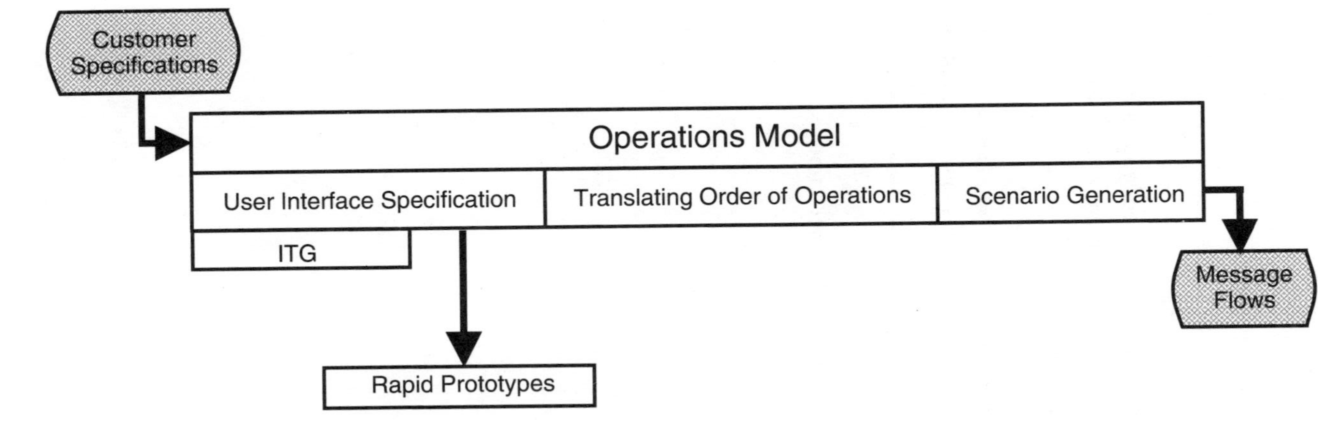

Figure B.2 Operations Model Generation

1. Specify user interfaces and order of operation of user interaction;

2. Translate order of operations of user interaction into an initial message sequence;

3. Expand the message sequence into detailed operational scenarios involving sensors, actuators, and other interfaces; and

4. Divide the detailed message sequence into a detailed event/response pattern indicating inputs and outputs.

Figure B.3 Operations Model Generation

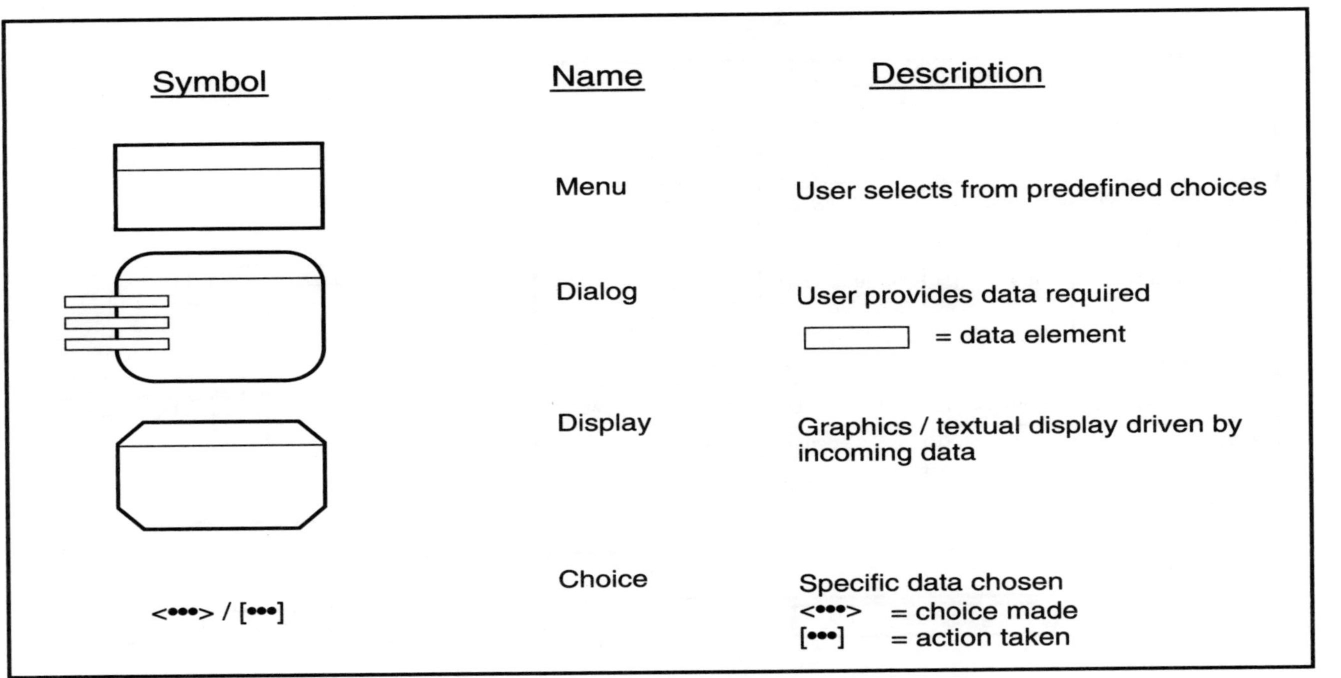

Figure B.4 User Interface Specification Notation

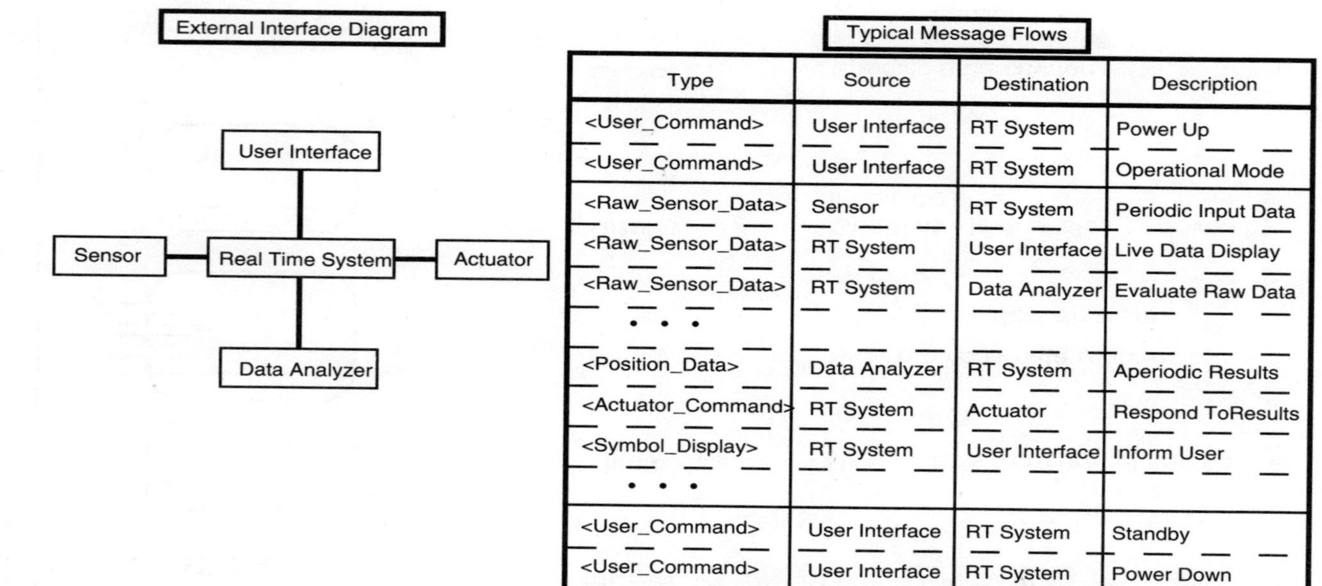

Type	Source	Destination	Description
<User_Command>	User Interface	RT System	Power Up
<User_Command>	User Interface	RT System	Operational Mode
<Raw_Sensor_Data>	Sensor	RT System	Periodic Input Data
<Raw_Sensor_Data>	RT System	User Interface	Live Data Display
<Raw_Sensor_Data>	RT System	Data Analyzer	Evaluate Raw Data
• • •			
<Position_Data>	Data Analyzer	RT System	Aperiodic Results
<Actuator_Command>	RT System	Actuator	Respond ToResults
<Symbol_Display>	RT System	User Interface	Inform User
• • •			
<User_Command>	User Interface	RT System	Standby
<User_Command>	User Interface	RT System	Power Down

Figure B.5 Typical Operational Scenario Generation

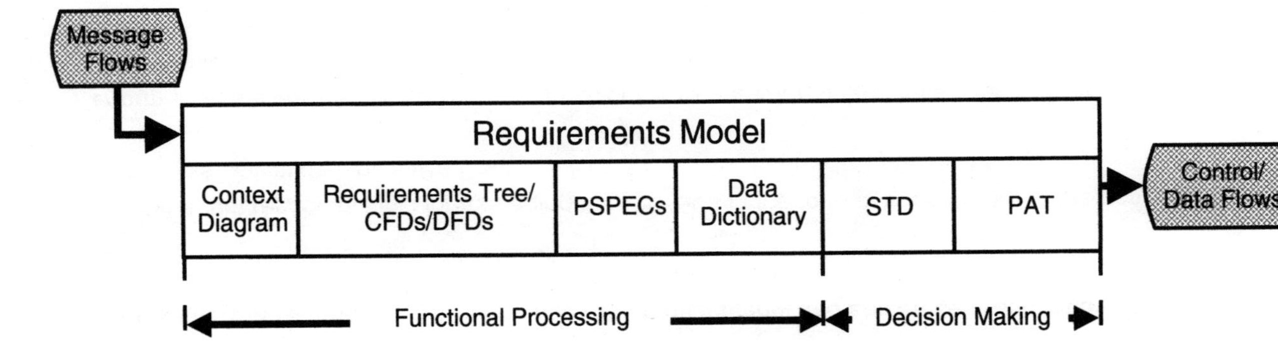

Figure B.6 Requirements Model Generation

1. Generate a context diagram using the detailed message sequence;
2. Construct functional requirements in the form of a requirements tree and process specifications (PSPECs);
3. Describe event/response logic for managing the PSPECs in the form of state transition diagrams (STD) and process activation tables (PAT);
4. Perform a consistency and completeness check of implementor requirements against operational requirements;
5. Use data dictionary to determine an initial set of data abstractions and operations on abstractions; and
6. Allocate timing requirements to PSPECs.

Figure B.7 Requirements Model Generation

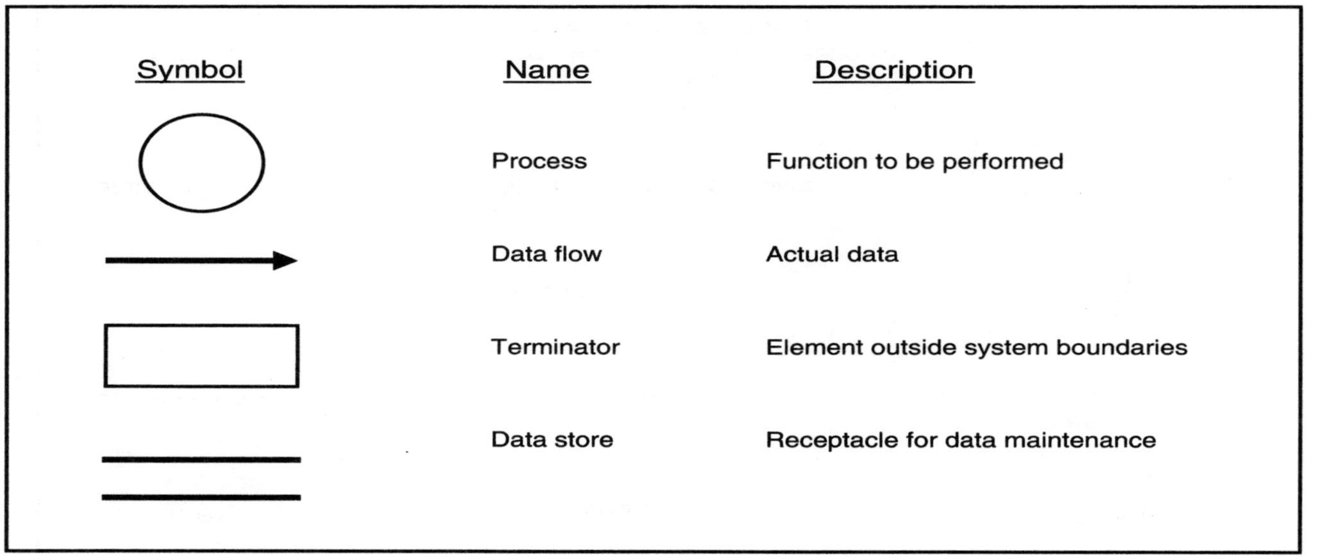

Symbol
Name
Description
Process
Function to be performed
Data flow
Actual data
Terminator
Element outside system boundaries
Data store
Receptacle for data maintenance

Figure B.8 Functional Specification Notation

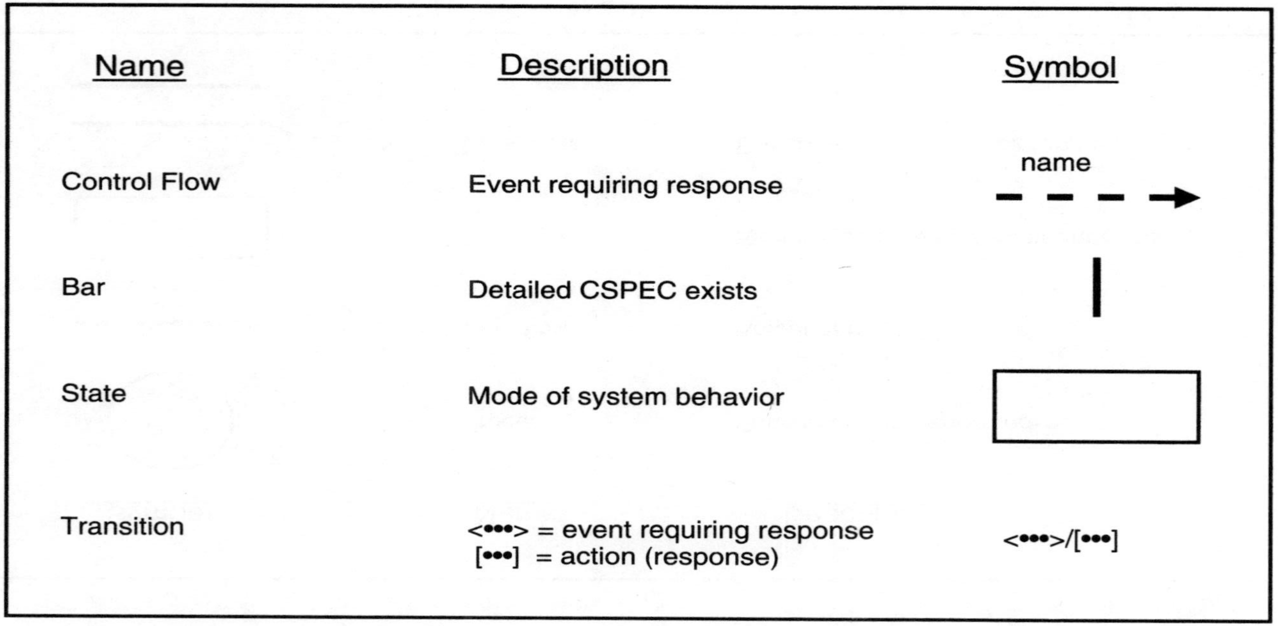

Name	Description	Symbol
Control Flow	Event requiring response	name
Bar	Detailed CSPEC exists	
State	Mode of system behavior	
Transition	<•••> = event requiring response [•••] = action (response)	<•••>/[•••]

Figure B.9 Control Flow Specification Notation

Actions \ Leaf Requirements	P_1	P_2	•••	P_m
A_1		0 (deactivated)		
A_2	1 (in parallel)		1 (in parallel)	
⋮				
A_n		1 (sequential)		2 (sequential)

Figure B.10 Process Activation Table

Description	Symbol	Is	Comment
Is equivalent to	:: =	Composed of	Equal in math sense (Also, →, ⇒)
And (sequence)	+	Together with	Imply addition or ordered grouping
Iteration (repetition)	{ }	Iterations of	No index or 0 to
Either-or (selection)	[ ]	Select 1 of	At least (2) expressions
Optional	( )	Optional	Expression may/may not be included
	* *	Comment	
	' '	Literal	
	\ \	Description/comment	

- Hierarchical data structure combines some set of sequence, selection, and/or iteration [nested!]
- Avoid overly hierarchical/nested data structures

Figure B.11 Requirements Dictionary Notation

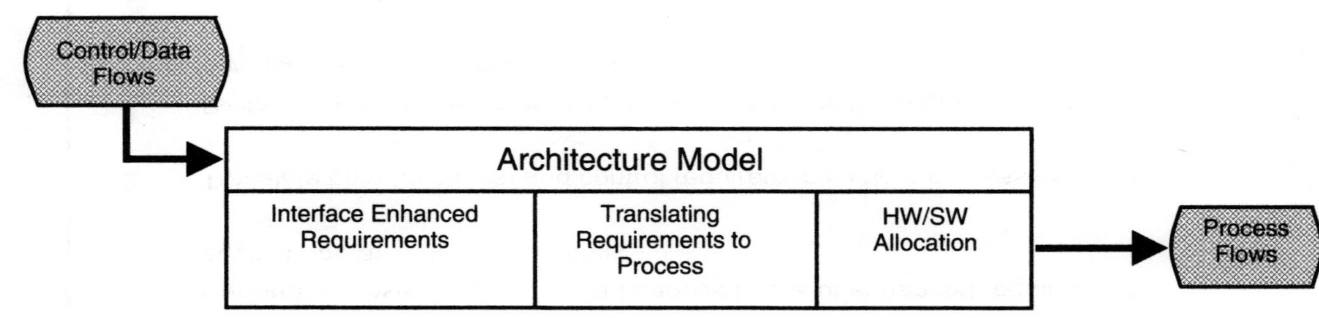

Figure B.12 Architecture Model Generation

1. Enhance both functional and control requirements to accommodate specifc hardware/technological interfaces;

2. Perform a consistency and completeness check of enhanced requirements against operational requirements;

3. Translate both functional and control requirements into a process architecture;

4. Perform a consistency and completeness check of the process architecture against operational requirements;

5. Evaluate architecture performance against timing constraints based on combining timing allocations for requirements mapped into each architecture process; and

6. Allocate requirements within each architecture process to hardware and to software.

Figure B.13 Architecture Model Generation

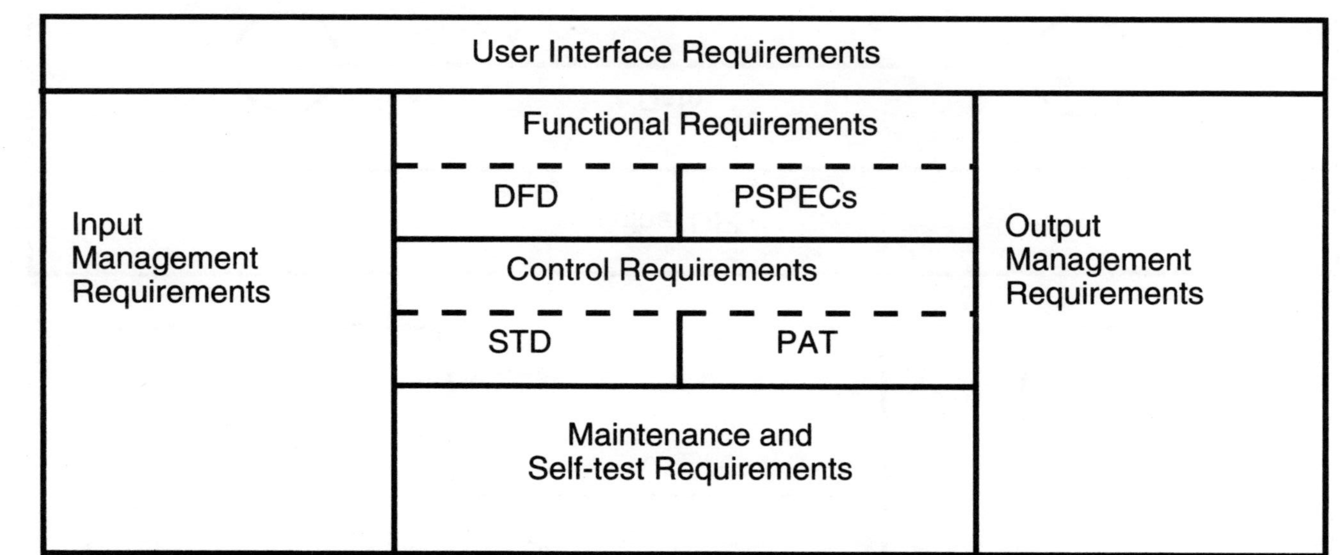

Figure B.14 Notation for Requirements Enhancement

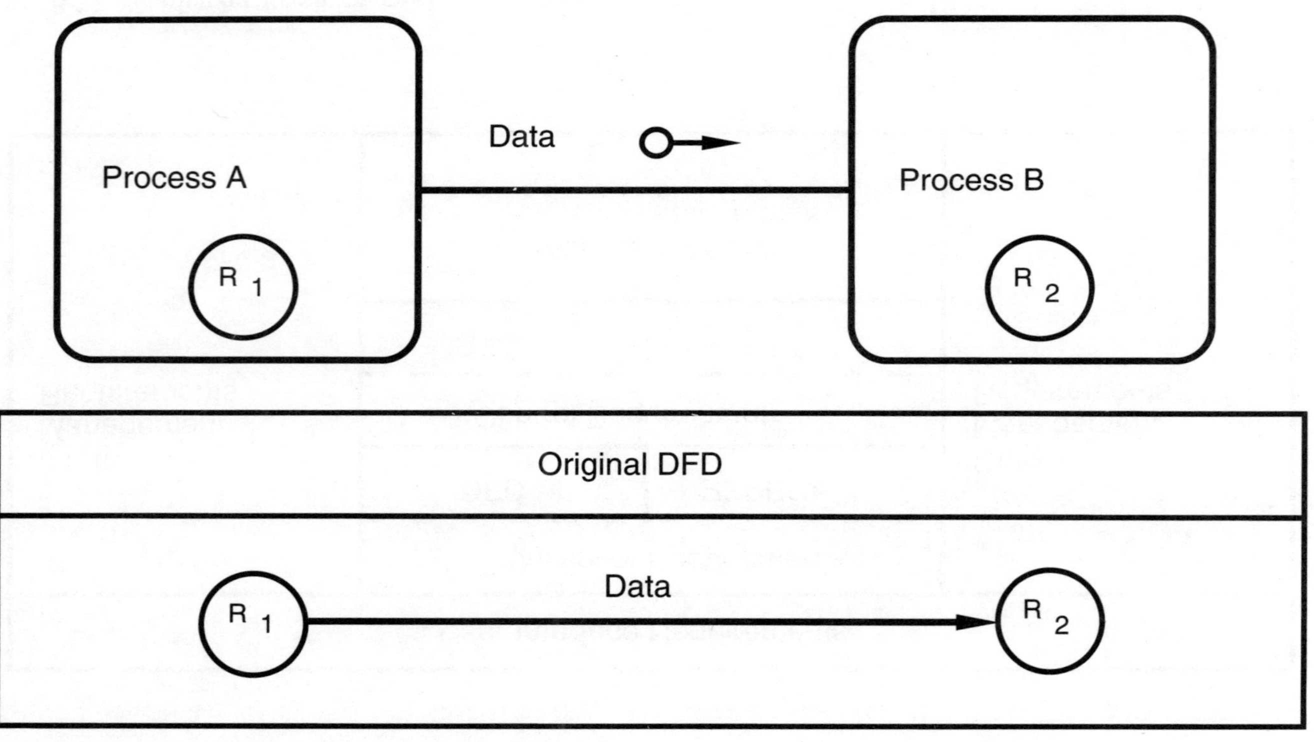

Figure B.15 Typical Process Graph

General Justification:	Motivation for Selection of Processes
Performance:	Effects on Throughput/Response Times
Integration and Test Impacts:	Level of Effort, Frustration Involved
Reliability:	Job Performance on a Stable, Repetitive Basis
Control Concept:	Extent to which Control Manages Workload
Traceability:	Level of Effort Required to Maintain
Flexibility:	Ability to Easily Modify in Face of Evolving Requirements
Portability:	Independence from Underlying Target Platform
HW Dependence:	Impact on Allocation of Requirements to HW
SW Dependence:	Impact on Allocation of Requirements to SW

Figure B.16 Criteria for Process Architecture Evaluation

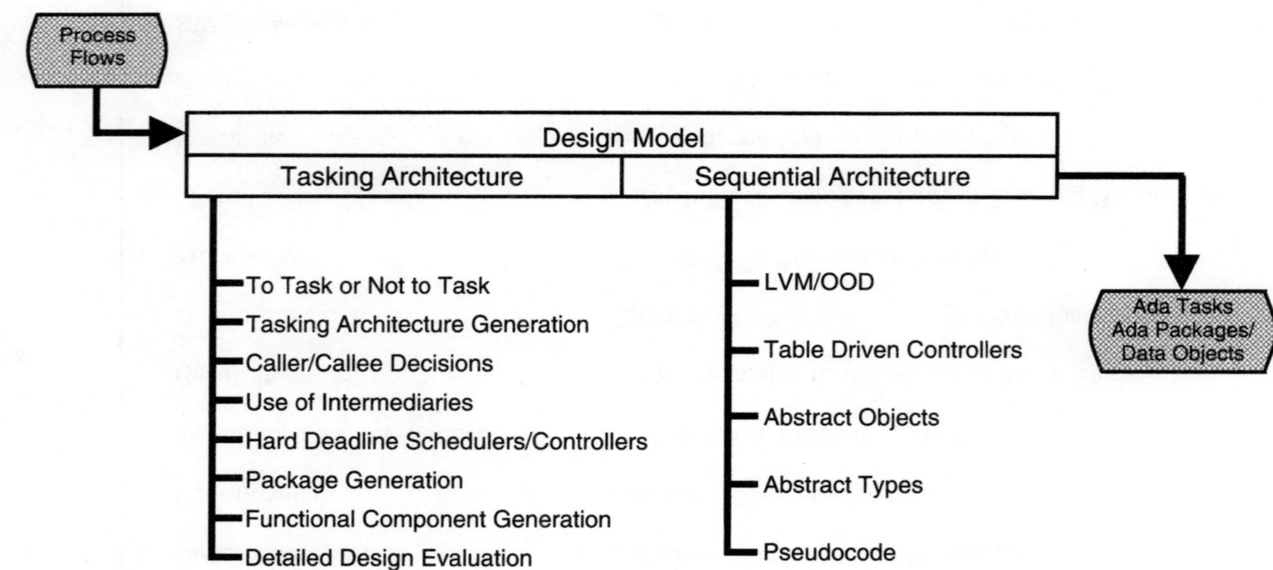

Figure B.17 Design Model Generation

1. Generate an initial tasking architecture;
2. Establish caller/callee relationships;
3. Employ (or do not employ) intermediaries;
4. Perform a consistency and completeness check of the tasking architecture against operational requirements;
5. Allocate tasks to packages;
6. Generate functional components of the packages;
7. Use layered abstractions, table driven controllers, data objects, and data types to construct the sequential design of each task; and
8. Evaluate the detailed design to assess its quality.

Figure B.18 Design Model Generation

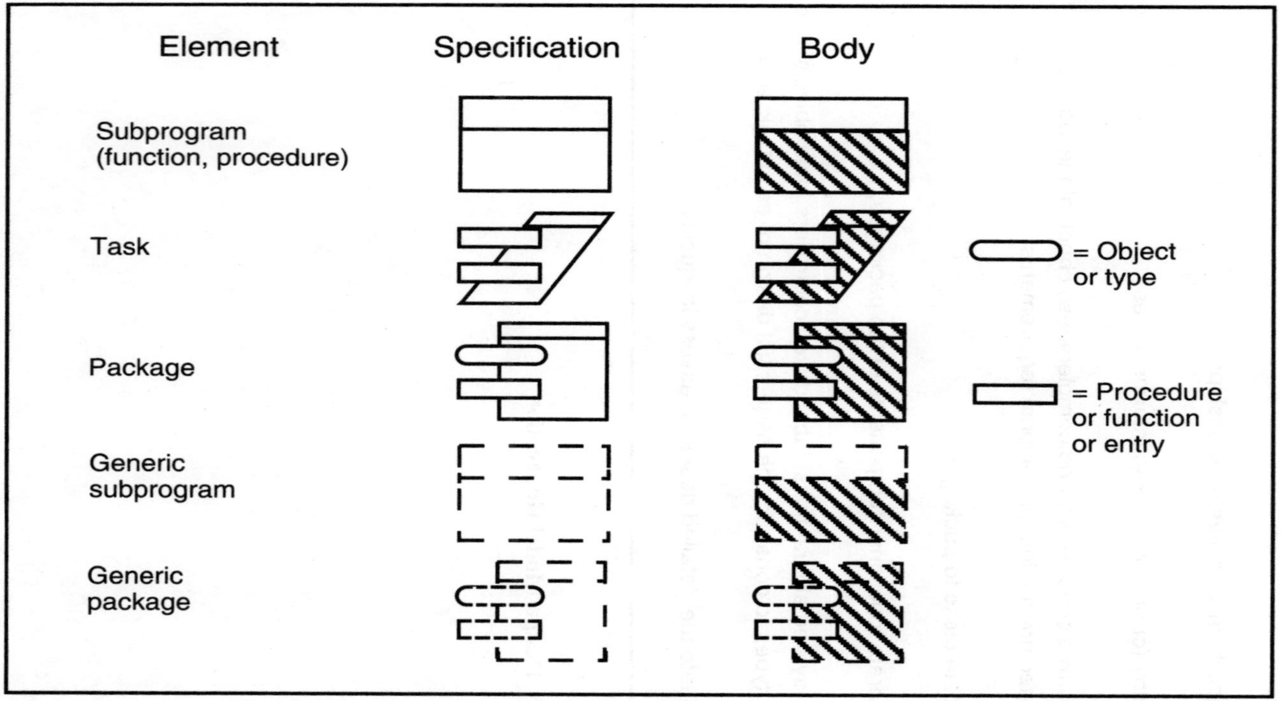

Element	Specification	Body
Subprogram (function, procedure)		
Task		
Package		
Generic subprogram		
Generic package		

= Object or type

= Procedure or function or entry

Figure B.19 Design Model Notation

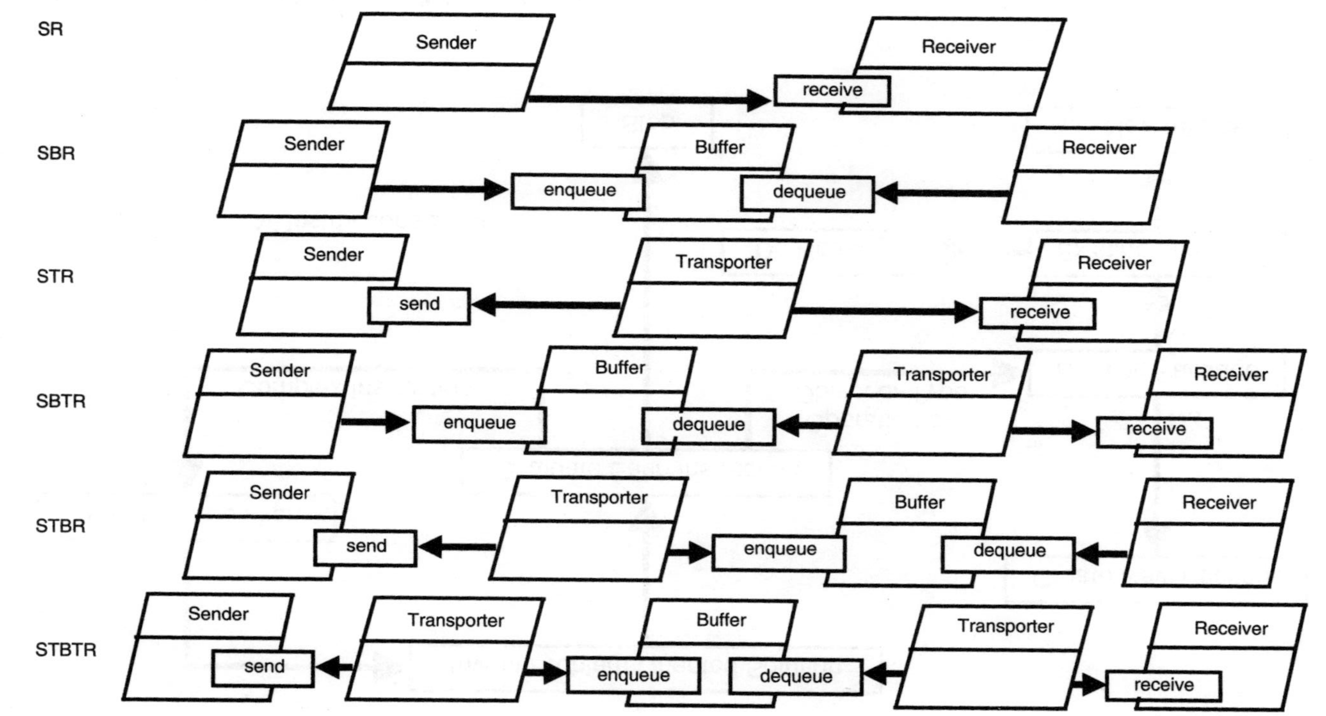

Figure B.20 Tasking Intermediary Alternatives

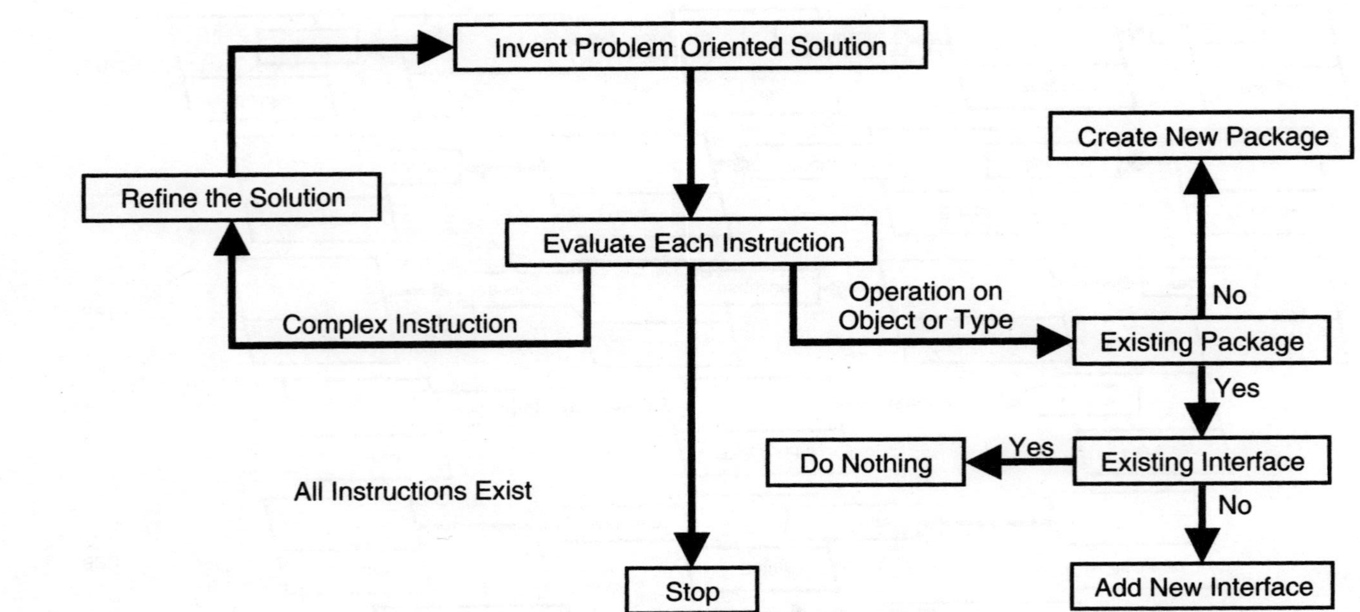

Figure B.21 Layered Virtual Machines/Object-Oriented Design

Index

H

I

L

M

S

OpenAda

OpenAda PC

- Requirements: IBM PC, PS/2 or compatible, MS-DOS version 3.0 or higher, 640K RAM, 5MB hard disk space.
- Fully Validated Ada Compiler/Linker (ACVC Version 1.11) for Real Mode Applications
- Fully integrated, menu driven interface in windowed programming environment with mouse support
- Built-in language sensitive editor
- Ada specific source level debugger with split screen debugging capabilities
- High-level optimizer
- On-line "Hypertext" Ada Language Reference Manual
- DOS environment library
- Library management tools
- Amake support tool
- On-line help utility
- Graphics, numerics and utility libraries
- Complete User Documentation
- Provided in either 5.25" or 3.5" disks
- Software floating point and 80x87 hardware floating point supported

OpenAda Macintosh

- Requirements: Mac SE, Mac II, or Mac Plus, Finder Version 6.1 or higher, 2MB RAM, 5MB hard disk space.
- Fully Validated Ada Compiler (ACVC Version 1.11)
- Linker
- Macintosh Environment Library (MEL) which provides a binding to the operating system and applications such as Mac Toolbox
- Ada specific source level debugger
- High-level optimizer
- Macintosh Programmers Workshop (MPW) provides Apple Computer's software development environment for the Macintosh including:
    - Quick Draw graphics operations
    - Amake
    - Spelling checker
    - Power user scripting language
    - Multi-windowed text editor and command interpreter
    - Multi-user source code control system
- Utility library
- Concise, easy-to-follow, complete User Documentation
- Software floating point and 68881 hardware floating point supported
- OPTIONAL: MPW complete documentation set

Features and Technical Specifications

OpenAda/OpenSELECT CASE Order Form

	Quantity	Subtotal
❒ OpenAda PC - 3.5" diskettes $99	______	______
❒ OpenAda PC - 5.25" diskettes $99	______	______
❒ OpenAda Macintosh $99	______	______
❒ OpenSELECT CASE - 3.5" diskettes $129	______	______
❒ OpenSELECT CASE - 5.25" diskettes $129	______	______
Shipping and Handling $10 per unit	______	______
(California residents add 7.75% for tax)	______	______
TOTAL	______	______

Please Print

Name ______________________

Address ______________________

City/State/Zip ______________________

Phone ______________________

School (If Applicable) ______________________

Class/Instructor ______________________

☐ *Check enclosed*

☐ *Charge my credit card*

Please do not send cash.
Allow four weeks for delivery.

Mastercard# ______________________
or
VISA# ______________________

Expiration Date ______________________

Name on Card ______________________

Signature ______________________

Complete all information to speed processing.
Prices subject to change with introduction of new products.

Mail To:

MERIDIAN

SOFTWARE SYSTEMS INC

10 Pasteur Street, Irvine, CA 92718

Thank You for Your Order!!